Frommer's®

Washington State

5th Edition

by Karl Samson

Here's what the critics say about Frommer's:

"Amazingly easy to use. Very portable, very complete."

—*Booklist*

"Detailed, accurate, and easy-to-read information for all price ranges."
—*Glamour Magazine*

"Hotel information is close to encyclopedic."

—*Des Moines Sunday Register*

"Frommer's Guides have a way of giving you a real feel for a place."
—*Knight Ridder Newspapers*

Wiley Publishing, Inc.

About the Author

Karl Samson lives in Oregon, where he spends his time juggling his obsessions with traveling, gardening, outdoor sports, and wine. Each winter, to dry out his webbed feet, he flees the soggy Northwest to update the *Frommer's Arizona* guide. However, he always looks forward to his return to the land of good espresso. Karl is also the author of *Frommer's Seattle*.

Published by:

Wiley Publishing, Inc.

111 River St.
Hoboken, NJ 07030-5774

ISBN-13: 978-0-471-76389-5
ISBN-10: 0-471-76389-6

Editor: Shelley Bance
Production Editor: Katie Robinson
Cartographer: Andrew Dolan
Photo Editor: Richard Fox
Production by Wiley Indianapolis Composition Services

Front cover photo: Tatoosh Range Beargrass
Back cover photo: Olympic National Park, Hoh Rainforest

For information on our other products and services or to obtain technical support, please contact our Customer Care Department within the U.S. at 800/762-2974, outside the U.S. at 317/572-3993 or fax 317/572-4002.

Wiley also publishes its books in a variety of electronic formats. Some content that appears in print may not be available in electronic formats.

Manufactured in the United States of America

5 4 3 2

Contents

List of Maps

An Invitation to the Reader

In researching this book, we discovered many wonderful places—hotels, restaurants, shops, and more. We're sure you'll find others. Please tell us about them, so we can share the information with your fellow travelers in upcoming editions. If you were disappointed with a recommendation, we'd love to know that, too. Please write to:

Frommer's Washington State, 5th Edition
Wiley Publishing, Inc. • 111 River St. • Hoboken, NJ 07030-5774

An Additional Note

Please be advised that travel information is subject to change at any time—and this is especially true of prices. We therefore suggest that you write or call ahead for confirmation when making your travel plans. The authors, editors, and publisher cannot be held responsible for the experiences of readers while traveling. Your safety is important to us, however, so we encourage you to stay alert and be aware of your surroundings. Keep a close eye on cameras, purses, and wallets, all favorite targets of thieves and pickpockets.

Other Great Guides for Your Trip:

Frommer's Seattle
Irreverent Guide to Seattle & Portland
Frommer's Vancouver & Victoria

Frommer's Star Ratings, Icons & Abbreviations

Every hotel, restaurant, and attraction listing in this guide has been ranked for quality, value, service, amenities, and special features using a **star-rating system.** In country, state, and regional guides, we also rate towns and regions to help you narrow down your choices and budget your time accordingly. Hotels and restaurants are rated on a scale of zero (recommended) to three stars (exceptional). Attractions, shopping, nightlife, towns, and regions are rated according to the following scale: zero stars (recommended), one star (highly recommended), two stars (very highly recommended), and three stars (must-see).

In addition to the star-rating system, we also use **seven feature icons** that point you to the great deals, in-the-know advice, and unique experiences that separate travelers from tourists. Throughout the book, look for:

Finds	Special finds—those places only insiders know about
Fun Fact	Fun facts—details that make travelers more informed and their trips more fun
Kids	Best bets for kids and advice for the whole family
Moments	Special moments—those experiences that memories are made of
Overrated	Places or experiences not worth your time or money
Tips	Insider tips—great ways to save time and money
Value	Great values—where to get the best deals

The following **abbreviations** are used for credit cards:

AE	American Express	DISC	Discover	V	Visa
DC	Diners Club	MC	MasterCard		

Frommers.com

Now that you have the guidebook to a great trip, visit our website at **www.frommers.com** for travel information on more than 3,000 destinations. With features updated regularly, we give you instant access to the most current trip-planning information available. At Frommers.com, you'll also find the best prices on airfares, accommodations, and car rentals—and you can even book travel online through our travel booking partners. At Frommers.com, you'll also find the following:

- Online updates to our most popular guidebooks
- Vacation sweepstakes and contest giveaways
- Newsletter highlighting the hottest travel trends
- Online travel message boards with featured travel discussions

What's New in Washington

I live in the Northwest and spend much of every year scouring Washington state in search of what's new and noteworthy. There are always great new hotels and restaurants to be discovered, new tour companies and museums. Occasionally, new parks or other natural areas have opened to the public. Inevitably, a few favorite old restaurants or shops have gone out of business. Worse still, sometimes the places I once liked no longer make the grade and have to be taken out of this guide. Following are some of my discoveries.

SEATTLE Orientation Budget travelers have several new options for getting to Seattle this year. First of all, you no longer have to arrive home from your Seattle trip with red eyes when you fly **Jet-Blue** (℗ **800/JETBLUE;** www.jetblue. com) from New York's JFK Airport. Jet-Blue added daytime flights to and from Seattle in 2005. Delta's **Song** (℗ **800/ 359-7664;** www.flysong.com) also has flights between New York's JFK and Seattle.

The **Seattle-Tacoma International Airport** (℗ **206/431-4444;** www.port seattle.org/seatac) finally opened its beautiful new glassed-in Central Terminal, and flyers are really excited that so many great local shops and restaurants have outlets in the new terminal.

Perhaps to make up for all these great new transportation options, Seattle has closed its bus tunnel, which for many years has channeled public buses under city streets instead of through above-ground traffic congestion. The reason for closing this marvel of urban planning is that it will be retrofitted to handle light rail trains that will use it in a few years.

Where to Stay The new **Inn at El Gaucho,** 2502 First Ave. (℗ **866/354-2824** or 206/728-1133; inn.elgaucho. com), upstairs from the city's poshest steakhouses, is a retro-swank boutique hotel that makes a perfect base for a Seattle visit with lots of nightclubbing and dining out.

The **Hotel Ändra,** 2000 Fourth Ave. (℗ **877/448-8600** or 206/448-8600; www.hotelandra.com), is a swank and stylish place cut from the same cloth as the W hotel chain. Not only is the Hotel Ändra gorgeous, but it's located on the edge of the hip Belltown neighborhood, which makes it an excellent base for club-goers and foodies alike.

Dining Local celebrity chef Tom Douglas has done it again. His latest restaurant, **Lola,** 2000 Fourth Ave. (℗ **206/441-1430;** www.tomdouglas.com), in the hip Hotel Ändra, was an instant hit when it opened. Lola puts a creative spin on Greek food, adding dishes rarely found in the U.S., as well as regional ingredients. Yum!

One of my favorite new Seattle restaurants, **Lark,** 926 12th Ave. (℗ **206/323-5275**), is in an odd little building on an unlikely street on the back side of Capitol Hill. It's well worth searching out for chef Jonathan Sundstrom's creative small plates.

Sports fans should not miss an opportunity to have a meal or drink at the coolest sports bar/restaurant in the city. **Sport Restaurant & Bar,** 140 Fourth Ave. N., Suite 130 (© 206/404-7767; www.sportrestaurant.com), directly across the street from the Space Needle, has a huge, wall-hung plasma TV between the bar and the restaurant, and booths in the dining room have their own little wall-hung TVs, as well. The booth TVs are a big hit with families.

Seeing the Sights   If you travel to Seattle anytime before January 2007, you can forget about visiting the **Seattle Art Museum,** 100 University St. (© 206/654-3100; www.seattleartmuseum.org). As part of a major expansion, the museum plans to close its doors for a year. However, if all goes according to plan, by spring 2006, the museum's new Olympic Sculpture Park will have opened. The 8.5-acre park will be wedged between Western Avenue and the waters of Elliott Bay at the north end of the Seattle waterfront. The sculpture park will be free to the public, and one of the highlights will be Alexander Calder's massive *Eagle* sculpture. The Seattle Art Museum is also in the middle of a big expansion, but its new wing won't open until 2007.

Microsoft co-founder Paul Allen has been at it again. At the Frank Gehry–designed colorful blob of a building that houses the Experience Music Project rock-'n'-roll museum, you can now gaze upon Captain Kirk's command chair from the starship *Enterprise.* Plenty of other pieces of science fiction memorabilia are also on display at Allen's new **Science Fiction Museum and Hall of Fame,** 325 Fifth Ave. N. (© 877/SCI-FICT or 206/SCI-FICT. www.sfhomeworld.org).

By the time you read this, the **Klondike Gold Rush National Historical Park,** 319 Second Ave. S. © 206/553-7220; www.nps.gov/klse), should be

happily ensconced in its new Pioneer Square home at the address here. By the way, the historical park's visitor center/museum is now directly across from Zeitgeist Art/Coffee.

The **Burke Museum,** University of Washington, 17th Ave. NE and NE 45th St. (© 206/543-5590; www.burkemuseum.org), is a little gem of a museum with fascinating and eclectic collections. In the summer of 2005, the museum doubled the size of one of its galleries and planned to bring in larger traveling exhibitions.

Public libraries usually aren't big tourist attractions, but the new **Seattle Central Library,** 1000 Fourth Ave. (© 206/386-4636; www.spl.org), in downtown Seattle is such an architectural oddity that it became an instant must-see when it opened in the summer of 2004. Built of glass and steel, the building is all gravity-defying angles and vast, light-filled spaces. Yes, there are plenty of books, too.

If you're trying to find the **Russian submarine** that was parked at the south end of the waterfront for the past few years, it's no longer there, since it headed to the sunnier climes of Southern California. Likewise, you can abandon ideas of taking in an IMAX film on the waterfront. The **IMAXDome Theater** that for years was housed in the same building as the Seattle Aquarium has darkened its screen permanently, due to a major renovation project on the pier that was its home. Also, if you go looking for the **Seahawks Stadium,** you might miss your football game. The team finally sold the rights to its shiny new digs, so you'll now be catching the NFL action at **Qwest Field.**

THE SAN JUAN ISLANDS, WHIDBEY ISLAND & THE EMERALD COAST   The San Juan Islands   The new little **Island Museum of Art,** 314

Spring St. (© **360/370-5050;** www. wbay.org), is affiliated with San Juan Island's Westcott Bay Sculpture Park & Nature Reserve and, though small, has interesting exhibitions by regional artists.

Foodies and wine lovers heading to San Juan Island should be sure to plan on having a meal at Friday Harbor's **Steps Wine Bar and Cafe,** Friday Harbor Center, First Street between Spring and East streets (© **360/370-5959;** www.steps winebarandcafe.com). This tucked-away little restaurant is a big hit with locals and a great place for a light meal and a glass of wine.

Bellingham Families visiting Bellingham should be sure to visit **Mindport,** 210 W. Holly St. (© **360/647-5614;** Mindport.org), an interactive art-and-science museum primarily for kids. The **Bellingham Railway Museum,** 1320 Commercial St. (© **360/393-7540;** www.bellinghamrailwaymuseum.org), is another hit with kids.

THE OLYMPIC PENINSULA Port Townsend Manresa Castle, 651 Cleveland St. (© **800/732-1281** or 360/385-5750; www.manresacastle.com), the most impressive of Port Townsend's historic hotels, has undergone a renovation and is looking better than it has in years.

Olympic National Park East & Hood Canal Although well off the usual Olympic Peninsula tourist route, the new **Alderbrook Resort & Spa,** 10 E. Alderbrook Dr., Union (© **800/622-9370** or 360/898-2200; www.alderbrookresort. com), is such a beautiful waterfront lodge that it is worth planning a trip around a stay here.

THE CASCADES Lake Chelan Vineyards continue to replace apple orchards in the hills above Lake Chelan and, consequently, wineries are proliferating. New area wineries include **Benson Vineyards Estate Winery,** 754 Winesap

Ave., Manson (© **509/687-0313;** www. bensonvineyards.com); **Big Pine Winery,** 280 Summit Blvd. (© **509/687-0889;** www.bigpinewinery.com); **C. R. Sandidge Wines,** 137 E. Woodin Ave., Chelan (© **509/682-3704;** www.cr sandidgewines.com); and **Tildio Winery,** 70 E Wapato Lake Rd., Manson (© **509/ 687-8463;** www.tildio.com).

Leavenworth & The Wenatchee Valley The Bavarian theme town of Leavenworth has seen a proliferation of winery tasting rooms that have opened all over the state. Wineries with tasting rooms in Leavenworth now include Glen Fiona, Gold Digger Cellars, Kestrel Vintners, Maison de Padgett, Pasek Cellars, Silver Lake Winery, and Willow Crest Winery.

Snoqualmie Pass Want to play some golf in the piney woods on the east side of Snoqualmie Pass? Book a room at the new **Prospector Inn at Suncadia,** Roslyn (© **866/904-6300;** www.prospectorat suncadia.com), a small luxury lodge at the heart of a big golf resort community now under development.

The Columbia Gorge If you're touring the Washington side of the Columbia Gorge, you no longer have to cross the river to Hood River, Oregon, to find good food. In the little town of Bingen, **Viento,** 216 W. Steuben St. (Wash. 14), Bingen (© **509/493-0049;** www.viento kitchen.com), has brought an eclectic mélange of flavors to the hungry foodies on the north side of the river. Just want a pizza and a great microbrew? Head to Stevenson's **Walking Man Brewery,** 240 SW First St. (© **509/427-5520**), for an impressive selection of beers brewed on the premises.

EASTERN WASHINGTON Ellensburg Cave B Inn at Sagecliffe, 344 Silica Rd. NW, Quincy (© **888/785-2283** or 509/785-2283; www.cavebinn. com), one of Washington's most impressive new lodges, sits on 900-foot cliffs above the Columbia River in the middle of the state. Vineyards surround this fascinating inn and a winery is on the premises.

Yakima & the Wine Country New Yakima Valley wineries to search out include **Alexandria Nicole Cellars,** 717 Sixth St., Prosser (© 509/786-3497; www.alexandrianicolecellars.com); **Kana Winery,** 10 S. Second St., Yakima (© 509/453-6611; www.kanawinery. com); and **Sheridan Vineyard,** 2980 Gilbert Rd., Zillah (© 509/829-3205; www.sheridanvineyard.com). A couple of area wineries—Bookwalter and Alexandria Nicole—serve light meals.

Walla Walla Wineries continue to pop up in Walla Walla like champagne corks on New Year's Eve. Some to make note of include **Fort Walla Walla,** 127 E. Main St. (© 509/520-1095; www.fortwalla wallacellars.com); **Morrison Lane,** 201 W. Main St. (© 509/526-0229; www. morrisonlane.com); **Whitman Cellars,** 1015 W. Pine St. (© 509/529-1142; www.whitmancellars.com); **Five Star Cellars,** 840 C St. (© 509/527-8400; www.fivestarcellars.com); **Basel Cellars,** 2901 Old Milton Hwy. (© 509/522-0200; www.baselcellars.com); **Dusted Valley Vintners,** 1248 Old Milton Hwy. (© 509/525-1337; www.dustedvalley. com); and **Saviah Cellars,** 1979 JB George Rd. (© 509/520-5166; www. saviahcellars.com).

The caliber of Walla Walla restaurants ratcheted up another notch with the opening of **26brix,** 207 W. Main St. (© 509/526-4075; www.twentysixbrix. com), the quintessential wine-country restaurant.

Palouse How do you get people in one small eastern Washington town to drive 20 miles to another small town for dinner? You open the **Whoopemup Hollow Café,** 120 Main St., Waitsburg (© 509/337-9000), a pretty little place serving southern and Cajun food.

Spokane If you've got the kids along when you visit Spokane, be sure to take them to **Mobius Kids,** 808 W. Main Ave. (© 509/624-5437; www.mobiusspokane. org), a fun interactive children's museum. If the weather is hot, children will also enjoy spending time playing in the water at the Rotary Riverfront Fountain in Spokane's Riverfront Park. While you're in this downtown park, don't miss the new Spokane Falls SkyRide, with lilac-colored gondolas that swing out over Spokane Falls.

A couple of new wineries in Spokane are worth visiting. **Barrister Winery,** 1213 W. Railroad Ave. (© 509/465-3591; www.barristerwinery.com), is one of the best new wineries in the state. Don't miss it. **Robert Karl Cellars,** 115 W. Pacific Ave. (© 509/363-1353; www. robertkarl.com), also produces some good wines.

Spokane added another renovated historic hotel this past year. The **Montvale Hotel,** 1005 W. First Ave. (© 866/668-8253 or 509/747-1919; www.montvale hotel.com), was originally opened in 1899 to house miners. Today it is a luxurious boutique hotel with the feel of an urban lodge.

1

The Best of Washington

Despite what you might have heard to the contrary, there is more to Washington state than lattes, rain, and Microsoft. Washington is actually such a diverse state that it could have served as a model for the song "America the Beautiful." Out in the eastern high desert country, beautiful spacious skies are as big as Montana's (part of the Rocky Mountains even reaches into Washington). In the Cascades, mountains turn majestically purple at sunset. In the Palouse country of the southeastern corner of the state, amber waves of grain stripe the steep hillsides. In the Yakima, Wenatchee, and Chelan valleys, the fruited plains produce the world's most familiar apples (and some pretty good wine, too). The Pacific Coast has beaches white with foam, and with an inland sea across the Olympic Peninsula from the Pacific, the sun in Washington shines from sea to shining sea. Washington is indeed beautiful country.

The diversity of this state goes far beyond mere song lyrics, however. There's an island archipelago as beautiful as the coast of Maine (without the harsh winters). Beaches are long and sandy (though the waters are too cold for swimming). There are granite mountains as rugged as the Sierra Nevada (but with fewer hikers). Desert canyons are like those of the Southwest (though not as hot). Vineyard-covered hillsides resemble those of the Napa Valley (without the crowds). There's even a bayfront city with dauntingly steep streets (but no cable cars).

With such a complex and diverse landscape to be explored, planning a trip can be a daunting task. Where should we go? Where should we stay? Where should we eat? Planning a trip involves a lot of decisions, and, if you only have a week or two for your entire trip, you'll want to get the most from it. To help you get a better grip on the state's highlights, its not-to-be-missed attractions and activities, we've put together this list of the best in the state. Keep in mind that most are written up in more detail elsewhere in this book, but this chapter will give you an overview and get you started.

1 The Best Natural Attractions

- **The San Juan Islands:** Forested mountains rise up from the cold waters north of Puget Sound to form the archipelago known as the San Juan Islands. Bald eagles circle overhead while orca whales dive for salmon below. Such natural beauty is a powerful magnet and despite hordes of tourists in summer, the San Juans are the best summer vacation spot. See section 3 in chapter 6.

- **Olympic National Park:** This park has the only rainforests in the contiguous United States, and they make up a fascinating ecosystem. Living plants stake out every square inch of space, from towering Sitka spruce trees to mosses and lush ferns. The park preserves miles of pristine, fog-shrouded beaches and beautiful alpine and subalpine scenery with lush meadows. See chapter 8.

- **The North Cascades National Park Complex:** Comprised of one national park and two national recreation areas, this remote, rugged region is among the least explored. Most visitors view the park from the North Cascades Scenic Highway that has stupendous views on clear days, but is closed by snow nearly half the year. See section 1 in chapter 10.

- **Mount Rainier National Park:** With its glaciers and easily accessible alpine meadows, Mount Rainier is Washington's favorite mountain. Sunrise and Paradise are the two best vantage points for viewing the massive bulk of Mount Rainier, and in these two areas of the park, you'll also find some of the best hiking trails. See section 6 in chapter 10.

- **Mount St. Helens National Volcanic Monument:** Mount St. Helens is slowly recovering from the 1980 volcanic blast that turned one of the Cascades' most beautiful peaks into a scarred landscape of fallen trees and fields of ash, but it remains the only active volcano in the contiguous U.S. Several visitor centers portray the events of the 1980 eruption and what has happened since. See section 7 in chapter 10.

- **Columbia Gorge National Scenic Area:** Carved by ice-age floods 1,200 feet deep, the Columbia Gorge is a unique feature of the Northwest landscape. Waterfalls by the dozen cascade from the basalt cliffs on the Oregon side of the gorge, but the best wide-angle views are from the Washington side, which has one of the largest monoliths in the world. See section 8 in chapter 10.

2 The Best Outdoor Activities

- **Sea Kayaking in the San Juan Islands:** Emerald islands, clear water, orca whales, bald eagles, and remote campsites that are only reached by boat lure sea kayakers to the San Juan Islands. Paddle the islands on your own (if you're experienced) or go out with a guide for a few hours or a few days. See section 3 in chapter 6.

- **Hiking the Olympic Coast:** Within the contiguous U.S., very few miles of wilderness coastline are left. Among the longest, and most spectacular, are those of Olympic National Park on the west side of the Olympic Peninsula. Whether you want to do a good daylong hike, or several days of backpacking along the beach, you've got several options along this coast. See chapter 8.

- **Cross-Country Skiing in the Methow Valley:** This valley on the east side of Washington's North Cascades has more than 100 miles of immaculately groomed trails, making it one of the premier cross-country ski destinations in the country. Ski from one lodge to the next down the valley, or use one of the luxurious lodges as a base for daylong ski treks. See section 2 in chapter 10.

- **Hiking on Mount Rainier:** Fed by huge amounts of melting snow each summer, the meadows of wildflowers on the flanks of Mount Rainier burst into bloom each year in July. Through these colorful hillsides meander miles of hiking trails that are among the most memorable in the state. Sure, you'll encounter crowds, but the wildflower displays and Mount Rainier for a backdrop far outweigh the inconvenience of dealing with hordes of other hikers. See section 6 in chapter 10.

- **Climbing Mount St. Helens:** Though it isn't the highest peak in the Washington Cascades, Mount St.

Washington

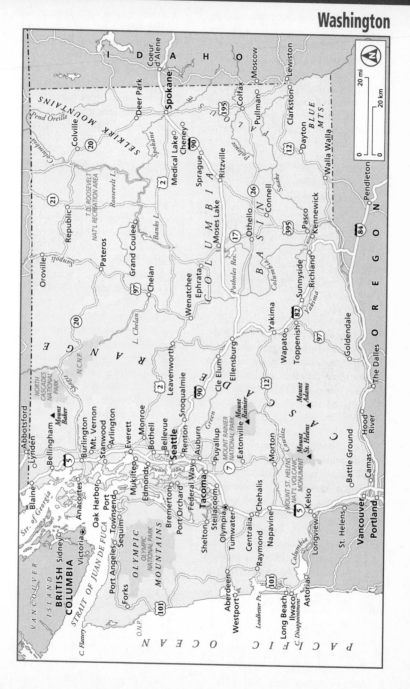

Helens is the most interesting mountain to climb (you'll need a permit, and numbers of climbers are limited). You don't need technical climbing skills, just lots of stamina and a tolerance for hiking in dusty conditions (if the snow has melted, you'll be hiking in volcanic ash). At press time, the summit was closed to climbers due to volcanic activity. See section 7 in chapter 10.

- **Windsurfing at Hood River:** Winds that blow through the Columbia Gorge whip up white-capped standing waves and have turned this area into the windsurfing capital of the United States, attracting boardsailors from around the world. See section 8 in chapter 10.

3 The Best Beaches

- **Alki Beach** (Seattle): In West Seattle, this is the closest Washington comes to a Southern California–style beach scene. There's a sandy beach and a paved path crowded with in-line skaters, walkers, and cyclists. Across the street are lots of cheap restaurants and places to buy sunglasses. See chapter 5.

- **Obstruction Pass State Park** (Orcas Island): Set at the end of a half-mile-long trail through the woods, this tiny cove is barely big enough for a dozen sea kayakers to beach their boats, but therein lies its charm. This is the quintessential little San Juan Islands cove beach, and you don't need a boat to get to it. See section 3 in chapter 6.

- **Deception Pass State Park Beaches** (Whidbey Island): This is the most popular state park in Washington, and the miles of beaches along two sides of Deception Pass are among the prettiest in the Puget Sound area. See section 1 in chapter 6.

- **Dungeness Spit** (Dungeness): With 6 miles of windswept sand stretching out to a lighthouse in the Strait of Juan de Fuca, Dungeness is a beach for hikers whose reward is the sight of the area's resident harbor seals. See section 2 in chapter 8.

- **Rialto Beach** (Olympic National Park outside Forks): Located on the north side of the Quillayute River, this beach is the southern terminus of a 29-mile-long stretch of wilderness beach. However, most visitors simply walk a mile up the beach to Hole in the Wall, a huge monolith through which the ocean's waves have bored a tunnel. See section 4 in chapter 8.

- **Second Beach & Third Beach** (Olympic National Park outside Forks): It's difficult to pick the best beach in the national park, since almost all are ruggedly beautiful, but these two beaches just outside the community of La Push are my personal favorites. Here you can hear the calls of eagles and gulls and contemplate the sheer vastness of the Pacific. See section 4 in chapter 8.

4 The Best Hikes

- **Trails Out of Hurricane Ridge** (Olympic National Park): Hurricane Ridge is the most easily accessible alpine region of Olympic National Park. From here and nearby Obstruction Peak, several hikes will give you a glimpse of a superb part of the Olympic wilderness. See section 3 in chapter 8.

- **Hall of Mosses Trail/Hoh River Trail** (Hoh River Valley): Whether you're up for a short walk in the woods or a multi-day backpacking trip, this is the best place to experience the Olympic Peninsula's famed rainforest. Don't forget your rain gear. See section 4 in chapter 8.
- **Chain Lakes Loop Trail** (Mount Baker): This 9-mile trail circling Table Mountain is one of the most breathtaking and rewarding hikes. With streams, lakes, cliffs, meadows, huckleberries, and plenty of views, this trail packs in everything that makes the Mount Baker area special. See section 1 in chapter 10.
- **The Maple Pass Loop Trail** (North Cascades Scenic Highway): Along the North Cascades Scenic Highway, you won't find a more rewarding hike. The trail climbs nearly 2,000 feet from Rainy Pass to a ridge with an astounding view of the mountains. See section 1 in chapter 10.
- **Trails Out of Sunrise** (Mount Rainier National Park): The Sunrise area, on the northeast flanks of Washington's Mount Rainier, has fabulous, unobstructed views of both the mountain and Emmons Glacier, the largest glacier in the contiguous 48 states. From Sunrise, pick from more than a dozen trails of different lengths heading to viewpoints and lakes. See section 6 in chapter 10.
- **The Beacon Rock Trail** (Columbia Gorge): Although this hike is less than 2 miles long, it makes up for the short length with its steep pitch. In fact, much of the trail is on metal stairs bolted to the sheer cliff face of Beacon Rock, a massive monolith that rivals the Rock of Gibraltar in size. The view from the top is superb. See section 8 in chapter 10.

5 The Best Scenic Drives

- **Chuckanut Drive:** This road winds south from Bellingham through the Chuckanut Mountains that rise straight up from the waters of Chuckanut and Samish bays. Across the water lie the San Juan Islands, and sunsets are spectacular. Larrabee State Park provides a chance to get out of your car and walk down to a pretty little beach. See section 5 in chapter 6.
- **The North Cascades Scenic Highway:** Passing through the most rugged and spectacular mountains in the Northwest, this highway did not open until 1972 due to the difficulty of building any road through Washington's glacier-carved North Cascades. It is closed for half the year due to snows and avalanches. See section 1 in chapter 10.
- **The Columbia River Scenic Highway:** Wash. 14 parallels the Columbia River from Vancouver, Washington, eastward through the Columbia Gorge, and it has some of the most awe-inspiring vistas in the Northwest. Visible across the river in Oregon are not only the waterfalls and basalt cliffs of the gorge, but also the snow-clad summit of Mount Hood. See section 8 in chapter 10.
- **The Yakima River Canyon:** Wash. 821, which connects Ellensburg with Yakima, is a little-known gem of a road. This route follows the Yakima River through a deep canyon bounded by rolling sagebrush hills and is a memorable alternative to I-82, which also connects Ellensburg and Yakima. See chapter 11.
- **The Palouse:** This wheat-farming region in southeastern Washington is a convoluted landscape of steep hills and narrow valleys, and a meandering drive through the region is a trip back

in time. Small towns and boldly striped hillsides make it the most fascinating farm country in the state. See section 4 in chapter 11.

- **Soap Lake to the Grand Coulee Dam:** The landscape of central Washington is that of a desert, but vast floodwaters once poured across it. A drive through the coulee country gives a glimpse at one of the most fascinating events in Northwest geologic history, with canyons, mineral lakes, caves, and a waterfall. See section 6 in chapter 11.

6 The Best B&Bs & Inns

- **The Gaslight Inn** (Seattle; ✆ 206/325-3654): Beautifully decorated with lots of original Stickley furniture, this inn consists of two houses in the Capitol Hill neighborhood. One house is done in a contemporary style, while the other will appeal to fans of the Arts-and-Crafts style. There's a swimming pool. See p. 85.

- **Spring Bay Inn** (Orcas Island; ✆ 360/376-5531): This secluded waterfront inn is a luxurious island retreat, and a stay includes not only a bed and breakfast, but brunch and a daily sea-kayak excursion. In-room fireplaces and a hot tub right on the beach add romance. See p. 178.

- **Inn on Orcas Island** (✆ 888/886-1661 or 360/376-5227): On the edge of a small bay and looking as if it were brought here from Martha's Vineyard or Nantucket, this luxurious inn is in a modern building that seems to have been built 100 years ago. See p. 178.

- **Willcox House** (The Kitsap Peninsula; ✆ 800/725-9477 or 360/830-4492): This 1930s Art Deco mansion on the shore of Hood Canal is straight from an old Hollywood movie (movie stars stayed here back in the '30s and '40s). See p. 203.

- **Chinaberry Hill** (Tacoma; ✆ 253/272-1282): Located in Tacoma's Stadium Historic District, this grand Victorian is as impressive as any of the historic B&Bs in Port Townsend. The inn is steeped in classic Northwest

elegance and abounds in beautiful woodwork. See p. 212.

- **Thornewood Castle Inn** (Lakewood; ✆ 253/584-4393): Few B&Bs in America can claim to be castles, but Thornewood, built in 1909, certainly can. With 28 bedrooms and 22 bathrooms, this sprawling mansion is as close as you'll come to a European manor home in the U.S. See p. 213.

- **Hoquiam's Castle** (Hoquiam; 360/533-2005): Built in 1897 by a local timber baron, this stately Victorian inn is an amazing assemblage of turrets and gables, balconies and bay windows. The town of Hoquiam isn't a major tourist destination, but this inn is reason enough to spend a weekend in the area. See p. 260.

- **Abendblume Inn** (Leavenworth; ✆ 800/669-7634 or 509/548-4059): Of the many alpine chalet accommodations in Leavenworth, this is the most luxurious. The attention to detail in the construction of this chalet makes the inn an especially enjoyable place to spend a romantic weekend. See p. 299.

- **Run of the River Inn & Refuge** (Leavenworth; ✆ 800/288-6491 or 509/548-7171): Set amid beautiful rock gardens on a side channel of the Icicle Creek, this rustic, yet contemporary log inn is a tranquil place to stay. The innkeepers are quite helpful and eager to share their love of the area. See p. 300.

- **Cave B Inn at Sagecliffe** (Ellensburg; © **888/785-2283** or 509/785-2283): Set atop 900-foot cliffs overlooking the Columbia River in central Washington, this inn offers luxury in a remote location, and is worth the drive. See p. 327.

7 The Best Mountain Lodges & Resorts

- **Lake Crescent Lodge** (Olympic National Park west of Port Angeles; © **360/928-3211**): On the shore of Lake Crescent, a landlocked fjord in Olympic National Park, this lodge is the best base for exploring the park's north side. It has simple rooms in the old lodge building, larger rooms in newer buildings, and rustic cabins. See p. 243.

- **Lake Quinault Lodge** (Lake Quinault; © **800/562-6672** or 360/288-2900): This gracefully aging lodge on the shore of Lake Quinault has the most character of any of the lodges scattered around the perimeter of Olympic National Park. It's a cross between a mountain lodge and a classic lake resort. See p. 250.

- **Sun Mountain Lodge** (Winthrop; © **800/572-0493** or 509/996-2211): Perched atop a mountain and overlooking the remote Methow Valley, this is the premier mountain resort. Luxurious and rustic, it's a base for cross-country skiing in winter and hiking and mountain biking in summer. See p. 283.

- **Freestone Inn** (Mazama; © **800/639-3809** or 509/996-3906): This impressive log lodge beside a small trout lake at the west end of the Methow Valley is not as extensive a place as nearby Sun Mountain Lodge, but the guest rooms are among the most luxurious in the state. See p. 283.

- **Mountain Home Lodge** (Leavenworth; © **800/414-2378** or 509/548-7077): Set in the middle of a large pasture high on the slopes above the town of Leavenworth, this lodge enjoys a breathtaking view of the Stuart Range, and in winter it's only accessible by snow coach (complimentary transport provided by the lodge). See p. 299.

- **Sleeping Lady** (Leavenworth; © **800/574-2123** or 509/548-6344): Although primarily a conference resort, this place on the outskirts of Bavarian Leavenworth is far too pleasant to be reserved for those in town on business. With the feel of an upscale summer camp, the lodge is tucked amid granite boulders and ponderosa pines. See p. 299.

- **Salish Lodge & Spa** (Snoqualmie Falls; © **800/272-5474** or 425/888-2556): Perched on the brink of Snoqualmie Falls near the town of North Bend, this elegant country lodge is a favorite weekend getaway for Seattleites who come to be pampered at the spa and to enjoy the nearby farm country, mountain trails, and ski slopes. See p. 304.

- **Paradise Inn** (Mount Rainier National Park; © **360/569-2275**): Perched high on the slopes of Washington's Mount Rainier, this classic mountain lodge was built in 1917. Because the lodge is only open May through October, it books up early in the year and stays packed throughout the summer. You just can't beat the location. Unfortunately, this inn will be closed for major rehabilitation and structural improvements in 2006 and 2007. See p. 311.

- **Skamania Lodge** (Stevenson; © **800/221-7117** or 509/427-7700): Set amid the grandeur of the Columbia Gorge, this modern mountain resort makes the ideal base for exploring the gorge. The resort's golf course has a very distracting view of the Oregon side of the Columbia Gorge. See p. 322.

- **Bonneville Hot Springs Resort** (© **866/459-1678** or 509/427-7767): Tucked amid the trees not far from Bonneville Dam, this hot springs resort has a traditional elegance. There are no great views, but the spa and warm-springs-fed pool make up for it. See p. 322.

8 The Best Waterfront Resorts & Lodges

- **Woodmark Hotel on Lake Washington** (Kirkland; © **800/822-3700** or 425/822-3700): Set on spacious grounds on the eastern shore of Lake Washington, this luxurious hotel is the Seattle area's finest waterfront hotel and has a resort feel. See p. 90.
- **Friday Harbor House** (Friday Harbor; © **866/722-7356** or 360/378-8455): This one isn't right on the water, but it still has the most luxurious accommodations on San Juan Island, and guest rooms have views of the water and distant island peaks. See p. 170.
- **Rosario Resort & Spa** (Orcas Island; © **800/562-8820** or 360/376-2222): With an elegant, historic mansion as its focal point and activities and amenities to keep you busy for a week's vacation, this is the premier resort in the San Juan Islands. See p. 178.
- **La Conner Channel Lodge** (La Conner; © **888/466-4113** or 360/466-1500): Set on the shore of the Swinomish Channel, this inn is steeped in Northwest styling. River rocks and weathered wood siding lend an air of age to the exterior, brightened by lovely perennial gardens. Guest rooms have balconies and fireplaces, fir accents and slate floors, for an unexpected sophistication. See p. 187.
- **The Inn at Langley** (Whidbey Island; © **360/221-3033**): The setting alone, overlooking Saratoga Passage, may be enough to rank this place firmly among the best small inns in the region. However, Japanese-influenced styling, soaking tubs with water views, and fireplaces are all uncommon luxuries at this romantic retreat. See p. 158.
- **Semiahmoo Resort** (Blaine; © **800/770-7992** or 360/318-2000): On a spit of land across the water from Canada, this is Washington's premier golf and beach resort. Its long stretch of beachfront makes it a great place to escape, whether you want to play golf or tennis or just take a walk on the sand. See p. 193.
- **The Captain Whidbey Inn** (Whidbey Island; © **800/366-4097** or 360/678-4097): This unusual inn was built in 1907 of local madrona-tree logs, which give it a thoroughly unique appearance. The island's seafaring history is evoked throughout the inn, and the seat in front of the lobby's beach-stone fireplace is a wonderful spot to spend a gray afternoon. See p. 158.
- **The Resort at Ludlow Bay** (Port Ludlow; © **877/805-0868** or 360/437-7000): Located a few miles south of Port Townsend, this small, luxury inn offers all the best aspects of the San Juan Islands without the hassles of the ferries. An adjacent golf course adds to the resort's appeal. See p. 229.
- **Kalaloch Lodge** (Forks; © **866/525-2562** or 360/962-2271): Comprised primarily of aging bluff-top cabins overlooking a wild and

windswept beach, this is Olympic National Park's only oceanfront lodge. Although rustic, it is extremely popular due to its beachside setting. See p. 250.

- **Alderbrook Resort & Spa** (Union; ✆ 800/622-9370 or 360/898-2200):

Although it's way off the main tourist routes, this recently opened waterfront resort on Hood Canal is the most luxurious lodge in the Olympic Peninsula area. See p. 253.

9 The Best Off-the-Beaten-Path Restaurants

- **The Herbfarm Restaurant** (Woodinville; ✆ 425/485-5300): This restaurant northeast of Seattle is adjacent to several wineries. Once little more than a roadside farmstand specializing in herbs, over the years it has become the most highly acclaimed (and most expensive) restaurant in the state. See p. 104.
- **The Chef's Kitchen Restaurant** (Langley; ✆ 360/221-3033): Set in a quintessentially Northwestern inn on Whidbey Island, this is one of the state's most memorable restaurants. It serves some of the best (and most expensive) multi-course gourmet dinners in Washington. See p. 159.
- **Christina's** (Orcas Island; ✆ 360/ 376-4904): For more than 25 years, this has been the premier restaurant on Orcas Island. The food is innovative, the ingredients fresh and seasonal, and the water view unforgettable. See p. 180.
- **Bay Café** (Lopez Island; ✆ 360/468-3700): Classy and casual, this epitomizes the Lopez Island experience— quiet, comfortable, and unpretentious. Even if you aren't staying on Lopez, meals are so good that it's worth catching the ferry to dine here. See p. 184.
- **Molly Ward Gardens** (Poulsbo; ✆ 360/779-4471): Housed in an old barn in a small rural valley outside the Scandinavian theme town of Poulsbo, this restaurant sums up Northwest lifestyles with its country

gardens, eclectic decor, and creative cuisine. See p. 204.
- **The Ajax Cafe** (Port Hadlock; ✆ 360/385-3450): With excellent food, live old-time music on the weekends, and silly hats hanging from the ceiling (and frequently worn by dinner guests), this hidden gem of a restaurant is south of Port Townsend. Housed in an old wooden waterfront building, it's a favorite for those with something to celebrate. See p. 231.
- **The Ark Restaurant & Bakery** (Nahcotta; ✆ 360/665-4133): Oyster lovers note: This restaurant on the Long Beach Peninsula is just down the road from Oysterville, adjacent to oyster farms and an oyster packing plant, so the shellfish is as fresh as it gets. See p. 267.
- **Sun Mountain Lodge** (Winthrop; ✆ 800/572-0493 or 509/996-4707): If you get vertigo easily, you may want to forego meals at this precipitously perched dining room overlooking the Methow Valley. However, if you relish creative cooking accompanied by dizzying mountain views, this restaurant should not be missed. See p. 284.
- **26brix** (Walla Walla; ✆ 509/526-4075): Foie gras? Caviar? Veal sweetbreads? Walla Walla has broken into the culinary big time with this winecountry restaurant. Chef Mike Davis was formerly executive chef at the Seattle area's luxurious Salish Lodge. See p. 346.

- **Whitehouse-Crawford Restaurant** (Walla Walla; ☎ 509/525-2222): In downtown Walla Walla, at the heart of Washington's fastest-growing wine region, this restaurant in a former mill building shares space with a winery. The scene and menu have a true Seattle feel. See p. 347.

10 The Best Wineries (Open to the Public)

- **Portteus Vineyards** (Yakima Valley; ☎ 509/829-6970): Intensely flavored, full-bodied red wines are the specialty at this winery about midway down the Yakima Valley. Prices are moderate and the red table wine is also a great value. See p. 331.

- **Sheridan Vineyard** (Yakima Valley; 509/829-3205): Focusing production on bordeaux blends and syrah, this little winery produces some highly distinctive fruit-driven wines from estate-grown grapes. See p. 331.

- **Wineglass Cellars** (Yakima Valley; ☎ 509/829-3011): This small, unassuming, family-run winery produces some of the state's most awesome red wines. In addition, it's one of the most underrated and little known wineries in the Yakima Valley. See p. 332.

- **Amavi Cellars** (Walla Walla; ☎ 509/525-3541): One of the newer wineries in Walla Walla, this is a sister winery to the celebrated Pepper Bridge Winery. The syrah here is among the finest in the region and prices are under $25. See p. 342.

- **Five Star Cellars** (Walla Walla; ☎ 509/527-8400): Producing rich, dark, fully extracted red wines with soft tannins, this little Walla Walla winery produces stellar and very drinkable wines. Definitely a rising star on the local wine scene. See p. 344.

- **Rulo Winery** (Walla Walla; ☎ 509/525-7856): Small and family-owned, Rulo crafts complex, full-bodied syrah, creamy chardonnay, and aromatic viognier. Reasonable prices and high quality make it truly memorable. See p. 345.

- **Tamarack Cellars** (Walla Walla; ☎ 509/526-3533): Winemaker Ron Colvin crafts a small number of lush, memorable red wines at his little winery at the Walla Walla airport. The emphasis is on red wines with silky tannins and big fruit character. See p. 344.

- **Woodward Canyon Winery** (Walla Walla; ☎ 509/525-4129): This winery produces some of Washington's premier red wines, yet surprisingly, it offers great wines at $20 or less (and plenty of more expensive bottles). See p. 343.

- **Barrister Winery** (Spokane; ☎ 509/465-3591; www.barristerwinery.com): Started by two lawyers (thus the name), this winery in the up-and-coming warehouse district of downtown Spokane produces delicious red wines with a perfect blend of fruit, tannin, and oakiness. See p. 353.

- **Townshend Cellar** (Spokane; ☎ 509/238-1400; www.townshendcellar.com): Quite a few Washington wineries are now making port, but few make them as good as this little, out-of-the-way winery north of Spokane. The huckleberry port is pure ambrosia. See p. 354.

11 The Best Family Attractions & Activities

- **Seattle Center** (Seattle): As the site of the Space Needle, Seattle Center is one of the city's required stops. However, families will also find here a children's museum, a children's theater, an interactive science museum, amusement park rides, and an arcade area. See p. 113.

- **Museum of Flight:** Airplanes may not be quite as fascinating to kids as fire engines and trains, but this museum has so many cool airplanes and things to do that kids usually don't want to leave. See p. 119.

- **Whale-Watching Tours in the San Juan Islands:** Sure, you can see orca whales perform at marine parks, but in the San Juan Islands during the summer, you can see genuinely free Willies, and lots of them. During whale-watching tours, minke whales, harbor seals, and even bald eagles may be spotted. See section 3 in chapter 6.

- **Fort Worden State Park** (Port Townsend): With a beach, old gun batteries, a science center with tidepool touch tanks, and hiking trails, this park is a big entertainment center for kids. See p. 226.

- **Point Defiance Park** (Tacoma): This gigantic city park at the north end of Tacoma packs in more fun stuff for kids than they could hope to do in a day. It has a zoo, a replica of a historic trading fort, and an old-time logging camp. See p. 209.

- **Long Beach:** With minigolf, horseback riding, miles of wide beaches, and perfect winds for kite flying, this beach community on the southern Washington coast is the state's best family beach. See section 2 in chapter 9.

12 The Best Small Towns

- **La Conner:** Surrounded by tulip fields and filled with art galleries and interesting shops, this former fishing and farming town gets jammed on weekends, but stop by on a weekday or in the off season, and you'll be easily seduced by its vintage charm. See section 4 in chapter 6.

- **Langley:** Near the south end of Whidbey Island, this former fishing village is now something of an upscale arts community. Art galleries, antiques and fashion shops, and several good restaurants are all right on the shore of Saratoga Passage, and some buildings even rise straight out of the water. See section 1 in chapter 6.

- **Port Townsend:** Late in the 19th century, this town on the Olympic Peninsula was poised to become the region's most important city, but when the railroad passed it by, it slipped into obscurity. Today, Port

Townsend is obscure no more. With block after block of Victorian homes and a waterfront setting, it is now a favorite weekend destination for Seattleites. See section 1 in chapter 8.

- **Leavenworth:** Lederhosen? Dirndls? Polka parties? Sounds like someplace to avoid, but actually, the Bavarian theme town of Leavenworth works. Maybe there are too many cuckoo clocks and nutcrackers for sale, but those mountains on the edge of town are the real thing. See section 4 in chapter 10.

- **Winthrop:** If you saw an 1890s photo of Winthrop and then visited this remote community in north central Washington, you would think the town was caught in a time warp. It just doesn't look much different than it did back then. See section 2 in chapter 10.

2

Planning Your Trip to Washington

Planning your trip before you leave home can make all the difference between enjoying your vacation and wishing you'd stayed home. In fact, for many people, planning a trip is half the fun of going. If you're one of those people, then this chapter should prove useful. When should I go? What is this trip going to cost me? Can I catch a festival during my visit? Where should I head to pursue my favorite sport? These are some questions we'll answer in this chapter. Additionally, you can contact information sources listed to find out more about Washington and to take a look at photos (in brochures or on the Web) that will get you excited about your upcoming trip.

1 The Regions in Brief

The state of Washington covers 68,139 square miles—roughly the same area as all of New England. Within this large area can be found surprising geographical diversity, including an inland sea dotted with hundreds of islands, temperate rainforests where rainfall is measured in feet, an arid land of sagebrush and junipers, several distinct mountain ranges, an active volcano, the West's most important river, and, of course, hundreds of thousands of acres of coniferous forests (hence the state's nickname—the Evergreen State).

Puget Sound Puget Sound, a convoluted maze of waterways, is a vast inland sea that stretches for more than 80 miles, from north of Seattle south to Olympia. Created when glaciers receded at the end of the last ice age, Puget Sound is characterized by deep waterways surrounded by hilly, forested terrain. Because the sound's protected waters make such good harbors and are so full of fish and shellfish, this area has been the most densely populated region of the state since long before the first Europeans sailed into these waters.

Today, the eastern shore of the sound has become the largest metropolitan area in the state—one huge Pugetopolis that includes Seattle, Tacoma, Olympia, and dozens of smaller cities and bedroom communities. The western and southernmost reaches of the sound are much less developed.

The San Juan Islands Lying just to the north of Puget Sound, the San Juan Islands are a lush, mountainous archipelago, home to orca whales, harbor seals, and bald eagles. Of the 175 or so named San Juan Islands, only four are accessible by public ferry and, of these, only three—San Juan, Orcas, and Lopez—have accommodations (although the fourth, Shaw, has a campground). The mild climate, watery vistas, and quiet, rural character of these islands have made the San Juans the state's favorite summer vacation destination. As such, the islands are packed to overflowing throughout the summer and it can be impossible to get a hotel reservation at the last minute. A summer trip to the San Juans definitely requires plenty of advance planning. It also requires a great deal of patience, as waits for ferries can stretch into hours. To avoid the crowds, visit in spring or fall, when the weather is often just as good as in the summer. Because the San Juans lie within the rain shadow of the Olympic Mountains, they get far less rain than Seattle.

The Olympic Peninsula   Aside from a thin necklace of private land around its perimeter, this huge peninsula, wedged between Puget Sound and the Pacific Ocean, is almost entirely public land. At the heart of the peninsula is Olympic National Park, which encompasses almost the entirety of the Olympic Mountains. Surrounding the park is Olympic National Forest, which is distinguishable from the park by its many clear-cut areas. Due primarily to the immensity of the forests and the size of the trees here, the forests of the Olympic Peninsula have, over the past 100 years, seen some of the most intensive logging in the nation. The gigantic size of the trees here is due to the astounding amount of rain that falls on parts of the peninsula. The western slopes of the Olympic Mountains contain some of the only temperate rainforests in the contiguous United States, and in these forests, the annual rainfall often exceeds 150 inches. Rugged, remote beaches separated by rocky headlands characterize the Pacific shore of the peninsula, while along the north coast, there are a number of large towns, including the historic Victorian seaport of Port Townsend.

Southwest Washington   The southwest corner of the state is, for the most part, a sparsely populated region of huge tree farms. However, along the southern coast, there are long sandy beaches and numerous beach resorts and towns, which, though popular with Portlanders and the residents of Puget Sound, lack a distinctly Northwest character. Inland,

up the Columbia River, lies the city of Vancouver (not to be confused with Vancouver, British Columbia), which is rich in regional history, but overshadowed by Portland, Oregon, across the Columbia River.

The Cascade Range   Dividing the state into eastern and western regions, the Washington Cascades are actually two very distinct mountain ranges. The North Cascades are jagged, glaciated granite peaks, while the central and southern Washington Cascades are primarily volcanic in origin. Mount St. Helens, which erupted with awe-inspiring force in 1980, is the only one of these volcanoes to be active in recent years, but even Mount Rainier, the highest mountain in the state, is merely dormant and is expected to erupt again sometime in the next few hundred years (probably with devastating effect, considering the large population that now resides at the foot of the mountain). Within this mountain range are North Cascades National Park, Mount Rainier National Park, Mount St. Helens National Volcanic Monument, the third deepest lake in the country (Lake Chelan), a half-dozen ski areas, and a couple of interesting little theme towns. If you're thinking about a summer vacation in these mountains, keep in mind that the snow at higher elevations often doesn't melt until well into July.

Eastern Washington   While to the west of the Cascade Range, all is gray skies and green forests, to the east the sun shines 300 days a year and less than 10 inches of rain falls in an average year. Although this sun-drenched and sparsely populated shrub steppe is highly valued by waterlogged residents of western Washington, it is, with the exception of its wine country, of little interest to out-of-state visitors. Irrigation waters from the Columbia River have allowed the region to become an agricultural powerhouse. From the Yakima Valley to the Walla Walla area, large areas of wine-grape vineyards have helped make Washington the second-largest producer of wine in the country. Also, in the Yakima, Wenatchee, and Chelan valleys, apple orchards produce the bulk of the nation's apple crop. Out in the southeast corner of the state lie the rolling Palouse Hills, where rich soils sustain the most productive wheat fields in the nation. Spokane is the region's largest metropolitan area.

2 Visitor Information

For information on Washington, contact the **Washington State Tourism Office,** P.O. Box 42525, Olympia, WA 98504 (✆ **800/544-1800;** www.experience washington.com). For information on Seattle and vicinity, contact the **Seattle's Convention and Visitors Bureau,** 701 Pike St., Suite 800, Seattle, WA 98101 (✆ **206/461-5840;** www.seeseattle.org), which operates a Citywide Concierge Center inside the Washington State Convention and Trade Center, Eighth Avenue and Pike Street, main level (✆ **206/461-5888**). If you're surfing the Net to search for information on the Seattle area, check out **www.ci.seattle.wa.us/html/visitor,** the city of Seattle's visitor information site.

Also, keep in mind that most cities and towns in Washington have either a tourist office or a chamber of commerce that can provide you with information. When approaching cities and towns, watch for signs along the highway directing you to these information centers. See the individual chapters for specific addresses.

To get information on outdoor recreation in national parks and national forests of Washington, contact the **Outdoor Recreation Information Center,** Seattle REI Building, 222 Yale Ave. N., Seattle, WA 98109 (✆ **206/470-4060;** www.nps.gov/ccso/oric.htm).

For information on Washington state parks, contact **Washington State Parks and Recreation Commission,** 7150 Cleanwater Lane (P.O. Box 42650), Olympia, WA 98504-2650 (✆ **360/902-8844;** www.parks.wa.gov).

3 Money

ATMS

The easiest and best way to get cash away from home is from an ATM (automated teller machine). The **Cirrus** (✆ **800/424-7787;** www.mastercard.com) and **PLUS** (✆ **800/843-7587;** www.visa.com) networks span the globe; look at the back of your bank card to see which network you're on, then call or check online for ATM locations at your destination. Be sure you know your personal identification number (PIN) and daily withdrawal limit before you depart. *Note:* Remember that many banks impose a fee every time you use a card at another bank's ATM. In addition, the bank from which you withdraw cash may charge its own fee. To compare banks' ATM fees within the U.S., use **www.bankrate.com**.

You can use your credit card to receive cash advances at ATMs. Keep in mind that credit card companies protect themselves from theft by limiting maximum withdrawals outside their home country, so call your credit card company before you leave home. And keep in mind that you'll pay interest from the moment of your withdrawal.

TRAVELER'S CHECKS

Traveler's checks are something of an anachronism from the days before the ATM made cash accessible at any time. Given the fees you'll pay for ATM use at banks other than your own, however, you might be better off with traveler's checks if you'll be withdrawing money often.

You can get traveler's checks at almost any bank. **American Express** offers denominations of $20, $50, $100, $500, and (for cardholders only) $1,000. You'll pay a service charge ranging from 1% to 4%. You can also get American Express traveler's checks over the phone by calling ✆ **800/221-7282;** Amex gold and platinum cardholders who use this number are exempt from the 1% fee.

Visa offers traveler's checks at Citibank locations nationwide, as well as at several other banks. The service charge ranges between 1.5% and 2%; checks come in denominations of $20, $50, $100, $500, and $1,000. Call ✆ **800/732-1322** for information. AAA members can obtain Visa checks for a $9.95 fee (for checks up to $1,500) at most AAA offices or by calling ✆ **866/339-3378. MasterCard** also offers traveler's checks. Call ✆ **800/223-9920** for a location near you.

CREDIT CARDS

Credit cards are another safe way to carry money. They also provide a convenient record of all your expenses and generally offer relatively good exchange rates. You can also withdraw cash advances from your credit cards at banks or ATMs, provided you know your PIN. If you don't know yours, call the number on the back of your credit card and ask the bank to send it to you. It usually takes 5 to 7 business days, though some banks will provide the number over the phone if you tell them your mother's maiden name or some other personal information. Keep in mind that many banks now assess a 1% to 3% transaction fee on all charges you incur abroad (whether you're using the local currency or U.S. dollars). However, credit cards still may be the smart way to go when you factor in things like exorbitant ATM fees and the higher exchange rates and service fees you'll pay with traveler's checks.

4 When to Go

If you're reading this section, there's probably one question on your mind: When can I visit and not get rained on? The answer, of course, is never. Although the Northwest's infamous rains fall primarily between October and early July, it can rain any month of the year, so be sure to bring an umbrella or rain gear of some sort with you. This is especially important if you plan on visiting the Olympic Peninsula, parts of which receive more than 150 inches of rain each year. In fact, if you visit any part of the coast, expect grayer, wetter weather than in the Seattle area. From the coast to the Cascade Range, moist winds off the Pacific Ocean keep temperatures mild year-round, so you'll likely need a sweater or light jacket at night, even if you visit in August.

July and August are the most reliably rainless months of the year and, consequently, are the most popular times of the year to visit Washington. It is during these 2 months that the sun is seen most often and rain is almost unheard of (though not unknown). During these dry summer months, Washington families flock to the San Juan Islands to, among other things, watch the region's famous orca whales feeding in the waters off San Juan Island. July and August are also the state's main festival months, and several of the big festivals in the Seattle area can make finding a hotel room on a festival weekend difficult.

Labor Day weekend aside, September is one of the best months to visit. Skies are often still cloudless, and kids are back in school (the crowds at popular destinations, like the San Juan Islands and Mount Rainier, are really bad only on weekends). In the mountains, wildflowers often still bloom (though peak bloom in the Cascade Range and Olympic Mountains is July–Aug).

With the coming of the rains, Washingtonians begin spending far more time indoors and consequently, the performing arts in Seattle and other major cities begin their annual seasons. So, if you're keen on catching the Seattle Opera or some of Seattle's fringe theater, you'll need to plan a rainy season visit. This may not be as bad as it sounds considering the fact that hotels in Seattle offer substantial discounts during the dreary winter months. Keep in mind, though, that winters usually include one or two blasts of Arctic air that bring snow and freezing weather to the Seattle area.

Winter also brings the ski season and sometimes record-setting snowfalls, such as that of the winter of 1998–99, which dumped close to 100 feet of snow on Mount Baker. While the snow in Washington can be heavy and rains often fall in the mountains in the middle of winter, there are several very popular ski areas in the Cascades, as well as some smaller ski areas in eastern Washington.

Note that the preceding discussion applies to the west side of the Cascades. East of the Cascades, the climate is very different and some regions, sometimes referred to as the high desert, are characterized by temperature extremes and a lack of rain. These areas can be very cold in the winter and can get moderate amounts of snow in the foothill regions. In summer, the weather can be blazing hot, though nights are often cool enough to require a sweater or light jacket. The dry lands of eastern Washington are primarily agricultural regions, and it is here that most of the state's wine grapes are grown. In winter, most wineries that are open to the public cut their hours or close down completely.

Seattle's Average Temperature & Days of Rain

Jan	Feb	Mar	Apr	May	June	July	Aug	Sept	Oct	Nov	Dec
Temp. (°F)	46	50	53	58	65	69	75	74	69	60	52	47
Temp. (°C)	8	10	11	15	18	21	24	23	21	16	11	8
Rain (days)	19	16	17	14	10	9	5	7	9	14	18	20

WASHINGTON CALENDAR OF EVENTS

For additional information on events in Washington State, check the calendar section on the Washington State Tourism Office website at **www.experiencewashington.com**.

February

Northwest Flower & Garden Show (© 800/229-6311 or 206/789-5333; www.gardenshow.com), Washington State Convention and Trade Center. This massive show for avid gardeners has astonishing floral displays. Second week of February.

Red Wine and Chocolate (© 800/258-7270; www.yakimavalleywine.com), Yakima Valley. Sample Yakima Valley reds, accompanied by tastings of decadent chocolate desserts. Presidents' Weekend.

April

Skagit Valley Tulip Festival (© 360/428-5959; www.tulipfestival.org), La Conner. An hour north of Seattle, acres of tulips and daffodils cover the Skagit Valley with broad swaths of color, creating an enchanting landscape. Very festive. All month.

Spring Barrel Tasting (© 800/258-7270; www.yakimavalleywine.com), Yakima Valley. Straight-from-the-barrel wine tasting and spring-release wines at Yakima Valley wineries. Last full weekend in April.

Washington State Apple Blossom Festival (© 509/662-3616; www.appleblossom.org), Wenatchee. Many different events, including a parade and activities for families. End of April to early May.

May

Opening Day of Boating Season (℗ 206/325-1000; www.seattleyacht club.org), Lake Union and Lake Washington. A parade of boats and much fanfare take place as Seattle boaters bring out everything from kayaks to yachts. First Saturday in May.

Irrigation Festival (℗ 360/683-6197; www.irrigationfestival.com), Sequim. More than 110 years old, this is the oldest continuously held festival in Washington, and it has a grand parade, dancing, and arts and crafts. Early May.

Seattle Maritime Festival (℗ 206/728-3163; www.portseattle.org). Tugboat races are the highlight of this annual Port of Seattle event. Festivities are centered on the Bell Street Pier (Pier 66) on the Seattle waterfront. Mid-May.

Viking Fest (℗ 360/779-FEST; vikingfest.org), Poulsbo. Norwegian heritage on display in picturesque Poulsbo, with a parade and entertainment. Mid-May.

Spokane Lilac Festival (℗ 509/535-4554; www.lilacfestival.org), Spokane. For nearly 70 years, this event has celebrated the blooming of the lilacs. Don't miss the lilac gardens at Manito Park. Mid-May.

Seattle International Film Festival (℗ 206/324-9996; www.seattlefilm.com), at theaters around town. New foreign and independent films are screened over several weeks during this highly regarded film festival. Mid-May to mid-June.

Northwest Folklife Festival (℗ 206/684-7300; www.nwfolklife.org), Seattle Center. This is the largest folk festival in the country, with dozens of national and regional folk musicians performing on numerous stages. In addition, there are crafts vendors from all over the Northwest, with lots of good food and dancing. Memorial Day weekend.

June

Mural-in-a-Day (℗ 800/569-3982 or 509/865-3262), Toppenish. The small town of Toppenish has covered its blank walls with murals, and each June, one more is added in a day of intense painting. Early June.

July

Fourth of Jul-Ivar's (℗ 206/587-6500; www.ivars.net), Myrtle Edwards Park, north end of Seattle waterfront. Fireworks over Elliott Bay. July 4th.

Washington Mutual Family Fourth at Lake Union (℗ 206/281-7788; www.onereel.org), Lake Union. This is Seattle's other main Fourth of July fireworks display. July 4th.

Lake Union Wooden Boat Festival and Classic Speedboat Show (℗ 206/382-2628; www.cwb.org), Center for Wooden Boats. Featured are classic speedboats and wooden boats, both old and new, from all over the Northwest. Races, demonstrations, food, and entertainment. July 4th weekend.

Walla Walla Sweet Onion Festival (℗ 509/525-1031; www.sweetonions.org), Walla Walla. Onion-themed entertainment and food booths feature the delicious local onion. Mid-July.

Bellevue Arts & Crafts Fair (℗ 415/519-0742; www.bellevueart.org), Bellevue Square, Bellevue. This is the largest arts-and-fine-crafts fair in the Northwest. Last weekend in July.

Seafair (℗ 206/728-0123; www.seafair.com). This is the biggest Seattle event of the year, with daily festivities—parades, hydroplane boat races, an air show with the Navy's Blue Angels, the Torchlight Parade, ethnic festivals, sporting events, and open house on naval ships. Events take place all over Seattle. Early July to early August.

Pilchuck Glass School Open House (© 206/621-8422; www.pilchuck.com), Stanwood. If you're a fan of glass artist Dale Chihuly, you won't want to miss an opportunity to visit the school that helped him make a name for himself. The open house is immensely popular, so buy tickets early. Mid-July.

August

Chief Seattle Days (© 360/598-3311), at Suquamish tribal headquarters. Celebration of Northwest Native American culture across Puget Sound from Seattle. Third weekend in August.

Washington State International Kite Festival (© 800/451-2542; www.kitefestival.com), Long Beach. World-class kite-flying competition. Third week in August.

Makah Days (© 360/645-2201; www.makah.com), Neah Bay. Canoe races, Native American arts, and salmon bake presented by the Makah tribe in the northwest corner of the Olympic Peninsula. End of August.

September

Bumbershoot, the Seattle Arts Festival (© 206/281-7788; www.bumbershoot.org). Seattle's second most popular festival derives its peculiar name from a British term for an umbrella—an obvious reference to the rainy weather. Lots of rock music and other events pack Seattle's youthful set into Seattle Center and other venues. You'll find plenty of arts and crafts on display, too. Labor Day weekend.

Ellensburg Rodeo (© 800/637-2444 or 509/962-7831; www.ellensburgrodeo.com), Ellensburg. The state's biggest rodeo, with a carnival and both country music and rock bands. Labor Day weekend.

Wooden Boat Festival (© 360/344-3436; www.woodenboat.org), Port Townsend. Historic boats on display, with demonstrations. Early September.

Western Washington Fair (© 253/841-5045; www.thefair.com), Puyallup. One of the largest fairs in the nation. Third week in September.

October

Issaquah Salmon Days Festival (© 425/392-0661; www.salmondays.org). This festival in Issaquah, 15 miles east of Seattle, celebrates the annual return of salmon that spawn within the city limits. First full weekend in October.

Kinetic Sculpture Race (© 888/365-6978; www.kineticrace.info), Port Townsend. The two rules of this race are (1) the vehicle must be people-powered; and (2) the wackier the contraption, the better. First Sunday in October.

Oktoberfest (© 509/548-5807; www.leavenworth.org), Leavenworth. A traditional Oktoberfest in this Bavarian town comes complete with kegs of beer shipped in from Munich and traditional German dancing. First and second weekend in October.

Cranberrian Fair (© 800/451-2542 or 360/642-3446), Ilwaco, Long Beach Peninsula. Cranberry bog tours, cranberry products, arts and crafts. Mid-October.

November

Thanksgiving in the Wine Country (© 800/258-7270; www.yakimavalleywine.com), Yakima Valley. Foods and the wines that complement them are offered for tasting by Yakima area wineries. Thanksgiving weekend.

Zoolights (© 253/591-5337; www.pdza.org), Tacoma. The Point Defiance Zoo is decorated with thousands of sparkling lights, creating colorful fantasy scenes. Day after Thanksgiving to January 1.

Christmas Lighting (© **509/548-5807**; www.leavenworth.org), Leavenworth. This Bavarian village was practically made for Christmas, and looks most photogenic when surrounded by snow and decorated with twinkling lights. Sleigh rides, roasted chestnuts, and all the traditional Bavarian trimmings. Day after Thanksgiving through the first three weekends of December.

December

Argosy Cruises Christmas Ships Festival (© **800/642-7816** or 206/623-1445; www.argosycruises. com), various locations. Boats decked out with imaginative Christmas lights parade past various waterfront locations. Argosy Cruises offers tours; see section 6, "Organized Tours," in chapter 5. Throughout December.

AT&T New Year's at the Needle (© **206/905-2100** or 206/684-7200; www.seattlecenter.com), Seattle Center. The Space Needle ushers in the new year by bursting into light when midnight strikes. December 31.

5 Travel Insurance, Health & Safety

Check your existing insurance policies and credit card coverage before you buy travel insurance. You may already be covered for lost luggage, cancelled tickets, or medical expenses.

The cost of travel insurance varies widely, depending on the cost and length of the trip, your age and health, and the type of trip you're taking, but expect to pay between 5% and 8% of the vacation itself. You can get estimates from various providers through **InsureMyTrip.com**.

TRIP-CANCELLATION INSURANCE Trip-cancellation insurance will help retrieve your money if you have to back out of a trip or depart early, or if your travel supplier goes bankrupt. Permissible reasons for trip cancellation can range from sickness to natural disasters to the State Department declaring a destination unsafe for travel. In this unstable world, trip-cancellation insurance is a good buy if you're purchasing tickets well in advance. Who knows what the state of the world, or of your airline, will be in 9 months? Insurance policy details vary, so read the fine print—and make sure that your airline or cruise line is on the list of carriers covered in case of bankruptcy. A good resource is **"Travel Guard Alerts,"** a list of companies considered high-risk by Travel Guard

International (see website below). Protect yourself further by paying for the insurance with a credit card. By law, consumers can get their money back on goods and services not received if they report the loss within 60 days after the charge is listed on their credit card statement.

For more information, contact one of the following recommended insurers: **Access America** (© 866/807-3982; www.accessamerica.com); **Travel Guard International** (© 800/826-4919; www.travelguard.com); **Travel Insured International** (© 800/243-3174; www.travelinsured.com); and **Travelex Insurance Services** (© 888/457-4602; www.travelex-insurance.com).

MEDICAL INSURANCE Most health insurance policies cover you if you get sick away from home—but verify that you're covered before you depart, particularly if you're insured by an HMO. If you require additional medical insurance, try **MEDEX Assistance** (© 410/453-6300; www.medexassist.com) or **Travel Assistance International** (© 800/821-2828; www.travelassistance.com; for general information on services, call the company's **Worldwide Assistance Services, Inc.,** at © 800/777-8710).

LOST-LUGGAGE INSURANCE On domestic flights, checked baggage is covered up to $2,500 per ticketed passenger. On international flights (including U.S. portions of international trips), baggage coverage is limited to approximately $9.07 per pound, up to approximately $635 per checked bag. If you plan to check items more valuable than what's covered by the standard liability, see if your homeowner's policy covers your valuables, get baggage insurance as part of your comprehensive travel-insurance package, or buy Travel Guard's "BagTrak" product. Be sure to take any valuables or irreplaceable items with you in your carry-on luggage, because many valuables are simply not covered by airline policies.

If your luggage is lost, immediately file a lost-luggage claim at the airport, detailing the luggage contents. Most airlines require that you report delayed, damaged, or lost baggage within 4 hours of arrival. The airlines are required to deliver luggage, once found, directly to your house or destination free of charge.

STAYING HEALTHY

If you're worried about getting sick while away from home, consider purchasing **medical travel insurance** (see below) and remember to carry your ID card in your purse or wallet at all times. In most cases, your existing health plan will provide the coverage you need.

WHAT TO DO IF YOU GET SICK AWAY FROM HOME

If you get sick, consider asking your hotel concierge to recommend a local doctor— even his or her own. You can also try an urgent-care facility or a local hospital, many of which have walk-in clinics for emergency cases that are not life-threatening. You may not get immediate attention, but you won't pay the high price of an emergency room visit.

If you suffer from a chronic illness, consult your doctor before your departure. For conditions like epilepsy, diabetes, or heart problems, wear a **MedicAlert identification tag** (© 888/ 633-4298; www.medicalert.org), which will immediately alert doctors to your condition and give them access to your records through MedicAlert's 24-hour hot line.

Pack **prescription medications** in your carry-on luggage, and carry prescription medications in their original containers, with pharmacy labels—otherwise, they won't make it through airport security. Also carry copies of your prescriptions in case you lose your pills or run out. Don't forget an extra pair of your contact lenses or prescription glasses.

For domestic trips, most reliable health-care plans provide coverage if you get sick away from home. See "Medical Insurance," above.

6 The Active Vacation Planner

The abundance of outdoor recreational activities is one reason why people choose to live in Washington. With mountains and beaches within an hour's drive of major metropolitan areas, there are many choices for active vacationers.

ACTIVITIES A TO Z
BICYCLING/MOUNTAIN BIKING

The San Juan Islands, with their winding country roads and Puget Sound vistas, are the most popular bicycling locales in the state. Of the four main San Juan Islands (San Juan, Orcas, Lopez, and Shaw), Lopez has the easiest and Orcas the most challenging terrain for bikers. Here you can pedal for as few or many days as you like, stopping at parks, inns, and quaint villages.

Other popular road-biking spots include Bainbridge and Vashon islands, with their easy access to Seattle; the

Olympic Peninsula, with its scenic vistas and campgrounds; and the Long Beach Peninsula, with its miles of flat roads. Seattle, Tacoma, Spokane, and Yakima also all have many miles of easy paths for bicycle riding.

The region's national forests provide miles of logging roads and single-track trails for mountain biking. However, the state's premier mountain-biking destination is the Methow Valley, where miles of cross-country ski trails are opened to bicycles in the summer.

If you're interested in participating in an organized bicycle tour, there are a couple of companies you might want to contact. **Backroads,** 801 Cedar St., Berkeley, CA 94710-1800 (**©** **800/462-2848** or 510/527-1555; www.backroads.com), offers road bike trips in the San Juan Islands and on the Olympic Peninsula. Tour prices range from $1,698 to $2,698. **Bicycle Adventures,** P.O. Box 11219, Olympia, WA 98508 (**©** **800/443-6060** or 360/786-0989; www.bicycleadventures. com) offers biking trips in the San Juan Islands, on the Olympic Peninsula, to the volcanoes of Washington, and through the Columbia Gorge. Tour prices range from $1,044 to $2,668.

BIRD-WATCHING   With a wide variety of habitats, Washington offers many excellent bird-watching spots. Each winter in January, bald eagles flock to the Skagit River, north of Seattle, to feast on salmon. Birders can observe from shore or on a guided raft trip. Outside the town of Hoquiam, migratory shorebirds make annual stops at the Gray's Harbor Wildlife Refuge in the Bowerman Basin area. One of Washington's best birding excursions is a ride through the San Juan Islands on one of the state-run ferries. From these floating observation platforms, birders can spot bald eagles and numerous pelagic birds.

CAMPING   Public and private campgrounds abound all across Washington,

with those in Mount Rainier National Park and Olympic National Park being the most popular. North Cascades National Park has campgrounds, as well. At North Cascades National Park Complex, camping is on a first-come, first-served basis, while at one campground in Olympic National Park and two campgrounds within Mount Rainier National Park, reservations are taken. To get information on outdoor recreation in Washington's national parks and forests, contact the **Outdoor Recreation Information Center,** Seattle REI Building, 222 Yale Ave. N., Seattle, WA 98109 (**©** **206/470-4060;** www.nps.gov/ccso/ oric.htm). The Forest Service's regional Web page (**www.fs.fed.us/r6**) is a good source, too.

Washington also has more than 80 state parks with campgrounds. Moran State Park on Orcas Island and Deception Pass State Park have two of the most enjoyable campgrounds. For information on Washington state parks, contact **Washington State Parks and Recreation Commission,** 7150 Cleanwater Lane (P.O. Box 42650), Olympia, WA 98504-2650 (**©** **360/902-8844;** www.parks.wa.gov).

For state campsite reservations, contact **Washington State Parks Reservations** (**©** **888/226-7688;** www.parks.wa.gov). To make campsite reservations at national forest campgrounds, contact the **National Recreation Reservation Service** (**©** **877/444-6777** or 518/885-3639; www.reserve usa.com). For reservations at Mount Rainier or Olympic National Park, contact the **National Park Reservation Service** (**©** **800/365-2267** or 301/722-1257; reservations.nps.gov).

One economical way to tour the Northwest is with a recreational vehicle. They can be rented for a weekend, a week, or longer. RVs can be rented in Washington from **Western Motorcoach Rentals,** 19303 Hwy. 99, Lynnwood, WA 98036 (**©** **800/800-1181;** www.westernrv.com).

FISHING   For information on freshwater fishing in Washington, contact the **Department of Wildlife,** Natural Resources Building, 1111 Washington St. SE, Olympia, WA 98501 (℗ **360/902-2200;** wdfw.wa.gov); mailing address: 600 Capitol Way N., Olympia, WA 98501-1091.

HIKING & BACKPACKING   Washington has an abundance of hiking trails, including a section of the Pacific Crest Trail, which runs along the spine of the Cascades from Canada to the Oregon state line (and onward through Oregon and California to Mexico). In the Olympic National Park, you'll find hikes along the beach, through valleys in rainforests, and through alpine meadows; at Mount Rainier National Park, you can hike through forests and the state's most beautiful meadows (hikes from Sunrise and Paradise are the most spectacular); and in North Cascades National Park, there are hiking trails through the state's most rugged scenery. The Alpine Lakes region outside Leavenworth is breathtakingly beautiful, but so popular that advance-reservation permits are required. In the past, another popular hike has been to the top of Mount St. Helens. However, after Mount St. Helens became more active in the autumn of 2004, the summit was closed to hikers. Lesser known are the hiking trails on Mount Adams in Washington's southern Cascades. In the Columbia Gorge, the hike up Dog Mountain is strenuous, but rewarding. For general information on hiking in the Northwest and for information on the Northwest Forest Pass, which is required at most national forest trailheads in Washington, contact **Nature of the Northwest,** 800 NE Oregon St., Suite 177, Portland, OR 97232 (℗ **503/872-2750;** www.naturenw.org).

If you'd like to hike the wild country of Washington state with a knowledgeable guide, you have a couple of good options.

The **Olympic Park Institute,** 111 Barnes Point Rd., Port Angeles, WA 98363 (℗ **360/928-3720;** www.yni.org/opi), offers a variety of hiking and backpacking trips, as does the **North Cascades Institute,** 810 State Rte. 20, Sedro-Woolley, WA 98284-1239 (℗ **360/856-5700,** ext. 209; www.ncascades.org).

SEA KAYAKING   Sea kayaks differ from river kayaks in that they are much longer, more stable, and able to carry gear, as well as a paddler or two. There are few places in the country with better sea kayaking than the waters of Puget Sound and around the San Juan Islands, and, therefore, this sport is especially popular in the Seattle area. The protected waters of Puget Sound offer numerous spots for a paddle of a few hours or a few days. A water trail called the **Cascadia Marine Trail** even links camping spots throughout the sound. For more information about this trail, contact the Washington Water Trails Association (℗ **206/545-9161;** www.wwta.org).

The San Juan Islands are by far the most popular sea-kayaking spot in the region, and several tiny islands, accessible only by boat, are designated state campsites. In the Seattle area, Lake Union and Lake Washington are both popular kayaking spots. Willapa Bay, on the Washington coast, is another popular paddling spot.

If you'd like to explore Puget Sound or Seattle's Lake Union in a sea kayak, contact the **Northwest Outdoor Center,** 2100 Westlake Ave. N., Suite 1, Seattle, WA 98109 (℗ **800/683-0637** or 206/281-9694; www.nwoc.com). This center rents kayaks and also offers various classes and guided trips. Day trips are $70 and 3-day trips are $295.

In the San Juan Islands, **San Juan Kayak Expeditions** (℗ **360/378-4436;** www.sanjuankayak.com) offers multi-day kayak trips, charging $380 for a 3-day trip and $480 for a 4-day trip. **Orcas**

Outdoors (© 360/376-4611; www.orcasoutdoors.com) offers 3-day trips for $350. **Crystal Seas Kayaking** (© 877/SEAS-877 or 360/378-4223; www.crystalseas.com) runs kayak camping trips ranging from 2 days ($299) to 6 days ($849), and inn-to-inn trips ranging from 2 days ($780) to 6 days ($2,280). **Sea Quest Expeditions/Zoetic Research** (© 888/589-4253 or 360/378-5767; www.sea-quest-kayak.com), is a non-profit organization that sponsors educational sea-kayaking trips through the San Juans. The 3-day trips are $419 and 5-day trips are $599.

SKIING & SNOWBOARDING

Washington has about a half-dozen major ski areas and about the same number of lesser areas. The major ski areas are all located in the Cascade Range. These include Mount Baker, a snowboarding mecca near Bellingham; Mission Ridge, which is located near Wenatchee and is known for its powder snow; Stevens Pass, which is near the Bavarian-theme town of Leavenworth; the Summit at Snoqualmie, which is located less than an hour from Seattle; Crystal Mountain near the northeast corner of Mount Rainier National Park; and White Pass, which is southeast of Mount Rainier National Park. For information on all of these ski areas, see chapter 10. Tiny locals-only ski areas with only a handful of runs include Hurricane Ridge, in Olympic National Park (see chapter 8); Loup Loup, near Winthrop (see chapter 10); and Echo Valley, near Lake Chelan (see chapter 10). Heli-skiing is also available in the Methow Valley (see chapter 10).

Many downhill ski areas also offer groomed cross-country ski trails. The best cross-country areas in Washington include the Methow Valley (one of the largest trail systems in the country), Leavenworth, the Summit at Snoqualmie, White Pass, and Stevens Pass.

WHALE-WATCHING

Orca whales, commonly called killer whales, are a symbol of the Northwest and are often seen in Puget Sound and around the San Juan Islands, especially during the summer. Dozens of companies offer whale-watching trips from the San Juans. You can also spot orcas from San Juan Island's Lime Kiln State Park. For information on orca-watching opportunities, see chapter 6. Out on the Washington coast, migrating gray whales can be seen from March through May. In the town of Westport, there are both viewing areas and companies operating whale-watching excursions. For more information, see chapter 9.

WHITEWATER RAFTING

Plenty of rain and lots of mountains combine to produce dozens of good whitewater-rafting rivers, depending on the time of year and water levels. In the Washington Cascades, some of the popular rafting rivers include the Wenatchee outside Leavenworth, the Methow near Winthrop, the Skagit and Skykomish rivers north of Seattle, and the White Salmon River near the Columbia Gorge. On the Olympic Peninsula, the Queets, Hoh, and Elwha rivers are the main rafting rivers. See the respective chapters for information on rafting companies operating on these rivers. Rates generally range from about $50 to $89 for a half-day of rafting.

Many companies offer trips on several different rivers. Among these companies are Alpine Adventures Wild & Scenic River Tours (© 800/RAFT-FUN or 206/323-1220; www.alpineadventures.com), DownStream River Runners (© 800/234-4644 or 360/805-9899; www.riverpeople.com), North Cascades River Expeditions (© 800/634-8433; www.riverexpeditions.com), Osprey Rafting Company (© 888/548-6850; www.shoottherapids.com), River Riders (© 800/448-RAFT; www.riverrider.com), and Wildwater River Tours (© 800/522-WILD or 253/939-2151; www.wildwater-river.com).

7 Educational & Volunteer Vacations

On the Olympic Peninsula, the **Olympic Park Institute,** 111 Barnes Point Rd., Port Angeles, WA 98363 (℗ **360/928-3720;** www.yni.org/opi), offers a wide array of summer field seminars ranging from painting classes to bird-watching trips to multi-day backpacking trips.

The North Cascades Institute, 810 State Rte. 20, Sedro-Woolley, WA 98284-1239 (℗ **360/856-5700,** ext. 209; www.ncascades.org), is a nonprofit organization that offers field seminars focusing on natural and cultural history in the North Cascades. The institute has a beautiful new campus on the shore of Diablo Lake in the North Cascades.

The Nature Conservancy is a nonprofit organization dedicated to the global preservation of natural diversity, and to this end it operates educational field trips and work parties to its own nature preserves and those of other agencies. For information about field trips in Washington, contact **The Nature Conservancy,** 217 Pine St., Suite 1100, Seattle, WA 98101 (℗ **206/343-4344;** nature.org).

If you enjoy the wilderness and want to get more involved in preserving it, consider a Sierra Club Service Trip. These trips are for the purpose of building, restoring, and maintaining hiking trails in wilderness areas. It's a lot of work, but it's also a lot of fun. For more information on Service Trips, contact **Sierra Club Outdoor Activities Department,** 85 Second St., Second Floor, San Francisco, CA 94105 (℗ **415/977-5500;** www. sierraclub.org). Alternatively, you can call your local chapter of the Sierra Club or Washington's Cascade Chapter (℗ **206/ 523-2147;** cascade.sierraclub.org).

Earth Watch Institute, 3 Clock Tower Place, Suite 100 (Box 75), Maynard, MA 01754 (℗ **800/776-0188** or 978/461-0081; www.earthwatch.org), sends volunteers on scientific research projects. Contact the institute for a catalog listing trips and costs. Projects have included studies of salmon in Washington's Skagit River and archaeological programs in the same area of the state.

8 Specialized Travel Resources

TRAVELERS WITH DISABILITIES

Always be sure to mention your disability at the same time that you make airline reservations. Policies often differ among airlines regarding wheelchairs and Seeing Eye dogs.

Most hotels now provide wheelchair-accessible rooms, and some of the larger and more expensive hotels also have TDD telephones and other amenities for the hearing- and sight-impaired.

If you plan to visit any of Washington's three national parks (Mount Rainier, Olympic, and North Cascades), do avail yourself of the **Golden Access Passport,** which gives free lifetime entrance to all national parks, monuments, wildlife refuges, historic sites, and recreation areas for persons who are visually impaired or permanently disabled, regardless of age. You may pick up a Golden Access Passport at any NPS visitor center by showing proof of medically determined disability and eligibility for receiving benefits under federal law. For more information, go to www.nps.gov/fees_passes.htm or call ℗ **888/467-2757.**

Many travel agencies have customized tours and itineraries for travelers with disabilities. **Flying Wheels Travel** (℗ **507/ 451-5005;** www.flyingwheelstravel.com) offers escorted tours and cruises that emphasize sports and private tours in minivans with lifts. **Access-Able Travel Source** (℗ **303/232-2979;** www.access-able.com) has extensive access information and advice for traveling around the world with disabilities. **Accessible Journeys** (© 800/846-4537 or 610/521-0339; www.disabilitytravel.com) caters specifically to slow walkers and wheelchair travelers, their families and friends.

Avis Rent a Car has an "Avis Access" program that offers such services as a dedicated 24-hour toll-free number (© **888/879-4273**) for customers with special travel needs; special car features such as swivel seats, spinner knobs, and hand controls; and accessible bus service.

Organizations that give assistance to disabled travelers include **MossRehab** (www.mossresourcenet.org), which provides a library of accessible-travel resources online; the **American Foundation for the Blind** (AFB; © **800/232-5463**; www.afb.org), a referral resource for the blind or visually impaired that includes information on traveling with Seeing Eye dogs; and **SATH (Society for Accessible Travel & Hospitality;** © **212/447-7284;** www.sath.org; annual membership fees: $45 adults, $30 seniors and students), which offers a wealth of travel resources for all types of disabilities and informed recommendations on destinations, access guides, travel agents, tour operators, vehicle rentals, and companion services.

For more information specifically targeted to travelers with disabilities, the community website **iCan** (www.icanonline.net/channels/travel) has destination guides and several regular columns on accessible travel.

GAY & LESBIAN TRAVELERS

Seattle is one of the most gay-friendly cities in the country, with a large gay and lesbian community centered around Capitol Hill. Here in this neighborhood, you'll find numerous bars, nightclubs, stores, and bed-and-breakfasts catering to the gay community. Broadway, Capitol Hill's main drag, is also the site of the annual Seattle Pride march (www.seattlepride.org), held each year in late June.

The *Seattle Gay News* (© 206/324-4297; www.sgn.org) is the community's newspaper, available at area bookstores and gay bars and nightclubs.

Beyond the Closet, 518 E. Pike St. (© 206/322-4609), and **Bailey Coy Books,** 414 Broadway E. (© 206/323-8842), are the two main gay bookstores and good sources of information for what's going on within the community.

The **Lesbian Resource Center,** 227 S. Orcas St. (© **206/322-3953;** www.lrc.net), provides community and business resource information, as well as a calendar of upcoming events and various activities.

The **Gaslight Inn** is a gay-friendly bed-and-breakfast in the Capitol Hill area; see p. 85 for a full review. For information on gay and lesbian bars and nightclubs, see p. 149.

The **International Gay and Lesbian Travel Association** (IGLTA; © **800/448-8550** or 954/776-2626; www.iglta.org) is the trade association for the gay and lesbian travel industry, and has an online directory of gay- and lesbian-friendly travel businesses; go to its website and click on "Members."

SENIOR TRAVEL

Mention the fact that you're a senior citizen when you make travel reservations. Although all the major U.S. airlines except America West have cancelled their senior discount and coupon book programs, many hotels still offer lower rates for seniors. In most cities, people over the age of 60 qualify for reduced admission to theaters, museums, and other attractions, and discounted fares on public transportation.

Members of **AARP** (formerly known as the American Association of Retired Persons), 601 E St. NW, Washington, DC 20049 (© **888/687-2277;** www.aarp.org), get discounts on hotels, airfares, and car rentals. AARP provides a wide range of benefits, including *AARP: The Magazine* and a monthly newsletter. Anyone over age 50 can join.

If you plan to visit any of the national parks (Mount Rainier, Olympic, or North Cascades) while in the Seattle area, you can save on entry fees by getting a **Golden Age Passport,** available for a one-time processing fee of $10 to U.S. citizens and permanent residents 62 and older. This federal government pass allows lifetime entrance privileges to all national parks, monuments, historic sites, recreation areas, and wildlife refuges. You can apply in person at any NPS facility that charges an entrance fee, as long as you can show reasonable proof of age. For more information, go to www.nps.gov/fees_passes.htm or call © **888/467-2757.**

Many reliable agencies and organizations target the 50-plus market. **Elderhostel** (© **877/426-8056;** www.elder hostel.org) arranges study programs for those ages 55 and over (and a spouse or companion of any age). **ElderTreks** (© **800/741-7956;** www.eldertreks. com), restricted to travelers ages 50 and older, has small-group tours to off-the-beaten-path or adventure-travel locations.

FAMILY TRAVEL

If you have enough trouble simply getting your kids out of the house in the morning, dragging them thousands of miles away may seem like an insurmountable challenge. But family travel can be immensely rewarding, giving you new ways of seeing the world through smaller pairs of eyes.

To locate those accommodations, restaurants, and attractions that are particularly kid-friendly, refer to the "Kids" icon throughout this guide.

Families traveling in Washington should be sure to take note of family admission fees at many museums and other attractions. These admission prices are often less than what it would cost for individual tickets for the whole family. At hotels and motels, children usually stay free if they share their parent's room and no extra bed is required, and sometimes they also get to eat for free in the hotel dining room. Be sure to ask.

Recommended family travel Internet sites include **Family Travel Forum** (www.familytravelforum.com), a comprehensive site that provides customized trip planning; and **Family Travel Network** (www.familytravelnetwork.com), an award-winning site that gives travel features, deals, and tips.

Frommer's National Parks with Kids (Wiley Publishing, Inc.) has tips for enjoying your trip to Olympic National Park.

Note: If you plan to travel on to Canada during your Washington vacation, be sure to bring your children's birth certificates or passports with you.

9 Planning Your Trip Online

SURFING FOR AIRFARES

The "big three" online travel agencies, **Expedia.com, Travelocity.com,** and **Orbitz.com** sell most of the air tickets bought on the Internet. (Canadian travelers should try expedia.ca and Travelocity.ca; U.K. residents can go for expedia.co.uk and opodo.co.uk.). **Kayak.com** is also gaining popularity and uses a sophisticated search engine (developed at MIT). Each has different business deals with the airlines and may offer different fares on the same flights, so it's wise to shop around.

Also remember to check **airline websites,** especially those for low-fare carriers such as Southwest and JetBlue, whose fares are often misreported or simply missing from travel agency websites. Even with major airlines, you can often shave a few bucks from a fare by booking directly through the airline. But you'll get these discounts only by **booking online:** Most airlines now offer online-only fares that even their phone agents know nothing about. For the websites of airlines that fly to and from Washington state, check out "Getting There," p. 34.

Great **last-minute deals** are available through free weekly e-mail services provided directly by the airlines. Most of these are announced on Tuesday or Wednesday and must be purchased online. Most are only valid for travel that weekend, but some (such as Southwest's) can be booked weeks or months in advance. Sign up for weekly e-mail alerts at airline websites or check megasites that compile comprehensive lists of last-minute specials, such as **Smarter Travel** (smartertravel.com). For last-minute trips, **site59.com** and **lastminutetravel.com** in the U.S. and **lastminute.com** in Europe often have better air-and-hotel package deals than the major-label sites.

If you're willing to give up some control over your flight details, use what is called an **"opaque" fare service** like **Priceline** (www.priceline.com; www.priceline.co.uk for Europeans) or its smaller competitor **Hotwire** (www.hotwire.com). Both offer rock-bottom prices in exchange for travel on a "mystery airline" at a mysterious time of day, often with a mysterious change of planes en route. The mystery airlines are all major, well-known carriers. Your chances of getting a 6am or 11pm flight, however, are still pretty high. Hotwire tells you flight prices before you buy; Priceline usually has better deals than Hotwire, but you have to play their "name our price" game or pick exact flights, times, and airlines from a list of offers. If you're new at this, **BiddingForTravel** (www.biddingfortravel.com) does a good job of demystifying Priceline's prices and also its strategies.

SURFING FOR HOTELS

Shopping online for hotels is generally done one of two ways: by booking through the hotel's own website or through an independent booking agency (or a fare-service agency like Priceline; see below).

Frommers.com: The Complete Travel Resource

For an excellent travel-planning resource, we highly recommend **Frommers. com** (www.frommers.com), voted Best Travel Site by *PC Magazine*. We're a little biased, of course, but we guarantee that you'll find the travel tips, reviews, monthly vacation giveaways, bookstore, and online-booking capabilities thoroughly indispensable. Among the special features are our popular **Destinations** section, where you'll get expert travel tips, hotel and dining recommendations, and advice on the sights to see for more than 3,500 destinations around the globe; the **Frommers.com Newsletter,** with the latest deals, travel trends, and money-saving secrets; our **Community** area featuring **Message Boards,** where Frommer's readers post queries and share advice (sometimes even our authors show up to answer questions); and our **Photo Center,** where you can post and share vacation tips. When your research is finished, the **Online Reservations System** (www.frommers.com/book_a_trip) takes you to Frommer's preferred online partners for booking your vacation at affordable prices.

Of the big three sites, **Expedia** offers a long list of special deals and virtual tours or photos of available rooms so you can see what you're paying for. **Travelocity** posts unvarnished customer reviews and ranks its properties according to the AAA rating system. **Trip Advisor** (www.tripadvisor.com) is another excellent source of unbiased user reviews of hotels. While even the finest hotels can inspire misleading and poor reviews from picky or crabby travelers, the body of user opinions is usually a more reliable indicator.

Other reliable online booking agencies include **Hotels.com** and **Quikbook.com**. An excellent free program, **TravelAxe** (www.travelaxe.net), can help you search multiple hotel sites at once, even ones you might never have heard of—and conveniently lists the total price of the room, including the taxes and service charges. Another booking site, **Travelweb** (www.travelweb.com), is partly owned by the hotels it represents (including the Hilton, Hyatt, and Starwood chains) and is, therefore, plugged directly into the hotels' reservations systems. Be sure to **get a confirmation number** and **make a printout** of any online booking transaction you make.

In the opaque website category, **Priceline** and **Hotwire** are even better for hotels than for airfares; through both, you're allowed to pick the neighborhood and quality level of your hotel before paying. Priceline's hotel product is much better at getting five-star lodging for three-star prices than at finding anything at the bottom of the scale. On the downside, many hotels stick Priceline guests in the least desirable rooms. Be sure to go to the BiddingforTravel website (see above) before bidding on a hotel room on Priceline; it has a fairly up-to-date list of hotels that Priceline uses in major cities.

10 The 21st-Century Traveler

INTERNET ACCESS AWAY FROM HOME

Travelers have any number of ways to check e-mail and access the Internet on the road. Of course, using your own laptop—or even a PDA (personal digital assistant) or electronic organizer with a modem—gives you the most flexibility. However, if you don't have a computer, you can still access e-mail and even your office computer from cybercafes.

WITHOUT YOUR OWN COMPUTER

It's hard nowadays to find a city that *doesn't* have a few cybercafes. Although there's no definitive directory for cybercafes—these are independent businesses, after all—two places to start looking are at **www.cybercaptive.com** and **www.cybercafe.com**.

Aside from formal cybercafes, most **public libraries** offer access free or for a small charge.

To retrieve your e-mail, ask your **Internet Service Provider (ISP)** if it has a Web-based interface tied to your existing e-mail account. If your ISP doesn't have such an interface, you can use the free **mail2web** service (www.mail2web.com) to view and reply to your home e-mail. For more flexibility, you may want to open a free, Web-based e-mail account with **Yahoo! Mail** (http://mail.yahoo.com). (Microsoft's Hotmail is another popular option, but Hotmail has severe spam problems.) Your home ISP may also be able to forward your e-mail to the Web-based account automatically.

WITH YOUR OWN COMPUTER

More and more hotels, cafes, and retailers are signing on as Wi-Fi (wireless fidelity)

Online Traveler's Toolbox

Veteran travelers usually carry some essential items to make their trips easier. Following is a selection of handy online tools to bookmark and use:

- **Mapquest** (www.mapquest.com). This best of the mapping sites lets you choose a specific address or destination and, in seconds, returns a map and detailed directions.
- *Seattle Times* (www.seattletimes.com). A solid virtual version of Seattle's print stalwart, this site offers many of the paper's stories online. There's also an entertainment section with information on movies, theater, and concerts around town.
- *Seattle Weekly* (www.seattleweekly.com). *Seattle Weekly* is the city's main arts-and-entertainment weekly and provides detailed information on what's happening in film, music, theater, and the arts. It also features an extensive dining guide and database of restaurant reviews.
- **Visa ATM Locator** (www.visa.com), for locations of PLUS ATMs worldwide, or **MasterCard ATM Locator** (www.mastercard.com), for locations of Cirrus ATMs worldwide.
- **Intellicast** (www.intellicast.com) and **Weather.com** (www.weather.com), for weather forecasts for all 50 states and for cities around the world.

"hotspots," from where you can get high-speed connection without cable wires, networking hardware, or a phone line (see below). You can get Wi-Fi connection one of several ways. Many laptops sold in the last year have built-in Wi-Fi capability (an 802.11b wireless Ethernet connection). Mac owners have their own networking technology, Apple AirPort. For those with older computers, you can plug in an 802.11b/**Wi-Fi card** (around $50). You sign up for wireless access service much as you do for cellphone service, through a plan offered by one of several commercial companies that have made wireless service available in airports, hotel lobbies, and coffee shops, primarily in the U.S. (followed by the U.K. and Japan). **T-Mobile Hotspot** (www.t-mobile.com/hotspot) serves up wireless connections at more than 1,000 Starbucks coffee shops nationwide. **Boingo** (www.boingo.com) and **Wayport** (www.wayport.com) have

set up networks in airports and high-class hotel lobbies. To locate other hotspots providing **free wireless networks,** visit **www.personaltelco.net/index.cgi/WirelessCommunities**.

For dial-up access, most business-class hotels have dataports for laptop modems, and many hotels provide free high-speed Internet access using an Ethernet network cable. **Call your hotel in advance** to see what your options are.

In addition, major Internet Service Providers (ISPs) have **local access numbers,** allowing you to go online by placing a local call. Check your ISP's website for information.

Wherever you go, bring a **connection kit** of the right power and phone adapters, a spare phone cord, and a spare Ethernet network cable—or find out whether your hotel supplies them to guests.

11 Getting There

BY PLANE

THE MAJOR AIRLINES

The **Seattle-Tacoma International Airport** (☎ 206/431-4444; www.portseattle.org/seatac) is served by about 30 airlines. The major carriers include: **Air Canada** (☎ 888/247-2262; www.aircanada.ca), **Alaska Airlines** (☎ 800/252-7522; www.alaskaair.com), **American Airlines** (☎ 800/433-7300; www.aa.com), **America West** (☎ 800/235-9292; www.americawest.com), **Continental** (☎ 800/523-3273; www.continental.com), **Delta** (☎ 800/221-1212; www.delta.com), **Frontier** (☎ 800/432-1359; www.frontierairlines.com), **Horizon Air** (☎ 800/547-9308; www.horizonair.com), **Independence Air** (☎ 800/359-3594; www.flyi.com), **JetBlue Airways** (☎ 800/JET-BLUE; www.jetblue.com), **Northwest/KLM** (☎ 800/225-2525; www.nwa.com), **Song** (☎ 800/359-7664; www.flysong.com); **Southwest** (☎ 800/435-9792; www.southwest.com), **United** (☎ 800/864-8331; www.united.com), and **US Airways** (☎ 800/428-4322; www.usair.com).

For information on flights to the United States from other countries, see section 3, "Getting Around," in chapter 3.

Seaplane service between Seattle and the San Juan Islands and Victoria, British Columbia, is provided by **Kenmore Air** (☎ **800/543-9595** or 425/486-1257; www.kenmoreair.com), with its Seattle terminals at the south end of Lake Union and the north end of Lake Washington.

GETTING THROUGH THE AIRPORT

With the federalization of airport security, screening procedures at U.S. airports are more stable and consistent than ever. Generally, you'll be fine if you arrive at the airport **1 hour** before a domestic flight and **2 hours** before an international flight.

Bring a **current, government-issued photo ID** such as a driver's license or passport. Keep your ID at the ready to present at check-in, the security checkpoint, and sometimes even the gate. (Children under 18 do not need government-issued photo IDs for domestic flights, but they do for international flights to most countries.)

Passengers with e-tickets, which have made paper tickets nearly obsolete, can beat the ticket-counter lines by using airport **electronic kiosks** or even **online check-in** from their home computers. Online check-in involves logging onto your airline's website, accessing your reservation, and printing out your boarding pass.

If you have trouble standing for long periods of time, tell an airline employee; the airline will provide a wheelchair. Speed up security by **not wearing metal objects** such as big belt buckles. If you've got metallic body parts, a note from your doctor can prevent a long chat with the security screeners.

Federalization has stabilized **what you can carry on** and **what you can't.** The general rule is that sharp things are out. Bring food in your carry-on rather than checking it, as explosive-detection machines used on checked luggage have been known to mistake food (especially chocolate, for some reason) for bombs. Travelers in the U.S. are allowed one carry-on bag, plus a "personal item" such as a purse, briefcase, or laptop bag. The Transportation Security Administration (TSA) has issued a list of restricted items; check its website (www.tsa.gov/public/index.jsp) if you'd like more details.

Airport screeners may decide that your checked luggage warrants a hand search. You can now purchase luggage locks that allow screeners to open and relock a checked bag if hand searching is necessary. Look for Travel Sentry certified locks at luggage or travel shops and Brookstone stores (you can buy them online at www.brookstone.com). Luggage inspectors can open these TSA-approved locks with a special code or key—rather than having to cut them off the suitcase, as they normally do to conduct a hand search. For more information on the locks, visit www.travelsentry.org.

FLY FOR LESS: TIPS ON GETTING THE BEST AIRFARES

Passengers sharing the same airplane cabin rarely pay the same fare. Travelers who need to purchase tickets at the last minute, change their itinerary at a moment's notice, or fly one-way often get stuck paying the premium rate. Here are several good ways to keep your airfare costs down.

- Passengers who can book their ticket either **long in advance or at the last minute,** or who **fly midweek** or **at less-trafficked hours** may pay a fraction of the full fare. If your schedule is flexible, say so, and ask if you can secure a cheaper fare by changing your flight plans.
- Keep an eye on local newspapers for **promotional specials or fare wars,** when airlines lower prices on their most popular routes. You rarely see fare wars offered for peak travel times, but if you can travel in the off-months, you may snag a bargain.
- **Consolidators,** also known as bucket shops, are great sources for international tickets, although they usually can't beat Internet fares within North America. Start by looking in Sunday newspaper travel sections; U.S. travelers should focus on the *New York Times, Los Angeles Times,* and *Miami Herald.* For less-developed destinations, small travel agents who cater to immigrant communities in large cities often have the best deals. Several reliable consolidators are worldwide and available online. STA Travel has

been the world's leading consolidator for students since purchasing Council Travel, but its fares are competitive for travelers of all ages. Air Tickets Direct (© 800/778-3447; www.airticketsdirect.com) is based in Montreal and leverages the currently weak Canadian dollar for low fares.

- **Join frequent-flier clubs.** Frequent-flier membership doesn't cost a cent, but it does entitle you to better seats, faster response to phone inquiries, and prompter service if your luggage is stolen or your flight is canceled or delayed, or if you want to change your seat.

BY CAR

Seattle is 110 miles from Vancouver, British Columbia, 175 miles from Portland, 810 miles from San Francisco, 1,190 miles from Los Angeles, and 285 miles from Spokane.

I-5 is the main north-south artery through Washington, running south to Portland and north to the Canadian border. I-405 is Seattle's east-side bypass and accesses the cities of Bellevue, Redmond, and Kirkland on the east side of Lake Washington. I-90 connects Seattle to Spokane in eastern Washington. Wash. 520 connects I-405 with Seattle just north of downtown and also ends at I-5. Wash. 99, the Alaskan Way Viaduct, is a major north-south highway that passes right through the Seattle waterfront.

See section 2, "Getting Around," in chapter 5 for details on driving, parking, and car rentals in Seattle.

BY TRAIN

Amtrak (© 800/872-7245; www.amtrak.com) service runs from Vancouver, British Columbia, to Seattle and from Portland and as far south as Eugene, Oregon, on the *Cascades* (a high-speed, European-style Talgo train). The train takes about 4 hours from Vancouver to Seattle and 3½ to 4 hours from Portland to Seattle. One-way fares from Vancouver to Seattle or from Portland to Seattle are usually between $27 and $32. Booking earlier will get you a less expensive ticket.

There is also Amtrak service to Seattle from San Diego, Los Angeles, San Francisco, and Portland on the *Coast Starlight,* and from Spokane and points east on the *Empire Builder.* Amtrak also operates a bus between Vancouver and Seattle, so be careful when making a reservation since you might be on a bus, rather than a train.

Like the airlines, Amtrak has several discounted fares; although they're not all based on advance purchase, you'll have more discount options by reserving early. The discount fares can be used only on certain days and during certain hours; be sure to find out exactly what restrictions apply. Tickets for children ages 2 to 15 cost half the price of a regular coach fare when the children are accompanied by a fare-paying adult. Also inquire about money-saving packages.

BY FERRY

If you're traveling between Victoria, British Columbia, and Seattle, several options are available through **Victoria Clipper,** Pier 69, 2701 Alaskan Way (© **800/888-2535,** 206/448-5000, or 250/382-8100 in Victoria; www.victoria clipper.com). Ferries make the 2- or 3-hour trip throughout the year, at prices ranging from $70 to $133 round-trip for adults (the lower fare is for advance-purchase tickets). Some scheduled trips also make stops in the San Juan Islands.

Bellingham, north of Seattle, is the port for Alaska ferries.

PACKAGE TOURS

Gray Line of Seattle (© 800/426-7532 or 206/624-5077; www.graylineofseattle. com) offers 2- to 7-day bus and cruise tours that include Seattle, Mount Rainier, Vancouver, and Victoria. Prices range from about $120 for a 3-day trip in the winter to $525 for a 4-day trip in summer.

If you prefer traveling on your own, but would like to have a custom itinerary planned for your trip to Washington or the Northwest, consider consulting **Pacific Northwest Journeys** (© **800/935-9730** or 206/935-9730; www.pnwjourneys. com). This company can tailor a trip that suits your personal traveling style.

12 Getting Around

BY CAR

A car is by far the best way to see the state of Washington. There just isn't any other way to get to the more remote natural spectacles or to fully appreciate such regions as the Olympic Peninsula.

All of the major car-rental agencies have offices in Seattle and at or near Seattle-Tacoma International Airport. Companies with a desk and cars inside the terminal include **Alamo** (© 800/327-9633 or 206/433-0182; www.goalamo. com), **Avis** (© 800/831-2847 or 206/433-5232; www.avis.com), **Budget** (© 800/527-0700 or 206/431-8800; www.budget.com), **Hertz** (© 800/654-3131 or 206/248-1300; www.hertz.com),

and **National** (© 800/227-7368 or 206/433-5501; www.nationalcar.com). Companies with desks inside the terminal, but cars parked off the airport premises, include **Advantage** (© 800/777-5500 or 206/824-0161; www.arac.com), **Dollar** (© 800/800-3665 or 206/433-5825; www.dollar.com), **Enterprise** (© 800/261-7331 or 206/246-1953; www.enterprise.com), and **Thrifty** (© 800/847-4389 or 206/246-7565; www.thrifty.com).

Gasoline Washington is a big state, so keep your gas tank as full as possible when traveling in the mountains or on the sparsely populated east side of the Cascades.

Washington Driving Distances

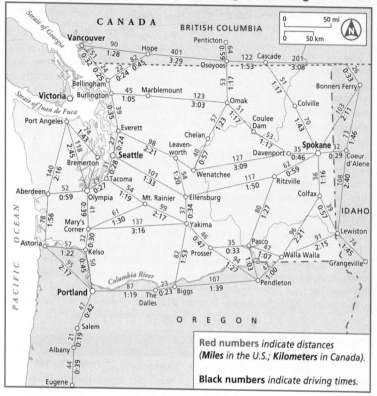

Red numbers *indicate distances*
(**Miles** *in the U.S.;* **Kilometers** *in Canada*).

Black numbers *indicate driving times.*

Maps   Maps are available at most highway tourist information centers, at the tourist information offices listed earlier in this chapter, and at gas stations throughout the region. For a free map of Washington, call the **Washington State Tourism Office** (© 800/544-1800).

Driving Rules   A right turn on red is permitted after first coming to a complete stop. You may also turn left on a red light if you're in the far left lane of a one-way street and are turning into another one-way street. Seat belts are required, as are car seats for children.

Breakdowns/Assistance   In the event of a breakdown, stay with your car, lift the hood, turn on your emergency flashers, and wait for a police patrol car.

BY PLANE
Washington is a large state, and if you're trying to see every corner of it in a short time, you may want to consider flying. There are airports with regularly scheduled commercial flights at Bellingham, Whidbey Island, Port Angeles, Wenatchee, Yakima, Walla Walla, and Spokane. Fares vary, but at press time, a one-way flight between Bellingham and Spokane (with a stop in Seattle) on Alaska Airlines was quoted at $124 with a 7-day advance purchase, and $237 with no advance purchase. Airlines operating short hops

between many of these towns and cities include **Alaska Airlines** (📞 **800/252-7522;** www.alaskaair.com) and the affiliated **Horizon Air** (📞 **800/547-9308;** www.horizonair.com).

Seaplane service between Seattle and the San Juan Islands and Victoria, British Columbia, is provided by **Kenmore Air** (📞 **800/543-9595** or 425/486-1257; www.kenmoreair.com), with its Seattle terminals at the south end of Lake Union and the north end of Lake Washington. **San Juan Airlines** (📞 **800/874-4434;** www.sanjuanairlines.com) flies to the San Juans from Seattle's Boeing Field and from Bellingham and Anacortes.

BY TRAIN

There is **Amtrak** service from Seattle to Spokane and points east, and service between Vancouver, British Columbia, Seattle, Portland, and points south, but otherwise, the train isn't a viable way of getting around Washington state. If you do decide to take the train, booking early will save you money.

BY FERRY

Washington State Ferries (📞 **800/84-FERRY** or 888/808-7977 within Washington, or 206/464-6400; www.wsdot.wa.gov/ferries) is the most extensive ferry system in the United States. See specific destinations in chapters 5, 6, 7, and 8 for information on routes and fares.

There are also several smaller ferries. **Black Ball Transport** (📞 **360/457-4491,** or 250/386-2202 in Victoria; www.cohoferry.com) and **Victoria Express** (📞 **360/452-8088** or 250/361-9144; www.victoriaexpress.com) ferries operate between Port Angeles and Victoria, British Columbia. There's also passenger-ferry service between Seattle and Victoria, British Columbia, and, in summer, between Seattle and San Juan Island on the **Victoria Clipper** ferries (📞 **800/888-2535,** 206/448-5000, or 250/382-8100; www.victoriaclipper.com).

13 Cruises

While Washington is not a big cruise-ship destination per se, several companies offer Alaska cruises that start in Washington and spend a little time in the waters of Puget Sound and the San Juan Islands. Several smaller cruise lines provide voyages on small ships. Rates below are per person and based on double occupancy.

In the big-ship category, several companies operate Alaska cruises out of Seattle. There are 7-day trips offered by **Norwegian Cruise Lines** (📞 **800/327-7030;** www.ncl.com), with fares starting at $983. **Holland America Line** (📞 **877/SAIL-HAL;** www.hollandamerica.com) has similar cruises starting at $1,099. **Princess Cruises** (📞 **800/PRINCESS;** www.princess.com) has 7-day trips.

Cruises on smaller ships are provided by several other companies. **Lindblad**

Expeditions (📞 **800/397-3348** or 212/765-7740; www.expeditions.com) has a 12-day voyage through the San Juan Islands to Alaska, with fares starting at $5,390. **Cruise West** (📞 **888/851-8133;** www.cruisewest.com) offers an 11-day trip from Seattle to Alaska. Fares start at $3,279 per person. **Catalyst Cruises** (📞 **800/670-7678;** www.cruise-nw.com) has 7-day San Juan Island voyages on a 62-foot yacht. The fare is $1,750 per person.

There are also cruises up the Columbia River. Most of these play up the Lewis and Clark history. If you prefer a voyage aboard a small vessel, consider a trip with **Cruise West** (📞 **888/851-8133;** www.cruisewest.com), which has an 8-day trip from Portland on the Columbia and Snake rivers. Fares start at $1,799. Seven-to 13-day cruises with naturalists and historians are offered by **Lindblad Expeditions** (✆ **800/397-3348** or 212/765-7740;www.expeditions.com), starting at $2,490.

The *Queen of the West* and the *Empress of the North,* two modern paddle-wheel ships operated by the **American West Steamboat Company** (✆ **800/434-1232;** www.columbiarivercruise.com), go on the Columbia. The 7-night fares range from $1,389 to $5,169. The *Empress of the North* also cruises from Seattle to Alaska. **Great American Journeys** (✆ **800/901-9152** or 206/388-0444; www.greatamericanriver journeys.com) also has riverboat trips, starting at $1,989.

FAST FACTS: Washington

American Express In Seattle, the Amex office is in the Plaza 600 building at 600 Stewart St. (✆ **206/441-8622**). The office is open Monday through Friday from 8:30am to 5:30pm. For card member services, phone ✆ **800/528-4800**. Call ✆ **800/AXP-TRIP** or go to **www.americanexpress.com** for other locations or general information.

Car Rentals See "Getting Around," above.

Area Code The area code is **206** in Seattle, **425** for the Eastside (including Kirkland and Bellevue), and **253** for south King County (near the airport). The area code east of the Cascade Range is **509**.

Business Hours The following are general guidelines; specific establishments' hours may vary. Banks are open Monday through Friday from 9am to 5pm (some also on Sat 9am–noon). Stores are open Monday through Saturday from 10am to 6pm and Sunday from noon to 5pm (malls usually stay open until 9pm Mon–Sat). Bars generally open around 11am, but are legally allowed to be open Monday through Saturday from 6am to 1am and Sunday from 10am to 1am.

Driving Rules See "Getting Around," above.

Drugstores Rite-Aid (**800/748-3243**; www.riteaid.com for locations) and Walgreens (✆ **800/WALGREENS** for locations) are two large pharmacy chains found in the Northwest.

Embassies & Consulates See "Fast Facts: For the International Traveler," in chapter 3.

Emergencies Call ✆ **911** for fire, police, and ambulance.

Holidays See "Washington Calendar of Events," earlier in this chapter.

Information See "Visitor Information," earlier in this chapter, and individual city chapters for local information offices.

Liquor Laws The legal minimum drinking age in Washington state is 21. Aside from on-premise sales of cocktails in bars and restaurants, hard liquor can only be purchased in liquor stores. Beer and wine are available in convenience stores and grocery stores. Brewpubs tend to sell only beer and wine, but some also have licenses to sell hard liquor.

Lost & Found Be sure to tell all of your credit card companies the minute you discover your wallet has been lost or stolen and file a report at the nearest police precinct. Your credit card company or insurer may require a police report number or record of the loss. Most credit card companies have an emergency toll-free number to call if your card is lost or stolen; they may be able to wire you a cash advance immediately or deliver an emergency credit card in a day or two. Visa's U.S. emergency number is ⓒ **800/847-2911** or 410/581-9994. American Express cardholders and traveler's check holders should call ⓒ **800/ 221-7282**. MasterCard holders should call ⓒ **800/307-7309** or 636/722-7111. For other credit cards, call the toll-free number directory at ⓒ **800/555-1212**.

If you need emergency cash over the weekend when all banks and American Express offices are closed, you can have money wired to you via **Western Union** (ⓒ **800/325-6000**; www.westernunion.com).

Identity theft and fraud are potential complications of losing your wallet, especially if you've lost your driver's license along with your cash and credit cards. Notify the major credit-reporting bureaus immediately; placing a fraud alert on your records may protect you against liability for criminal activity. The three major U.S. credit-reporting agencies are **Equifax** (ⓒ **800/766-0008**; www. equifax.com), **Experian** (ⓒ **888/397-3742**; www.experian.com), and **TransUnion** (ⓒ **800/680-7289**; www.transunion.com). Finally, if you've lost all forms of photo ID, call your airline and explain the situation; they may allow you to board the plane if you have a copy of your passport or birth certificate and a copy of the police report you've filed.

Maps See "Getting Around," above.

Police To reach the police, dial ⓒ **911.**

Safety See "Insurance, Health & Safety," earlier in this chapter.

Smoking Although many of the restaurants listed in this book are smoke-free establishments, there are also many restaurants that do allow smoking. At most high-end places, the smoking area is usually in the bar/lounge.

Taxes The state of Washington makes up for its lack of an income tax with its heavy sales tax, and counties add on their own as well. In Seattle you'll pay 8.8%. Hotel-room tax in the Seattle metro area ranges from 10% to 16%. On rental cars, you'll pay not only an 18.5% car-rental tax, but also, if you rent at the airport, an additional 10% to 12% airport concession fee, for a whopping total of around 30%! You eliminate 10% of this by renting your car somewhere other than the airport.

Time Zone Washington state is on Pacific Standard Time (PST) and observes daylight saving time, which usually lasts from the first Sunday in April to the last Sunday in October, making it consistently 3 hours behind the U.S. East Coast. In 2007, daylight saving time will be extended from the second Sunday in March to the first Sunday in November.

3

For International Visitors

Whether it's your 1st visit or your 10th, a trip to the United States may require an additional degree of planning. This chapter will provide essential information, helpful tips, and advice for the more common problems that visitors encounter.

1 Preparing for Your Trip

ENTRY REQUIREMENTS

Check at any U.S. embassy or consulate for current information and requirements. You can also obtain a visa application and other information online at the **U.S. State Department**'s website, at **www.travel.state.gov**.

VISAS The U.S. State Department has a **Visa Waiver Program** allowing citizens of the following countries (at press time) to enter the United States without a visa for stays of up to 90 days: Andorra, Australia, Austria, Belgium, Brunei, Denmark, Finland, France, Germany, Iceland, Ireland, Italy, Japan, Liechtenstein, Luxembourg, Monaco, the Netherlands, New Zealand, Norway, Portugal, San Marino, Singapore, Slovenia, Spain, Sweden, Switzerland, and the United Kingdom. Citizens of these nations need only a valid passport and a round-trip air or cruise ticket upon arrival. If they first enter the United States, they may also visit Mexico, Canada, Bermuda, and/or the Caribbean islands and return to the United States without a visa. Further information is available from any U.S. embassy or consulate. Canadian citizens may enter the United States without visas; they need only proof of residence.

Citizens of all other countries must have (1) a valid passport that expires at least 6 months later than the scheduled end of their visit to the United States, and (2) a tourist visa, which may be obtained without charge from any U.S. consulate.

To obtain a visa, the traveler must submit a completed application form, with a 1½-inch-square photo, and demonstrate binding ties to a residence abroad. Usually you can obtain a visa at once or within 24 hours, but it may take longer during the summer rush from June through August. If you cannot go in person, ask the nearest U.S. embassy or consulate about applying by mail. Your travel agent or airline office may be able to provide you with visa applications and instructions. The U.S. consulate or embassy that issues your visa will determine whether it will be a multiple- or single-entry visa and set restrictions regarding the length of your stay.

British subjects can obtain up-to-date visa information by calling the **U.S. Embassy Visa Information Line** (✆ **0891/200-290**) or by visiting the "Visas to the U.S." section of the American Embassy London's website at www. usembassy.org.uk.

Irish citizens can obtain up-to-date visa information through the **Embassy of the USA Dublin,** 42 Elgin Rd., Dublin 4, Ireland (✆ **353/1-668-8777**) or consult the "Consular Services" section of the website at http://dublin.usembassy.gov.

Australian citizens can obtain up-to-date visa information from the **U.S. Embassy Canberra,** Moonah Place, Yarralumla, ACT 2600 (© **02/6214-5600**) or check the U.S. Diplomatic Mission's website at http://usembassy-australia.state.gov/consular.

Citizens of **New Zealand** can obtain up-to-date visa information by contacting the **U.S. Embassy New Zealand,** 29 Fitzherbert Terrace, Thorndon, Wellington (© **644/472-2068**), or get the information directly from the "For New Zealanders" section of the website at http://usembassy.org.nz.

MEDICAL REQUIREMENTS Unless you're arriving from an area known to be suffering from an epidemic (particularly cholera or yellow fever), inoculations or vaccinations are not required for entry into the United States. If you have a medical condition that happens to require **syringe-administered medications,** carry a valid signed prescription from your physician—the Federal Aviation Administration (FAA) no longer allows airline passengers to pack syringes in their carry-on baggage without documented proof of medical need. If you have a disease that requires treatment with **narcotics,** you should also carry documented proof with you—smuggling narcotics aboard a plane is a serious offense with severe penalties in the U.S.

For **HIV-positive visitors,** requirements for entering the United States are somewhat vague and change frequently. According to the latest publication of *HIV and Immigrants: A Manual for AIDS Service Providers,* the Immigration and Naturalization Service (INS) doesn't require a medical exam for entry into the United States, but INS officials may stop individuals because they look sick or because they are carrying AIDS/HIV

medicine. For up-to-the-minute information, contact **AIDSinfo** (© **800/448-0440** or 301/519-6616 outside the U.S.; www.aidsinfo.nih.gov) or the **Gay Men's Health Crisis** (© **212/367-1000;** www.gmhc.org).

DRIVER'S LICENSES Foreign driver's licenses are usually recognized in the U.S., but you should get an international one if your home license is not in English.

PASSPORT INFORMATION

Safeguard your passport in an inconspicuous, inaccessible place like a money belt. Make a copy of the critical pages, including the passport number, and store it in a safe place, separate from the passport itself. If you lose your passport, visit the nearest consulate of your native country as soon as possible for a replacement. Passport applications are downloadable from the websites listed below.

Many countries are now requiring that even children have their own passports to travel internationally.

FOR RESIDENTS OF CANADA

You can pick up a passport application at any of 28 regional passport offices or most travel agencies. Canadian children who travel must have their own passport. However, if you hold a valid Canadian passport issued before December 11, 2001, that bears the name of your child, the passport remains valid for you and your child until it expires. Passports cost C$87 for those 16 years and older (valid 5 years), C$37 children ages 3 to 15 (valid 5 years), and C$22, children under 3 (valid 3 years). Applications, which must be accompanied by two identical passport-size photographs and proof of Canadian citizenship, are available at travel agencies throughout Canada or from the central **Passport Office,** Department of Foreign Affairs and International Trade, Ottawa, ON K1A 0G3 (© **800/567-6868;** www.dfait-maeci.gc.ca/passport).

Processing takes 5 to 10 days if you apply in person, or about 3 weeks by mail.

FOR RESIDENTS OF THE UNITED KINGDOM

To pick up an application for a standard 10-year passport (5-year passport for children under 16), visit the nearest Passport Office, major post office, or travel agency. You can also contact the **United Kingdom Passport Service** at ☏ **0870/571-0410** or visit its website at www.passport.gov.uk. Passports are £42 for adults and £25 for children under 16, with another £30 fee if you apply in person at a Passport Office. Processing takes about 2 weeks (1 week if you apply at the Passport Office).

FOR RESIDENTS OF IRELAND

You can apply for a 10-year passport, costing (€57), at the **Passport Office,** Setanta Centre, Molesworth Street, Dublin 2 (☏ **01/671-1633;** www.irlgov.ie/iveagh). Those under age 18 and over 65 must apply for a €12 3-year passport. You can also apply at 1A South Mall, Cork (☏ **021/272 525**) or over the counter at main post offices.

FOR RESIDENTS OF AUSTRALIA

You can get an application from any local post office or branch of Passports Australia, but must schedule an interview at the passport office to present your application materials. Consult the **Australian Passport Information Service** at ☏ **131-232** or the website at www.passports.gov.au. Passports cost A$150 for adults, A$75 for under 18.

FOR RESIDENTS OF NEW ZEALAND

You can pick up a passport application at any New Zealand Passports Office or download it from the website. Contact the **Passports Office** at ☏ **0800/225-050** in New Zealand or 04/474-8100, or log onto www.passports.govt.nz. Passports

for adults are NZ$71 and for children under 16 NZ$36.

CUSTOMS
WHAT YOU CAN BRING IN

Every visitor more than 21 years of age may bring in, free of duty, the following: (1) 1 liter of wine or hard liquor; (2) 200 cigarettes, 100 cigars (but not from Cuba), or 3 pounds of smoking tobacco; and (3) $100 worth of gifts. These exemptions are offered to travelers who spend at least 72 hours in the United States and who have not claimed them within the preceding 6 months. It is altogether forbidden to bring into the country foodstuffs (particularly fruit, cooked meats, and canned goods) and plants (vegetables, seeds, tropical plants, and the like). Foreign tourists may carry in or out up to $10,000 in U.S. or foreign currency with no formalities; larger sums must be declared to U.S. Customs and Border Protection on entering or leaving, which includes filing form CM 4790. For details regarding U.S. Customs and Border Protection (CBP), consult your nearest U.S. embassy or consulate, or contact the **CBP** office at (☏ **202/927-1770** or www.cbp.gov).

WHAT YOU CAN TAKE HOME

U.K. citizens returning from a non-E.U. country have a customs allowance of: 200 cigarettes; 50 cigars; 250g of smoking tobacco; 2 liters of still table wine; 1 liter of spirits or strong liqueurs (over 22% volume); 2 liters of fortified wine, sparkling wine or other liqueurs; 60cc (ml) perfume; 250cc (ml) of toilet water; and £145 worth of all other goods, including gifts and souvenirs. People under 17 cannot have the tobacco or alcohol allowance. For more information, consult **HM Customs & Excise** at ☏ **0845/010-9000** (from outside the U.K., 020/8929-0152), or http://customs.hmrc.gov.uk.

For a clear summary of **Canadian rules,** request the booklet *I Declare,* from the **Canada Customs and Revenue Agency** (© **800/461-9999** in Canada, or 204/983-3500; www.cra-arc.gc.ca). Canada allows its citizens a C$750 exemption, and you're allowed to bring back duty-free one carton of cigarettes, one can of tobacco, 40 imperial ounces of liquor, and 50 cigars (Canadian citizens under 18 or 19, depending on their province, cannot have the tobacco or alcohol allowance). In addition, you're allowed to mail gifts to Canada valued at less than C$60 a day, if they're unsolicited and don't contain alcohol or tobacco (write on the package "Unsolicited gift, under $60 value"). All valuables should be declared on the Y-38 form before departure from Canada, including serial numbers of valuables you already own, such as expensive foreign cameras. *Note:* The C$750 exemption can only be used once a year and only after an absence of 7 days.

The duty-free allowance in **Australia** is A$900 or, for those under 18, A$450. Citizens age 18 and over can bring in 250 cigarettes or 250 grams of loose tobacco, and 2.25 liters of alcohol. If you're returning with valuables you already own, such as foreign-made cameras, you should file form B263. A helpful brochure available from Australian consulates or Customs offices is *Know Before You Go*. For details, consult the **Australian Customs Service** at © **1300/363-263** or www.customs.gov.au.

The duty-free allowance for **New Zealand** is NZ$700. Citizens over 17 can bring in 200 cigarettes, 50 cigars, or 250 grams of tobacco (or a mixture of all three if their combined weight doesn't exceed 250g); plus 4.5 liters of wine and beer, or 1.125 liters of liquor. New Zealand currency does not carry import or export restrictions. Fill out a certificate of export, listing the valuables you are taking out of the country; that way, you can bring them back without paying duty.

Most questions are answered in a free pamphlet available at New Zealand consulates and Customs offices: *New Zealand Customs Guide for Travellers, Notice no. 4.* For more information, contact **New Zealand Customs,** The Customhouse, 17–21 Whitmore St., Box 2218, Wellington (© **0800/428-786** or 04/473-6099; www.customs.govt.nz).

HEALTH INSURANCE

Although it's not required of travelers, health insurance is highly recommended. Unlike many European countries, the United States does not usually offer free or low-cost medical care to its citizens or visitors. Doctors and hospitals are expensive, and in most cases will require advance payment or proof of coverage before they render their services. Policies can cover everything from the loss or theft of your baggage and trip cancellation to the guarantee of bail in case you're arrested. Good policies will also cover the costs of an accident, repatriation, or death. Packages such as **Europ Assistance's "Worldwide Healthcare Plan"** are sold by European automobile clubs and travel agencies at attractive rates. **Worldwide Assistance Services, Inc.** (© **800/777-8710;** www.worldwide assistance.com) is the U.S. agent for Europ Assistance.

Though lack of health insurance may prevent you from being admitted to a hospital in nonemergencies, don't worry about being left on a street corner to die: The American way is to fix you now and bill you later.

INSURANCE FOR BRITISH TRAVELERS Most big travel agents offer their own insurance and will probably try to sell you their package when you book a holiday. Think before you sign. **Britain's Consumers' Association** recommends that you insist on seeing the policy and reading the fine print before buying travel insurance. **The Association**

of British Insurers (© 020/7600-3333; www.abi.org.uk) gives advice by phone and publishes *Holiday Insurance,* a free guide to policy provisions and prices. You could also shop around for better deals: Try **Columbus Direct** (© 0870/033-9988; www.columbusdirect.net).

INSURANCE FOR CANADIAN TRAVELERS Canadians should check with their provincial health plan offices or call **Health Canada** (© 866/225-0709; www.hc-sc.gc.ca) to find out the extent of its coverage and what documentation and receipts they must take home in case they are treated in the United States.

MONEY

CURRENCY The U.S. monetary system is very simple: The most common **bills** are the $1 (a "buck"), $5, $10, and $20 denominations. There are also $2 bills (seldom encountered), $50 bills, and $100 bills (the last two are usually not welcome as payment for small purchases). All the paper money was recently redesigned, making the faces on them disproportionately large, but the old-style bills are still legal tender.

Coins come in seven denominations: 1¢ (1 cent, or a penny); 5¢ (5 cents, or a nickel); 10¢ (10 cents, or a dime); 25¢ (25 cents, or a quarter); 50¢ (50 cents, or a half-dollar); the gold-colored Sacagawea coin, worth $1; and the rare silver dollar.

Note: The "foreign-exchange bureaus" so common in Europe are rare even at airports in the U.S., and nonexistent outside major cities. It's best not to change foreign money (or traveler's checks denominated in a currency other than U.S. dollars) at a small-town bank, or even a branch in a big city; in fact, leave any currency other than U.S. dollars at home.

TRAVELER'S CHECKS Traveler's checks are widely accepted, but make sure that they're denominated in U.S. dollars; foreign-currency checks are often difficult to exchange. The three traveler's checks that are most widely recognized—and least likely to be denied—are **Visa, American Express,** and **Thomas Cook.** Be sure to record the numbers of the checks, and keep that information in a separate place in case they get lost or stolen. Most Washington businesses are pretty good about taking traveler's checks, but you're better off cashing them in at a bank and paying in cash. *Remember:* You'll need identification, such as a driver's license or passport, to change a traveler's check.

CREDIT CARDS & ATMs Credit cards are the most widely used form of payment in the United States: **Visa** (Barclaycard in Britain), **MasterCard** (EuroCard in Europe, Access in Britain, Chargex in Canada), **American Express, Diners Club,** and **Discover.** There are, however, a handful of stores and restaurants in Washington that do not take credit cards, so be sure to ask in advance. Most businesses display a sticker near their entrance to let you know which cards they accept. (*Note:* Businesses may require a minimum purchase, usually around $10, to use a credit card.)

It's highly recommended that you bring at least one major credit card. You must have one to rent a car, and hotels and airlines usually require a credit card imprint as a deposit against expenses. In an emergency, a credit card is invaluable.

You'll find automated teller machines (ATMs) in just about every town in Washington, and on every block in the business districts of the big cities. Some ATMs will allow you to draw U.S. currency against your bank and credit cards. Check with your bank before leaving home, and remember that you will need your personal identification number (PIN) to do so. Most accept Visa, MasterCard, and American Express, as well as ATM cards from other U.S. banks. Expect to be charged up to $3 per transaction if you're not using your bank's ATM.

Travel Tip

Keep a copy of all your travel papers separate from your wallet or purse, and leave a copy with someone at home in case of an emergency.

One way around these fees is to ask for "cash back" at grocery stores that accept ATM cards and don't charge usage fees. Of course, you'll have to purchase something first.

ATM cards with major credit card backing, known as "debit cards," are a commonly accepted form of payment in most stores and restaurants. Debit cards draw money directly from your checking account. Some stores allow you to receive "cash back" on your purchases.

SAFETY

GENERAL SUGGESTIONS Washington's tourist areas are generally safe, though U.S. urban areas tend to be less safe than those in Europe or Japan. You should always stay alert. This is particularly true of large American cities. If you're in doubt about which neighborhoods are safe, don't hesitate to make inquiries with the hotel front desk staff or the local tourist office.

Avoid deserted areas, especially at night, and don't go into public parks after dark unless there's a concert or similar occasion that will attract a crowd.

Avoid carrying valuables with you on the street, and keep expensive cameras or electronic equipment bagged up or covered when not in use. If you're using a map, do try to consult it inconspicuously—or better yet, study it before you leave your room. Hold on to your pocketbook, and place your billfold in an inside pocket. In theaters, restaurants, and other public places, keep your possessions in sight.

Always lock your room door—don't assume that once you're inside the hotel,

you are automatically safe and no longer need to be aware of your surroundings.

DRIVING SAFETY Driving safety is important, too, and carjacking is not unprecedented. Question your rental agency about personal safety and ask for a traveler-safety brochure when you pick up your car. Obtain written directions—or a map with the route clearly marked—from the agency showing how to get to your destination. (Many agencies now offer the option of renting a cellphone for the duration of your car rental. Otherwise, contact **InTouch USA** at ℂ **800/872-7626** or www.intouchusa.com for short-term cellphone rental.) If possible, arrive and depart during daylight hours.

If you drive off a highway and end up in a risky neighborhood, leave the area as quickly as possible. If you have an accident, even on the highway, stay in your car with the doors locked until you assess the situation or the police arrive. If you're bumped from behind on the street or involved in a minor accident with no injuries, and the situation appears to be suspicious, motion to the other driver to follow you. Never get out of your car in such situations. Go directly to the nearest police precinct, well-lit service station, or 24-hour store.

Park in well-lit, busy areas when possible. Always keep your car doors locked, even if the vehicle is attended. Never leave any packages or valuables in sight. If someone attempts to rob you or steal your car, don't try to resist the thief/carjacker. Report the incident to the police department immediately by calling ℂ **911.**

2 Getting to the U.S.

BY PLANE For an extensive listing of airlines that fly into Seattle, see section 11, "Getting There," in chapter 2.

A number of U.S. airlines offer service from Europe to the United States. If they do not have direct flights from Europe to Seattle, they can book you straight through on a connecting flight.

In Great Britain, you can make reservations by calling the following numbers: **Air Canada** (© 0871/220-1111; www.air canada.ca), **American** (© 020/7365-0777 in London, or 0845/7789-789 outside London; www.aa.com), **British Airways** (© 0870/850-9850; www.british airways.com), **Continental** (© 0129/377-6464; www.continental.com), **Delta** (© 0800/414-767; www.delta.com), **Northwest/KLM** (© 08705/074-074; www.nwa.com), **United** (© 0845/8444-777; www.ual.com), and **US Airways** (© 0845/600-3300; www.usairways.com).

International carriers that fly from Europe to Los Angeles and/or San Francisco include **Aer Lingus** (© 0818/365-000 in Ireland; www.aerlingus.com) and **British Airways** (© 0870/850-9850; www.britishairways.com), which also flies direct to Seattle from London.

From New Zealand and Australia, there are flights to Los Angeles on **Qantas** (© 13 13 13 in Australia; www.qantas.com.au) and **Air New Zealand** (© 0800/737-000 in Auckland; www.airnew zealand.co.nz). From Los Angeles, you can continue on to Seattle on a regional carrier, such as **Alaska Airlines** (© 02/9244-2317 in Sydney, or 09/308-3358 in Auckland; www.alaskaair.com) or **Southwest** (© 800/435-9792 in the U.S.; www.southwest.com).

From Toronto, there are nonstop flights to Seattle on **Air Canada** (© 888/247-2262; www.aircanada.ca).

From Vancouver, British Columbia, there are flights to Seattle on **Air Canada**

(© 888/247-2262; www.aircanada.ca), **Alaska Airlines** (© 800/252-7522; www.alaskaair.com), and **Horizon Air** (© 800/547-9308; www.horizonair.com).

AIRLINE DISCOUNTS Smart travelers can reduce the price of a plane ticket by shopping around. Overseas visitors, for example, can take advantage of the APEX (Advance Purchase Excursion) reductions offered by major U.S. and European carriers. For more money-saving airline advice, see section 11, "Getting There," in chapter 2. For the best rates, be flexible with travel dates and times.

BY TRAIN Amtrak (© 800/872-7245; www.amtrak.com) offers service from Vancouver, British Columbia, to Seattle, a trip that takes about 4 hours. One-way fares from Vancouver to Seattle are usually around $27 to $32. Booking earlier will get you a less expensive ticket. Amtrak also operates a high-speed European-style train between Vancouver and Eugene, Oregon.

Like the airlines, Amtrak offers several discounted fares; although they're not all based on advance purchase, you'll have more discount options by reserving early.

BY FERRY If you're traveling between Victoria, British Columbia, and Seattle, several options are available through **Victoria Clipper,** Pier 69, 2701 Alaskan Way (© **800/888-2535,** 206/448-5000, or 250/382-8100 in Victoria; www.victoriaclipper.com). Ferries make the 2- or 3-hour trip year-round at prices ranging from $70 to $133 round-trip for adults (the lower fare is for advance-purchase tickets). Some trips also stop in the San Juan Islands.

IMMIGRATION & CUSTOMS CLEARANCE Visitors arriving from another country should cultivate patience and resignation before setting foot on U.S.

soil. Clearing immigration control can take as long as 2 hours, especially on summer weekends, so carry this guidebook or other reading material. People traveling by air from Canada, Bermuda, and certain Caribbean countries can sometimes clear U.S. Customs and Border Protection (CBP) at the point of departure.

3 Getting around the U.S.

For specific information on traveling to and around Washington state, see sections 11 and 12 in chapter 2 and sections 1 and 2 in chapter 5.

BY PLANE Some large airlines offer transatlantic or transpacific passengers special discount tickets under the name **Visit USA,** which allows mostly one-way travel from one U.S. destination to another at very low prices. Unavailable in the U.S., these discount tickets must be purchased abroad in conjunction with your international fare. This system is the easiest, fastest, cheapest way to see the country. Obtain information well in advance from your travel agent or airline, since the conditions attached to discount tickets can be changed without advance notice.

BY CAR Unless you plan to spend the bulk of your vacation in a city where walking is the best way to get around (read: New York City or New Orleans), the most cost-effective way to travel the United States is by car. The interstate highway system connects cities and towns all over the country, with an extensive network of federal, state, and local highways and roads as well. Some of the national car-rental companies with offices in Washington include **Alamo** (© 800/462-5266; www.alamo. com), **Avis** (© 800/230-4898; www.avis. com), **Budget** (© 800/527-0700; www. budget.com), **Dollar** (© 800/800-3665; www.dollar.com), **Hertz** (© 800/654-3131; www.hertz.com), and **National** (© 800/227-7368; www.nationalcar.com).

If you plan to rent a car in the United States, you probably won't need the services of an additional automobile organization. If you're planning to buy or borrow a car, automobile-association membership is recommended. **AAA,** the **American Automobile Association** (© **800/222-4357;** travel.aaa.com), is the country's largest auto club and supplies its members with maps, insurance, and, most important, emergency road service. The cost of joining runs from $63 for singles to $87 for two members, but if you're a member of a foreign auto club with reciprocal arrangements, you can enjoy free AAA service in America. See section 11, "Getting There," in chapter 2 for more information.

BY TRAIN International visitors (excluding Canadians) can also buy a **USA Rail Pass,** good for 15 or 30 days of unlimited travel on **Amtrak** (© **800/ USA-RAIL;** www.amtrak.com). The pass is available through many overseas travel agents. Prices valid for travel across the United States in 2005 for a 15-day pass were $295 off-peak, $440 peak; a 30-day pass costs $385 off-peak, $550 peak. Fares are significantly cheaper, however, within particular regions. See Amtrak's website for the cost of travel within the western, eastern, or northwestern United States. With a foreign passport, you can also buy passes direct from some Amtrak locations, including San Francisco, Los Angeles, Chicago, New York, Miami, Boston, and Washington, D.C. Reservations are generally required and should be made as early as possible. Regional rail passes are also available.

BY BUS Bus travel is often the most economical form of public transit for short hops between U.S. cities, but it can also be extremely slow and rather uncomfortable—certainly not an option for everyone (particularly when Amtrak, which is far more luxurious, offers similar rates). **Greyhound/Trailways** (© **800/231-2222;** www.greyhound.com), the sole nationwide bus line, offers an **International Ameripass** that must be purchased before coming to the United States, or by phone through the Greyhound International Office at the Port Authority Bus Terminal in New York City (© **212/971-0492**). The pass can be obtained from foreign travel agents or through Greyhound's website (order at least 21 days before your departure to the U.S.) and costs less than the domestic version. 2005 passes cost as follows: 4 days ($179), 7 days ($239), 10 days ($289), 15 days ($349), 21 days ($419), 30 days ($479), 45 days ($529), or 60 days ($639). You can get more info on the pass at the website, or by calling © **402/330-8552.** In addition, special rates are available for seniors, students, and children.

FAST FACTS: For the International Traveler

Automobile Organizations Auto clubs will supply maps, suggested routes, guidebooks, accident and bail-bond insurance, and emergency road service. The **American Automobile Association (AAA)** is the major auto club in the United States. If you belong to an auto club in your home country, inquire about AAA reciprocity before you leave. You may be able to join AAA even if you're not a member of a reciprocal club; to inquire, call AAA (© **800/222-4357**). AAA is actually an organization of regional auto clubs, so look under "AAA Automobile Club" in the White Pages of the telephone directory. AAA has a nationwide emergency road service telephone number (© 800/AAA-HELP).

Business Hours Offices are usually open weekdays from 9am to 5pm. Banks are open weekdays from 9am to 3pm or later and sometimes Saturday mornings. Stores typically open between 9 and 10am and close between 5 and 6pm from Monday through Saturday. Stores in shopping complexes or malls tend to stay open late: until about 9pm on weekdays and weekends, and many malls and larger department stores are open on Sundays.

Climate See section 4, "When to Go," in chapter 2.

Currency & Currency Exchange See "Entry Requirements" and "Money" under "Preparing for Your Trip," earlier in this chapter.

Drinking Laws The legal age for purchase and consumption of alcoholic beverages is 21; proof of age is required and often requested at bars, nightclubs, and restaurants, so it's always a good idea to bring ID when you go out. Beer and wine often can be purchased in supermarkets, but liquor laws vary from state to state.

Do not carry open containers of alcohol in your car or any public area that isn't zoned for alcohol consumption. The police can fine you on the spot. Nothing will ruin your trip faster than getting a citation for DUI (driving under the influence), so don't drive while intoxicated.

Electricity Like Canada, the United States uses 110 to 120 volts AC (60 cycles), compared to 220 to 240 volts AC (50 cycles) in most of Europe, Australia, and New Zealand. If your small appliances use 220 to 240 volts, you'll need a 110-volt transformer and a plug adapter with two flat parallel pins to operate them here. Downward converters that change 220 to 240 volts to 110 to 120 volts are difficult to find in the United States, so bring one with you.

Embassies & Consulates All embassies are located in the nation's capital, Washington, D.C. Some consulates are located in major U.S. cities, and most nations have a mission to the United Nations in New York City. If your country isn't listed below, call for directory information in Washington, D.C. (② 202/555-1212) or log on to **www.embassy.org/embassies**.

The embassy of **Australia** is at 1601 Massachusetts Ave. NW, Washington, DC 20036 (② 202/797-3000; www.austemb.org). There are consulates in New York, Honolulu, Houston, Los Angeles, and San Francisco.

The embassy of **Canada** is at 501 Pennsylvania Ave. NW, Washington, DC 20001 (② 202/682-1740; www.canadianembassy.org). Other Canadian consulates are in Buffalo (NY), Detroit, Los Angeles, New York, and Seattle.

The embassy of **Ireland** is at 2234 Massachusetts Ave. NW, Washington, DC 20008 (② 202/462-3939; www.irelandemb.org). Irish consulates are in Boston, Chicago, New York, San Francisco, and other cities. See website for complete listing.

The embassy of **Japan** is at 2520 Massachusetts Ave. NW, Washington, DC 20008 (② 202/238-6700; www.embjapan.org). Japanese consulates are located in many cities including Atlanta, Boston, Detroit, New York, San Francisco, and Seattle.

The embassy of **New Zealand** is at 37 Observatory Circle NW, Washington, DC 20008 (② 202/328-4800; www.nzemb.org). New Zealand consulates are in Los Angeles, Salt Lake City, San Francisco, and Seattle.

The embassy of the **United Kingdom** is at 3100 Massachusetts Ave. NW, Washington, DC 20008 (② 202/588-7800; www.britainusa.com). Other British consulates are in Atlanta, Boston, Chicago, Cleveland, Houston, Los Angeles, New York, San Francisco, and Seattle.

Emergencies Call ② 911 to report a fire, call the police, or get an ambulance anywhere in the United States. This is a toll-free call. (No coins are required at public telephones.)

If you encounter serious problems, contact the **Traveler's Aid International** (② 202/546-1127; www.travelersaid.org) to help direct you to a local branch. This nationwide, nonprofit, social-service organization geared to helping travelers in difficult straits offers services that might include reuniting families separated while traveling, providing food and/or shelter to people stranded without cash, or even emotional counseling. If you're in trouble, seek them out.

Gasoline (Petrol) Petrol is known as gasoline (or simply gas) in the United States, and petrol stations are known as both gas stations and service stations. At press time, the cost of gasoline in the U.S. is around $2.50 a gallon and fluctuating drastically. Taxes are already included in the printed price. One U.S. gallon equals 3.8 liters or .85 imperial gallons.

Holidays Banks, government offices, post offices, and many stores, restaurants, and museums are closed on the following legal national holidays: January 1 (New Year's Day), the third Monday in January (Martin Luther King, Jr. Day), the third Monday in February (Presidents' Day, Washington's Birthday), the last Monday in May (Memorial Day), July 4 (Independence Day), the first Monday in September (Labor Day), the second Monday in October (Columbus Day), November 11 (Veterans' Day/Armistice Day), the fourth Thursday in November (Thanksgiving Day), and December 25 (Christmas). Also, the Tuesday following the first Monday in November is Election Day and is a federal government holiday in presidential-election years (held every 4 years, and next in 2008).

Legal Aid If you are "pulled over" for a minor infraction (such as speeding), never attempt to pay the fine directly to a police officer; this could be construed as attempted bribery, a much more serious crime. Pay fines by mail, or directly into the hands of the clerk of the court. If accused of a more serious offense, say and do nothing before consulting a lawyer. Here the burden is on the state to prove a person's guilt beyond a reasonable doubt, and everyone has the right to remain silent, whether he or she is suspected of a crime or actually arrested. Once arrested, a person can make one telephone call to a party of his or her choice. Call your embassy or consulate.

Mail If you aren't sure what your address will be in the United States, mail can be sent to you, in your name, c/o General Delivery at the main post office of the city or region where you expect to be. (Call © **800/275-8777** for information on the nearest post office.) The addressee must pick up mail in person and must produce proof of identity (driver's license, passport, and so on). Most post offices will hold your mail for up to one month, and are open Monday to Friday from 8am to 6pm, and Saturday from 9am to 3pm.

Generally found at intersections, mailboxes are blue with a red-and-white stripe and carry the inscription U.S. MAIL. If your mail is addressed to a U.S. destination, don't forget to add the five-digit postal code (or zip code), after the two-letter abbreviation of the state to which the mail is addressed. This is essential to prompt delivery.

At press time, domestic postage rates were 24¢ for a regular postcard and 39¢ for a large postcard or a letter. For international mail, a first-class letter of up to 1 ounce costs 84¢ (63¢ to Canada and Mexico); a first-class postcard costs 75¢ (55¢ to Canada and Mexico); and a preprinted postal aerogramme costs 75¢. For more information, see usps.com.

Measurements See the chart on the inside front cover of this book for details on converting metric measurements to U.S. equivalents.

Taxes The United States has no value-added tax (VAT) or other indirect tax at the national level. Every state, county, and city has the right to levy its own local tax on all purchases, including hotel and restaurant checks, airline tickets, and so on.

In Washington, the sales tax rate is around 8.8% in most places. Also, you'll pay around 30% in taxes and concession fees when you rent a car at Seattle-Tacoma International Airport. (You'll save 10%–11% by renting somewhere other than the airport.) Hotel-room taxes generally range from around 10% to 16%. Travelers on a budget should keep both car-rental and hotel-room taxes in mind when planning a trip.

Telephone, Telegraph, Telex, & Fax The telephone system in the United States is run by private corporations, so rates, especially for long-distance service and operator-assisted calls, can vary widely. Generally, hotel surcharges on long-distance and local calls are astronomical, so you're usually better off using a **public pay telephone,** which you'll find clearly marked in most public buildings and private establishments, as well as on the street. Convenience grocery stores and gas stations always have them. Many convenience groceries and packaging services sell **prepaid calling cards** in denominations up to $50; these can be the least expensive way to call home. Many public phones at airports now accept American Express, MasterCard, and Visa credit cards. **Local calls** made from public pay phones in most locales cost either 25¢ or 35¢. Pay phones do not accept pennies, and few will take anything larger than a quarter.

You may want to look into leasing a cellphone for your trip.

Most long-distance and international calls can be dialed directly from any phone. **For calls within the United States and to Canada,** dial 1 followed by the area code and the seven-digit number. **For other international calls,** dial 011 followed by the country code, city code, and the telephone number of the person you are calling.

Calls to area codes **800, 888, 877,** and **866** are toll-free. However, calls to numbers in area codes **700** and **900** (chat lines, bulletin boards, "dating" services, and so on) can be very expensive—usually a charge of 95¢ to $3 or more per minute, and they sometimes have minimum charges that can run as high as $15 or more.

For **reversed-charge or collect calls,** and for person-to-person calls, dial 0 (zero, not the letter O) followed by the area code and number you want; an operator will then come on the line, and you should specify that you are calling collect, or person-to-person, or both. If your operator-assisted call is international, ask for the overseas operator.

For **local directory assistance** ("information"), dial 411; for long-distance information, dial 1, then the appropriate area code and 555-1212.

Telegraph and telex services are provided primarily by Western Union. You can bring your telegram into the nearest Western Union office (there are hundreds across the country) or dictate it over the phone (© **800/325-6000**). You can also telegraph money, or have it telegraphed to you, very quickly over the Western Union system, but this service can cost as much as 15% to 20% of the amount sent.

Most hotels have **fax machines** available for guest use (be sure to ask about the charge to use it). Many hotel rooms are even wired for guests' fax machines. A less expensive way to send and receive faxes may be at stores such as **The UPS Store** (formerly Mail Boxes Etc.), a national chain of retail packing service shops. (Look in the Yellow Pages directory under "Packing Services.")

There are two kinds of telephone directories in the United States. The so-called **White Pages** list private households and business subscribers in alphabetical order. The inside front cover lists emergency numbers for police, fire, ambulance, the Coast Guard, poison-control center, crime-victims hot line, and so on. The first few pages will tell you how to make long-distance and international calls, complete with country codes and area codes. Government numbers are usually printed on blue paper within the White Pages. Printed on yellow paper, the so-called **Yellow Pages** list all local services, businesses, industries, and houses of worship according to activity with an index at the front or back. The Yellow Pages also include city plans or detailed area maps and public transportation routes.

Time The continental United States is divided into **four time zones:** Eastern Standard Time (EST), Central Standard Time (CST), Mountain Standard Time (MST), and Pacific Standard Time (PST). Alaska and Hawaii have their own zones. For example, noon in New York City (EST) is 11am in Chicago (CST), 10am in Denver (MST), 9am in Los Angeles (PST), 8am in Anchorage (AST), and 7am in Honolulu (HST).

Daylight saving time takes effect at 2am the first Sunday in April until 2am the last Sunday in October, except in Arizona, Hawaii, the U.S. Virgin Islands, and Puerto Rico. (Indiana will begin observing daylight saving time in April 2006.) Daylight saving moves the clock 1 hour ahead of standard time. (A new law will extend daylight saving in 2007; clocks will change the second Sun in Mar and the first Sun in Nov.)

Tipping Tips are a very important part of certain workers' income, and gratuities are the standard way of showing appreciation for services provided. (Tipping is certainly not compulsory if the service is poor!) In hotels, tip **bellhops** at least $1 per bag ($2–$3 if you have a lot of luggage) and tip the **chamber staff** $1 to $2 per day (more if you've left a disaster area for him or her to clean up). Tip the **doorman** or **concierge** only if he or she has provided you with some specific service (for example, calling a cab for you or obtaining difficult-to-get theater tickets). Tip the **valet-parking attendant** $1 every time you get your car.

In restaurants, bars, and nightclubs, tip **service staff** 15% to 20% of the check, tip **bartenders** 10% to 15%, tip **checkroom attendants** $1 per garment, and tip **valet-parking attendants** $1 per vehicle.

As for other service personnel, tip **cab drivers** 15% of the fare; tip **skycaps** at airports at least $1 per bag ($2–$3 if you have a lot of luggage); and tip **hairdressers** and **barbers** 15% to 20%.

Toilets You won't find public toilets or "restrooms" on the streets in most U.S. cities, but they can be found in hotel lobbies, bars, restaurants, museums, department stores, railway and bus stations, and service stations. Large hotels and fast-food restaurants are probably the best bet for good, clean facilities. Restaurants and bars in resorts or heavily visited areas may reserve their restrooms for patrons. Some establishments display a notice indicating this.

4

Suggested Washington Itineraries

Where should I go? What should I see? What's the best route? How do I maximize my time? I know all these questions well, having asked them myself when planning vacation itineraries, and I've been asked them by other people planning trips to Washington state. This chapter should help you answer those questions. I'm not going to get down to the nitty-gritty details like where to get gas, but I do mention below the occasional not-to-be-missed or out-of-the-way restaurant or mountain lodge.

If you read through all these itineraries, you'll notice a bit of overlap. There are some destinations and attractions that just should not be missed on any visit to the state. Almost any visit to Washington should include at least a day in Seattle, and to really get a feel for what the state is all about, you have to get out amid the big trees. There's a good reason why they call this the Evergreen State.

1 Washington in 1 Week

Washington is a big state, so don't expect to see it all in a single week's vacation. However, for most people who don't live in the Northwest, Washington is that rainy region of towering evergreens, sparkling waters, and free-flowing espresso. This 1-week itinerary will allow you to explore the Washington that you've probably conjured up in your mind.

Days ❶ & ❷: Seattle ★★

Spend your first 2 days exploring Seattle. Start your days at the bustling **Pike Place Market** (p. 111). On the waterfront, visit the **Seattle Aquarium** (p. 111) and take a short boat tour. My favorite boat tours are the sailboat excursions offered by **Emerald City Charters** (p. 126). Don't miss the fun **Underground Tour** (p. 113) in the Pioneer Square neighborhood. At Seattle Center, catch the view from atop the Space Needle and, if rock music and science fiction appeal to you, spend a few

hours at the **Experience Music Project** (p. 114) and the **Science Fiction Museum** (p. 114). For the chance to see migrating salmon, visit the **Hiram M. Chittenden Locks** (p. 118).

Days ❸ & ❹: The San Juan Islands ★★

Depending on the time of year, take a passenger ferry or a floatplane to Friday Harbor in the San Juan Islands. Either way, you'll be in for quite an adventure. If you fly and it happens to be summer, be sure to do a whale-watching tour

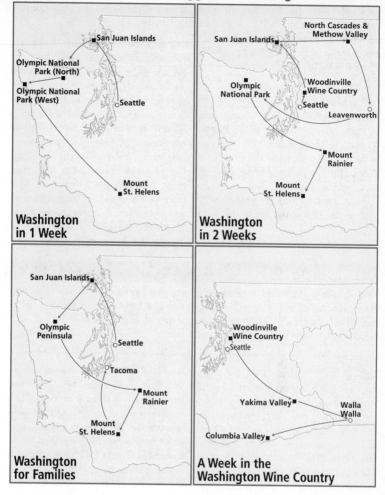

Washington in 1 Week

- San Juan Islands
- Olympic National Park (North)
- Olympic National Park (West)
- Seattle
- Mount St. Helens

Washington in 2 Weeks

- San Juan Islands
- North Cascades & Methow Valley
- Olympic National Park
- Woodinville Wine Country
- Seattle
- Leavenworth
- Mount Rainier
- Mount St. Helens

Washington for Families

- San Juan Islands
- Olympic Peninsula
- Seattle
- Tacoma
- Mount Rainier
- Mount St. Helens

A Week in the Washington Wine Country

- Woodinville Wine Country
- Seattle
- Yakima Valley
- Walla Walla
- Columbia Valley

while you're in the islands. Visit the **Whale Museum** (p. 166) to learn more about the region's orca whales. To learn about the island's forgotten Pig War, visit the 2 units of San Juan Island's **San Juan Island National Historical Park** (p. 167). If you're a cyclist, rent a bike 1 day and explore San Juan Island or catch a ferry to **Lopez Island** (p. 181), the flattest of the ferry-serviced San Juans.

Day ❺: Olympic National Park North ✿✿✿

From the San Juans, fly back to Seattle, rent a car and catch a ferry across Puget Sound to begin a journey out to **Olympic National Park** (p. 235). This sprawling park preserves not only glacier-carved peaks and alpine meadows, but also wild beaches and rainforests. Spend the night either in Port Angeles or at **Lake**

Crescent Lodge (p. 243). If you have time, be sure to visit the Victorian port town of **Port Townsend** (p. 221). In July and August, you can see lavender fields near the town of Sequim.

Day ❻: Olympic National Park West ✯✯✯

Drive out to the wilderness beaches near La Push. After a stroll or hike on **Rialto, Second,** or **Third Beach** (p. 247), head to the mossy rainforest of the Hoh River Valley. Hike the **Hall of Mosses Trail** (p. 248), and if you have time and have planned ahead, go for a short **raft trip** (p. 241) on the Hoh River. Spend the night

at one of the lodges on **Lake Quinault** (p. 250 and 251).

Day ❼: Mount St. Helens National Volcanic Monument ✯✯✯

Because today will require the most driving of any day in this itinerary, get an early start. Continue around the Olympic Peninsula and then head southeast to **Mount St. Helens National Volcanic Monument** (p. 314), which preserves the only active volcano in the contiguous United States. After visiting the monument, drive back north to Tacoma, where there are lots of good lodging options and several excellent museums, including the **Museum of Glass** (p. 208) and the **Tacoma Art Museum** (p. 208).

2 Washington in 2 Weeks

Plan on spending 2 weeks in Washington and you'll get a good sense of this state's diverse landscapes. Not only will you be able to spend more time relaxing in the San Juan Islands, but you'll also get to explore the rugged North Cascades and wildflower meadows of Mount Rainier National Park.

Days ❶ & ❷: Seattle ✯✯

Start your Washington state vacation in Seattle, where you should make a coffeehouse your first stop. After your hands are wrapped around a genuine Seattle latte, you're ready to take on the city. Start your first day at **Pike Place Market** (p. 111), where you can stuff yourself with all kinds of tasty food samples and snacks. From the market, head down to the **waterfront** (p. 108), where you should be sure to visit the **Seattle Aquarium** (p. 111) and go for a **boat excursion** (p. 125). The next day, spend time at **Seattle Center** (p. 113), which is home to the Space Needle, the Experience Music Project, and the Science Fiction Museum.

Day ❸: Woodinville Wine Country ✯

Washington is second only to California in wine production, and no visit to the state

would be complete without sampling a little fruit of the vine. The most convenient place to do some wine tasting is 30 minutes north of Seattle near the town of Woodinville. Here you should be sure to visit **Chateau Ste. Michelle** (p. 150) and **Columbia Winery** (p. 150), the area's two biggest producers. Afterward, check out some of the smaller wineries in the area.

Days ❹, ❺, ❻ & ❼: San Juan Islands ✯✯✯

Next head north to the emerald islands known as the San Juans. These idyllic islands are way out of the mainstream and home to quaint villages, delightful bed-and-breakfast inns, and excellent restaurants. Plan on staying on Orcas Island and San Juan Island, or, if you're a cyclist, quiet Lopez Island. While you're in the islands, be sure to try **sea kayaking**

(p. 157, p. 169, p. 177, and p. 182), and, if it's summer, be sure to go **whale-watching** (p. 169). The mountain-top views and hiking trails at **Moran State Park** (p. 177) also should not be missed.

Day ❽: The North Cascades & the Methow Valley ⭐⭐⭐

From the San Juans, drive east over the North Cascades Scenic Highway, which passes through the most grandly rugged landscape in the state. Jagged snow-capped peaks rise all around, and tucked amid the mountain slopes are lakes of astonishing colors. Much of the region is preserved in the various units of the **North Cascades National Park Complex** (p. 6). En route, be sure to stop at **Diablo Lake Overlook** (p. 277), **Rainy Pass** (p. 277), and **Washington Pass** (p. 277). Spend the night in the Methow Valley, which is home to two of the state's finest mountain lodges.

Day ❾: Leavenworth ⭐⭐

From the Methow Valley, get an early start and take a **boat tour** (p. 287) on gla-cier-carved **Lake Chelan** (p. 285), which is the third deepest lake in the country. Boat tours go more than 50 miles up this lake to the remote community of Ste-hekin, which is so isolated that it has no roads leading to it. From Lake Chelan, continue to the self-consciously quaint Bavarian theme town of **Leavenworth** (p. 292). Sure, this town can be tacky, but the natural setting is breathtaking in its ruggedness, and residents have done an impressive job of reproducing an alpine village here in the mountains of Washington.

Days ❿, ⓫ & ⓬: Olympic National Park ⭐⭐⭐

From Leavenworth, drive back up and over the Cascade Range, and first take the ferry to Whidbey Island from Mukilteo and then the ferry from Whidbey Island to **Port Townsend** (p. 221), a Victorian port town on the Olympic Peninsula. With its many B&Bs and historic commercial district full of galleries and eclectic shops, Port Townsend makes a good place to spend your first night on the peninsula. The next day, begin your explorations of **Olympic National Park** (p. 235) with a hike through the alpine meadows at **Hurricane Ridge** (p. 8). Continue on to the Forks area, where you can walk on the Olympic coast's wilderness beaches. South of Forks, head up the **Hoh River Valley** (p. 247) to explore one of the national park's rainforest valleys.

Day ⓭: Mount Rainier National Park ⭐⭐⭐

Today get an early start, since it is a long drive to **Mount Rainier National Park** (p. 306). Mount Rainier is a dormant volcano, and its massive bulk dominates the horizon from all over the state. Popular with mountain climbers, the mountain is also known for its gorgeous displays of alpine wildflowers in July and August. The best place to see these wild-flowers is in **Paradise** (p. 309).

Day ⓮: Mount St. Helens National Volcanic Monument ⭐⭐⭐

While Mount Rainier is a dormant volcano, not far away you can visit the only active volcano in the contiguous United States. **Mount St. Helens** (p. 314), which erupted with unimaginable force in May 1980, began another period of activity in the fall of 2004. Today you can see a new lava dome building within the massive crater left after the 1980 eruption. Several interpretive centers provide loads of information about the first big blast and the current state of things within this fascinating national volcanic monument.

3 Washington for Families

While Washington doesn't have a major amusement park to attract families, it does have lots of great, child-oriented museums in Seattle, a park full of fun attractions in Tacoma, national parks, and an active volcano (how cool is that?).

Days ❶ & ❷: Seattle 🌟🌟

Spend the first 2 days of your trip exploring all the kid-friendly attractions of Seattle. Spend time on the waterfront visiting the **Seattle Aquarium** (p. 111) and going for a boat tour. At Seattle Center, originally built for the 1962 World's Fair, you'll find enough cool attractions to keep kids of all ages busy for a day or more. Kids' favorites include the **Space Needle** (p. 114), the **Children's Museum** (p. 123), the **Pacific Science Center** (p. 114), the **Experience Music Project** (p. 114), the **Science Fiction Museum** (p. 114), a small amusement park, and the **Seattle Children's Theatre** (p. 123).

Days ❸, ❹ & ❺: The San Juan Islands 🌟🌟🌟

From Seattle, head north to the San Juan Islands, home to orca whales and bald eagles. With its beaches, state parks, scooter rentals, and summertime whale-watching tours, the San Juans have long been a favorite summer destination of Washington families. Visit the **Whale Museum** (p. 166) and the **San Juan Island National Historical Park** (p. 167) on San Juan Island, and **Moran State Park** (p. 177) on Orcas Island. The San Juans are also a great place to introduce the kids to sea kayaking; there are lots of tour companies here that will take the whole family out on the water.

Days ❻, ❼ & ❽: Olympic Peninsula 🌟🌟🌟

If you've brought along passports, you could travel from the San Juans to the Olympic Peninsula by way of Victoria, British Columbia. Otherwise, head back to Anacortes, drive south to the Keystone ferry landing on Whidbey Island, and cross over to **Port Townsend** (p. 221) on the Olympic Peninsula. In Olympic National Park, visit **Hurricane Ridge** (p. 8), **Sol Duc Hot Springs** (p. 238), the **beaches near La Push** (p. 247), and the **Hoh River Valley rainforest** (p. 247). At Hurricane Ridge, you're likely to see nearly tame deer. In the Hoh River Valley, keep an eye out for elk. Spend your last night on the peninsula at a lodge on Lake Quinault.

Days ❾ & ❿: Mount Rainier National Park 🌟🌟🌟

From Lake Quinault, drive to Mount Rainier National Park. En route, be sure to stop at **Northwest Trek Wildlife Park** (p. 217), a drive-through zoo filled with wild animals from around North America. At Mount Rainier National Park, wander the wildflower meadows at **Paradise** (p. 309), visit the 1,000-year-old western red cedars at **Grove of the Patriarchs** (p. 309), and look for mountain goats on the trails at **Sunrise** (p. 309).

Day ⓫: Mount St. Helens National Volcanic Monument 🌟🌟🌟

You may not see red-hot lava pouring down the side of the volcano, but since late 2004, **Mount St. Helens** (p. 314) has been spewing ash and smoke, and a new lava dome has been building in the crater left by the volcano's huge 1980 eruption. Although operated as a sort of promotional facility for the logging industry, the **Charles W. Bingham Forest Learning Center** (p. 315) has a playground and hands-on exhibits that kids love. At the end of the day, drive north to Tacoma to spend the night.

Day ⑫: Tacoma ✿✿

Tacoma's Point Defiance Park is one of the best places in the state to bring the family. Start at **Point Defiance Zoo & Aquarium** (p. 210) and then visit the **Fort Nisqually Living History Museum** (p. 210), where interpreters dress up in 19th-century fur-traders' attire, and the **Camp 6 Logging Museum** (p. 209), where the family can hop aboard an old logging train. The park also has lots of hiking trails and good waterfront restaurants nearby.

4 A Week in the Washington Wine Country

Washington state is the second-largest producer of wine in the United States, after California, and as in California, wineries are all over the state. However, the biggest concentrations are in eastern Washington's Yakima Valley and Walla Walla areas. Spend a week driving through the state's various wine regions and you'll get a good feel for the diversity of wines produced.

Day ①: Seattle & the Woodinville Wine Country ✿✿

Start your wine tour in Seattle, and head north of the city 30 minutes to the Woodinville area. Here you'll find a couple of the state's largest wine producers— **Chateau Ste. Michele** (p. 150) and **Columbia Winery** (p. 150)—as well as some of its smallest. For the ultimate wine country experience, stay at the **Willows Lodge** (p. 90) and have dinner at **The Herbfarm** (p. 104).

Days ② & ③: Yakima Valley ✿

From the Seattle area, head 140 miles east on I-90 and I-82 to **Yakima** (p. 328), which marks the start of the state's main wine-grape-growing region. The Yakima Valley wine region stretches for 70 miles between the city of Yakima and the Tri-Cities area (Richland, Kennewick, and Pasco). There are so many wineries in the valley that you can easily spend 2 days wine tasting in the area and still leave plenty of wineries for a return visit. The biggest concentrations of wineries are near Zillah, at the west end of the valley, and near Prosser, at the east end. Spend a night in Yakima and the next night in the Tri-Cities area.

Days ④, ⑤ & ⑥: Walla Walla ✿✿

Walla Walla (p. 340) is Washington's hottest wine region, and I'm not talking about the climate. This little college town is packed with great wineries, excellent restaurants and good places to stay. All in all, Walla Walla is the best place in the state to taste wine. Keep an eye out for memorable syrahs and viogniers. Many of the best little wineries are only open to the public on Saturdays, so be sure to plan your schedule accordingly. You won't want to miss these gems, many of which are tiny operations near the airport.

Day ⑦: The Columbia Valley ✿✿

From Walla Walla, head back west by way of the Columbia River Gorge. This hot, windy region produces some of the best wines in the state. Be sure to visit **Maryhill Winery** (p. 321), which has one of the most spectacular settings of any winery in the state and also produces a wide range of decent wines. Plan to picnic on the winery's terrace overlooking the Columbia River. As you continue west, you'll pass several more small wineries. Spend the night at a B&B or luxury lodge in the Columbia Gorge and then continue on to Portland or back to Seattle to fly home.

5 The Cascade Loop

Although this itinerary doesn't take in the San Juan Islands, Mount Rainier, or Olympic National Park, it visits some of the most beautiful places in western Washington. The route stretches from Puget Sound to the Cascade Range and takes in a little bit of everything. There are quaint old fishing villages, waterfront walks, rugged mountains, a Wild West theme town, a Bavarian theme town, the third deepest lake in the United States, and, of course, the Seattle urban experience.

Day ❶: Seattle ★★

Spend your first day in Seattle getting a quick feel for this city on the shores of Puget Sound. Walk the **waterfront** (p. 108) and take a short **boat tour** (p. 125), poke around the stalls at **Pike Place Market** (p. 111), take the **Underground Tour** (p. 113), and survey the city from atop the **Space Needle** (p. 114). If this seems like a lot to do in one day, don't worry, there are plenty of espresso bars to keep you on your feet.

Day ❷: Whidbey Island ★★

From Seattle, it's fewer than 30 miles to the town of Mukilteo and the ferry to Whidbey Island. While this island is bigger than any of the San Juans, it offers similar island vistas, beaches, and quaint small towns. Plus, it is easier to get on and off, which makes it a convenient island experience for anyone short on time. Spend time strolling around the old fishing village of **Langley** (p. 156) and then head north to **Whidbey Island Greenbank Farm** (p. 156), **Ebey's Landing National Historic Reserve** (p. 157) near **Coupeville** (p. 156), and **Deception Pass State Park** (p. 157).

Days ❸ & ❹: Bellingham ★★

Leaving Whidbey Island by bridge at the north end of the island, visit **La Conner** (p. 185), the cutest little restored fishing village in the state. Be sure to visit its **Museum of Northwest Art** (p. 187). In spring, tulips and daffodils blanket the farm fields around La Conner. From

there, drive north to Bellingham by way of scenic **Chuckanut Drive** (p. 191) and be sure to stop at **Larrabee State Park** (p. 192). Bellingham is one of my favorite cities in Washington. It's small but has lots to offer. Stroll around the historic **Fairhaven Historic District** (p. 190), walk along the waterfront, and visit the downtown museums. Take a day trip to **Mount Baker** (p. 272) and do some hiking in alpine meadows.

Day ❺: The North Cascades Scenic Highway ★★★

From Bellingham, drive east over the North Cascades Scenic Highway, which passes through the most grandly rugged landscape in the state. Jagged, snow-capped peaks rise all around, and tucked amid the mountain slopes are lakes of stunning colors. Much of the region is preserved in the various units of the **North Cascades National Park Complex** (p. 6). En route, be sure to stop at the **Diablo Lake Overlook** (p. 277), **Rainy Pass** (p. 277), and **Washington Pass** (p. 277). Spend the night in the Methow Valley, which is home to two of the state's finest mountain lodges.

Days ❻ & ❼: Chelan & Stehekin ★★★

From the Methow Valley, get an early start and head up 55-mile-long glacier-carved **Lake Chelan** (p. 285) on one of the tour boats operated by the **Lake Chelan Boat Company** (p. 287). This is the third deepest lake in the country and

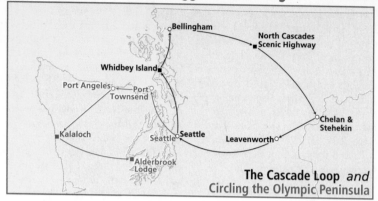

The Cascade Loop *and*
Circling the Olympic Peninsula

is basically a landlocked fjord with rugged mountains rising straight up from the waters of the lake. For an unforgettable experience, spend 2 nights in Stehekin, a community so isolated that no roads lead to it. You can hike, bicycle, and go swimming or fishing. Alternatively, spend a night or two in Chelan and do some wine tasting at area wineries.

Days ❽ & ❾: Leavenworth

From Lake Chelan, continue to the self-consciously quaint, Bavarian-theme town of **Leavenworth** (p. 292). Sure, this town can be tacky, but the natural setting is breathtakingly rugged, and residents have done an impressive job of reproducing an alpine village here in the mountains of Washington. In summer, there is good hiking in the area, and in winter, there is downhill and cross-country skiing. In town, you'll find tasting rooms for numerous Washington state wineries.

Day ❿: Seattle

On your last day, head back to Seattle for one more night. En route, you can do some hiking at Stevens Pass or in the Lake Wenatchee area. If you're interested in wine, detour to the **Woodinville** (p. 150) area north of Seattle and stop in at some wineries.

6 Circling the Olympic Peninsula

There may not be another drive in Washington that so aptly captures all this state offers in a single journey. Starting in Seattle, this loop drive takes in Puget Sound, the Olympic Mountains, and the wild Washington coast. Along the way, you'll enjoy ferry rides, a Victorian port town, lavender fields, wilderness beaches, mountain meadows, rainforests, glacier-carved lakes, and rustic lodges.

Day ❶: Seattle

Spend your first day in Seattle getting a quick feel for this city on the shores of Puget Sound. Walk the **waterfront** (p. 108) and take a short **boat tour** (p. 125), poke around the stalls at **Pike Place Market** (p. 111), take the **Underground Tour** (p. 113), and survey the city from atop the **Space Needle** (p. 114). If this seems like a lot to do in one day, don't worry, there are plenty of espresso bars to keep you on your feet.

Day ❷: Port Townsend ✦✦

From Seattle, catch the Bainbridge Island ferry and head northwest to the Victorian port town of **Port Townsend** (p. 221). This is one of the prettiest little towns in the state and is full of good restaurants and interesting shops. Stay in one of the town's Victorian B&Bs or hotels for the full experience. Do visit **Fort Worden State Park** (p. 226), with its beaches, trails, and the great little **Port Townsend Marine Science Center** (p. 226).

Days ❸, ❹ & ❺: Port Angeles & Northern Olympic National Park ✦✦✦

Next head on around the north side of the Olympic Peninsula toward Port Angeles. In July and August, be sure to explore the **lavender fields** (p. 233) surrounding the town of Sequim. From Port Angeles, drive up to **Hurricane Ridge** (p. 8), the most easily accessible area of alpine meadows in **Olympic National Park** (p. 235). The next day, if you've brought your passport, you can take a ferry to Victoria, British Columbia, which preserves a bit of jolly old England. Alternatively, visit **Dungeness Spit** (p. 232), where you can hike for miles along the beach. West of Port Angeles, rent a boat on **Lake Crescent** and have a soak at **Sol Duc Hot Springs Resort** (p. 244). Stay either in Port Angeles or at nearby **Lake Crescent Lodge** (p. 243).

Days ❻ & ❼: Kalaloch ✦

For your next 2 nights, use the cabins at Kalaloch Lodge as a base. En route from the Port Angeles area, be sure to make the long drive out to Neah Bay and hike the short trail to Cape Flattery. This is by far the most scenic view on the coast. From here you can visit the **wilderness beaches** (p. 247) that stretch for miles north and south of the Native American community of La Push, due west of the town of Forks. For short hikes, I like Rialto Beach and Third Beach. Spend your second day exploring the rainforests of the Hoh River Valley. Hike the **Hall of Mosses Trail** (p. 248) and go for a short rafting trip with **Rainforest Paddlers** (p. 248). There are also many more miles of easily accessible national park beaches stretching north from Kalaloch Lodge.

Day ❽: Alderbrook Lodge ✦✦

For your last night on the Olympic Peninsula, stay at the luxurious **Alderbrook Resort & Spa** (p. 253), and be sure to arrive early enough to do some relaxing. The resort is built on the shore of Hood Canal, a long, fishhook-shaped bay off Puget Sound. If you aren't already hiked out, there are some strenuous, but very rewarding hikes along the eastern edge of Olympic National Park. Check with the park to make sure your chosen trail is open. Winter storms in the area tend to do a lot of damage to trails and forest-service roads.

Seattle

Imagine yourself sitting in a park on the Seattle waterfront, a double-tall latte and an almond croissant close at hand. The snowy peaks of the Olympic Mountains shimmer on the far side of Puget Sound, while the ferryboats come and go across Elliott Bay. It's a summer day, and the sun is shining. (Hey, as long as we're dreaming, why not dream big?) It just doesn't get much better than this, unless, of course, you swap the latte for a microbrew and catch a 9:30pm summer sunset. No wonder people love this town so much.

Okay, so the waterfront is as touristy as San Francisco's Fisherman's Wharf, but what a view! Seattle is a city of views, and for many visitors, the must-see vista is the panorama atop the Space Needle. With the 21st century in full swing, this image of the future may look decidedly 20th-century retro, but still, it's hard to resist an expensive elevator ride in any city. You can even take a monorail straight out of *The Jetsons* to get there (and pass right through the Frank Gehry–designed Experience Music Project en route).

EMP, as the Experience Music Project is known, is yet another of Seattle's handful of architectural oddities. Its swooping, multicolored, metal-skinned bulk rises at the foot of the Space Needle, proof that real 21st-century architecture looks nothing like the vision of the future people dreamed of when the Space Needle was built for the 1962 World's Fair. EMP is the brainchild of Microsoft cofounder Paul Allen, who built this rock 'n' roll cathedral to house his vast collection of Northwest rock memorabilia. After revenues from the rock museum failed to meet his expectations, Allen even added a Science Fiction Museum and Hall of Fame (is this town a computer nerd's dream come true, or what?).

Paul Allen's money has also been hard at work changing the architectural face of the south end of downtown Seattle, which is where you'll find the state-of-the-art Qwest Field—home to Allen's Seattle Seahawks NFL football team. Together with the Seattle Mariners' Safeco Field, Qwest Field has created a massive sports-arena district at the south end of downtown. Next up for Allen is to develop the under-utilized, yet very accessible area between downtown Seattle and Lake Union.

Allen projects aside, Seattle has been for many years one of the nation's most popular cities, and life in recent years has undergone dramatic changes. An influx of urban residents has brought a new vibrancy to the downtown area, and the city has grown wealthier and more sophisticated. It has built a new football stadium and retractable-roof baseball stadium, along with a new opera house, an architecturally avant-garde main library, a symphony hall, glittering new hotels, and upscale restaurants and shops. Still in the works are a controversial light-rail system and an extension of Seattle's monorail.

It's clear that Seattle has not grown complacent. Sure, it has traffic congestion to rival that of L.A., and the weather really is lousy for most of the year. However,

Seattleites manage to overcome these minor inconveniences, in large part by spilling out into the streets and parks whenever the sun shines. To visit Seattle in the summer is to witness an exodus, so follow the lead of the locals and head for the great outdoors. Should you brave a visit in the rainy season, don't despair: There are compensations for such misfortune, including a roof on Pike Place Market and an espresso bar on every block.

1 Orientation

ARRIVING
BY PLANE

Seattle-Tacoma International Airport (© **206/433-5388;** www.portseattle.org/seatac), most commonly referred to simply as Sea-Tac, is located about 14 miles south of Seattle.

Inside the Main Terminal, you'll find a **Visitor Information Desk** (© **206/433-5218**) in the baggage-claim area across from carousel no. 11. It is open daily from 9am to 5pm. (*Note:* This desk cannot make hotel reservations for you.)

Travelex (© **206/248-0401** or 206/248-7848; www.travelex.com) currency exchange desks are located in the Main Terminal's B Concourse and in the North Satellite at the N gates.

Also at the airport are branches of all the major car-rental companies (for further details, see p. 72).

GETTING INTO THE CITY BY CAR   There are two main exits from the airport: From the loading/unloading area, take the first exit if you're staying near the airport. Take the second exit (Wash. 518) if you're headed to downtown Seattle. Driving east on Wash. 518 will connect you to I-5, where you'll then follow the signs for Seattle. Generally, allow 30 minutes for the drive between the airport and downtown, or 45 minutes to an hour during rush hour.

During rush hour, it's sometimes quicker to take Wash. 518 west to Wash. 509 north to Wash. 99 to Wash. 519 (which becomes the Alaskan Way Viaduct running along the Seattle waterfront).

GETTING INTO THE CITY BY TAXI, SHUTTLE, OR BUS   A **taxi** into downtown Seattle will cost you about $34 to $36 (expect to pay around $28 for the return ride to the airport). There are usually plenty of taxis around, but if not, call **Yellow Cab** (© **206/622-6500**) or **Farwest Taxi** (© **206/622-1717**). The flag-drop charge is $2.50; after that, it's $2 per mile.

Gray Line Airport Express (© **800/426-7532** or 206/626-6088; www.grayline ofseattle.com) is your best bet for getting downtown. These shuttle vans provide service between the airport and downtown Seattle daily, every 30 minutes from about 5am to 11pm. Passengers are picked up from outside the baggage-claim area, at Door 00 just past baggage carousel 1. Shuttles stop at the following downtown hotels: Madison Renaissance, Crowne Plaza, Fairmont Olympic, Seattle Hilton, Sheraton Seattle, Grand Hyatt, Westin, and Warwick. Fares are $10 one-way for adults and $7.25 one-way for children ages 2 to 12. Connector service to and from the above hotels is also provided from numerous other downtown hotels, as well as from the Amtrak station, the Washington State Ferries terminal (Pier 52), and the Greyhound station. Connector service is free from some downtown hotels, but from other locations it costs $2.50 one-way; call for details. The main drawback of this shuttle service is that you may have to stop at several hotels before getting dropped off, so it could take you 45 minutes to get from the airport to your hotel. However, if you're traveling by yourself or with just one other person, this is your most economical choice other than a public bus.

Shuttle Express (© **800/487-7433** or 425/981-7000; www.shuttleexpress.com) provides 24-hour service between Sea-Tac and the Seattle, North Seattle, and Bellevue areas. Rates for scheduled shuttles to University District hotels are $26 for one adult, $32 for two, $39 for three, and $44 for four. Rates to downtown Seattle are $23 for one or two adults, $27 for three, and $30 for four. Children ages 12 and under ride free. You need to make a reservation to get to the airport, but to leave the airport, simply follow the red-and-black signs to the Ground Transportation Center on the third floor of the parking garage. If there are three or more of you traveling together, this will be your cheapest option for getting into town other than a public bus.

Metro Transit (© **800/542-7876** in Washington, or 206/553-3000; http://transit.metrokc.gov) operates two public buses between the airport and downtown. These buses leave from near Door 6 (close to carousel no. 1) of the baggage-claim area. It's a good idea to call for the current schedule when you arrive in town. Bus no. 194 runs every 15 to 30 minutes to Third Avenue and Union Street; it operates Monday through Friday from about 6am to 9pm, Saturday from about 6:30am to 9pm, and Sunday from about 6:30am to 7:30pm. Bus no. 174 runs every 25 to 30 minutes to Ninth Avenue and Stewart Street; it operates Monday through Friday from about 4:45am to 2:45am, Saturday from about 5:45am to 2:45am, and Sunday from about 6:45am to 2:45pm. Bus trips to downtown take 40 to 50 minutes, depending on conditions. The fare is $1.25 during off-peak hours, $2 during peak hours.

BY TRAIN OR BUS

Amtrak (© **800/872-7245;** www.amtrak.com) trains stop at King Street Station, 303 S. Jackson St., within a few blocks of the historic Pioneer Square neighborhood. Any bus running north through downtown will take you to within a few blocks of most downtown hotels. The Waterfront Streetcar also stops within a block of King Street Station and can take you to the Edgewater hotel.

Greyhound (© **800/231-2222** or 206/628-5526; www.greyhound.com) buses arrive at 811 Stewart St., a few blocks northeast of downtown Seattle, not far from Lake Union and Seattle Center. Several budget chain motels are located only a few blocks from the bus station.

BY CAR

See section 11 in chapter 2 and "Getting Around," below.

VISITOR INFORMATION

Visitor information on Seattle and the surrounding area is available by contacting **Seattle's Convention and Visitors Bureau Citywide Concierge Center,** Washington State Convention and Trade Center, Eighth Avenue and Pike Street, main level (© **206/461-5888;** www.seeseattle.org). To find it, walk up Pike Street to the convention center (the street is covered by a huge arched glass ceiling out in front of the convention center).

CITY LAYOUT

Although downtown Seattle is fairly compact and can be easily navigated on foot, finding your way by car can be frustrating. The Seattle area has experienced phenomenal growth for more than 15 years, thus creating severe traffic-congestion problems. Here are some guidelines to help you find your way around.

MAIN ARTERIES & STREETS Three interstate highways serve Seattle. Seattle's main artery is I-5, which runs through the middle of the city. Take the James Street exit west if you're heading for the Pioneer Square area, take the Seneca Street exit for Pike Place Market, or take the Olive Way exit for Capitol Hill. I-405 is the city's north-south bypass and travels up the east shore of Lake Washington through Bellevue and Kirkland (Seattle's high-tech corridor). I-90 comes in from the east, crossing one of the city's two floating bridges, and ends at the south end of downtown.

Downtown is roughly defined as extending from the stadium district (just south of the Pioneer Square neighborhood) on the south to Denny Way on the north, and from Elliott Bay on the west to I-5 on the east. Within this area, most avenues are numbered, whereas streets have names. Exceptions to this rule are the first two roads parallel to the waterfront (Alaskan Way and Western Ave.) and avenues east of Ninth Avenue.

Many downtown streets and avenues are one-way. Spring, Pike, and Marion streets are all one-way eastbound, while Seneca, Pine, and Madison streets are all one-way westbound. Second and Fifth avenues are both one-way southbound, while Fourth and Sixth avenues are one-way northbound. First and Third avenues are two-way streets.

To get from downtown to Capitol Hill, take Pike Street or Olive Way. Madison Street, Yesler Way, or South Jackson Street will get you over to Lake Washington on the east side of Seattle. If you're heading north across town, Westlake Avenue will take you to the Fremont neighborhood, while Eastlake Avenue will take you to the University District. These two roads diverge at the south end of Lake Union. To get to the arboretum from downtown, take Madison Street.

FINDING AN ADDRESS After you become familiar with the streets and neighborhoods of Seattle, there is really only one important thing to remember: Pay attention to the compass point of an address. Most downtown streets have no directional designation attached, but once you cross I-5 going east, most streets and avenues are designated "East." South of Yesler Way, which runs through Pioneer Square, streets are designated "South." West of Queen Anne Avenue, streets are designated "West." The University District is designated "NE" (Northeast), and the Ballard neighborhood "NW" (Northwest). If you're looking for an address on First Avenue South, head south of Yesler Way.

Another helpful hint is that odd-numbered addresses are likely to be on the west and south sides of streets, whereas even-numbered addresses will be on the east and north sides. Also, in the downtown area, address numbers increase by 100 with each block as you move away from Yesler Way going north or south and as you go eastward from the waterfront.

STREET MAPS If the streets of Seattle seem totally unfathomable, rest assured that even longtime residents sometimes have a hard time finding their way around. Don't be afraid to ask directions. Obtain a free map of the city from Seattle's Convention and Visitors Bureau Citywide Concierge Center (see above).

You can buy a decent map of Seattle at most convenience stores and gas stations. For a greater selection, stop in at **Metsker Maps,** 1511 First Ave. (© **800/727-4430** or 206/623-8747; www.metskers.com).

Remembering Seattle's Streets

Locals use an irreverent little mnemonic device for remembering the names of Seattle's downtown streets, and since most visitors spend much of their time downtown, this phrase could be useful to you as well. It goes like this: "Jesus Christ made Seattle under protest." This stands for all the downtown east-west streets between Yesler Way and Olive Way/Stewart Street—Jefferson, James, Cherry, Columbia, Marion, Madison, Spring, Seneca, University, Union, Pike, and Pine.

If you're a member of AAA, you can get free maps of Seattle and Washington State either at your local AAA office or at the Seattle branch in the University District at 4554 Ninth Ave. NE (© **206/448-5353**).

THE NEIGHBORHOODS IN BRIEF

DOWNTOWN This is Seattle's main business district and can roughly be defined as the area from Pioneer Square in the south to around Pike Place Market in the north, and from First Avenue to Eighth Avenue. It's characterized by steep streets, high-rise office buildings, luxury hotels, and a high density of retail shops (primarily national chains). This is also where you'll find the Seattle Art Museum and Benaroya Hall, which is home to the Seattle Symphony. Hotels are convenient to both Pioneer Square and Pike Place Market, so this is a good neighborhood in which to stay. Unfortunately, hotels here are the most expensive in the city.

FIRST HILL Because it is home to several large hospitals, this hilly neighborhood just east of downtown and across I-5 is called "Pill Hill" by Seattleites. First Hill is home to the Frye Art Museum and a couple of good hotels.

THE WATERFRONT The Seattle waterfront stretches along Alaskan Way from roughly Washington Street in the south to Broad Street and Myrtle Edwards Park in the north. The most touristy neighborhood in Seattle, it has tacky gift shops, greasy fish-and-chips windows, and tour-boat docks. You'll also find the city's only waterfront hotel (the Edgewater), the Seattle Aquarium, and a few excellent seafood restaurants. The waterfront is also residential, and at the north end of Alaskan Way, there are water-view condominiums.

PIONEER SQUARE The Pioneer Square Historic District, known for its restored 1890s buildings, is centered around the corner of First Avenue and Yesler Way. The tree-lined streets and cobblestone plazas make this one of the prettiest downtown neighborhoods. Pioneer Square (which refers to the neighborhood, not a specific square) is full of antiques shops, art galleries, restaurants, bars, and nightclubs. Because of the number of bars in this neighborhood, late nights are not a good time to wander, and the street people are off-putting to many visitors.

THE INTERNATIONAL DISTRICT Known to locals as the I.D., this is the most distinctive of Seattle's neighborhoods and home to a large Asian population. Here is the Wing Luke Asian Museum, Hing Hay Park (a small park with an ornate pagoda), Uwajimaya (an Asian supermarket), and other small shops and restaurants.

The Chinatown/International District begins around Fifth Avenue South and South Jackson Street. This neighborhood is good for a stroll.

BELLTOWN In the blocks north of Pike Place Market between Western and Fourth avenues, this area once held mostly warehouses, but over the past decade and a half it has become gentrified. Today Belltown is ground zero for upscale Seattle restaurants. Keeping the restaurants in business are the residents of the neighborhood's many high-rise condominiums. Belltown's numerous nightclubs and bars attract crowds of the young, the hip, and the stylish—who, in turn, attract nighttime panhandlers.

QUEEN ANNE HILL Queen Anne is just northwest of Seattle Center and has great views of the city. This affluent neighborhood, one of the most prestigious in Seattle proper, is where you'll find some of Seattle's oldest homes. Today the neighborhood is divided into the Upper Queen Anne and Lower Queen Anne neighborhoods. Upper Queen Anne has a very peaceful neighborhood feel and abounds in moderately priced restaurants. Lower Queen Anne, adjacent to the theaters and Marion Oliver McCaw Hall at Seattle Center, is something of a theater district with a more urban character.

CAPITOL HILL To the northeast of downtown, centered along Broadway near Volunteer Park, Capitol Hill is Seattle's main gay neighborhood as well as a popular youth-culture shopping district. Broadway sidewalks are always crowded, and it is nearly impossible to find a parking space. There are lots of inexpensive restaurants in the area, but few are really worth recommending. This is also Seattle's main hangout for runaways and street kids,

many of whom have become involved in the city's drug scene. Despite the youthful orientation, Capitol Hill is where you'll find many bed-and-breakfast establishments housed in some of the neighborhood's impressive old homes and mansions.

UNIVERSITY DISTRICT As the name implies, this neighborhood in the northeast section of the city surrounds the University of Washington. The U District, as it's known to locals, provides all the amenities of a college neighborhood: cheap ethnic restaurants, pubs, clubs, espresso bars, and music stores. The neighborhood has several good hotels that offer substantial savings over comparable downtown Seattle accommodations.

FREMONT North of the Lake Washington Ship Canal between Wallingford and Ballard, Fremont is home to Seattle's best-loved piece of public art—*Waiting for the Interurban*—as well as the famous *Fremont Troll* sculpture. This is Seattle's wackiest neighborhood, filled with eclectic shops and ethnic restaurants. In the summer, there's a Sunday flea market, and outdoor movies are screened on Saturday nights. If you visit only one neighborhood outside of downtown, make it Fremont.

BALLARD In northwest Seattle, bordering the Lake Washington Ship Canal and Puget Sound, you'll find Ballard, a former Scandinavian community that retains visible remnants of its past. Now known for its busy nightlife, Ballard is one of Seattle's up-and-coming neighborhoods and is undergoing a pronounced change in character. You'll find art galleries and a few interesting boutiques and shops along the tree-shaded streets of the neighborhood's old commercial center. It's worth a stroll to see what's happen-

Greater Seattle Orientation

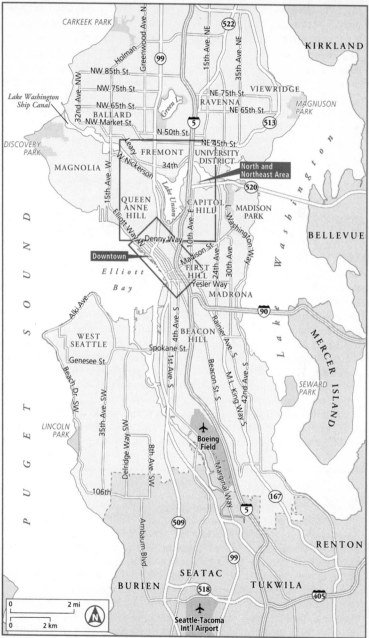

ing. The Nordic Heritage Museum often has interesting art exhibits.

THE EASTSIDE Home to Bill Gates, Microsoft, countless high-tech spinoff companies, and seemingly endless suburbs, the Eastside lies across Lake Washington from Seattle proper and comprises such fast-growing cities as **Kirkland, Bellevue, Redmond,** and a few other smaller communities. As the presence of Bill Gates's media-hyped mansion attests, there are some wealthy neighborhoods here. Wealth doesn't necessarily equal respect, however, and the Eastside is still much derided by Seattle citizens, who perceive it as an uncultured bedroom community.

WEST SEATTLE West Seattle, across the wasteland of the port facility from downtown Seattle, is the site of the ferry terminal for trips to Vashon Island and the Kitsap Peninsula. It also has Seattle's favorite beach, Alki, which is as close to a Southern California beach experience as you'll find in the Northwest. The waterfront restaurant with the best view of Seattle is Salty's on Alki Beach.

2 Getting Around

BY PUBLIC TRANSPORTATION

BY BUS   The best thing about Seattle's **Metro** (© **800/542-7876** in Washington or 206/553-3000; http://transit.metrokc.gov) bus system is that as long as you stay within the downtown area, you can ride for free between 6am and 7pm. The **Ride Free Area** is between Alaskan Way (the waterfront) to the west, Sixth Avenue and I-5 to the east, Battery Street to the north, and South Jackson Street to the south. Within this area are Pioneer Square, the waterfront attractions, Pike Place Market, the Seattle Art Museum, and almost all of the city's major hotels. Two blocks from South Jackson Street is Qwest Field (where the Seahawks play), 3 long blocks from South Jackson Street is Safeco Field (where the Mariners play), and 6 blocks from Battery Street is Seattle Center. Keeping this in mind, you can see a lot of Seattle without having to spend a dime on transportation.

If you travel outside the Ride Free Area, fares range from $1.25 to $2, depending on distance and time of day. (The higher fares are incurred during commuter hours.) *Note:* When traveling out of the Ride Free Area, you pay when you get off the bus;

Value Discount Passes

On Saturday, Sunday, and holidays, you can purchase an **All-Day Pass** for $2.50; it's available on any Metro bus as well as on the Waterfront Streetcar, and it's good anywhere outside the Ride Free Area. On other days of the week, you can purchase a **Visitor Pass,** for $5, which can be used on buses, the water taxi, and the Waterfront Streetcar. Visitor Passes are available at Metro Customer Service offices at King Street Center, 201 S. Jackson St., and at Rainier Square's Transportation Connection, which can be entered from Fourth Avenue, between University and Union streets. These passes can also be purchased at Seattle's Convention and Visitors Bureau, Eighth Avenue and Pike Street, and at Uwajimaya, an Asian supermarket, 600 Fifth Ave. S. For more information, contact **Metro** (© **206/624-7277;** http://transit.metrokc.gov).

when traveling into the Ride Free Area, you pay when you get on the bus. Exact change is required; dollar bills are accepted.

BY WATERFRONT STREETCAR   In addition to the bus system, **Metro** (© **800/542-7876** in Washington or 206/553-3000; http://transit.metrokc.gov) also operates old-fashioned streetcars that follow a route along the waterfront from Pier 70 to Pioneer Square and then east to the corner of Fourth Avenue South and South Jackson Street, which is on the edge of the International District. These streetcars are more tourist attraction than commuter transportation, and are actually much more useful to visitors than are most of the city's buses. Tourist sites along the streetcar route include the International District, Pioneer Square, the Seattle Aquarium, and Pike Place Market. In the summer, streetcars operate Monday through Friday from around 6:30am to 11:10pm, departing every 20 to 30 minutes; on Saturday, Sunday, and holidays, they operate from 8:45am to 11:40pm (shorter hours in other months). The one-way fare for adults is $1.25 in off-peak hours and $1.50 in peak hours; youths ages 5 to 17 pay 50¢. Exact change is required. If you plan to transfer to a Metro bus, you can get a transfer good for 90 minutes. Streetcars are wheelchair accessible.

BY MONORAIL   If you are planning a visit to Seattle Center, there is no better way to get there from downtown than on the **Seattle Monorail** (© **206/905-2620;** www.seattlemonorail.com), which leaves from Westlake Center shopping mall (Fifth Ave. and Pine St.). The elevated train covers the 1¼ miles in 2 minutes and passes right through the middle of the Experience Music Project as it arrives at and departs from Seattle Center. The monorail currently operates Monday through Thursday from 11am to 7pm, Friday from 11am to 9pm, Saturday from 9am to 9pm, and Sunday from 9am to 7pm. However, these operating hours, which are based on one train being out of commission for repairs, should be expanded by the time you visit Seattle. Departures are every 10 minutes. The one-way fare is $1.50 for adults and 75¢ for seniors and children ages 5 to 12.

BY WATER TAXI   A water taxi operates between the downtown Seattle waterfront (Pier 55) and Seacrest Park in West Seattle, providing access to West Seattle's popular Alki Beach and adjacent paved path. For a service schedule, check with Metro (© **206/205-3866;** http://transit.metrokc.gov). The one-way fare is $3 (free for children under 5), free with a valid bus transfer or all-day pass.

BY FERRY   **Washington State Ferries** (© **800/84-FERRY,** 888/808-7977 in Washington, or 206/464-6400; www.wsdot.wa.gov/ferries) is the most extensive ferry system in the United States, and while these ferries won't help you get around Seattle, they offer scenic options for getting out of town (and cheap "cruises," too). From downtown, car ferries sail to Bremerton (1-hr. crossing) and Bainbridge Island (35-min. crossing). From West Seattle, car ferries go to Vashon Island (15-min. crossing) and Southworth (35-min. crossing), on the Kitsap Peninsula. One-way fares between Seattle and Bainbridge Island or Bremerton, or between Edmonds and Kingston via car ferry, are $11 ($13 from early May to mid-Oct) for a car and driver, $6.10 for adult car passengers or walk-ons, $3 for seniors, and $4.90 for children ages 5 to 18. Car passengers and walk-ons only pay fares on westbound car ferries. One-way fares between Fauntleroy (West Seattle) and Vashon Island or between Southworth and Vashon Island are $14 ($17 from early May to mid-Oct) for a car and driver, $4 for car passengers or walk-ons, $2 for seniors, and $3.20 for children ages 5 to 18. Passenger-only ferry service goes to Vashon Island from Pier 50 on the Seattle waterfront.

BY CAR

Before you venture into downtown Seattle by car, keep in mind that traffic congestion is bad, parking is limited (and expensive), and streets are almost all one-way. You'll avoid a lot of frustration and aggravation by leaving your car in your hotel's parking garage or by not bringing a car into downtown.

Depending on your plans for a visit, you may not need a car at all. If you plan to spend your time in downtown Seattle, a car is a liability. The city center is well served by public transportation, with free buses in the downtown area, the monorail from downtown to Seattle Center, and the Waterfront Streetcar connecting Pike Place Market and Pioneer Square by way of the waterfront. You can even take the ferries over to Bainbridge Island or Bremerton for an excursion out of the city. Most Seattle neighborhoods of interest to visitors are also well served by public buses. However, if your plans include any excursions out of the city, say to Mount Rainier or the Olympic Peninsula, you'll definitely need a car.

CAR RENTALS   Car-rental rates vary as widely and as wildly as airfares, so it pays to do some comparison shopping. In Seattle, daily rates for a compact car average between $30 and $40, with weekly rates averaging around $175 to $200. Rates are highest in the summer and lowest in the winter, but you'll almost always get lower rates the further ahead you reserve. Be sure to budget for the 18.5% car-rental tax (and, if you rent at the airport, an additional 10%–12% airport concession fee and other charges will increase your cost by a whopping 30%!).

All of the major car-rental agencies have offices in Seattle and at or near Seattle-Tacoma International Airport. Companies with a desk and cars inside the terminal include **Alamo** (© 800/327-9633 or 206/433-0182; www.goalamo.com), **Avis** (© 800/831-2847 or 206/433-5232; www.avis.com), **Budget** (© 800/527-0700 or 206/431-8800; www.budget.com), **Hertz** (© 800/654-3131 or 206/248-1300; www.hertz.com), and **National** (© 800/227-7368 or 206/433-5501; www.nationalcar.com). Companies with desks inside the terminal but cars parked off the airport premises include **Advantage** (© 800/777-5500 or 206/824-0161; www.arac.com), **Dollar** (© 800/800-3665 or 206/433-5825; www.dollar.com), **Enterprise** (© 800/261-7331 or 206/246-1953; www.enterprise.com), and **Thrifty** (© 800/847-4389 or 206/246-7565; www.thrifty.com).

PARKING   On-street parking in downtown Seattle is expensive, extremely limited, and, worst of all, rarely available near your destination. Most downtown parking lots (either above or below ground) charge from $12 to $20 per day, though many lots offer early-bird specials that allow you to park all day for around $8 if you arrive before a certain time in the morning (usually around 9am).

You can save money by leaving your car near the Space Needle, where parking lots charge $5 to $6 per day. The lot at Fifth Avenue North and North Republican Street, on the east side of Seattle Center, charges only $5 for all-day parking. The Pike Place Market parking garage, accessed from Western Avenue under the sky bridge, offers free parking if you park for less than an hour (just enough time to run in and grab a quick bite). Also, some market merchants validate parking permits, as do many market restaurants if you're dining after 5pm. In the International District, the Lower Queen Anne neighborhood, and a few streets south of Seattle Center, you'll find free 2-hour on-street parking.

Value **Driving a Bargain in Seattle**

For the best deal on a rental car, make your reservation at least a week in advance. It also pays to call several times over a period of a few weeks just to check prices. You're likely to be quoted different rates every time you call, since prices fluctuate based on demand and availability. Remember the old Wall Street adage: Buy low!

Always ask about special weekend rates, promotional rates, or discounts for which you may be eligible (AAA, AARP, corporate, Entertainment Book, military, and so on). Also make sure you clarify whether there is a charge for mileage. And don't forget to mention that you're a frequent flier: You may be able to get miles for your car rental.

If you have your own car insurance, you might already have collision coverage. If you do not hold your own policy, your credit card may provide collision coverage, allowing you to decline the collision-damage waiver, which can add a bundle to the cost of a rental. (Gold and platinum cards usually offer this perk, but check with your card issuer before relying on it. Note that while many cards provide collision coverage, they do not provide liability coverage.)

If there's any way you can arrange to pick up your car somewhere other than the airport, you can save the 10% to 12% airport concession fee.

It's always smart to decline the gasoline plans offered by rental agencies and simply plan on returning your rental car with a full tank of gas. The prices charged by the rental companies to fill your tank are usually a rip-off.

DRIVING RULES A right turn at a red light is permitted after coming to a full stop. A left turn at a red light is permissible from a one-way street onto another one-way street after coming to a full stop.

If you park your car on a sloping street, be sure to turn your wheels to the curb—you may be ticketed if you don't. When parking on the street, be sure to check the time limit on your parking meter. Some allow only as little as 15 minutes of parking, while others are good for up to 4 hours. Also be sure to check whether or not you can park in a parking space during rush hour.

Stoplights in the Pioneer Square area are particularly hard to see, so be alert when approaching all intersections.

BY TAXI
If you decide not to use the public transit system, call **Yellow Cab** (© 206/622-6500) or **Farwest Taxi** (© 206/622-1717). Taxis can be difficult to hail on the street in Seattle, so it's best to call or wait at the taxi stands at major hotels. The flag-drop charge is $2.50; after that, it's $2 per mile. A maximum of four passengers can share a cab; the third and fourth passengers will each incur an extra charge of 50¢.

ON FOOT
Seattle is a surprisingly compact city. You can easily walk from Pioneer Square to Pike Place Market and take in most of downtown. Remember, though, that the city is also

very hilly. When you head in from the waterfront, you will be climbing a very steep hill. If you get tired while strolling downtown, remember that between 6am and 7pm, you can always catch a bus for free as long as you stay within the Ride Free Area. Cross the street only at corners and only with the lights in your favor. Jaywalking, especially in the downtown area, is a ticketable offense.

3 Where to Stay

Seattle is close on the heels of San Francisco as a West Coast summer-in-the-city destination, so its hotels are usually booked solid for July and August. Not only do the hotels here stay full during the summer, but if you aren't on an expense account, you may be faced with sticker shock when you see what Seattle's downtown hotels charge. However, if you're willing to head out a bit from downtown, you'll find prices a little easier to swallow.

Be sure to make reservations as far in advance as possible, especially if you plan a visit during Seafair or another major festival. See the "Washington Calendar of Events" on p. 20 for the dates of major festivals.

In the following listings, price categories are based on rates for a double room in high season (most hotels charge the same for a single or double room). The rates listed do not include taxes, which add up to around 16% in Seattle.

Note: For comparison purposes, we list what hotels call "rack rates" or walk-in rates—but you should rarely have to pay these highly inflated prices. Various discounts and specials are often available, so make it a point to ask if any are being offered during your stay (and be sure to check the hotel's website for Internet specials). At inexpensive chain motels, discounted rates are almost always available for AAA members and seniors.

Room rates can be considerably lower from October through April (the rainy season), and downtown hotels often offer substantially reduced prices on weekends year-round (while budget hotels often charge more on weekends).

A few hotels include breakfast in their rates; others offer complimentary breakfast only on certain deluxe floors. Most Seattle hotels offer nonsmoking rooms, while most bed-and-breakfast inns are exclusively nonsmoking establishments. Most hotels, but few inns, also offer wheelchair-accessible rooms.

If you're having a hard time finding a room in your price range, consider using the services of **Pacific Northwest Journeys** (© 800/935-9730 or 206/935-9730; www.pnwjourneys.com). This company specializes in itinerary planning, but also has a reservations service. The charge is $45 per reservation; however, you can usually make that up in savings on just a 2-night stay. If you're going to be in town for longer than that, you'll definitely save money. Last-minute reservations are often possible, too. A consultation service is also available for people who would like a little assistance with their itinerary.

Every year from November through March, more than two dozen area hotels offer deep-cut discounts through **Seattle Super Saver** (© 800/535-7071; www.seattle supersaver.com). Rates under this plan are generally 50% of what they would be in the summer months. Anytime of year, you can contact Seattle Super Saver to make hotel reservations at rates comparable to what you will find at other online booking sites.

Seattle is a city of diverse neighborhoods, and in many of those neighborhoods you'll discover fine B&Bs. Often less expensive than downtown hotels, these B&Bs provide an opportunity to see what life is like for the locals. I've listed some of my favorites in the pages that follow, but to find out about other good options, contact the **Seattle Bed & Breakfast Association** (② 800/348-5630 or 206/547-1020; www.seattlebandbs.com). A **Pacific Reservation Service** (② 800/684-2932 or 206/439-7677; www.seattle bedandbreakfast.com), books rooms at dozens of accommodations in the Seattle area, including B&Bs and houseboats. A wide range of rates is available.

DOWNTOWN & FIRST HILL

Downtown Seattle is the heart of the city's business community and home to numerous business hotels. Although these properties are among the most conveniently located Seattle hotels, they are also the most expensive choices and are designed primarily for business travelers on expense accounts, not vacationers. Many of these hotels do offer discounted weekend and winter rates, however. The area has plenty of good restaurants, but they tend to fall into one of two categories—cheap lunch spots or expense-account dinner places.

VERY EXPENSIVE

Alexis Hotel ⭐⭐   The Alexis is a sparkling gem in an enviable location halfway between Pike Place Market and Pioneer Square and only 3 blocks from the waterfront, the Seattle Art Museum, and Benaroya Hall. In the middle of the lobby is a massive Dale Chihuly chandelier, and throughout the hotel is an extensive art collection. The pleasant mix of contemporary and antique furnishings, and cheerful and personalized service, gives the Alexis a very special atmosphere. In the guest rooms, classic styling with a European flavor prevails. Almost half of the rooms are suites, including comfortable fireplace suites with whirlpool baths. The spa suites are the real winners, with whirlpool tubs in exceedingly luxurious bathrooms. The hotel has complimentary evening wine tastings.

1007 First Ave. (at Madison St.), Seattle, WA 98104. ② 800/426-7033 or 206/624-4844. Fax 206/621-9009. www.alexishotel.com. 109 units. $299–$319 double; $355–$549 suite. Rates include evening wine reception. Children under 18 stay free in parent's room. AE, DC, DISC, MC, V. Valet parking $26. Pets accepted. **Amenities:** Restaurant (New American); 2 lounges; exercise room; access to nearby health club; Aveda day spa; steam room; concierge; 24-hr. room service; massage; laundry service; dry cleaning. *In room:* A/C, TV, dataport, minibar, hair dryer, iron, Wi-Fi.

Fairmont Olympic Hotel ⭐⭐⭐   If nothing but classically elegant surroundings will do, then head straight for the Fairmont Olympic Hotel, a gorgeous facsimile of an Italian Renaissance palace. Without a doubt, this hotel has the grandest lobby in Seattle. Gilt-and-crystal chandeliers hang from the arched ceiling, while ornate moldings grace the glowing hand-burnished oak walls and pillars. Although many of the guest rooms tend to be rather small (with either two twin beds or one king bed), all are very elegant. If you crave extra space, opt for one of the suites, of which there are more than 200 (however, be aware that the executive suites aren't much bigger than the hotel's deluxe rooms). The Georgian is the most elegant restaurant in Seattle. For plush surroundings, excellent service, and great amenities, this hotel can't be beat.

411 University St., Seattle, WA 98101. ② 800/223-8772, 800/821-8106 (in Washington), 800/268-6282 (in Canada), or 206/621-1700. Fax 206/682-9633. www.fairmont.com/seattle. 450 units. $299–$429 double; $369–$3,000 suite. Children 18 and under stay free in parent's room. AE, DC, DISC, MC, V. Valet parking $30. Small pets accepted. **Amenities:** 2 restaurants (Continental/Northwest, Seafood); lounge; health club with indoor pool; exercise machines; spa; Jacuzzi; saunas; children's programs; concierge; downtown courtesy car; business center; shopping arcade; 24-hr. room service; massage; babysitting; laundry service; dry cleaning. *In room:* A/C, TV, dataport, minibar, hair dryer, iron, safe, high-speed Internet access.

Seattle Accommodations & Dining—Downtown including First Hill

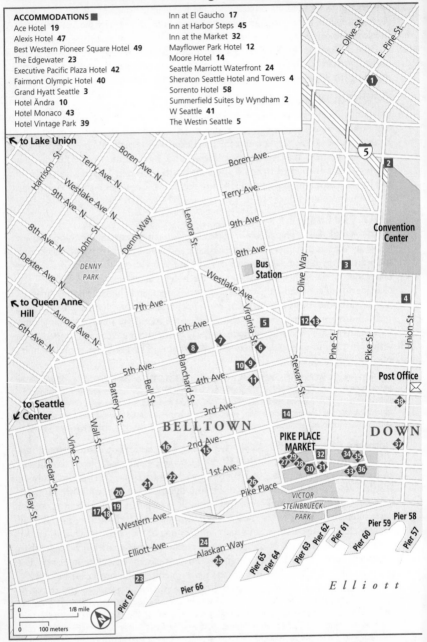

ACCOMMODATIONS ■
Ace Hotel **19**
Alexis Hotel **47**
Best Western Pioneer Square Hotel **49**
The Edgewater **23**
Executive Pacific Plaza Hotel **42**
Fairmont Olympic Hotel **40**
Grand Hyatt Seattle **3**
Hotel Ändra **10**
Hotel Monaco **43**
Hotel Vintage Park **39**

Inn at El Gaucho **17**
Inn at Harbor Steps **45**
Inn at the Market **32**
Mayflower Park Hotel **12**
Moore Hotel **14**
Seattle Marriott Waterfront **24**
Sheraton Seattle Hotel and Towers **4**
Sorrento Hotel **58**
Summerfield Suites by Wyndham **2**
W Seattle **41**
The Westin Seattle **5**

↖ to Lake Union

Boren Ave. N.
Boren Ave.
Harrison St.
Terry Ave. N.
Westlake Ave. N.
9th Ave. N.
8th Ave. N.
Dexter Ave. N.
John St.
Denny Way
Terry Ave.
Lenora St.
9th Ave.
8th Ave.

DENNY PARK

↖ to Queen Anne Hill

Aurora Ave. N.
6th Ave. N.
7th Ave.
6th Ave.
5th Ave.
Battery St.
Blanchard St.
Bell St.
4th Ave.
3rd Ave.
2nd Ave.
1st Ave.
Virginia St.
Westlake Ave.
Olive Way
Stewart St.
Pine St.
Pike St.
Union St.

Bus Station

Convention Center

to Seattle Center ↙

Wall St.
Vine St.
Cedar St.
Clay St.
Western Ave.
Elliott Ave.
Alaskan Way

BELLTOWN

PIKE PLACE MARKET

VICTOR STEINBRUECK PARK

DOWN

Post Office ✉

Pier 67
Pier 66
Pier 65
Pier 64
Pier 63
Pier 62
Pier 61
Pier 60
Pier 59
Pier 58
Pier 57

Elliott

0   1/8 mile
0   100 meters

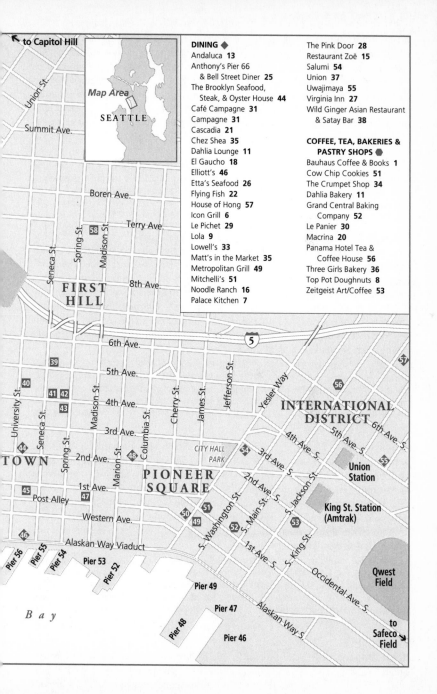

to Capitol Hill

Map Area

SEATTLE

DINING ◆
Andaluca **13**
Anthony's Pier 66
& Bell Street Diner **25**
The Brooklyn Seafood,
Steak, & Oyster House **44**
Café Campagne **31**
Campagne **31**
Cascadia **21**
Chez Shea **35**
Dahlia Lounge **11**
El Gaucho **18**
Elliott's **46**
Etta's Seafood **26**
Flying Fish **22**
House of Hong **57**
Icon Grill **6**
Le Pichet **29**
Lola **9**
Lowell's **33**
Matt's in the Market **35**
Metropolitan Grill **49**
Mitchelli's **51**
Noodle Ranch **16**
Palace Kitchen **7**

The Pink Door **28**
Restaurant Zoë **15**
Salumi **54**
Union **37**
Uwajimaya **55**
Virginia Inn **27**
Wild Ginger Asian Restaurant
& Satay Bar **38**

**COFFEE, TEA, BAKERIES &
PASTRY SHOPS ●**
Bauhaus Coffee & Books **1**
Cow Chip Cookies **51**
The Crumpet Shop **34**
Dahlia Bakery **11**
Grand Central Baking
Company **52**
Le Panier **30**
Macrina **20**
Panama Hotel Tea &
Coffee House **56**
Three Girls Bakery **36**
Top Pot Doughnuts **8**
Zeitgeist Art/Coffee **53**

Union St.

Summit Ave.

Boren Ave.

Terry Ave.

Seneca St.

Spring St.

Madison St.

58

8th Ave.

**FIRST
HILL**

6th Ave.

5

39

5th Ave.

40

41 **42**

4th Ave.

43

3rd Ave.

University St.

Seneca St.

Spring St.

Madison St.

Marion St.

Columbia St.

Cherry St.

James St.

Jefferson St.

Yesler Way

56

**INTERNATIONAL
DISTRICT**

4th Ave. S.

5th Ave. S.

6th Ave. S.

57

44

2nd Ave.

48

TOWN

_CITY HALL
PARK_

54

3rd Ave. S.

55

Union
Station

**PIONEER
SQUARE**

1st Ave.

47

45

Post Alley

Western Ave.

50

51

49

S. Washington St.

52

2nd Ave. S.

S. Main St.

S. Jackson St.

King St. Station
(Amtrak)

53

46

Alaskan Way Viaduct

1st Ave. S.

S. King St.

Pier 56

Pier 55

Pier 54

Pier 53

Pier 52

Pier 49

Pier 47

Pier 48

Pier 46

Alaskan Way S.

Occidental Ave. S.

Qwest
Field

to
Safeco
Field

_B a y_

77

Grand Hyatt Seattle ★★★ If you're accustomed to staying in only the finest hotels, book your room here. For classic luxury, contemporary styling, modern amenities, and attentive service, this hotel simply can't be beat. A Willem de Kooning sculpture outside the front door and a spacious lobby full of regionally inspired glass art set the tone the moment you arrive. You may wonder whether this is a hotel or an art museum. There is, however, one catch. Unless you spring for something pricier than the basic "deluxe guest room," you're going to be a bit cramped; the least expensive rooms here are designed for solo business travelers. The health club is well outfitted, but there's no swimming pool.

721 Pine St., Seattle, WA 98101. ℂ 800/233-1234 or 206/774-1234. Fax 206/774-6120. www.grandseattle. hyatt.com. 425 units. $199–$340 double; $1,250–$3,000 suite. Children 18 and under stay free in parent's room. AE, DC, DISC, MC, V. Valet parking $29; self-parking $22. **Amenities:** Restaurant (Steakhouse); lounge; health club with Jacuzzi, sauna, and steam room; concierge; 24-hr. room service; massage; laundry service; dry cleaning. *In room:* A/C, TV, dataport, fridge, coffeemaker, hair dryer, iron, safe, high-speed Internet access, Wi-Fi.

Sorrento Hotel ★★★ With its wrought-iron gates, palm trees in the entrance courtyard, and plush seating in the octagonal lobby, the Sorrento, which first opened in 1909, has a classic elegance and old-world atmosphere. The hotel boasts commanding views of downtown Seattle from its setting high on First Hill, yet downtown is only a few (steep) blocks away (complimentary limousine service is available). The guest rooms are among the finest in the city, and although more than half the units are suites, many provide little more space than the standard rooms. Ask for a room on the hotel's west side, where you'll have a view of the city and Puget Sound. The hotel's dining room is a dark, clubby place.

900 Madison St., Seattle, WA 99104-1297. ℂ 800/426-1265 or 206/622-6400. Fax 206/343-6155. www.hotel sorrento.com. 76 units. $250–$295 double; $340–$2,500 suite. Children under 18 stay free in parent's room. AE, DC, DISC, MC, V. Valet parking $24. Pets accepted. **Amenities:** Restaurant (Northwest/Mediterranean); lounge; exercise room and access to nearby health club; concierge; courtesy downtown shuttle; business center; 24-hr. room service; massage; babysitting; laundry service; dry cleaning. *In room:* A/C, TV, fax, dataport, minibar, coffeemaker, hair dryer, iron, high-speed Internet access, Wi-Fi.

W Seattle ★★ Here in the land of espresso and high-tech, the ultra-hip W Seattle is a natural. The lobby has the look and feel of a stage set, with dramatic lighting and sleek furniture, and in the evenings, the space transforms into a trendy lounge. Rooms are not only beautifully designed and filled with plush amenities, but tend to be larger than those at other W hotels. They're full of great perks, such as Bliss Spa bath products, goose-down comforters, and CD players. The -09 and -02 "Cool Corner" rooms cost more than regular units, but are worth it. The Earth & Ocean restaurant is one of downtown's best. Definitely the coolest hotel in Seattle.

1112 Fourth Ave., Seattle, WA 98101. ℂ 877/W-HOTELS or 206/264-6000. Fax 206/264-6100. www.whotels. com/seattle. 426 units. $199–$409 double; from $750 suite. Children under 18 stay free in parent's room. AE, DC, DISC, MC, V. Valet parking $27. Pets accepted ($25 per day). **Amenities:** Restaurant (New American); lounge; exercise room; access to nearby health club; concierge; business center; 24-hr. room service; in-room massage; babysitting; laundry service; dry cleaning. *In room:* A/C, TV/VCR, dataport, minibar, coffeemaker, hair dryer, iron, safe, high-speed Internet access.

EXPENSIVE

Hotel Monaco ★★ The Monaco is one of downtown Seattle's hippest business hotels, attracting a young and affluent clientele. If you appreciate cutting-edge style, you'll go for the eclectic, over-the-top, retro-contemporary design here. The lobby has reproductions of ancient Greek murals; in the guest rooms, you'll find wild color schemes, bold striped wallpaper, stereos with CD players, and leopard-print terry-cloth robes. For a view of Mount Rainier, ask for room nos. 1019, 1119, or 1219. Miss your pet back home? Call the front desk, and a staff member will send up a pet goldfish for the night. **Sazerac,** the hotel's New American restaurant, is as boldly designed as the rest of the place. Be sure to order the restaurant's namesake cocktail at the adjacent bar.

1101 Fourth Ave., Seattle, WA 98101. (C) **800/945-2240** or 206/621-1770. Fax 206/621-7779. www.monaco-seattle. com. 189 units. $155–$299 double; $185–$329 suite. Rates include evening wine tasting. Children under 18 stay free in parent's room. AE, DC, DISC, MC, V. Valet parking $26. Pets accepted. **Amenities:** Restaurant (New American); lounge; exercise room and access to nearby health club; concierge; business center; 24-hr. room service; massage; babysitting; laundry service; dry cleaning. In room: A/C, TV, dataport, minibar, coffeemaker, hair dryer, iron, high-speed Internet access, Wi-Fi.

Hotel Vintage Park ☞☞
Small, classically elegant, and exceedingly romantic, the Vintage Park is a must for both lovers and wine lovers. The guest rooms, all of which are named for Washington wineries, are perfect for romantic getaways, and each evening in the librarylike lobby, the hotel hosts a complimentary wine tasting. Throughout the hotel are numerous references to grapes and wine—even the mini-bars are stocked with Washington wines. When you see the plush draperies framing the beds and the neo-Victorian furnishings in the deluxe units, you'll likely want to spend your days luxuriating amid the sumptuous surroundings. Deluxe rooms have the best views (including views of Mount Rainier), but bathrooms are small. Standard rooms, though smaller and less luxuriously appointed, are still very comfortable, and surprisingly, the bathrooms are larger than those in the deluxe rooms.

1100 Fifth Ave., Seattle, WA 98101. (C) **800/624-4433** or 206/624-8000. Fax 206/623-0568. www.hotelvintagepark. com. 126 units. $159–$299 double; $575–$795 suite. Children under 18 stay free in parent's room. AE, DC, DISC, MC, V. Valet parking $26. Pets accepted. **Amenities:** Restaurant (Italian); lounge; access to nearby health club; concierge; 24-hr. room service; laundry service; dry cleaning. In room: A/C, TV, dataport, minibar, hair dryer, iron, Wi-Fi.

Inn at Harbor Steps ☞☞
Situated on the lower floors of a modern apartment building across the street from the Seattle Art Museum, this inn has an excellent location that's convenient to all of downtown Seattle's major attractions. The guest rooms, overlooking a courtyard garden, are spacious enough to feel like apartments. The furnishings are surprisingly classical and lend these rooms a comfortable, homey feel. Every unit has a gas fireplace; the largest rooms have whirlpool tubs. The only real drawback here is the lack of views.

1221 First Ave., Seattle, WA 98101. (C) **888/728-8910** or 206/748-0973. Fax 206/748-0533. www.innatharborsteps. com. 28 units. $165–$230 double. Rates include full breakfast and afternoon tea and appetizers. Children under 5 stay free in parent's room. AE, DC, MC, V. Parking $15. **Amenities:** Restaurant (Brazilian); lounge; indoor pool; health club with Jacuzzi, sauna, and basketball court; concierge; business center; laundry service; dry cleaning. In room: A/C, TV, dataport, minibar, coffeemaker, hair dryer, iron, free local calls, high-speed Internet access.

Sheraton Seattle Hotel and Towers ☞☞☞
At 35 stories, this is one of the two largest hotels in Seattle. Because it's so large, it does a brisk convention business, and the building is almost always buzzing with activity. Don't let the crowds put you off, however. There's a reason so many people want to stay here: The hotel does things right and captures much of the essence of Seattle in its many features. It has a 35th-floor exercise room and swimming pool with great views of the city. You also get good views from guest rooms on the higher floors. All units are fairly spacious.

For even more space, book one of the king rooms, which are designed for business travelers.

1400 Sixth Ave., Seattle, WA 98101. © 800/325-3535 or 206/621-9000. Fax 206/621-8441. www.sheraton.com/seattle. 840 units. $169–$385 double; $300–$5,000 suite. Children under 18 stay free in parent's room. AE, DC, DISC, MC, V. Valet parking $26; self-parking $24. Pets accepted. **Amenities:** Restaurant (American); 2 lounges (including wine bar); indoor pool; health club; Jacuzzi; sauna; concierge; business center; room service; massage; babysitting; laundry service; dry cleaning; concierge-level rooms. *In room:* A/C, TV, dataport, minibar, coffeemaker, hair dryer, iron, safe, high-speed Internet access.

The Westin Seattle ★★★ (Kids   With its distinctive cylindrical towers, the 47-story Westin is the tallest hotel in Seattle and consequently provides the best views of any hotels in the city. From rooms on the upper floors of the north tower's northwest side, you'll get breathtaking vistas of the Space Needle, Puget Sound, and the Olympic Mountains. Guest rooms here are some of the nicest in town. Couple those great views with the Westin's plush "Heavenly Beds," and you'll be sleeping on clouds, both literally and figuratively. Although the pool doesn't have any views, keep in mind that few downtown hotels have pools at all. There are also two excellent restaurants.

1900 Fifth Ave., Seattle, WA 98101. © 800/WESTIN-1 or 206/728-1000. Fax 206/728-2007. www.westin.com/seattle. 891 units. $169–$345 double; from $419 suite. Children under 18 stay free in parent's room. AE, DC, DISC, MC, V. Valet parking $29; self-parking $26. Pets accepted ($50 deposit). **Amenities:** 2 restaurants (Seafood, American); lounge; large indoor pool; exercise room; Jacuzzi; concierge; business center; 24-hr. room service; laundry service; dry cleaning. *In room:* A/C, TV, dataport, minibar, coffeemaker, hair dryer, iron, safe, high-speed Internet access.

MODERATE

Executive Pacific Plaza Hotel ★   There aren't too many reasonably priced choices left in downtown Seattle, but this hotel, built in 1928, offers not only moderately priced rooms but also a prime location—halfway between Pike Place Market and Pioneer Square, and just about the same distance from the waterfront. Over the past few years, the hotel has undergone extensive renovations that have updated the rooms and given the lobby a very stylish and contemporary look. However, the rooms are still small (verging on tiny). Consequently, I recommend this place primarily for solo travelers. Rates have been slowly creeping up lately, and, by the time you visit, this hotel may not be as great a deal as it once was.

400 Spring St., Seattle, WA 98104. © 800/426-1165 or 206/623-3900. Fax 206/623-2059. www.pacificplazahotel.com. 155 units. $119–$149 double; $299 suite. Children under 12 stay free in parent's room. AE, DC, DISC, MC, V. Parking $18. Pets accepted. **Amenities:** 2 restaurants (Pan-Asian, coffee shop); concierge; car-rental desk; business center; laundry service; dry cleaning. *In room:* A/C, TV, dataport, coffeemaker, hair dryer, iron.

Mayflower Park Hotel ★★   If your favorite recreational activities include shopping or sipping martinis, the Mayflower Park is for you. Built in 1927, this historic hotel is connected to a shopping mall and is within a block of both Nordstrom and Macy's. Most rooms are furnished with an eclectic blend of contemporary Italian and traditional European pieces. Some units still have small, old-fashioned bathrooms, but all have been recently renovated. The smallest guest rooms are cramped. If you crave space, ask for one of the larger corner rooms or a suite. Martini drinkers should spend time at **Oliver's** lounge (p. 147), with the best martinis in Seattle. The hotel's Andaluca restaurant is a plush, contemporary spot serving creative cuisine.

405 Olive Way, Seattle, WA 98101. © 800/426-5100, 206/382-6990, or 206/623-8700. Fax 206/382-6997. www.mayflowerpark.com. 171 units. $119–$229 double; $139–$365 suite. Children 18 and under stay free in parent's room. AE, DC, DISC, MC, V. Valet parking $21. **Amenities:** Restaurant (Mediterranean/Northwest); lounge; exercise room and access to nearby health club; Jacuzzi; concierge; business center; shopping arcade; 24-hr. room service; laundry service; dry cleaning. *In room:* A/C, TV, dataport, coffeemaker, hair dryer, iron.

Summerfield Suites by Wyndham ✦ *Value*   Just a block uphill from the Washington State Convention and Trade Center, this hotel caters primarily to business travelers. At the same time, the hotel is about equidistant between the waterfront and the hip Capitol Hill shopping and nightlife district, so it's a good choice if you're just here for fun. The suites are well laid out and have full kitchens, so you can save on restaurant bills (maybe do some shopping at Pike Place Market). Many rooms have good views that take in the Space Needle, but be aware that many rooms get traffic noise from both the freeway and Pike Street. A tiny pool is on a pleasant terrace.

1011 Pike St., Seattle, WA 98101. ⓒ 800/996-3426 or 206/682-8282. Fax 206/682-5315. www.wyndham.com. 193 units. $109–$169 double. Rates include continental breakfast. Children 17 and under stay free in parent's room. AE, DC, DISC, MC, V. Valet parking $24. **Amenities:** Small outdoor pool; exercise room; Jacuzzi; concierge; downtown courtesy shuttle; coin-op laundry; dry cleaning. *In room:* A/C, TV, dataport, fridge, coffeemaker, hair dryer, iron, high-speed Internet access.

THE WATERFRONT

Seattle's most touristy neighborhood, the waterfront also has the city's finest views and is home to several worthwhile attractions and activities. Seattle's only actual waterfront hotel, The Edgewater, is here (see below), and it should be the top choice of anyone desiring a Seattle vacation in the thick of things.

VERY EXPENSIVE

Seattle Marriott Waterfront ✦✦   Across Alaskan Way from Elliott Bay, this hotel doesn't have the superb views of the nearby Edgewater, but it's adjacent to the waterfront. The hotel seems to do a brisk business putting up people heading out on cruises (some cruise ships dock right across the street). The best views are from the large junior suites at the northwest corner of the hotel. Because of the way the hotel is designed, many standard rooms have only limited views, but there are little balconies where you can stand and breathe the salt air.

2100 Alaskan Way, Seattle, WA 98121. ⓒ 800/228-9290 or 206/443-5000. Fax 206/256-1000. www.seattlemarriottwaterfront.com. 358 units. $199–$419 double. Children under 18 stay free in parent's room. AE, DC, DISC, MC, V. Valet parking $26. **Amenities:** 2 restaurants (Seafood, American); 2 lounges; indoor/outdoor pool; exercise room and access to nearby health club; Jacuzzi; concierge; courtesy downtown shuttle; business center; 24-hr. room service; massage; coin-op laundry; laundry service; dry cleaning. *In room:* A/C, TV, dataport, coffeemaker, hair dryer, iron, safe, high-speed Internet access.

EXPENSIVE

The Edgewater ✦✦ *Value*   On a pier at the north end of the waterfront, the Edgewater is Seattle's only hotel directly on the bay and is designed to resemble a deluxe fishing lodge. The views out the windows are among the best in Seattle, and sunsets can be mesmerizing. On a clear day, you can see the Olympic Mountains across Puget Sound, which is why this easily is one of my favorite Seattle hotels. The mountain-lodge theme continues in the rooms, which have rustic fireplaces and lodgepole-pine furniture. The least expensive units here overlook the city (and the parking lot). The rooms with balconies are a bit smaller than other rooms, but are my top choice, although the new premium water-view rooms are pretty hard to beat. Beatles fans can stay in the same suite as the Fab Four when they first visited Seattle back in 1964.

Pier 67, 2411 Alaskan Way, Seattle, WA 98121. ⓒ 800/624-0670 or 206/728-7000. Fax 206/441-4119. www.edgewaterhotel.com. 223 units. $169–$539 double; $575–$2,500 suite. Children under 18 stay free in parent's room. AE, DC, DISC, MC, V. Valet parking $22. Pets accepted. **Amenities:** Restaurant (Northwest/Seafood); lounge; exercise room and access to nearby health club; courtesy bikes; concierge; business center; room service; massage; babysitting; laundry service; dry cleaning. *In room:* A/C, TV, dataport, minibar, coffeemaker, hair dryer, iron, high-speed Internet access, Wi-Fi.

PIONEER SQUARE & THE INTERNATIONAL DISTRICT

The historic Pioneer Square area is Seattle's main nightlife district and can be a pretty rowdy place on a Saturday night. By day, however, the area's many art galleries and antiques stores attract a very different clientele. Still, even in the daylight, be prepared to encounter a lot of street people. Warnings aside, this is one of the prettiest corners of Seattle and the only downtown neighborhood with historic flavor. The International District lies but a few blocks away from Pioneer Square—again, a good place to explore by day, but less appealing at night.

EXPENSIVE

Best Western Pioneer Square Hotel   This hotel, listed on the National Register of Historic Places, is right in the heart of the Pioneer Square historic district, Seattle's nightlife and art gallery neighborhood. As such, things get especially raucous on weekend nights, and this hotel is only recommended for urban dwellers accustomed to dealing with street people and noise. However, if you're in town to party (or to attend a Mariners or Seahawks game), there's no more convenient location in the city. However, be careful on the surrounding streets late at night. Guest rooms are fairly small (some are positively cramped), but are furnished in an attractive classic style.

77 Yesler Way, Seattle, WA 98104. ✆ 800/800-5514 or 206/340-1234. Fax 206/467-0707. www.pioneersquare.com. 75 units. July–Sept $169–$299 double; Oct–June $129–$229 double. Rates include continental breakfast. Children 12 and under stay free in parent's room. AE, DC, DISC, MC, V. Parking $20–$25. **Amenities:** Access to nearby health club; concierge; business center; room service; babysitting; laundry service; dry cleaning. *In room:* A/C, TV, dataport, coffeemaker, hair dryer, iron, free local calls, high-speed Internet access, Wi-Fi.

BELLTOWN & PIKE PLACE MARKET

Belltown, which extends north from Pike Place Market, is Seattle's fastest-growing urban neighborhood, with dozens of restaurants, an equal number of nightclubs, and several good hotels. If your Seattle travel plans include lots of eating out at hip restaurants or staying out late partying, then Belltown is the place to stay.

VERY EXPENSIVE

Hotel Ändra   In the trendy Belltown neighborhood and only a few blocks from downtown shopping and Pike Place Market, this hotel melds a vintage building with bold contemporary styling and manages to succeed even better than the local W hotel. Located near lots of good restaurants and hot nightclubs, this is a great place to stay if you're in Seattle to make the scene. Rooms are done in cool blues and kelp greens, with lots of wood and stainless-steel accents, Swedish modern furniture, ergonomic desk chairs, genuine alpaca headboards, retro clocks, and flat-screen TVs. Lights are on dimmers, so you can create just the right mood. The hotel's restaurant is the newest offering from Tom Douglas, one of my favorite Seattle chefs.

2000 Fourth Ave., Seattle, WA 98121. ✆ 877/448-8600 or 206/448-8600. Fax 206/441-7140. www.hotelandra.com. 118 units. $219–$249 double; $309–$1,300 suite. Children under 17 stay free in parent's room. AE, DISC, MC, V. Valet parking $24. Pets accepted. **Amenities:** Restaurant (New American); lounge; exercise room and access to nearby health club; concierge; business center; massage and spa services; laundry service; dry cleaning. *In room:* A/C, TV, dataport, coffeemaker, hair dryer, iron, safe, high-speed Internet access, Wi-Fi.

Inn at the Market   For romance, convenience, and the chance to immerse yourself in the Seattle aesthetic, it's hard to beat this small hotel in Pike Place Market. To make the most of a stay, be sure to ask for one of the water-view rooms that have wide bay windows overlooking Puget Sound. Even if you don't get a water-view room, you'll still find spacious accommodations, with mold-to-your-body Tempur-Pedic beds, large bathrooms, and elegant decor for the feel of an upscale European beach resort. **Campagne** serves excellent southern French fare, while **Café Campagne** offers country-style French food amid casual surroundings. (See p. 95 and p. 97 for full reviews of both restaurants.)

86 Pine St., Seattle, WA 98101. ⓒ 800/446-4484 or 206/443-3600. www.innatthemarket.com. 70 units. $210–$350 double; $575 suite. Children 18 and under stay free in parent's room. AE, DC, DISC, MC, V. Parking $23. **Amenities:** 3 restaurants (French, country French, juice bar and cafe); access to nearby health club; concierge; courtesy downtown shuttle; room service; laundry service; dry cleaning. *In room:* A/C, TV, dataport, minibar, coffeemaker, hair dryer, iron, safe, high-speed Internet access, Wi-Fi.

EXPENSIVE

Inn at El Gaucho ⓡⓡ
While low-budget hipsters have the Ace hotel, those who are more flush with cash can opt for this plush little Belltown inn directly above, and affiliated with, the retro-swanky El Gaucho steakhouse. The nondescript front door does nothing to prepare you for the luxurious little lobby up on the second floor, which makes this place a real find. After a night on the town, have breakfast in the plush feather bed. Leather chairs and sofas and plasma screen TVs all make rooms well worth lingering in. Throw in fresh flowers and you have a great place for a romantic weekend on the town. *One caveat:* The inn is up a flight of stairs.

2502 First Ave., Seattle, WA 98121. ⓒ 866/354-2824 or 206/728-1133. inn.elgaucho.com. 18 units. $155–$345 suite. Rates include continental breakfast. AE, MC, V. Valet parking $20. **Amenities:** Restaurant (Steakhouse); lounge; access to nearby health club; concierge; room service; laundry service; dry cleaning. *In room:* A/C, TV, dataport, coffeemaker, hair dryer, high-speed Internet access, Wi-Fi.

INEXPENSIVE

Ace Hotel
The Ace is the city's hippest economy hotel. White-on-white and stainless steel are the hallmarks of the minimalist decor. There are white TVs, and even the brick walls and wood floors have been painted white. Wall decorations are minimal, except in those rooms with 1970s photomurals of the great outdoors. Platform beds and blankets salvaged from foreign hotels add to the chic feel, as do the tiny stainless-steel sinks in the rooms with shared bathrooms. Basically, aside from the eight large rooms with private bathrooms, this place is a step above a hostel and is aimed at the 20- and 30-something crowd. Be aware that some walls are paper-thin and the clientele here tend to keep late hours.

2423 First Ave., Seattle, WA 98101. ⓒ 206/448-4721. Fax 206/374-0745. www.acehotel.com. 28 units, 14 with shared bathroom. $65–$99 double with shared bathroom; $130–$199 double with private bathroom. Children 13 and under stay free in parent's room. AE, DC, DISC, MC, V. Parking $17. Pets accepted. *In room:* TV, dataport, coffeemaker, Wi-Fi.

Moore Hotel
In a historic building two blocks from Pike Place Market, this hotel has benefited from recent room renovations, making it a good choice for young, adventurous travelers. The Moore is not fancy, and if you aren't in a renovated room on a floor with renovated hallways, the place can seem a bit dreary. However, if you request one of the updated suites, you'll be pleasantly surprised by the stylishly modern, large rooms with hardwood floors, full kitchens, and big windows. The lobby hints at the Moore's historic character, but this place is a budget, rather than historic, hotel. If you want to be in the heart of town at budget rates, this is the place.

1926 Second Ave., Seattle, WA 98101. ⓒ 800/421-5508 or 206/448-4851. Fax 206/728-5668. www.moorehotel.com. 140 units (45 with shared bathroom). $55 double with shared bathroom; $69–$79 double with private bathroom; $95–$130 suite. Children under 10 stay free in parent's room. MC, V. Parking $15. **Amenities:** Restaurant (American); lounge. *In room:* TV.

QUEEN ANNE & SEATTLE CENTER

The Queen Anne neighborhood is divided into Upper Queen Anne and Lower Queen Anne. The upper neighborhood is an upscale residential area with an attractive shopping district. The hotels listed here are in the lower neighborhood, which conveniently flanks Seattle Center and also offers lots of inexpensive restaurants for the budget-minded.

EXPENSIVE

MarQueen Hotel *Kids* *Finds*   This Lower Queen Anne hotel is in a renovated 1918 brick building that will appeal to travelers who enjoy lodgings with historic character. Seattle Center is only 3 blocks away, and from there you can take the monorail into downtown. Although the MarQueen is geared toward business travelers, it's a good choice for vacationers as well. Guest rooms are spacious, though a bit oddly laid out, due to the hotel's previous incarnation as an apartment building. Lots of dark-wood trim and hardwood floors give a genuinely old-fashioned feel. Many units have separate little seating areas and full kitchens, which makes this a good choice for families. An espresso bar is in the building and good restaurants are nearby.

600 Queen Anne Ave. N., Seattle, WA 98109. **C** **888/445-3076** or 206/282-7407. Fax 206/283-1499. www.marqueen.com. 56 units. $145–$175 double; $180–$315 suite. Children 12 and under stay free in parent's room. AE, DC, DISC, MC, V. Valet parking $15. **Amenities:** Access to nearby health club; concierge; courtesy downtown shuttle; room service; laundry service; dry cleaning. *In room:* A/C, TV, dataport, kitchen, minibar, fridge, coffeemaker, hair dryer, iron, free local calls, high-speed Internet access.

MODERATE

Comfort Suites Downtown/Seattle Center *Kids*   Although it's none too easy to find this place, the bargain rates and spacious rooms make the Comfort Suites worth searching out. Since it's located only 3 blocks from Seattle Center, you could feasibly park your car at the hotel and walk or use public transit to get around. If you've brought the family, the suites are a good deal, and the proximity to Seattle Center will help keep the kids entertained. Ask for a room away from the busy highway that runs past the hotel. The accommodations here are quite a bit nicer than at the nearby Holiday Inn, but otherwise the two hotels are comparable.

601 Roy St., Seattle, WA 98109. **C** **800/517-4000** or 206/282-2600. Fax 206/282-1112. www.comfortsuites.com. 158 units. Late May to mid-Sept $99–$149 double; other months $74–$119 double. Rates include continental breakfast. Children 18 and under stay free in parent's room. AE, DC, DISC, MC, V. Free parking. **Amenities:** Exercise room; downtown courtesy shuttle; coin-op laundry. *In room:* A/C, TV, dataport, fridge, coffeemaker, hair dryer, iron, free local calls, high-speed Internet access.

Inn at Queen Anne   In the Lower Queen Anne neighborhood close to Seattle Center and numerous restaurants and espresso bars, this inn is housed in a converted older apartment building. Though the rooms here aren't as nice as those at the nearby Mar-Queen, they're comfortable enough, albeit sometimes a bit cramped and not entirely modern. Deluxe units have air-conditioning and high-speed Internet access. The convenient location and economical rates are the big pluses here, but there's also a pleasant garden surrounding the hotel. In summer, you should opt for a deluxe room with air-conditioning.

505 First Ave. N., Seattle, WA 98109. **C** **800/952-5043** or 206/282-7357. Fax 206/217-9719. www.innatqueenanne.com. 68 units. July 1–Aug 31 $109–$129 double; Apr 16–Jun 30 and Sept 1–Oct 15 $89–$129 double; Oct 16–Apr 15 $69–$119 double. Rates include continental breakfast. Children 12 and under stay free in parent's room. AE, DC, DISC, MC, V. Parking $10. **Amenities:** Courtesy downtown shuttle; coin-op laundry; laundry service; dry cleaning. *In room:* TV, kitchenette, fridge, free local calls.

LAKE UNION

Less than a mile from downtown and lined with houseboats, marinas, and waterfront restaurants, Lake Union has a quintessentially Seattle character. Floatplanes use the lake as a runway, and you can rent a kayak, canoe, or rowboat from several places around the lake. If you're happiest when close to the water but want to avoid the Seattle waterfront crowds, this is an excellent alternative.

MODERATE

Silver Cloud Inns Seattle–Lake Union ★★ _Kids_ _Value_   Across the street from Lake Union, this hotel has good views (some of which take in the Space Needle). The rooms are big and filled with lots of amenities, which makes them convenient for long stays and family vacations. The two swimming pools (one indoor and one outdoor) should also appeal to kids. Although the hotel doesn't have a restaurant of its own, there are plenty of waterfront options within walking distance. Floatplane tours also leave from right across the street. This is a good value for such a great location.

1150 Fairview Ave. N., Seattle, WA 98109. ⓒ 800/330-5812 or 206/447-9500. Fax 206/812-4900. www.silvercloud. com. 184 units. June–Sept $129–$230 double; Oct–May $99–$179 double. Rates include continental breakfast. Children under 18 stay free in parent's room. AE, DC, DISC, MC, V. Free parking. **Amenities:** Indoor and outdoor pools; exercise room and access to nearby health club; 2 Jacuzzis; courtesy local shuttle; business center; guest laundry; laundry service; dry cleaning. _In room:_ A/C, TV, dataport, fridge, coffeemaker, hair dryer, iron, free local calls, high-speed Internet access.

CAPITOL HILL & EAST SEATTLE

A mile or so uphill and to the east of downtown Seattle, Capitol Hill is a neighborhood with a split personality. It's a hangout for the 20-something crowd and the city's main gay neighborhood, yet it's also home to numerous large restored homes, many of which have been converted into bed-and-breakfast inns. If you prefer B&Bs to corporate hotels, this is the best neighborhood in which to base yourself. Although Capitol Hill is a bit of a walk from downtown, the neighborhood has good public bus connections to the city center.

MODERATE

Gaslight Inn ★   Anyone enamored of Craftsman bungalows and the Arts-and-Crafts movement should enjoy a stay in this 1906 home. Throughout the inn are numerous pieces of Stickley furniture and oak trim at every turn. The common rooms are spacious and attractively decorated with a combination of Western and Northwestern flair. In summer, guests can swim in the backyard pool. Guest rooms have lots of oak furnishings and some rooms have peeled-log beds. An annex next door has a studio and six suites. One suite, done in a contemporary style with an art-glass chandelier, has a fireplace and an outstanding view of the city.

1727 15th Ave., Seattle, WA 98122. ⓒ 206/325-3654. Fax 206/328-4803. www.gaslight-inn.com. 15 units, 3 with shared bathroom. $78–$98 double with shared bathroom; $98–$148 double with private bathroom; $128 studio; $148–$178 suite. Rates include continental breakfast. AE, MC, V. Off-street parking for suites. No children allowed. **Amenities:** Small seasonal heated outdoor pool; concierge; laundry service. _In room:_ TV, dataport, hair dryer, iron, free local calls.

Salisbury House   On tree-lined 16th Avenue East, this grand old house has a wide wraparound porch from which you can enjoy one of Seattle's prettiest residential streets. Inside, there's plenty to admire as well. Two living rooms (one with a wood-burning fireplace) and a second-floor sun porch provide great spots for relaxing and meeting other guests. On sunny summer days, breakfast may even be served in the

Seattle Accommodations & Dining—Capitol Hill, Lake Union, Queen Anne & North Seattle

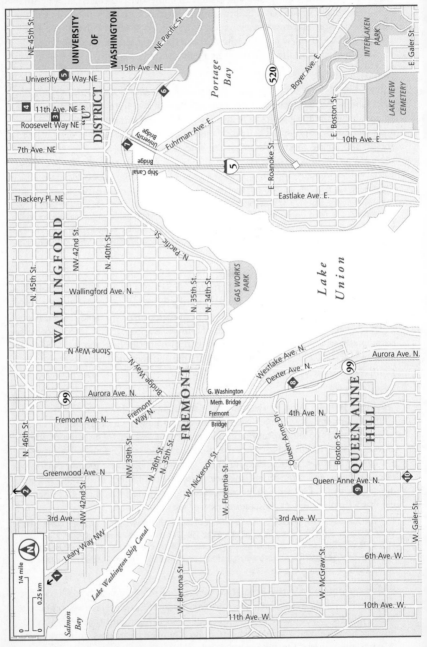

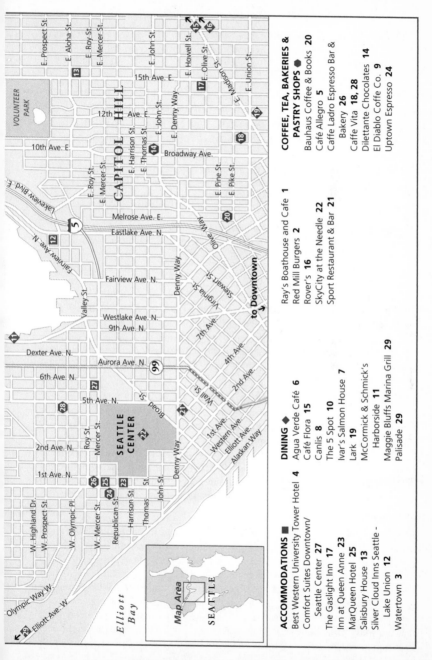

ACCOMMODATIONS ■

Best Western University Tower Hotel **4**
Comfort Suites Downtown/
Seattle Center **27**
The Gaslight Inn **17**
Inn at Queen Anne **23**
MarQueen Hotel **25**
Salisbury House **13**
Silver Cloud Inns Seattle -
Lake Union **12**
Watertown **3**

DINING ◆

Agua Verde Café **6**
Café Flora **15**
Canlis **8**
The 5 Spot **10**
Ivar's Salmon House **7**
Lark **19**
McCormick & Schmick's
Harborside **11**
Maggie Bluffs Marina Grill **29**
Palisade **29**

Ray's Boathouse and Cafe **1**
Red Mill Burgers **2**
Rover's **16**
SkyCity at the Needle **22**
Sport Restaurant & Bar **21**

**COFFEE, TEA, BAKERIES &
PASTRY SHOPS** ●

Bauhaus Coffee & Books **20**
Café Allegro **5**
Caffe Ladro Espresso Bar &
Bakery **26**
Caffe Vita **18, 28**
Dilettante Chocolates **14**
El Diablo Coffe Co. **9**
Uptown Espresso **24**

Kids Family-Friendly Hotels

Comfort Suites Downtown/Seattle Center (p. 84)   The suites make this a good family choice, and the location near the Seattle Center will make the kids happy.

MarQueen Hotel (p. 84)   Located within a few blocks of Seattle Center and its many attractions, this converted apartment building provides a convenient location for families and spacious suites with kitchenettes.

Seattle Marriott Sea-Tac Airport (p. 89)   With a huge jungley atrium containing a swimming pool and whirlpool spas, kids can play Tarzan and never leave the hotel. A tiny game room has a few video games.

Silver Cloud Inns Seattle–Lake Union (p. 85)   Located right across the street from Lake Union and several reasonably priced restaurants, this modern hotel is a good choice for families. It also has two pools and spacious rooms.

The Westin Seattle (p. 80)   Parents will love the views from the tallest hotel in Seattle, while the kids will enjoy the pool—a rarity in downtown hotels.

small formal garden in the backyard. Guest rooms all have queen-size beds with down comforters; one has a fireplace and a whirlpool tub, while another has a claw-foot tub.

750 16th Ave. E., Seattle, WA 98112. © **206/328-8682.** Fax 206/720-1019. www.salisburyhouse.com. 5 units. $95–$155 double (lower rates Nov–Apr). Rates include full breakfast. 2-night minimum in summer; 3-night minimum on holiday weekends. Children over 12 are welcome and stay free in parent's room. AE, MC, V. *In room:* Dataport, coffeemaker, hair dryer, iron, free local calls, Wi-Fi.

NORTH SEATTLE (THE UNIVERSITY DISTRICT)

Located 10 to 15 minutes north of downtown Seattle, the University District (more commonly known as the U District) appeals primarily to younger travelers, but it offers less expensive accommodations than downtown and is still fairly convenient to Seattle's major attractions. Also nearby are the Burke Museum, Henry Art Gallery, Museum of History and Industry, Woodland Park Zoo, and, of course, the University of Washington. As you would expect in a university neighborhood, there are lots of cheap restaurants, making this an all-around good choice for anyone on a budget.

EXPENSIVE

Watertown ✸✸   Watertown is one of Seattle's U District entries in the hip-hotel market. Only blocks from the University of Washington, this beautifully designed hotel is well placed for a young, hip clientele. If you're into contemporary styling, you'll love it, even if you aren't in town on university business. Platform beds, streamlined built-ins, desks with frosted-glass tops and ergonomic chairs, and huge full-length mirrors are just a few of the interesting features in the guest rooms. Bathrooms are large and have granite countertops; when you see the frosted-glass portal on the door, you'll imagine you're on a cruise ship. Guests enjoy a complimentary wine tasting during their stay, as well as access to the pool and hot tub at the nearby University Inn, which is under the same management. Be sure to check out the hotel's "A la Cart" program, which will send you a Spa Cart, a Movie Cart, or a Surf Cart (for surfing the Internet).

4242 Roosevelt Way NE, Seattle, WA 98105. ℂ **866/944-4242** or 206/826-4242. Fax 206/315-4242. www. watertownseattle.com. 100 units. $145–$165 double; $165–$185 suite. Rates include continental breakfast. Children under 18 stay free in parent's room. AE, DC, DISC, MC, V. Free parking. **Amenities:** Restaurant/lounge (wine bar); exercise room and access to nearby health club; bikes; courtesy shuttle to downtown; coin-op laundry; laundry service; dry cleaning. *In room:* A/C, TV, dataport, fridge, coffeemaker, hair dryer, iron, safe, free local calls, high-speed Internet access.

MODERATE
Best Western University Tower Hotel ✦✦ *Value*   Despite its location away from downtown, this is one of Seattle's hippest hotels, with excellent value. For these reasons, it's one of my favorite hotels in the city. You're surrounded by Art Deco style, and the retro look is both elegant and playful. You even get views of downtown Seattle, distant mountains, and various lakes and waterways. Every room here is a corner unit, which means plenty of space to spread out and plenty of views from the higher floors. Small bathrooms are the biggest drawback. This hotel is considerably cheaper than comparable downtown options.

4507 Brooklyn Ave. NE, Seattle, WA 98105. ℂ **800/899-0251** or 206/634-2000. Fax 206/545-2103. www.university towerhotel.com. 155 units. June–Sept $129–$169 double; Oct–May $109–$139 double. Rates include continental breakfast. Children under 18 stay free in parent's room. AE, DC, DISC, MC, V. Free parking. **Amenities:** Restaurant (Eclectic, coffee shop); lounge; exercise room; business center. *In room:* A/C, TV, dataport, coffeemaker, hair dryer, iron.

NEAR SEA-TAC AIRPORT
The airport is 30 to 45 minutes south of downtown Seattle (depending on traffic), but other than that, there's little to recommend this area as a place to stay.

MODERATE
Seattle Marriott Sea-Tac Airport ✦✦ *Kids*   With a steamy atrium garden and plenty of tropical plants, a swimming pool, and two whirlpool tubs, this resortlike hotel is an excellent choice if you're visiting during the rainy season. There are even waterfalls and totem poles for that Northwest outdoorsy feeling; best of all, it's always sunny and warm in here (which is more than you can say for the real Northwest outdoors). In the lobby, big aquaria perpetuate the tropical feel. Meanwhile, the hotel's restaurant, with its stone pillars, rough-hewn beams, and deer-antler chandeliers, conjures up a lodge feel. Guest rooms are comfortable, with good beds and pillows.

3201 S. 176th St., Seattle, WA 98188. ℂ **800/314-0925** or 206/241-2000. Fax 206/248-0789. www.marriott.com. 459 units. $99–$189 double; $225–$450 suite. Children under 18 stay free in parent's room. AE, DC, DISC, MC, V. Parking $12. **Amenities:** Restaurant (American); lounge; indoor atrium pool; exercise room; Jacuzzi; game room; concierge; car-rental desk; courtesy airport shuttle; business center; room service; laundry service; dry cleaning; concierge-level rooms. *In room:* A/C, TV, dataport, coffeemaker, hair dryer, iron, high-speed Internet access.

THE EASTSIDE
The Eastside (a reference to this area's location on the east side of Lake Washington) is Seattle's main high-tech suburb and comprises the cities of Bellevue, Kirkland, Issaquah, and Redmond. Should you be out this way on business, you may find an Eastside hotel to be more convenient than one in downtown Seattle. Surprisingly, two of the most luxurious hotels in the entire Seattle area are here on this side of the lake. If it isn't rush hour, you can usually get from the Eastside to downtown in about 20 minutes via the famous floating I-90 and Wash. 520 bridges. During rush hour, however, it can take much longer.

VERY EXPENSIVE

Bellevue Club Hotel ✻✻✻   With its gardens, architecture, and interior design, this hotel epitomizes contemporary Northwest style. Beautiful landscaping surrounds the entrance, and works of contemporary art can be found throughout public areas. The "club" in this hotel's name refers to the health club and full-service spa that share the building with the hotel. You won't find more elegant rooms anywhere in the Seattle area. Accommodations are extremely plush, with the high-ceilinged garden rooms among my favorites. These have floor-to-ceiling walls of glass, massive draperies, and private patios facing a beautiful garden. Luxurious European fabrics lend a romantic feel. Bathrooms are resplendent in granite and glass, and most have whirlpool tubs.

11200 SE Sixth St., Bellevue, WA 98004. ℂ 800/579-1110 or 425/454-4424. Fax 425/688-3101. www.bellevueclub. com. 67 units. $255–$315 double ($195–$250 weekends); $575–$1,650 suite. Children under 18 stay free in parent's room. AE, DC, DISC, MC, V. Pets accepted ($35 fee). Parking $5–$10. **Amenities:** 3 restaurants (Pacific Rim, family cafe, coffee shop); lounge; 2 indoor pools and 1 outdoor pool; expansive health club with Jacuzzis, saunas, steam rooms, 11 tennis courts, racquetball courts, squash courts, and aerobics studios; spa; children's programs; game room; concierge; business center; 24-hr. room service; massage; babysitting; laundry service; dry cleaning. *In room:* A/C, TV, dataport, minibar, hair dryer, iron, safe, high-speed Internet access, Wi-Fi.

Willows Lodge ✻✻✻ *Finds*   From the moment you turn into the lodge's parking lot, you'll recognize this as someplace special. In the heart of the Woodinville wine country about 30 minutes north of Seattle and adjacent to the much-celebrated Herbfarm Restaurant (see later in this chapter), this lodge is a beautiful blend of rustic and contemporary. The abundance of polished woods (some salvaged from an old building in Portland) gives this hotel something of a Japanese aesthetic. It's all very soothing and tranquil, an ideal retreat from which to visit nearby wineries. Guest rooms have beds with European linens and down duvets.

14580 NE 145th St., Woodinville, WA 98072. ℂ 877/424-3930 or 425/424-3900. Fax 425/424-2585. www. willowslodge.com. 86 units. $260–$340 double; $550–$750 suite. Rates include continental breakfast. Children under 18 stay free in parent's room. AE, DC, DISC, MC, V. Pets accepted with $200 refundable deposit. **Amenities:** 2 restaurants (Northwest); 2 lounges; exercise room; full-service spa; Jacuzzi; sauna; bike rentals; concierge; room service; massage; dry cleaning. *In room:* A/C, TV/DVD, dataport, minibar, coffeemaker, hair dryer, iron, safe, free local calls, high-speed Internet access, Wi-Fi.

Woodmark Hotel on Lake Washington ✻✻   Although Kirkland's Woodmark Hotel is 20 minutes from downtown Seattle (on a good day), it is the metro area's premier waterfront lodging. Surrounded by a luxury residential community, the Woodmark has the feel of a beach resort and looks out over the very same waters that Bill Gates views from his nearby Xanadu. There are plenty of lake-view rooms here, and you'll pay a premium for them. For less expensive lodging, try the creek-view rooms, which have a pleasant view of an attractively landscaped little stream. Floor-to-ceiling windows that open are a nice feature on sunny summer days. The hotel's dining room is pricey, but several less-expensive restaurants are in the same complex of buildings. Guests can also go out for a complimentary cruise on the hotel's restored 1956 Chris-Craft boat.

1200 Carillon Point, Kirkland, WA 98033. ℂ 800/822-3700 or 425/822-3700. Fax 425/822-3699. www.thewoodmark. com. 100 units. $215–$285 double; $330–$1,800 suite. Children under 18 stay free in parent's room. AE, DC, MC, V. Valet parking $12; self-parking $10. Pets accepted. **Amenities:** Restaurant (New American); lounge; exercise room; access to nearby health club; full-service spa; watersports equipment rentals; concierge; business center; salon; 24-hr. room service; massage; laundry service; dry cleaning. *In room:* A/C, TV, dataport, minibar, coffeemaker, hair dryer, iron, safe, high-speed Internet access, Wi-Fi.

MODERATE

Extended StayAmerica–Bellevue ✪   Just off I-405 near downtown Bellevue, this modern, off-ramp motel caters primarily to long-term guests. To this end, the rooms are all large, have kitchenettes, and offer free local calls. However, you won't get daily maid service unless you are staying only a few days and pay extra for it. If you stay for a week, rates drop considerably. This is about the most expensive of the Seattle area's Extended StayAmerica hotels, so if you don't mind staying in a different, less upscale suburb, you can find even lower rates.

11400 Main St., Bellevue, WA 98004. ✆ **800/398-7829** or 425/453-8186. Fax 425/453-8178. www.extendedstay. com. 148 units. $95–$105 double ($406–$455 weekly). Children under 18 stay free in parent's room. AE, DC, DISC, MC, V. Free parking. Pets accepted ($25 per day). **Amenities:** Coin-op laundry. *In room:* A/C, TV, dataport, kitchenette, fridge, coffeemaker, iron, free local calls, high-speed Internet access.

4 Where to Dine

The fact that **Pike Place Market,** a public market filled with food stalls, is one of Seattle's top attractions should clue you in to the fact that this city takes food seriously. Throughout the summer, and other times of year as well, the market overflows with a marvelous bounty of fresh salmon, Dungeness crabs, artisanal cheeses, Northwest berries, locally grown organic vegetables, wild mushrooms, and a wide variety of other produce. Best of all, this bounty makes it onto the tables of lots of great Seattle restaurants, and plenty are right in the Pike Place Market neighborhood.

Of course, as everyone on earth seems to know by now, Seattle takes coffee very seriously. This is where **Starbucks** got its start, and though the stylish espresso bars are now ubiquitous all across the country and around the world, there was a time when there was only one Starbucks—and, of course, it was (and still is) located in the Pike Place Market.

While the market neighborhood gets my vote for best dining district in the city, nearby **Belltown,** which begins just a few blocks from Pike Place Market, also abounds in great restaurants. Be aware that most of these places are not cheap: Entree prices at most restaurants in these two neighborhoods average around $20 or more, and there are a few places where you'll pay quite a bit more. However, if you happen to visit in spring or fall, keep an eye out for special prix-fixe menus. Over the past few years, even the most expensive restaurants around the city have been offering $25 fixed-price dinners.

If those prices seem discouraging, rest assured that you can also find plenty of less expensive restaurants in the Pike Place Market neighborhood. In fact, because the market is such a tourist attraction, it has scads of cheap places to eat. Just don't expect haute cuisine at diner prices. There are, however, a few gems, which I have listed in this chapter. Even the trendy Belltown neighborhood has a handful of good, inexpensive eateries.

DOWNTOWN & FIRST HILL
EXPENSIVE

The Brooklyn Seafood, Steak & Oyster House ✪✪ SEAFOOD   This classic seafood restaurant looks as if it's been here since the Great Seattle Fire and is, in fact, housed in one of the city's oldest buildings. The specialty is definitely oysters, with close to a dozen different types piled up at the oyster bar on any given night. If

oysters on the half shell don't appeal to you, there are plenty of other tempting appetizers, ranging from cilantro-battered calamari to Dungeness crab cakes with wasabi
aioli. For a classic Northwest dish, try the alder-planked king salmon (roasted on a
slab of alder wood); for something a bit more unusual, opt for the sautéed prawns with
brandy, garlic, chili, and tomatoes.

1212 Second Ave. ⓒ 206/224-7000. Reservations recommended. Main courses $11–$14 at lunch, $16–$37 at dinner. AE, DC, DISC, MC, V. Mon–Fri 11am–3pm; Mon–Thurs 5–10pm; Fri 5–10:30pm; Sat 4:30–10:30pm; Sun 4–10pm
(oyster bar open later every night).

Metropolitan Grill ⓡⓡ STEAK   Fronted by massive granite columns that make it
look more like a bank than a restaurant, the Metropolitan Grill is a very traditional
steakhouse that attracts a well-heeled clientele, primarily men in suits. When you walk
in the front door, you'll immediately encounter a case full of meat that ranges from
filet mignon to triple-cut lamb chops (with the occasional giant lobster tail tossed in).
Perfectly cooked dry-aged steaks are the primary attraction; a baked potato and a pile
of thick-cut onion rings complete the ultimate carnivore's dinner. Financial matters
are a frequent topic of discussion here, and the bar even has a "Guess the Dow" contest. I hope you sell stocks high, since it'll take some capital gains to finance a dinner
for two here.

820 Second Ave. ⓒ 206/624-3287. www.themetropolitangrill.com. Reservations recommended. Main courses
$9–$39 at lunch, $19–$60 at dinner. AE, DC, DISC, MC, V. Mon–Fri 11am–3pm; Mon–Thurs 5–10:30pm; Fri 5–11pm;
Sat 4–11pm; Sun 4–10pm.

Union ⓡⓡ NEW AMERICAN   Across the street from the Seattle Art Museum's
new wing (still under construction), this beautiful, minimalist space houses one of
Seattle's finest restaurants. Chef Ethan Stowell has assembled a kitchen crew with
impeccable credentials, and it shows on the highly creative, constantly changing
menu. Basically, this is a don't-miss spot on any foodies' visit to Seattle. The tasting
menus that allow you to sample various delicious small plates are the way to go; they
allow chef Stowell to show off his chops. The quality of ingredients is incomparable
and the presentation gorgeous. Keep an eye out for the potato soup with truffle oil
and roasted sweetbreads with braised morels. Try the creamy chocolate-espresso pot de
crème if it's on the dessert menu.

1400 First Ave. ⓒ 206/838-8000. www.unionseattle.com. Reservations recommended. Main courses $18–$22; tasting menu $60 ($105 with wine). AE, DISC, MC, V. Daily 5–11pm.

MODERATE

Wild Ginger Asian Restaurant & Satay Bar ⓡⓡ PAN-ASIAN   This Pan-Asian
restaurant has long been a Seattle favorite. It's across the street from Benaroya Hall, so
it's perfect for dinner before a symphony performance. I like to pull up a comfortable
stool at the large satay bar and watch the cooks grill little skewers of everything from
chicken to scallops to prawns to lamb. Each skewer is served with a small cube of
sticky rice and pickled cucumber; order three or four satay sticks and you'll have a
meal. If you prefer to sit at a table for a more traditional dinner, Wild Ginger can also
accommodate you. Try the Panang beef curry (rib-eye steak in pungent curry sauce of
cardamom, coconut milk, Thai basil, and peanuts). The restaurant also operates the
Triple Door, a classy live-music club down in the basement, so be sure to check the
performance schedule.

1401 Third Ave. ⓒ 206/623-4450. Reservations recommended. Satay sticks $2.95–$5.65; main courses $7.25–$14
at lunch, $9–$24 at dinner. AE, DC, DISC, MC, V. Mon–Sat 11:30am–2am; Sun 4:30pm–2am.

Kids Family-Friendly Restaurants

Ivar's Salmon House (p. 101)   This restaurant is built to resemble a Northwest Coast Native American longhouse and is filled with artifacts that kids will find fascinating. If they get restless, they can go out to the floating patio and watch the boats passing by.

Maggie Bluffs Marina Grill (p. 100)   Located at a marina overlooking Elliott Bay and downtown Seattle, this economical place has food the kids will enjoy and provides crayons to keep them occupied while they wait. Before or after a meal, you can take a free boat ride across the marina to an observation deck atop the breakwater.

Mitchelli's (p. 94)   This Pioneer Square restaurant is a good bet if you've been to a ball game or wandering the waterfront. Not only is there a kids' menu, but the restaurant will provide some drawing materials to keep the kids occupied during your meal. Best of all, on Monday nights, kids eat free with their parents.

Sport (p. 101)   Located directly across the street from the Space Needle, this restaurant is a big hit with sports fans, young and old, and it's a great place for lunch if you're spending the day at Seattle Center. For the full-on family experience, get one of the booths that has its own wall-hung plasma TV.

THE WATERFRONT
EXPENSIVE

Elliott's ★★ SEAFOOD   While most of its neighbors are content to coast along on tourist business, Elliott's aims to keep the locals happy by serving some of the best seafood in Seattle. The quality of the food here may be in inverse proportion to the view, since the restaurant is right on the waterfront, but the view isn't that great. If you're looking for superbly prepared fresh seafood, however, Elliott's is an excellent bet. Salmon and Dungeness crab are usually prepared several different ways. Meanwhile, the oyster bar can have as many as 20 varieties available, so this is definitely the place to get to know your Northwest oysters.

Pier 56, 1201 Alaskan Way. ⓒ **206/623-4340.** Reservations recommended. Main courses $9–$40 at lunch, $18–$38 at dinner. AE, DC DISC, MC, V. Sun–Thurs 11am–10pm; Fri–Sat 11am–11pm.

MODERATE

Anthony's Pier 66 & Bell Street Diner ★★ SEAFOOD   The Anthony's chain has several outposts around the Seattle area, but this complex is the most convenient and versatile. It not only has an upper-end, stylish seafood restaurant with good waterfront views, but also a moderately priced casual restaurant and a walk-up counter. The bold contemporary styling and abundance of art glass set Anthony's apart from most waterfront restaurants. The upscale crowd heads upstairs for Asian-inspired seafood dishes, while the more cost-conscious stay downstairs at the Bell Street Diner, where meals are easier on the wallet (though far less creative). For higher prices, you get better views. In summer the decks are the place to be.

2201 Alaskan Way. ℂ 206/448-6688. www.anthonys.com. Reservations recommended at Pier 66, not taken at Bell Street Diner. Pier 66 main courses $9–$24; Bell Street Diner main courses $7–$19. AE, MC, V. Pier 66 Mon–Thurs 5–9:30pm, Fri–Sat 5–10pm, Sun 5–9pm; Bell Street Diner Mon–Thurs 11am–10pm, Fri–Sat 11am–10:30pm, Sun 11am–9pm.

PIONEER SQUARE & THE INTERNATIONAL DISTRICT

In addition to the International District restaurant listed below, you'll find a large food court at **Uwajimaya,** 600 Fifth Ave. S. (ℂ **206/624-6248;** www.uwajimaya.com), a huge Asian supermarket. Its stalls serve foods of different Asian countries. It all smells great, and everything is inexpensive, which makes this a great place for a quick meal.

MODERATE

Mitchelli's ℞ *Kids* ITALIAN/LATE-NIGHT   In the heart of Pioneer Square, Mitchelli's serves good, basic Italian food in a cozy spot with friendly, old-world atmosphere. The vintage wooden-topped lunch counter in a room with classic hexagonal-tile floors is a popular after-work and late-night gathering spot, and the conversation is lively. You can't go wrong with the lasagna or pizza from the wood-fired oven. Better yet, build your own custom pasta dish with your choice of seafood or meat. For a rich dessert, dig into a caramello—creamy caramel with toasted walnuts and whipped cream. If you're a night owl, keep Mitchelli's in mind. Full meals are served until 4am on Friday and Saturday nights, catering to the starving hordes that pour out of the area's many bars after last call.

84 Yesler Way. ℂ 206/623-3883. www.mitchellis.com. Reservations recommended. Main courses $6–$17. AE, DC, MC, V. Mon–Thurs 11:30am–11pm; Fri 11:30am–4am; Sat 8am–4am; Sun 8am–11pm.

INEXPENSIVE

House of Hong ℞ *Value* CHINESE   If you're in the International District anytime between 10am and 4:30pm and want to sample the best dim sum in Seattle, head for the House of Hong. It's located at the uphill end of the neighborhood in a big yellow building. All of the little dumplings, pot stickers, and stuffed won tons that comprise the standards of dim sum are done to perfection here—not too greasy, not too starchy, with plenty of meat in the fillings. Try the whole fried shrimp, crunchy on the outside and moist and meaty inside. There's lots of variety to the offerings, so pace yourself and keep an eye out for whatever looks particularly appetizing. The House of Hong has free parking.

409 Eighth Ave. ℂ 206/622-7997. www.houseofhong.com. Reservations not necessary. Dim sum $2.30–$5.60; main courses $6.75–$28. AE, DISC, MC, V. Mon–Sat 9am–2am; Sun 9am–midnight; dim sum served daily 10am–4:30pm.

Salumi ℞ *Finds* ITALIAN   For many folks, salami is a guilty pleasure. We all know it has way too much fat, but it tastes too good to resist. Now, raise the bar on salami, and you have the artisan-cured meats of this closet-size eatery near Pioneer Square. The owner, Armandino Batali, who happens to be the father of New York's famous chef Mario Batali, makes all his own salami (as well as traditional Italian-cured beef tongue). Order up a meat plate with a side of cheese and some roasted red bell peppers, pour yourself a glass of wine from the big bottle on the table, and you have a perfect lunchtime repast in the classic Italian style. Did I mention the great breads and tapenades? Wow! If you're down in the Pioneer Square area at lunch, don't miss this place (even if there's a long line).

309 Third Ave. S. ℂ 206/621-8772. Reservations not accepted. Main courses $6.50–$13. AE, MC, V. Tues–Fri 11am–4pm.

BELLTOWN & PIKE PLACE MARKET
VERY EXPENSIVE

Campagne ❀❀ FRENCH   With large windows that look out over the top of Pike Place Market to Elliott Bay, Campagne is an unpretentious yet elegant French restaurant. With such a prime location, it shouldn't be surprising that Campagne relies heavily on the wide variety of fresh ingredients from the market. Consequently, the menu changes with the seasons. There are always several interesting salads as well. Don't expect to find coq au vin or boeuf bourguignon on the menu that tends to focus on French dishes that may not be familiar to American diners: lamb shoulder marinated in anchovies and garlic, rib-eye steak with roasted marrow bone, salt cod and curry fritters with aioli.

In the Inn at the Market, 86 Pine St. ℂ 206/728-2800. www.campagnerestaurant.com. Reservations recommended. Main courses $20–$33. AE, MC, V. Daily 5:30–10pm (late-night menu Fri–Sat until midnight).

Cascadia Restaurant ❀❀❀ NORTHWEST   Chef Kerry Sear first made a name for himself in Seattle at the Georgian, the opulent restaurant at what is now the Fairmont Olympic Hotel. Here, at his own restaurant, he celebrates all foods Northwestern in an elegant, understated space in Belltown. For the full Cascadia experience, indulge in one of Sear's seven-course tasting menus. For the ultimate Northwest dinner, try the menu of dishes prepared with seasonal ingredients from around the Cascadia region, which stretches from British Columbia to Northern California. Because the menu changes with the seasons, you never know what you might find, but rest assured it will be memorable. There's also a seven-course vegetarian dinner. Want the dining experience but can't afford the prices? Try the bar, which has a menu of 10 dishes for $10 or under and serves a delicious martini with a scoop of Douglas fir sorbet in it.

2328 First Ave. ℂ 206/448-8884. www.cascadiarestaurant.com. Reservations highly recommended. Main courses $25–$48; 3-course prix-fixe dinner $25; 7-course tasting menu $55–$85. AE, DC, MC, V. Mon–Thurs 5–10pm; Fri–Sat 5–10:30pm.

El Gaucho ❀❀ LATE-NIGHT/STEAK   Conjuring up the ghosts of dinner clubs of the 1930s and 1940s, this high-end Belltown steakhouse looks like it could be a Fred Astaire film set. The pure theatrics make this place a must if you're in the mood to spend big bucks on a thick, juicy steak. Sure, you may find a better steak at one of the other high-end steakhouses in town, but you just can't duplicate the experience of dining at El Gaucho. Stage-set decor aside, the real stars of the show here are the 28-day dry-aged Angus beefsteaks, definitely some of the best in town—but know that the perfect steak doesn't come cheap. There's also a classy bar off to one side, a separate cigar lounge, and, for after-dinner dancing, the affiliated **Pampas Room** nightclub.

2505 First Ave. ℂ 206/728-1337. www.elgaucho.com. Reservations recommended. Main courses $17–$98 (steaks $38–$59). AE, DC, DISC, MC, V. Mon–Sat 5pm–1am; Sun 5–11pm.

EXPENSIVE

Chez Shea ❀❀ NORTHWEST   Quiet, dark, and intimate, Chez Shea has long been one of Seattle's top restaurants, and with only a dozen candlelit tables and views across Puget Sound to the Olympic Mountains, it's an ideal setting for romance. The menu changes with the season, and ingredients come primarily from the market below. On a recent spring evening, dinner started with gravlax carpaccio, followed by an asparagus bisque and sea scallops with truffled pea purée and a carrot-ginger purée. Among the half-dozen nightly entrees were pan-seared veal chops with morel mushrooms and truffled mashed potatoes; duck confit with herb crepes; and halibut with a pistachio crust. Though dessert is a la carte, you'll find it impossible to let it pass. The city may have equally fine restaurants, but none with such a romantic atmosphere. Attached to this restaurant is the casual Shea's Lounge, with a similar atmosphere but lower prices.

Corner Market Building, 94 Pike St., Suite 34. ℂ 206/467-9990. www.chezshea.com. Reservations highly recommended. Prix-fixe 4-course dinner $44. AE, MC, V. Tues–Sun 5–10pm.

Dahlia Lounge 🦀🦀 PAN-ASIAN/NORTHWEST   The neon chef holding a flapping fish may suggest that the Dahlia is little more than a roadside diner. However, a glimpse of the stylish interior will have you thinking otherwise, and one bite of any dish will convince you that this is one of Seattle's finest restaurants. Mouthwatering Dungeness crab cakes, a bow to chef Tom Douglas's Delaware roots, are the house specialty and should not be missed. The menu—influenced by the far side of the Pacific Rim—changes regularly, and the lunch menu has some of the same offerings at lower prices. It's way too easy to fill up on the restaurant's breads, which are baked in the adjacent Dahlia Bakery, and for dessert, it takes a Herculean effort to resist the crème caramel.

2001 Fourth Ave. ℂ 206/682-4142. www.tomdouglas.com. Reservations highly recommended. Main courses $11–$22 at lunch, $18–$30 at dinner. AE, DC, DISC, MC, V. Mon–Fri 11:30am–2:30pm; Mon–Thurs 5–10pm; Fri–Sat 5–11pm; Sun 5–9pm.

Flying Fish 🦀🦀 LATE-NIGHT/NORTHWEST/SEAFOOD   In business for more than a decade now, Flying Fish is the main stage for local celebrity chef Christine Keff. Not only does Flying Fish offer the bold combinations of vibrant flavors demanded by the city's well-traveled palates, but the hip Belltown restaurant also serves dinner until 1am every night. Every dish here is a work of art, and with small plates, large plates, and platters for sharing, diners are encouraged to sample a wide variety of the kitchen's creations. The menu changes daily, but keep an eye out for the smoked shrimp spring rolls, which are positively sculptural (and delicious). The festive desserts are almost a miniature party on the plate. There's also a huge wine list.

2234 First Ave. ℂ 206/728-8595. www.flyingfishseattle.com. Reservations recommended. Main courses $9–$16 at lunch; $17–$25 at dinner. AE, DC, MC, V. Mon–Fri 11:30am–2pm; daily 5pm–1am.

Icon Grill 🦀 AMERICAN   With colorful art glass hanging from chandeliers, overflowing giant vases, and every inch of wall space covered with framed artwork, this place goes way overboard with its decor, but that's exactly what makes it so fun. Basically, it's an over-the-top rendition of a Victorian setting gone 21st century. The menu leans heavily to well-prepared comfort foods, such as a molasses-glazed meatloaf that locals swear by and a macaroni-and-cheese unlike anything your mother made. Liven things up with a grilled pear salad. The food here is consistent, and the Icon is both a Seattle and a culinary experience.

1933 Fifth Ave. ℂ 206/441-6330. www.icongrill.net. Reservations recommended. Main courses $8.75–$17 at lunch, $16–$30 at dinner. AE, MC, V. Mon–Fri 11:30am–2pm; Mon–Thurs 5:30–10pm; Fri 5:30–11pm; Sat 5–11pm; Sun 5–10pm.

Le Pichet 🦀 FRENCH   Seattle seems to have a thing for French restaurants. They're all over the place in this city, with a surprising number clustered around Pike Place Market. Le Pichet is one of my favorites. The name is French for "pitcher" and refers to the traditional ceramic pitchers used for serving inexpensive French wines. This should clue you in to the casual nature of the place, the sort of spot where you can drop by anytime of day, grab a stool at the bar, and have a light meal. The menu is rustic French, and almost everything is made fresh on the premises. With many small plates and appetizers, it's fun to assemble a light meal of shared dishes. On Sunday afternoons, there's live music.

1933 First Ave. ⓒ **206/256-1499.** Reservations recommended. Small plates $8–$11; main courses $17–$18. MC, V. Sun–Thurs 8am–midnight; Fri–Sat 8am–2am.

Matt's in the Market ★★ *Finds* AMERICAN REGIONAL/INTERNATIONAL This is a real Pike Place Market experience. Quite possibly the smallest gourmet restaurant in Seattle, Matt's is a tiny cubbyhole of a place in the Corner Market Building, directly across the street from the information booth at First and Pike. There are only a handful of tables and a few stools at the counter, and the kitchen takes up almost half the restaurant, giving the cooks little more than the space of a walk-in closet in which to work their culinary magic. The menu changes regularly, with an emphasis on fresh ingredients from the market stalls that are only steps away. There's also a good selection of reasonably priced wines. The food reveals whatever influences and styles happen to appeal to the chef at that moment—perhaps Moroccan, perhaps Southern. If you spot anything with smoked catfish on the menu, try it.

Corner Market Building, 94 Pike St. ⓒ **206/467-7909.** Reservations highly recommended. Main courses $9–$10 at lunch, $16–$21 at dinner. MC, V. Mon–Sat 11:30am–2:30pm; Tues–Sat 5:30–9:30pm.

Restaurant Zoë ★★ NORTHWEST Belltown is packed with trendy, upscale restaurants where being seen is often more important than the food being served. This is definitely *not* one of those places, although the huge windows facing Second Avenue provide plenty of people-watching opportunities. The decor is subtly stylish and the waitstaff (dressed in black) lacks the attitude that mars the experience at many other trendy restaurants. Chef/owner Scott Staples mines the bounties of the Northwest for his seasonal fare, preparing such dishes as pan-seared sweetbreads with smoked bacon, pickled pear, honey-roasted onion, greens and a sherry dressing. Risotto is reliably good and changes with the seasons. Be sure to start your meal with the restaurant's signature Zoë cocktail.

2137 Second Ave. ⓒ **206/256-2060.** www.restaurantzoe.com. Reservations highly recommended. Main courses $16–$30. AE, MC, V. Sun–Thurs 5–10pm; Fri–Sat 5–11pm.

MODERATE

Café Campagne ★★ *Value* FRENCH This little cafe is an offshoot of the popular Campagne, a much more formal French restaurant (see above), and though it's in the heart of the Pike Place Market neighborhood, it's a world away from the market madness. I like to duck in here for lunch and escape the shuffling crowds. What a relief—so civilized, so very French. The dark and cozy place has a hidden feel to it, and most people leave thinking they've discovered some secret hideaway. The menu changes with the seasons. The cafe doubles as a wine bar that has a good selection of reasonably priced wines by the glass or bottle.

1600 Post Alley. ⓒ **206/728-2233.** www.campagnerestaurant.com. Reservations recommended. Main courses $11–$20 at lunch, $14–$20 at dinner; 3-course prix-fixe menu $25. AE, MC, V. Mon–Thurs 11am–10pm; Fri 11am–5pm; Sat–Sun 8am–4pm; Fri–Sat 5:30–11pm; Sun 5–10pm.

Etta's Seafood ★★ SEAFOOD Seattle chef Tom Douglas's strictly seafood (well, almost) restaurant, Etta's, is located smack in the middle of the Pike Place Market area and, of course, serves Douglas's signature crab cakes (crunchy on the outside, creamy on the inside), which are not to be missed (and if they're not on the menu, just ask). Don't ignore your side dishes, either; they can be exquisite and are usually enough to share around the table. In addition to the great seafood dishes, the menu always has a few other fine options, including several that date from Douglas's Café Sport days in the early 1980s. Stylish contemporary decor sets the mood, making this place as popular with locals as it is with tourists.

2020 Western Ave. ⓒ 206/443-6000. www.tomdouglas.com. Reservations recommended. Main courses $11–$30. AE, DC, DISC, MC, V. Mon–Thurs 11:30am–9:30pm; Fri 11:30am–10pm; Sat–Sun 9am–3pm; Sat 4–10pm; Sun 4–9pm.

Lola 🌶🌶 GREEK   Local celeb chef Tom Douglas celebrates his wife's/partner's Greek heritage with his latest restaurant, which is located in the über-hip Hotel Ändra. More akin to Douglas's Palace Kitchen than his plush Dahlia Lounge, Lola is a loud, lively, casual place. Rest assured, this is not your standard Greek place. In fact, other than the words kabob, tzatziki, and dolmades, you won't find much common ground here with other Greek restaurants. Start things out with the super-garlicky *skordalia* (made with potatoes and lots of garlic) spread and pita bread. I always have the octopus and pork belly braised in red wine, but you should also try the salmon kabobs with fennel or the prawn kabobs with curried muscat glaze. For the full-on family-dinner treatment, go for the Lola Big Dinner, which will give you tastes of the less adventurous dishes on the menu. Not up for a big meal? Get the lamb burger; it's fabulous!

2000 Fourth Ave. ⓒ 206/441-1430. www.tomdouglas.com. Reservations highly recommended. Main courses $9–$14 at lunch; $11–$38 at dinner. AE, DC, DISC, MC, V. Mon–Fri 6–10am and 11am–4pm; Sat–Sun 7am–3pm; Sun–Thurs 4–10pm; Fri–Sat 4–11pm (late-night menu served until midnight).

Palace Kitchen 🌶🌶 AMERICAN REGIONAL/LATE-NIGHT/MEDITERRANEAN   This is the most casual of chef Tom Douglas's four Seattle establishments, with a bar that attracts nearly as many customers as the restaurant. The atmosphere is urban chic, with cement pillars, simple wood booths, and a few tables in the front window, which overlooks the monorail tracks. The menu is short and features a nightly selection of unusual cheeses and different preparations from the apple-wood grill. I like to begin a meal here with the creamy goat-cheese fondue. Entrees are usually simple and delicious, ranging from the Palace burger royale (a strong contender for best burger in Seattle) to Walla Walla onion tarts and handmade saffron linguine. For dessert, the coconut cream pie is an absolute must.

2030 Fifth Ave. ⓒ 206/448-2001. www.tomdouglas.com. Reservations accepted only for parties of 6 or more. Main courses $12–$30. AE, DC, DISC, MC, V. Daily 5pm–1am.

The Pink Door 🌶 ITALIAN/LATE-NIGHT   Pike Place Market's better restaurants tend to be well hidden, and if I didn't tell you about this one, you'd probably never find it. There's no sign out front—only the pink door for which the restaurant is named (look for it between Stewart and Virginia). On the other side of the door, stairs lead to a cellarlike space, which is almost always empty on summer days when folks forsake it to dine on the deck with a view of Elliott Bay. What makes this place so popular is as much the fun atmosphere as the reliable Italian food. You may encounter a tarot-card reader or a magician, and most nights in the bar there's some sort of Felliniesque cabaret performer (accordionists, trapeze artists, and the like). Be sure to start your meal with the tangy olive tapenade. From there, you might move on to an Italian classic such as lasagna or a dish made with fresh seafood from the market.

1919 Post Alley. ⓒ 206/443-3241. Reservations recommended. Main courses $9.50–$16 at lunch; $14–$20 at dinner. AE, MC, V. Mon–Sat 11:30am–2:30pm and 5:30–10pm; Sun 5:30–10pm.

INEXPENSIVE

Lowell's ✿ AMERICAN   Everyone in Seattle seems to have a favorite budget place to eat at Pike Place Market. Most of the time I like to grab little bites here and there and savor lots of flavors, but when I've been on my feet for too many hours and just have to sit down, I head to Lowell's. Although the counter-service restaurant is nothing to e-mail home about, this place is a market institution. I like the fish tacos, but there are also good steamer clams, decent fish and chips, salmon dishes, chowder, and burgers. However, what makes this place truly special is the view. Big walls of glass look out to Elliott Bay and the Olympic Mountains. It's so quintessentially Seattle and so unforgettable that you can't help wondering why you aren't being asked to pay a king's ransom to eat with this view. Also, you should know that this place has three floors (with a bar on the second floor), all of which have those same superb vistas.

Main Arcade, 1519 Pike Place. ✆ 206/622-2036. Reservations not accepted. Main courses $7.50–$16. AE, DC, DISC, MC, V. Mon–Fri 7am–5pm; Sat–Sun 7am–6pm (open later in summer).

Noodle Ranch ✿ *Finds* PAN-ASIAN   This Belltown hole in the wall serves Pan-Asian cuisine for the hip-yet-financially challenged crowd. It's a lively, boisterous scene, and the food is packed with intense, and often unfamiliar, flavors. Don't miss the fish grilled in grape leaves with its nice presentation and knockout dipping sauce. In fact, all of the dipping sauces here are delicious. Another dish not to be missed is the Mekong grill—rice noodles with a rice-wine/vinegar-and-herb dressing topped with grilled pork, chicken, beef, or tofu. You'll also find the likes of Laotian cucumber salad and Japanese-style eggplant. In fact, you'll find lots of vegetarian options. Although the place is frequently packed, you can usually get a seat without waiting too long.

2228 Second Ave. ✆ 206/728-0463. www.thenoodleranch.com. Reservations not accepted. Main courses $8–$12. AE, MC, V. Mon–Thurs 11am–10pm; Fri 11am–11pm; Sat noon–10pm.

QUEEN ANNE & SEATTLE CENTER
VERY EXPENSIVE

Canlis ✿✿✿ CONTINENTAL/NORTHWEST   This is one of Seattle's most formal and traditional restaurants, the perfect place to celebrate a very special occasion. A local institution, Canlis has been in business since 1950 but has managed to keep up with the times. Its very stylish interior mixes contemporary decor with Asian antiques; its Northwest cuisine, with Asian and Continental influences, keeps both traditionalists and more adventurous diners content. Steaks from the copper grill are perennial favorites here, as are the spicy Peter Canlis prawns. To finish, why not go all the way and have the Grand Marnier soufflé? Canlis has one of the best wine lists in Seattle.

2576 Aurora Ave. N. ✆ 206/283-3313. www.canlis.com. Reservations highly recommended. Main courses $25–$75; chef's tasting menu $75 ($120 with wines). AE, DC, DISC, MC, V. Mon–Thurs 5:30–9pm; Fri–Sat 5–10pm.

SkyCity at the Needle ✿✿ NORTHWEST   Both the restaurant and the prices are sky high at this revolving restaurant, located just below the observation deck at the top of Seattle's famous Space Needle. However, because you don't have to pay extra for the elevator ride if you dine here, the high prices are a bit more in line with other Seattle splurge restaurants. Okay, maybe you can get better food elsewhere, and maybe you can dine with a view at other Seattle restaurants, but you won't get as spectacular a panorama as here. The menu works hard at offering some distinctly Northwestern flavor combinations, but still has plenty of familiar fare for those who aren't into culinary adventures. Simply prepared steaks and seafood make up the bulk of the offerings, with a couple of vegetarian options as well. I recommend coming here for lunch; the menu includes some of the same dishes, prices are considerably more reasonable, and the views, encompassing the city skyline, Mount Rainier, and the Olympic Mountains, are unsurpassed.

Space Needle, 400 Broad St. ✆ 800/937-9582 or 206/905-2100. www.spaceneedle.com. Reservations highly recommended. Main courses $20–$29 at lunch, $29–$52 at dinner; weekend brunch $39 adults, $16 children 10 and under. AE, DC, DISC, MC, V. Mon–Fri 11am–3:30pm; Sat–Sun 9am–3:30pm; daily 5–10pm.

EXPENSIVE

Palisade NORTHWEST   With a panorama that sweeps from downtown to West Seattle and across the sound to the Olympic Mountains, Palisade has one of the best views of any Seattle waterfront restaurant. It also happens to have fine food and inventive interior design (incorporating a saltwater pond, complete with fish, sea anemones, and starfish, right in the middle of the dining room). The menu features both fish and meats prepared in a wood-fired oven and in a wood-fired rotisserie. The three-course sunset dinners, served before 6pm, cost $24 to $30 and are a great way to enjoy this place on a budget. Palisade also has an excellent and very popular Sunday brunch. If I were going to splurge on dinner at a waterfront restaurant, I'd make it here. *Note:* The restaurant is not easy to find, but it's more than worth the search. Call for directions or to have the restaurant's complimentary limo pick you up at your hotel.

Elliott Bay Marina, 2601 W. Marina Place. ✆ 206/285-1000. www.palisaderestaurant.com. Reservations recommended. Main courses $19–$69; Sun brunch $19–$25. AE, DC, DISC, MC, V. Mon–Thurs 5–9pm; Fri 4:30–10pm; Sat 4–10pm; Sun 9:30am–2pm and 4–9pm.

INEXPENSIVE

The 5 Spot AMERICAN REGIONAL/LATE-NIGHT   Every 3 months or so, this restaurant, one of Seattle's favorite diners, changes its menu to reflect a different regional U.S. cuisine. You may find Brooklyn comfort food featured, or perhaps Cuban-influenced Miami-style meals, but you can bet that whatever's on the menu will be filling and fun. The atmosphere here is pure kitsch—whenever the theme is Florida, the place is adorned with palm trees and flamingos and looks like the high-school gym done up for prom night. This bustling diner is popular with all types who appreciate that they won't go broke eating here. To find it, look for the sign depicting neon coffee pouring into a giant coffee cup, right at the top of Queen Anne Hill.

1502 Queen Anne Ave. N. ✆ 206/285-7768. www.chowfoods.com. Reservations accepted only for parties of 6 or more. Main courses $8.75–$18. MC, V. Mon–Fri 8:30am–midnight; Sat–Sun 8:30am–3pm and 5pm–midnight.

Maggie Bluffs Marina Grill   AMERICAN   It's never easy to find affordable waterfront dining in any city, and Seattle is no exception. However, if you're willing to drive a few miles from downtown, you can save quite a few bucks at this casual marina restaurant located at the foot of Magnolia Bluff (northwest of downtown Seattle). The patio dining area is very popular on sunny summer days, but it's worth waiting for a table. The menu is fairly simple, offering the likes of burgers and fish and chips, but it also includes a few dishes that display a bit more creativity. The restaurant overlooks a marina full of pleasure boats; though the view is partially obstructed by a breakwater, you can still see Elliott Bay, West Seattle, downtown, and even the

Space Needle. Crayons are on hand to keep the kids entertained. After your meal, walk out on Pier G and take a free shuttle boat a few yards through the marina to an observation deck atop the breakwater.

Elliott Bay Marina, 2601 W. Marina Place. ℂ 206/283-8322. Reservations not accepted. Main courses $8.50–$11. AE, DC, DISC, MC, V. Sun–Thurs 11:15am–9:30pm; Fri–Sat 11:15am–10pm.

Sport Restaurant & Bar ℛ ℳids AMERICAN   A friend's teenage son came back from a recent family trip to Seattle raving about this restaurant. If you've got sports fans for kids (or you're one yourself), this big restaurant right across the street from the Space Needle is a must. While the food is decent enough (especially the "Kobe" beef burgers), it's the in-booth plasma TVs that won over my friend's son. Be fore-warned, however, that you can't reserve one of these way-cool booths, so arrive early or plan on a wait for one of these in-demand tables. For adults, there's a bar with a huge wall-hung TV, in addition to standard screens.

140 Fourth Ave. N., Suite 130. ℂ 206/404-7767. www.sportrestaurant.com. Reservations not accepted. Main courses $6–$16. AE, DISC, DC, MC, V. Sun–Thurs 11:30am–1pm; Fri–Sat 11:30am–midnight.

LAKE UNION
MODERATE

Ivar's Salmon House ℛℛ ℳids SEAFOOD   With a view of the Space Needle on the far side of Lake Union, flotillas of sea kayaks silently slipping by, sailboats racing across the lake, and powerboaters tying up at the dock out back, this restaurant on the north side of Lake Union is quintessential Seattle. Add to the scene an award-winning building designed to resemble a Northwest Coast Indian longhouse, and you have what may be the best place in town for a waterfront meal. Okay, so maybe you can find better food at a few other waterfront places, but none has the unequivocally Seat-tle atmosphere you'll find here. This place is a magnet for weekend boaters who aban-don their own galley fare in favor of Ivar's clam chowder and famous alder-smoked salmon. Lots of artifacts, including long dugout canoes and historic photos of Native American chiefs, make Ivar's a hit with both kids and adults. Bear in mind that this restaurant's popularity means that service can be slow; just relax and keep enjoying the great views.

401 NE Northlake Way. ℂ 206/632-0767. www.ivars.net. Reservations recommended. Main courses $8–$18 at lunch, $13–$27 at dinner. AE, MC, V. Mon–Thurs 11am–9pm; Fri–Sat 11am–10pm; Sun 10am–2pm and 3:30–9pm.

McCormick & Schmick's Harborside ℛ SEAFOOD   With its waterfront setting and views of the marinas on the west side of Lake Union, this restaurant has the best location of any of Seattle's McCormick & Schmick's. The menu, which changes daily, includes seemingly endless choices of appetizers, sandwiches, salads, and creative entrees. Just be sure to order something with seafood, such as seared rare ahi with Cajun spices, Parmesan-crusted petrale sole, or salmon roasted on a cedar plank and served with a berry sauce. Sure, there are meat dishes on the menu, but why bother (unless you've only come here for the excellent view)? Bar specials for $1.95 are available in the late afternoon and evening, and there are always plenty of varieties of oysters on the half-shell.

1200 Westlake Ave. N. ℂ 206/270-9052. www.mccormickandschmicks.com. Reservations recommended. Main courses $7–$30. AE, DC, DISC, MC, V. Mon–Thurs 11:30am–10pm; Fri 11:30am–11pm; Sat noon–11pm; Sun noon–9:45pm.

CAPITOL HILL & EAST SEATTLE
VERY EXPENSIVE

Rover's ✿✿✿ NORTHWEST/VEGETARIAN   Tucked away in a quaint clapboard house behind a chic little shopping center in the Madison Valley neighborhood east of downtown, Rover's is one of Seattle's most acclaimed restaurants. Thierry Rautureau, the restaurant's much-celebrated and award-winning chef, received classical French training before falling in love with the Northwest and all the wonderful ingredients it offers. *Voilà!* Northwest cuisine with a French accent. The delicacies on the frequently changing menu are enough to send the most jaded of gastronomes into fits of indecision. Luckily, you can simply opt for one of the fixed-price dinners and leave the decision making to a professional—the chef. Culinary creations include scrambled eggs with lime crème fraîche and caviar, foie gras terrine sometimes served with preserved bing cherry relish, hibiscus-infused sorbet, and squab breast with onion confit, chanterelles, and lemon-thyme sauce. *Vegetarians, take note:* You won't often find a vegetarian feast that can compare with the ones served here.

2808 E. Madison St. ✆ 206/325-7442. www.rovers-seattle.com. Reservations required. Main courses $18–$20 at lunch, $35 3-course prix fixe lunch; 5-course degustation menu $80 (vegetarian) and $90; chef's 8-course grand menu $125. AE, MC, V. Fri noon–1:30pm; Tues–Thurs 6–9:30pm; Fri–Sat 5:30–9:30pm.

MODERATE

Lark ✿✿ NORTHWEST/MEDITERRANEAN   You wouldn't think to look at it, but this little neighborhood restaurant on a somewhat run-down back street on Capitol Hill has an impressive pedigree. Chef Jonathan Sundstrom formerly headed the kitchen at the W Seattle's Earth & Ocean restaurant. From the downtown financial district, he headed for the 'hoods and opened this far more casual bistro. The menu consists of dozens of small plates that you should assemble into a meal to fit your appetite. On a recent night, the carpaccio of yellowtail with fennel and truffled green peaches and the seared foie gras with caramelized turnips were two of the standouts ordered by my table. Cheese lovers take note: The cheese list is one of the best in the city, and whether you order some as an appetizer of as an end to your meal, be sure to try something off this list. Unfortunately, dishes sometimes don't taste as good as they sound on the menu.

926 12th Ave. ✆ 206/323-5275. Reservations only for parties of 6 or more. Main courses $9–$20. MC, V. Tues–Sun 5–10:30pm.

INEXPENSIVE

Cafe Flora ✿ VEGETARIAN   Big, bright, and airy, this Madison Valley cafe will dispel any ideas you may have about vegetarian food being boring. This meatless gourmet cooking draws on influences from around the world—it's a vegetarian's dream come true. One of the house specialties is a portobello Wellington made with mushroom-pecan pâté and sautéed leeks in a puff pastry. Keep an eye out for unusual pizzas made with strawberries and brie or eggplant and pine nuts. On weekends, a casual brunch has interesting breakfast fare.

2901 E. Madison St. ✆ 206/325-9100. www.cafeflora.com. Reservations accepted only for parties of 8 or more. Main courses $9.25–$17; 3-course prix fixe menu $25. MC, V. Tues–Fri 11:30am–10pm; Sat–Sun 9am–2pm; Sat 5–10pm; Sun 5–9pm (open on Mon in summer).

NORTH SEATTLE (INCLUDING FREMONT, WALLINGFORD & THE UNIVERSITY DISTRICT)

MODERATE

Ray's Boathouse and Cafe ★★ SEAFOOD   When Seattleites want to impress visiting friends and relatives, this restaurant often ranks right up there with the Space Needle, the ferries, and Pike Place Market. The view across Puget Sound to the Olympic Mountains is superb. You can watch the boat traffic coming and going from the Lake Washington Ship Canal, and bald eagles can often be seen fishing just offshore. Then there's Ray's dual personality—Ray's Cafe upstairs is a lively (and loud) cafe and lounge, while Ray's Boathouse downstairs is a more formal, sedate scene. The downstairs menu is more creative, while the upstairs menu is less expensive (but even upstairs you can order from the downstairs menu). The crab cakes are delicious and packed full of crab. If you see any sort of fish in *sake kasu* (a typically Northwest/Pacific Rim preparation made from a paste that is a byproduct of sake brewing), order it. Whatever your mood, Ray's has you covered. Be sure to take a peek in the crab tanks in front of the restaurant.

6049 Seaview Ave. NW. ⓒ **206/789-3770** for Boathouse or 206/782-0094 for Cafe. www.rays.com. Reservations recommended. Main courses $18–$36 at Boathouse, $9–$18 at Cafe. AE, DC, DISC, MC, V. Boathouse Sun–Thurs 5–9pm, Fri–Sat 5–9:30pm; Cafe Sun–Thurs 11:30am–10pm, Fri–Sat 11:30am–10:30pm.

INEXPENSIVE

Agua Verde Café ★ (Finds MEXICAN   Set on the shore of Portage Bay, which lies between Lake Union and Lake Washington, this casual Mexican restaurant is very popular with college students from the adjacent University of Washington. Consequently, there's often a line out the door as customers wait to give their orders at the counter. The menu is limited to tacos, Mexican-style sandwiches, empanadas, quesadillas, and, at dinner, a handful of more substantial entrees. It's hard to go wrong here, but I recommend the tacos that come three to an order. Try the grilled halibut or yam tacos, both topped with a delicious avocado sauce. Add a couple of sides—cranberry slaw, pineapple-jicama salsa, or creamy chile potatoes—for a filling and inexpensive meal. Agua Verde also serves pretty good margaritas and rents kayaks for $15 to $18 per hour.

1303 NE Boat St. ⓒ **206/545-8570**. www.aguaverde.com. Reservations not accepted. Main courses $2.50–$9 at lunch; $5.75–$13 at dinner. MC, V. Mon–Thurs 11am–9pm; Fri–Sat 11am–10pm; Sun noon–6pm.

Red Mill Burgers ★ AMERICAN   Just a little north of Woodland Park Zoo, this retro burger joint is tiny and always hoppin' because everyone knows it does one of the best burgers in Seattle. Try the verde burger, made with Anaheim peppers for just the right amount of fire. Don't miss the onion rings, and don't come dressed in your finest attire—the burgers are definitely multi-napkin affairs.

A second Red Mill Burgers is at 1613 W. Dravus St. (ⓒ **206/284-6363**), which is midway between downtown Seattle and Ballard.

312 N. 67th St. ⓒ **206/783-6362**. www.redmillburgers.com. Burgers $2.90–$5.25. No credit cards. Tues–Sat 11am–9pm; Sun noon–8pm.

WEST SEATTLE

EXPENSIVE

Salty's on Alki Beach ★★ SEAFOOD   Although the prices are almost as out of line as those at the Space Needle, and the service is unpredictable, this restaurant has *the* waterfront view in Seattle, and the food is usually pretty good. Because Salty's is set on the northeast side of the Alki Peninsula, it faces downtown Seattle on the far side of Elliott Bay. Come at sunset for dinner and watch the sun sparkle off skyscraper windows as the lights of the city twinkle. On sunny summer days, lunch on one of the two decks is a sublimely Seattle experience. Don't be discouraged by the ugly industrial/port area through which you drive to get here; Salty's marks the start of Alki Beach, the closest Seattle comes to a Southern California beach scene. Just watch for the giant rusted salmon sculptures swimming amid rebar kelp beds and the remains of an old bridge. Hey, Seattle even recycles when it comes to art!

1936 Harbor Ave. SW. © **206/937-1600.** www.saltys.com. Reservations recommended. Main courses $10–$20 at lunch, $19–$44 at dinner. AE, DC, DISC, MC, V. Mon–Thurs 11am–3pm and 5–9pm (9:30pm in summer); Fri 11am–3pm and 5–9:30pm (10pm in summer); Sat 10am–2pm and 4–9:30pm (10pm in summer); Sun 9am–2pm (1pm in summer) and 4–9pm (9:30pm in summer).

INEXPENSIVE

Alki Crab & Fish SEAFOOD   Sure, there are plenty of places on the Seattle waterfront to get fish and chips, but for an unforgettable cheap meal, catch the water taxi over to Alki Beach. Here, right at the Alki Beach water-taxi dock, this little fish-and-chips joint boasts one of the best views in Seattle. In fact, next-door-neighbor Salty's on Alki Beach has made its reputation almost solely based on this same vista. So if you want the city's best view of the Seattle skyline, but don't want to blow your budget, this is the place. You can ride the water taxi over from the Seattle waterfront, spring for the halibut and chips, and not come close to what you would spend on a meal at Salty's. If you're just coming over to eat, you request a transfer and get back to Seattle without having to pay for the return ride!

1660 Harbor Ave. SW. © **206/938-0975.** Main dishes $2.75–$10. MC, V. Summer: Mon–Thurs 10am–8pm, Fri 10am–9pm, Sat 9am–9pm, Sun 9am–8pm; reduced hours other months.

THE EASTSIDE (INCLUDING BELLEVUE & KIRKLAND)
VERY EXPENSIVE

The Herbfarm Restaurant NORTHWEST   The Herbfarm, the most highly acclaimed restaurant in the Northwest, is known across the nation for its extraordinarily lavish meals. The menu changes throughout the year, with themes to match the seasons. Wild gathered vegetables, Northwest seafood and meats, organic produce, wild mushrooms, and, of course, the generous use of fresh herbs from the Herbfarm gardens are the ingredients from which the chef, Jerry Traunfeld, creates his culinary extravaganzas. Dinners are paired with complementary Northwest wines (and occasionally something particularly remarkable from Europe). Dinners here are so popular that you should plan well in advance if you want to be sure of a wonderful Herbfarm experience.

14590 NE 145th St., Woodinville. © **425/485-5300.** www.theherbfarm.com. Reservations required. Fixed-price 9-course dinner $159–$189 per person with 5 or 6 matched wines ($50 per-person deposit required). AE, MC, V. Seatings Thurs–Sat at 7pm; Sun at 4:30pm.

EXPENSIVE

Yarrow Bay Grill NORTHWEST   The combination of Northwest cuisine and a view across Lake Washington to Seattle has made this restaurant, in the upscale Carillon Point retail, office, and condo development, a favorite of Eastside diners (we've heard even Bill Gates eats here). The setting is decidedly nouveau riche and about as close to a Southern California setting as you'll find in the Northwest. The menu is not so long that you can't make a decision, but long enough to provide some serious options. To start, the curried crab cake with cilantro chutney is a favorite, as is the seven-spice calamari. Entrees are usually equally divided between seafood and meats, with at least one vegetarian dish on the menu. Keep in mind that the menu is short and changes daily. Nearly every table has a view, and there's a great deck for good weather. Downstairs from this restaurant is the affiliated, but less expensive, Beach Café.

1270 Carillon Point, Kirkland. ℂ 425/889-9052. www.ybgrill.com. Reservations recommended. Main courses $20–$39. AE, DC, DISC, MC, V. Mon–Thurs 5:30–9:30pm; Fri–Sat 5:30–10pm; Sun 5–9pm.

COFFEE, TEA, BAKERIES & PASTRY SHOPS
CAFES, COFFEE BARS & TEA SHOPS

Unless you've been on Mars for the past decade, you're likely aware that Seattle has become the espresso capital of America. Seattleites are positively rabid about coffee, which isn't just a hot drink or a caffeine fix anymore, but rather a way of life. Wherever you go in Seattle, you're rarely more than about a block from your next cup. There are espresso carts on the sidewalks, drive-through espresso windows, espresso bars, espresso counters at gas stations, espresso milkshakes, espresso chocolates, even eggnog lattes at Christmas.

Starbucks (www.starbucks.com), the ruling king of coffee, is seemingly everywhere you turn in Seattle. It sells some 30 types and blends of coffee beans. **Seattle's Best Coffee/SBC** (www.seattlesbest.com), another of Seattle's favorite espresso-bar chains, is also owned by Starbucks. Close on the heels of Starbucks and SBC in popularity and citywide coverage is the **Tully's** chain, which seems to have an espresso bar on every corner that doesn't already have a Starbucks or an SBC. Serious espresso junkies, however, swear by **Caffe Ladro** (www.caffeladro.com) and **Caffe Vita** (www.caffe vita.com). If you see one of either of these chains, check it out and see what you think.

Coffee bars and cafes are as popular as bars and pubs for places to hang out and visit with friends. Among my favorite Seattle cafes are the following (organized by neighborhoods):

Pioneer Square & the International District

Zeitgeist Art/Coffee ⊙, 171 S. Jackson St. (ℂ 206/583-0497), with its big windows and local artwork, is popular with the Pioneer Square art crowd.

In the International District, don't miss the atmospheric **Panama Hotel Tea & Coffee House** ⊙, 607 S. Main St. (ℂ **206/515-4000;** www.panamahotelseattle.com), which is filled with historic photos and offers a fascinating glimpse into the neighborhood's past. This is a great place to relax over a pot of rare Chinese tea and a slice of the cafe's unusual green-tea cake.

Belltown & Pike Place Market

Seattle is legendary as a city of coffeeholics, and Starbucks is the main reason. This company has coffeehouses all over town (and all over the world), but the **Starbucks** in Pike Place Market, at 1912 Pike Place (ℂ **206/448-8762**), was once the only Starbucks anywhere. Today this is the only chain store allowed in the market. Although you won't find any tables or chairs here, Starbucks fans shouldn't miss an opportunity to get their coffee at the source.

The Seattle Center & Queen Anne Areas

Caffe Ladro Espresso Bar & Bakery ☕☕, 2205 Queen Anne Ave. N. (© **206/ 282-5313**), in the heart of the pleasant Upper Queen Anne area, has the feel of a cozy neighborhood coffeehouse. There's another Caffe Ladro in the MarQueen Hotel building in Lower Queen Anne at 600 Queen Anne Ave. N. (© **206/282-1549**). Other Caffe Ladros can be found downtown at 801 Pine St. (© **206/405-1950**) and at 108 Union St. (© **206/267-0600**); and in the Fremont neighborhood at 452 N. 36th St. (© **206/675-0854**).

Uptown Espresso, 525 Queen Anne Ave. N. (© **206/285-5663**), with its crystal chandelier, gilt-framed classical painting, and opera music on the stereo, has a very theatrical, European feel. It has good baked goodies, too.

Caffe Vita is one of Seattle's finest coffee roasters. In the Lower Queen Anne neighborhood, you can sample these superb coffees at Caffe Vita's own coffeehouse, at 813 Fifth Ave. N. (© **206/285-9662**).

If you've tired of tall-double-raspberry mochas and are desperately seeking a new coffee experience, make a trip to Upper Queen Anne's **El Diablo Coffee Co.,** 1811 Queen Anne Ave. N. (© **206/285-0693**), a Latin-style coffeehouse. The Cubano, made with two shots of espresso and caramelized sugar, and the *café con leche* (a Cubano with steamed milk) are both devilishly good drinks. *Viva la revolución!*

Capitol Hill & East Seattle

Bauhaus Coffee & Books ☕, 301 E. Pine St. (© **206/625-1600**), on the downtown edge of Capitol Hill, is a great place to hang out and soak up the atmosphere of Seattle's main gay neighborhood. There are always lots of interesting 30-something types (mostly men) hanging out reading or carrying on heated discussions.

Caffe Vita, 1005 E. Pike St. (© **206/709-4440**), has a devoted following of espresso fanatics who swear by the perfectly roasted coffee beans and lovingly crafted lattes served here.

North Seattle

Café Allegro, 4214 University Way NE (© **206/633-3030**), down an alley around the corner from University Way in the U District, is Seattle's oldest cafe and a favored hangout of University of Washington students. Keep looking; you'll find it.

BAKERIES & PASTRY SHOPS

Pioneer Square & the International District

Grand Central Baking Company ☕, 214 First Ave. S. (© **206/622-3644**; www. grandcentralbakery.com), in Pioneer Square's Grand Central Arcade, is responsible for awakening Seattle to the pleasures of rustic European-style breads. This bakery not only turns out great bread, but also makes good pastries and sandwiches.

Although the name is none too appealing, **Cow Chip Cookies,** 102A First Ave. S. (© **206/292-9808**), bakes Seattle's best chocolate-chip cookies, which come in different sizes, depending on the size of your craving.

Belltown & Pike Place Market

The **Crumpet Shop** ☕, 1503 First Ave. (© **206/682-1598**), specializes in its British namesake pastries, but does scones as well. It's almost a requirement that you accompany your crumpet or scone with a pot of tea.

Le Panier, 1902 Pike Place (© **206/441-3669**), is a great place to get a croissant and a latte and watch the market action.

With a wall of glass cases filled with baked goods and a window facing onto one of the busiest spots in the market, **Three Girls Bakery,** 1514 Pike Place, stall no. 1 (© 206/622-1045), is a favorite place to grab a few pastries or other goodies to go.

For some of the best baked goodies in the city, head to **Macrina** ✿✿, 2408 First Ave. (© **206/448-4032;** www.macrinabakery.com), a neighborhood bakery/cafe that's a cozy place for a quick, cheap breakfast or lunch. In the morning, the smell of baking bread wafts down First Avenue and draws in many a passerby.

Tom Douglas's restaurants—Dahlia Lounge, Palace Kitchen, Etta's, and Lola—are all immensely popular, and there was such a demand for the breads and pastries served at these places that Douglas opened his own **Dahlia Bakery,** 2001 Fourth Ave. (© **206/441-4540;** www.tomdouglas.com). The croissants here are the best in Seattle—and you can get Douglas's fabled coconut cream pie to go.

Leave it to Seattle to take the doughnut craze and turn it into something sophisticated. **Top Pot Doughnuts,** 2124 Fifth Ave. (© **206/728-1966**), is housed in a former showroom building with big walls of glass. Books now line the walls; doughnuts fill the display cases. This place was created by the same folks who gave Seattle the Zeitgeist and Bauhaus coffeehouses.

Capitol Hill & East Seattle

Basically, **Dilettante Chocolates** ✿✿, 416 Broadway E. (© **206/329-6463**), is a chocolate restaurant that happens to be Seattle's leading proponent of cocoa as the next drink to take the country by storm. If you don't order something with chocolate here, you're missing the point.

MARKET MUNCHING

Few Seattle activities are more fun than munching your way through Pike Place Market. With dozens of fast-food vendors, it's nearly impossible to resist the array of finger foods and quick bites. Here are some of my favorite places:

If you're planning a picnic, **DeLaurenti** ✿✿, 1435 First Ave. (© **206/622-0141**), near the market's brass pig, is a perfect spot for pâté, sandwiches, and wine.

For more substantial picnic fare, perhaps some wild salmon with ginger-orange salsa or wild-mushroom risotto, head to **Dish D'Lish** (© **206/223-1848**), just a few steps away from *Rachel* (the brass pig) and the flying fish at Pike Place Fish. This little gourmet-to-go place is the brainchild of local celeb chef Kathy Casey, who helped start the whole Northwest cuisine trend more than 15 years ago.

If you're a fan of the stinking rose, don't miss the **Garlic Garden** (© 877/207-5166 or 206/405-4022; www.garlicgarden.com), just around the corner from the pig statue. The Lebanese Breeze garlic dip/spread is so good, you're only allowed one free sample. Buy a container to spread on some bread from Le Panier.

At **Beecher's Handmade Cheese,** 1600 Pike Place (© **206/956-1964;** www.beecherscheese.com), you can watch cheese being made and sample some of the products. But what brings me back here again and again is the awesome macaroni-and-cheese; get some to go and have a picnic down on the waterfront.

The **Spanish Table,** 1427 Western Ave. (© **206/682-2827;** www.tablespan.com), is a specialty food shop on one of the lower levels of the market. You can get simple Spanish-style sandwiches, great soups, cheeses, and other light meal items, and then shop for a paella pan. This quiet corner of the market is a great place to get away from the crowds and try some food you might never have encountered before.

World Class Chili ☞, inside the market's Economy Building, 93 Pike St. (© **206/ 623-3678**), really lives up to its name. Chili connoisseurs should not pass it by.

When you just have to have something sweet, cold, and creamy, try the much-lauded gelato at **Bottega Italiana,** 1425 First Ave. (© **206/343-0200;** www.bottega italiana.com).

5 What to See & Do

I hope you've got a good pair of walking shoes and a lot of stamina (a double latte helps), because Seattle is a walking town. The city's two biggest attractions—the waterfront and Pike Place Market—are the sorts of places where you'll spend hours on your feet. When your feet are beat, you can relax on a tour boat and enjoy views of the city from the waters of Puget Sound, or you can take a 2-minute rest on the monorail, which links downtown with Seattle Center, home of the Space Needle. If your energy level sags, don't worry; an espresso bar is always nearby.

By the way, that monorail ride takes you right through the middle of Paul Allen's Experience Music Project, the Frank Gehry–designed rock-music museum also located in Seattle Center. Paul Allen, who made his millions as one of the cofounders of Microsoft, has spent many years changing the face of Seattle. He has renovated Union Station and developed the area adjacent to Qwest Field, which was built for the Seattle Seahawks football team, whose owner is—you guessed it—Paul Allen. The new stadium is adjacent to the Seattle Mariners' Safeco Field, which is one of the few ballparks in the country with a retractable roof.

Despite Seattle's many downtown diversions, however, the city's natural surroundings are still its primary attraction. You can easily cover all of Seattle's museums and major sights in 2 or 3 days. Once you've seen what's indoors, you can begin exploring the city's outdoor life.

ON THE WATERFRONT

The Seattle waterfront, which lies along Alaskan Way between Yesler Way in the south and Bay Street and Myrtle Edwards Park in the north, is the city's most popular attraction. Yes, it's very touristy, with tacky gift shops, saltwater taffy, T-shirts galore, and lots of overpriced restaurants, but it's also home to the Seattle Aquarium, Odyssey Maritime Discovery Center, and Ye Olde Curiosity Shop (king of the tacky gift shops). Ferries to Bainbridge Island and Bremerton, as well as several different boat tours, also operate from the waterfront. This is also the best place to hire a horse-drawn carriage for a spin around downtown.

You'll find the Washington State Ferries terminal at **Pier 52,** which is at the south end of the waterfront near Pioneer Square. (A ferry ride makes for a cheap cruise.) At **Pier 55,** there are excursion boats offering harbor cruises and trips to Tillicum Village on Blake Island. At **Pier 56,** cruise boats leave for trips through the Chittenden (Ballard) Locks to Lake Union. See section 6, later in this chapter, for details on these excursions.

At **Pier 57,** you'll find both the **Bay Pavilion,** which has a vintage carousel and a video arcade to keep the kids busy, and **Pier 57 Parasail** (© **206/622-5757**), which straps a parasail on your back, hooks you to a long rope, and then tows you around Elliott Bay. The view from above the water is almost as good as the view from the

Seattle Attractions

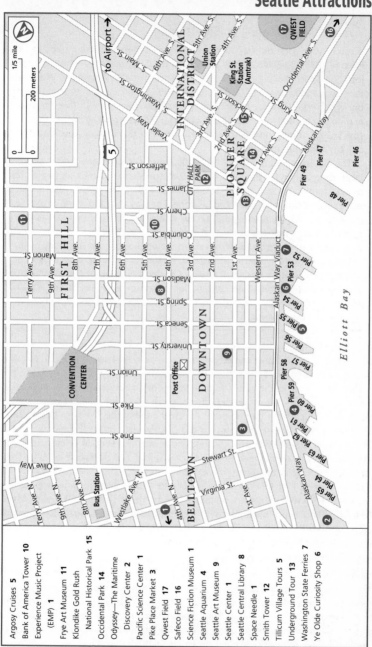

Argosy Cruises **5**

Bank of America Tower **10**

Experience Music Project (EMP) **1**

Frye Art Museum **11**

Klondike Gold Rush National Historical Park **15**

Occidental Park **14**

Odyssey—The Maritime Discovery Center **2**

Pacific Science Center **1**

Pike Place Market **3**

Qwest Field **17**

Safeco Field **16**

Science Fiction Museum **1**

Seattle Aquarium **4**

Seattle Art Museum **9**

Seattle Center **1**

Seattle Central Library **8**

Space Needle **1**

Smith Tower **12**

Tillicum Village Tours **5**

Underground Tour **13**

Washington State Ferries **7**

Ye Olde Curiosity Shop **6**

Value Saving Money on Sightseeing

If you're a see-it-all, do-it-all kind of person, you'll definitely want to buy a **City-Pass** (© 888/330-5008 or 208/787-4300; http://citypass.com), which gets you into the Space Needle, Pacific Science Center, Seattle Aquarium, Woodland Park Zoo, and Museum of Flight, and also lets you take a boat tour of the harbor with Argosy Cruises, all at a savings of 50% if you visit all five attractions and do the harbor tour. The passes, good for 9 days from the date of first use, cost $42 for adults and $25 for children ages 4 to 13. Purchase your CityPass at any participating attractions.

The **Go Seattle Card** (© 800/887-9103; www.goseattlecard.com) is another interesting option for the see-it-all, do-it-all travelers who are able to plan out a daily tour route in advance. It takes careful planning to get your money's worth out of this card, but it can be done. The way this card works is that you pay $49 ($29 for children ages 3–12) for a card that will get you into as many participating attractions as you can visit in one day. There's a discount for 2-, 3-, 5-, and 7-day cards, and your best bet would probably be the 3-day card.

Before visiting any Seattle attractions, be sure to first stop by **Seattle's Convention and Visitors Bureau Citywide Concierge Center,** at the Washington State Convention and Trade Center, Eighth Avenue and Pike Street (© 206/461-5888; www.seeseattle.org), where you can pick up a booklet full of two-for-one and other coupons.

Space Needle, and, because you take off and land from the back of the boat, you won't even get wet. Rides are $49 to $54 for one person and $89 to $95 for a tandem ride.

Pier 59 is home to the Seattle Aquarium (see below for details) and a small waterfront park. Continuing up the waterfront, you'll find **Pier 66,** also called the Bell Street Pier, which has a rooftop park. This is the site of the Odyssey–The Maritime Discovery Center (see below), which is dedicated to the history of shipping and fishing in Puget Sound. Anthony's (p. 93), one of the best seafood restaurants on the waterfront, is also on this pier. At **Pier 67,** you'll find The Edgewater hotel (p. 81), a great place to take in the sunset over a drink or dinner.

Next door, at **Pier 69,** you'll see the dock for ferries that ply the waters between Seattle and Victoria, British Columbia. Just north of this pier is grassy **Myrtle Edwards Park,** a nice finale to a very pleasant waterfront. This park has a popular bicycling-and-skating trail and is the northern terminus for the **Waterfront Streetcar,** which can take you back to your starting point.

Odyssey–The Maritime Discovery Center   Sort of an interactive promotion for modern fishing and shipping, this facility at the north end of the Seattle waterfront is aimed primarily at kids and has more than 40 hands-on exhibits highlighting Seattle's modern working waterfront and its links to the sea. Exhibits include a kid-size fishing boat, a virtual kayak trip through Puget Sound, and a live radar center that allows you to track the movement of vessels in Elliott Bay. In another exhibit, you get to use a simulated crane to practice loading a scale model of a cargo ship.

Pier 66 (Bell St. Pier), 2205 Alaskan Way. © **206/374-4000.** www.ody.org. Admission $7 adults, $5 seniors and students 5–18, $2 children 2–4, free for children under 2. Tues–Sat 10am–5pm; Sun noon–5pm. Closed day before

Thanksgiving, Thanksgiving, Dec 24–25, and New Year's Day. Bus: 15, 18, 21, 22, or 56 to Bell St. Waterfront Trolley: Bell St. Station.

Seattle Aquarium 𝓡𝓡   Although not nearly as large and impressive as the Monterey Bay Aquarium or the Oregon Coast Aquarium, the Seattle Aquarium is still quite enjoyable and has well-designed exhibits dealing with the water worlds of the Puget Sound region. Star attractions here are the playful river otters and sea otters, as well as the giant octopus. There's also an underwater viewing dome from which you get a fish's-eye view of life beneath the waves, and each September you can watch salmon return up a fish ladder to spawn. Of course, there are also plenty of small tanks that allow you to familiarize yourself with the many fish of the Northwest, a beautiful coral-reef tank, and several smaller tanks that exhibit fish from distant waters. *Life on the Edge* focuses on tidepool life along Washington's Pacific Ocean and Puget Sound shores, while *Life of a Drifter* highlights jellyfish.

Pier 59, 1483 Alaskan Way. ⓒ **206/386-4300.** www.seattleaquarium.org. Admission $12 adults, $8 children 6–12, $5 children 3–5. Mid-Sept through Mar daily 10am–5pm; Apr through late May daily 9:30am–5pm; Memorial Day weekend to mid-Sept daily 9:30am–7pm. Bus: 16 or 10, 12, 15, or 18 and then walk through Pike Place Market to the waterfront. Waterfront Streetcar: Pike St. Station.

PIKE PLACE MARKET TO PIONEER SQUARE
Pike Place Market and the Pioneer Square historic district lie at opposite ends of First Avenue; midway between the two is the Seattle Art Museum.

The **Pioneer Square** area, with its historic buildings, interesting shops, museum, and Underground Tour (see "Good Times in Bad Taste," below), is worth a morning or afternoon of exploration.

Klondike Gold Rush National Historical Park   "At 3 o'clock this morning, the steamship *Portland,* from St. Michaels for Seattle, passed up (Puget) Sound with more than a ton of gold on board and 68 passengers." When the *Seattle Post-Intelligencer* published that sentence on July 17, 1897, it started a stampede. Would-be miners heading for the Klondike goldfields in the 1890s made Seattle their outfitting center and helped turn it into a prosperous city. When they struck it rich up north, they headed back to Seattle, the first U.S. outpost of civilization, and unloaded their gold, making Seattle doubly rich. Although this place isn't in the Klondike (that's in Canada) and isn't really a park (it's more of a museum in a historic building), it's still a fascinating little museum, and it seems only fitting that it should be here in Seattle. (Another unit of the park is in Skagway, Alaska.)

319 Second Ave. S. ⓒ **206/553-7220.** www.nps.gov/klse. Free admission. Daily 9am–5pm. Closed Thanksgiving, Christmas, and New Year's Day. Bus: 15, 16, 18, 21, or 22. Waterfront Streetcar: Occidental Park stop.

Pike Place Market 𝓡𝓡𝓡   Pike Place Market, originally a farmers' market, was founded in 1907 when housewives complained that middlemen were raising the prices of produce. The market allowed shoppers to buy directly from producers and thus save on grocery bills. By the 1960s, however, the market was no longer the popular spot it had been. World War II had deprived it of nearly half its farmers when Japanese Americans were moved to internment camps. The postwar flight to the suburbs almost spelled the end of the market, and the site was being eyed for a major redevelopment project. Fortunately, a grass-roots movement to save the 9-acre market culminated in it being declared a National Historic District.

Today the market is once again bustling, but the 100 or so farmers and fishmongers who set up shop on the premises are only a small part of the attraction. More than 150 local craftspeople and artists can be found here, selling their creations as street performers serenade milling crowds. There are also hundreds of small specialty shops throughout the market, plus dozens of restaurants, including some of the city's best. At the **information booth** almost directly below the large PIKE PLACE MARKET sign, you can pick up a free map and guide to the market. Keep an eye out for low-flying fish at the **Pike Place Fish** stall, and be sure to save some change for *Rachel*, the market's giant piggy bank, which has raised more than $100,000 over the years.

Victor Steinbrueck Park, at the north end of the market at the intersection of Pike Place, Virginia Street, and Western Avenue, is a popular lounging area for both the homeless and those just looking for a grassy spot in the sun. In the park, you'll see two 50-foot-tall totem poles.

To get a glimpse behind the scenes at the market and learn all about its history, you can take a 1-hour guided **Market Heritage Tour** (℃ **206/774-5249** for information and reservations). Tours are offered Wednesday through Sunday at 11am and 2pm; the cost is $7 for adults and $5 for seniors and children under 18. Reservations are required and should be made at least a day in advance. They depart from the market's **Heritage Center,** 1531 Western Ave., an open-air building filled with interesting historical exhibits (take the Skybridge to the Market Garage and then take the elevator to the Western Ave. level).

See "Market Munching," earlier in this chapter, for a rundown of some of my favorite market food vendors. Also, if you're going to be in town in October, consider attending the annual Feast at the Market (℃ **206/461-6935,** ext. 161; www. pikemed.org/feast), a showcase for food from market restaurants.

Between Pike and Pine sts. at First Ave. ℃ 206/682-7453. www.pikeplacemarket.org. Most businesses Mon–Sat 10am–6pm, Sun 11am–5pm; many produce vendors open at 8am in summer; restaurant hours vary. Closed Easter, Thanksgiving, Christmas, and New Year's Day. Bus: 10, 12, 15, 18, 21, or 22. Waterfront Streetcar: Pike St. Station.

Seattle Art Museum ☆☆

You simply can't miss this downtown art museum. Just look for Jonathon Borofsky's *Hammering Man,* an animated three-story steel sculpture that pounds out a silent beat in front of the museum. Inside, you'll find one of the nation's premier collections of Northwest Coast Indian art and artifacts and an equally large collection of African art. Exhibits cover European and American art ranging from ancient Mediterranean works to pieces from the medieval, Renaissance, and baroque periods. A large 18th-century collection and a smaller 19th-century exhibition lead up to a 20th-century collection that includes a room devoted to Northwest contemporary art. (There's also a smattering of Asian art at this museum, but the city's major collection of Asian art is at the affiliated Seattle Asian Art Museum in Volunteer Park; see p. 116 for details.) *Note:* The Seattle Art Museum will be closed until January 2007.

100 University St. ℃ 206/654-3100. www.seattleartmuseum.org. Admission $7 adults, $5 seniors and students, free for children 12 and under (for some special exhibitions, higher admissions are charged). Regular exhibits, free for all 1st Thurs of each month; free for seniors 1st Fri of each month (special exhibitions discounted). Admission ticket also valid at Seattle Asian Art Museum for 1 week. Tues–Wed and Fri–Sun 10am–5pm; Thurs 10am–9pm. Closed Thanksgiving and Christmas (open some holiday Mon). Bus: 10, 12, 15, 18, 21, 22, 39, or 42.

Seattle Central Library ☆☆

It isn't often that the library is considered one of the coolest joints in town, but Seattle's downtown library, which opened in 2004, is such an architectural wonder that it's now one of the city's highlights. The design of this building left much of the city's populace polarized—you either loved it or hated it.

Good Times in Bad Taste

If you love bad jokes and are fascinated by the bizarre (or perhaps this describes your children), you won't want to miss the Underground Tour and a visit to Ye Olde Curiosity Shop. Together, these two attractions should reassure you that espresso, traffic jams, and Microsoft aside, Seattle does have a sense of humor.

If you have an appreciation for off-color humor and are curious about the seamier side of Seattle history, the **Underground Tour,** 608 First Ave. (② **206/682-4646;** www.undergroundtour.com), will likely entertain and enlighten you. The tours lead down below street level in the Pioneer Square area, where you can still find the vestiges of Seattle businesses built just after the great fire of 1889. Learn the lowdown dirt on early Seattle, a town where plumbing was problematic and a person could drown in a pothole. Tours are held daily. The cost is $10 for adults, $8 for seniors and students ages 13 to 17 or with college ID, and $5 for children ages 7 to 12; children ages 6 and under are discouraged.

Ye Olde Curiosity Shop, Pier 54, 1001 Alaskan Way (② **206/682-5844;** www.yeoldecuriosityshop.com), is a cross between a souvenir store and *Ripley's Believe It or Not!* It's weird! It's tacky! It's always packed! The collection of oddities was started in 1899 by Joe Standley, who developed a more-than-passing interest in strange curios. See Siamese-twin calves, a natural mummy, the Lord's Prayer on a grain of rice, a narwhal tusk, shrunken heads, a 67-pound snail, fleas in dresses—all the stuff that may have fascinated you as a kid.

There isn't much of a middle ground with this giant glass cube and its diamond-patterned steel girders and strange angles. Regardless of your reaction to architect Rem Koolhaas's design, you can't help but notice that in a town known for its gray skies, this library abounds in natural light. If you need to use the Internet, this place has hundreds of computer terminals, too.

1000 Fourth Ave. ② 206/386-4636. www.spl.org. Free admission. Mon–Wed 10am–8pm; Thurs–Sat 10am–6pm; Sun 1–5pm. Closed New Year's Day, Martin Luther King Day, Presidents' Day, Easter, Memorial Day, July 4th, Labor Day, Veterans Day, Thanksgiving, and Dec 24–25. Bus: Any Fourth Ave. bus.

SEATTLE CENTER ATTRACTIONS

Built in 1962 for the World's Fair, Seattle Center is today not only the site of Seattle's famous Space Needle but also a cultural and entertainment park that doubles as the city's favorite festival grounds. Within Seattle Center's boundaries, you'll find the Experience Music Project (EMP), the Pacific Science Center, the Seattle Children's Museum, the Seattle Children's Theatre, Key Arena (home of the NBA's Seattle Supersonics), the Marion Oliver McCaw Hall, the Intiman Theatre, the Bagley Wright Theatre, a children's amusement park, and a fountain that's a favorite summertime hangout. See "Especially for Kids," later in this chapter, for further details on Seattle Center attractions that young travelers will enjoy. Not far away is Lake Union, where there are a couple of nautical attractions.

Experience Music Project (EMP) ✿✿ The brainchild of Microsoft cofounder Paul Allen and designed by avant-garde architect Frank Gehry, who is known for pushing the envelope of architectural design, this rock 'n' roll museum is a massive multicolored blob at the foot of the Space Needle. Originally planned as a memorial to Seattle native Jimi Hendrix, the museum grew to encompass not only Hendrix, but all of the Northwest rock scene (from "Louie Louie" to grunge) and the general history of American popular music.

The most popular exhibits here (after the Jimi Hendrix room) are the interactive rooms. In one room you can play guitars, drums, keyboards, or even DJ turntables. In another, you can experience what it's like to be onstage performing in front of adoring fans. Another exhibit focuses on the history of guitars and has some of the first electric guitars, which date from the early 1930s. Give yourself plenty of time to explore here.

Seattle Center, 325 Fifth Ave. N. ✆ **877/EMPLIVE** or 206/EMPLIVE. www.emplive.org. Admission $20 adults, $16 seniors, $15 children 7–17, free for children 6 and under. Memorial Day to Labor Day daily 10am–8pm; Labor Day to Memorial Day Tues–Thurs, Sun 10am–6pm, Fri–Sat 10am–8pm. Bus: 1, 2, 3, 4, 13, 15, 16, 18, 24, or 33. Monorail: From Westlake Center at Pine St. and Fourth Ave.

Pacific Science Center ✿✿ _Kids_ Although its exhibits are aimed primarily at children, the Pacific Science Center is fun for all ages. The main goal of this sprawling complex at Seattle Center is to teach kids about science and instill a desire to study it. To that end, there are life-size robotic dinosaurs, a butterfly house and insect village (with giant robotic insects), a Tech Zone where kids can play virtual-reality soccer or challenge a robot to tic-tac-toe, and dozens of other fun hands-on exhibits addressing the biological sciences, physics, and chemistry. The August Bubble Festival is always a big hit. There's a planetarium for learning about the skies (with laser shows for the fun of it), plus an IMAX theater. Be sure to check the schedule for special exhibits when you're in town.

Seattle Center, 200 Second Ave. N. ✆ **206/443-2001**; 206/443-IMAX for IMAX information, or 206/443-2850 for laser show information. www.pacsci.org. Admission $10 adults, $8.50 seniors, $7 ages 3–12, free for children under 3. IMAX $8–$10 adults, $7.50–$9 seniors, $7–$8 ages 3–12, free for children under 3. Laser show $5–$7.50. Various discounted combination tickets available. Mon–Fri 10am–5pm; Sat–Sun and holidays 10am–6pm. Closed Thanksgiving and Christmas. Bus: 1, 2, 3, 4, 13, 15, 16, 18, 24, or 33. Monorail: Seattle Center.

Science Fiction Museum and Hall of Fame (SFM) ✿ Inside the Experience Music Project, this little exhibit is another project of Seattle's own billionaire nerd Paul Allen. Just as in EMP, this museum is packed with pop-culture icons, this time from the world of science fiction. With displays of actual props and costumes from such historic sci-fi films and TV shows as _Star Trek, Star Wars, Alien, Dr. Who_, and _Terminator_, this place is an absolute must for devoted fans of one of literature's least-respected, yet best-loved genres. The museum spends a lot of time chronicling the history of science fiction, with displays of 1930s and 1940s pulp fiction magazines. Other displays focus on the fans themselves (and the conventions they stage), as well as the connections to science. However, for most visitors, the movie props are the real draws. From robots to jet packs to space suits and ray guns, it's all here.

Seattle Center, 325 Fifth Ave. N. ✆ **877/367-5483** or 206/SCI-FICT. www.sfhomeworld.org. Admission $13 adults, $8.95 seniors and children 7–17. Memorial Day to Labor Day 10am–8pm; other months Tues–Thurs, Sun 10am–6pm, Fri–Sat 10am–8pm. Bus: 1, 2, 3, 4, 13, 15, 16, 18, 24, or 33. Monorail: From Westlake Center at Pine St. and Fourth Ave.

Space Needle ✿✿ From a distance it resembles a flying saucer on top of a tripod, and when it was built for the 1962 World's Fair, the 605-foot-tall Space Needle was

Space Needle Alternatives

If you don't want to deal with the crowds at the Space Needle but still want an elevated downtown view, you have some alternatives. One is the big, black **Bank of America Tower** (℡ 206/386-5151), at the corner of Fifth Avenue and Columbia Street. At 943 feet, this is the tallest building in Seattle (twice as tall as the Space Needle), with more stories (76, to be exact) than any other building west of the Mississippi. Up on the 73rd floor, you'll find an observation deck with views that dwarf those from the Space Needle. Admission is only $5 for adults and $3 for seniors and children. It's open on Monday through Friday from 8:30am to 4:30pm.

Not far from the Bank of America Tower is the **Smith Tower,** 506 Second Ave. (℡ 206/622-4004; www.smithtower.com). Opened in 1914, this was Seattle's first skyscraper and, for 50 years, the tallest building west of Chicago. Although the Smith Tower has only 42 stories, it still offers excellent views from its 35th-floor observation deck, which surrounds the ornate Chinese Room, a banquet hall with a carved ceiling. A lavish lobby and original manual elevators make this a fun and historic place to take in the Seattle skyline. Deck hours vary with the time of year and scheduled events in the Chinese Room; check in advance to be sure it will be open when you want to visit. Admission is $6 for adults, $5 for seniors and students, and $4 for children ages 6 to 12.

If you've ever seen a photo of the Space Needle framed by Mount Rainier and the high-rises of downtown Seattle, it was probably taken from **Kerry Viewpoint,** on Queen Anne Hill. If you want to take your own drop-dead gorgeous photo of the Seattle skyline from this elevated perspective, head north from Seattle Center on Queen Anne Avenue North and turn left on West Highland Drive. When you reach the park, you'll immediately recognize the view.

Another great panorama is from the water tower in **Volunteer Park,** on Capitol Hill at East Prospect Street and 14th Avenue East. (See p. 116 for details.)

meant to suggest future architectural trends. Today the Space Needle is the quintessential symbol of Seattle, and at 520 feet above ground level, its observation deck provides superb views of the city and its surroundings. Displays identify more than 60 sites and activities in the Seattle area, and high-powered telescopes let you zoom in on distant sights. You'll also find a pricey restaurant, SkyCity (p. 99), atop the tower. If you don't mind standing in line and paying quite a bit for an elevator ride, make this your first stop in Seattle so that you can orient yourself. There are, however, cheaper alternatives if you just want a view of the city (see "Space Needle Alternatives," above).

Seattle Center, 400 Broad St. ℡ 206/905-2100. www.spaceneedle.com. Admission $13 adults, $11 seniors, $6 ages 4–13, free for children under 4. No charge if dining in the SkyCity restaurant. Sun–Thurs 9am–11pm; Fri–Sat 9am–midnight. Valet parking $13 for all-day parking. Bus: 1, 2, 3, 4, 13, 15, 16, 18, 24, or 33. Monorail: From Westlake Center at Pine St. and Fourth Ave.

THE NEIGHBORHOODS
THE INTERNATIONAL DISTRICT

Seattle today boasts of its strategic location on the Pacific Rim, but its ties to Asia are nothing new. This is evident in the International District, Seattle's main Asian neighborhood, which is centered between Fifth Avenue South and 12th Avenue South (between S. Washington St. and S. Lane St.). Called the International District rather than Chinatown because so many Asian nationalities have made the area home, this neighborhood has been the center of the city's Asian communities for more than 100 years. You can learn about the district's history at the **Wing Luke Museum,** 407 Seventh Ave. S. (© **206/623-5124;** www.wingluke.org).

At the corner of Maynard Avenue South and South King Street, you'll find **Hing Hay Park,** the site of an ornate and colorful pavilion given to Seattle by the city of Taipei, Taiwan.

There are many restaurants, import stores, and food markets in the I.D. The huge **Uwajimaya** (p. 138) is all of these rolled up in one.

FIRST HILL (PILL HILL) & CAPITOL HILL

Seattle is justly proud of its parks, and **Volunteer Park** ☆☆ on Capitol Hill at 14th Avenue East and East Prospect Street (drive north on Broadway and watch for signs), is one of the most popular. Here you'll find not only acres of lawns, groves of trees, and huge old rhododendrons, but also an old water tower that provides one of the best panoramas in the city. A winding staircase leads to the top of the water tower, from which you get 360-degree views. On the observatory level, there is also an interesting exhibit about the Olmsted Brothers and the system of parks they designed for Seattle. To find the water tower, park near the Seattle Asian Art Museum if you can; then walk back out of the parking lot to where the road splits.

Frye Art Museum ☆   On First Hill not far from downtown Seattle, this museum is primarily an exhibit space for the extensive personal art collection of Charles and Emma Frye, Seattle pioneers who began collecting art in the 1890s. The collection focuses on late-19th-century and early-20th-century representational art by European and American painters, with works by Andrew Wyeth, Thomas Hart Benton, Edward Hopper, Albert Bierstadt, and Pablo Picasso, as well as a large collection of engravings by Winslow Homer.

704 Terry Ave. (at Cherry St.). © 206/622-9250. www.fryeart.org. Free admission. Tues–Wed and Fri–Sat 10am–5pm; Thurs 10am–8pm; Sun noon–5pm. Closed July 4th, Thanksgiving, Christmas, and New Year's Day. Bus: 3, 4, 10, 12, or 60.

Seattle Asian Art Museum ☆   Housed in an Art Deco building in Volunteer Park, the Asian art collection places an emphasis on Chinese and Japanese art, but also includes works from Korea, Southeast Asia, South Asia, and the Himalayas. Among the museum's most notable pieces are the works of Chinese terra-cotta funerary art, Chinese snuff bottles, and Japanese *netsukes* (belt decorations). One room is devoted to Japanese ceramics, while three rooms are devoted to Chinese ceramics. The central hall contains stone religious sculptures of South Asia (primarily India). The museum hosts frequent lectures and concerts.

Volunteer Park, 1400 E. Prospect St. © 206/654-3100. www.seattleartmuseum.org. Admission $3 adults, free for children 12 and under. Free to all 1st Thurs and 1st Sat of each month; free for seniors 1st Fri of each month. Admission ticket valid for $3 off admission to the Seattle Art Museum if used within 1 week. Wed and Fri–Sun 10am–5pm, Thurs 10am–9pm; Tues 10am–5pm between Memorial Day and Sept 1. Closed Mon holidays, Thanksgiving, Christmas, and New Year's Day. Bus: 7 or 10.

Volunteer Park Conservatory ⚘   This stately old Victorian conservatory, built in 1912, houses a large collection of tropical and desert plants, including palm trees, orchids, and cacti. There are also seasonal floral displays.

Volunteer Park, 1400 E. Galer St. ℂ **206/684-4743**. Free admission. Memorial Day to Labor Day daily 10am–7pm; other months daily 10am–4pm. Bus: 7 or 10.

NORTH SEATTLE (INCLUDING THE U DISTRICT, FREMONT & MONTLAKE)

The **Fremont District,** which begins at the north end of the Fremont Bridge near the intersection of Fremont Avenue North and North 36th Street, is one of Seattle's funkiest and most unusual neighborhoods. Even livelier, though not nearly as eclectic or artistic, the **University District** (known locally as the U District) has loads of cheap restaurants and the types of shops you would associate with a college-age clientele. However, the main attractions for visitors are the two excellent museums on the university campus and the nearby Museum of History and Industry, which is just across the Montlake Bridge.

Burke Museum ⚘   At the northwest corner of the University of Washington campus, the Burke Museum features exhibits on the natural and cultural heritage of the Pacific Rim. Permanent exhibits include *Life & Times of Washington State,* which covers 500 million years of Washington history (and prehistory) with lots of fossils, including a complete mastodon, on display. The second permanent exhibit, *Pacific Voices,* focuses on the many cultures of the Pacific Rim and their connections to Washington State. There is also a smaller temporary-exhibit gallery. In front of the museum stand three totem poles that are replicas of totem poles that were carved in the 1870s and 1880s.

University of Washington, 17th Ave. NE and NE 45th St. ℂ **206/543-5590** or 206/543-7907. www.burkemuseum. org. Admission $6.50 adults, $5 seniors, $4 children 5–18, free for children under 5 (higher ticket prices in effect for special exhibits). For $1 more, you can get admission to the nearby Henry Art Gallery. Free 1st Thurs of each month. Daily 10am–5pm (1st Thurs of each month until 8pm). Closed July 4th, Thanksgiving, Christmas, and New Year's Day. Bus: 7, 43, 70, 71, 72, or 73.

Future of Flight Aviation Center & Boeing Tour ⚘   Boeing has long been a major economic presence in Seattle, and it still does much of its manufacturing in the area. The company's Everett assembly plant, 30 miles north of Seattle, is the largest building, by volume, in the world and could easily hold 911 basketball courts, 74 football fields, 2,142 average-size homes, or all of Disneyland (with room left over for covered parking). Tours of the building let you see how they assemble huge passenger jets, while hands-on interactive exhibits about commercial jet aviation and manufacturing provide interesting background information on the industry. The tours of the assembly plant are the main event here, but the new exhibits provide plenty to entertain you while waiting for your tour to begin. You can design your own jet on a computer, go for a ride in a flight simulator, or head up to the roof to check out the action at Paine Field. Guided 1-hour tours are offered on the hour from 9am to 4pm, and tickets for same-day use are sold on a first-come, first-served basis beginning at 8:30am; in summer, tickets for any given day's tours usually sell out by noon. To make reservations in advance, call one of the numbers below or visit the website.

8415 Paine Field Blvd., Mukilteo. ℂ **800/464-1476** or 360/756-0086. www.futureofflight.org. Admission $15 adults, $14 seniors, $8 children 5–17, free for children under 5. Daily 8:30am–5:30pm. Closed Thanksgiving, Christmas, and New Year's Day. From I-5 north of Seattle, take exit 189 to Wash. 526 W.; continue 4 miles to the intersection of Paine Field Blvd. and 84th St. SW.

Henry Art Gallery   The focus of the Henry Art Gallery, located on the west side of the UW campus, is on contemporary art with retrospectives of individual artists, as well as exhibits focusing on specific themes or media. The museum benefits from large, well-lit gallery spaces illuminated by pyramidal and cubic skylights that can be seen near the main entrance. Photography and video are both well represented, and for the most part, the exhibits are the most avant-garde in the Seattle area. The museum's latest cutting-edge installation is Skyspace, by James Turrell, who uses light to create his artwork. The Skyspace is a small room with an oval opening in the ceiling to frame the sky. At night, the outside of the glass Skyspace is illuminated by an ever-changing light show. The museum also has a cafe and a small sculpture courtyard. Parking is often available at the Central Parking Garage, at NE 41st Street and 15th Avenue NE. Expect the unexpected here—and prepare to be challenged in your concept of what constitutes art.

> **Insider Tip**
> Parking on the University of Washington campus is expensive on weekdays and Saturday mornings, so try to visit the Burke Museum or Henry Art Gallery on a Saturday afternoon or a Sunday, when parking is free.

University of Washington, 15th Ave. NE and NE 41st St. ✆ **206/543-2280.** www.henryart.org. Admission $8 adults, $6 seniors, free for students and children under 14; free for all Thurs. For $1 more, you can get admission to the nearby Burke Museum. Tues–Wed and Fri–Sun 11am–5pm; Thurs 11am–8pm. Closed July 4th, Thanksgiving, Dec 24–25, and New Year's Day. Bus: 7, 43, 70, 71, 72, or 73.

Hiram M. Chittenden Locks 🅐🅐   There is something oddly fascinating about locks. No, not the locks on doors—the locks that raise and lower boats. Locks don't provide panoramic views and aren't nearly as dramatic as waterfalls, but for some strange reason, a lot of people are intrigued by the concept of two side-by-side bodies of water on two different levels. Consequently, the Hiram M. Chittenden Locks in the Ballard neighborhood are among the most popular attractions in the city. These locks, operated by the Army Corps of Engineers, consist of a small lock and a large lock. The latter accommodates barges, commercial fishing vessels, and the like, while the small lock stays busy shuttling small private boats (including sea kayaks) between the saltwater of Puget Sound and the freshwater of the Lake Washington Ship Canal, which connects to both Lake Union and Lake Washington. It's a slow process locking boats back and forth, but none of the onlookers seem to mind, and people onshore and those on the boats often strike up conversations.

When the gates of the lock are closed, it's possible to continue to the far side of the ship canal to the fish ladders and fish-viewing windows that provide opportunities for salmon viewing during the summer months. The chance to see salmon in a fish ladder is as much of a draw as the locks themselves, and in the past, the fish runs have also attracted hungry sea lions that sometimes become regular salmon-swallowing pests.

Also here at the locks, you can stroll the grounds of the Carl S. English, Jr., Botanical Gardens, a city park filled with rare and unusual shrubs and trees. March through November, there are free tours of the grounds on Monday through Friday at 1 and 3pm, Saturday and Sunday at 11am and 1 and 3pm.

The locks are a 10- to 15-minute drive north of downtown. Follow Elliott Avenue north along the waterfront from downtown Seattle; after crossing the Ballard Bridge, drive west on NW Market Street.

3015 NW 54th St. ℂ 206/783-7059. Free admission. Daily 7am–9pm. Visitor center: May–Sept daily 10am–6pm; Oct–Apr Thurs–Mon 10am–4pm. Closed Thanksgiving, Christmas Day, and New Year's Day. Bus: 17.

Museum of History and Industry (MOHAI)

If the Seattle Underground Tour's vivid description of life before the 1889 fire has you curious about what the city's more respectable citizens were doing back in those days, you can find out here, where re-created storefronts provide glimpses into their lives. Located at the north end of the Washington Park Arboretum, this museum explores Seattle's history with frequently changing exhibits on more obscure aspects of the city's past. While many of the displays will be of interest only to local residents, anyone wishing to gain a better understanding of the history of the city and the Northwest may also enjoy the exhibits here. There's a Boeing mail plane from the 1920s, plus an exhibit on the 1889 fire that leveled the city. MOHAI also hosts touring exhibitions that address Northwest history. Although not actually in north Seattle, this museum is just across the Montlake Bridge from the University District.

McCurdy Park, 2700 24th Ave. E. ℂ 206/324-1126. www.seattlehistory.org. Admission $7 adults, $5 seniors and youths 5–17, free for children under 5; free 1st Thurs of each month. Daily 10am–5pm (sometimes until 8pm Thurs or 1st Thurs of each month). Closed Thanksgiving and Christmas. Bus: 43. From I-5, take Wash. 520 east (exit 168B) to the Montlake exit, go straight through the stoplight to 24th Ave. E, and turn left.

Woodland Park Zoo

In north Seattle, this sprawling zoo has outstanding exhibits focusing on Alaska, tropical Asia, the African savanna, and the tropical rainforest. The brown-bear enclosure, one of the zoo's best exhibits, is a very realistic reproduction of an Alaskan stream and hillside. In the savanna, zebras gambol and giraffes graze contentedly near a reproduction of an African village. An elephant forest provides plenty of space for the zoo's pachyderms, and the gorilla and orangutan habitats are also very well done. There's even a large walk-through butterfly house ($1 additional fee) during the summer months. A farm animal area and petting zoo are big hits with the little ones.

750 N. 50th St. ℂ 206/684-4800. www.zoo.org. Admission $10 adults, $7 children 3–12, free for children 2 and under. Mar 15–Apr 30 and Sept 15–Oct 14 daily 9:30am–5pm; May 1–Sept 14 daily 9:30am–6pm; Oct 15–Mar 14 daily 9:30am–4pm. Parking $3.50. Bus: 5.

SOUTH SEATTLE

Museum of Flight

Right next door to Boeing Field, an active airport 15 minutes south of downtown Seattle, this museum will have aviation buffs walking on air. Housed inside the six-story glass-and-steel repository are some of history's most famous planes. Suspended in the Great Hall are more than 20 planes, including a 1935 DC-3, the first Air Force F-5 supersonic fighter, and the *Gossamer Condor*, a human-powered airplane. The Personal Courage Wing houses 28 World War I and World War II fighter planes. You'll also see one of the famous Blackbird spy planes, as well as a rare World War II Corsair fighter that was rescued from Lake Washington and restored to its original glory. Visitors also get to board a retired British Airways Concorde supersonic airliner. An exhibit on the U.S. space program features an Apollo command module. The museum also incorporates part of Boeing's old wooden factory building from its early years.

9404 E. Marginal Way S. ℂ 206/764-5720. www.museumofflight.org. Admission $14 adults, $13 seniors, $7.50 children 5–17, free for children under 5. Free 1st Thurs of each month 5–9pm. Daily 10am–5pm (until 9pm 1st Thurs of each month). Closed Thanksgiving and Christmas. Bus: 174. Take exit 158 off I-5.

BEACHES, PARKS & PUBLIC GARDENS
BEACHES

Because the waters of **Puget Sound** stay chilly year-round, the saltwater beaches in the Seattle area are not really swimming beaches. They are primarily places to play in the sand, gaze across the water at the Olympic Mountains, and enjoy a picnic. Seattle is also bordered on the east by **Lake Washington,** a large lake with numerous parks and small beaches along its shores. Even though the waters never get truly warm, the lake is still popular for swimming. There is, however, one caveat. A parasite spread by geese and known as swimmer's itch is commonplace in the waters of Lake Washington. Consequently, you should always change out of your bathing suit and shower as soon after swimming as possible.

Alki Beach ✪, across Elliott Bay from downtown Seattle, is the city's most popular beach and is the nearest approximation you'll find in the Northwest to a Southern California beach scene. The paved path that runs along this 2½-mile beach is popular with skaters, walkers, and cyclists; the road that parallels the beach is lined with shops, restaurants, and beachy houses and apartment buildings. But the views across Puget Sound to the Olympic Mountains confirm that this is indeed the Northwest. (Despite those views, this beach lacks the greenery that makes some of the city's other beaches so much more appealing.) A water taxi operates between the downtown Seattle waterfront and Alki Beach; (see section 2, earlier in this chapter, for details. By the way, Alki rhymes with sky, not key.

For a more Northwestern beach experience (which usually includes a bit of hiking or walking), head to one of the area's many waterfront parks. **Lincoln Park,** 8011 Fauntleroy Way SW (✆ **206/684-4075**), south of Alki Beach in West Seattle, has bluffs and forests backing the beach. Northwest of downtown Seattle in the Magnolia area, you'll find **Discovery Park** ✪✪, 3801 W. Government Way (✆ **206/386-4236**), where miles of beaches are the primary destination of most park visitors. To reach Discovery Park, follow Elliott Avenue north along the waterfront from downtown Seattle, then take the Magnolia Bridge west toward the Magnolia neighborhood, and follow Grayfield Street to Galer Street to Magnolia Boulevard.

Golden Gardens Park ✪✪, 8499 Seaview Place NW (✆ **206/684-4075**), located north of Ballard and Shilshole Bay, is my favorite Seattle beach park. Although the park isn't very large and is backed by railroad tracks, the views of the Olympic Mountains are magnificent, and on summer evenings people build fires on the beach. Lawns and shade trees make Golden Gardens ideal for a picnic.

PARKS

Seattle's many parks are part of what make this such a livable city. In the downtown area, **Myrtle Edwards Park** ✪, 3130 Alaskan Way W. (✆ **206/684-4075**), at the north end of the waterfront, is an ideal spot for a sunset stroll with views of Puget Sound and the Olympic Mountains. The park includes a 1¼-mile paved pathway.

Freeway Park, at Sixth Avenue and Seneca Street, is one of Seattle's most unusual parks. Built right on top of busy I-5, this green space is more like a series of urban plazas, with terraces, waterfalls, and cement planters creating walls of greenery. You'd never know that a roaring freeway lies beneath your feet. Unfortunately, although the park is convenient, the isolated nature of its many nooks and crannies often gives it a deserted and slightly threatening feel.

My, what an inefficient way to fish.

Ring toss, good. Horseshoes, bad.

Faster! Faster! Faster!

We take care of the fiddly bits, from providing over 43,000 customer reviews of hotels, to helping you find our best fares, to giving you 24/7 customer service. So you can focus on the only thing that matters. Goofing off.

travelocity®
You'll never roam alone.™

travelocity.com   **1-888-TRAVELOCITY**   AOL Keyword: Travel

For serious communing with nature, however, nothing will do but **Discovery Park** ☆☆, 3801 W. Government Way (© **206/386-4236**). Occupying a high bluff and sandy point jutting into Puget Sound, this is Seattle's largest and wildest park. You can easily spend a day wandering the trails and beaches here. The park's visitor center is open Tuesday through Sunday from 8:30am to 5pm. Discovery Park is a 15-minute drive from downtown; to get here, follow the waterfront north from downtown Seattle toward the Magnolia neighborhood and watch for signs to the park. When you reach the park, follow signed trails down to the beach and out to the lighthouse at the point. Although the lighthouse is not open to the public, the views from the beach make this a good destination for an hour's walk. The beach and park's bluff-top meadows make good picnic spots.

Up on Capitol Hill, at East Prospect Street and 14th Avenue East, you'll find **Volunteer Park** ☆☆, 1247 15th Ave. E. (© **206/684-4555**), which is surrounded by the elegant mansions of this old neighborhood. It's a popular spot for sunning and playing Frisbee, and it's home to the Seattle Asian Art Museum (p. 116), an amphitheater, a water tower with a superb view of the city, and a conservatory filled with tropical and desert plants. With so much variety, you can easily spend a morning or afternoon exploring this park.

On the east side of Seattle, along the shore of Lake Washington, you'll find not only swimming beaches but also **Seward Park** ☆, 5902 Lake Washington Blvd. S. (© **206/ 684-4075**). This large park's waterfront areas may be its biggest attraction, but it also has a dense forest with trails winding through it. Keep an eye out for the bald eagles that nest here. The park is south of the I-90 floating bridge off Lake Washington Boulevard South. From downtown Seattle, follow Madison Street northeast and turn right onto Lake Washington Boulevard.

Fish Gotta Swim

It's no secret that salmon in the Puget Sound region have dwindled to dangerously low numbers in recent years. But it's still possible to witness the annual return of salmon in various spots around the sound.

In the autumn, on the waterfront, you can see returning salmon at the **Seattle Aquarium** (p. 111), which has its own fish ladder. But the very best place to see salmon is at the **Hiram M. Chittenden Locks**, 3015 NW 54th St. (© **206/783-7059**; see p. 118 for directions and hours). Between June and September (July–Aug are the peak months), you can view salmon through underwater observation windows as they leap up the locks' fish ladder. These locks, which are used primarily by small boats, connect Lake Union and Lake Washington with the waters of Puget Sound, and depending on the tides and lake levels, there is a difference of 6 to 26 feet on either side of the locks.

East of Seattle, in downtown Issaquah, salmon can be seen year-round at the **Issaquah Salmon Hatchery,** 125 W. Sunset Way (© **425/391-9094**). However, it is in the fall that adult salmon can be seen returning to the hatchery. Each year on the first weekend in October, the city of Issaquah holds the Issaquah Salmon Days Festival to celebrate the return of the natives.

In north Seattle, you'll find several parks worth visiting. These include the unique **Gasworks Park** ☆, 2101 N. Northlake Way, at Meridian Avenue North (✆ **206/ 684-4075**), at the north end of Lake Union. In the middle of its green lawns, this park holds the rusting hulk of an old industrial plant, and the park's small Kite Hill is the city's favorite kite-flying spot. North of here, on Green Lake Way North near the Woodland Park Zoo, you'll find **Green Lake Park** ☆☆, 7201 East Green Lake Dr. N. (✆ **206/684-4075**), which is a center for exercise buffs who jog, bike, and skate around the park on a 2.8-mile paved path. It's also possible to swim in the lake (there are changing rooms and a beach with summer lifeguards) and picnic on the many grassy areas. For information on renting in-line skates or a bike for riding the path here, see p. 129 and p. 128 respectively.

PUBLIC GARDENS

See also the listings for Volunteer Park Conservatory on p. 117 and Hiram M. Chittenden Locks on p. 118.

Bellevue Botanical Garden ☆

Any avid gardener should be sure to make a trip across one of Seattle's two floating bridges to the city of Bellevue and its Bellevue Botanical Garden. Although this 36-acre garden opened only in 1992, it has matured very quickly to become one of the Northwest's most-talked-about perennial gardens. The summertime displays of flowers, in expansive mixed borders, are absolutely gorgeous. You can also see a Japanese garden, a shade border, and a water-wise garden (designed to conserve water). April through October, free guided tours of the garden are offered Saturday and Sunday at 2pm.

Wilburton Hill Park, 12001 Main St., Bellevue. ✆ 425/452-2750. www.bellevuebotanical.org. Free admission. Daily dawn–dusk; visitor center daily 9am–4pm. Take the NE Eighth St. exit east off I-405.

Japanese Garden

Situated on 3½ acres of land, the Japanese Garden is a perfect little world unto itself, with babbling brooks, a lake rimmed with Japanese irises and filled with colorful koi (Japanese carp), and a cherry orchard (for spring color). A special tea garden encloses a teahouse, where on the third Saturday of each month between April and October, you can attend a traditional tea ceremony ($10). Unfortunately, noise from a nearby road can be distracting.

Washington Park Arboretum, 1075 Lake Washington Blvd. E. (north of E. Madison St.). ✆ 206/684-4725. Admission $5 adults, $3 seniors and youths 6–18, free for children under 6. Mar–Nov Tues–Sun 10am to dusk. Closed Dec–Feb. Bus: 11.

Kubota Garden ☆

In South Seattle in a working-class neighborhood not far from the shores of Lake Washington, this 20-acre Japanese-style garden was the life's work of garden designer Fujitaro Kubota. Today the gardens are a city park, and the mature landscaping and hilly setting make this the most impressive and enjoyable Japanese garden in the Seattle area. Kubota began work on this garden in 1927, and over the years built a necklace of ponds, a traditional stroll garden, and a mountainside garden complete with waterfalls. Between April and October, free tours of the gardens are offered at 10am on the fourth Saturday of the month.

9817 55th Ave. S. (at Renton Ave. S.). ✆ 206/684-4584. www.kubota.org. Free admission. Daily dawn–dusk. From downtown, take I-5 south to exit 158 (Pacific Hwy. S/E. Marginal Way), turn left toward Martin Luther King Jr. Way, and continue uphill on Ryan Way; turn left on 51st Ave. S., right on Renton Ave. S., and right on 55th Ave. S. Bus: 106.

Washington Park Arboretum ☆

Acres of trees and shrubs stretch from the far side of Capitol Hill all the way to the Montlake Cut (a canal connecting Lake

Washington to Lake Union). Within the 230-acre arboretum are 5,000 varieties of plants and quiet trails that are pleasant throughout the year but become most beautiful in spring, when the azaleas, cherry trees, rhododendrons, and dogwoods are all in bloom. The north end of the arboretum, a marshland that is home to ducks and herons, is popular with bird-watchers as well as kayakers and canoeists. (See p. 129 in "Outdoor Pursuits," later in this chapter, for places to rent a canoe or kayak.) A boardwalk with views across Lake Washington meanders along the waterside in this area (though noise from the adjacent freeway detracts considerably from the experience).

2300 Arboretum Dr. E. ℭ 206/543-8800. http://depts.washington.edu/wpa/general.htm. Free admission. Daily dawn–dusk; Graham Visitors Center daily 10am–4pm. Bus: 11, 43, or 48. Enter on Lake Washington Blvd. off E. Madison St.; or take Wash. 520 off I-5 north of downtown, take the Montlake Blvd. exit, and go straight through the 1st intersection.

ESPECIALLY FOR KIDS

In addition to the listings below, kids will also enjoy many of the attractions described earlier in this chapter, including the **Odyssey Maritime Discovery Center** (p. 110), **Seattle Aquarium** (p. 111), **Pacific Science Center** (p. 114), and **Woodland Park Zoo** (p. 119).

Adolescent and preadolescent boys seem to unfailingly love **Ye Olde Curiosity Shop** and the **Underground Tour** (see p. 113 for both). Younger kids also love the **Museum of Flight** (p. 119).

And even the surliest teenagers will think you're pretty cool for taking them to the **Experience Music Project** (p. 114).

Kids need to burn off some energy? Earlier in this chapter, see "Beaches, Parks & Public Gardens" for descriptions of Seattle's best beaches and recreational areas; "Outdoor Pursuits" for the lowdown on biking and in-line skating; and "Spectator Sports" for details on Seattle's professional football, basketball, and baseball teams.

You might also be able to catch a performance at the **Seattle Children's Theatre** (ℭ **206/441-3322;** www.sct.org), in Seattle Center (see below); or at the **Northwest Puppet Center,** 9123 15th Ave. NE (ℭ **206/523-2579;** www.nwpuppet.org).

Children's Museum ⓀⒾⒹⓈ The Children's Museum is located in the basement of the Center House at Seattle Center, which is partly why Seattle Center is such a great place to spend a day with the kids. The museum includes plenty of hands-on cultural exhibits, a child-size neighborhood, a Discovery Bay for toddlers, a mountain wilderness area, a global village, and other special exhibits to keep the little ones busy learning and playing for hours.

Seattle Center, Center House, 305 Harrison St. ℭ **206/441-1768.** www.thechildrensmuseum.org. Admission $7.50 adults and children, $6.50 seniors, free for children under 1. Mon–Fri 10am–5pm; Sat–Sun 10am–6pm. Closed Thanksgiving, Christmas Eve, Christmas Day, and New Year's Day. Bus: 1, 2, 3, 4, 13, 15, 16, 18, 24, or 33. Monorail: From Westlake Center at the corner of Pine St. and Fourth Ave.

Seattle Center Ⓡ ⓀⒾⒹⓈ If you want to keep the kids entertained all day long, head to Seattle Center. This 74-acre cultural center and amusement park stands on the northern edge of downtown at the end of the monorail line. The most visible building at the center is the **Space Needle** (p. 114), which provides an outstanding panorama of the city from its observation deck. However, of much more interest to children are the **Fun Forest** (ℭ **206/728-1585;** www.funforest.com), with its roller coaster, log flume, merry-go-round, Ferris wheel, arcade games, and minigolf; the

Children's Museum (see above); and **Seattle Children's Theatre** (© **206/441-3322;** www.sct.org). This is also Seattle's main festival site, and in the summer months hardly a weekend goes by without some special event filling its grounds. On hot summer days the **International Fountain** is a great place for kids to keep cool (bring a change of clothes).

305 Harrison St. © **206/684-7200.** www.seattlecenter.com. Free admission; pay per ride or game (various multiride tickets available). Fun Forest outdoor rides: early June to Labor Day daily noon–10 or 11pm; reduced days and hours other months (call for hours). Indoor attractions open year-round at 11am. Bus: 1, 2, 3, 4, 13, 15, 16, 18, 24, or 33. Monorail: From Westlake Center at the corner of Pine St. and Fourth Ave.

6 Organized Tours

For information on the **Underground Tour,** see the box titled "Good Times in Bad Taste" on p. 113.

WALKING TOURS

In addition to the walking tours mentioned here, there are Pike Place Market tours offered by the market itself. See the Pike Place Market listing on p. 111 for details.

If you'd like to explore downtown Seattle with a knowledgeable guide, join one of the informative walking tours offered by **See Seattle Walking Tours** (© **425/ 226-7641;** www.see-seattle.com), which visit Pike Place Market, the waterfront, the Pioneer Square area, and the International District. Tours cost $20 and can last a half-day or a full day, depending on how much stamina you have.

You can also learn a lot about local history and wander through hidden corners of the city on the 2-hour tours run by **Duse McLean/Seattle Walking Tour** (© **425/ 885-3173;** www.seattlewalkingtours.com). These tours take in historic buildings, public art, and scenic vistas. Tours are $15 and are held year-round by reservation.

For an insider's glimpse of life in Seattle's International District, hook up with **Chinatown Discovery Tours** (© **425/885-3085;** www.seattlechinatowntour.com). On these walking tours, which last from 1½ to 3¼ hours, you'll learn the history of this colorful and historic neighborhood. Options include "A Touch of Chinatown," a brief introduction to the area; "Chinatown by Day," which includes a six-course lunch; "Nibble Your Way through Chinatown," which provides a sampling of flavors from around the I.D.; and "Chinatown by Night," which includes an eight-course banquet. Rates (for four or more on a tour) range from $15 to $40 per person (slightly higher for fewer than four people).

BUS TOURS

If you'd like an overview of Seattle's main tourist attractions, or if you're pressed for time during your visit, you can pack in a lot of sights on a city tour with **Gray Line of Seattle** (© **800/426-7532** or 206/624-5077; www.graylineofseattle.com). Half-day tours cost $29 for adults, $15 for children. Many other options, including tours to Mount Rainier National Park and to the Boeing plant in Everett, are also available.

Gray Line also operates a **Double-Decker Tour** in open-top buses. These city tours run from late May through mid-Oct and cost $17 for adults and $9 for children. Buses depart from a half-dozen stops around the city; call for details or keep an eye out for a parked double-decker bus.

To glimpse a bit more of Seattle on a guided van tour, try the "Explore Seattle Tour" offered by **Customized Tours and Charter Service** (© **800/770-8769** or

Seattle by Duck

Paul Revere would have had a hard time figuring out what to tell his fellow colonists if the British had arrived by Duck. A Duck, if you didn't know, is a World War II amphibious vehicle that can arrive by land or by sea, and these odd-looking things are now being used to provide tours of Seattle on both land and water. Duck tours take in the standard city sights, but then plunge right into Lake Union for a tour of the Portage Bay waterfront, with its many houseboats and great views. The 90-minute tours leave from a parking lot across from the Space Needle; they cost $23 for adults and $13 for kids. Contact **Seattle Duck Tours** ☞, 516 Broad St. (© **800/817-1116** or 206/441-DUCK; www.seattleducktours.net). Because these tours encourage visitors to get a little daffy, they're very popular; reservations are recommended.

206/878-3965; www.customizedtours.net), which charges $36 per person. This tour stops at Pike Place Market, the Hiram M. Chittenden Locks and Fish Ladder, and the Klondike Gold Rush Historical Park. The company also offers a Boeing plant tour ($40 per person) and a Snoqualmie Falls and wineries tour ($45 per person).

BOAT TOURS

In addition to the boat tours and cruises mentioned below, you can do your own low-budget "cruise" simply by hopping on one of the ferries operated by **Washington State Ferries** (© **800/84-FERRY** or 888/808-7977 in Washington, or 206/464-6400; www.wsdot.wa.gov/ferries). Try the Bainbridge Island or Bremerton ferries out of Seattle for a 1½- to 2½-hour round-trip. For more information on these ferries, see p. 71.

If you don't have enough vacation time scheduled to fit in an overnight trip to the San Juan Islands, it's still possible to get a feel for these picturesque isles by riding the San Juan Islands ferry from Anacortes to Friday Harbor. These boats depart from Anacortes, 75 miles north of Seattle. If you get off in Friday Harbor, you can spend a few hours exploring this town before returning to Anacortes. Alternatively, if you have more money to spend (and even less time), boat tours of the San Juans depart from the Seattle waterfront. For information on ferries and boat excursions to the San Juan Islands, see chapter 6.

For a boat excursion that includes a salmon dinner and Northwest Coast Indian masked dances, consider coughing up the cash for the **Tillicum Village Tours** ☞☞, Pier 55 (© **800/426-1205** or 206/933-8600; www.tillicumvillage.com). Located at Blake Island State Park across Puget Sound from Seattle and only accessible by tour boat or private boat, Tillicum Village was built in conjunction with the 1962 Seattle World's Fair. The "village" is actually just a large restaurant and performance hall fashioned after a traditional Northwest Coast longhouse, but with the totem poles standing vigil out front, the forest encircling the longhouse, and the waters of Puget Sound stretching out into the distance, Tillicum Village is a beautiful spot. After the dinner and dances, you can strike out on forest trails to explore the island (you can return on a later boat if you want to spend a couple of extra hours hiking). There are even beaches on which to relax. Tours are $69 for adults, $62 for seniors, $25 for children ages 5 to 12, and free for children under 5. They're offered daily from May to September, and on a more limited basis (usually weekends only) during other months. If you opt for only one tour while in Seattle, this should be it—it's unique and truly Northwestern, the salmon dinner is pretty good, and the traditional dances are fascinating (though more for the craftsmanship of the masks than for the dancing itself). You can also just opt to ride the boat out to Blake Island and skip the meal and dancing. This option costs $35 for adults, $32 for seniors, and $10 for children ages 5 to 12.

Seattle is a city surrounded by water; so to see it from various aquatic perspectives, head out with **Argosy Cruises** ⚐ (© **800/642-7816** or 206/623-1445; www.argosy cruises.com). It offers a 1-hour harbor cruise that departs from Pier 55 ($14–$17 adults, $6.25–$7.75 for children ages 5–12) and a 2½-hour cruise from Lake Union through the Hiram M. Chittenden Locks to Elliott Bay that departs (by bus to Lake Union) from Pier 56 ($25–$32 for adults, $9.50–$10 for children). Argosy also operates two cruises around Lake Washington that will take you past Bill Gates's fabled waterfront Xanadu; the 2-hour cruise departs from the AGC Marina at the south end of Lake Union, while the 1½-hour cruise departs from downtown Kirkland on the east side of the lake ($21–$26 for adults, $8.25–$9.25 for children). However, of these options, I recommend the cruise through the

---

⟨Value Money-Saving Tip

The **Ticket/Ticket** booth under the big clock at Pike Place Market sometimes has boat-tour tickets available at discounted prices. If your schedule is flexible, be sure to check here first.

---

locks; it may be the most expensive, but you get good views and a chance to navigate the locks. Reservations are recommended; the higher rates are for April through September.

Want a meal with your cruise? Try one of Argosy's lunch, brunch, or dinner cruises aboard the *Royal Argosy* (www.argosycruises.com). Lunch and brunch cruises are $39 to $45 for adults and $20 to $22 for children ages 5 to 12; dinner cruises are $65 to $85 for adults and $25 to $35 for children. These cruises get my vote for best dinners afloat.

Looking for a quieter way to see Seattle from the water? From May to mid-October, **Emerald City Charters,** Pier 54 (© **800/831-3274** or 206/624-3931; www.sailing seattle.com), offers 1½- and 2½-hour sailboat cruises. The longer excursions are at sunset. The cruises cost $25 to $40 for adults, $20 to $35 for seniors, and $18 to $30 for children under 12.

VICTORIA EXCURSIONS

Among Seattle's most popular boat tours are daylong excursions to Victoria. These trips are operated by **Victoria Clipper** ⚐⚐, Pier 69, 2701 Alaskan Way (© **800/888-2535,** 206/448-5000, or 250/382-8100 in Victoria; www.victoriaclipper.com), several times a day during the summer (once or twice a day in other months). The high-speed catamaran passenger ferry takes 2 to 3 hours to reach Victoria. If you leave on the earliest ferry, you can spend the better part of the day exploring Victoria and be back in Seattle for a late dinner. Round-trip fares range from $70 (with 7-day advance purchase) to $133 for adults, $70 to $123 for seniors, and $55 to $67 for children ages 1 to 11 (between mid-Sept and mid-June, one child travels free with each adult paying for a 7-day advance-purchase round-trip fare). Some scheduled trips

Seattle Noir

If your tastes run to the macabre, you may be interested in the tours offered by **Private Eye on Seattle** ✦ (© 206/365-3739; www.privateeyetours.com). These somewhat bizarre van tours are led by a private eye named Jake, who shares stories of interesting and unusual cases from the Emerald City. Tours are $25 per person. Another option is a unique tour of some of the city's haunted locales.

---

also stop in the San Juan Islands during the summer. Various tour packages are available, including an add-on tour to Butchart Gardens. Overnight trips can also be arranged.

You can also fly to Victoria from Seattle in a floatplane operated by **Kenmore Air** (© 800/543-9595 or 425/486-1257; www.kenmoreair.com). Flights take only 45 minutes, which leaves plenty of time to explore Victoria and still make it back to Seattle in time for dinner. The round-trip fare is $205 to $249 per person. You can opt to add on a whale-watching excursion or a tour of Butchart Gardens.

For more complete information on Victoria, pick up a copy of *Frommer's Vancouver & Victoria.*

SCENIC FLIGHTS

Seattle is one of the few cities in the United States where floatplanes are a regular sight in the skies and on the lakes. If you want to see what it's like to take off and land from the water, you've got a couple of options.

Seattle Seaplanes ✦, 1325 Fairview Ave. E. (© 800/637-5553 or 206/329-9638; www.seattleseaplanes.com), has 20-minute flights that take off from the southeast corner of Lake Union and fly over the city for $68. This company also offers flights to nearby waterfront restaurants for dinner.

If you'd rather pretend you're back in the days of *The English Patient,* you can go up in a vintage biplane with **Olde Thyme Aviation** ✦ (© 206/730-1412; www.olde thymeaviation.com), which operates from Boeing Field. Flights are offered on sunny weekends. A 20-minute flight along the Seattle waterfront to the Space Needle costs $125 for two people; other flights range in price from $149 to $495 for two people.

A RAILWAY EXCURSION

If you're a fan of riding the rails, consider the **Spirit of Washington Dinner Train,** 625 S. Fourth St., Renton (© 800/876-7245 or 425/227-7245; www.spiritof washingtondinnertrain.com). Running from Renton, at the south end of Lake Washington, to the Columbia Winery near Woodinville, at the north end of Lake Washington, this train rolls past views of the lake and Mount Rainier. Along the way, you're served a filling lunch or dinner. At the turnaround point, you get to tour a winery and taste some wines. There are also Mystery Trains that include staged whodunits. Rates are $60 to $75 for dinner tours, $50 to $65 for lunch/brunch tours, and $80 for Mystery Trains. The higher prices are for seating in the dome car, which definitely offers finer views. Between November and April, children ages 12 and under ride free with a paying adult.

7 Outdoor Pursuits

See "Beaches, Parks & Public Gardens," earlier in this chapter, for a rundown of great places to play.

BIKING

Gregg's Greenlake Cycle, 7007 Woodlawn Ave. NE (© **206/523-1822;** www.greggs cycles.com), and the **Bicycle Center,** 4529 Sand Point Way NE (© **206/523-8300;** www.bicyclecenterseattle.com), both rent bikes by the hour, day, or week. Rates range from $3 to $7 per hour and $15 to $42 per day. These shops are both convenient to the **Burke-Gilman/Sammamish River Trail** ᴪᴪ, a 27-mile paved pathway created mostly from an old railway bed. This immensely popular path is a great place to take the family for a bike ride or to get in a long, vigorous ride without having to deal with traffic. The Burke-Gilman portion of the trail starts in the Ballard neighborhood of North Seattle, but the most convenient place to start a ride is at **Gas Works Park,** on the north shore of Lake Union. From here, you can ride north and east, by way of the University of Washington, to **Kenmore Logboom Park,** at the north end of Lake Washington. Serious riders can continue on from Kenmore Logboom Park on the Sammamish River portion of the trail, which leads to **Marymoor Park,** at the north end of Lake Sammamish. Marymoor Park is the site of a velodrome (bicycle race-track). This latter half of the trail is my favorite part; it follows the Sammamish River and passes through several pretty parks. Riding the entire trail out and back is a 54-mile round-trip popular with riders in training for races. Plenty of great picnicking spots can be found along both sections of the trail.

The West Seattle bike path along **Alki Beach** is another good place to ride; it offers great views of the sound and the Olympics. If you'd like to pedal this pathway, you can rent single-speed bikes at **Alki Crab & Fish Co.,** 1660 Harbor Ave. SW (© **206/ 938-0975**), which charges $10 for 3 hours. This place has a limited number of bikes, so do call ahead and make a reservation. You can then take the water taxi from the downtown waterfront to West Seattle; the dock is right at Alki Crab & Fish Co.

GOLF

While Seattle isn't a name that springs immediately to mind when folks think of golf, the sport is a passion here, just as it is all across the country. Should you wish to get in a round while you're in town, Seattle has three conveniently located municipal golf courses: **Jackson Park Golf Course,** 1000 NE 135th St. (© **206/363-4747**); **Jefferson Park Golf Course,** 4101 Beacon Ave. S. (© **206/762-4513**); and **West Seattle Golf Course,** 4470 35th Ave. SW (© **206/935-5187**). This latter course has great views of the Seattle skyline and gets my vote as the best of the city's municipal courses. All three charge very reasonable greens fees of between $26 and $31.

HIKING

Within Seattle itself, several large nature parks are laced with enough trails for a few good long walks. Among these are **Seward Park,** 5898 Lake Washington Blvd., southeast of downtown; and **Lincoln Park,** 8011 Fauntleroy Ave. SW, south of Alki Beach in West Seattle. However, the city's largest natural park and Seattleites' favorite quick dose of nature is **Discovery Park,** 3801 W. Government Way (© **206/386-4236**), northwest of downtown at the western tip of the Magnolia neighborhood. This park covers more than 500 acres and has many miles of trails and beaches to hike—not to mention gorgeous views, forest paths, and meadows for lazing in after a long walk. To reach Discovery Park, follow Elliott Avenue north along the waterfront from downtown Seattle, then take the Magnolia Bridge west toward the Magnolia neighborhood and follow Grayfield Street to Galer Street to Magnolia Boulevard.

IN-LINE SKATING

The city has dozens of miles of paved paths that are perfect for skating. In North Seattle you can rent in-line skates at **Gregg's Greenlake Cycle,** 7007 Woodlawn Ave. NE (© 206/523-1822; www.greggscycles.com), for $5 per hour. The trail around **Green Lake** and the **Burke-Gilman/Sammamish River Trail** (see the description under "Biking," above) are both good places for skating that are convenient to Gregg's.

Other favorite skating spots to try include the paved path in **Myrtle Edwards Park** just north of the Seattle waterfront, the paved path along **Lake Washington Boulevard** north of Seward Park, and the **Alki Beach** pathway in West Seattle.

JOGGING

The **waterfront,** from Pioneer Square north to Myrtle Edwards Park, where a paved path parallels the water, is a favorite downtown jogging route. The residential streets of **Capitol Hill,** combined with roads and sidewalks through **Volunteer Park,** are another good choice. If you happen to be staying in the University District, you can access the 27-mile **Burke-Gilman/Sammamish River Trail** or run the ever-popular trail around **Green Lake.** Out in West Seattle, the **Alki Beach** pathway is also very popular and provides great views of the Olympics.

SEA KAYAKING, CANOEING, ROWING & SAILING

If you'd like to try your hand at **sea kayaking** , head to the **Northwest Outdoor Center** , 2100 Westlake Ave. N. (© **800/683-0637** or 206/281-9694; www.nwoc.com), located on the west side of Lake Union. Here you can rent a sea kayak for between $12 and $17 per hour. You can also opt for guided tours lasting from a few hours to several days, and there are plenty of classes available for those who are interested.

Moss Bay Rowing and Kayak Center, 1001 Fairview Ave. N. (© **206/682-2031;** www.mossbay.net), rents sea kayaks (as well as canoes, pedal boats, and sailboats) at the south end of Lake Union near Chandler's Cove. Rates range from $12 per hour for a single to $17 per hour for a double. Because this rental center is a little closer to downtown Seattle, it's a better choice if you are here without a car.

If you're interested in renting a wooden rowboat or sailboat on Lake Union, head to the **Center for Wooden Boats** , 1010 Valley St. (Waterway 4, south end of Lake Union; © **206/382-2628;** www.cwb.org), an unusual little museum that rents exhibited boats at rates ranging from $10 to $46 per hour. (Call for hours of availability.)

In this same general area, you can rent kayaks at the **Agua Verde Paddle Club,** 1303 NE Boat St. (© **206/545-8570,** ext. 101; www.aguaverde.com), at the foot of Brooklyn Avenue on Portage Bay (the body of water between Lake Union and Lake Washington). Kayaks can be rented from March through October, for $15 to $20 per hour. Best of all, this place is part of the Agua Verde Café, a great Mexican restaurant! Before or after a paddle, get an order of tacos. See p. 103 for details.

At **Green Lake Boat Rental,** 7351 E. Green Lake Way N. (© **206/527-0171**), in North Seattle not far from Woodland Park Zoo, you can rent canoes, paddleboats, sailboats, and rowboats for a bit of leisurely time on the water. There is also a paved path around the park, which is one of the most popular in Seattle (it's a great place to join crowds of locals enjoying one of the city's nicest green spaces). Kayaks, canoes, rowboats, and paddleboats all rent for $12 per hour, and sailboats go for $20 per hour.

8 Spectator Sports

With professional football, baseball, basketball, ice hockey, and women's basketball teams, as well as the various University of Washington Huskies teams, Seattle is definitely a city of sports fans.

Ticketmaster (© 206/628-0123; www.ticketmaster.com) sells tickets to almost all sporting events in the Seattle area. You'll find Ticketmaster outlets at area Fred Meyer stores and Tower Records.

BASEBALL

Of all of Seattle's major league sports teams, none is more popular than the American League's **Seattle Mariners** (© 206/346-4000 or 206/346-4001; www.seattlemariners. com). The team has a devoted following, so you can expect tickets to be hard to find, unless you buy them well in advance.

The Mariners' retro-style **Safeco Field** is indisputably one of the most beautiful ballparks in the country. It's also one of a handful of stadiums with a retractable roof (which can open or close in 10–20 min.), allowing the Mariners a real grass playing field without worrying about getting rained out.

Ticket prices range from $7 to $55. Though you may be able to get a single ticket on game day at the Safeco Field box office, it would be tough to get two seats together. Mariners tickets are a hot commodity, so if you want to ensure that you get good seats, order in advance at **Mariners Team Stores** (there are locations at Fourth and Stewart sts. downtown and in the Bellevue Square shopping mall) or through **Ticketmaster** (© 206/622-HITS; www.ticketmaster.com), which has outlets at Fred Meyer and Tower Records. Parking is next to impossible in the immediate vicinity of Safeco Field, so plan to leave your car behind.

If you'd like a behind-the-scenes look at the ballpark, take a **1-hour tour** that costs $7 for adults, $6 for seniors, and $5 for kids ages 3 to 12. Tickets can be purchased at the Mariners Team Store at Safeco Field, at other Mariners Team Stores around the city, or through Ticketmaster. Tour times vary, and tours are not offered when day games are scheduled.

BASKETBALL

The NBA's **Seattle SuperSonics** (© 800/4NBA-TIX, 800/743-7021, or 206/283-3865; www.supersonics.com) play in the Key Arena at Seattle Center, and though they always seem to trail behind the Portland Trailblazers, they generally put in a good showing every season. Tickets cost $10 to $129 and are available at the arena box office or through **Ticketmaster** (© 206/628-0888). Tickets can generally be had even on short notice, except for games against the Lakers and Blazers, which are always well attended.

Seattle is also home to the 2004 WNBA champion women's pro basketball team, the **Seattle Storm** (© 877/WNBA-TIX or 206/217-WNBA; www.storm.wnba. com), which also plays in Key Arena. Ticket prices range from $10 to $39, and they are available either at the arena box office or by calling Ticketmaster (© 206/628-0888).

The **University of Washington Huskies** women's basketball team has been pretty popular for years. For information on both the women's and men's Huskies basketball games, call © 206/543-2200 or go to www.gohuskies.com.

FOOTBALL

The NFL's **Seattle Seahawks** (© **888/635-4295** or 206/381-7816; www.seahawks.com) play at **Qwest Field,** 800 Occidental Ave. S. (© 206/381-7582; www.qwestfield.com), which stands on the site of the old Kingdome and is adjacent to the Seattle Mariners' Safeco Field. Tickets to games run from $33 to $315 and are sold through **Ticketmaster** (© **206/622-HAWK;** www.ticketmaster.com). An impressive winning streak in the 2005 season turned Seahawks tickets into some of the hottest and hardest-to-find tickets in town. Unless the team starts losing again, you can expect games to keep selling out, so try to get your tickets as soon as possible after they go on sale in August. Traffic and parking in the vicinity of Seahawks Stadium is a nightmare on game days, so take the bus if you can. Between June and September, tours of the stadium are available daily (except on game days) at 12:30 and 2:30 pm; they cost $7 for adults and $5 for seniors and children ages 4 to 12. In other months, tours are offered 2 or 3 days a week; call for details.

Not surprisingly, the **University of Washington Huskies** (© **206/543-2200;** www.gohuskies.com), who play in Husky Stadium on the university campus, have a loyal following. Big games (Nebraska or Washington State) sell out as soon as tickets go on sale in the summer. Other games can sell out in advance, but obstructed-view tickets are usually available on game day. Ticket prices range from $40 to $60 for reserved seats and from $20 to $30 for general admission.

9 Shopping

Nordstrom, Eddie Bauer, REI—these names are familiar to shoppers all across the country. They're also the names of stores that got their start here in Seattle, which has long been *the* place to shop in the Northwest. Throw in such regional favorites as Pendleton, Nike, and Filson, and you'll find that Seattle is a great place to shop, especially if you're in the market for recreational and outdoor gear and clothing.

As the Northwest's largest city, Seattle has also become home to all of the national retail chains you would expect to find in a major metropolitan area. These chains have opened flashy stores and taken over many of the storefronts in downtown Seattle. The names and merchandise at these stores should be familiar: Banana Republic, Old Navy, Levi Strauss, Ann Taylor, Coach, St. John, Louis Vuitton, Tiffany, Barneys New York. These and many others now have stores in Seattle, so if you forgot to pick up that dress in Chicago or those running shoes in New York, have no fear—you can find them here.

Seattle does, however, have one last bastion of local merchandising, **Pike Place Market.** Whether shopping is your passion or an occasional indulgence, you shouldn't miss this historic market, which is one of Seattle's top tourist attractions. Once the city's main produce market (and quite a few produce stalls remain), this sprawling collection of buildings is today filled with hundreds of unusual shops. See also the listing for Pike Place Market on p. 111.

THE SHOPPING SCENE

Although Seattle is a city of neighborhoods, many of which have great little shops, ground zero of the Seattle shopping scene is the corner of **Pine Street and Fifth Avenue.** Within 2 blocks of this intersection are two major department stores (**Nordstrom** and **Macy's**) and two upscale urban shopping malls (**Westlake Center** and

Pacific Place). There's even a sky bridge between Nordstrom and Pacific Place to make your shopping that much easier. Fanning out east and south from this intersection are blocks of upscale stores that have begun to take on a very familiar look. Small local shops have been replaced by national and international boutiques and megastores; here in this neighborhood, you'll now find Ann Taylor, Banana Republic, Barneys New York, Coach, Gap, Max Mara, and Niketown. However, you'll still find a few local independents in the area as well.

Within this downtown shopping district, you'll also find the loosely affiliated shops of **Rainier Square** (www.rainier-square.com). Although not actually a shopping mall, Rainier Square, which is bordered by University and Union streets and Fourth and Sixth avenues, is packed with great upscale shops and boutiques, including Brooks Brothers, Louis Vuitton, Northwest Pendleton, and St. John.

The city's main tourist shopping district is the **Pike Place Market** neighborhood. Here you'll find dozens of T-shirt and souvenir shops, as well as import shops and stores appealing to teenagers and 20-somethings. Pike Place Market is a fascinating warren of cubbyholes that pass for shops. While produce isn't usually something you stock up on while on vacation, several market shops sell ethnic cooking supplies that are less perishable than a dozen oysters or a king salmon. You may not find anything here you really need, but it's fun to look (at least that's what millions of Seattle visitors each year think).

Just west of Pike Place Market is the Seattle **waterfront,** where you'll find many more gift and souvenir shops. This is the most touristy and tackiest neighborhood in the city. Save your money for somewhere else.

South of downtown, in the historic **Pioneer Square** area, is the city's greatest concentration of art galleries, some of which specialize in Native American art. This neighborhood has several antiques stores, but is also home to a dozen or more bars and attracts a lot of homeless people. It's fun to explore by day but strictly for young partyers by night.

As the center of both the gay community and the city's youth culture, **Capitol Hill** has the most eclectic selection of shops in Seattle. Beads, imports, CDs, vintage clothing, politically correct merchandise, and gay-oriented goods fill the shops along Broadway. Capitol Hill's main shopping plaza is the Broadway Market, which has lots of small shops.

The **Fremont** neighborhood, just north of Lake Union, is filled with retro stores selling vintage clothing, curious crafts, and mid-20th-century furniture and collectibles. As of this writing, however, the neighborhood is undergoing a fairly rapid gentrification that is forcing out many smaller, more unusual shops.

A couple of miles east of Fremont is the **Wallingford** neighborhood, which is anchored by an old school building that has been converted into a shopping arcade with boutiques selling interesting crafts, fashions, and gifts.

The **University District,** also in North Seattle, has everything necessary to support a student population—and also goes upscale at the University Village shopping center.

SHOPPING A TO Z
ANTIQUES & COLLECTIBLES

If antiques are your passion, you won't want to miss the opportunity to spend a day browsing the many antiques stores in the historic farm town of **Snohomish,** located roughly 30 miles north of Seattle. The town has more than 400 antiques dealers and is, without a doubt, the antiques capital of the Northwest. There are also plenty of antiques stores right in Seattle. The following are some of our favorites.

Honeychurch Antiques   For high-quality Asian antiques, including Japanese woodblock prints, textiles, furniture, and ivory and woodcarvings, few Seattle antiques stores can approach Honeychurch Antiques. Regular special exhibits give this shop the feel of a tiny museum. The store's annex, called **Glenn Richards,** 964 Denny Way (✆ **206/287-1877;** glennrichards.com), specializes in "entry-level" antiques. 411 Westlake Ave. N. ✆ **206/622-1225. www.honeychurch.com.**

Jean Williams Antiques   If your taste in antiques runs to 18th- and 19th-century French and English formal or country furniture, this Pioneer Square antiques dealer may have something to add to your collection. 115 S. Jackson St. ✆ **206/622-1110. www. jeanwilliamsantiques.com.**

Laguna   Twentieth-century art pottery is the specialty of this shop in Pioneer Square. Pieces by such mid-century pottery factories as Fiesta, Roseville, Bauer, Weller, and Franciscan fill the shelves here. This is a great place to look for dinnerware and vintage tiles. 116 S. Washington St. ✆ **206/682-6162. www.lagunapottery.com.**

ANTIQUES MALLS & FLEA MARKETS

Antiques at Pike Place   Located in the Pike Place Market area, this antiques and collectibles mall is one of the finest in Seattle. There are more than 80 dealers, and much of what's available here is fairly small, which means you might be able to fit your find into a suitcase. 92 Stewart St. ✆ **206/441-9643.**

Fremont Sunday Market 🖈🖈   Crafts, imports, antiques, collectibles, and fresh produce combine to make this Seattle's second-favorite public market (after Pike Place Market). From April through October the market is open on Sunday from 10am to 5pm; other months, it's open on Sunday from 10am to 4pm. N. 34th St. (1 block west of the Fremont Bridge). ✆ **206/781-6776. www.fremontmarket.com/fremont.**

Pioneer Square Antique Mall   This underground antiques mall is in the heart of Pioneer Square, right beside the ticket booth for the Seattle Underground Tour. It has more than 60 stalls selling all manner of antiques and collectibles. Look for glass, old jewelry, and small collectibles. 602 First Ave. ✆ **206/624-1164.**

ART GALLERIES

The **Pioneer Square** area has long been Seattle's main gallery district. Although it still has quite a few galleries, in the past few years many have moved to other parts of the metropolitan area, including the two wealthy Eastside suburbs of Bellevue and Kirkland. Still, enough galleries are left around Pioneer Square that anyone interested in art should wander south of Yesler Way. Some galleries are closed on Monday.

General Art Galleries

Carolyn Staley Fine Japanese Prints 🖈   This Pioneer Square gallery specializes in Japanese prints, both old and new. The highlight is the large collection of 19th- and 20th-century woodblock prints. 314 Occidental Ave. S. ✆ **206/621-1888. www.carolynstaleyprints.com.**

Davidson Galleries 🖈🖈   In the heart of the Pioneer Square neighborhood, this gallery focuses on three different areas—contemporary paintings and sculptures (often by Northwest artists), contemporary prints by American and European artists, and antique prints, some of which date from the 1500s. 313 Occidental Ave. S. ✆ **206/624-7684. www.davidsongalleries.com.**

Kimzey Miller Gallery ★★ The evocative Northwest landscape paintings of Z. Z. Wei are always a highlight of a visit to this downtown gallery not far from the Seattle Art Museum. Also keep an eye out for the sculptural glass-and-steel constructions of David Gignac. 1225 Second Ave. © 206/682-2339.

Art Glass

Foster/White Gallery ★★ If you are enamored of art glass, be sure to stop by one or both of the Foster/White galleries in Seattle. These galleries represent Dale Chihuly and always have works by this master glass artist. Some of Chihuly's pieces even sell for less than $10,000! Foster/White also represents top-notch Northwest artists in the disciplines of painting, ceramics, and sculpture. 123 S. Jackson St. © 206/622-2833. www.fosterwhite.com. Also at 1331 Fifth Ave. (© 206/583-0100).

Glasshouse Studio In the Pioneer Square area and founded in 1972, Glasshouse claims to be the oldest glassblowing studio in the Northwest. In the studio, you can watch handblown art glass being made, and then, in the gallery, you can check out the works of numerous local glass artists. 311 Occidental Ave. S. © 206/682-9939. www.glasshouse-studio.com.

Phoenix Rising Gallery Artists from around the country are represented here, and there is always some highly imaginative decorative work on display. Phoenix Rising also sells ceramic pieces and wooden crafts. 2030 Western Ave. © 206/728-2332. www.prgallery.com.

Vetri ★ Vetri, which is affiliated with the prestigious William Traver Gallery, showcases innovative work primarily from emerging glass artists and local area studios, but also sells works by artists from other countries. It's all high-quality and riotously colorful. Prices are relatively affordable. 1404 First Ave. © 206/667-9608. www.vetriglass.com.

William Traver Gallery ★★ In business for more than 25 years, this is one of the nation's top art-glass galleries and showcases the work of dozens of glass artists. The pieces shown here are on the cutting edge of glass art, so to speak, and will give you a good idea of the broad spectrum of work being created by contemporary glass artists. You'll find the gallery on the second floor. 110 Union St. © 206/587-6501. www.travergallery.com.

Native American Art

Ancient Grounds ★ This eclectic downtown antiques shop and natural-history gallery sells not only quality Northwest Coast Indian masks but also Japanese masks, rare mineral specimens, and a wide variety of other rare and unusual pieces from all over the world. There's even an espresso bar on the premises. 1220 First Ave. © 866/749-0747 or 206/749-0747.

Flury & Company Ltd. ★ This Pioneer Square gallery specializes in prints by famed Seattle photographer Edward S. Curtis, who is known for his late-19th- and early-20th-century portraits of Native Americans. The gallery also has an excellent selection of antique Native American art and artifacts. 322 First Ave. S. © 206/587-0260. www.fluryco.com.

The Legacy Ltd. ★★ In business since 1933, this is Seattle's oldest and finest gallery of contemporary and historic Northwest Coast Indian and Alaskan Eskimo art and artifacts. You'll find a large selection of masks, boxes, bowls, baskets, ivory artifacts, jewelry, prints, and books for the serious collector. 1003 First Ave. © 800/729-1562 or 206/624-6350. www.thelegacyltd.com.

Stonington Gallery   This is another of Seattle's top galleries specializing in contemporary Native American arts and crafts. It offers a good selection of Northwest Coast Indian masks, totem poles, mixed-media pieces, prints, carvings, and Northwest Coast–style jewelry. 119 S. Jackson St. © 866/405-4485 or 206/405-4040. www.stonington gallery.com.

BOOKS

In addition to the stores listed below, you'll find more than a half-dozen locations of **Barnes & Noble** around the metro area, including one downtown at 600 Pine St. (© **206/264-0156**). A **Borders** is downtown at 1501 Fourth Ave. (© **206/622-4599**).

Elliott Bay Book Company ☝☝   With battered wooden floors, a maze of rooms full of books, and frequent readings and in-store appearances by authors, this Pioneer Square bookstore feels as if it has been around forever. It has an excellent selection of titles on Seattle and the Northwest, so if you want to learn more about the region or are planning further excursions, stop by. There is also a good little cafe down in the basement. 101 S. Main St. © 800/962-5311 or 206/624-6600. www.elliottbaybook.com.

Flora & Fauna Books ☝ *Finds*   Gardeners, bird-watchers, and other naturephiles, take note: Down below street level in what passes for the active Seattle underground of the Pioneer Square area, you'll find a store filled with books that'll have you wishing you were in your garden or out in the woods identifying birds and flowers. 121 First Ave. S. © 206/623-4727. www.ffbooks.net.

COFFEE

All over the city, on almost every corner, you'll find espresso bars, cafes, and coffeehouses. Even though you can get coffee back home, you may want to stock up on whichever local coffee turns out to be your favorite. If you're a latte junkie, you can even make a pilgrimage to the shop that started it all: the Pike Place Market Starbucks, listed below, that was once the only Starbucks in the world.

Starbucks   Seattle is well known as a city of coffeeholics, and Starbucks is the main reason. This company has coffeehouses all over town (and all over the world), but this was once the only Starbucks in the world. Although you won't find any tables or chairs here, Starbucks fans shouldn't miss an opportunity to get their coffee at the source. Pike Place Market, 1912 Pike Place. © 206/448-8762. www.starbucks.com.

CRAFTS

The Northwest is a magnet for skilled craftspeople, and shops all around town sell a wide range of high-quality and imaginative crafts. At Pike Place Market, you can see what area craftspeople are creating and meet the artisans themselves.

Fireworks Fine Crafts Gallery   Playful, outrageous, bizarre, beautiful—these are just some of the adjectives used to describe the eclectic collection of Northwest crafts on sale at this Pioneer Square gallery. Cosmic clocks, wildly creative jewelry, and artistic picture frames are some of the fine and unusual items here. 210 First Ave. S. © 800/ 505-8882 or 206/682-9697. www.fireworksgallery.net. Also at Westlake Center, 400 Pine St. (© 206/682-6462); University Village, 2617 NE Village Lane (© 206/527-2858); and Bellevue Square, 196 Bellevue Sq., Bellevue (© 425/688-0933).

Northwest Craft Center ☝ *Finds*   This large gallery at Seattle Center is the city's premier ceramics showcase—it sells art ceramics that push the envelope of what can be made from clay. There's a gallery space, as well as a gift shop selling less expensive pieces. Seattle Center, 305 Harrison St. © 206/728-1555.

Northwest Fine Woodworking 🍂🍂 This store is a showcase for some of the most amazing woodworking you'll ever see. Be sure to stroll through here while in the Pioneer Square area, even if you aren't in the market for a one-of-a-kind piece of furniture. The warm hues of the exotic woods are soothing, and the designs are beautiful. Furniture, boxes, sculpture, vases, bowls, and much more are created by more than 20 Northwest artisans. 101 S. Jackson St. © 206/625-0542. www.nwfinewoodworking.com.

Twist 🍂 This store is filled with items such as unusual artist-created jewelry, Adirondack chairs made from recycled water skis, twisted glass vases, candlesticks, and ceramics. All are slightly offbeat, yet tasteful objets d'art. 600 Pine St. © 206/315-8080. www.twistonline.com.

DEPARTMENT STORES

Macy's 🍂 Seattle's "other" department store, formerly the Bon Marché, which was established in 1890 and only recently became a Macy's, is every bit as well stocked as the neighboring Nordstrom. With such competition nearby, this large department store tries hard to keep its customers happy. 1601 Third Ave. © 206/506-6000. www.macys.com.

Nordstrom 🍂🍂🍂 Known for personal service, Nordstrom stores have gained a reputation for being among the premier department stores in the United States. The company originated here in Seattle (opening its first store in 1901), and its customers are devotedly loyal. This is a state-of-the-art store, with all sorts of little boutiques, cafes, live piano music, and other features to make your shopping excursion a memorable experience.

Best of all, whether it's your 1st visit or your 50th, the knowledgeable staff will help you in any way they can. Prices may be a bit higher than those at other department stores, but for your money you get the best service available. The store is packed with shoppers during the half-yearly sale in June and anniversary sale in July. Nordstrom is also at area shopping malls. 500 Pine St. © 206/628-2111. www.nordstrom.com.

DISCOUNT SHOPPING

Nordstrom Rack 🍂 *Value* This is the Nordstrom overflow shop where you'll find three floors of discontinued lines as well as overstock, all at greatly reduced prices. Women's fashions make up the bulk of the merchandise here, but there is also a floor full of men's clothes and shoes, plus plenty of kids' clothes. 1601 Second Ave. © 206/448-8522. Also at 3920 124th St. SE, Bellevue (© 425/746-7200), and 19500 Alderwood Mall Pkwy., Lynnwood (© 425/774-6569).

FASHION

In addition to the stores listed below, you'll find quite a few familiar names in downtown Seattle, including Ann Taylor, Banana Republic, Barneys New York, Eddie Bauer, Gap, and Max Mara.

Men's & Women's Clothing

Eddie Bauer Eddie Bauer got his start here in Seattle back in 1920, and today the chain is one of the country's foremost purveyors of outdoor fashions—although these days, outdoor fashion is looking quite a bit more urban. 600 Pine St. © 206/622-2766. www.eddiebauer.com.

Ex Officio ⊛ *Value*   If you've already started planning your next trip, be sure to stop by this travel-clothing store up toward the north end of Belltown. It's an outlet for the Seattle-based Ex Officio and is packed full of lightweight, easy-care clothes designed for world travelers. 114 Vine St. ℂ **206/283-4746. www.exofficio.com.**

Northwest Pendleton ⊛⊛   For Northwesterners, and for many other people across the nation, Pendleton is and always will be *the* name in classic wool fashions. This store features tartan plaids and Indian-pattern separates, accessories, shawls, and blankets. 1313 Fourth Ave. ℂ **800/593-6773** or 206/682-4430. www.nwpendleton.com.

Women's Clothing

Alhambra   Alhambra stocks an eclectic collection of women's clothing and jewelry. There are purses from France, shoes from Italy, and fashions from Turkey and the U.S. These add up to a unique European look that's a little more refined than what you'll find at Baby and Co. 101 Pine St. ℂ **206/621-9571. www.alhambranet.com.**

Baby and Co. ⊛⊛   Claiming stores in Seattle and on Mars, this up-to-the-minute store stocks fashions that can be trendy, outrageous, or out of this world. The designs are strictly French, so you aren't likely to find these fashions in too many other places in the U.S. Whether you're into earth tones or bright colors, you'll likely find something you can't live without. 1936 First Ave. ℂ **206/448-4077.**

Endless Knot ⊛   If you've ever had a thing for funky fashions from Asia, you'll be amazed at how tasteful and upscale such styles can be. The racks of this Belltown boutique are lined with drapey natural-fiber fashions in bold colors—plus there are lots of accessories to accompany the clothes. 2300 First Ave. ℂ **206/448-0355.**

Passport Clothing ⊛   Soft and easygoing is the current style at this large store near Pike Place Market. Velvet, linen, cotton, rayon, and other natural fibers are the fabrics of choice here. 123 Pine St. ℂ **206/628-9799. www.passportclothing.com.**

Ragazzi's Flying Shuttle ⊛⊛   Fashion becomes art and art becomes fashion at this chic boutique-cum-gallery on Pioneer Square. Hand-woven fabrics and hand-painted silks are the specialties here, but, of course, such sophisticated fashions require equally unique body decorations in the form of exquisite jewelry creations. Designers and artists from the Northwest and the rest of the nation find an outlet for their creativity at the Flying Shuttle. 607 First Ave. ℂ **206/343-9762. www.ragazzisflyingshuttle.com.**

GIFTS/SOUVENIRS

Pike Place Market is the Grand Central Station of Seattle souvenirs, with stiff competition from Seattle Center and Pioneer Square.

Made in Washington   Whether it's salmon, wine, or Northwest crafts, you'll find a varied selection of Washington State products in this shop. This is an excellent place to pick up gifts for all those friends and family members who didn't get to come to Seattle with you. Pike Place Market, 1530 Post Alley (at Pine St.). ℂ **206/467-0788. www.madein washington.com. Also at Westlake Center, 400 Pine St. (ℂ 206/623-9753).**

Ye Olde Curiosity Shop *Kids*   If you can elbow your way into this waterfront institution, you'll find every inch of space, horizontal and vertical, covered with souvenirs and crafts, both tacky and tasteful (but mostly tacky). Surrounding this merchandise are the weird artifacts that have made this one of the most visited shops in Seattle. Pier 54, 1001 Alaskan Way. ℂ **206/682-5844. www.yeoldecuriosityshop.com.**

JEWELRY

Unique artist-crafted jewelry can be found at **Ragazzi's Flying Shuttle** (p. 137) and **Twist** (p. 136).

Facèré Jewelry Art Gallery ☆   A big rock on a gold band? How uninspired. At this tiny shop inside the City Centre shopping gallery, rings, earring, necklaces, and brooches are miniature works of contemporary art made from a fascinating range of materials. If you're searching for unique items to adorn your body, don't miss this shop. City Centre, 1420 Fifth Ave. ☏ 206/624-6768. www.facerejewelryart.com.

Fox's Gem Shop   Seattle's premier jeweler, Fox's has been around for more than 90 years and always has plenty of a girl's best friends. Colorless or fancy colored diamonds available here are of the finest cut. 1341 Fifth Ave. ☏ 800/733-2528 or 206/623-2528. www. foxsgem.com.

MALLS/SHOPPING CENTERS

City Centre ☆☆   This upscale downtown shopping center is the Seattle address of such familiar retailers as Barneys New York and Ann Taylor. There are works by Dale Chihuly and other Northwest glass artists on display throughout City Centre, as well as a very comfortable lounge where you can rest your feet and escape from the Seattle weather. 1420 Fifth Ave. ☏ 206/624-8800. www.shopcitycentre.com.

Pacific Place ☆☆   This downtown mall, located adjacent to Nordstrom, contains five levels of upscale shop-o-tainment, including Cartier, Tiffany & Co., bebe, Coach, Max Mara, seven restaurants, and a multiplex movie theater. A huge skylight fills the interior space with much-appreciated natural light, and an adjoining garage ensures that you'll find a place to park (maybe). 600 Pine St. ☏ 206/405-2655. www.pacificplaceseattle.com.

Westlake Center ☆   In the heart of Seattle's main shopping district, this upscale, urban shopping mall has more than 80 specialty shops, including Godiva, Crabtree & Evelyn, and Made in Washington, along with an extensive food court. The mall is also the southern terminus for the monorail to Seattle Center. 400 Pine St. ☏ 206/467-1600. www.westlakecenter.com.

MARKETS

Pike Place Market ☆☆☆   Pike Place Market is one of Seattle's most famous landmarks and tourist attractions. It shelters not only produce vendors, fishmongers, and butchers, but also artists, craftspeople, and performers. Hundreds of shops and dozens of restaurants (including some of Seattle's best) are tucked away in nooks and crannies on the numerous levels of the market. With so much to see and do, a trip to Pike Place Market can easily turn into an all-day affair. See also the sightseeing listing on p. 111. Pike St. and First Ave. ☏ 206/682-7453. www.pikeplacemarket.org.

Uwajimaya ☆☆   Typically, your local neighborhood supermarket probably has a section of Chinese cooking ingredients that's about 10 feet long, with half that space taken up by various brands of soy sauce. Now imagine your local supermarket with nothing but Asian foods, housewares, produce, and toys. That's Uwajimaya, Seattle's Asian supermarket in the heart of the International District. A big food court here serves all kinds of Asian food. 600 Fifth Ave. S. ☏ 206/624-6248. www.uwajimaya.com.

RECREATIONAL GEAR

Filson ☆☆   This Seattle company has been outfitting people headed outdoors ever since the Alaskan gold rush at the end of the 1890s. You won't find any high-tech fabrics here—just good old-fashioned wool, and plenty of it. Filson's clothes are meant to last a lifetime (and have the prices to prove it), so if you demand only the best, even when it comes to outdoor gear, be sure to check out this local institution. 1555 Fourth Ave. S. ✆ **800/297-1897** or 206/622-3147. www.filson.com.

REI ✫✫✫   Recreational Equipment, Inc. (REI), was founded here in Seattle back in 1938 and today is the nation's largest co-op selling outdoor gear. The company's impressive flagship, located just off I-5 not far from Lake Union, is a cross between a high-tech warehouse and a mountain lodge. This massive store sells almost anything you could ever need for pursuing your favorite outdoor sport. It also has a 65-foot climbing pinnacle, a rain room for testing rain gear, a mountain-bike trail for test-riding bikes, a footwear test trail, even a play area for kids. Up on the top floor is a cafe with an outstanding view of downtown. With all this under one roof, who needs to go outside? 222 Yale Ave. N. ✆ **888/873-1938** or 206/223-1944. www.rei.com.

SALMON

If you think that the fish at Pike Place Market looks great, but you could never get it home on the plane, think again. Any of the seafood vendors in Pike Place Market will pack your fresh salmon or Dungeness crab in an airline-approved container that will keep it fresh for up to 48 hours. Alternatively, you can buy vacuum-packed smoked salmon that will keep for years without refrigeration.

Pike Place Fish ✫✫   Located behind *Rachel,* Pike Place Market's life-size bronze pig, this fishmonger is just about the busiest spot in the market most days. What pulls in the crowds are the antics of the workers here. Order a big silvery salmon and you'll have employees shouting out your order and throwing the fish over the counter. Crowds are always gathered around the stall hoping to see some of the famous "flying fish." Pike Place Market, 86 Pike Place. ✆ **800/542-7732** or 206/682-7181. www.pikeplacefish.com.

Totem Smokehouse ✫   Northwest Coast Indians relied heavily on salmon for sustenance, and to preserve the fish, they used alder-wood smoke. The tradition is carried on today to produce smoked salmon, one of the Northwest's most delicious food products. This store, located at street level in Pike Place Market, sells vacuum-packed smoked salmon that will keep without refrigeration for several years if the package remains unopened. Pike Place Market, 1906 Pike Place. ✆ **800/972-5666** or 206/443-1710. www. totemsmokehouse.com.

TOYS

Archie McPhee ✫✫ *(Kids)*   You may already be familiar with this temple of the absurd through its mail-order catalog or website. Now imagine the fun of wandering through aisles full of goofy gags and all that other wacky stuff. Give yourself plenty of time and take a friend. You'll find Archie's place in the Ballard neighborhood. 2428 NW Market St. ✆ **206/297-0240.** www.mcphee.com.

Magic Mouse ✫ *(Kids)*   Adults and children alike have a hard time pulling themselves away from this, the wackiest toy store in downtown Seattle. It's conveniently located in Pioneer Square and has a good selection of European toys. 603 First Ave. ✆ **206/ 682-8097.**

Market Magic Shop ✫✫   No magic mice here, but if you want to learn how to pull a rabbit out of a hat, this is the place. This little Pike Place Market shop is a must for aspiring magicians. You'll find all kinds of great tricks and all the tools of the trade.

There are also juggling supplies and plenty of cool posters. Pike Place Market, 1501 Pike Place, no. 427. ℂ **206/624-4271.** www.speakeasy.org/magic.

10 After Dark

It's true that Seattleites spend much of their free time enjoying the city's natural surroundings, but that doesn't mean they overlook the more cultured evening pursuits. In fact, the winter weather that keeps people indoors, combined with a longtime desire to be the cultural mecca of the Northwest, has fueled a surprisingly active and diverse nightlife scene. Music lovers will find a plethora of classical, jazz, and rock offerings. The Seattle Opera is ranked one of the top companies in the country, and its stagings of Wagner's *Ring* series have achieved near-legendary status. The Seattle Symphony also receives frequent accolades. Likewise, the Seattle Repertory Theatre has won Tony awards for its productions, and a thriving fringe-theater scene keeps lovers of avant-garde theater discoursing for hours in cafes about the latest hysterical or thought-provoking performances.

Much of Seattle's evening entertainment scene is clustered in the **Seattle Center** and **Pioneer Square** areas. The former hosts theater, opera, and classical-music performances; the latter is a bar-and-nightclub district. Other concentrations of nightclubs can be found in **Belltown,** where crowds of the young and hip flock to the neighborhood's many trendy clubs, and **Capitol Hill,** with its ultracool gay scene. **Ballard,** formerly a Scandinavian enclave in North Seattle, attracts a primarily middle-class, not-too-hip, not-too-old crowd, including lots of college students and techies. It's not the hipster Belltown scene, it's not the PBR-swilling blues scene of Pioneer Square, and it's not the sleek gay scene of Capitol Hill. It's just a comfortable neighborhood nightlife scene.

While winter is a time to enjoy the performing arts, summer brings an array of outdoor festivals. They take place during daylight hours as much as after dark, and information on such festivals and performance series is found in this chapter.

To find out what's going on when you're in town, pick up a free copy of *Seattle Weekly* (www.seattleweekly.com), Seattle's arts-and-entertainment newspaper. You'll find it in bookstores, convenience stores, grocery stores, newsstands, and newspaper boxes around downtown and other neighborhoods. On Friday, the *Seattle Times* includes a section called "Ticket," and it's a handy guide to the week's arts-and-entertainment offerings.

THE PERFORMING ARTS

While the Seattle Symphony performs in downtown's Benaroya Hall, the main venues for the performing arts are primarily clustered at **Seattle Center,** the special events complex built for the 1962 World's Fair. Here, in the shadow of the Space Needle, you'll find Marion Oliver McCaw Hall, Bagley Wright Theater, Intiman Playhouse, Seattle Children's Theatre, Seattle Center Coliseum, Memorial Stadium, and Experience Music Project's Sky Church performance hall.

OPERA & CLASSICAL MUSIC

The **Seattle Opera** (ℂ **800/426-1619** or 206/389-7676; www.seattleopera.org), which performs at Seattle Center's Marion Oliver McCaw Hall, is considered one of the finest opera companies in the country. It is *the* Wagnerian opera company in the United States. The stagings of Wagner's four-opera *The Ring of the Nibelungen* are breathtaking spectacles that draw crowds from around the country. However, because the cycle was just staged in 2005, it will be a few years before Wagner's magnum opus is performed again. In addition to such classical operas as *Carmen* and *Parsifal,* the regular season usually includes a more contemporary production. Ticket prices range from $41 to $144.

The 90-musician **Seattle Symphony** (ⓒ **866/833-4747** or 206/215-4747; www. seattlesymphony.org), which performs at the acoustically superb Benaroya Hall, offers an amazingly diverse season that runs from September to July. With several different series, there's something for every classical-music fan, including evenings of classical, light classical, and pops music, plus afternoon concerts, children's concerts, guest artists, and more. Ticket prices range from $15 to $85.

THEATER
Mainstream Theaters
The **Seattle Repertory Theatre** (ⓒ **877/900-9285** or 206/443-2222; www.seattlerep. org), which performs at the Bagley Wright and Leo K. theaters at Seattle Center, 155 Mercer St., is Seattle's top professional theater and stages the most consistently entertaining productions in the city. The Rep's season runs from September to June, with six plays performed in the main theater and two in the more intimate Leo K. Theatre. Productions range from classics to world premieres. Tickets go for $15 to $46. When available, rush tickets are distributed a half-hour before showtime for $20.

With a season that runs from April to December, the **Intiman Theatre** (ⓒ **206/ 269-1900;** www.intiman.org), which performs at the Intiman Playhouse, Seattle Center, 201 Mercer St., fills in the gap left by those months when the Seattle Rep's lights are dark. Ticket prices range from $27 to $46.

A Contemporary Theater (ACT), Kreielsheimer Place, 700 Union St. (ⓒ **206/ 292-7676;** www.acttheatre.org), performing in the historic Eagles Building theater adjacent to the Washington State Convention and Trade Center, offers slightly more adventurous productions than the other major theater companies in Seattle, though it's not nearly as avant-garde as some of the smaller companies. ACT also puts on Seattle's annual staging of *A Christmas Carol.* The season runs from May to December. Ticket prices usually range from $25 to $50.

Ticket, Please
Full-price advance-purchase tickets to the Seattle Symphony and to many performing-arts events are handled by **Ticketmaster** (ⓒ **206/292-ARTS;** www. ticketmaster.com). For half-price, day-of-show tickets (and 1-day advance tickets for matinees) to a wide variety of performances all over the city, stop by **Ticket/Ticket** (ⓒ **206/324-2744**), which has three sales booths in the Seattle area: one in Pike Place Market, one on Capitol Hill, and one in Bellevue. The Pike Place Market location, in the Pike Place Market information booth at First Avenue and Pike Street, is open Tuesday through Sunday from noon to 6pm. The Capitol Hill booth is in the Broadway Market, 401 Broadway E., and is open Tuesday through Saturday from noon to 7pm and Sunday from noon to 6pm. The Bellevue booth is in the Meydenbauer Center, NE Sixth Street and 112th Avenue, and is open Tuesday through Sunday from noon to 6pm. Ticket/Ticket charges a small service fee, the amount of which depends on the ticket price.

Fringe Theater

Not only does Seattle have a healthy mainstream performing-arts community, it also has the sort of fringe theater life once only associated with such cities as New York, Los Angeles, London, and Edinburgh. The city's more avant-garde performance companies frequently grab their share of the limelight with daring, outrageous, and thought-provoking productions.

Check the listings in *Seattle Weekly* or the Friday *Seattle Times* "Ticket" entertainment guide to see what's going on during your visit. The following venues are some of Seattle's more reliable places for way-off-Broadway productions, performance art, and spoken-word performances:

- **Book-It Repertory Theater,** Seattle Center, 305 Harrison St. (*©* **206/216-0833;** www.book-it.org). This theater company specializes in adapting literary works for the stage; it also stages works by local playwrights. Most performances are held at Seattle Center.
- **Empty Space Theatre,** 3509 Fremont Ave. N. (*©* **206/547-7500;** www.empty space.org). One of Seattle's biggest little theaters, Empty Space stages mostly comedies and is popular with a young crowd.
- **Re-Bar,** 1114 Howell St. (*©* **206/233-9873**). Although this is primarily a nightclub popular with the Seattle gay crowd, it is also a performance-art center that stages the sorts of unusual productions that may appeal to the city's gay community. In other words, some pretty outrageous stuff makes it to the stage.
- **Seattle Public Theater at the Bathhouse on Green Lake,** 7312 W. Green Lake Dr. N. (*©* **206/524-1300;** www.seattlepublictheater.com). Seattle Public Theater stages wacky performances at the old Green Lake bathhouse. Shows range from original musicals to updated versions of Shakespeare. The location right on the lake makes this a great place to catch some live theater.
- **Theater Schmeater,** 1500 Summit Ave. (*©* **206/324-5801;** www.schmeater.org). Lots of weird and sometimes wonderful comedy, including ever-popular live, late-night stagings of episodes from The Twilight Zone.

DANCE

Although it has a well-regarded ballet company and a theater dedicated to contemporary dance and performance art, Seattle is not nearly as devoted to dance as to theater and classical music. That said, hardly a week goes by without some sort of dance performance being staged somewhere in the city. Touring companies of all types, the University of Washington Dance Department faculty and student performances, the UW World Series (see below for details), and the Northwest New Works Festival (see below for details) all bring plenty of creative movement to the stages of Seattle. Check *Seattle Weekly* or the *Seattle Times* for a calendar of all upcoming performances.

The **Pacific Northwest Ballet,** Marion Oliver McCaw Hall, 301 Mercer St. (*©* **206/441-2424;** www.pnb.org), is Seattle's premier dance company. During the season, which runs from September to June, the company presents a wide range of classics, new works, and (the company's specialty) pieces choreographed by George Balanchine. This company's performance of *The Nutcracker,* with outstanding dancing and sets, plus costumes by children's book author Maurice Sendak, is the highlight of every season. The Pacific Northwest Ballet performs at Marion Oliver McCaw Hall at Seattle Center. Ticket prices range from $20 to $137.

Much more adventurous choreography is the domain of **On the Boards,** Behnke Center for Contemporary Performance, 100 W. Roy St. (© **206/217-9888;** www. ontheboards.org), which, although it stages a wide variety of performance art, is best known as Seattle's premier modern-dance venue. In addition to dance performances by Northwest artists, there are a variety of productions each year by internationally known performance artists. Tickets go for $7 to $25.

MAJOR PERFORMANCE HALLS

With ticket prices for shows and concerts so high these days, it pays to be choosy about what you see, but sometimes *where* you see it is just as important. Benaroya Hall, the Seattle Symphony's downtown home, has such excellent acoustics that a performance here is worth attending just for the sake of hearing how a good symphony hall should sound. Seattle also has two restored historic theaters that are as much a part of a performance as what happens onstage.

Benaroya Hall (© **206/215-4747**), on Third Avenue between Union and University streets in downtown Seattle, is the home of the Seattle Symphony. This state-of-the-art performance hall houses two concert halls—the main hall and a smaller recital hall. It's home to the Watjen concert organ, a magnificent pipe organ, as well as a Starbucks, a cafe, a symphony store, and a pair of Dale Chihuly chandeliers. Amenities aside, the main hall's excellent acoustics are the big attraction.

The **5th Avenue Theatre,** 1308 Fifth Ave. (© **206/625-1900** for information, or 206/292-ARTS for tickets; www.5thavenuetheatre.org), which first opened its doors in 1926 as a vaudeville house, is a loose re-creation of the imperial throne room in Beijing's Forbidden City. Today the astounding interior is as good a reason as any to see a show here. Don't miss an opportunity to attend a performance. Broadway shows are the theater's mainstay; ticket prices usually range from $20 to $70.

The **Paramount Theatre,** 911 Pine St. (© **206/682-1414;** www.theparamount. com), one of Seattle's few historic theaters, has been restored to its original beauty and today shines with all the brilliance as when it first opened. New lighting and sound systems have brought the theater up to contemporary standards. The theater hosts everything from rock concerts to Broadway musicals. Tickets are available through Ticketmaster.

Affiliated with the Paramount Theatre, the **Moore Theatre,** 1932 Second Ave. (© **206/682-1414;** www.themoore.com), in Belltown, gets lots of national rock acts that won't likely draw as many people as bands that play at the Paramount.

PERFORMING ARTS SERIES

The **UW World Series** (© **800/859-5342** or 206/543-4880; www.uwworldseries. org), held at Meany Hall on the University of Washington campus, is actually several different series that include chamber music, classical piano, dance, and world music and theater. Together these four series keep the Meany Hall stage busy between October and May. Special events are also scheduled. Tickets go for $29 to $60. The box office is at 4001 University Way NE, which is off campus.

Seattle loves the theater, including fringe works. Avant-garde performances are the specialty of the **Northwest New Works Festival** (© **206/217-9888;** www.ontheboards. org), an annual barrage of contemporary dance and performance art staged each spring by On the Boards.

Summer is a time of outdoor festivals and performance series in Seattle, and should you be in town during the sunny months, you'll have a wide variety of alfresco performances from which to choose. The city's biggest summer music festivals are the **Northwest Folklife Festival,** over Memorial Day weekend, and **Bumbershoot,** over Labor Day weekend. See the "Washington Calendar of Events" (p. 20) for details.

Cingular Summer Nights at South Lake Union Park, 860 Terry Ave. N. (℡ 206/ 281-7788 for information, or 206/628-0888 for tickets; www.summernights.org), presents a summer's worth of big-name acts at a park at the south end of Lake Union. Blues, jazz, rock, and folk acts generally pull in a 30- to 50-something crowd. Ticket prices range from $32 to $56.

At **Woodland Park Zoo** (℡ 206/615-0076; www.zoo.org), the **Zoo Tunes** concert series brings in more big-name performers from the world of jazz, easy listening, blues, and rock. Tickets go for $16 to $21; bear in mind that they usually sell out as soon as they go on sale in early May.

North of Seattle in Woodinville, **Summer Concerts at Chateau Ste. Michelle,** 14111 NE 145th St. (℡ 425/415-3300 for information, or 206/628-0888 for tickets; www.ste-michelle.com), is the area's most enjoyable outdoor summer concert series. It's held at the winery's amphitheater, which is surrounded by beautiful estate-like grounds. Chateau Ste. Michelle is Washington's largest winery, so plenty of wine is available. The lineup is calculated to appeal to the 30- to 50-something crowd (past performers have included Mark Knopfler, Gipsy Kings, Steve Winwood, and regional favorite Pink Martini). Ticket prices range from $30 to $80, with a few shows priced higher in summer. See p. 150 for more on Woodinville and Chateau Ste. Michelle.

THE CLUB & MUSIC SCENE

If you have the urge to do a bit of clubbing and barhopping, there's no better place to start than **Pioneer Square.** Good times are guaranteed, whether you want to hear a live band, hang out in a good old-fashioned bar, or dance. Keep in mind that this neighborhood tends to attract a very rowdy crowd (lots of frat boys) and can be pretty rough late at night.

Belltown, north of Pike Place Market, is another good place to club-hop. Clubs here are way more style-conscious than those in Pioneer Square and tend to attract 20- and 30-something trendsetters.

Seattle's other main nightlife district is the former Scandinavian neighborhood of **Ballard,** where you'll find more than a half-dozen nightlife establishments, including taverns, bars, and live-music clubs.

Capitol Hill, a few blocks uphill from downtown Seattle, is the city's main gay nightlife neighborhood, with much of the action centered around the corner of East Madison Street and 15th Avenue East.

FOLK, ROCK & REGGAE
Downtown
The Triple Door ✈✈ Popular music for adults? What a concept! This swanky new nightclub is a total novelty in the Seattle club world. It isn't geared toward the 20-something crowd. The music is diverse—from jazz to world beat to flamenco to Maria Muldaur, the Tubes, and Ottmar Liebert. You'll find the club in the basement below the ever-popular Wild Ginger restaurant, across the street from Benaroya Hall. 216 Union St. ℡ 206/838-4333. www.thetripledoor.net. Cover none–$50 (mostly $20–$25).

Pioneer Square

The Pioneer Square area is Seattle's main live-music neighborhood, and the clubs have banded together on Friday and Saturday nights to make things easy for music fans. The **Pioneer Square Club Stamp** plan lets you pay one admission to get into nine clubs. The charge is $12 ($10 from 8–9pm). Participating clubs currently include Doc Maynard's, the Central Saloon, Fenix Underground, the Last Supper Club, the New Orleans Creole Restaurant, Tiki Bob's, Howl at the Moon, Juan O'Reilly's, and the J & M Cafe. Most of these clubs are short on style and hit-or-miss when it comes to music (which makes the joint cover a great way to find out where the good music is on any given night).

Central Saloon   Established in 1892, the Central is the oldest saloon in Seattle. As a local institution, it's a must-stop during a night out in Pioneer Square. You might catch sounds ranging from funk to reggae. 207 First Ave. S. ☎ **206/622-0209**. www.central saloon.com. Cover $5–$12 (Pioneer Square Club Stamp).

Fenix Underground   This Fenix didn't rise from its own ashes; it rose from the rubble of its earthquake-damaged former location. This underground club, located right in Occidental Park, is the most happening place in the neighborhood. There's also a Fenix Aboveground upstairs. 109 S. Washington St. ☎ **206/405-4323**. www.fenixunderground. com. Cover none–$12 (Pioneer Square Club Stamp); special shows $15–$25.

Belltown & Environs

The Crocodile Café☆   With its rambunctious decor, this Belltown establishment is a combination nightclub, bar, and restaurant. There's live rock Tuesday through Saturday nights, and the music calendar here is always eclectic, with everything from rock to folk to jazz. However, alternative rock dominates, as it has since the heyday of Seattle grunge. 2200 Second Ave. ☎ **206/441-5611**. www.thecrocodile.com. Cover $6–$20.

EMP   The Experience Music Project, Seattle's humongous lump o' color rock museum, isn't just some morgue for dead rockers. This place is a showcase for real live rockers, too. **Liquid Lounge,** a small club with no cover and a wide range of musical sensibilities, is a good place to catch anything from a reggae dance party to a hip-hop or acoustic show. 325 Fifth Ave. N. ☎ **206/770-2702**. www.emplive.com. No cover.

Showbox   Across the street from Pike Place Market, this club books a wide variety of local and name rock acts. Definitely *the* downtown rock venue for performers with a national following. 1426 First Ave. ☎ **206/628-3151**. www.showboxonline.com. Cover $5–$25.

Capitol Hill

Baltic Room   This swanky Capitol Hill hangout for the beautiful people stages a wide range of music (mostly DJs) encompassing everything from dancehall reggae to hip-hop and *bhangra* (contemporary Indian disco). 1207 Pine St. ☎ **206/625-4444**. www. balticroom.com. Cover $3–$10.

Century Ballroom   With a beautiful wooden dance floor, this is *the* place in Seattle for a night out if you're into swing, salsa, or tango. Every week, there are a couple of nights of swing and salsa dancing, complete with lessons early in the evening. Tuesday nights are currently tango night. The crowd here is very diverse, with patrons of all ages. 915 E. Pine St. ☎ **206/324-7263**. www.centuryballroom.com. Cover $3–$15.

Ballard
Tractor Tavern   For an ever-eclectic schedule of music for people whose tastes go beyond the latest rap artist, the Tractor Tavern is the place to be. You can catch almost anything from rockabilly to Hawaiian slack-key guitar to singer-songwriters to banjo music to Celtic to folk to zydeco. Sound like your kind of place? 5213 Ballard Ave. NW. © 206/789-3599. www.tractortavern.citysearch.com. Cover $5–$20.

JAZZ & BLUES
Dimitriou's Jazz Alley ♠♠   Cool and sophisticated, this Belltown establishment is reminiscent of a New York jazz club and has been around for more than 20 years. Seattle's premier jazz venue, it books only the best performers, including many name acts. 2033 Sixth Ave. © 206/441-9729. www.jazzalley.com. Cover usually $19–$27.

New Orleans Creole Restaurant   If you like your food and your jazz hot, check out the New Orleans in Pioneer Square. Throughout the week, there's Cajun, Dixieland, R&B, jazz, and blues. 114 First Ave. S. © 206/622-2563. Cover none–$12 (Pioneer Square Club Stamp).

The Pampas Room   You'll know you're in the right spot when you can smell the cigar smoke wafting up from this basement nightclub. The big-money crowd claims this retro-swank upscale jazz club as its very own on Friday and Saturday nights, which features live jazz. 90 Wall St. © 206/728-1337. No cover.

Tula's ♠   This is the real thing: a jazz club that's a popular jazz musicians' after-hours hangout and a good place to catch up-and-coming performers. American and Mediterranean food is served. 2214 Second Ave. © 206/443-4221. www.tulas.com. Cover $5–$15.

CABARET
Cabaret at Crepe de Paris Restaurant   Throughout the year, this club stages a wide variety of entertaining programs of music, dance, and humor. Updated torch songs and numbers from classic musicals assure that the shows here will appeal to young and old alike. Reservations are required. Rainier Square, 1333 Fifth Ave. © 206/623-4111. Cover $15–$20 show only; $42–$44 dinner and show.

The Pink Door ♠♠   Better known as Pike Place Market's unmarked restaurant, The Pink Door has a hopping after-work bar scene that tends to attract a 30-something crowd. It also doubles as a cabaret featuring Seattle's most eclectic lineup of performers, including cross-dressing tango dancers, trapeze artists, and the like. Lots of fun and not to be missed. 1919 Post Alley. © 206/443-3241. No cover.

DANCE CLUBS
Bada Lounge   If Swedish modern, molded plastic, and techno are your scene, this place is for you. With its retro-futurist decor and wall of monitors projecting video wallpaper, this club/restaurant is as stylin' as they come here in Seattle. The white-on-white decor is calculated to make people in black look their very best. Early in the evening, this is a Pan-Asian restaurant; later on, there's dancing to beat-driven dance tracks. 2230 First Ave. © 206/374-8717. www.badalounge.com. Cover none–$5.

Contour   A few blocks up First Avenue from Pioneer Square, this modern dance club attracts a more diverse crowd than most Pioneer Square clubs. The music ranges from deep house to trance to drum and bass, and the partying on Friday and Saturday goes on until 7am the next day. Laser-light shows, fire dancers—this joint is one wild party! 807 First Ave. © 206/447-7704. www.clubcontour.com. Cover none–$10.

Tia Lou's/Lico Lounge   With its open-air deck atop a covered parking lot, this second-floor bar provides not only a great spot for a few drinks on a warm summer evening, but also a primo people-watching perspective on the busiest bar block in Belltown. Margaritas are the drink of choice here. There's DJ dance music Friday and Saturday nights. 2218 First Ave. ℂ **206/733-8226.** Cover $10.

THE BAR & PUB SCENE
BARS
The Waterfront
Six-Seven Lounge ✴   If you get any closer to the water, you'll have wet feet. Located inside downtown Seattle's only waterfront hotel, this bar boasts what just may be the best bar view in the city. Watch the ferries come and go, or see the sun set over Puget Sound and the Olympics. In the Edgewater, Pier 67, 2411 Alaskan Way. ℂ **206/269-4575.**

Downtown
The Bookstore—A Bar   Just off the lobby of the posh Alexis Hotel, this cozy little bar is—surprise—filled with books. There are plenty of interesting magazines on hand as well, so if you want to sip a single malt and smoke a cigar but don't want to deal with crowds and noise, this is a great option. Very classy. In the Alexis Hotel, 1007 First Ave. ℂ **206/382-1506.**

Oliver's   Maybe you've seen one too many places that claim to make the best martini and you're feeling dubious. Here at Oliver's, they've repeatedly put their martinis to the test and come out on top. The atmosphere is classy and the happy-hour appetizers are good, but in the end, only you can decide whether these martinis are the best in Seattle. In the Mayflower Park Hotel, 405 Olive Way. ℂ **206/623-8700.**

Belltown
Axis   This is where it all begins most weekend nights for the black-clad crowds of ultrahip Seattle singles who crowd the sidewalks and bars of Belltown. Get here early enough and maybe you'll even snag one of the coveted sidewalk tables. If you're too late, don't worry: The front walls roll up and there's still the second row. It's a serious singles scene with good food. 2214 First Ave. ℂ **206/441-9600.**

See Sound Lounge   With walls of colored lights and a front wall that swings open to let in the summer air, this retro-mod bar on a pretty street is one of Belltown's hottest hangouts. The cool scene here is a required stop during a night out in this trendy neighborhood. 115 Blanchard St. ℂ **206/374-3733.** www.seesoundlounge.com.

The Virginia Inn   Although the Virginia Inn is located in *très chic* Belltown, this bar/restaurant has a decidedly Old Seattle feel, due in large part to the fact that this place has been around since 1903. Best of all, this is a nonsmoking bar and it serves French food! 1937 First Ave. ℂ **206/728-1937.**

Pike Place Market
Alibi Room   If you've been on your feet all day in Pike Place Market and have had it with the crowds of people, duck down the alley under the market clock and slip through the door of this hideaway. The back-alley setting gives this place an atmospheric speakeasy feel. Popular with artists and other creative types. 85 Pike St. ℂ **206/623-3180.**

The Tasting Room ✴   In the Pike Place Market area, this cozy wine bar has the feel of a wine cellar and is cooperatively operated by several small Washington State wineries. You can taste the wines of Apex Cellars, Camaraderie Cellars, Harlequin Wine

Cellars, JM Cellars, Wilridge Winery, and Wineglass Cellars, or buy wine by the glass or bottle. Light snacks are also available. 1924 Post Alley. © **206/770-9463**. www.winesof washington.com.

Pioneer Square

FX McRory's Right across the street from the Seattle Seahawks' Qwest Field and not far from Safeco Field, this bar attracts well-heeled sports fans (with the occasional Mariners and Seahawks players thrown in for good measure). You'll find Seattle's largest selection of bourbons here. There's also an oyster bar and good food. 419 Occidental Ave. S. © **206/623-4800**. www.fxmcrorys.com.

Ibiza Dinner Club ⊛ Pioneer Square is mostly all about dive bars, which really makes this swanky restaurant/bar stand out in the crowd. This place is just gorgeous, the sort of place that you might expect to find in Belltown, not here in Pioneer Square. The decor and patrons are beautiful, and the food and cocktails are very creative. 528 Second Ave. © **206/381-9090**. www.ibizadinnerclub.com.

BREWPUBS

Big Time Brewery & Alehouse Big Time, Seattle's oldest brewpub, is located in the University District and is done up to look like a turn-of-the-20th-century tavern, complete with a 100-year-old back bar and a wooden refrigerator. The pub serves as many as 12 of its own brews at any given time, and some of these can be pretty unusual. 4133 University Way NE. © **206/545-4509**. www.bigtimebrewery.com.

Elysian Brewing Company ⊛ Although the brewery at this Capitol Hill brewpub is one of the smallest in the city, the pub itself is quite large and has an industrial feel that says "local brewpub." The stouts and strong ales are especially good, and the brewers' creativity here just can't be beat. Hands-down the best brewpub in Seattle. There's a second Elysian at 2106 N. 55th St. (© **206/547-5929**). 1221 E. Pike St. © **206/ 860-1920**. www.elysianbrewing.com.

The Pike Pub & Brewery Located in an open, central space inside Pike Place Market, this brewpub makes excellent stout and pale ale. With its comfortable couches, the Pike is a great place to get off your feet after a day of exploring the market. 1415 First Ave. © **206/622-6044**. www.pikebrewing.com.

Pyramid Ale House This pub, south of Pioneer Square in a big old warehouse, is part of the brewery that makes the Northwest's popular Pyramid beers and ales. It's a favorite spot for dinner and drinks before or after baseball games at Safeco Field and football games at Qwest Field. There's good pub food, too. 1201 First Ave. S. © **206/682-3377**. www.pyramidbrew.com.

IRISH PUBS

Fadó This Irish pub is part of a national chain, but has the feel of an independent pub. Lots of antiques, old signs, and a dark, cozy feel make it a very comfortable place for a pint. There's live Irish music several nights a week, a weekly pub quiz, and of course you can watch soccer matches on the telly. 801 First Ave. © **206/264-2700**. www.fado irishpub.com. Cover none–$5.

Kells At one time, the space now occupied by this pub was the embalming room of a mortuary. These days, the scene is much more lively and has the feel of a casual Dublin pub. Kells pulls a good pint of Guinness, serves traditional Irish meals, and features live Irish music 7 nights a week. Pike Place Market, 1916 Post Alley. ℂ 206/728-1916. www.kellsirish.com. Cover $5 Fri–Sat only.

The Owl & Thistle Pub   Right around the corner from Fadó is this equally authentic-feeling pub. The Post Alley entrance gives this place the ambience of a back-street Dublin pub. There's live music most nights, with the house band playing Irish music on Friday and Saturday nights. 808 Post Alley. ℂ 206/621-7777. www.owlnthistle.com.

THE GAY & LESBIAN SCENE

Capitol Hill is Seattle's main gay neighborhood; consequently, it has the city's greatest concentration of gay and lesbian bars and clubs. Look for the readily available *Seattle Gay News* (ℂ 206/324-4297; www.sgn.org), where you'll find ads for many of the city's gay bars and nightclubs.

BARS

C. C. Attle's   Perched high on Capitol Hill, this bar is a local gay landmark and primarily attracts an older crowd; it can be something of a regulars' scene. It's also well known for its cheap, strong cocktails. There are a couple of patios and three separate bars. 1501 E. Madison St. ℂ 206/726-0565.

The Cuff Complex Seattle   A virtual multiplex of gay entertainment, this place has no fewer than three separate bars. There's a quiet bar, a dance club, and a patio for those rain-free nights. It's primarily a leather-and-Levis crowd, but you're still welcome even if you forgot to pack your leather pants. 1533 13th Ave. ℂ 206/323-1525. www.thecuff. com. Cover none–$10.

Manray Video Bar   This retro-futuristic Capitol Hill bar is well known for attracting Seattle's beautiful people, at least the gay ones. High-priced designer martinis are the specialty. In the summer you can hang out on the patio, but it's all the video monitors that make this such an unusual place to see and be seen. 514 E. Pine St. ℂ 206/568-0750. www.manrayvideo.com.

R Place Bar & Grill   With three floors of entertainment, you hardly need to go anywhere else for a night on the town. There's a video bar on the ground floor, pool tables and video games on the second floor, and a dance floor up on the top level. 619 E. Pine St. ℂ 206/322-8828. www.rplaceseattle.com.

Thumpers   Across the street from C. C. Attle's, Thumpers is a classy bar/restaurant done up in oak, and it's been a favorite of Seattle's gay community for more than 20 years. The seats by the fireplace are perfect on a cold and rainy night, while for sunny days there are two decks with great views. There's live music several nights each week (maybe even a Judy & Liza show). 1500 E. Madison St. ℂ 206/328-3800.

Wildrose   This friendly restaurant/bar is a longtime favorite of the Capitol Hill lesbian community and claims to be the oldest lesbian bar on the West Coast. In spring and summer there is an outdoor seating area. Pool tournaments and karaoke are mainstays here. 1021 E. Pike St. ℂ 206/324-9210. www.thewildrosebar.com. Cover none–$4.

DANCE CLUBS

Neighbours   This has been the favorite dance club of Capitol Hill's gay community for years. As at other clubs, different nights of the week feature different styles of music. You'll find this club's entrance down the alley. 1509 Broadway. ℂ 206/324-5358. www.neighboursonline.com. Cover none –$12.

Re-Bar   Each night there's a different theme, with the DJs spinning everything from funk to punk. This club isn't exclusively gay, but it's still a favorite of Seattle's gay community. 1114 Howell St. ⟨ 206/233-9873. www.rebarseattle.com. Cover none–$10.

AT THE MOVIES

Summertime in the Fremont neighborhood brings **Fremont Saturday Nite Outdoor Movies** (⟨ 206/781-4230; fremontoutdoormovies.com), a series that features modern classics, B movies (sometimes with live overdubbing by a local improv comedy company), and indie shorts. Films are screened on Saturday nights in the parking lot at North 35th Street and Phinney Avenue North. The parking lot opens at 7:30pm; there is a $5 suggested donation.

Want to sip a martini while watching the latest indie film hit? Find out what's playing at Belltown's **Big Picture Seattle,** 2505 First Ave. (⟨ 206/256-0566 or 206/256-0572; www.thebigpicture.net). This cool little basement theater below El Gaucho steakhouse is a favorite of indie film fans.

11 Easy Excursions: Seattle's Wine Country

SEATTLE'S WINE COUNTRY

Washington is the fastest-growing wine region in the country and today produces more wine than any other state except California. Although the main wine country lies hundreds of miles to the east in central and eastern Washington, a small winery region is but a 30-minute drive north of Seattle outside the town of Woodinville. A number of wineries in the Woodinville area are open to the public on a regular basis (with several others open only by appointment or not open to the public at all), and the proximity to Seattle makes this an excellent day's outing. Woodinville is also home to the Northwest's top restaurant and a gorgeous modern lodge, which together with the wineries add up to a great place for a romantic getaway.

To reach this miniature wine country, head north on I-5, take the NE 124th Street exit, and drive east to 132nd Avenue NE. Turn left here and continue north to NE 143rd Place/NE 145th Street. Turn right and drive down the hill. At the bottom of the hill, you will be facing the first of the area's wineries.

The **Columbia Winery,** 14030 NE 145th St. (⟨ 800/488-2347 or 425/488-2776; www.columbiawinery.com), has Washington's largest tasting bar and produces a wide range of good wines. It's open daily from 10am to 7pm in summer (closes at 5pm on Mon in other months). This place is crowded on weekends, so try to arrive early.

Directly across NE 145th Street from the Columbia Winery, you'll find the largest and most famous of the wineries in the area, **Chateau Ste. Michelle** ⟨, 14111 NE 145th St. (⟨ 800/267-6793 or 425/488-1133; www.ste-michelle.com). Open daily from 10am to 5pm, this is by far the most beautiful one in the Northwest, located in a grand mansion on a historic 1912 estate. It's also the largest one in the state and is known for its consistent quality. If you take the free tour, you can sample several of the less expensive wines. For a $5 tasting fee, you can try some older reserve vintages. For $8, you can have a private tasting of older wines (reservations suggested; call ⟨ 425/415-3633). Because this place is so big and produces so many different wines, you never know what you may find being poured in the tasting room. An amphitheater on the grounds stages big-name music performances in summer.

If you drive north from Chateau Ste. Michelle, NE 145th Street becomes Wood-inville-Redmond Road (Wash. 202) and you soon come to **Silver Lake Winery,** 15029 Woodinville-Redmond Rd. NE (© **425/485-2437;** www.silverlakewinery. com). This winery crafts good reds, but can be hit-or-miss. It's open daily from noon to 5pm.

Next up the road heading north is a hidden gem, the small **Facelli Winery,** 16120 Woodinville-Redmond Rd. NE (© **425/488-1020;** www.facelliwinery.com), which is open Saturday and Sunday from noon to 4pm and produces excellent reds.

Continue a little farther to **DiStefano Winery,** 12280 Woodinville Dr. SE (© **425/487-1648;** www.distefanowinery.com), which is best known for its full-bodied red wines, but also produces some memorable whites. The tasting room is open Saturday and Sunday from noon to 5pm.

From DiStefano, drive east on NE 175th Street/NE Woodinville-Duvall Road, turn left on NE North Woodinville Way, and then turn right on 144th Avenue NE to reach **Austin Robaire Vintners,** 19501 144th Ave. NE (© **206/406-0360;** www.austin robaire.com), which produces superb (and expensive) red wines made from grapes grown at some of Washington's top vineyards. The tasting room here is open only the first and third Saturdays of each month from 1 to 4pm.

Nearby, **Mathews Cellars,** 16116 140th Place NE (© **425/487-9810;** www. matthewscellars.com), is open to the public, only on Saturday from noon to 4pm. To find this winery, drive south from Woodinville on Wash. 202/140th Place NE.

FAST FACTS: Seattle

Airport See chapter 2, "Getting There," and "Arriving," earlier in this chapter.

Car Rentals See "Getting Around," earlier in this chapter.

Dentist Contact the Dental Referral Service (© 800/510-7315).

Doctor To find a physician, check at your hotel for a referral, contact **Swedish Medical Center** (© 800/SWEDISH; www.swedish.org), or call the referral line of the **Virginia Mason Medical Center** (© 888/862-2737).

Emergencies For police, fire, or medical emergencies, phone © 911.

Hospitals Hospitals convenient to downtown include **Swedish Medical Center,** 747 Broadway (© 206/386-6000; www.Swedish.org), and **Virginia Mason Medical Center,** 1100 Ninth Ave. (© 206/583-6433 for emergencies, or 206/624-1144 for information).

Information See "Visitor Information," earlier in this chapter.

Internet Access First, ask at your hotel to see if it provides Internet access. Alternatively, you can head to the **Seattle Central Library,** 1000 Fourth Ave., (© 206/386-4636), which has hundreds of online computer terminals.

Newspapers & Magazines The *Seattle Post-Intelligencer* and *Seattle Times* are Seattle's two daily newspapers. *Seattle Weekly* is the city's free arts-and-entertainment weekly.

Pharmacies Conveniently located downtown pharmacies include **Rite Aid,** with branches at 319 Pike St. (© 206/223-0512) and 2603 Third Ave. (© 206/441-8790).

You can also call Rite Aid (© **800/748-3243**) for the location nearest you. For 24-hour service, try **Bartell Drug Store,** 600 First Ave. N. (© **206/284-1353**), in the Lower Queen Anne neighborhood.

Photographic Needs **Cameras West,** 1908 Fourth Ave. (© **206/622-0066**), is downtown and has 1-hour film processing. It's open Monday to Friday from 9:30am to 6pm, Saturday from 10am to 6pm, and Sunday from noon to 5pm.

Police For police emergencies, phone © **911.**

Restrooms Public restrooms are in Pike Place Market, Westlake Center, Pacific Place, Seattle Center, and the Washington State Convention and Trade Center. Restrooms are in most hotel lobbies and coffee bars in downtown Seattle.

Safety Although Seattle is a relatively safe city, it has its share of crime. The most questionable neighborhood you're likely to visit is the Pioneer Square area, which is home to more than a dozen bars and nightclubs. By day, this area is quite safe (though it has a large contingent of street people), but late at night, when the bars are closing, stay aware of your surroundings and keep an eye out for suspicious characters and activities. Also take extra precautions with your wallet or purse when you're in the crush of people at Pike Place Market. Whenever possible, try to park your car in a garage at night. If you must park on the street, make sure there are no valuables in view—or anything that even looks like it might contain something of worth. I once had my car broken into because I left a shopping bag full of trash on the back seat.

Taxes Seattle has an 8.8% sales tax. In restaurants there's an additional 5% food-and-beverage tax on top of the sales tax. The hotel-room tax in the metro area ranges from around 10% to 16%. On rental cars, you'll pay not only an 18.5% car-rental tax, but also, if you rent at the airport, an additional 10% to 12% airport concession fee, for a whopping total of around 30%!

Taxis See "Getting Around," earlier in this chapter.

Transit Info For 24-hour information on Seattle's Metro bus system, call © **206/ 553-3000.** For information on the Washington State Ferries, call © **800/84-FERRY** or 888/808-7977 in Washington, or 206/464-6400.

Weather Check the *Seattle Times* or *Seattle Post-Intelligencer* newspapers for forecasts. If you want to know what to pack before you depart, go to **www.wrh. noaa.gov/seattle, www.cnn.com/weather,** or **www.wunderground.com/US/WA.**

6

The San Juan Islands &
Washington's Northwest Coast

Water, water everywhere, and quite a few islands, too. That about sums up the landscape of the north Puget Sound and San Juan Islands region. Here, within a vast inland sea, lie hundreds of islands both large and small, and the lure of these emerald isles is powerful. There may not be any turquoise waters, white-sand beaches, or palm trees swaying in the breeze, but an island is a getaway no matter where it is—and these islands are no exception. The fact that many of the region's islands bear Spanish names seems to further add to the romance of a trip to the San Juans.

When English explorer Capt. George Vancouver first sailed down the Strait of Juan de Fuca in 1792, he discovered a vast inland sea and named it Puget Sound. To the north of this sound, within a convolution of twisting channels, narrow straits, and elongated bays, lay an archipelago of islands, and rising to the east in a magnificent backdrop stood a range of snowcapped peaks. Several of the archipelago's islands—San Juan, Lopez, Fidalgo, Guemes, Sucia, and Matia—had already been named by earlier Spanish explorers, but Vancouver's 2 months of exploring and charting the waters of the region left Northwest maps with many new names—Deception Pass, Whidbey Island, Bellingham Bay, and Mount Baker.

From the mid–19th century to the mid–20th century, this region was primarily a fishing, farming, and logging region, but as early as the first decade of the 20th century, Washingtonians from the mainland had begun to discover the charms of island life. Today, the northern Puget Sound and San Juan Islands are Washington's favorite summer playgrounds and weekend getaways. Shimmering waters, mountain vistas, and tranquil islands are the ingredients of the tonic that revives the weary souls of vacationers from densely populated and industrialized southern Puget Sound. Though it's only 30 miles from Seattle to Whidbey Island and 85 miles to the San Juans, the distance is multiplied by the serenity that descends as you cross the sound by ferry.

However, this corner of the state isn't all about island life. On the mainland, the historic fishing village of La Conner has become the most charming little town in the state. Surrounding La Conner are the Skagit Valley bulb fields, which burst into bloom each spring with acres and acres of tulips and daffodils.

Farther north, the town of Bellingham serves as a base for exploring Washington's northwest coast. There are few crowds here, and the vistas (and the oysters) are as good as any you'll find in the islands. It is also on this coast that you'll find the state's premier waterfront golf resort.

1 Whidbey Island ★★

30 miles N of Seattle, 40 miles S of Bellingham

While the San Juan Islands are beautiful, their beauty has become something of a liability—during the summer, they're just too crowded. If you don't relish the hours-long waits for ferries, you can still have an island experience here on Whidbey Island. At 45 miles in length, Whidbey is one of the largest islands in the continental United States. Only 30 miles from Seattle, it's also a popular weekend getaway for Seattleites who come here seeking tranquillity and relaxation. However, outside of Washington, Whidbey Island isn't nearly as well known as the San Juans, which is why it is less crowded in the summer.

Never more than a few miles wide, Whidbey offers views of the water at seemingly every turn of its winding country roads. Farms, forests, bluffs, and beaches provide the foregrounds to the aquatic vistas, and two historic villages, Langley and Coupeville, offer the same sort of quaint settings people expect from the San Juans. Old wooden commercial buildings have been restored and now house excellent restaurants, art galleries, and unique shops. Charming bed-and-breakfast inns (and one of the state's most luxurious small hotels) pamper visitors to the island and provide the romantic surroundings that are so much a part of the Whidbey experience.

But what, you wonder, is there to do on Whidbey Island? Next to nothing, and that is the island's main appeal. This is an island you visit in order to rest and rejuvenate. You don't have to do anything, just sit back and relax. However, there are a few options for burning off excess energy: wine tasting, shopping, garden touring, hiking in state parks and a national historic reserve, walking on beaches, and sea kayaking. Sounds a lot like the San Juans, doesn't it?

Lest you get the impression that Whidbey Island is heaven on earth, let me make you aware of the Whidbey Island Naval Air Station, which, with its thundering jets, has considerably altered the idyllic atmosphere of the island's northern half. Oak Harbor, the island's largest community, is located just outside the base and is characterized by the sort of strip-mall sprawl that surrounds most military bases. For this reason, the vast majority of the island's B&Bs are located in central and south Whidbey. It's partly because of what has happened to Oak Harbor that Ebey's Landing National Historic Reserve was created. When people who had moved to the island because of its tranquil atmosphere saw the sprawl that was spreading around Oak Harbor, they acted quickly to preserve some of the island's rural beauty, the very essence of Whidbey Island.

ESSENTIALS

GETTING THERE   From I-5, take Wash. 20 west at Burlington. The highway turns south before you reach Anacortes and crosses over the Deception Pass Bridge to reach the north end of Whidbey Island.

Washington State Ferries (© **800/84-FERRY** or 888/808-7977 in Washington, or 206/464-6400; www.wsdot.wa.gov/ferries) operates ferries between Mukilteo and Clinton at the south end of the island and from Port Townsend to Keystone near Coupeville. Fares are $6.30 to $7.90 for a car and driver and $3.60 for passengers between Mukilteo and Clinton; $8.20 to $10 for a car and driver and $2.35 for passengers between Port Townsend and Keystone. The **Airporter Shuttle** (© **866/ 235-5247** or 360/380-8800; www.airporter.com) provides daily service from Sea-Tac International Airport to Oak Harbor. The fare is $36 one-way and $65 round-trip.

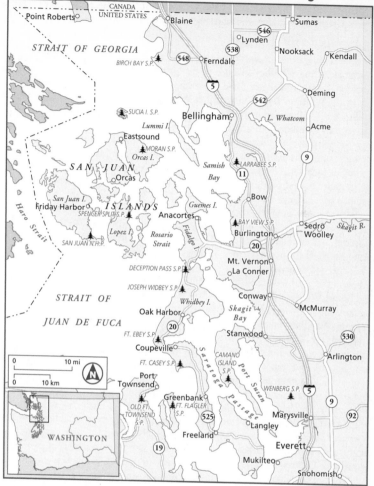

VISITOR INFORMATION Contact **Island County Tourism,** P.O. Box 365, Coupeville, WA 98239-0365 (© **888/747-7777;** www.donothinghere.com); **Central Whidbey Chamber of Commerce,** 107 S. Main St. (P.O. Box 152), Coupeville, WA 98239 (© **360/678-5434;** www.centralwhidbeychamber.com); or the **Langley South Whidbey Chamber of Commerce,** 208 Anthes St. (P.O. Box 403), Langley, WA 98260 (© **360/221-5676;** langleychamb.whidbey.com).

GETTING AROUND Island Transit (© 800/240-8747 or 360/321-6688; www. islandtransit.org) provides free public bus service on Whidbey Island.

FESTIVALS On the first weekend of March, you can eat your fill of mussels at the **Penn Cove Mussel Festival,** and in mid-July, Langley celebrates the visual and performing arts with the **Choochokam** street festival. In early August, there's the **Historic Coupeville Arts and Crafts Festival.** In late February, aspiring private detectives descend on Whidbey Island for the **Langley Mystery Weekend,** during which participants wander around trying to figure out "who done it."

EXPLORING THE ISLAND

If you're coming from the south and take the ferry from Mukilteo, then the best place to start exploring Whidbey Island is in the historic fishing village of **Langley,** which is reached by taking Langley Road off Wash. 525. Before you ever reach town, you'll pass by the **Whidbey Island Vineyard & Winery,** 5237 S. Langley Rd. (© 360/221-2040; www.whidbeyislandwinery.com), where you can taste a few wines. Many of the white wines are made from grapes grown here on the island, while the reds are made from grapes grown in eastern Washington. The tasting room is open Wednesday through Sunday from noon to 5pm (in July and Aug, open Mon also).

Langley today is a compact little village with a mix of sophisticated shops, interesting art galleries, and good, moderately priced restaurants occupying restored wooden commercial buildings along the waterfront. **First Street Park,** right in downtown, provides access to a narrow, rocky beach and offers views of Saratoga Passage and the distant Cascades. A couple of blocks away, you'll find the **South Whidbey Historical Museum,** 312 Second St. (© 360/221-2101), a small museum housing displays on local history. The museum is open Saturday and Sunday from 1 to 4pm; admission is a $2 suggested donation.

Four miles northwest of **Freeland,** which is the narrowest point of the island, you'll find **South Whidbey State Park** (© 360/902-8844), with 2 miles of shoreline, hiking trails through some old-growth forest, and a campground. Continuing north, you come to **Whidbey Island Greenbank Farm** (© 360/678-7700; www.greenbank farm.com), at Wash. 525 and Wonn Road in **Greenbank.** This former loganberry farm is now a community park. For many years, the farm was known for its loganberry liqueur, and today, in the farm's tasting room, you can still sample loganberry wine, as well as other wines from around the region. In summer, you can even pick your own loganberries. In the farm's main building, you'll find both the tasting room and a small cafe known for its delicious loganberry pies. With its big red barns and rolling farmlands, Greenbank Farm is as picture-perfect a farm as you'll find anywhere in western Washington. A network of trails meanders around the farm property, making this a good place to stretch your legs. Not far away, you can sample more wines at **Greenbank Cellars,** 3112 Day Rd., Greenbank (© **360/678-3964;** www.whidbey. com/wine). The winery is open Thursday through Monday from 11am to 5pm. To reach the winery from Greenbank Farm, drive south on Wash. 525 and then take Bakken Road west to Day Road.

Also in Greenbank (just off Wash. 525) is **Meerkerk Rhododendron Gardens,** 3531 Meerkerk Lane (© **360/678-1912;** www.meerkerkgardens.org), which was originally a private garden, but is now operated by the Seattle Rhododendron Society as a display and test garden. It's open daily from 9am to 4pm (peak bloom is Apr–May). Admission is $5.

Coupeville, located in central Whidbey Island just north of the turnoff for the ferry to Port Townsend, is another historic waterfront village. This town was founded in 1852 by Capt. Thomas Coupe, and the captain's 1853 home is among those in town that have been restored. The quiet charm of yesteryear is Coupeville's greatest appeal, and many of its old wooden commercial buildings now house antiques stores. At the north end of downtown, a gravel path leads up a bluff to the Coupeville Town Park, which is a good spot for a picnic. At the end of the Coupeville Wharf, you can see the skeleton of Rosie the gray whale, which hangs from the ceiling of the building at the end of the wharf.

In Coupeville you'll find the **Island County Historical Museum,** 908 NW Alexander St. (© **360/678-3310;** www.islandhistory.org), which is the best place to learn about the island's seafaring, farming, and military history. Between May and September, the museum is open Wednesday through Monday from 10am to 5pm; October through April, it's open Friday through Monday from 10am to 4pm. Admission is $3 for adults, and $2.50 for seniors and students.

Much of the land around Coupeville is now part of the **Ebey's Landing National Historic Reserve.** The reserve, one of the first of its kind in the nation, was created "to preserve and protect a rural community which provides an unbroken historic record from the nineteenth century exploration and settlement of Puget Sound to the present time." There is no visitor center for the reserve, but there is an information kiosk near the dock in Coupeville, and the adjacent museum has copies of an informative brochure about the reserve, as well as a brochure that outlines a driving and bicycling tour of the preserve.

Three miles south of Coupeville, adjacent to the Keystone ferry landing, is **Fort Casey State Park,** 1280 Engle Rd. (© **360/902-8844**), a former military base that was built in the 1890s to guard Puget Sound; it still has its gun batteries. In addition to the fort, the park includes beaches, hiking trails, a campground, and the 1897 **Admiralty Head lighthouse** (© **360/679-7391**), which is now an interpretive center that is open daily from 11am to 5pm in summer. Park admission is $5. Just south of Fort Casey State Park near the Keystone Ferry landing (Port Townsend ferries) is **Keystone State Park,** which is a designated underwater park for scuba divers. A few miles north of Fort Casey is the smaller **Fort Ebey State Park,** Libbey Road (© **360/ 902-8844**), another former military site built to protect the sound. Here there are excellent views of the Strait of Juan de Fuca, as well as a campground, hiking and mountain biking trails, and a lake for swimming and fishing.

Deception Pass State Park (© **360/902-8844**), at the northern tip of the island has miles of beaches, quiet coves, freshwater lakes, dark forests, hiking trails, camping, and views of Deception Pass, the churning channel between Whidbey Island and Fidalgo Island. A high bridge connects these two large islands by way of a smaller island in the middle of Deception Pass, and overlooks at the bridge allow you to gaze down on the tidal waters that surge and swirl between the islands.

SPORTS & OUTDOOR ACTIVITIES

BOAT CHARTERS   Between May and September, the *Cutty Sark* operates out of the Captain Whidbey Inn, 2072 W. Captain Whidbey Inn Rd. (© **800/366-4097** or 360/678-4097; www.captainwhidbey.com), with scheduled day-sail cruises for $30 per person. Multi-day excursions are also provided.

SEA KAYAKING   One of the best ways to get a feel for Whidbey Island is from water level in a sea kayak. Tours originating in Langley are offered by **Whidbey Island Sea Kayaking** (© **800/233-4319;** www.whidbeyislandkayaking.com), which charges $49 for a 2-hour tour. These tours operate between March and October.

WHERE TO STAY
IN LANGLEY

Boatyard Inn ★★   Right on Langley's little marina and designed to look like an old cannery building, this three-story inn is clad in a combination of wood, cedar shingles, and corrugated metal. Guest rooms are huge and have full kitchens, water views, gas fireplaces, and small balconies. There are also four two-bedroom loft suites. Downtown Langley is a few hundred yards uphill, and there's a small adjacent beach as well as the marina. This is a good choice if you like lots of space or need a kitchen.

200 Wharf St. (P.O. Box 866), Langley, WA 98260. © 360/221-5120. Fax 360/221-5124. www.boatyardinn.com. 10 units. $185–$230 double (lower midweek winter rates). AE, DC, DISC, MC, V. **Amenities:** Massage. *In room:* TV, kitchenette, fridge, coffeemaker, hair dryer, iron, free local calls, Wi-Fi.

The Inn at Langley 🏵🏵   This is one of the most luxurious and romantic inns in the Northwest. With its weathered cedar shingles, exposed beams, works of contemporary art, and colorful garden, the inn evokes all the best of life in the region, and the guest rooms have a Zen-like quality that soothes and relaxes. The inn's four floors jut out from a bluff overlooking Saratoga Passage, and with 180-degree views from every room, you'll have plenty of opportunities to spot orca whales and bald eagles. While the bedrooms and balconies are luxurious enough, the bathrooms are the star attractions. Each comes with an open shower and a double whirlpool tub that looks out over the water. Pull back an opaque sliding window and you also get a view of the room's fireplace. From Friday through Sunday (and Thurs in summer), the Chef's Kitchen Restaurant serves a gourmet six-course fixed-price dinner focusing on creative Northwest flavors ($80 per person).

400 First St. (P.O. Box 835), Langley, WA 98260. © 360/221-3033. www.innatlangley.com. 26 units. $195–$275 double; $395 suite; $495 cottage. Rates include continental breakfast. 2-night minimum on weekends. AE, MC, V. Children over 12 accepted. **Amenities:** Restaurant (Northwest); access to nearby health club; spa; massage. *In room:* TV/VCR, dataport, fridge, coffeemaker, hair dryer.

IN COUPEVILLE

The Captain Whidbey Inn 🏵🏵   Three miles west of Coupeville off Madrona Way stands one of the Northwest's most unusual inns. Shady, quiet grounds offer a tranquil setting that has revived flagging spirits for almost a century. Built in 1907 of small madrona logs, the historic inn is architecturally fascinating, a bit of American folk art. I love the character of this place, though it is not for everyone. The rooms in the main building are small and lack private bathrooms, but they manage to capture the feel of the island's seafaring past. Suites, cottages, and cabins are available for those who need more space (though none of these have as much character as the inn rooms despite the considerably higher room rates). The inn's dining room and adjacent bar both overlook Penn Cove. Try the mussels, which are fresh from the bay out front.

2072 W. Captain Whidbey Inn Rd., Coupeville, WA 98239. © 800/366-4097 or 360/678-4097. www.captainwhidbey. com. 32 units, 12 with shared bathroom. $85–$95 double with shared bathroom, $150 double with bathroom; $155 suite; $175 cabin; $275–$285 cottage. 2-night minimum on weekends. MC, V. **Amenities:** Restaurant (Northwest) and lounge. *In room:* No phone.

WHERE TO DINE

For baked goods and espresso, drop by the **Langley Village Bakery,** 221 Second St. (© 360/221-3525).

Café Langley 🏵🏵 MEDITERRANEAN/NORTHWEST   Romantic and intimate, this restaurant seamlessly fuses Northwest and Middle Eastern flavors and aesthetics and has long been one of Langley's most popular restaurants. The cafe has been around for years and serves up familiar dishes such as spanakopita and shish kabobs, but also is known for its flank steak marinated in sherry and herbs. The prawns à la Greque are another good choice, as are the Penn Cove mussels. The latter are available as either an appetizer or an entree. Weekly specials add yet another dimension to the reliable menu. Café Langley is a good bet for a romantic dinner.

113 First St. ℂ **360/221-3090**. www.langley-wa.com/cl. Reservations recommended. Main courses $14–$19. AE, MC, V. Mon–Thurs 11:30am–2:30pm and 5–9pm; Fri–Sat 11:30am–3pm and 5–9pm; Sun 11:30am–3pm and 5–8:30pm.

The Chef's Kitchen Restaurant ✸✸✸ NORTHWEST   The bounty of Whidbey Island, which produces a mouth-watering variety of seafood and produce, serves as the basis for the gourmet meals served at this tiny restaurant. Complex sauces, unexpected flavor combinations, and impeccably fresh ingredients all add up to memorable meals. A recent meal began with an egg filled with divine white-truffle custard and then moved on to a sweet corn consommé with tomatoes and cherries and a salad of chanterelle mushrooms and lentils. Entrees included roast quail with zucchini blossom stuffing and halibut with honey-drizzled Penn Cove mussels. Although dinners don't come with matched wines for each course, there is a superb wine list that includes lots of excellent half-bottles of wine. All in all, meals here are unforgettable and are best paired with a stay at the Inn at Langley.

At the Inn at Langley, 400 First St. ℂ **360/221-3033**. www.innatlangley.com. Reservations required. Six-course prix fixe meal $80. Seatings Fri–Sat 7pm; Sun 6pm.

The Edgecliff ✸ MEDITERRANEAN/NORTHWEST   Although the cliff on which this restaurant is built is more of a bluff, the views are still the best of any restaurant in Langley. The food is also quite good, and the setting, up the hill from the heart of the village, is quite tranquil. If you like oysters, then you'll love the way they're prepared here. They're done with an unusual sesame-seed crust and come accompanied by Thai peanut sauce. Also keep an eye out for the butternut squash ravioli with brown butter–brandy sauce, caramelized walnuts, roasted garlic, and fresh sage. Delicious! The restaurant has a small lounge in case you'd like to simply enjoy the setting over a cocktail or glass of wine.

510 Cascade Ave. ℂ **360/221-8899**. Main courses $8–$11 lunch, $14–$28 dinner. DISC, MC, V. Mon–Thurs 11:30am–2:30pm and 5–9pm; Fri 11:30am–2:30pm and 5–10pm; Sat noon–3pm and 5–10pm; Sun noon–3pm and 5–9pm.

IN COUPEVILLE

For gourmet picnic fare, stop by **Bayleaf,** 901 Grace St. (ℂ **360/678-6603**).

Christopher's ✸ NORTHWEST   In a warehouse-style building in downtown Coupeville, Christopher's may not have water views, but it does serve some of the best food in town. Chef/owner Andreas Wurzrainer is from Austria, and occasionally dishes from the home country show up on the menu. For the most part the menu sticks to familiar fare such as shrimp scampi and cioppino, though you'll also find dishes such as barbecued salmon with raspberry barbecue sauce. It would be foolish to pass up the Penn Cove mussels, which are steamed with white wine, garlic, and herbs.

23 Front St. ℂ **360/678-5480**. www.christophersonwhidbey.com. Reservations recommended. Main courses $7.25–$10 lunch, $13–$20 dinner. AE, DISC, MC, V. Mon–Fri 11:30am–2pm and 5–9pm; Sat–Sun noon–2:30pm and 5–9pm (closed Wed Sept–May).

The Oystercatcher ✸✸ NORTHWEST   A block off the waterfront at the back of a small building, this tiny restaurant is the best in town. Chef and owner Susan Vanderbeek has 3 decades of experience at Northwest restaurants, and looks over her handful of tables with great care. The menu changes every few weeks and usually includes three appetizers and three or four entrees. With such a short menu, you can be sure every dish is perfectly done. On a recent menu, appetizers included oysters with a basil-lemon mayonnaise, as well as local mussels. Among the entrees were a pan-roasted chicken served with Moroccan spice rub and seared rack of lamb marinated in lemon, rosemary, and pomegranate juice.

901 Grace St. ⓒ 360/678-0683. Reservations highly recommended. Main courses $18–$28. MC, V. Wed–Sat 5–9pm.

2 Anacortes

75 miles N of Seattle, 39 miles S of Bellingham, 92 miles S of Vancouver, B.C.

For most people, Anacortes is little more than that town you drive through on the way to the San Juan Islands ferry terminal. Actually, Anacortes has much more to offer than a driver late for the ferry could ever know. The route to the ferry sticks to roads that are fine examples of commercial and suburban sprawl—strip malls, gas stations, aging motels, housing developments. However, if you have time to detour off the main road, you'll find a town that, while not nearly as quaint as those on the San Juans, does have some historic character and, perhaps best of all, plenty of good places to eat. The restored downtown business district, residential neighborhoods full of old Victorian homes, a large, forested waterfront park, and a mountain-top viewpoint are all worth a look. So, if you can, slow down and take a look at Anacortes before or after a trip to the San Juans.

Anacortes made its early fortunes on lumbering and fishing, and today commercial fishing, as well as boat building, are still important to the town's economy. This marine orientation has given the town its character, which can be seen in the many restored buildings along Commercial Avenue.

Anacortes also makes a good base for exploring the San Juans if you either can't get or can't afford a room on the islands. Using Anacortes as a base and leaving your car here on the mainland, you can travel as a passenger on the ferries and, by using public transit, mopeds, or bicycles, still manage to see plenty of the San Juans. In any event, Anacortes is also on an island, Fidalgo Island, with plenty of water views, the best of which are from Washington Park near the ferry terminal, from atop Mount Erie in the middle of the island, and from Deception Pass State Park at the south end of the island.

ESSENTIALS

GETTING THERE   From I-5 at Burlington, take Wash. 20 west to the Wash. 20 Spur. South of Anacortes, Wash. 20 connects to Whidbey Island by way of the Deception Pass Bridge.

See "Getting There" under "The San Juan Islands," below, for details on airport shuttle service to Anacortes from Seattle–Tacoma International Airport and for information on ferry connections to Anacortes from the islands and Vancouver Island, British Columbia.

VISITOR INFORMATION   For information on Anacortes, contact the **Anacortes Chamber of Commerce,** 819 Commercial Ave., Anacortes, WA 98221 (ⓒ **360/293-3832;** www.anacortes.org).

EXPLORING ANACORTES

If you want to learn more about local history, stop by the **Anacortes Museum,** 1305 Eighth St. (ⓒ **360/293-1915;** www.anacorteshistorymuseum.org), housed in a former Carnegie Library. It's open Thursday through Monday from 1 to 5pm;

The Name Game

Founded in the 1850s by Amos Bowman, Anacortes was named after Bowman's wife, Annie Curtis, but over the years the spelling and pronunciation were slowly corrupted to its current Spanish-sounding pronunciation (in keeping with such local Spanish names as San Juan, Lopez, and Guemes).

admission is a suggested $2 donation. Across the street from the museum is **Causland Memorial Park,** the town's most unusual attraction. Built in 1919 to honor servicemen who died in World War I, the park contains rock walls constructed as giant mosaics. It's a piece of folk art that reflects a simpler era. **Murals** are a mainstay of the Northwest's historic towns, and here in Anacortes they take the shape of more than 50 life-size cutouts of the town's forefathers.

Any walking tour of downtown should include a visit to the historic **W. T. Preston Snagboat,** 713 R Ave. (© 360/293-1915), a sternwheeler that was built in the 1890s to clear logjams on Puget Sound and now sits on dry land in a little park at the corner of Seventh Street and R Avenue. June through August, the sternwheeler is open daily from 11am to 5pm; April, May, September, and October, it's open on weekends only. Admission is $2 adults and $1 for seniors and children ages 6 to 16. Next door, at the corner of Seventh Street and R Avenue, is **The Depot Arts Center,** 611 R Ave. (© 360/293-3663; www.depotartscenter.com), a restored 1911 railway depot that now serves as an arts center, with a collection of work by regional artists.

For a glimpse of an old-fashioned hardware store, stop by **Marine Supply and Hardware Co.,** 202 Commercial St. (© 360/293-3014), which is the oldest continuously operating marine supply store on the West Coast.

Nature lovers can head to **Washington Park,** just a short distance past the ferry terminal. The park contains not only a campground and several miles of hiking trails, but tranquil **Sunset Beach,** which looks out across Rosario Strait to the San Juan Islands. For even more spectacular views, head up to **Mount Erie Park** ★★ on the summit of 1,270-foot Mount Erie. From here, on a clear day you can see Mount Rainier, Mount Baker, and the Olympic Mountains. You'll find this park by heading south out of Anacortes on Commercial Avenue, turning right on 32nd Street and then left on H Avenue (which becomes Heart Lake Rd.), and then taking Erie Mountain Drive to the top of the mountain.

You don't have to go all the way to the San Juans if you want to do some whalewatching. Orca-viewing excursions are offered by **Island Adventures** (© **800/465-4604** or 360/293-2428; www.islandadventurecruises.com), which charges $45 to $69, and also by **Mystic Sea Charters** (© **800/308-9387**; www.mysticseacharters. com), which charges $59 to $69. It's also possible to do a little sea kayaking here in the Anacortes area. Sea-kayak rentals are available at **Eddyline Watersports Center,** 2403 Commercial Ave. (© **866/445-7506** or 360/299-2300; www.seakayakshop. com), which charges $30 to $45 for a half-day rental and $45 to $65 for a full-day rental. Guided kayak tours are also offered throughout the year.

WHERE TO STAY

Ship Harbor Inn ★ Immediately adjacent to the ferry terminal for San Juan Islands ferries and overlooking a wetland with good bird-watching, this inn is a good choice if you weren't able to get a room on the islands or are planning on taking the early ferry all the way to Vancouver Island, Canada. This is also a good choice if you are planning to explore the islands by bicycle. Rooms are large and most have balconies and views of the water. If you plan to spend more than 1 night here, you might want to opt for one of the "cabin" rooms, which have full kitchens. There's also a Jacuzzi suite.

5316 Ferry Terminal Rd., Anacortes, WA 98221. © **800/852-8568** or 360/293-5177. www.shipharborinn.com. 26 units. $99–$169 double (lower rates in winter). Rates include continental breakfast. AE, DC, DISC, MC, V. **Amenities:** Coin-op laundry. *In room:* TV, fridge, free local calls.

WHERE TO DINE

For good pastries and baked goodies, be sure to drop by **La Vie En Rose** *✺*, 418 Commercial Ave. (© **360/299-9546;** www.laviebakery.com), a great little French pastry shop that also serves interesting light meals. For healthy, light meals, fresh juices, and smoothies, try the **Star Bar Café,** 416½ Commercial Ave. (© **360/299-2120**). Before leaving town, you should also be sure to pick up some smoked salmon at **Seabear Smokehouse and Store** *✺*, 605 30th St. (© **800/645-FISH** or 360/293-4661; www. seabear.com).

Adrift *✺* INTERNATIONAL   With its dark interior and urban vibe, Adrift is an unexpected treat in this retirement community. The restaurant is sort of a de facto artists' community center for Anacortes and serves not only good food (often organic and usually locally sourced), but generous helpings of art and music. The menu is highly eclectic and leans toward Asian and Mediterranean influences. At lunch, I go for the oyster burger, and at dinner, it's the crab cakes with spicy ginger-garlic sauce or the seared scallops with citrus butter.

510 Commercial Ave. © 360/588-0653. www.adriftrestaurant.com. Reservations recommended. Main courses $7.50–$18. AE, DISC, MC, V. Mon–Fri 11am–9pm; Sat 8am–9pm.

Gere-a-Deli DELI   Many places claim to be New York–style delis, but this is the only one in the Northwest that comes close to duplicating the genuine feel of a deli in Manhattan. Big and bustling, Gere-a-Deli is *the* place for lunch in Anacortes, and while the sandwiches may not be as good as those in the Big Apple, the urban feel, vintage signs, huge windows, and lively chatter of conversation all add up to a classic deli experience.

502 Commercial Ave. © 360/293-7383. Reservations required for Fri dinner. Sandwiches $5–$8.25. MC, V. Mon–Sat 7am–4pm.

Rockfish Grill and Anacortes Brewery AMERICAN   Although you can get good fish and chips, pizzas, and burgers in this brewpub, the menu also includes plenty of dishes that are unexpectedly imaginative. For a starter, try the tequila-lime shrimp cocktail or the double oyster "martini." Among the entrees, the wood-fired raviolis are a good bet. Wash it all down with one of the brewery's excellent beers.

320 Commercial Ave. © 360/588-1720. www.anacortesrockfish.com. Main courses $9–$18. AE, MC, V. Sun–Thurs 11:30am–10pm; Fri–Sat 11:30am–midnight.

3 The San Juan Islands *✺✺✺*

On a late afternoon on a clear summer day, the sun slants low, suffusing the scene with a golden light. The fresh salt breeze and the low rumble of the ferry's engine lull you into a dream state. All around you, rising from a shimmering sea, are emerald-green islands, the tops of glacier-carved mountains inundated with water at the end of the

The San Juan Islands

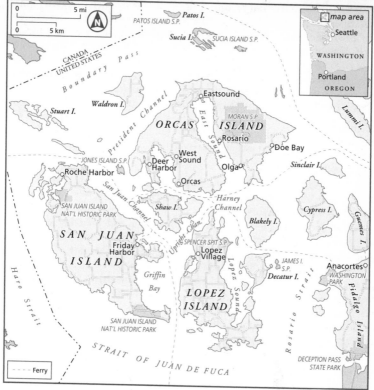

last ice age. A bald eagle swoops from its perch on a twisted madrona tree. Off the port bow, you spot several fat harbor seals lounging on a rocky islet. As the engine slows, you glide toward a narrow wooden dock with a simple sign above it that reads ORCAS ISLAND. With a sigh of contentment, you step out onto the San Juan Islands and into a slower pace of life.

There's something magical about traveling to the San Juans. Some say it's the light, some say it's the sea air, some say it's the weather (temperatures are always moderate, and rainfall is roughly half that of Seattle). Whatever it is that so entrances, the San Juans are the favorite getaway of urban Washingtonians, and if you visit these idyllic islands, I think you, too, will fall under their spell.

There is, however, one caveat: The San Juans have been discovered. In summer, if you're driving a car, you may encounter waits of several hours to get on the ferries. One solution is to leave your car on the mainland and come over either on foot or by bicycle. If you choose to come over on foot, you can then rent a car, moped, or bike; take the San Juan island shuttle bus; or use taxis to get around. Then again, you can just stay in one place and relax.

Along with crowded ferries come hotels, inns, and campgrounds that can get booked up months in advance and restaurants that can't seat you without a reservation. If it's summer, don't expect to find a place to stay if you arrive without a room reservation.

In other seasons, it's a different story. Spring and fall are often clear, and in spring, the islands' gardens and hedgerows of wild roses burst into bloom, making this one of the nicest times of year to visit. Perhaps best of all, room rates in spring and fall are much lower than in summer.

No one seems to agree on how many islands there actually are in the San Juans; there may be as few as 175 or as many as 786. The lower number represents those islands large enough to have been named, while the larger number includes all of the islands, rocks, and reefs that poke above the water at the lowest possible tide. Of all these islands, only four (San Juan, Orcas, Lopez, and Shaw) are serviced by the Washington State Ferries, and of these, only three (San Juan, Orcas, and Lopez) have anything in the way of tourist accommodations.

ESSENTIALS

VISITOR INFORMATION   For information on all the islands, contact the **San Juan Islands Visitors Bureau,** P.O. Box 1330, Friday Harbor, WA 98250 (© **888/ 468-3701;** www.guidetosanjuans.com).

For specific information on San Juan, contact the **San Juan Island Chamber of Commerce,** P.O. Box 98, Friday Harbor, WA 98250 (© **360/378-5240;** www. sanjuanisland.org). For Orcas, contact the **Orcas Island Chamber of Commerce,** P.O. Box 252, Eastsound, WA 98245 (© **360/376-8888;** www.orcasisland.org). And for Lopez, contact the **Lopez Island Chamber of Commerce,** 6 Old Post Rd. (P.O. Box 102), Lopez, WA 98261 (© **877/433-2789** or 360/468-4664; www.lopezisland. com).

Also, check out www.orcasisle.com and www.thesanjuans.com.

GETTING THERE   **Washington State Ferries** (© **800/84-FERRY,** 888/808- 7977 in Washington, or 206/464-6400; www.wsdot.wa.gov/ferries) operates ferries between Anacortes and four of the San Juan Islands (Lopez, Shaw, Orcas, and San Juan) and Sidney, British Columbia (on Vancouver Island near Victoria).

The round-trip fare for a vehicle and driver from Anacortes to Lopez is $22 to $33, to Shaw or Orcas $26 to $40, to San Juan $31 to $47, and to Sidney $40 to $50. The higher fares listed here reflect a summer surcharge, and the lower ones (except for trips to Sidney) are Sunday-through-Tuesday fares.

The round-trip fare for passengers from Anacortes to any of the islands ranges from $10 to $12 ($15 from Anacortes to Sidney). The fare for a vehicle and driver on all westbound inter-island ferries is $14 to $17; walk-on passengers and passengers in cars ride free. Except for service from Sidney, fares are not collected on eastbound ferries, nor are walk-on passengers charged for inter-island ferry service. If you plan to explore the islands by car, you'll save some money by starting your tour on San Juan Island and making your way back east through the islands.

During the summer you may have to wait several hours to get on a ferry, so arrive early. If you plan to leave your car on the mainland, any time between mid-May and mid-September, you'll pay $10 to park it overnight at the Anacortes ferry terminal ($20 for 3 days, $30 for 1 week).

There are also passenger-ferry services from several cities around the region. **Victoria Clipper** (© **800/888-2535,** 206/448-5000, or 250/382-8100; www.victoriaclipper. com) operates excursion boats between Seattle and Friday Harbor on San Juan Island. There are also boats that go to Victoria. The round-trip fare to Friday Harbor is $60 to $100, depending on the time of year. One-day advance-purchase discounts of $10 to $30 are available on round-trip tickets, with one child under 12 traveling free with each paying adult. Without the advance booking, children pay half price.

Between Port Townsend and Friday Harbor, passenger service is available from mid-April to early October from **P.S. Express** (© 360/385-5288; www.pugetsoundexpress.com), which will also carry bicycles and sea kayaks. One-way fares are $40 to $50 for adults and $30 to $40 for children; round-trip fares are $60 to $67 for adults and $41 to $49 for children.

From Bellingham, there is passenger service to Friday Harbor (San Juan Island) on the **San Juan Island Commuter,** Bellingham Cruise Terminal, 335 Harris Ave. (© 800/443-4552 or 360/738-8099; www.islandcommuter.com). The round-trip adult fare is $49 for adults and $25 for children. These passenger ferries operate between mid-May and early September.

If you're short on time, you can fly to the San Juans. **Kenmore Air** (© 800/543-9595 or 425/486-1257; www.kenmoreair.com) offers floatplane flights that take off from either Lake Union or the north end of Lake Washington. Round-trip fares to the San Juans are between $176 and $212 (lower for children). Flights go to Friday Harbor and Roche Harbor on San Juan Island; Rosario Resort and Deer Harbor, and West Sound on Orcas Island; and the Lopez Islander on Lopez Island. You can also get from Seattle to the San Juans on **San Juan Airlines** (© 800/874-4434; www.sanjuan airlines.com), which flies from Boeing Field.

You can also get from Sea-Tac Airport to the San Juan Islands ferry terminal in Anacortes on the **Airporter Shuttle** (© 866/235-5247 or 360/380-8800; www.airporter.com), which charges $33 one-way and $61 round-trip.

GETTING AROUND   Car rentals are available on San Juan Island from **M&W Auto Sales,** 725 Spring St. (© 800/323-6037 or 360/378-2886; www.interisland.net/mandw), which charges between $50 and $80 per day during the summer. Cars can also be rented from **Susie's Mopeds,** at the top of the ferry lanes in Friday Harbor (© 800/532-0087 or 360/378-5244; www.susiesmopeds.com), for $96 per day. Susie's rents scooters and mopeds as well, for $20 to $40 per hour or $60 to $120 per day.

For a cab on San Juan Island, call **Bob's Taxi** (© 360/378-6777; www.bobstaxi andtours.com).

San Juan Transit (© 800/887-8387 or 360/378-8887; www.sanjuantransit.com) operates a shuttle bus on San Juan Island during the summer. This shuttle can be boarded at the ferry terminal and operates frequently throughout the day, stopping at the island's major attractions, which makes this a great way to get around if you come out without a car. Day passes are $10 for adults, $9 for seniors, and $5 for children ages 5 to 12, and 2-day passes are also available. One-way ($4–$5 adults, $2 children) and round-trip ($7 adults, $3 children) tickets are also available. Children ages 4 and under always ride free.

SAN JUAN ISLAND

San Juan Island is not the largest of these islands, but it is the most populous, and is home to the county seat, Friday Harbor, which is the biggest and most developed town in the islands. As the hub of island activity, San Juan Island is home to more whale-watching and sea-kayaking companies than any of the other islands. It also has charter boats, fishing boats, moped rentals, and lots of souvenir shops. This all adds up to crowds in the summer, so if you're looking for an idyllic island getaway, you might want to try Orcas or Lopez.

However, what San Juan Island has going for it is lots of history, plus great views of the Olympic Mountains across the Strait of Juan de Fuca, and the only place in the islands where you can reliably see orca whales from shore.

EXPLORING FRIDAY HARBOR

Friday Harbor is the only real town on all of the islands, and as such it is home to numerous tourist-oriented shops, restaurants, motels, and B&Bs, as well as such island necessities as grocery and hardware stores. With its well-protected, large marina, it's also one of the most popular places in the islands for boaters to drop anchor.

If you arrive by car, you'll first want to find a parking space, which can be difficult in the summer. Once on foot, take a stroll around **Friday Harbor** to admire the simple wood-frame shop buildings constructed in the early 20th century. At that time, Friday Harbor was thought of as the southernmost port in Alaska and was a busy harbor. Schooners and steamships hauled the island's fruit, livestock, and lime (for cement) off to more populous markets. Today such pursuits have all died off, but reminders of the island's rural roots linger on, and these memories have fueled the island's new breadwinner: tourism.

Whale-watching is one of the most popular summer activities in the San Juans, and no one should visit the islands at this time of year without going out to see the area's orca whales. Before you head out, stop by the **Whale Museum** ⚓, 62 First St. N. (© **360/378-4710;** www.whale-museum.org), where you can see whale skeletons and models of whales and learn all about the area's pods of orcas (also known as killer whales). The museum is open daily from 10am to 5pm (July–Aug 9am–6pm); admission is $6 for adults, $5 for seniors, and $3 for students and children ages 5 to 18.

If you're interested in learning more about island history, stop by the **San Juan Historical Museum,** 405 Price St. (© **360/378-3949;** www.sjmuseum.org), housed in an 1894 farmhouse. It also includes several other historic buildings on its grounds. From May to September, the museum is open Tuesday through Thursday from 10am to 3pm and Saturday and Sunday from 1 to 4pm. In October, March, and April, the museum is open Saturday from 1 to 4pm. Open by appointment in other months. Admission is $2 for adults, $1 for children ages 6 to 18; free to children under 6.

Many of the town's old buildings now house art galleries and interesting shops. At **Waterworks Gallery,** 315 Spring St. (© **360/378-3060;** www.waterworksgallery. com), you'll find fine art and contemporary crafts by local and regional artists. **Arctic Raven Gallery,** 130 S. First St. (© **888/378-3222** or 360/378-3433; www.arctic ravengallery.com), specializes in contemporary Native American arts and crafts. **The Garuda & I,** 60 First St. (© **888/675-7039** or 360/378-3733), carries fascinating items from throughout the world, with an emphasis on Asian imports. Up at the top of Spring Street behind an amazingly contorted Camperdown elm tree, you can also visit the little **Island Museum of Art,** 314 Spring St. (© **360/370-5050;** www. wbay.org), which is affiliated with the Westcott Bay Sculpture Park & Nature Reserve. The museum highlights local and regional artists. The museum is open Tuesday through Saturday from 11am to 5pm. Admission is free.

If you need some wine for your vacation or want to take some home with you, stop by the tasting room at **Island Wine Company,** 2 Cannery Landing (© **800/248-WINE** or 360/378-3229; www.sanjuancellars.com), which is the only place you can buy wine from San Juan Cellars. However, these wines are made from grapes grown in eastern Washington, not grapes grown on the islands. You'll find the wine shop on the immediate left as you leave the ferry.

If you walk over to the other side of the ferry landing and then out on the pier that serves as the dock for passenger ferries, you can take a peak at the **Spring Street Landing Aquarium,** a modest tank full of local denizens of the deep. The tank is in an open-air building at the end of the pier. Also keep an eye out for wildlife here. I've seen an otter swimming around by this pier.

Continuing along the waterfront toward the marina, you'll come to **Fairweather Park,** where you'll find artist Susan Point's traditional Northwest Coast Indian house post sculpture, which is similar to a totem pole. The sculpture represents the human-animal relationship and the marine ecosystem. Here in the park, you'll also find some covered picnic tables. At the adjacent marina, there are free concerts on Sunday afternoons in July. Concerts currently start at 2pm.

SEEING THE REST OF THE ISLAND

Most of the island's main attractions can be seen on a long loop drive around the perimeter of San Juan. Start the drive by following Roche Harbor signs north out of Friday Harbor (take Spring St. to Second St. to Tucker Ave.).

In about 3 miles, you'll come to **San Juan Vineyards** ⭑, 3136 Roche Harbor Rd. (© **360/378-9463;** www.sanjuanvineyards.com), which makes wines both from grapes grown off the island and from its own estate-grown Siegerrebbe and Madeline Angevine grapes. The tasting room is housed in an old schoolhouse built in 1896. It's open daily from 11am to 5pm in summer, Wednesday through Sunday from 11am to 5pm in spring and fall, and by appointment in other months.

A little farther north, you'll come to **Roche Harbor Village,** once the site of large limestone quarries that supplied lime to much of the West Coast. Many of the quarries' old structures are still visible, giving this area a decaying industrial look, but amidst the abandoned machinery stands the historic **Hotel de Haro,** a simple white-washed wooden building with verandas across its two floors. Stop to admire the old-fashioned marina and colorful gardens; the deck of the hotel's lounge is one of the best places on the island to linger over a drink. In an old pasture on the edge of the resort property, you'll find the **Westcott Bay Sculpture Park & Nature Reserve** (© **360/370-5050;** www.wbay.org), a sculpture park that includes more than 100 works of art set in grassy fields and along the shores of a small pond. Back in the woods near the resort is a **mausoleum,** which was erected by the founder of the quarries and the Hotel de Haro.

South of Roche Harbor, on West Valley Road, you'll come to the **English Camp** unit of **San Juan Island National Historical Park** ⭑ (© **360/378-2902;** www.nps.gov/sajh). This park commemorates the San Juan Island Pig War, one of North America's most unusual and least remembered confrontations. Way back in 1859, San Juan Island nearly became the site of a battle between the British and the Americans. The two countries had not yet agreed upon the border between the United States and Canada when a British pig on San Juan Island decided to have dinner in an American garden. Not taking too kindly to this, the owner of the garden shot the pig. The Brits, rather than welcome this succulent addition to their evening's repast, threatened redress. In less time than it takes to smoke a ham, both sides were calling in reinforcements. Luckily, this pigheadedness was defused, and a more serious confrontation was avoided.

This English Camp unit of the historical park is set on picturesque Garrison Bay, and, with its huge old shade trees, wide lawns, and white wooden buildings, is the picture of British civility. There's even a formal garden surrounded by a white picket fence. You can look inside the reconstructed buildings and imagine the days when this was one of the most far-flung corners of the British Empire. If you're full of energy, hike the 1.25-mile trail to the top of 650-foot **Mount Young** for a beautiful panorama of the island. There's also an easier 1-mile shoreline-hugging hike out to the end of **Bell Point.** The grounds are open daily from dawn to 11pm, and the visitor center is open from early June through early September, daily from 9am to 5pm. Throughout the summer, there is a variety of living history programs here on Saturday afternoons.

South of English Camp, watch for the Mitchell Bay Road turnoff. This connects to the Westside Road, which leads down the island's west coast. Along this road, you'll find **San Juan County Park,** a great spot for a picnic. A little farther south, you'll come to **Lime Kiln State Park** ⟨★★⟩ (*©* **360/378-2044**), the country's first whale-watching park and a great place to spot these gentle giants in summer. This latter park is open daily from 8am to dusk and admission is $5. On either side of the state park are Deadman Bay Nature Preserve and Lime Kiln Nature Preserve, two properties acquired for public use by the San Juan County Land Bank. Between the state park and two preserves, there are more than 3 miles of hiking trails, which makes this the best hiking spot on the island.

As Westside Road moves inland, a left onto Wold Road will bring you to **Pelindaba Lavender Farms,** 33 Hawthorne Lane (*©* **866/819-1911** or 360/378-4248; www.pelindaba.com). The farm has roughly 5 acres of lavender plants, including a cutting field where visitors can cut their own lavender stems. It's open daily from 10am to 5pm between May and September. The gift shop is packed with lavender-scented products, and at the Lavendera Day Spa, you can get a massage or other skin or body treatment. There's another gift shop and tearoom in the Friday Harbor Center shopping plaza, in downtown Friday Harbor. The farm has a Lavender Harvest Festival each year in mid-July.

At the far south end of the island is the wind-swept promontory on which **American Camp** stood during the Pig War. Here you'll find a visitor center (open daily 8am–5pm in summer and 8am–4:30pm in other months) and two reconstructed buildings; before American Camp was built here, this was the site of a Hudson's Bay Company farm. The meadows sweeping down to the sea were once grazed by sheep and cattle, but today you'll see only rabbits browsing amid the high grasses and wild-flowers (and the occasional red fox stalking the rabbits). Hiking trails here lead along the bluffs and down to the sea. My favorites are the **Mount Finlayson Trail,** which leads to the top of a grassy hill, and the **Lagoon Trail,** which leads through a dark forest of Douglas fir to **Jackle's Lagoon,** a great spot for bird-watching. Keep your eyes peeled for bald eagles, which are relatively plentiful around here. If you'd just like to picnic at a pleasantly secluded beach, head to the park's **Fourth of July Beach.** During summer months, there are Saturday afternoon living history programs at American Camp.

Continuing past American Camp will bring you to Cattle Point, site of a lighthouse and the **Cattle Point Interpretive Area.** This latter spot served, in the 1920s, as a Navy Radio Compass Station that helped ships navigate the nearby waters. Today there are rock outcrops, two tiny beaches, great views of Lopez Island, interpretive signs, and a few picnic tables that make this one of the best picnic spots on the island. Cattle Point is also a good destination for a bike ride from Friday Harbor.

BOAT & BUS TOURS

If you come over to San Juan Island without a car and want to see as much of the island as possible in a short amount of time, consider taking a narrated bus tour through **San Juan Transit,** Cannery Landing building, Front and East streets (℃ **800/ 887-8387** or 360/378-8887; www.sanjuantransit.com), which has its office right at the ferry landing and charges $17 for adults, $15 for seniors, $10 for kids ages 4 to 17 with adult, free for children under 4 with adult.

SPORTS & OUTDOOR ACTIVITIES

BICYCLING   Bicycling is a favorite sport of island visitors. Winding country roads are ideal for leisurely trips. If you didn't bring your own wheels, you can rent a bike in Friday Harbor from **Island Bicycles,** 380 Argyle St. (℃ **360/378-4941;** www. islandbicycles.com), which charges $7 to $14 per hour (2-hr. minimum) or $35 to $70 per day. Here on San Juan Island you can also rent scooters and mopeds. They're available in Friday Harbor by the hour or by the day from **Susie's Mopeds** (℃ **800/ 532-0087** or 360/378-5244; www.susiesmopeds.com), which is located at the top of the ferry lanes. Expect to pay $20 to $40 per hour or $60 to $120 per day for a moped or scooter.

BOAT CHARTERS   If you and a few friends would just like to get out on the water for a leisurely cruise, there are always boats to be chartered in Friday Harbor. Check around the marina for notices. If you're looking for a weeklong bareboat charter, contact **Charters Northwest** (℃ **360/378-7196;** www.chartersnw.com).

FISHING   If you want to try catching some salmon, contact **Buffalo Works by Nash Brothers** (℃ **360/378-4612;** www.sanjuansalmon.com).

SCUBA DIVING   Believe it or not, scuba diving is also popular in the San Juans. Though the water stays frigid year-round, it's also exceedingly clear. If you're a diver and want to rent equipment or go on a guided dive, or if you want to take a diving class while you're here, contact **Island Dive & Watersports,** 2A Spring St. Landing, Friday Harbor (℃ **800/303-8386** or 360/378-2772; www.divesanjuan.com). A two-tank dive will cost you $79.

SEA KAYAKING 🐾   The 3- and 5-hour sea-kayak tours out of Roche Harbor Village are offered by **San Juan Safaris** (℃ **800/450-6858** or 360/378-1323; www. sanjuansafaris.com), which also operates out of Friday Harbor. The cost is $59 to $75. Tours are offered mid-April through September. I prefer the trips that originate at Roche Harbor Village.

Moments Thar She Blows!

While summer visitors to San Juan have a plethora of ways to go whale-watching, as far as I'm concerned, the best way to search for orcas is from a sea kayak, and the best kayaking company for such an outing is **Outdoor Odysseys** (℃ **800/ 647-4621** or 206/361-0717; www.outdoorodysseys.com), which has been operating here in the San Juans for 20 years. This company's trips start from San Juan County Park and head out through the local orca pods' favorite feeding grounds near Lime Kiln State Park. In the summer, you stand a good chance of seeing orcas, and any time of year, you're likely to see harbor seals and bald eagles. Day tours, offered May through September, cost $75 and include lunch.

Crystal Seas Kayaking (© 877/SEAS-877 or 360/378-4223; www.crystalseas. com) does anything from 3-hour tours ($59) to sunset tours ($59) to all-day tours ($75) and multi-day trips.

There are 3- and 4-day trips offered by **San Juan Kayak Expeditions** (© **360/ 378-4436;** www.sanjuankayak.com), which charges $380 and $480, respectively, for its outings.

WHALE-WATCHING 🦈🦈   When it's time to spot some whales, you have two choices. You can take a whale-watching cruise, or you can head over to **Lime Kiln State Park** 🦈🦈, where a short trail leads down to a rocky coastline from which orca whales, minke whales, Dall's porpoises, and sea lions can sometimes be seen. The best months to see orcas are June through September, but it's possible to see them throughout the year.

In the summer, 3-hour whale-watching cruises from Roche Harbor Village, on the north side of the island, are offered by **San Juan Safaris** (© **800/450-6858** or 360/378-1323; www.sanjuansafaris.com), which charges $59 for adults and $39 for children ages 12 and under. This company also has tours from Friday Harbor. Similar cruises are offered by **San Juan Excursions** (© **800/80-WHALE** or 360/378-6636; www.watchwhales.com), which operates out of Friday Harbor. Cruises are $59 for adults and $39 for children ages 4 to 12.

For a speedier, more personalized whale-watching excursion, **Maya's Whale Watch Charters** (© **360/378-7996;** www.mayaswhalewatch.biz), has the fastest whale-watching boat in the islands. It takes six people at a time; a 3-hour tour is $59.

WHERE TO STAY

In addition to the hotels, B&Bs, and inns listed here, there are also lots of vacation rentals available on San Juan Island through **Windermere San Juan Island,** 100 First St. (P.O. Box 488), Friday Harbor, WA 98250 (© **800/391-8190** or 360/378-3601; www.windermerevacationrentals.com). Rates range from $800 to $3,800 per week.

EXPENSIVE

Friday Harbor House 🦈🦈   With its contemporary yet distinctly Northwest architecture, this luxurious little boutique hotel brings urban sophistication to Friday Harbor. From the hotel's bluff-top location, you have excellent views of the ferry landing, the Friday Harbor marina, and, in the distance, Orcas Island. Guest rooms come complete with fireplaces and oversized whirlpool tubs, making this place a great choice for a romantic getaway. In some rooms, you can relax in your tub and gaze at both the view out the window and your own crackling fire. A few units have small balconies. These are some of the best rooms in the San Juan Islands, and if you enjoy contemporary styling, you'll love this place. The dining room serves Northwest cuisine and is one of the best restaurants on the island. At press time, there were plans to expand this inn and add two or three new suites.

130 West St. (P.O. Box 1385), Friday Harbor, WA 98250. © **866/722-7356** or 360/378-8455. Fax 360/378-8453. www.fridayharborhouse.com. 20 units. Memorial Day weekend to Sept $240–$310 double, $340 suite; Oct to day before Memorial Day weekend $150–$200 double, $265 suite. Rates include continental breakfast. Children under 12 stay free in parent's room. AE, DISC, MC, V. **Amenities:** Restaurant (Northwest); access to nearby health club; concierge; massage; babysitting; laundry service. *In room:* TV/VCR, dataport, minibar, fridge, coffeemaker, hair dryer, iron, free local calls.

Lakedale Resort at Three Lakes 🦈🦈 *(Kids)*   Although best known as the island's favorite private campground, Lakedale Resort at Three Lakes also has six very attractive modern cabins and a 10-room lodge that is a luxurious rendition of a classic log

All about Orcas

Although once known as killer whales and much maligned as the wolves of the deep, orca whales are actually highly intelligent, family-oriented animals. Orcas can be found in every ocean, but one of their highest concentrations is in the waters stretching north from Puget Sound along the coast of British Columbia. Consequently, this has become one of the most studied and most publicized populations of orcas in the world.

These whales, which can grow to 30 feet long and weigh almost 9,000 pounds, are the largest members of the porpoise family. In the wild, they can live up to 80 years, and female orcas usually live 20 to 30 years longer than males.

Orcas are among the most family-oriented animals on earth, and related whales will often live together their entire lives, sometimes with three generations present at the same time. Family groups frequently band together with other closely related groups into extended families known as pods. A community of orcas consists of several pods, and in this region the community numbers around 100 individuals. There are three distinct populations of orcas living in the waters off Vancouver Island, British Columbia. They are referred to as the northern and southern resident communities and the transient community. It's the southern resident community that whale-watchers in the San Juan Islands are most likely to encounter.

As predators, orcas do live up to the name "killer whale," and have been known to attack other whales much larger than themselves. Some orcas off the coast of Argentina even swim up onto the shore, beaching themselves to attack resting sea lions, then thrashing and twisting their way back into the water. However, not all orcas feed on other marine mammals. Of the three communities in this area, only the transients feed on mammals. The two resident communities feed primarily on salmon, which are abundant in these waters, especially off the west side of San Juan Island during the summer.

mountain lodge. The cabins are attractively and individually decorated, with large cedar porches overlooking the forest. All have two bedrooms, two bathrooms, a full kitchen, and a gas fireplace. There's a hot tub in a gazebo, and guests have access to the resort's 82 acres, which include trails, several lakes for swimming, canoeing (boat rentals are also available), and trout fishing. Think of this as a sort of summer camp for the entire family. Lots of fun and very woodsy. Guests staying in the lodge get a continental breakfast.

4313 Roche Harbor Rd., Friday Harbor, WA 98250. ✆ **800/617-2267** or 360/378-2350. Fax 360/378-0944. www.lakedale.com. 16 units. $137–$209 lodge double; $177–$279 cabin; $400–$425 house. 2- to 3-night minimum. MC, V. Children over 12 welcome in lodge; children under 4 stay free in parent's cabin. **Amenities:** Jacuzzi; canoe rentals. *In room:* No phone in cabins.

Roche Harbor 🐾🐾 *Kids*   Situated at the north end of San Juan, Roche Harbor is steeped in island history, with the historic Hotel de Haro, established in 1886, serving as its centerpiece. A brick driveway and manicured gardens provide the foreground for the white two-story hotel, which overlooks the marina and has porches running the length of both floors. Although the rooms in the Hotel de Haro are quite basic (all but four have shared bathrooms) and have not been updated in years, the building has loads of character (sloping floors, log walls, vintage wallpaper, a fireplace in the lobby). The condominiums, although a bit dated, are good bets for families. The best accommodations here, however, are the Company Town cottages and the four luxury McMillin suites, in a restored home adjacent to the historic hotel. These latter suites are among the finest rooms on the island. The waterfront dining room has a view of the marina, and the deck makes a great spot for a sunset cocktail. Besides the amenities listed, there are whale-watching cruises, sea-kayak tours, and a marina.

248 Reuben Memorial Dr. (P.O. Box 4001), Roche Harbor, WA 98250. ✆ **800/451-8910** or 360/378-2155. Fax 360/378-6809. www.rocheharbor.com. Historic hotel: 20 units (16 with shared bathroom); modern accommodations: 25 condos, 9 cottages, 4 suites. $85–$99 double with shared bathroom; $160–$299 suite; $199–$360 condo; $229–$249 cottage (lower rates Oct to mid-May). AE, MC, V. **Amenities:** 3 restaurants (Continental/Northwest, American); lounge; outdoor pool; 2 tennis courts; bike and moped rentals; shopping arcade; coin-op laundry. *In room:* Coffeemaker, hair dryer, iron.

San Juan Suites ✦ On the second floor of a new building a block from the ferry landing in Friday Harbor, these suites make a great base for an extended stay in the islands. There are large kitchens, big living rooms, balconies, and luxurious beds. Because staying here is a bit like having your own apartment in the islands, this place is for travelers who are pretty self-sufficient. You even check yourself in when you arrive. Several good restaurants are within walking distance, as is a grocery store.

150-A Spring St., Friday Harbor, WA 98250. ✆ **800/722-2939** or 360/378-8773. Fax 360/378-8775. www.sanjuan islandsuites.com. 5 units. Summer $165–$340 double; fall–spring $130–$270 double. MC, V. *In room:* TV/DVD, dataport, kitchen, fridge, coffeemaker, hair dryer.

MODERATE

Friday's Historic Inn ✦ In downtown Friday Harbor 2 blocks from the ferry landing, this small hotel offers a few affordable rooms. The less expensive guest rooms are small and simply furnished, with the occasional antique and unusual driftwood headboards in some rooms. A few of the rooms have kitchenettes and eight have double whirlpool tubs. The best rooms are the ground-floor rooms, including a two-bedroom suite that's a good choice for families. Most rooms have a TV and VCR, and many also have in-room Jacuzzi tubs, kitchenettes, or fireplaces.

35 First St. (P.O. Box 2023), Friday Harbor, WA 98250. ✆ **800/352-2632** or 360/378-5848. Fax 360/378-2881. www.friday-harbor.com. 18 units, 4 with shared bathroom. $99–$129 double with shared bathroom; $149–$299 double with private bathroom. Lower rates in winter. Rates include continental breakfast (except in 3 vacation rentals). MC, V. **Amenities:** Massage. *In room:* No phone.

Juniper Lane Guest House ✦ *Value* This cedar-shingled house, with its colorful trim, sits on the outskirts of Friday Harbor with views of pastures just over the back fence. Constructed primarily from salvaged wood, this guesthouse is a labor of love for young owner Juniper Maas, who patterned her lodging after places she's visited in her world travels. The interior is a bold blend of burnished wood and bright colors, with eclectic artwork on display throughout. Some guest rooms have shared bathrooms, others have private bathrooms, and a couple of units are designed as dorm rooms (good choices for families). My personal favorite is the Regal Royale room, with its claw-foot tub. Although breakfast is not included in the rates, guests have use of the kitchen. Young travelers, and the young at heart, should like this place as much as I do.

1312 Beaverton Valley Rd., Friday Harbor, WA 98250. © 360/378-7761. www.juniperlaneguesthouse.com. 6 units. $30 per person in dorm; $80 double with shared bathroom; $120 double with private bathroom; $150 family room; $175 cabin. Children under 10 stay free in parent's room. MC, V. *In room:* Hair dryer, no phone.

Olympic Lights Bed & Breakfast ✵✵   At San Juan's dry southwestern tip, the Olympic Lights is a Victorian farmhouse surrounded by wind-swept meadows, and if it weren't for the sight of Puget Sound out the window, you could easily mistake the setting for the prairies of the Midwest. There are colorful flower gardens, an old barn, and even some hens to lay the eggs for your breakfast. The ocean breezes, nearby beach, and friendliness of innkeepers Christian and Lea Andrade lend a special feel to this American classic. My favorite room here is the Ra Room, which is named for the Egyptian sun god and features a big bay window. The view out the windows is enough to settle the most stressed-out soul.

146 Starlight Way, Friday Harbor, WA 98250. © 888/211-6195 or 360/378-3186. Fax 360/378-2097. www.olympic lights.com. 4 units. May–Oct $130–$140 double; Nov–Apr $99 double. Rates include full breakfast. 2-night minimum July–Sept. No credit cards. *In room:* Hair dryer, no phone.

CAMPGROUNDS

Lakedale Campground ✵✵, 4313 Roche Harbor Rd., Friday Harbor, WA 98250 (© 800/617-2267 or 360/378-2350; www.lakedale.com), is 4 miles north of Friday Harbor. With over 80 acres, several lakes, and campsites for tents as well as RVs, this private campground makes an ideal spot for a family vacation. Rates vary by season and number in party, but start at $26 in summer.

Our favorite campground on the island is **San Juan County Park** ✵✵, 380 Westside Rd. N. (© 360/378-8420 for information, or 360/378-1842 for reservations), which has unbeatable views and is set on the site of an old waterfront farm. Campsites are $25 to $34 per night, and reservations can be made up to 90 days in advance.

WHERE TO DINE

In addition to the restaurants listed below, Friday Harbor has several other places where you can get a quick, simple meal. About a block from the top of the ferry lanes is the **Market Chef,** 225 A St. (© 360/378-4546), a combination espresso bar and gourmet takeout restaurant that also bakes outrageously good chocolate-chip cookies. This place is open Monday through Friday from 10am to 6pm and sometimes on Saturday as well. Although it's a bit hard to find, **Backdoor Kitchen & Catering,** 400b A St. (© 360/378-9540), a great little lunch spot in the middle of a plant nursery and garden-design center, is worth searching out for its eclectic menu. The Backdoor is open Monday through Friday from 11am to 3pm, and in the summer also serves dinner Friday through Sunday nights. The **Garden Path Café,** 135 Second St. (© 360/ 378-6255), has a good selection of deli salads, soups, and baked goods. It's open Monday through Friday from 10am to 6:30pm. If you're staying someplace with a kitchen and want fresh seafood for dinner, stop by **Friday Harbor Seafood** (© 360/378-5779), on the main dock in the Friday Harbor marina. This seafood market also sells smoked fish (including succulent smoked scallops), great picnic fare.

For the best latte on the island, head to **The Doctor's Office,** 85 Front St. (© 360/ 378-8865) straight across from the ferry landing in an old Victorian house. For the most unusual coffee and tea, try the lavender-flavored beverages at **Pelindaba Downtown Gallery and Café,** First Street between Spring and East streets (© 360/378-6900; www.Pelindaba.com), in the Friday Harbor Center. Be sure to have a lavender scone with your lavender latte or tea. For fresh-baked bread, good cheeses, and other gourmet for an island picnic, stop in at **Kneadful Things,** 895 Spring St. (© 360/ 378-7089), which is on the edge of town. When it's time for beer, heft a pint of locally brewed ale at the **Front Street Ale House,** 1 Front St. (© 360/378-2337). The IPA is particularly good.

If you're up near the north end of the island at mealtime, you've got several good options at the Roche Harbor resort, marina, and historic hotel. **McMillin's Dining Room** (© 800/451-8910 or 360/378-5757) is the most formal option and serves the best food. For a more casual setting and a waterside deck, try the **Madrona Grill** (© 800/451-8910, ext. 400, or 360/378-5757), which is popular with the boating crowd that ties up in the marina. For lunch or a light dinner, try the **Lime Kiln Cafe** (© 360/378-2155), on the dock at Roche Harbor Village. This lively little cafe serves filling breakfasts and good chowder and fish and chips. Big windows allow you to gaze out at the boats in the marina.

Duck Soup Inn ✸✸ NORTHWEST/INTERNATIONAL   This restaurant, located 4½ miles north of Friday Harbor, sums up the San Juan Islands experience. It's rustic and casual, set in tranquil rural surroundings beside a small pond, and yet serves superb multi-course dinners. Inside the quintessentially Northwest building, you'll find lots of exposed wood and a fieldstone fireplace. The menu changes frequently, depending on the availability of fresh produce, but is always very creative (the chef has a penchant for the flavors of Asia and the Mediterranean). You might find seared scallops with fresh artichokes or braised spring rabbit. Of course, you're also likely to find duck, perhaps served in sour-cherry-and-juniper sauce.

50 Duck Soup Lane. © 360/378-4878. www.ducksoupinn.com. Reservations highly recommended. Main courses $15–$31. MC, V. Summer Tues–Sun 5–8:30 or 9pm; call for days and hours in other months. Closed Nov–Mar.

Friday Harbor House Dining Room ✸✸ NORTHWEST   In the luxurious Friday Harbor House boutique hotel, this is the most sophisticated restaurant on San Juan Island. Striking contemporary decor sets the tone, but doesn't distract diners from the harbor views out the glass walls. The chef draws on diverse inspirations for the dishes served here, which are always attractively presented and carefully prepared. The menu is short and relies heavily on local ingredients, including island-grown greens and Westcott Bay oysters. A recent menu included perfectly cooked wild salmon with herbed polenta and a chardonnay butter emulsion, as well as a succulent halibut baked in a mushroom crust and served with an arugula and shaved fennel salad, pomegranate syrup and basil oil.

130 West St. © 360/378-8455. Reservations highly recommended. Main courses $18–$34. AE, MC, V. Daily 5:30–9pm.

The Place Bar & Grill ✸✸ NORTHWEST/INTERNATIONAL   Just to the right as you get off the ferry and housed in a small wooden building that was once part of a U.S. Coast Guard station, this is San Juan Island's finest waterfront restaurant. The menu changes regularly, but a couple of my favorite dishes are almost always available. These include superb Asian-style crab cakes with sesame-ginger aioli and baked oysters with hazelnut-garlic butter. Best of all, these two dishes are both available as appetizers and entrees. Looking for something else? Try the Pacific Rim bouillabaisse. No matter what you order, be sure to start your meal with the mushroom sauté, which has been featured in *Bon Appetit* magazine.

1 Spring St. © 360/378-8707. Reservations highly recommended. Main courses $16–$30. MC, V. Daily 5–9pm.

Steps Wine Bar and Cafe ⟨⟨ NEW AMERICAN   This new restaurant down a pedestrian passage just uphill from the ferry landing became an instant hit with locals when it opened in 2005. There's no view and it's a bit hard to find, so most tourists never make it here, which is their loss. The food menu is short and changes frequently to take advantage of whatever is fresh, while the wine list is long, featuring excellent wines from all over the world. Whether you just need a few light snacks to go with a glass of wine or a filling dinner, you'll be happy with the menu. Small plates and sides make up the bulk of the menu, so you can piece together a dinner that fits your appetite. If you spot anything with the strawberry-soy vinaigrette, give it a try. Just don't order too many dishes before you make it to the dessert menu. I like to eat downstairs with a view of the open kitchen, but the loft level is quieter and makes a good place for a romantic dinner.

Friday Harbor Center, First St. between Spring and East sts. ⓒ 360/370-5959. www.stepswinebarandcafe.com. Reservations recommended. Main dishes $16–$18. MC, V. Wed–Mon 5:30–9:30pm (light menu available from 4–11pm).

Vinny's ⟨⟨ ITALIAN   From the name, you might think this place is some dark dive serving New York–style pizza. Not exactly. Located across the street from the Friday Harbor House and claiming the same good views of the marina, Vinny's is San Juan Island's premier Italian restaurant. With its great views and lively atmosphere, this is the perfect place for a celebratory dinner or a somewhat boisterous night out with friends. The calamari with pine nuts, tomatoes, raisins, lemon, and vinaigrette should not be missed. This is seafood country, for sure, but the charbroiled steaks are a big hit (try one with Gorgonzola-Parmesan butter), and the menu also features plenty of well-prepared standards such as lasagna and *penne alla puttanesca*.

165 West St. ⓒ 360/378-1934. Reservations recommended. Main courses $15–$34. AE, DISC, MC, V. Mon–Thurs 11:30am–2pm; Sun–Thurs 5–9pm; Fri–Sat 5–10pm.

ORCAS ISLAND

Orcas Island, the largest of the San Juans, is also the most beautiful of the islands. If you have time to visit only one island, make it Orcas. The island, which covers 58 square miles, is a particular favorite of nature lovers who come to enjoy the views of green rolling pastures, the hiking trails of Moran State Park, the forested mountains (at 2,409 ft. tall, Mount Constitution is the highest point in the islands), and fjord-like bays (Eastsound, West Sound, and Deer Harbor).

EXPLORING THE ISLAND

Shops worth checking out in East Sound include **The Darvill Gallery,** 296 Main St. (ⓒ 360/376-2351; www.darvillsrareprints.com), which sells antique prints and maps, and the adjacent **Darvill's Bookstore,** 296 Main St. (ⓒ 360/376-2135), which specializes in Northwest fiction, history, and guidebooks. Also be sure to stop by **Olga's Cabinet of Curiosities,** North Beach Road, in Eastsound Square (ⓒ 360/376-5863; www.olgasonorcas.com). This highly eclectic little gift shop is affiliated with Olga's Restaurant and Mercantile, my favorite restaurant on the island.

To learn a little about the history of Orcas Island, drop by the **Orcas Island Historical Museum,** 181 N. Beach Rd., Eastsound (ⓒ 360/376-4849; www.orcasisland. org/~history). Between late May and late September, the museum is open Tuesday through Sunday from 10am to 3pm (Fri until 6pm). At the **Lambiel Museum** (ⓒ 360/376-4544; www.lambielmuseum.com), on Horseshoe Highway southeast of Eastsound, you can view a private collection of artwork by more than 200 artists from around the San Juan Islands. The museum is open daily by appointment. Admission is $10 and tours take about 2 hours.

Just outside Eastsound, off Horseshoe Highway, you'll find **Howe Art,** 236 Double Hill Rd. (© 360/376-2945; www.howeart.net), a studio and gallery run by sculptor Anthony Howe, who fashions hanging kinetic sculptures from stainless steel.

Several interesting pottery shops are located around the island. A few miles west of Eastsound off Enchanted Forest Road is **Orcas Island Pottery,** 338 Old Pottery Rd. (© 360/376-2813; www.orcasislandpottery.com), the oldest pottery studio in the Northwest. Between Eastsound and Orcas on Horseshoe Highway is **Crow Valley Pottery,** 2274 Orcas Rd. (© 360/376-4260; www.crowvalley.com), housed in an 1866 log cabin. On the east side of the island in the community of Olga, **Orcas Island Artworks,** Horseshoe Highway (© 360/376-4408; www.orcasisland.com/artworks), is full of beautiful work by island artists.

SPORTS & OUTDOOR ACTIVITIES

Moran State Park (© 360/902-8844; www.parks.wa.gov), which covers 5,252 acres of the island, is the largest park in the San Juans and the main destination for most island visitors. If the weather is clear, you'll enjoy great views from the summit of Mount Constitution, which rises 2,409 feet above Puget Sound. There are also five lakes, 33 miles of hiking trails, and an environmental learning center. Popular park activities include fishing, hiking, boating, mountain biking, and camping (for campsite reservations, contact **Washington State Parks** at © 888/226-7688, or go to www.parks.wa.gov/reserve.asp). The park is off Horseshoe Highway, about 13 miles from the ferry landing; the parking fee is $5.

BIKING Although Orcas is considered the most challenging of the San Juan Islands for biking, plenty of cyclists pedal the island's roads. **Dolphin Bay Bicycles** (© 360/376-4157; www.rockisland.com/~dolphin), just to the right as you get off the ferry, has long been my favorite place in the islands to rent a bike. It's so close to the ferry dock that you can come to Orcas without a car, walk up the street to the shop, and hop on a bike. From here you can explore Orcas Island or take a free ferry to Lopez Island or Shaw Island. Bikes rent for $30 per day, $70 for 3 days, and $100 per week.

If you're already on the island and staying up near Eastsound, try **Wildlife Cycles,** 350 North Beach Rd., Eastsound (© 360/376-4708; www.wildlifecycles.com), where bikes rent for $30 to $40 per day.

BIPLANE RIDES For an overview of Orcas Island, try a scenic ride in a restored 1929 Travelair. The 30-minute flights with **Magic Air Tours** (© 800/376-1929 or 360/376-2733; www.magicair.com) cost $249 for two people ($199 for one person).

BOAT TOURS, RENTALS & CHARTERS Want to explore some of the outer islands? Contact **North Shore Charters** (© 360/376-4855; www.sanjuancruises. net), which offers a shuttle service to some smaller islands.

If you're interested in heading out on the water aboard a 1940s sloop, contact Captain Ward Fay at **Northwest Classic Day Sailing** (© 360/376-5581; www.classicday sails.com). Captain Fay sails out of Deer Harbor and charges $60 for adults and $45 for children under 13 for a 3-hour cruise. The season runs from May through September. At Rosario Resort, you can book a sailboat cruise aboard the *Morning Star,* a 56-foot, two-masted sailboat. Contact **Morning Star Charters** (© 360/376-2099; www.orcascharters.com). A 3-hour sail costs $50 to $60 per person.

At Rosario you can also rent a bareboat or skippered sailboat from **Orcas Sailing** (© **360/376-2113;** www.orcassailing.com), which charges $120 to $160 for a half-day bareboat rental and $220 to $260 for a full day. You can also rent small sailboats and powerboats at **Orcas Boat Rentals,** Deer Harbor Marina, Deer Harbor Road (© **360/376-7616;** www.orcasboats.com). The place charges between $200 and $250 for an 8-hour rental.

GOLF   Golfers can head to the 9-hole **Orcas Island Golf Club,** 2171 Orcas Rd. (© **360/376-4400**) near Eastsound. For 9 holes, it costs $22 and 18 holes cost $30. Golf carts are an additional $15 to $20.

HIKING   With 33 miles of trails, **Moran State Park** 🐸🐸 allows hikes ranging from short, easy strolls alongside lakes to strenuous, all-day outings. Alternatively, head south of the community of Olga, on the east arm of the island, where you'll find a .5-mile trail through **Obstruction Pass State Park** 🐸🐸. This trail leads to a quiet little cove that has a few walk-in/paddle-in campsites. The park is at the end of Obstruction Pass Road. There is a $5 day-use/parking fee at both of these parks. Right in Eastsound, you can go for a short but rewarding walk at **Madrona Point,** where the Lummi Indian Nation allows access to its Tsel Whi'sen sacred grounds. Trails wind past madrona trees and little meadows beside the water. To find the park, head away from the village on Haven Road, which is an extension of Prune Alley. You can learn all about the natural history and plant life of the islands on guided hikes offered by **Gnats Nature Hikes** (© **360/376-6629;** www.orcasislandhikes.com). Half-day hikes ($30) head out on the trails of Moran State Park.

SEA KAYAKING 🐸🐸   The best way to see the Orcas Island coast is by sea kayak. My favorite local kayaking company is **Shearwater Adventures** (© **360/376-4699;** www.shearwaterkayaks.com), which offers guided 3-hour tours ($49) and all-day tours ($85). These tours go out from several locations around the island, but I think those departing from Deer Harbor are the most scenic.

If you're on the island without a car, it's possible to go out from right at the ferry landing with **Orcas Outdoors Adventure Center** (© **360/376-4611;** www.orcasoutdoors.com), which offers guided sea-kayak tours lasting from 1 hour ($25) to overnight ($220).

Two-hour paddle tours ($25) and brunch tours ($40) are offered by **Spring Bay Inn** (© **360/376-5531;** www.springbayinn.com), on the east side of the island near the village of Olga. These trips are in an area where bald eagles nest in the summer.

WHALE-WATCHING 🐸🐸   If you want to see some of the orca whales for which the San Juans are famous, you can take a whale-watching excursion with **Deer Harbor Charters** (© **800/544-5758** or 360/376-5989; www.deerharborcharters.com), which operates out of both Deer Harbor and Rosario Resort and charges $55 for adults and $37 for children; or with **Orcas Island Eclipse Charters** (© **800/376-6566** or 360/376-6566; www.orcasislandwhales.com), which operates out of the Orcas Island ferry dock; cost is $56 for adults and $35 for children.

WHERE TO STAY
Expensive
The Inn at Ship Bay 🐸🐸   Set on a high bluff just outside the village of Eastsound, this inn boasts a tranquil setting and rooms that are both luxurious and comfortable. Pillow-top king beds and gas fireplaces make it easy to spend way too much of your visit just cozying up in the rooms here. If you sit back in the Adirondack chairs on

your balcony and gaze out over the water, you may never leave. Although guest rooms are in modern buildings that have been designed to look old, the inn's centerpiece is an 1869 home that serves as the restaurant.

326 Olga Rd. (P.O. Box 1374), Eastsound, WA 98245. ✆ **877/276-7296** or 360/376-5886. Fax 360/376-4675. www.innatshipbay.com. 11 units. Summer $150–$195 double, $250–$275 suite; fall–spring lower rates. MC, V. **Amenities:** Restaurant (Northwest). *In room:* TV, dataport, fridge, coffeemaker, free local calls.

Inn on Orcas Island   Looking as if it were transplanted directly from Cape Cod or Martha's Vineyard, this inn blends traditional styling with contemporary lines to create a classically inspired beauty. Situated on a meadow overlooking a small bay just off Deer Harbor, this elegant inn has luxurious rooms in the main house plus a cottage and a more casually decorated carriage house with its own kitchen. Some rooms have balconies; suites have jetted tubs. All of the accommodations feature water views, impeccable decor, and the plushest beds in the San Juans; they practically beg you to forget plans for the day's outing and just stay put so you can enjoy the posh surroundings. Innkeepers Jeremy Trumble and John Gibbs once owned a frame shop and spent years collecting and framing all the prints and original oil paintings that now hang in the inn. A sunroom in the main house is a wonderful place to while away the morning. Breakfasts are lavish affairs that will leave you full until dinner.

114 Channel Rd. (P.O. Box 309), Deer Harbor, WA 98243. ✆ **888/886-1661** or 360/376-5227. Fax 360/376-5228. www.theinnonorcasisland.com. 8 units. May–Oct $185 double, $225–$285 suite, cottage, or carriage house; Nov–Apr $145 double, $185–$245 suite, cottage, or carriage house. Rates include full breakfast. 2-night minimum May–Oct, holidays, and all weekends. AE, MC, V. Children not accepted. **Amenities:** Bikes. *In room:* Dataport, fridge.

Rosario Resort & Spa   This is the most luxurious lodging on Orcas Island and the only place in the San Juans that can actually claim to be a resort. Although Rosario has a wide variety of modern, comfortably appointed accommodations, the centerpiece remains the 1904 Moran Mansion, an imposing white-stucco building on the shore of Cascade Bay. This mansion houses the resort's main dining room, lounge, spa, and library. The larger, more luxurious guest rooms (with fireplaces and good views) are across the marina and up a steep hill from the main building. For the ultimate in luxury, stay in the Round House, a suite in an unusual round building on a rocky knoll near the marina.

1400 Rosario Rd., Eastsound, WA 98245. ✆ **800/562-8820** or 360/376-2222. Fax 360/376-2289. www.rosario resort.com. 116 units. July–Sept $199–$239 double, $239–$699 suite; Nov–Mar $89–$109 double, $119–$325 suite; Apr–June and Oct $149–$169 double, $189–$599 suite. Children under 16 stay free in parent's room. AE, DC, MC, V. Pets accepted ($25 per night). **Amenities:** 2 restaurants (American, Seafood); lounge, poolside bar; 1 indoor and 2 outdoor pools; exercise room; full-service spa; Jacuzzi; sauna; watersports equipment rentals; concierge; car-rental desk; room service; massage; coin-op laundry. *In room:* TV, coffeemaker, hair dryer, iron, free local calls.

Spring Bay Inn   This inn would deserve a recommendation by virtue of being one of the only waterfront B&Bs in the San Juans. However, innkeepers Sandy Playa and Carl Burger, both retired park rangers, have made this such a special place that it is one of the more memorable inns in the state of Washington. Stays here can be relaxing, fun, and educational, and the setting and the inn itself combine to make this a great place for a romantic getaway. You can soak in the hot tub on the beach and watch the sunset, spot bald eagles from just outside the inn's front door, hike on the nature trails, and, best of all, go for a guided sea-kayak tour each morning. All of the guest rooms have woodstoves, two have views from their tubs, and two have balconies.

P.O. Box 97, Olga, WA 98279. (© 360/376-5531. Fax 360/376-2193. www.springbayinn.com. 5 units. $220–$260 double. Rates include continental breakfast, brunch, daily kayak tour. 2-night minimum. DISC, MC, V. **Amenities:** 2 Jacuzzis; watersports equipment; concierge; business center; massage; laundry service. *In room:* Dataport, fridge, hair dryer, iron, free local calls, high-speed Internet access, Wi-Fi.

Turtleback Farm Inn ✪✪
Nowhere on Orcas will you find a more idyllic setting than this bright-green restored farmhouse overlooking 80 acres of farmland at the foot of Turtleback Mountain. Simply furnished with antiques, the guest rooms range from cozy to spacious, and each has its own special view. My favorite unit in the main house is the Meadow View Room, which has a private deck and a claw-foot tub. The four rooms in the Orchard House are among the biggest and most luxurious on the island (with gas fireplaces, claw-foot tubs, balconies, wood floors, and refrigerators). Days here start with a big farm breakfast served at valley-view tables that are set with bone china, silver, and linen. If you're staying in the Orchard House, breakfast is delivered to your room. Finish your day with a nip of sherry by the fire.

1981 Crow Valley Rd., Eastsound, WA 98245. (© 800/376-4914 or 360/376-4914. Fax 360/376-5329. www.turtle backinn.com. 11 units. Main house: June–Sept $100–$180 double; Orchard House: June–Sept $245 double; lower rates other months. Rates include full breakfast. 2-night minimum June–Sept, weekends, and holidays. DISC, MC, V. Children under 4 stay free in parent's room in Orchard House; in farmhouse, children over 8 are welcome. **Amenities:** Access to nearby health club; concierge; massage. *In room:* Hair dryer, iron.

Moderate

Cascade Harbor Inn ✪
Formerly a part of Rosario Resort, this hotel enjoys similar Eastsound views and is adjacent to both the Rosario marina and Moran State Park. Guest rooms range from standard motel rooms to studios with Murphy beds to spacious suites with kitchens. All the rooms have water views, though in some cases the view is somewhat hidden by trees. The lodge sits on a steep hillside above the water, and a path leads down to the Rosario marina.

1800 Rosario Rd., Eastsound, WA 98245. (© 800/201-2120 or 360/376-6350. Fax 360/376-6354. www.cascade harborinn.com. 45 units. Summer $129–$399 double; spring and fall $90–$279 double; winter $65–$199 double. Children 9 and under stay free in parent's room ($10 for children 10–17). Rates include continental breakfast (summer only). AE, DISC, MC, V. **Amenities:** Concierge. *In room:* TV, coffeemaker, free local calls.

The Kingfish Inn ✪ *Finds*
Housed in the old West Sound general store, this inn is about as quaint as they come. Downstairs, the old general store has been converted into a cozy little cafe, while upstairs, there are three rooms with views over West Sound. These views are among the best on the island. The fourth room is just off the cafe's deck. However, the upstairs rooms are much more attractively furnished, with a sort of Tuscan feel, and you should try to get one of these rooms. These rooms have rustic armoires and beautiful beds with fluffy duvets. One of the rooms has a woodstove and one has a picture-perfect porch. Bathrooms, however, are very basic and have showers only.

Deer Harbor and Crow Valley roads, West Sound (mailing address 4362 Crow Valley Rd., Eastsound, WA 98245). (© 360/376-4440. www.kingfishinn.com. 4 units. $100–$160 double. Rates include breakfast. MC, V. **Amenities:** Restaurant (American); massage. *In room:* TV/VCR, hair dryer, iron.

Orcas Hotel ✪
Right at the Orcas ferry landing, this attractive old Victorian hotel has been welcoming guests since 1904, and with its white picket fence and perennial gardens is the absolute picture of slow-paced island living. The guest rooms, done in a simple country style, vary in size, but all are carpeted and furnished with antiques. On the first floor of the three-story building, you'll find a quiet lounge, bakery, cafe, and restaurant. This place is a good choice for less-fussy travelers coming over without a car.

P.O. Box 369, Orcas, WA 98280. ⓒ 888/672-2792 or 360/376-4300. Fax 360/376-4399. www.orcashotel.com. 12 units (4 with shared bathroom). $89–$114 double with shared bathroom; $114–$208 double with private bathroom. Some rates include continental breakfast. AE, MC, V. **Amenities:** 2 restaurants; lounge. *In room:* No phone.

CAMPGROUNDS

With 151 sites, **Moran State Park** ☆☆ (ⓒ 360/902-8844) is the most popular camping spot on the island. Reservations are accepted (and highly recommended) May 15 through September 15 and can be made up to 9 months in advance through **Washington State Parks Reservations** (ⓒ 888/226-7688; www.parks.wa.gov/reserve.asp). Additional campsites are available at the **Doe Bay Resort & Retreat** ☆ (ⓒ 360/376-2291; www.doebay.com), a sort of Deadhead beach resort that charges $35 per night for campsites. If you enjoy roughing it, there are hike-in or paddle-in sites at **Obstruction Pass State Park** ☆ at the south end of the east arm of the island (near Olga). Keep in mind that there is no water available at this isolated and beautifully situated park.

WHERE TO DINE

For great cookies, don't miss **Teezer's Cookies,** at North Beach Road and A Street, Eastsound (ⓒ 360/376-2913). In West Sound, the **West Sound Cafe,** at Deer Harbor Road and Crow Valley Road (ⓒ 360/376-4440), housed in a former general store and with a great view of the water, serves good breakfasts, lunches, and the best fish and chips on the island. The deck here is great at sunset. Housed in a little cottage in Eastsound, **The Kitchen,** 249 Prune Alley (ⓒ 360/376-6958), is my favorite spot on the island for healthy light meals. This place isn't strictly vegetarian, but it does lots of great Asian-inspired wraps and rice and noodle dishes. The kitchen at The Kitchen is open Monday through Saturday from 11am to 7pm.

Cafe Olga ☆ *(finds)* INTERNATIONAL   Housed in an old strawberry-packing plant that dates from the days when these islands were known for their fruit, Cafe Olga is a good spot for reasonably priced breakfasts and lunches. Everything here is homemade, using fresh local produce whenever possible. The blackberry pie is a special treat, especially with Lopez Island Creamery ice cream. This building also houses Orcas Island Artworks, a gallery representing more than 65 Orcas Island artists.

Horseshoe Hwy., Olga. ⓒ 360/376-5098. Main courses $10–$17 at lunch; $13–$21 at dinner. MC, V. July 1–Sept 15 daily 9am–8pm; shorter hours other months. Closed Jan–Feb.

Christina's ☆☆ NORTHWEST   On the second floor of an old waterfront building in Eastsound, Christina's has been Orcas's premier fine dining establishment for more than 25 years now. The beautiful view down the sound is part of what makes this place special, but it's chef Christina's fresh, creative dishes that really make this place memorable. The menu here is short, changes regularly, and features innovative cuisine prepared with an emphasis on local ingredients. Christina's showcases its creativity in such tasty appetizers as creamy lovage soup with lemony shrimp toast. On a recent evening, the basil-glazed halibut with roasted vegetables was superb. Whether you crave the unusual or the familiar, you'll likely be satisfied here. Desserts, especially the chocolate torte, can be heavenly. This is the perfect place for a sunset dinner, and if the weather is pleasant, the deck is the place to be. If you're on a budget, you can eat in the bar, which, however, lacks those great views.

Porter Building, 310 Main St., Eastsound. ⓒ 360/376-4904. www.christinas.net. Reservations highly recommended. Main courses $27–$30. AE, DC, DISC, MC, V. Daily 4–9:30pm (closed Tues–Wed fall–spring). Closed 1st 3 weeks of Nov.

Inn at Ship Bay NORTHWEST   About midway between Eastsound and the turnoff for Rosario Resort, you'll spot the Inn at Ship Bay, a cluster of yellow farm-house-style buildings set behind an old orchard in a field high above the water. Inside, you'll find plenty of windows that let you gaze out to sea. Chef Geddes Martin worked at Rosario for many years and now brings his skills to his own kitchen. You can't miss with the local oysters on the half shell; the clam chowder (if it's on the menu) is also excellent. If the mussels in shallot-saffron broth are available, don't miss them either. There are always plenty of other great seafood dishes on the menu as well.

326 Olga Rd., Eastsound. *(C)* **877/276-7296** or 360/376-5886. www.innatshipbay.com. Reservations recommended. Main courses $19–$27. DISC, MC, V. Tues–Sat 5:30–9 or 9:30pm. Closed late Dec to mid-Feb.

Olga's Restaurant ECLECTIC   This is the sort of place you may at first find a tad pricey for breakfast or lunch, but later realize is your favorite restaurant on the islands. The menu changes regularly, but look for tiger-prawn pasta, halibut chowder, the fried-oyster Caesar salad, and the Monte Cristo sandwich made with fresh-baked brioche. If you're full, looking at the dessert menu is tantamount to self-flagellation. Right next door is a very eclectic gift shop associated with the restaurant.

Eastsound Square, North Beach Road, Eastsound. *(C)* **360/376-5862.** www.olgasonorcas.com. Main courses $8–$16. MC, V. Summer Thurs–Mon 9am–3pm; call for days and hours other months.

Rose's ECLECTIC   This started out as a hole-in-the-wall gourmet-food shop, but has now graduated into one of my favorite island eateries. With its Tuscan-influenced decor, big patio, and stone pizza oven, Rose's is both a casual and stylish place for inex-pensive lunches. Lunch features creative sandwiches, flavorful soups, designer pizzas, and a few more substantial entree specials. The dinner menu leans heavily toward Mediterranean flavors. Be sure to keep an eye out for the rose-scented ice cream. The restaurant still has an associated gourmet-food shop where you can pick up imported cheeses, baked goods, and wine.

382 Prune Alley, Eastsound. *(C)* **360/376-4292.** Reservations accepted only for parties of 6 or more. Main dishes $8–$17. MC, V. Summer Mon–Wed 10am–6pm, Thurs–Sat 10am–9pm. Closed Jan.

LOPEZ ISLAND

Of the three islands with accommodations, Lopez is the least developed, and although it is less spectacular than Orcas or San Juan, it is flatter, which makes it popular with bicyclists who prefer easy grades over stunning panoramas. Lopez maintains more of its agricultural roots than either Orcas or San Juan, and likewise has fewer activities for tourists. If you just want to get away from it all and hole up with a good book for a few days, Lopez may be the place for you.

EXPLORING THE ISLAND

Lopez Village is the closest thing to a town on this island, and it's where you'll find almost all the restaurants and shops.

At the **Lopez Island Historical Museum,** in Lopez Village (*(C)* **360/468-2049**), you can learn about the island's history and pick up a map of historic buildings. In July and August, the museum is open Wednesday through Sunday from noon to 4pm. In May, June, and September, it's open Friday through Sunday from noon to 4pm.

Lopez Island Vineyards *(★)*, 724B Fisherman Bay Rd. (*(C)* **360/468-3644;** www. lopezislandvineyards.com), located between the ferry landing and Lopez Village, was until recently the only winery that actually made wine from fruit grown here in the San Juans. Both its Siegerrebe and Madeleine Angevine are from local grapes, and its

Doing the Lopez Wave

Want to feel like a Lopez Island native? As you drive the island, give passing cars a quick wave of the hand. Among this island's friendly residents the greeting is so commonplace that it has come to be known as the Lopez Wave.

organic fruit wines are made from local fruit. Lopez Island Vineyards also makes wines from grapes grown in the Yakima Valley. In July and August, the winery tasting room is open Wednesday through Saturday from noon to 5pm; in May, June, and September, it's open on Friday and Saturday from noon to 5pm; and in April and October through mid-December, it's open on Saturday from noon to 5pm.

SPORTS & OUTDOOR ACTIVITIES

Eight county parks and one state park provide plenty of access to the woods and water on Lopez Island.

For a short, easy hike, head to **Upright Channel Park,** on Military Road (about a mile north of Lopez Village in the northwest corner of the island).

A little farther south and over on the east side of the island, you'll find **Spencer Spit State Park** ✹ (© 360/468-2251; www.parks.wa.gov), which has a campground. Here, the forest meets the sea on a rocky beach that looks across a narrow channel to Frost Island. You can hike the trails through the forest or explore the beach. There's a $5-per-day parking fee here.

South of Lopez Village on Bay Shore Road is the small **Otis Perkins Park,** between Fisherman Bay and open water. It has one of the island's longest beaches.

Down at the south end of the island, you'll find the tiny **Shark Reef Sanctuary** ✹✹, where a short trail leads through the forest to a rocky stretch of coast that is among the prettiest on all the ferry-accessible islands. Small offshore islands create strong currents that swirl past the rocks here. Seals and the occasional whale can be seen just offshore as well. It's a great spot for a picnic. To reach this natural area, drive south from Lopez Village on Fisherman Bay Road, turn right on Airport Road, and then turn left onto Shark Reef Road.

BIKING ✹✹   Because of its size, lack of traffic, numerous parks, and relatively flat terrain, Lopez is a favorite of cyclists. You can rent bikes for $5 to $20 an hour or $25 to $65 a day from **Lopez Bicycle Works,** 2847 Fisherman Bay Rd. (© 360/468-2847; www.lopezbicycleworks.com), at the marina on Fisherman Bay Road.

SEA KAYAKING ✹✹   If you want to explore the island's coastline by kayak, contact **Lopez Island Sea Kayaks,** at the marina on Fisherman Bay Road (© 360/468-2847; www.lopezkayaks.com), which is open May through October. A full-day tour costs $75, which includes lunch. A sunset paddle tour, offered in July and August only, goes for $35. Single kayaks can also be rented here for $15 to $25 per hour, $30 to $50 per half-day. Double kayaks rent for $25 to $35 per hour, $50 to $70 per half-day.

WHERE TO STAY

Lopez Farm Cottages and Tent Camping ✹✹ (Value   Set on 30 acres of pastures, old orchards, and forest between the ferry landing and Lopez Village, these modern cottages are tucked into a grove of cedar trees on the edge of a 2-acre meadow. From the outside, the board-and-batten cottages look like old farm buildings, but inside, you'll find a combination of Eddie Bauer and Scandinavian design. There are kitch-enettes, plush beds with lots of pillows, and, in the bathrooms of four of the cottages, showers with double shower heads. If showering together isn't romantic enough for you, there's a hot tub tucked down a garden path. Also on the property is a deluxe tents-only campground.

555 Fisherman Bay Rd., Lopez Island, WA 98261. ✆ 800/440-3556. www.lopezfarmcottages.com. 5 units. July–Sept $150–$175 double; Apr–June and Oct $125–$150 double; Nov–Mar $99–$125 double. Tent sites (available May–Oct) $33 double. Cottage rates include continental breakfast. MC, V. Children must be 14 or older. **Amenities:** Jacuzzi. *In room:* TV, kitchenette, fridge, coffeemaker, hair dryer, free local calls.

Lopez Islander Bay Resort ✿ *Kids*   About a mile south of Lopez Village, the Lopez Islander may not look too impressive from the outside, but it's actually a very comfortable lodging. All of the rooms have great views of Fisherman Bay; most have balconies as well. The more expensive rooms come complete with coffeemakers, wet bars, microwaves, and refrigerators. In addition to the amenities listed below, the Islander has a full-service marina with kayak rentals.

Fisherman Bay Rd. (P.O. Box 459), Lopez Island, WA 98261. ✆ 800/736-3434 or 360/468-2233. Fax 360/468-3382. www.lopezislander.com. 31 units. Late May to Sept $90–$143 double, $199–$260 suite; lower rates Oct to late May. Children under 18 stay free in parent's room. AE, DISC, MC, V. Pets accepted ($20 fee). **Amenities:** Restaurant (American); lounge; outdoor pool; exercise room; Jacuzzi; bike rentals; coin-op laundry. *In room:* TV, fridge, coffeemaker, hair dryer, iron, free local calls.

MacKaye Harbor Inn ✿   This former sea captain's home at the south end of the island was built in 1904 and was the first home on the island to have electric lights. Since that time, this old house has gone through many incarnations, and is today a very comfortable B&B with a mix of classic country styling and plenty of modern creature comforts. Located down at the south end of the island, the big white farm-house is set on a pretty little stretch of flat beach. There's a tea cottage out in the gar-den, and massages, as well as afternoon tea, can be taken in this sunny little building. With kayaks for rent and the calm water of MacKaye Harbor right across the road, this is a good place to give sea kayaking a try. There are also bikes available for guests and the innkeepers can direct you to good hikes in the area. The inn also rents two apartments in an adjacent carriage house.

949 MacKaye Harbor Rd., Lopez Island, WA 98261. ✆ 888/314-6140 or 360/468-2253. Fax 360/468-2393. www.mackayeharborinn.com. 7 units. $119–$195 double. 2-night minimum weekends and holidays. Rates include break-fast. MC, V. Pets accepted in carriage house ($200–$500 deposit). **Amenities:** Access to nearby health club; bikes; sea-kayak rentals/instruction. *In room:* Hair dryer.

CAMPGROUNDS

Spencer Spit State Park (✆ **360/468-2251**) is the island's largest and best camp-ground. This park has 37 campsites set amid tall fir trees. Campsites are $10 to $22 per night, and reservations can be made by contacting **Washington State Parks** (✆ **888/226-7688;** www.parks.wa.gov/reserve.asp). There are also campsites at **Odlin County Park** (✆ **360/378-8420** for information, or 360/378-1842 for reservations), which is just south of the ferry landing and has 30 campsites along the water. Athletic fields make this more of a community sports center than a natural area. Campsites are $11 to $19 per night. Tent campsites are also available at the privately owned **Lopez Farm Cottages and Tent Camping** ✿✿, 555 Fisherman Bay Rd. (✆ **800/440-3556;** www.lopezfarmcottages.com), which has 13 walk-in campsites about 2½ miles south of the ferry landing. These campsites have a very private feel, and both showers and a covered cooking area are provided. This campground is open May through October. Campsites are $33 per night for one or two people, and campers must be 14 or older.

WHERE TO DINE

When it's time for espresso, head to Lopez Village and drop by **Isabel's Espresso** (© 360/468-4114), a local hangout in the Village House Building on the corner of Lopez Road North, Lopez Road South, and Old Post Road. Across the street, you'll find divinely decadent pastries and other baked goods at **Holly B's Bakery** (© 360/ 468-2133). Note that this bakery is closed from December to March. For fresh-squeezed juices and healthy light meals, try **Vortex Juice Bar & Good Food,** Lopez Road South (© 360/468-4740), in Lopez Village in the Old Homestead.

Turn up Village Road North and you'll find **Vita's Wildly Delicious** (© 360/468-4268), which sells wines and delicious gourmet takeout food from a colorfully painted Victorian house. In summer, this place is open Tuesday through Saturday from 10am to 5pm. A little farther along this same street is the **Lopez Island Old-Fashioned Soda Fountain,** 157 Village Rd. (© 360/468-4511), which is located in the Lopez Island Pharmacy. During the summer, there's a Saturday farmers market across the street from these latter two businesses.

Bay Café ★★ NORTHWEST/INTERNATIONAL Housed in an eclectically decorated old waterfront commercial building with a deck that overlooks Fisherman Bay, the Bay Café serves some of the best food in the state. This is the sort of place where diners animatedly discuss what that other flavor is in the molé sauce on the pork tenderloin, and where people walk through the door and exclaim, "I want whatever it is that smells so good." The menu, though short, spans the globe and changes frequently. Come with a hearty appetite; meals include soup and salad, and the desserts are absolutely to die for (and often come decorated with colorful flower petals). For the quintessential Lopez dinner, accompany your meal with a bottle of wine from Lopez Island Vineyards.

Village Center, Lopez Village. © 360/468-3700. www.bay-cafe.com. Reservations highly recommended. Main courses $18–$30. AE, DISC, MC, V. Summer, Mon–Fri 5:30–8pm, Sat–Sun 5–8pm; spring and fall Sun and Wed–Thurs 5:30–7:30pm, Fri–Sat 5:30–8pm; winter hours may vary.

Bucky's ★ AMERICAN With a laid-back island feeling and an outside deck with a distant view of the water, this tiny place is where the locals hang out. The food, though simple, is consistently good—nothing fancy, just well-made familiar fare. The black-and-blue burger with blue cheese and Cajun spices definitely gets my vote for best burger in the islands. If you feel more like seafood, there are fish tacos and fish and chips.

Lopez Village Plaza. © 360/468-2595. Reservations taken only for parties of 5 or more. Main courses $7–$16. MC, V. Apr–Sept daily 11:30am–8pm. Closed Oct–Mar.

SHAW ISLAND

Shaw Island is the least developed of the four San Juan Islands served by regular ferries. The island is home to a few hundred tranquillity-loving residents who like the solitude of the island and want to keep it undeveloped. If you enjoy leisurely drives (or bike rides) in the country, Shaw Island makes a good day trip from any of the other three islands. However, there are no hotels, B&Bs, or restaurants, only a general store at the ferry landing and one small county park down at the south end of the island. The park, **Shaw Island County Park** (© 360/378-1842 or 360/378-8420), does, however, have a small campground (that takes summer reservations) and is popular with sea kayakers.

THE OTHER SAN JUAN ISLANDS: SEA-KAYAK TRIPS & CHARTER BOAT CRUISES

If you want to explore some of the other 168 islands that are not served by the ferries, you'll need a boat. Sailboats, powerboats, and sea kayaks are all popular vessels for exploring these other San Juans, and during the summer months, the waters are full of vessels of all shapes and sizes. Although many of the islands are private property, a few are, or have on them, state parks with campsites. If you want to find out about these marine parks, contact the **Washington State Parks Information Center** (© 360/902-8844; www.parks.wa.gov). Those without their own boat can still visit some of these islands either on a multi-day kayak tour, on a boat excursion, or on a charter boat cruise.

See section 6 in chapter 2 for information on companies offering multi-day sea-kayak tours in the San Juan Islands.

Charter boats, both motorboats and sailboats, can also be hired for multi-day cruises around the San Juan Islands. This is the easiest (not the cheapest) way to see some of these outer islands. Anchoring in secluded coves, exploring marine parks, scanning the skies for bald eagles, spying on orcas, porpoises, and sea lions—these are the activities that make a charter cruise through the San Juans such a memorable experience.

Fantasy Cruises (© 800/234-3861 or 360/378-1874; www.sanjuanislandcruises. com) offers 7-day, 6-night cruises through the San Juan Islands. These cruises, aboard a 130-foot cruise ship that carries fewer than 30 passengers, stop not only in the San Juans, but at other picturesque area ports including La Conner and Port Townsend. Boats can also be chartered through **Anacortes Yacht Charters** (© 800/233-3004; www.ayc.com), which has both powerboats and sailboats in its fleet.

4 La Conner & the Skagit Valley ★★

70 miles N of Seattle, 10 miles E of Anacortes, 32 miles S of Bellingham

In a competition for quaintest town in Washington, La Conner would leave the other contenders wallowing in the winter mud. This town, a former fishing village, has a waterfront street lined with restored wooden commercial buildings, back streets of Victorian homes, and acres of tulip and daffodil fields stretching out from the town limits. Add to this three museums, numerous plant nurseries and gardening-related stores, art galleries, luxurious inns, and good restaurants, and you have a town almost too good to be true.

La Conner does, however, have a couple of shortcomings. In the springtime, when the tulips blossom, the town and surrounding country roads are so jammed with cars that it can make a Seattle rush-hour commute seem pleasant. The other drawback is that La Conner is so close to the San Juans that it is hard to justify spending more than a day here when the islands are calling. If, however, you have some free time in your schedule, this town should not be missed.

La Conner dates from a time when Puget Sound towns were connected by water and not by road, and consequently, the town clings to the shore of Swinomish Channel. The town reached a commercial peak around 1900 (when steamers made the run to Seattle) and continued as an important grain- and log-shipping port until the Great

Depression. La Conner never recovered from the hard times of the 1930s, and when the highways bypassed the town, it became a neglected backwater. The wooden false-fronted buildings built during the town's heyday were spared the waves of progress that swept the Northwest during the latter half of the 20th century, and today these quaint old buildings give the town its charm.

Beginning in the 1940s, La Conner's picturesque setting attracted several artists and writers. By the 1970s, La Conner had become known as an artists' community, and tourism began to revive the economy. The town's artistic legacy eventually led to the building here of the Museum of Northwest Art, which is dedicated to the region's many contemporary artists.

Adding still more color to this vibrant little town are the commercial flower farms of the surrounding Skagit Valley. In the spring, tulips and daffodils carpet the surrounding farmlands with great swaths of red, yellow, and white. These flowers are grown to supply the fall bulb-planting needs of gardeners across the country, and heartbreaking as it sounds, the flowers are cut off in their prime to channel energy into the bulbs.

One more thing: Although the name sounds as if it's a combination of Spanish and Irish, La Conner is actually named for Louisa A. (LA) Conner, who helped found the town in the 1870s.

ESSENTIALS

GETTING THERE From I-5, take U.S. 20 west toward Anacortes. La Conner is south of U.S. 20 on La Conner–Whitney Road. Alternatively, take exit 221 off I-5 and head west on Fir Island Road to a left onto Chilberg Road, which leads into La Conner.

The **Airporter Shuttle** (© **866/235-5247** or 360/380-8800; www.airporter.com) operates between Sea-Tac Airport and the Anacortes ferry terminal, stopping at the Farmhouse Inn, which is at the junction of Wash. 20 and La Conner–Whitney Road, north of La Conner ($32 one-way, $58 round-trip).

VISITOR INFORMATION Contact the **La Conner Chamber of Commerce,** 413 Morris St. (P.O. Box 1610), La Conner, WA 98257 (© **888/642-9284** or 360/ 466-4778; www.laconnerchamber.com).

FESTIVALS For a few short weeks each year, from late March to mid-April, the countryside around La Conner is awash with color as hundreds of acres of Skagit Valley tulip and daffodil fields burst into bloom in a floral display that rivals that of the Netherlands. These flowers are grown for their bulbs, which each fall are shipped to gardeners all over the world. The **Skagit Valley Tulip Festival** (© **360/428-5959;** www.tulipfestival.org), held each year during bloom time, is La Conner's biggest annual festival and includes dozens of events. Contact the festival office or stop by the La Conner Chamber of Commerce (see above), for a map of the flower fields.

Whether you're here in tulip time or not, you might want to stop by some of the area's farms, gardens, and nurseries. **Roozengaarde Flowers & Bulbs,** 15867 Beaver Marsh Rd. (© **800/732-3266** or 360/424-8531; www.tulips.com), is the largest grower of tulips, daffodils, and irises in the country and has a gift shop. At **Christianson's Nursery & Greenhouse,** 15806 Best Rd., Mount Vernon (© **800/585-8200** or 360/466-3821; www.christiansonsnursery.com), you'll find hundreds of varieties of roses and lots of other plants as well. Nearby you can tour the beautiful English country gardens of **La Conner Flats,** 15920 Best Rd. (© **360/466-3190**), where high tea is served by reservation. Both of these nurseries are northeast of town off McLean Road (the main road to Mount Vernon).

EXPLORING LA CONNER & ITS ENVIRONS

The **Museum of Northwest Art** ☆☆, 121 S. First St. (ⓒ **360/466-4446**; www.museumofnwart.org), occupies a large contemporary building in downtown La Conner. The museum, which mounts a variety of exhibits throughout the year, features works by Northwest artists, including Morris Graves, Mark Tobey, and Guy Anderson, all of whom once worked in La Conner. This museum would be right at home in downtown Seattle, so it comes as a very pleasant surprise to find it in this tiny town. It's open Tuesday through Sunday from 10am to 5pm; admission is $5 for adults, $4 for seniors, and $2 for students and children ages 12 and over, free for children under 12 (free for all on first Tues of each month). You can also see art around the streets of downtown La Conner where more than a dozen sculptures (all for sale) are set up each year in the spring.

High atop a hill in the center of town, you can learn about the history of this area at the **Skagit County Historical Museum,** 501 S. Fourth St. (ⓒ **360/466-3365;** www.skagitcounty.net/museum). It's open Tuesday through Sunday from 11am to 5pm; admission is $4 for adults, $3 for seniors and children ages 6 to 12, free for children 5 and under. A few blocks away, you'll find the **La Conner Quilt Museum,** 703 S. Second St. (ⓒ **360/466-4288;** www.laconnerquilts.com), which is housed in the historic Gaches Mansion. On the first floor of this museum, you'll find rooms furnished with antiques, while on the second floor there are quilt displays. The museum is open Wednesday through Saturday from 11am to 4pm and Sunday from noon to 4pm; admission is $4.

There is excellent bird-watching around the Skagit Valley, especially during the winter months when migratory waterfowl, including trumpeter swans, snow geese, and various raptors, including peregrine falcons and bald eagles, flock to the area's marshes, bays, and farm fields. Eight miles north of La Conner at the **Padilla Bay National Estuarine Research Reserve and Breazeale Interpretive Center,** 10441 Bayview-Edison Rd. (ⓒ **360/428-1558;** www.padillabay.gov), you can bird-watch along 3 miles of trails through fields and along a dike. Interpretive exhibits explain the importance of estuaries and allow visitors to explore life in Padilla Bay and its salt marshes. The reserve is open daily; the interpretive center, Wednesday through Sunday from 10am to 5pm. Admission is free. The Skagit Wildlife Area, south of La Conner and west of Conway, is another good winter birding area.

Shopping is the most popular pastime in La Conner, and up and down First Street, you'll find lots of great galleries, boutiques, and gift shops filled with an eclectic assortment of must-have objects.

If you are heading north to Bellingham, consider driving the scenic Chuckanut Drive that begins about 15 miles north of La Conner. For details, see section 5, below.

WHERE TO STAY

La Conner Channel Lodge ☆☆   Luxurious accommodations, Northwest styling, and views of Swinomish Channel from all but seven of the rooms make this a truly memorable lodge. A flagstone entry and woodsy garden, cedar-shake siding, and a river-rock fireplace in the lobby set the tone for the rest of the lodge, and the lobby, with its small library alcove, has the sort of nautical feel you'd expect to find in a home built by a ship's captain 100 years ago. Most guest rooms are large and all have small balconies and gas fireplaces. Fir accents and a combination of slate flooring and carpeting give the rooms a natural richness.

205 N. First St., La Conner, WA 98257. (*✆*) **888/466-4113** or 360/466-1500. Fax 360/466-1525. www.laconner lodging.com. 40 units. Apr and July–Sept $140–$290 double; Oct–Mar and May–June $130–$290 double. Rates include continental breakfast. AE, DC, DISC, MC, V. **Amenities:** Access to nearby health club; massage. *In room:* TV, fridge, coffeemaker, hair dryer, iron, free local calls, Wi-Fi.

White Swan Guest House *✿*   If you're here for the tulip blossoms or if you're a gardener, make this your first choice. Located out in the country, this yellow 1898 Victorian farmhouse is set beneath ancient poplar trees and is surrounded by stunning perennial gardens. Of the guest rooms in the main house, we like the one with the turret, though all are comfortable enough. For more space and privacy, opt for the rustic little cottage set on the far side of the gardens. Peter Goldfarb, the owner, bakes up some of the best chocolate chip cookies around.

15872 Moore Rd., Mount Vernon, WA 98273. www.thewhiteswan.com. (*✆*) **360/445-6805**. 4 units, including 1 (cottage) with private bathroom. $75–$85 double; $160–$175 cottage. Rates include continental breakfast. MC, V. *In room:* No phone.

The Wild Iris *✿✿*   The Wild Iris is a modern Victorian inn on the edge of town, and most second-floor rooms have views of distant Mount Baker (these rooms are definitely worth asking for). The inn was designed for romantic weekends, and many of the rooms have double whirlpool tubs. In some the whirlpool tub is in the room, while in others it's on the balcony. This is a good bet for a romantic getaway.

121 Maple Ave. (P.O. Box 696), La Conner, WA 98257. (*✆*) **800/477-1400** or 360/466-1400. www.wildiris.com. 16 units. $109–$129 double; $149–$199 suite. Rates include full breakfast. AE, MC, V. **Amenities:** Concierge. *In room:* TV/DVD, dataport, Wi-Fi.

WHERE TO DINE

On a dark, rainy night, there's no better place in town to heft a pint of ale than at the **La Conner Brewing Company,** 117 S. First St. ((*✆*) **360/466-1415**), which is located right next door to the Museum of Northwest Art.

Kerstin's *✿✿* NORTHWEST   In a tall, narrow building across the street from the water, this contemporary restaurant and wine bar is your best bet in the area for a romantic dinner. Kerstin's also serves the most creative menu in town. While it looks from the street as though this restaurant only has a couple of tables, you'll find a larger dining room on the second floor. The local Samish Bay oysters, baked on the half shell, should not be missed. You'll also find plenty of other well-prepared local seafood, including wild salmon (perhaps with a pine nut and rosemary crust and a lime-butter sauce). Lamb shanks, prepared various ways, also show up regularly.

505 S. First St. (*✆*) **360/466-9111**. Reservations recommended. Main courses $9–$12 lunch, $18–$32 dinner. AE, MC, V. Daily noon–9pm.

Nell Thorn Restaurant & Pub *✿✿* INTERNATIONAL   Some of La Conner's finest meals are to be had at this cozy little restaurant attached to the La Conner Country Inn. The emphasis is on fresh, local, and organic, and the menu in the main dining room is limited. You might start with a wild-prawn salad or local oysters dusted with local herbs. For a main course, the beach bowl, which is packed with local fish and shellfish, is delicious. If you're in the mood for a more casual meal, dine in the tiny downstairs pub, where you can get soups, salads, and sandwiches. The abundance of wood and cramped quarters of the pub give it the feel of an old sailing ship.

La Conner Country Inn, 205 E. Washington Ave. ℂ **360/466-4261**. www.nellthorn.com. Reservations recommended. Main courses $11–$22. AE, DISC, MC, V. Tues–Thurs noon–9 or 10pm; Fri–Sat noon–10 or 11pm; Sun noon–9 or 10pm (fall–spring, no lunch Tues–Thurs).

5 Bellingham & Environs ★★

90 miles N of Seattle, 55 miles S of Vancouver

Perhaps best known outside of Washington state as the southern terminus for ferries heading north to Alaska, Bellingham is a vibrant little city that boasts excellent views of the San Juan Islands. Still an active shipping port, Bellingham has, at Squalicum Harbor, a large commercial and private boat marina, a hotel and commercial complex, and a park that together provide residents and visitors with a chance to enjoy the bay. South of downtown Bellingham, near the Bellingham Cruise Terminal, which is where Alaska ferries dock, is the historic community of Fairhaven. Fairhaven's old brick commercial buildings and interesting shops are a highlight of a visit to Bellingham.

Bellingham is in Whatcom County, which extends from the coast to the top of 10,778-foot Mount Baker and beyond. The county is still primarily rural in character, and near the coast, farming predominates. The nearby farm towns of Ferndale and Lynden are worth visiting for a glimpse of local history and a chance to explore the countryside. At Mount Baker there is a popular downhill skiing and snowboarding area in winter, while in summer, hiking trails lead through meadows and forests and up mountains for spectacular views. South of the city, the mountains and saltwater come together along one of Washington's most scenic stretches of coastline. Winding along this coastline is Chuckanut Drive, with glimpses of rugged shores, expansive waters, and the San Juan Islands.

ESSENTIALS

GETTING THERE   I-5 connects Bellingham with Seattle to the south and Vancouver to the north. Wash. 20, the North Cascades Scenic Highway, connects Bellingham with eastern Washington by way of Winthrop, while Wash. 542 leads to Mount Baker.

Bellingham International Airport (ℂ **360/671-5674**; www.portofbellingham. com/airport), 5 miles northwest of downtown Bellingham, is served by Horizon Airlines and Allegiant Air. The **Airporter Shuttle** (ℂ **866/235-5247** or 360/380-8800; www.airporter.com) runs between Sea-Tac Airport and Bellingham ($34 one-way, $60 round-trip).

Both **Amtrak** trains and **Greyhound** buses stop in Bellingham at the Fairhaven Station, which is adjacent to the Bellingham Cruise Terminal on Harris Avenue in the Fairhaven district.

VISITOR INFORMATION   Contact the **Bellingham/Whatcom County Convention & Visitors Bureau,** 904 Potter St., Bellingham, WA 98229 (ℂ **800/487-2032** or 360/671-3990; www.bellingham.org), just east of I-5 at exit 253.

GETTING AROUND   Rental cars are available at Bellingham International Airport from Avis, Budget, Enterprise, and Hertz. If you need a taxi, contact **Yellow Cab** (ℂ **360/734-8294**). Public bus service around the Bellingham area is provided by the **Whatcom Transportation Authority** (ℂ **360/676-7433**; www.ridewta.com).

WHAT TO SEE & DO
MUSEUMS

If you're interested in art, you shouldn't miss the **Western Washington University Outdoor Sculpture Collection,** off the Bill McDonald Parkway south of downtown.

With more than 20 large sculptures, including one by Isamu Noguchi, this is the largest collection of monumental sculptures on the West Coast. You can pick up a map and guide to the collection at the university's visitor center, or at **Western Gallery** (© **360/650-3900;** www.westerngallery.wwu.edu), which is also on the campus and features exhibits of contemporary art. When the university is in session, the gallery is open Monday, Tuesday, Thursday, and Friday from 10am to 4pm, Wednesday from 10am to 8pm, and Saturday from noon to 4pm.

American Museum of Radio & Electricity ★★ Nowadays, I-Pods, MP3s, and DVDs are so much a part of everyday life that it is easy to forget that sound recording is barely 100 years old. At this not-to-be-missed museum in downtown Bellingham, you can examine more than 800 antique radios (mostly pre-1930s wooden table-top models) and lots of other unusual instruments of early electrical technology. Among the displays is a mock-up of the radio room from the *Titanic,* and if you're lucky, a curator might demonstrate the Tesla coil, which can generate enough electricity to light up a fluorescent light several feet away. There's an original Theremin, sort of a forerunner to modern electronic synthesizers.

1312 Bay St. © **360/738-3886.** www.americanradiomuseum.org. Admission $4 adults, $2 children 12 and under. Wed–Sat 11am–4pm.

Mindport ★ (Kids) If you're traveling with the kids, be sure to check out the fascinating exhibits at this unusual little museum/gallery/learning center. The interactive exhibits blend art with science to create works of art that are hands-on examples of scientific principles. Science was never this fun when I was a kid.

210 W. Holly St. © **360/647-5614.** mindport.org. Admission $2. Wed–Fri noon–6pm. Sat 10am–5pm, Sun noon–4pm.

Whatcom Museum of History and Art ★★ This museum is housed in the former city hall building, which was built in 1892 and is one of Washington's finest examples of Victorian municipal architecture. Most of the museum is taken up by changing exhibits, but up on the third floor, you can see cases full of clocks, tools, and toys. You'll also find, in a big glass case, the old mechanism for the clock in this building's tower. A building across the street houses the gift shop and a gallery that often is used for unusual art installations and special-interest exhibits. This museum is worth a visit for its architecture alone.

121 Prospect St. © **360/676-6981.** www.whatcommuseum.org. Admission by donation. Tues–Sun noon–5pm.

FAIRHAVEN HISTORIC DISTRICT

Though downtown Bellingham has a fair number of restaurants and a few galleries, the **Fairhaven Historic District** is the most interesting neighborhood in town (and is also the site of the Bellingham Cruise Terminal, the southern terminus for ferries to Alaska). Fairhaven was once a separate town, and many of its brick buildings, built between 1880 and 1900, have now been restored and house interesting shops, art galleries, and several good restaurants. Around the neighborhood, you'll find more than two dozen historical markers, many of which commemorate the seamier side of life in Fairhaven in the 1890s. **Fairhaven Haunts and History Tours** (© **360/650-9691**), offers 1-hour walking tours of the neighborhood. These tours, which cost $4, are a fun way to learn about the neighborhood's history.

Today, **Village Books,** 1200 11th St. (© **360/671-2626;** www.villagebooks.com), serves as the cultural anchor for the neighborhood and has readings and book signings.

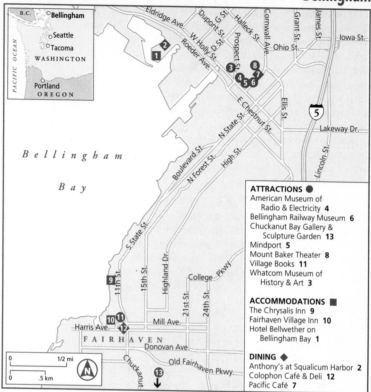

Here in Fairhaven, you'll also find several cafes and bakeries and even an old double-decker British bus that serves fish and chips. Several walking paths begin in Fairhaven. My favorite, the **South Bay Trail,** heads north along the shore and is actually built over the water on the Taylor Dock for part of its length. You'll find the start of this path near the northwest corner of **Fairhaven Common,** which is the little park at the center of Fairhaven. In summer, outdoor movies are shown in this little park.

CHUCKANUT DRIVE

Chuckanut Drive (Wash. 11), which begins on the southern edge of the Fairhaven Historic District and heads south for almost a dozen miles to the Samish farmlands, is one of the most scenic stretches of road in northwestern Washington. The road clings to the shoreline of Chuckanut and Samish bays as it winds south through the Chuckanut Mountains, which rise straight out of the water. Though most of the way is through dense woods, there are several pull-offs where you can gaze out to the San Juan Islands or up and down the rugged coastline. There are also numerous trailheads that allow you to head down to the shore or up into the Chuckanut Mountains, which are home to an extensive network of hiking and mountain-biking trails. Chuckanut Drive is particularly popular at sunset, and several good restaurants are at the southern end (see "Where to Dine," below).

At the northern end of the drive, be sure to stop in at the **Chuckanut Bay Gallery and Sculpture Garden,** 700 Chuckanut Dr. (© **877/734-4885** or 360/734-4885; www.chuckanutbaygallery.com), which is full of interesting artworks by Northwest artists and craftspeople. Continuing south, watch for the **North Chuckanut Mountain Trailhead,** which provides access to **Teddy Bear Cove** 👀, where you'll find a pair of tiny beaches separated by a small, rocky promontory. It's about a 2-mile round-trip hike to the cove. Although part of the trail is quite steep, part of the route follows the **Interurban Trail** 👀, a 6-mile-long hiking and mountain-biking trail that follows the route of an old trolley line and extends from Fairhaven Parkway and 20th Street in Fairhaven to **Larrabee State Park** 👀 (© **360/ 902-8844**). This latter park is the most popular stop along Chuckanut Drive and can be quite crowded in summer. The pretty little beach and access to miles of hiking trails make this park a required stop along the scenic drive. Admission is $5.

OTHER ATTRACTIONS & ACTIVITIES

If you're a fan of riding the rails, check the schedule of the **Lake Whatcom Railway** (© **360/595-2218;** www.lakewhatcomrailway.com), which operates a historic excursion train from the town of Wickersham southeast of Bellingham. There are Saturday and Tuesday trips from early July to early September, as well as runs around Valentine's Day, on Easter, and in October and December. Along the route, you'll get occasional glimpses of Mount Baker. The trips last 1½ hours and the fare is $14 for adults and $7 for children under age 18. Railroad buffs will also want to visit the **Bellingham Railway Museum,** 1320 Commercial St. (© **360/393-7540;** www.bellingham railwaymuseum.org), which has model railroad layouts and is open Tuesday and Thursday through Saturday from noon to 5pm. Admission is $3 for adults and $1 for students.

To explore Chuckanut Bay from a sea kayak, contact **Moondance Sea Kayak Adventures** (© **360/738-7664;** www.moondancekayak.com). It has half-day ($45 per person) and full-day ($80 per person) excursions starting at Larrabee State Park.

Sailboat excursions are another of my favorite ways to experience Bellingham. **Shawmanee Charters** (© **360/734-9849;** www.bellinghamsailing.com), has 3-hour Wednesday evening sailings during the summer for $45 per person. **Gatro Verde** (© **360/220-3215;** www.gatoverde.com), is a 42-foot catamaran that offers sailboat outings of 1½ to 6 hours. The shorter outings are $30 per person and the longer outings are $85 per person.

WHERE TO STAY

The Chrysalis Inn & Spa 👀 *Finds*   The Chrysalis is the most luxurious hotel in Bellingham, and, with its contemporary lodge styling, perfectly captures the essence of the Northwest today. In the lobby, big walls of glass focus the attention on the waters of Bellingham Bay, but the slate floors, burnished wood beams, and fireplace all give the views stiff competition. Guest rooms have water views, and double tubs, gas fireplaces, and window seats make these rooms the ideal place to hide away on a rainy Northwest weekend. To make a getaway even better, there is a full-service spa and a wine bar serving excellent food. About the only drawback to this inn is the presence of a railroad track between the inn and the water. However, excellent insulation keeps the train noises to a minimum and earplugs are provided free of charge.

804 10th St., Bellingham, WA 98225. © **888/808-0005** or 360/756-1005. www.thechrysalisinn.com. 43 units. Mid-May to Sept $179–$189 double, $249–$279 suite; Oct to mid-May $160–$179 double, $209–$259 suite. Rates include full breakfast. AE, DC, DISC, MC, V. Pets accepted ($50 fee). **Amenities:** Restaurant (Continental); lounge; full-service spa; concierge; room service; massage; laundry service; dry cleaning. *In room:* A/C, TV, dataport, minibar, coffeemaker, hair dryer, iron, free local calls, high-speed Internet access.

Fairhaven Village Inn ★★

This modern hotel in the heart of Fairhaven was designed to resemble a historic hotel and blends in perfectly with the adjacent historic buildings. There's even a cashier's cage for a front desk. Guest rooms are, however, quite modern and are tastefully traditional in their decor and furnishings. The balcony rooms, which also have fireplaces, are the most luxurious rooms and have views of the bay, but I actually prefer the rooms that overlook the Fairhaven village green. The location, amid Fairhaven's shops and restaurants—only a few blocks from the Alaska ferry terminal—makes this one of Bellingham's best hotel choices.

1200 Tenth St., Bellingham, WA 98225. © **877/733-1100** or 360/733-1311. Fax 360/756-2797. www.fairhaven villageinn.com. 22 units. Summer $149–$169 double, $279 suite; other months $119–$169 double, $239 suite. Rates include continental breakfast. Children 12 and under stay free in parent's room. AE, DC, DISC, MC, V. Pets accepted ($20). **Amenities:** Access to nearby health club, dry cleaning. *In room:* A/C, TV, dataport, coffeemaker, hair dryer, iron, free local calls, high-speed Internet access.

Hotel Bellwether on Bellingham Bay ★★

This hotel is the centerpiece of Squalicum Harbor, which also includes several restaurants, shops, a marina, and grassy Zuanich Park. The marina setting served as the design theme for this hotel, which has a distinct yacht-club feel. Dark wood paneling abounds, and a traditional styling predominates. Guest rooms are large and have soaking tubs (for one person), fireplaces, and balconies. The hotel's most unusual room is a three-story "lighthouse" suite that was designed to resemble a lighthouse and has a viewing deck on its third floor. This hotel seems designed to appeal to an older and more conservative crowd.

1 Bellwether Way, Bellingham, WA 98225. © **877/411-1200** or 360/392-3100. Fax 360/392-3101. www.hotel bellwether.com. 66 units. $129–$275 double; $159–$799 suite. Rates include continental breakfast. AE, DC, DISC, MC, V. Pets accepted ($65 nonrefundable deposit). **Amenities:** Restaurant (Northwest); lounge; putting green; exercise room; access to nearby health club; bike rentals; concierge; room service; massage; laundry service; dry cleaning. *In room:* A/C, TV, dataport, minibar, coffeemaker, hair dryer, iron, safe, high-speed Internet access, Wi-Fi.

NEARBY ACCOMMODATIONS

Semiahmoo Resort ★★★   Located on 1,100 acres at the end of a long sandy spit that reaches almost to Canada, Semiahmoo Resort is, despite the remote location, Washington's premier golf resort and health spa. Gables and gray shingles give the resort a timeless look, and throughout the classically styled interior of the main lodge are numerous lounges overlooking the water. Artwork abounds, with Native American and nautical themes prevailing. Not all guest rooms have views, but those that do have beds facing out to sea. The main dining room overlooks the water and offers excellent Northwest-style meals and an extensive wine list. There's also an oyster bar and lounge in an old salmon-packing plant. In addition to amenities listed below, the resort has a marina and paved bike and running paths.

9565 Semiahmoo Pkwy., Blaine, WA 98230-9326. © **800/770-7992** or 360/318-2000. www.semiahmoo.com. 198 units. May–Sept $169–$269 double, $249–$409 suite; Oct–Apr $99–$199 double, $239–$319 suite (all rates plus $3 resort fee). Children 17 and under stay free in parent's room. AE, DC, DISC, MC, V. Pets accepted ($50 fee). **Amenities:** 4 restaurants (Northwest, American); lounge; indoor and outdoor pool; 2 18-hole golf courses; 4 tennis courts; health club and exercise room; full-service spa; Jacuzzi; sauna; kayak rentals; bike rentals; business center; room service; massage; laundry service; dry cleaning. *In room:* A/C, TV, dataport, minibar, coffeemaker, hair dryer, iron, high-speed Internet access.

WHERE TO DINE
IN TOWN

For great coffee, stop in at **Tony's Coffee House,** 1101 Harris Ave. (✆ **360/738-4710**), which has been a favorite Fairhaven hangout for many years. At downtown's **La Vie en Rose,** 111 W. Holly St. (✆ **360/715-1839**), you can start your day with a French pastry. For regional microbrews, imported beers, and pub fare, try the very atmospheric **Archer Ale House,** 1212 Tenth St. (✆ **360/647-7002;** www.archerale house.com), in a basement in Fairhaven; or, for locally brewed beers, try **Boundary Bay Brewery & Bistro,** 1107 Railroad Ave. (✆ **360/647-5593;** www.bbaybrewery. com), in downtown Bellingham.

Anthony's at Squalicum Harbor ☙☙ SEAFOOD   Almost every waterfront city from Bellingham to Olympia now boasts an outpost of Seattle's popular Anthony's seafood restaurant chain, and for good reason. These places just seem to do things right. This impressive, lodgelike, waterfront building has big walls of glass overlooking a marina, an open kitchen with an eating bar, a lounge, and a bi-level dining room that assures everyone a water view. There is always plenty of variety on the menu, but dishes to try include the crab cakes, pan-fried Willapa Bay oysters, and the alder-planked salmon (a preparation that is a Northwest classic). Monday through Friday, four-course sunset dinners ($17) are served from 4:30 to 6pm. On Sundays, enjoy the all-you-can-eat Dungeness crab feed!

25 Bellwether Way. ✆ **360/647-5588.** www.anthonys.com. Reservations recommended. Main courses $8–$25. AE, MC, V. Sun–Thurs 11:30am–9:30pm; Fri–Sat 11:30am–10:30pm.

Colophon Café & Deli ☙ SOUPS/SANDWICHES   The Colophon is a Bellingham institution. Chill out with ice cream in summer, warm up with an espresso in winter, or make a filling meal of the star attractions here—homemade soups. You'll always find African peanut soup on the menu, as well as big sandwiches, quiches, and salads. However, for many Bellingham residents, the Colophon's desserts, and in particular its chocolate-chunk cake, have long been the best reasons to eat here.

1208 11th St. ✆ **360/647-0092.** www.colophoncafe.com. Main courses $6–$12. AE, DISC, MC, V. Mon–Sat 9am–10pm; Sun 10am–8pm (summer, Sun 10am–10pm).

Pacific Café ☙☙ NORTHWEST   In the Mount Baker Theater building, this romantic little cafe is, of course, the perfect spot for dinner before the show, but it's also a good choice for a flavorful lunch or dinner even if you're not on the way to a performance. The menu is always eclectic and usually reflects current trends in flavor combinations, but you can be sure you'll find plenty of Asian and Mediterranean influences. The garlic-Parmesan prawns is a good bet, as is the Thai coconut curry chicken if you like Thai food. Also keep an eye out for the passion fruit sorbet. Lunches are among the most creative in the city, and many of the same dishes served at dinner are also served at lunch. There's also an excellent wine list.

100 N. Commercial St. ✆ **360/647-0800.** Reservations recommended. Main courses $9.50–$15 lunch, $15–$28 dinner. AE, MC, V. Mon–Thurs 11:30am–2pm and 5:30–8:30pm; Fri 11:30am–2pm and 5:30–9pm; Sat 5:30–9pm.

ON CHUCKANUT DRIVE
The Oyster Bar on Chuckanut Drive ☙☙ NORTHWEST   Near the south end of Chuckanut Drive, this restaurant is the most formal of the handful of restaurants along the scenic drive. Of course, as the name implies, fresh local oysters are one of the specialties here, but the restaurant also serves up a wide range of imaginative

dishes, the likes of which you aren't likely to find on any other area menus: buffalo with chanterelle mushrooms, truffle oil, and a cabernet reduction; cedar-plank salmon, abalone with hazelnut-lime butter. There are great views of Samish Bay and the San Juan Islands. Desserts feature local fruits and berries. There's an excellent wine cellar.

2578 Chuckanut Dr. © **360/766-6185.** www.theoysterbaronchuckanutdrive.com. Reservations highly recommended. Main courses $8.50–$25 lunch, $20–$52 dinner. AE, MC, V. Daily 11:30am–10pm.

Rhododendron Café ★★ *Finds* NORTHWEST/INTERNATIONAL At the southern end of Chuckanut Drive amid the Samish farmlands, this place looks from the outside like any other farm-country roadside diner. However, take one look at the menu, and you'll find that the farmers in this area are a lucky group. The menu melds creative Northwest cookery with influences from around the world, and each month there are specials from a different part of the world. You might find Vietnamese, Guatemalan, Turkish, or Caribbean food on the menu when you stop by, and these adventurous specials are always worth trying. The regular menu has lots of local produce, fresh herbs from the restaurant's garden, and oysters from Samish Bay.

5521 Chuckanut Dr., Bow. © **360/766-6667.** www.rhodycafe.com. Main courses $9–$15. AE, DISC, MC, V. Wed–Fri 11:30am–9pm; Sat–Sun 9am–9pm. Closed Thanksgiving–Jan 1.

BELLINGHAM NIGHTLIFE

The **Mount Baker Theatre,** 104 N. Commercial St. (© **360/733-5793;** www.mountbakertheatre.com), is downtown Bellingham's other major landmark and is the city's premier performing-arts venue. The theater's 110-foot-tall lighthouse tower is visible from all over the city, and though the exterior decor is quite subdued, inside is an extravagant lobby resembling a Spanish galleon.

7

South Puget Sound & West Sound

With more arms than an octopus, the southern reach of Puget Sound is a region of convoluted waterways, inlets, bays, and harbors. Tucked among the coves, peninsulas, and islands that separate all this saltwater are some of Washington's most charming little towns. Past glacial activity gave this region the look of Scandinavian fjords, and it was that very similarity that more than a century ago attracted Scandinavian fishermen who founded what are today two of the region's most picturesque towns: Poulsbo and Gig Harbor. However, this region is also home to a couple of the state's largest cities—Tacoma and Olympia. While few major attractions are in the area, there is an abundance of natural beauty (with plenty of parks to explore) and, in Tacoma, several interesting museums and attractions as well.

The people who choose to live in this region, as well as those who visit, tend to do so for the water. Forest-ringed waterways, old fishing villages turned yacht havens, idyllic rural settings, the romance of living on an island—these are the aspects of life that attract people to this area. However, down in the southern reaches of the sound,

a very different aesthetic rules in the cities of Tacoma and Olympia. The former, once derided as an industrial wasteland, is in the middle of a renaissance that has turned it into a very livable city. The latter, as the capital of the state and home of a particularly liberal, liberal-arts university, has a mellow, laid-back air and, when the state legislature and the university are shut down, it becomes one of the quietest cities in the Northwest.

While green forests and blue waters are this region's dominant characteristics, life here is ruled by ferries and bridges, and visitors are advised to keep this in mind as they explore the region. While distances here are not great, missed ferries and traffic backups at the Tacoma Narrows bridge can add significantly to travel time. Leave plenty of room in your travel schedule for unforeseen delays.

However, these transportation problems provide much of the region with its slower pace of life, which in turn allows Seattleites and others to make quick escapes to the country by simply crossing to the west side of Puget Sound, where island time prevails and the views of the Olympic Mountains are just that much better.

1 Bainbridge Island ⊛

10 miles W of Seattle (by ferry), 35 miles NE of Bremerton, 46 miles SE of Port Townsend

Bainbridge Island, popular for its miles of waterfront, sound-and-mountain views, and rural feel, is for the most part an affluent bedroom community for Seattle. However, with its bustling little downtown area (reminiscent of tony towns in the San

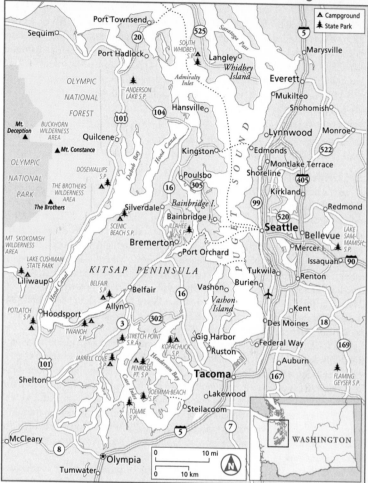

Francisco Bay area), excellent restaurants and B&Bs, many parks, and good bicycling and sea kayaking, it's also a great spot for a quick getaway.

Roughly 10 miles long and 3½ miles wide, Bainbridge Island had long been home to the Suquamish Indians when the island was first charted by Capt. George Vancouver in 1792. Within less than a century after Vancouver's visit, the island had become the site of the world's largest lumber mill (though this is now long gone). The island's early settlement centered around the ferry docks of what was known as the mosquito fleet, though eventually, when car ferries began using the community of Winslow (now known as downtown Bainbridge Island), that community became the island's business center. The island was not linked to the mainland by bridge until the Agate Pass Bridge was opened in 1950.

ESSENTIALS

GETTING THERE   Washington State Ferries (© **800/84-FERRY** or 888/808-7977 within Washington, or 206/464-6400; www.wsdot.wa.gov/ferries) operates a ferry service between Seattle's Pier 52 Colman Dock ferry terminal and Bainbridge Island. The trip takes 35 minutes and costs $11 ($13 from early May to mid-Oct) for a car and driver one-way, $6.10 for adult car passengers or walk-ons, $3 for seniors, and $4.90 for children ages 5 to 18; free for children 4 and under. Car passengers and walk-ons only pay fares on westbound ferries.

VISITOR INFORMATION   For more information on Bainbridge Island, contact the **Bainbridge Island Chamber of Commerce,** 590 Winslow Way E., Bainbridge Island, WA 98110 (© **206/842-3700;** www.bainbridgechamber.com).

EXPLORING BAINBRIDGE ISLAND

Just up the hill from the Bainbridge Island ferry terminal is the island's main shopping district, where you'll find interesting shops and restaurants. If you'd like to sample some local wines, drop by the **Bainbridge Island Vineyards and Winery,** 8989 Day Rd. E. (© **206/842-9463;** www.bainbridgevineyards.com), which is 4½ miles from the ferry landing (take Wash. 305 for 4 miles to the stoplight and turn right on Day Rd. E.). The winery specializes in European-style white wines made from estate-grown grapes. These wines are quite good and only available here and at a few select restaurants. The winery is open Wednesday through Sunday from noon to 5pm.

Down at the south end of the island is **Fort Ward State Park** (© **360/902-8844**), on the quiet shore of Rich Passage. The park offers picnicking, good bird-watching, and a 2-mile hiking trail. Admission is $5 per vehicle.

Garden enthusiasts will want to call ahead and make a reservation to visit the **Bloedel Reserve** ★, 7571 NE Dolphin Dr. (© **206/842-7631;** www.bloedelreserve. org), 6 miles north of the ferry terminal off Wash. 305 (turn right on Agate Point Rd.). The expansive and elegant grounds are the ideal place for a quiet stroll amid plants from around the world. Admission is $10 for adults, $8 for seniors, and $6 for children ages 5 to 12. The gardens are open Wednesday through Sunday from 10am to 4pm. Nearby, at the northern tip of the island, you'll find **Fay Bainbridge State Park** (© **206/842-3931**), which offers camping and great views across the sound to the Seattle skyline.

If you'd like to do a little paddling in a sea kayak or canoe, turn left as you get off the ferry and head to Waterfront Park, where you'll find **Back of Beyond Explorations** (© **206/842-9229**), located on a barge tied up to the city dock. Sea kayaks and canoes rent for $15 to $30 per hour depending on the type of boat you rent. Some unusual swan boats can be rented for $10 per half hour.

WHERE TO STAY

Island Country Inn ★   Right in downtown Bainbridge Island, this is the only motel-style lodging on the island, and with its convenient location, outdoor swimming pool and Jacuzzi, it makes a good choice for anyone coming to the island in summer. Guest rooms are just a cut above your usual motel room. For a longer stay, you may need the suites, which have kitchens.

920 Hildebrand Way NE, Bainbridge Island, WA 98110. © 800/842-8429 or 206/842-6861. www.nwcountryinns. com/Bainbridge.html. 44 units. $109–$119 double; $139–$159 suite. Rates include continental breakfast. Children 12 and under stay free in parent's room. AE, DISC, MC, V. Pets accepted ($20). **Amenities:** Small outdoor pool; Jacuzzi. *In room:* A/C, TV, dataport, coffeemaker, hair dryer, iron.

Waterfall Gardens ☞ This unusual B&B is on 5 acres of gardens and natural landscaping, with a wild salmon and trout stream that has been restored to a natural state by the inn's eco-friendly owners. Accommodations are in two buildings, one of which is designed to resemble an old farmhouse and has 15-foot ceilings and a suite with a full kitchen. The garden-level Waterfall and Weeping Cedars rooms, in the second building, are the smallest rooms here, but still very nice. The Waterfall Room has a double whirlpool tub. Note that breakfast is not included in the rates, so you might want to bring along some breakfast fare so that you don't have to leave this beautiful place too early. Also, be sure to play a round of "bobo" golf while you're here. It's played with a golf club and a tennis ball.

7269 Bergman Rd., Bainbridge Island, WA 98110. © **206/842-1434.** www.waterfall-gardens.com. 4 units. $119–$185 double. No credit cards. **Amenities:** Access to nearby health club. *In room:* TV, fridge, coffeemaker, hair dryer, iron.

WHERE TO DINE

If you're heading out to one of the island's state parks and need some rustic bread for a picnic, stop by **Blackbird Bakery,** 210 Winslow Way E. (© **206/780-1322**), where you can also get good cookies and pastries. When you need a steaming cup of espresso to warm and wake you, head to the **Pegasus Coffee House & Gallery,** 131 Parfitt Way SW (© **206/842-6725;** www.pegasuscoffeehouse.com), near the marina in Winslow. Soups, salads, sandwiches, and pastries are available. If you'd prefer a pint of ale in a cozy waterfront pub, drop in at the **Harbour Public House,** 231 Parfitt Way SW (© **206/842-0969;** www.harbourpub.com), which overlooks a marina about a block away from Pegasus Coffee. This place serves good pub food including burgers, fish and chips, and other seafood. For these latter two establishments, follow Winslow Way east through "downtown" Bainbridge Island and turn left onto Madison Avenue.

The Four Swallows ☞☞ ITALIAN/NORTHWEST Less than a block off Winslow Way in downtown Bainbridge Island, this casual, unpretentious restaurant is housed in a restored farmhouse built in 1889. Out front, under the shade trees, is a big deck for summer alfresco dining, and inside, rustic "primitive" antiques and old, high-backed wooden booths set the tone. The menu changes daily, but any month of the year, the antipasto plate, which showcases a wide range of seasonal specialties, makes a good starter. If you like seafood, order the delicious *brodetto,* a fish stew similar to bouillabaisse. Pizzas and pastas make up a good portion of the menu, and there are always plenty of fresh seafood dishes.

481 Madison Ave. © **206/842-3397.** www.fourswallows.com. Reservations recommended. Main dishes $12–$31. AE, MC, V. Tues–Sat 5:30–9pm.

Winslow Way Cafe ☞☞ MEDITERRANEAN/NORTHWEST Although pasta and pizzas dominate the menu here and prices are reasonable, this contemporary place oozes Seattle attitude. The big bar to one side fairly screams: "Have a martini!" The pizzas are just the sort of designer pies you would expect in such a setting and are generally excellent, but it is often hard to ignore the creative seafood dishes on the daily fresh sheet.

122 Winslow Way E. © **206/842-0517.** Reservations recommended. Main dishes $8.25–$22. MC, V. Mon–Thurs 11am–3:30pm and 4:30–10pm; Fri 11am–3:30pm and 4:30–10:30 or 11pm; Sat 10am–3:30pm and 4:30–10:30 or 11pm; Sun 10am–3:30pm and 4:30–10pm.

2 Poulsbo ★★ & the Kitsap Peninsula ★

Poulsbo: 15 miles NW of Bainbridge Island ferry dock, 35 miles S of Port Townsend, 45 miles N of Tacoma

Roughly 45 miles long and confusingly convoluted, the Kitsap Peninsula looks something like an arrowhead wedged between Seattle and the Olympic Peninsula. Tucked amid the folds of its many glacial hills and fjordlike waterways is an eclectic assortment of small towns, each with a very different character.

For thousands of years, this region was home to several Native American tribes, including the Suquamish, who once had a 900-foot-long longhouse on the shores of Agate Pass between the Kitsap Peninsula and Bainbridge Island. Chief Sealth (pronounced *see*-alth), for whom Seattle is named, was a member of the Suquamish tribe and today his grave can be visited near the town of Suquamish.

The region's earliest pioneer history is linked to the logging industry. At Port Gamble, on the north end of the peninsula, Andrew Pope and William Talbot chose to build their sawmill, which became the longest operating mill in the Northwest. Although the mill is now closed, Port Gamble remains a company town and still, for the most part, looks as if it hasn't changed in 100 years. However, it is currently undergoing development in the wake of the mill closing.

The state of Washington seems obsessed with theme towns; there's a Dutch town, a Wild West town, a Bavarian town, and here on the Kitsap Peninsula, a Scandinavian town. Though at first the town of Poulsbo seems merely a contrivance to sell tacky Scandinavian souvenirs, on closer inspection it proves to have much more character than that. The town's waterfront park, marinas, and picturesque setting on Liberty Bay have great appeal for the boating crowd.

The deep, protected harbors of the Kitsap Peninsula have, for more than a century, seen the comings and goings of the U.S. Navy, which has naval yards here in the town of Bremerton. Today the Bremerton Naval Yards are also home to a large fleet of mothballed navy ships, and these have become the town's greatest tourist asset in recent years, with two museums and a Vietnam-era destroyer open to the public. Not far away there is also a Trident nuclear submarine base, which, however, is not open to the public.

Across Sinclair Inlet from Bremerton, and accessible via the last privately owned passenger ferry still operating on Puget Sound, lies the small town of Port Orchard, which is filled with antiques malls.

ESSENTIALS

GETTING THERE   The Kitsap Peninsula lies between Puget Sound and the east side of the Olympic Peninsula and is bounded on its west side by Hood Canal (which is not a canal, but rather a long fjordlike extension of Puget Sound). Wash. 16 connects the peninsula with I-5 at Tacoma, while Wash. 3 connects the peninsula with U.S. 101 west of Olympia and continues north to the Hood Canal Bridge, a floating bridge that serves as the Kitsap Peninsula's northern link to the Olympic Peninsula. Bainbridge Island is connected to the Kitsap Peninsula by the Agate Pass Bridge on Wash. 305.

Washington State Ferries (© **800/84-FERRY** or 888/808-7977 in Washington, or 206/464-6400; www.wsdot.wa.gov/ferries) operates three ferries between the Kitsap Peninsula and the east side of Puget Sound: the Fauntleroy-Southworth ferry (a 35-min. crossing) from West Seattle, the Seattle-Bremerton ferry (a 60-min. crossing) from downtown Seattle, and the Edmonds-Kingston ferry (a 30-min. crossing) from

---

Finds **Chocolate to Take the Chill Off**

While in Port Gamble, don't miss **LaLa Land Chocolates,** 8 Rainier St. (© **360/ 297-4291**), which is across the street from the two museums. Its chili-chocolate truffles and its Mayan hot chocolate, made with habanero chili, are unforgettable. The shop also does a chocolate-inspired afternoon tea.

---

north of Seattle. Fares range between $11 and $13 for a car and driver on the Seattle-Bremerton or Edmonds-Kingston ferry and between $8.20 and $10 for a car and driver on the Fauntleroy-Southworth ferry. Passenger fare is $4.70. Car passengers and walk-ons only pay fares on westbound ferries.

VISITOR INFORMATION   For information on the Kitsap Peninsula, contact the **Kitsap Peninsula Visitor and Convention Bureau,** 32220 Rainier Ave. NE (P.O. Box 270), Port Gamble, WA 98364 (© **800/416-5615** or 360/297-8200; www.visit kitsap.com). For more information on Poulsbo, contact the **Greater Poulsbo Chamber of Commerce,** 19168-A Jensen Way (P.O. Box 1063), Poulsbo, WA 98370 (© **877/ 768-5726** or 360/779-4999; www.poulsbo.net).

FESTIVALS   In Poulsbo each May, the **Viking Fest** celebrates traditional Scandinavian culture, as does the October **First Lutheran Church Annual Lutefisk Dinner** (www.Poulsbo-lutefisk.com) and the December **Yul Fest.**

EXPLORING THE KITSAP PENINSULA

Just across the Agate Pass Bridge from Bainbridge Island lies the Kitsap Peninsula and the Suquamish Indian Reservation. Take your first right after crossing the bridge from Bainbridge Island, and in the village of **Suquamish,** you'll see signs for the grave of Chief Sealth, for whom Seattle was named. Nearby (turn at the Texaco station on the edge of town) you'll also find **Old Man House State Park,** which preserves the site of a large Native American longhouse. The Old Man House itself is long gone, but you'll find an informative sign and a small park with picnic tables. From Suquamish, head back to Wash. 305, continue a little farther west and watch for signs to the **Suquamish Museum,** 15838 Sandy Hook Rd. (© **360/598-3311,** ext. 422; www. suquamish.nsn.us/museum), on the Port Madison Indian Reservation. The museum houses a compelling history of Puget Sound's native people, with lots of historic photos and quotes from tribal elders about growing up in the area. From May through September the museum is open daily from 10am to 5pm; October through April, it's open Friday through Sunday from 11am to 4pm. Admission is $4 for adults, $3 for seniors, and $2.50 for children ages 12 and under. In this same general area, right on Wash. 305 at the west end of the Agate Pass Bridge, you'll also find the **Clearwater Casino,** 15374 Suquamish Way NW, Suquamish (© **800/375-6073** or 360/598-8700; www.clearwatercasino.com).

Continuing north on Wash. 305, you next come to the small town of **Poulsbo,** which overlooks fjordlike Liberty Bay. Settled in the late 1880s by Scandinavians, Poulsbo was primarily a fishing, logging, and farming town until the town decided to play up its Scandinavian heritage. Shops in the Scandinavian-inspired downtown sell all manner of Viking and Scandinavian souvenirs. Between downtown and the waterfront, you'll find Liberty Bay Park.

If you're interested in seeing Poulsbo from the water, you can rent a sea kayak from **Olympic Outdoor Center,** 18971 Front St. (© **800/592-5983** or 360/697-6095; www.olympicoutdoorcenter.com), which charges $13 to $18 per hour or $50 to $70 by the day.

If you have time and enjoy visiting historic towns, continue north from Poulsbo on Wash. 3 to **Port Gamble,** which looks like a New England village dropped down in the middle of the Northwest woods. This community was established in 1853 as a company town for the Pope and Talbot lumber mill. Along the town's shady streets are Victorian homes that were restored by Pope and Talbot. Stop by the Port Gamble Country Store, which now houses the **Port Gamble Historical Museum** (© **360/ 297-8074**), a collection of local memorabilia. Admission is $2.50 for adults and $1.50 for seniors and students (free for children ages 5 and under). From May through October the museum is open daily from 10:30am to 5pm; the rest of the year by appointment only. The same location is home to the **Of Sea and Shore Museum** (© **360/297-2426**), which houses an exhibit of seashells from around the world. This museum is open daily from 9am to 5pm; admission is free.

South of Port Gamble on Wash. 3, you can explore the Kitsap Peninsula's naval history. Between Poulsbo and Silverdale, you will be passing just east of the Bangor Navy Base, which is home port for a fleet of Trident nuclear submarines. The base is on Hood Canal. Near the town of Keyport, you can visit the **Naval Undersea Museum,** 610 Dowell St. (© **360/396-4148**), which is located 3 miles east of Wash. 3 on Wash. 308 near the town of Keyport. The museum examines all aspects of undersea exploration, with interactive exhibits, models, and displays that include a deep-sea exploration and research craft, a Japanese kamikaze torpedo, and a deep-sea rescue vehicle. The museum is open daily from 10am to 4pm (closed on Tues Oct–May), and admission is free.

Continuing south, you come to **Bremerton,** which is home to the Puget Sound Naval Shipyard, where mothballed U.S. Navy ships have included the aircraft carriers USS *Nimitz* and USS *Midway* and the battleships USS *Missouri* and USS *New Jersey.* There are always plenty of navy ships to be seen here in the harbor.

One mothballed destroyer, the USS *Turner Joy,* is open to the public as a memorial to those who served in the U.S. Navy and who helped build the navy's ships. Operated by the **Bremerton Historic Ships Association** (© **360/792-2457**), the *Turner Joy* is docked about 150 yards east of the Washington State Ferries terminal. From May through September, the ship is open daily from 10am to 5pm; October through April, it's open Saturday and Sunday from 10am to 4pm. Admission is $8 for adults, $7 for seniors, and $6 for children ages 5 to 12.

⟨Finds Bonsai by the Bay

Driving west from Tacoma on Wash. 16, just past the town of Port Orchard, you can't help but be curious about the odd collection of stunted trees and sculptures wedged between the highway and the waters of Sinclair Inlet. **Elandan Gardens,** Wash. 16, milepost 28, Gorst (© **360/373-8260;** www.elandangardens.com), is the result of one man's passion for bonsai. The collection includes trees that are more than 1,000 years old and have been trained for decades. There are also Japanese-style gardens to wander, open Tuesday through Sunday from 10am to 5pm (closed Jan); admission is $5 for adults and $1 for children under 12.

Nearby is the **Bremerton Naval Museum,** 402 Pacific Ave. (© **360/479-7447**), which showcases naval history and the historic contributions of the Puget Sound Naval Shipyard. The museum is open Monday through Saturday from 10am to 4pm and Sunday from 1 to 4pm. Admission is by donation.

Connecting all of these waterfront attractions is the Bremerton Boardwalk, which provides a pleasant place to stroll along the waters of Sinclair Inlet. Also here in Bremerton, you'll find the **Kitsap County Historical Society Museum,** 280 Fourth St. (© **360/479-6226;** www.waynes.net/kchsm), which is housed in a 1940s-era streamline modern bank building. The interesting architecture of the building is reason enough for a visit, but there are also historical photos by Edward S. Curtis and his brother Asahel, who at one time resided here in Kitsap County. The museum is open Tuesday through Saturday from 9am to 5pm (until 8pm first Fri of each month). Admission is by suggested donation ($2 adults, $1 seniors and students).

One of the last remaining private mosquito-fleet ferries still operates between Bremerton and **Port Orchard.** If you park your car on the waterfront in Bremerton, you can step aboard the little passenger-only ferry and cross the bay to Port Orchard. In this little waterfront town, you'll find several antiques malls that can provide hours of interesting browsing.

WHERE TO STAY

Manor Farm Inn 🐾🐾   Only about an hour from Seattle, between Poulsbo and the Hood Canal Bridge, Manor Farm Inn (which is actually a working farm) feels like a New England country inn. Whether you want to hide away in the comfort of your room or hang out with the farm animals, you'll feel content at this retreat from urban stress. If you crave lots of space, you might want to opt for the Carriage Room, which has the original carriage house doors on display. For a large bathroom, request The Loft, which is up a flight of stairs and has great views. In recent years, the Manor Farm Inn has become more of a retreat center than just a place to spend the night while exploring the area.

26069 Big Valley Rd. NE, Poulsbo, WA 98370. © **360/779-4628.** Fax 360/779-4876. www.manorfarminn.com. 6 units. $140–$170 double; Jan–Apr Sun–Thurs $125 double. Rates include full breakfast. Children over 12 are welcome. AE, MC, V. *In room:* Coffeemaker, hair dryer, iron, no phone.

Willcox House 🐾🐾   Set on the shore of Hood Canal and with a superb view of the Olympic Mountains, this 1930s Art Deco mansion is one of the state's finest inns. The inn was once a private estate and is surrounded by lush gardens of rhododendrons and azaleas that erupt into bloom each spring. There's a library where you can curl up in a leather chair beside the fire, a billiards room, a home theater with big-screen TV, and, of course, an elegant great room. Guest rooms are similarly elegant. Dinners are also served at the inn (reservation only) with fixed-price meals ranging in price from $27 on weeknights to $40 on Saturday nights. Regional cuisine and an excellent wine list make this one of the finest restaurants on the Kitsap Peninsula.

2390 Tekiu Rd. NW, Seabeck, WA 98380. © **800/725-9477** or 360/830-4492. www.willcoxhouse.com. 5 units. $139–$219 double. Rates include full breakfast. DISC, MC, V. **Amenities:** Dining room (Northwest). *In room:* Hair dryer, no phone.

WHERE TO DINE

The most elegant meals on the Kitsap Peninsula are served at the Willcox House, a luxurious inn overlooking the Hood Canal. Most of the diners are guests at the inn, but the fixed-price meals are open to the public by reservation. See above for details.

IN POULSBO

If you have a sweet tooth, don't miss **Sluys Poulsbo Bakery,** 18924 Front St. NE
(© **360/697-2253**), which bakes mounds of Scandinavian-inspired goodies (very
sweet), as well as stick-to-your-ribs breads. When you need a cup of espresso, head to
the **Poulsbohemian Coffeehouse,** 19003 Front St. (© **360/779-9199**), which has an
excellent view of Liberty Bay from atop the bluff on the edge of downtown.

Molly Ward Gardens ★★ *Finds* NORTHWEST   What a surprise to open the door
of this rambling old barn in a picturesque little valley and find a magical, hobbit-like
interior trimmed to the rafters with dried flowers and herbs. This is a husband-and-
wife-operation. Sam, the chef, turns out such dishes as pork tenderloin with homemade rhubarb chutney, rack of lamb with zinfandel sauce, and spaghetti squash with
Gorgonzola sauce. Lynn is the artist, and at Christmas the restaurant is decked out
with splendiferous garlands and arrangements created with bounty from woods and
field. In summer, there's outdoor seating among the flowers. Molly Ward Gardens is
located quite near the Manor Farm Inn.

27462 Big Valley Rd. © 360/779-4471. www.mollywardgardens.com. Reservations recommended. Main courses
$11–$15 lunch, $19–$37 dinner. AE, MC, V. Wed–Sat 11am–2:30pm and 6–9pm; Sun 10:30am–2:30pm and 6–9pm;
Tues 6–9pm.

Mor Mor Bistro and Bar ★★ NORTHWEST   You'll find Poulsbo's best and most
upscale restaurant partially hidden by a big magnolia tree. The space is sophisticated
and unpretentious, a description that fits the food as well. The menu changes daily,
but you can bet there will be simple comfort foods such as fish and chips, as well as
cedar-planked salmon. Personally, though, I like the prosciutto-wrapped halibut on
truffle-scented mashed potatoes. Raviolis are usually good bets as well. If you aren't
worried about putting on pounds, try snacking on the garlic-and-parmesan fries with
aioli (they also come with the fish and chips.

18820 Front St. © 360/697-3449. www.mormorbistro.com. Reservations recommended. Main courses $8–$14
lunch; $10–$26 dinner. AE, MC, V. Wed–Mon 11am–9pm.

3 Gig Harbor ★

45 miles S of Seattle, 30 miles S of Bremerton, 45 miles N of Olympia

On the far side of the Tacoma Narrows Bridge from Tacoma is the quaint waterfront
town of Gig Harbor. With its interesting little shops, art galleries, seafood restaurants,
fleet of commercial fishing boats, and marinas full of private pleasure craft, this town
is the quintessential Puget Sound fishing village. Framing this picture of Puget Sound's
past is the snowcapped bulk of Mount Rainier, which lends a near storybook quality.

Long the site of a Native American village, Gig Harbor was not discovered by Euro-
Americans until 1841, when sailors from an exploratory expedition who were charting the area from a gig (a small boat that had been launched from the expedition's
main ship) rowed into the bay. Settlers arrived here in 1867 and soon Gig Harbor was
a thriving fishing village of Scandinavians and Croatians.

ESSENTIALS

GETTING THERE   Gig Harbor lies just across the Tacoma Narrows Bridge from
Tacoma off Wash. 16.

VISITOR INFORMATION For more information on this area, contact the **Gig Harbor Peninsula Chamber of Commerce,** 3302 Harborview Dr., Gig Harbor, WA 98332 (© **888/553-5438** or 253/851-6865; www.gigharborchamber.com).

EXPLORING GIG HARBOR

Gig Harbor is a boaters' town. Up and down the length of the town's waterfront, marinas are crowded with sailboats and powerboats, and shops along the waterfront cater primarily to the boating crowd. However, all the boats, and the backdrop of Mount Rainier, also make this a very pleasant town for a leisurely stroll. You can also rent a boat and head out on the water.

On the waterfront, you'll find **Gig Harbor Rent-a-Boat,** 8829 N. Harborview Dr. (© **253/858-7341;** www.gigharborrentaboat.com), where you can rent a sailboat, powerboat, or sea kayak. Rates range from $12 an hour for a single sea kayak to $70 an hour for a 19-foot powerboat.

Most visitors to Gig Harbor come because of the boating opportunities, but landlubbers can stroll the town's main street, Harborview Drive, enjoy the view of the harbor, and stop to browse in dozens of interesting little shops and art galleries. Toward the south end of the waterfront, you'll find Jerisich Park, which has a public dock and is a good place for a picnic. At the north end, after the bend in the bay, you'll come to the Finholm area. Across from the water here stands the Finholm View Climb, a flight of 90 steps that lead up a steep hill. At the top of the hill, you'll find the quintessential Gig Harbor view of the bay and Mount Rainier.

If you're curious about the history of the area, visit the **Gig Harbor Peninsula Historical Society & Museum,** 4218 Harborview Dr. (© **253/858-6722;** www.gig harbormuseum.org), on the bend of the bay just before Finholm. The museum is open Tuesday through Saturday from 10am to 4pm, and admission is $2 for adults and $1 for seniors and children.

Within a short drive of Gig Harbor, you'll also find three waterfront state parks— **Penrose Point, Joemma,** and **Kopachuck**—all of which have beaches and campgrounds. Of these, Penrose Point (© **360/902-8844**) is the prettiest. This park is situated on Mayo Cove and has 2 miles of shoreline. To reach this park from Gig Harbor, drive north on Wash. 16 to Purdy, take Wash. 302 west and then follow signs to Key Center and the park. From both Joemma (which is about 4 miles beyond Penrose Point) and Kopachuck (from Wash. 16 in Gig Harbor, follow signs for the park) there are good spots to watch sunsets, with a nice sandy beach at Kopachuck.

WHERE TO STAY

The Maritime Inn 🎝🎝 Across from the waterfront in downtown Gig Harbor, this small, modern hotel manages to conjure up the image of an old beach resort cottage with its classic, simple styling. All the guest rooms have gas fireplaces and are romantic without being frilly. Pine furnishings lend a further air of classicism to the rooms. While most rooms have some sort of water view, the views are better from the few rooms on the second floor.

3212 Harborview Dr., Gig Harbor, WA 98335. © **888/506-3580** or 253/858-1818. Fax 253/858-1817. www.maritime inn.com. 15 units. $79–$149 double. Rates include continental breakfast. Children under 3 stay free in parent's room. AE, DC, DISC, MC, V. **Amenities:** Concierge. *In room:* A/C, TV, dataport, coffeemaker, hair dryer, iron, free local calls, high-speed Internet access.

WHERE TO DINE

When it's time for coffee, head to **Le Bistro Coffee House,** 4120 Harborview Dr. (**🕾 253/851-1033**), at the north end of downtown.

The Green Turtle 🕸🕸 PAN-ASIAN/INTERNATIONAL   With the hands-down best view in town (Mount Rainier is seen looming beyond the mouth of the harbor on clear days), this elegant little restaurant is tucked in an unlikely spot next door to a yacht sales office. Two walls of glass let everyone enjoy the views, and in summer there is a deck under a big old maple tree. The menu is almost entirely seafood, but you'll find a few chicken, duck, and steak dishes listed. Preparations lean toward the far side of the Pacific, with such dishes as fish and shellfish in a spicy Thai peanut sauce, pan-seared peppercorn-crusted ahi with a roasted garlic and ginger glaze, and curried halibut with artichoke hearts and basil.

2905 Harborview Dr. 🕾 **253/851-3167.** www.thegreenturtle.com. Reservations recommended. Main courses $6–$9 lunch, $18–$36 dinner. AE, DISC, MC, V. Tues–Thurs 11am–2:30pm and 4:30–9pm; Fri 11am–2:30pm and 4:30–10pm; Sat 4:30–10pm; Sun 4:30–9pm.

Tides Tavern 🕸 AMERICAN   This is basically just a tavern with an extensive menu, but with its great setting over the water at the east end of town, it's a good place for lunch or a casual dinner. The building that houses the tavern was originally constructed as a general store back in 1910, but has been the Tides Tavern since 1973. The menu is basic tavern fare—burgers, sandwiches, and pizzas—and if not entirely memorable, it can be tasty. On Saturday nights, there's live music. Because this is a tavern, you must be 21 or older to eat here.

2925 Harborview Dr. 🕾 **253/858-3982.** www.tidestavern.com. Reservations recommended for large parties. Main courses $7.50–$14. AE, MC, V. Daily 11am–closing.

4 Tacoma 🕸🕸

32 miles S of Seattle, 31 miles N of Olympia, 93 miles S of Port Townsend

Tacoma is a city that, in the words of Rodney Dangerfield, "just don't get no respect." For years its industrial image made it the brunt of jokes, many of which centered around the aroma of Tacoma. I'd like to be able to tell you that the skies over Tacoma are always clear and the air is fresh and clean, but it would be stretching the truth just a bit. However, it is definitely time to forget the old jokes and take a new look at this city in the midst of a profound transformation.

Things have changed a lot since the days when the city's waterfront was lined with smoke-belching lumber and paper mills, and, with a newfound commitment to the arts, Tacoma competes with Seattle as a city on the move. With its impressive museums and free downtown streetcar, Tacoma has made great strides toward reinventing itself.

Tacoma has also reclaimed much of its shoreline, and today a waterfront park runs the length of Ruston Way just north of downtown. Walkers, joggers, cyclists, and in-line skaters all flock to the paved trail that runs through this park, and along the park's length there are several good waterfront restaurants. Despite Tacoma's ongoing makeover, little has changed at Point Defiance Park, long a local favorite. With miles of trails, a world-class zoo and aquarium, numerous attractions, and great bicycling and in-line skating, this is one of the premier city parks in the Puget Sound region.

In between Point Defiance and downtown Tacoma lies one of the most impressive historic neighborhoods in the state. The streets of the Stadium Historic District are lined with beautiful mansions, most of which have been renovated and some of which

DINING ◆
Anthony's at Port Defiance **2**
Café Divino **4**
Harmon Pub & Brewery **14**
The Lobster Shop South **3**

ACCOMMODATIONS ■
Chinaberry Hill **7**
Silver Cloud Inn Tacoma **5**
The Villa Bed & Breakfast **6**

ATTRACTIONS ●
Camp 6 Logging Museum **1**
Fort Nisqually Living History Museum **1**
Karpeles Manuscript Library Museum **9**
Museum of Glass **12**
Port Defiance Park **1**
Port Defiance Zoo and Aquarium **1**
Tacoma Art Museum **11**
W.W. Seymour Botanical Conservatory **8**
Washington State History Museum **13**
Working Waterfront Maritime Museum **10**

are now B&Bs. These homes are a testament to the important role Tacoma played in Washington history. In 1883, Tacoma became the end of the line for the Northern Pacific Railroad, thus sealing the city's fate as the industrial center of Puget Sound. It was largely due to the railroad that Tacoma became a regional center of industry, a fate that the city is trying to overcome.

To see the past and the future of Tacoma, drop by downtown's Fireman's Park. From this small park, you can look down on smoke-belching mills and commercial port facilities, but if you then turn around, you'll be facing a new, revitalized Tacoma where the arts are flourishing and historic buildings are being preserved and renovated.

ESSENTIALS

GETTING THERE   Tacoma is on I-5 south of Seattle at the junction of Wash. 16, which is the main route north through the Kitsap Peninsula to Port Townsend and the Olympic Peninsula. Wash. 7 from the Mount Rainier area leads into downtown Tacoma from the south. Tacoma's city center is accessed by I-705, a short spur that leads from I-5 into the middle of downtown.

Seattle-Tacoma International Airport is 22 miles north of Tacoma. **ShuttleExpress** (© **800/487-7433** or 425/981-7000; www.shuttleexpress.com) operates an airport shuttle service; the fare is $26 one-way to downtown Tacoma.

Amtrak has service to Tacoma. The station is at 1001 Puyallup Ave.

VISITOR INFORMATION   For more information on this area, contact the **Tacoma Regional Convention & Visitor Bureau,** 1119 Pacific Ave., Fifth Floor, Tacoma, WA 98402 (© **800/272-2662** or 253/627-2836; www.traveltacoma.com), which has an information desk inside the gift shop at the Washington State History Museum, 1911 Pacific Ave.

GETTING AROUND   See section 2 in chapter 5 for information on renting cars at Sea-Tac International Airport. If you need a taxi, contact **Tacoma Orange Cab** (© **253/943-5555**). Public bus service is provided by **Pierce Transit** (© **800/ 562-8109** or 253/581-8000; www.piercetransit.org).

WHAT TO SEE & DO
MUSEUMS

Karpeles Manuscript Library Museum ❧   Housed in an imposing building across the street from Wright Park, this museum is dedicated to the preservation of original handwritten documents and letters. The founder of the libraries has amassed an astounding collection of original manuscripts, from musical scores by Beethoven to ancient papyrus texts to the cover letter for the Declaration of Independence.

407 South G St. © **253/383-2575.** Free admission. Tues–Sun 10am–4pm.

Museum of Glass ❧❧   Although it was Chihuly's work that inspired the construction of this museum, the Museum of Glass travels far and wide to bring the very best of art glass here to Tacoma, and art glass in all its myriad forms finds its way into the galleries of this high-style building on the waterfront. Whether it's stained glass in the style of Tiffany, a traveling exhibit from a European museum, or the latest thought-provoking installation by a cutting-edge glass artist, you'll find it here. The highlight is the hot shop, a huge cone-shaped studio space where visitors can watch glass artists work at several kilns. Connecting the museum to the rest of the city is the 500-foot-long Chihuly Bridge of Glass, which spans the I-705 freeway. Adjacent to this museum at 1821 E. Dock St. are two affiliated galleries that are outposts of the region's most highly respected art-glass gallery—the **William Traver Gallery** (© **253/ 383-3685;** www.travergallery.com) and **Vetri International Glass** (© **253/383-3692;** www.vetriglass.com).

1801 Dock St. © **866/4-MUSEUM** or 253/284-4750. www.museumofglass.org. Admission $10 adults, $8 seniors, $4 children 6–12, free for children under 6. Free to all on 3rd Thurs of each month. Memorial Day to Labor Day Mon–Sat 10am–5pm (until 8pm on 3rd Thurs of each month), Sun noon–5pm; other months closed Mon–Tues. Closed Thanksgiving, Christmas, and New Year's Day.

Tacoma Art Museum ❧❧   Housed in a modern building designed by noted architect Antoine Predock, the Tacoma Art Museum may not have as big a reputation as the Seattle Art Museum, but it mounts some impressive shows. The building, which only opened in 2003, is filled with beautiful galleries in which to display both the museum's own collections and traveling exhibitions. The museum is best known for its large collection of art by native son Dale Chihuly, and fans of the glass artist can sign up for a walking tour of many of his works both here in the museum and around downtown. Tours are offered Tuesday through Saturday, cost $8 to $10, include museum admission, and should be reserved 2 weeks in advance. The museum also has respectable collections of European Impressionism, Japanese woodblock prints, and American graphic art, and regularly brings in large traveling shows.

Tips **Wednesday Bargains**

With the Museum of Glass, the Tacoma Art Museum, and the Washington State History Museum all within 3 blocks of one another, Tacoma is an even better museum town than Seattle. You can save a little on the cost of visiting these three museums by visiting on a Wednesday when you can get into all three museums for $18 ($16 for seniors and $14 for students and children). For adults, this is a savings of $6.50, or, put another way, you get to visit the art museum for free!

1701 Pacific Ave. ℂ 253/272-4258. www.tacomaartmuseum.org. Admission $6.50 adults, $5.50 seniors and students, free for children under 6. Free to all on 3rd Thurs of each month. Tues–Sat 10am–5pm (until 8pm on 3rd Thurs of each month); Sun noon–5pm. Closed Thanksgiving, Christmas, and New Year's Day.

Washington State History Museum ★★ *Kids*   A massive archive of Washington state history, this impressive museum is like no other history museum in the Northwest. A full barrage of high-tech displays make history both fun and interesting. From a covered wagon to a sprawling HO-scale (3.5mm: 1 ft.) model railroad layout, a Coast Salish longhouse to a Hooverville shack, the state's history comes alive through the use of life-size mannequins, recorded narration, and "overheard" conversations. With loads of interactive exhibits and several films screened daily, it's obvious this museum is trying to appeal to the video-game generation, but older visitors will have fun, too.

1911 Pacific Ave. ℂ 888/238-4373 or 253/272-3500. www.wshs.org/wshm. Admission $8 adults, $7 seniors, $6 students 6–17, free for children 5 and under. Free for all Thurs 5–8pm. Mon–Wed and Fri–Sat 10am–5pm; Thurs 10am–8pm; Sun noon–5pm. Closed New Year's Day, Memorial Day, Labor Day, Thanksgiving, and Christmas.

Working Waterfront Maritime Museum ★   Although it isn't very large, this waterfront museum has some interesting exhibits and is a good introduction to Tacoma's maritime history. There are exhibits on the famous Foss tugboat company, a 27-foot Columbia River gillnetter, and a 1938 Chris-Craft. There are hands-on exhibits for kids, and a shop where you can see boats under construction and restoration.

705 Dock St. ℂ 253/272-2750. www.wwfrontmuseum.org. Admission $3 adults, $2 seniors and children 3–12. Mon–Fri 9am–5pm, Sat–Sun noon–5pm.

POINT DEFIANCE PARK

Point Defiance Park, on the north side of town at the end of Pearl Street, is Tacoma's center of activity and one of the largest urban parks in the country. In the park are several attractions, including the Point Defiance Zoo & Aquarium, Fort Nisqually Historic Site, and the Camp 6 Logging Museum. Founded in 1888, this park preserved one of the region's most scenic points of land. Winding through the wooded park is **Five Mile Drive,** which connects all the park's main attractions, as well as the picnic areas, and hiking and biking trails. Also in the park are a rose garden, a Japanese garden, a rhododendron garden, a dahlia test garden, and a native-plant garden. You can reach the park by following Ruston Way or Pearl Street north.

Camp 6 Logging Museum ★ *Kids*   This museum focuses on the days of steam power in Washington's logging history. Exhibits include plenty of steam equipment as well as old bunkhouses and a rail-car camp. The latter was a rolling logging camp with bunkhouses built on railroad cars. Indoor exhibits are closed November through March, but outdoor exhibits can be viewed year-round. On weekends in spring and summer and again in December, Camp 6 offers rides on an old logging train.

5400 N. Pearl St. © 253/752-0047. www.camp-6-museum.org. Free admission to museum; logging train rides $4 adults, $3 seniors, $2.50 children ages 3–12. Apr–Memorial Day and Oct Wed–Sun (and holidays) 10am–4pm; Memorial Day–Sept 30 Wed–Fri 10am–4pm, Sat–Sun (and holidays) 10am–7pm. Closed Nov–Mar.

Fort Nisqually Living History Museum 🦋 Fort Nisqually was a trading post founded in 1833 by the Hudson's Bay Company for the purpose of acquiring beaver pelts. However, it was established at a time when the fur trade was in decline and was soon moved to a new location and converted to a commercial farming business. This reconstruction, built in the 1930s, is based on the design of that second fort. Inside the stockade walls are two original buildings and several reconstructed buildings. Throughout the summer (and on weekends in other months), costumed interpreters are on hand. Numerous living-history events are staged throughout the year.

5400 N. Pearl St. © 253/591-5339. www.fortnisqually.org. Admission Mar–Oct $4 adults, $3 seniors and students, $2 children 5–12, free for children under 5; Nov–Feb $3 adults, $2 seniors and students, $1 children 5–12, free for children under 5 (weekend after Labor Day–Feb, admission charged on weekends only). Memorial Day to Labor Day daily 11am–5pm; Labor Day–Mar Wed–Sun 11am–4pm; Apr–Memorial Day Wed–Sun 11am–5pm. Closed Oct 9.

Point Defiance Zoo & Aquarium 🦋🦋 *Kids* In 2005, this combination zoo and aquarium celebrated its centennial by rebuilding 75% of the zoo. Among the additions were a children's zoo, an Asian Forest exhibit, and an outdoor theater with live-animal shows. The focus here is generally on the wildlife of Pacific Rim countries, and to that end, you'll find animals from such far-flung locations as the Arctic tundra, Southeast Asia, and the Andes Mountains. In the aquarium, the *Rocky Shores* exhibit features marine mammals, including beluga whales. Other exhibits include a northern Pacific aquarium, a tropical coral reef aquarium that's home to more than 40 sharks, and a seahorse exhibit. The zoo's biggest event of the year is its annual Zoolights program, which each December turns the grounds into a fantasy of Christmas lights.

5400 N. Pearl St. © 253/591-5337. www.pdza.org. Admission $8.75 adults, $8 seniors, $7 children 4–13, free for children under 4. Memorial Day weekend–Labor Day 9:30am–6pm; Apr–day before Memorial Day weekend and day after Labor Day–Sept 30 9:30am–5pm; Oct–Mar 9:30am–4pm and 6pm (hours vary with the season, call for details). Closed 3rd Fri in July, Thanksgiving, and Christmas.

TACOMA AREA PUBLIC GARDENS

Lakewold Gardens 🦋 Formerly a private estate, this 10-acre garden, designed by noted landscape architect Thomas Church, has extensive collections of Japanese maples and rhododendrons. There are also rose, fern, and alpine gardens that include numerous rare and unusual plants. The gardens are 10 miles south of Tacoma.

12317 Gravelly Lake Dr. SW, Lakewood. © 888/858-4106 or 253/584-4106. www.lakewold.org. Admission $5 adults, $3 seniors and students, free for children 12 and under. Apr–Sept Wed–Sun 10am–4pm; Oct–Mar Fri–Sun 10am–3pm. Take exit 124 off I-5.

Pacific Rim Bonsai Collection 🦋🦋 Assembled by the Weyerhaeuser Company in 1989 to honor trade relations with Pacific Rim nations, this includes more than 50 miniature trees from Japan, China, Korea, Taiwan, and Canada. It's the most impressive public bonsai collection in the state. Free guided tours are given on Sunday at noon. The collection is 8 miles north of Tacoma.

33663 Weyerhaeuser Way S., Weyerhaeuser corporate campus, Federal Way. © 253/924-5206. www.weyerhaeuser.com/bonsai. Free admission. Mar–Sept Fri–Wed 10am–4pm; Oct–Feb Sat–Wed 11am–4pm. Take exit 143 off I-5.

Rhododendron Species Foundation and Botanical Garden ★★   Covering 22 acres, this garden has one of the world's most extensive collections of species of wild rhododendrons and azaleas. More than 2,100 different varieties of plants put on an amazing floral display from March through May. There are collections of ferns, maples, heathers, and bamboos. For serious gardeners, this is one of the Northwest's garden musts, just 8 miles north of Tacoma.

2525 S. 336th St., Weyerhaeuser corporate campus, Federal Way. ✆ 253/838-4646. www.rhodygarden.org. Admission $3.50 adults, $2.50 seniors and students, children under 12 free. Free to all Nov–Feb. Mar–May Fri–Wed 10am–4pm; June–Feb Sat–Wed 11am–4pm. Take exit 143 off I-5.

W. W. Seymour Botanical Conservatory ★   Constructed in 1908, this elegant Victorian conservatory is one of only three of its kind on the West Coast and is listed on the National Register of Historic Places. More than 200 species of exotic plants (including plenty of orchids) are housed in the huge greenhouse, built of more than 3,500 panes of glass. The conservatory is in downtown Tacoma's Wright Park, which has more than 700 trees of 100 species, a shady retreat from downtown's pavement.

Wright Park, 316 S. G St. ✆ 253/591-5330. www.metroparkstacoma.org. Free admission. Tues–Sun 10am–4:30pm. Closed Thanksgiving, Nov 29–Dec 2, Christmas, and New Year's Day.

OTHER TACOMA PARKS

Although Point Defiance Park is Tacoma's premier park, the **Ruston Way Parks** rank a close second. Once jammed with smoking, decaying industrial buildings and piers, the Tacoma waterfront was an industrial area of national infamy. However, since the city of Tacoma reclaimed the shore of Commencement Bay and turned it into parkland, it has become one of the most attractive waterfront parks on Puget Sound. With grassy areas, a sandy beach, public fishing pier, and paved pathway, the waterfront is popular with strollers, cyclists, and in-line skaters.

Downtown at the corner of A Street and South Ninth, you'll find **Fireman's Park,** which has one of the world's tallest totem poles (carved in 1903) as well as a view of the Port of Tacoma below. After gazing down on the port, if you want to have a closer look, stop by the **Port of Tacoma Observation Tower** off East 11th Street. Here you can watch as ships from around the world are loaded and unloaded. To reach the port tower, take the 11th Street bridge from downtown.

HISTORIC DISTRICTS & BUILDINGS

Tacoma has quite a few historic buildings, the most notable of which is **Union Station,** 1717 Pacific Ave. Built in the Beaux Arts–style as the terminal for the first transcontinental railroad to reach the Northwest, the imposing building is now home to the federal courts and adjacent to the Washington State History Museum. In the building's lobby, you'll find a large glass installation by Dale Chihuly.

⟨Kids⟩ Wild Waves & an Enchanted Village

Wild Waves/Enchanted Village, 36201 Enchanted Parkway S., Federal Way (✆ 253/661-8000; www.sixflags.com), is a combination water park and amusement park with a large wooden roller coaster. When temperatures heat up in July and August, the waterslides here are the cool place to be. Bring your kids here on vacation, and they'll never forget their trip to Washington.

Stadium High School, 111 North E St., is a French château–style structure that was built as a hotel and later converted to a high school. The school is the centerpiece of the historic **Stadium District,** which is at the north end of Broadway and has more than 100 Victorian homes. This is one of the prettiest residential neighborhoods in the entire state, and many of the old homes verge on being mansions. At the south end of the Stadium District is the **Old City Hall Historic District,** which is the city's main antiques neighborhood. Along Broadway just north of Ninth Street, you'll find a dozen or so large antiques stores and malls. At the visitor center in the Washington State History Museum, you can pick up brochures on the city's historic districts.

Two miles north of downtown along the waterfront, you'll find Old Town Tacoma and the reconstructed **Job Carr Cabin Museum,** 2350 N. 30th St. (© 253/627-5405; www.jobcarrmuseum.org), where you can learn about the city's early history. The little museum is open Wednesday through Saturday from 1 to 4pm; admission is free. To reach it, follow Schuster Parkway/Ruston Way north.

VISITING HISTORIC STEILACOOM ✦

Founded in 1854 by a Maine sea captain, Steilacoom is Washington's oldest incorporated town. Once a bustling seaport, the quiet little community is today a National Historic District with 32 preserved historic buildings. To reach Steilacoom, take exit 125 off I-5 south between Tacoma and Olympia, drive to Lakewood and turn left on Steilacoom Boulevard.

The Steilacoom Museum, 112 Main St. (© **253/584-4133**), in the old town hall, houses exhibits on Steilacoom's pioneer history. The museum is open March through October, Wednesday through Sunday from 1 to 4pm; in February, November, and December, Friday through Sunday from 1 to 4pm (closed Jan). Suggested donation is $2. This museum is operated by the Steilacoom Historical Museum Association, which also maintains the nearby **Nathaniel Orr Pioneer Home and Orchard,** 1811 Rainier St., which was built between 1854 and 1857 and contains original furnishings. Between April and October, this house is open on Sunday from 1 to 4pm. The **Steilacoom Tribal Cultural Center and Museum,** 1515 Lafayette St. (© **253/584-6308**), has displays on the area's Steilacoom tribe. It's open Thursday through Saturday from 10am to 4pm; admission is $3 for adults and $1 for seniors and students.

WHERE TO STAY

Chinaberry Hill ✦✦   Amid the stately old homes of the Stadium Historic District, this grand Victorian home has luxurious guest rooms and commanding views of Commencement Bay. For sheer opulence, it's hard to beat the Pantages Suite, with its beautifully dressed bed, harbor views, and a whirlpool tub in an alcove under the eaves. The Carriage Suite, in the former carriage house, has a hot tub for two tucked into what was once a horse stall. Above this suite is a room in what was once the hayloft. Beautiful century-old trees shade the grounds. Classic Northwest elegance makes this one of the finest inns in the state.

302 Tacoma Ave. N., Tacoma, WA 98403. © **253/272-1282.** Fax 253/272-1335. www.chinaberryhill.com. 5 units. $135–$225 double; $265 2-bedroom suite; $295 cottage. Rates include full breakfast. AE, MC, V. Children 12 and over welcome in main house, all ages welcome in cottage. *In room:* A/C, TV/VCR, dataport, free local calls, high-speed Internet access, Wi-Fi.

Silver Cloud Inn Tacoma ✦✦   Built out over the waters of Commencement Bay, on a pier on the Ruston Way waterfront, this hotel has water views from every room. There's not a bad room in the hotel, but you should try to get a third-floor one to maximize your views. If you're in the mood for a splurge, the corner Jacuzzi suites are very romantic. The tub is in a corner with two walls of bay-view windows, and there are also gas fireplaces. Within 2 blocks of the hotel are restaurants of Old Town Tacoma, and along the Ruston Way waterfront pathway are good seafood restaurants.

2317 N. Ruston Way, Tacoma, WA 98402. © 866/820-8448 or 253/272-1300. www.silvercloud.com. 90 units. $149–$249 double; $179–$189 suite. Rates include full breakfast. AE, DC, DISC, MC, V. **Amenities:** Exercise room; courtesy local shuttle; business center; guest laundry; laundry service, Wi-Fi. *In room:* A/C, TV, dataport, fridge, coffeemaker, hair dryer, iron, free local calls, high-speed Internet access.

Thornewood Castle Inn 🏰🏰🏰 *Finds*   There may not be any real castles in the United States, but this imposing 30,000-square-foot manor house, located a few miles south of Tacoma, sure comes close. Built in 1909, Thornewood has 28 bedrooms and 22 bathrooms, and incorporated into its design is a 15th-century wood-paneled staircase and stained-glass windows dating from the 15th to 17th centuries. Guest rooms are, as you might expect, quite large, and if not quite as sumptuously appointed as the rest of the house, they are certainly grand in design. The mansion sits on the shore of American Lake, and the gardens were designed by the Olmsted Brothers. This is truly a one-of-a-kind inn. About the only drawback here is that nearby suburban homes dispel the fantasy that you are lord or lady of all you survey.

8601 N. Thorne Lane SW, Lakewood, WA 98498. © 253/584-4393. Fax 253/584-4497. www.thornewoodcastle.com. 10 units. $195–$400 double. Rates include full breakfast. AE, DISC, MC, V. No children under 12. *In room:* TV/VCR, dataport, fridge, coffeemaker.

The Villa Bed & Breakfast 🏰🏰   From the red roof tiles to the covered portico to the naiad statue in the garden pond, this inn cries out authentic Italianate villa. The only odd thing about this 1920s mansion is that it is in Tacoma and not Santa Barbara. Lovingly restored and filled with antiques, the inn feels for all the world like a villa in Italy. Designed for romantic getaways, all the rooms have either a whirlpool or antique soaking tub. All rooms but one also have gas fireplaces, and three of the rooms have their own private verandas. If you crave lots of space, opt for the Sorrento Suite, with its gas fireplace, a private veranda, a four-poster bed, and views of the Olympic Mountains and Commencement Bay.

705 N. Fifth St., Tacoma, WA 98403. © 888/572-1157 or 253/572-1157. www.villabb.com. 5 units. $150–$250 double. Rates include full breakfast. AE, DC, MC, V. Children over 12 welcome. **Amenities:** Jacuzzi; concierge; business center; massage. *In room:* TV, dataport, hair dryer, free local calls, Wi-Fi.

WHERE TO DINE
IN TACOMA

If too much time in museums leaves you sleepy, head to **Cutters Point,** 1936 Pacific Ave. (© **253/272-7101**), a coffee shop across the street from the Washington State History Museum.

Anthony's at Point Defiance 🏰🏰 SEAFOOD   Adjacent to the Vashon Island ferry landing on the edge of Point Defiance Park, this modern seafood restaurant, part of a very popular Seattle restaurant chain, has the best location of any of Tacoma's many waterfront restaurants. When the skies are clear, it's possible to see Mount Rainier rising beyond the adjacent marina (although the best views of the mountain are from the bar area), and then, of course, there are the comings and goings of the ferries. The prices are surprisingly reasonable considering both the location and the contemporary decor, and Anthony's stays pretty busy as a result. You'll find everything from clam chowder and pan-fried oysters to alder-planked salmon and cioppino. For a light meal, try the fish tacos.

5910 N. Waterfront Dr. © 253/752-9700. www.anthonys.com. Reservations accepted for 6 or more people. Main courses $5–$22. AE, DC, MC, V. Mon–Thurs 11am–9:30pm; Fri–Sat 11am–10:30pm; Sun 10am–9:30pm.

Café Divino ✦ *Finds* ITALIAN   This little hole-in-the-wall wine bar and restaurant is in the historic Old Town Tacoma neighborhood, which is north of present-day downtown Tacoma. The menu is short and the wines by the glass tend to be a bit pricey, but the food is good and the atmosphere is boisterously convivial. Some simple sandwiches (try the pesto chicken) and a few pasta dishes comprise the bulk of the menu, but most people end up assembling meals from the excellent salads and appetizers. Try the oven-roasted prawns and the smoked salmon quesadilla. Because this restaurant is only 2 blocks from the Ruston Way waterfront, you should try to get in a stroll before or after a meal.

2112 N. 30th St. © 253/779-4226. Reservations recommended. Main courses $8–$20. AE, DISC, MC, V. Mon–Thurs 11am–10pm; Fri 11am–11pm; Sat noon–11pm.

Harmon Pub & Brewery ✦ AMERICAN   In a renovated old commercial building across from the Washington State History Museum, this large pub is Tacoma's favorite downtown after-work hangout and business-lunch spot. The menu has primarily burgers and pizza, but there are usually interesting specials and, of course, plenty of good microbrews. The pub has adopted an outdoors theme, with various skiing-oriented special events in the winter season.

1938 Pacific Ave. © 253/383-2739. www.harmonbrewing.com. Reservations not accepted. Main courses $7–$16. AE, DC, DISC, MC, V. Mon–Thurs 11am–11pm; Fri 11am–midnight; Sat noon–midnight; Sun noon–8pm.

The Lobster Shop South ✦✦ SEAFOOD   This is the most upscale and expensive of the Ruston Way seafood places and has long been the city's top special-occasion seafood restaurant. The view's the thing here, and in summer there is lots of outdoor seating on the deck. Starters include a respectable New England–style clam chowder and a good lobster bisque. The appetizer not to miss is the hot lobster dip, made with lobster, artichoke hearts, onions, and Parmesan. Dishes on the main menu tend toward simple preparations made with lots of butter, but the daily fresh sheet has creative dishes. The crab cakes and the cioppino are always good bets, too. Sunday through Friday between 4:30 and 5:30pm, there are $17 three-course dinners.

4015 Ruston Way. © 253/759-2165. www.lobstershop.com. Reservations recommended. Main courses $9–$15 lunch, $15–$33 dinner. AE, DC, DISC, MC, V. Mon–Thurs 11:30am–2:30pm and 4:30–9:30pm; Fri 11:30am–2:30pm and 4:30–10:30pm; Sat 4:30–10:30pm; Sun 9:30am–1:30pm (brunch) and 4:30–9:30pm.

IN STEILACOOM

The Bair Restaurant ✦ *Finds* SODA FOUNTAIN/INTERNATIONAL   Perhaps the best reason to visit Steilacoom is to have a milkshake or ice-cream soda at this historic 1906 soda fountain. The interior of this old wooden building is how it might have looked back when it was a hardware store, making it part museum, part soda fountain. However, people no longer drop in for nails or tools, but they do line up for ice-cream sundaes. This is the oldest soda fountain we know of in the Northwest and is one of our favorites. Dinner is served on Friday and Saturday nights and afternoon tea on Monday through Saturday afternoons, but the real reason to come here is for an old-fashioned soda fountain experience.

1617 Lafayette St. © 253/588-9668. www.thebairrestaurant.com. Reservations recommended for dinner. Main courses $5–$11 breakfast and lunch, $16–$20 dinner. MC, V. Sun–Thurs 8am–3pm; Fri–Sat 8am–3pm and 5:30–9pm.

TACOMA AFTER DARK

Opened in 1983, the **Tacoma Dome,** 2727 East D St. (© **253/272-3663;** www.tacoma dome.org), which rises beside I-5 on the east side of the city, is Tacoma's most visible landmark and is the world's largest wood-domed arena. With seating for 28,000 people, it is the site of concerts, sporting events, and large exhibitions. Smaller productions take to the stages at the **Broadway Center for the Performing Arts,** 901 Broadway (© **800/291-7593** or 253/591-5894; www.broadwaycenter.org). This center consists of three theaters within a block of each other. The **Pantages,** a renovated vaudeville theater with a neoclassical terra-cotta facade, and the **Rialto Theatre,** a classic Italianate movie palace, were both built in 1918, while the **Theatre on the Square** was built in 1993. Together these three theaters present a wide variety of theater, music, and dance.

If you're just looking for someplace interesting to have a drink, check out **The Swiss,** 1904 S. Jefferson Ave. (© **253/572-2821;** www.theswisspub.com), which is located just uphill from the Washington State History Museum. The pub is at the top of a long flight of stairs that links the museum with the University of Washington Tacoma Campus. The pub not only has a great beer selection and decent food, but it also has a collection of Dale Chihuly glass sculptures. **The Spar,** 2121 N. 30th St. (© **253/627-8215;** www.the-spar.com), is another local favorite that has been around forever and is housed in a historic building in Old Town Tacoma. If martinis are more your style, head to downtown Tacoma's **21 Commerce,** 21 Commerce St. (© **253/ 272-6278;** www.21martinies.com), a swanky bar in a converted warehouse space. On weekends, DJs play acid jazz.

5 Olympia ★

60 miles S of Seattle, 100 miles N of Portland

At the southernmost end of Puget Sound, Olympia is the capital of Washington and a pleasant little city, though aside from the state capitol building and a few parks, it has little of interest to attract visitors. The city clings to the shores of Budd Inlet's twin bays and is further divided by Capitol Lake, above which, on a high bluff, stands the capitol building. Olympia boasts a fairly lively downtown and an attractive waterfront, but, despite the political importance of being the state capital, still has the air of a small town. The downtown is compact and low-rise, and when the legislature isn't in session, the city can be downright ghostly. Keeping things alive, however, are the students of Evergreen State College, a very progressive liberal arts college.

The Olympia area has a long history, and near here, in what is now the city of Tumwater, the first pioneers settled in 1844. A historic district and historical park along the Deschutes River in Tumwater preserve a bit of this history.

ESSENTIALS

GETTING THERE   Olympia is on I-5 at the junction with U.S. 101, which leads north around the Olympic Peninsula. Connecting the city to the central Washington coast and Aberdeen/Hoquiam is U.S. 12/Wash. 8.

The nearest airport with scheduled service is Seattle-Tacoma International Airport, 54 miles north. **Capital Aeroporter** (© **800/962-3579** or 360/754-7113; www. capair.com) provides a shuttle between the airport and Olympia.

There is **Amtrak** (© **800/872-7245;** www.Amtrak.com) rail service to Olympia; the station is at 6600 Yelm Hwy. SE.

Finds Land of the Giant Gophers?

Some 13 miles south of Olympia, near the town of Littlerock, you'll find the **Mima Mounds Natural Area Preserve,** which is an area of hundreds of small hills, each around 7 feet high. No one is sure how the mounds were formed, but their curious topography has produced much speculation over the years. The preserve is open daily, and in spring the wildflower displays here are quite impressive. To reach the preserve, take the Littlerock exit off I-5 and drive west on Wash. 121 to Waddell Creek Road. Turn right and continue 1½ miles.

VISITOR INFORMATION   Contact the **Olympia/Thurston County Visitor & Convention Bureau,** P.O. Box 7338, Olympia, WA 98507 (© 877/704-7500 or 360/704-7544; www.visitolympia.com), or the **State Capitol Visitor Information Center,** 416 14th Avenue SW (P.O. Box 41020), Olympia, WA 98504 (© 360/586-3460; www.ga.wa.gov/visitor).

GETTING AROUND   Public bus service is operated by **Intercity Transit** (© 360/786-1881; www.intercitytransit.com), with downtown shuttle buses.

THE CAPITOL CAMPUS

At 14th Avenue and Capitol Way, the neoclassical **Washington State Capitol building,** constructed between 1911 and 1928, is set amid a large and attractively landscaped campus known for its flowering cherry trees and rose gardens. At 267 feet tall, this is the tallest domed masonry state capitol in the country and bears a surprising resemblance to the Capitol in that other Washington. Around its campus, you'll see sculptures, the Tivoli fountain, and a conservatory (Mon–Fri 8am–3pm). The capitol is open daily with tours offered hourly between 10am and 3pm. For more information on tours of the grounds, contact the **State Capitol Visitor Center** (© 360/586-3460; www.ga.wa.gov/visitor).

OTHER AREA ATTRACTIONS

In downtown Olympia, you'll find the **Olympia Farmers Market,** 700 N. Capitol Way (© 360/352-9096; www.farmers-market.org), on the waterfront adjacent to Percival Landing Park. This is the second-largest open-air produce market in the state; it also has numerous prepared-food vendors and live music on the weekends. Between April and October, it's open Thursday through Sunday from 10am to 3pm; from November to December, it's open Saturday and Sunday only.

If you'd like to learn more about the area's history, especially that of the Native Americans who have called this region home for thousands of years, stop by the small **Washington State Capital Museum,** 211 W. 21st Ave. (© 360/753-2580; www.wshs.org/wscm). However, the building itself, an Italian Renaissance mansion built in the 1920s for a former mayor of Olympia, is the most interesting part of a visit here. The museum is open Tuesday through Friday from 10am to 4pm and Saturday from noon to 4pm. Admission is $2 for adults, $1.75 for seniors, and $1 for children ages 6 to 18; free for children under 6.

PRESERVES, PARKS & GARDENS

Lying at the edge of downtown Olympia, **Capitol Lake** and its surrounding parkland are favorites of area joggers, canoeists, and anglers. There is an excellent view of the

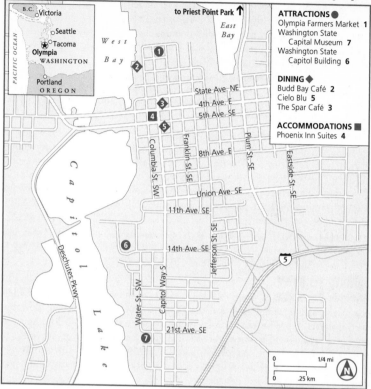

B.C. Victoria

Seattle

Tacoma

Olympia
WASHINGTON

Portland
OREGON

PACIFIC OCEAN

West Bay

East Bay

State Ave. NE

4th Ave. E

5th Ave. SE

8th Ave. E

Union Ave. SE

11th Ave. SE

14th Ave. SE

21st Ave. SE

Columbia St. SW

Franklin St. SE

Plum St. SE

Eastside St. SE

Jefferson St. SE

Water St. SW

S Capitol Way

Deschutes Pkwy.

Capitol Lake

ATTRACTIONS ●
Olympia Farmers Market **1**
Washington State
  Capital Museum **7**
Washington State
  Capitol Building **6**

DINING ◆
Budd Bay Café **2**
Cielo Blu **5**
The Spar Café **3**

ACCOMMODATIONS ■
Phoenix Inn Suites **4**

0   1/4 mi
0   .25 km

Capitol from the west side of the lake. Also in downtown is the 1½-mile-long **Percival Landing** boardwalk, which wanders along the shore of Budd Inlet past marinas, restaurants, public art, and interpretive panels. Between these two parks, you'll find Heritage Park and the Heritage Fountain, which has 47 choreographed water jets that are fun to watch. In summer, the fountain is a popular spot with local children who run through the fountains.

On the north side of Olympia, along the East Bay of Budd Inlet, are formal gardens, several miles of hiking trails, nice water views, and a beach at **Priest Point Park,** on East Bay Drive. The 3-mile round-trip Ellis Cove Trail provides beach access.

Nisqually National Wildlife Refuge (📞 **360/753-9467;** nisqually.fws.gov), located 8 miles north of Olympia at exit 114 off I-5, preserves the delta of the Nisqually River, which is a resting and wintering ground for large numbers of migratory birds. There are 7 miles of trails through the refuge. The visitor center is open Wednesday through Saturday from 9am to 4pm and Sunday from 12:30 to 4pm. A $3 vehicle admission fee is charged.

TWO NEARBY WILDLIFE ATTRACTIONS
Northwest Trek Wildlife Park ★★ (Kids)   The animals of North America are the focus of Northwest Trek, a wildlife park covering more than 715 acres near the town

of Eatonville. Bison roam, elk bugle, and moose munch contentedly knee-deep in the park's lake. Visitors are driven around the grounds in a naturalist-guided tram, and at certain spots, you can get out and walk to various enclosures. Residents include a grizzly bear, a wolf, cougars, lynx, and bobcats. There are also more than 5 miles of nature trails to wander after viewing the animals.

11610 Trek Dr. E., Eatonville. ℂ 360/832-6117. www.nwtrek.org. Admission $9.50 adults, $9.25 seniors, $7 children 5–17, $5 children 3–4. Mid-Feb to June and Sept Mon–Fri 9:30am–4pm, Sat–Sun 9:30am–5pm; July–Aug daily 9:30am–6pm; Oct to mid-Feb Fri–Sun and selected holidays 9:30am–3pm. Closed Thanksgiving and Christmas. To reach the park, take Wash. 510 southeast from I-5 (exit 111) to Yelm and continue west on Wash. 702.

Wolf Haven International 🌲 𝐾𝑖𝑑𝑠   Dedicated to the preservation of wolves and the education of the general public on the subject, Wolf Haven is a sanctuary for more than 30 wolves. During tours of the facility, you'll get to meet many of these canines, including a small pack that allows visitors to observe wolf-pack behavior in action. Throughout the summer, there are Saturday night Howl-Ins that are particularly popular with families. Advance reservations are required for Howl-Ins, which cost $12 for adults and $6 for children ages 3 to 12.

3111 Offut Lake Rd., Tenino. ℂ 800/448-9653 or 360/264-4695. www.wolfhaven.org. Admission $7 adults, $6 seniors, $5 children 3–12, free for children under 3. May–Sept Wed–Mon 10am–5pm; Apr and Oct Wed–Mon 10am–4pm; Mar and Nov–Jan Sat–Sun 10am–4pm. Last tour starts 1 hr. before closing. Closed Feb.

WHERE TO STAY

Phoenix Inn Suites 🌲 𝒱𝑎𝑙𝑢𝑒   Within 2 blocks of the water, the Percival Landing boardwalk, several restaurants, and the Olympia Farmers Market, this downtown hotel is a great choice for vacationers who like to leave their cars parked. Although the hotel is geared toward business travelers, the great location, large guest rooms, and many amenities make this an especially good value. Although the rooms are more junior suites than the sort of two-room suites you might find at an Embassy Suites hotel, they are quite large and well designed.

415 Capitol Way N., Olympia, WA 98501. ℂ 877/570-0555 or 360/570-0555. Fax 360/570-1200. www.phoenixinn suites.com. 102 units. $109–$199 double. Rates include continental breakfast. AE, DISC, MC, V. **Amenities:** Indoor pool; exercise room; Jacuzzi; business center; room service; coin-op laundry. *In room:* A/C, TV, dataport, fridge, coffeemaker, hair dryer, iron, free local calls.

WHERE TO DINE

If tea is your drink of choice, don't miss the **Tea Lady,** 430 Washington St. SE (ℂ **360/786-0350**), a shop that celebrates all things tea and always has several different hot teas available. If it's local microbrews you're after, drop by the **Fishbowl Brewpub,**

Finds So, Who Needs Starbucks?

When it's time for coffee, drop by **Batdorf & Bronson,** 516 S. Capitol Way (ℂ 360/786-6717), which is right downtown. This espresso bar pours the best Americano (espresso topped off with hot water) in the state. Java junkies should also be sure to stop by the **Batdorf & Bronson Tasting Room,** 200 Market St. NE (ℂ 360/753-4057; www.batdorf.com), which is at the company roastery and usually has several different coffees available to taste (and buy by the cup or the pound).

515 Jefferson St. SE ((C) **360/943-3650;** www.fishbrewing.com), which is very popular as an after-work gathering spot.

Budd Bay Café 🐠🐠 SEAFOOD   In downtown Olympia, the Budd Bay Café is the city's favorite waterfront restaurant and its lavish Sunday seafood brunch is always popular. The views from both the dining room and large deck take in the waters of Budd Bay as well as the state capitol. Just outside, the Percival Landing Waterfront Park boardwalk stretches for 1½ miles, ideal for that after-dinner stroll. The menu has such standards as seafood fettuccine, cedar-plank salmon, and pan-fried oysters, as well as good steaks and prime rib.

Percival Landing, 525 N. Columbia St. (C) **360/357-6963.** www.buddbaycafe.com. Reservations recommended. Main courses $8–$13 lunch, $10–$34 dinner. AE, DC, DISC, MC, V. Mon–Thurs 11am–9pm; Fri–Sat 11am–10pm; Sun 9:30am–9pm.

Cielo Blu 🐠 ECLECTIC   With flavors that span the globe from Barcelona to Tokyo, this is the most eclectic eatery in Olympia, and if you're in the mood for something more than pan-fried oysters or a burger, this is a good bet. The interior decor is as hip as it gets in Olympia; in fact, it's hard to tell if the dining room tables are surrounded by chairs or sculptures. All in all, this is a fun, hip place for a moderately priced meal. In a past incarnation, Cielo Blu was a Mediterranean restaurant, so you might want to stick with the pasta dishes and designer pizzas.

514 Capitol Way S. (C) **360/352-8007.** Main courses $6–$11 lunch; $10–$21 dinner. AE, DISC, MC, V. Tues–Fri 11:30am–2pm and 5–9pm; Sat 5–9pm.

The Spar Cafe 🐠 AMERICAN   In business since 1935, this downtown diner is a Northwest classic. On the walls are old black-and-white photos of period logging activities (the cafe's name refers to the spar trees used for rigging cables and pulleys), and along one wall is the original cigar counter, lined with glass-fronted humidor cabinets full of premium cigars. In back, through a swinging door, is a dark bar, but the cozy old booths out front are the main attraction. Breakfasts are some of the best in town (try the Fourth Avenue Mess). If it's genuine Olympia atmosphere you're looking for, this is the place.

114 E. Fourth Ave. (C) **360/357-6444.** Main courses $8–$15. AE, DISC, MC, V. Mon–Thurs 6am–8pm; Fri–Sat 6am–10pm; Sun 6am–8pm.

8

The Olympic Peninsula

The rugged and remote Olympic Peninsula, located in the extreme northwestern corner of Washington and home to Olympic National Park, was one of the last places in the continental U.S. to be explored. Its impenetrable, rain-soaked forests and steep, glacier-carved mountains effectively restricted settlement to the peninsula's more accessible coastal regions.

Though much of the Olympic Peninsula was designated a National Forest Preserve in 1897, and in 1909 became a national monument, it was not until 1938 that the heart of the peninsula—the jagged, snowcapped Olympic Mountains—became Olympic National Park. This region was originally preserved in order to protect the area's rapidly dwindling herds of Roosevelt elk, named for President Theodore Roosevelt (who was responsible for the area becoming a national monument). At that time, these elk herds were being decimated by commercial hunters.

Today, however, Olympic National Park, which is roughly the size of Rhode Island, is far more than an elk reserve. It is recognized as one of the world's most important wild ecosystems. The park is unique in the contiguous United States for its temperate rainforests, which are found in the west-facing valleys of the Hoh, Queets, Bogachiel, Clearwater, and Quinault rivers. In these valleys, rainfall can exceed 150 inches per year, trees (Sitka spruce, western red cedar, Douglas fir, and western hemlock) grow nearly 300 feet tall, and mosses enshroud the limbs of big-leaf maples.

Within a few short miles of the park's rainforests, the Olympic Mountains rise up to an alpine zone where no trees grow at all, and above these alpine meadows rises the 7,965-foot glacier-clad summit of Mount Olympus. Together, elevation and heavy snowfall (the rain of lower elevations is replaced by snow at higher elevations) combine to form the numerous glaciers within the park. It is these glaciers that have carved the Olympic Mountains into the jagged peaks that mesmerize visitors and beckon to hikers and climbers. Rugged and spectacular sections of the coast have also been preserved as part of the national park, and the offshore waters are designated as the Olympic Coast National Marine Sanctuary.

With fewer than a dozen roads, none of which leads more than a few miles into the park, Olympic National Park is, for the most part, inaccessible to the casual visitor. Only two roads penetrate the high country, and only one of these is paved. Likewise, only two paved roads lead into the park's famed rainforests. Although a long stretch of beach within the national park is paralleled by U.S. 101, the park's most spectacular beaches can only be reached on foot.

While the park is inaccessible to cars, it is a wonderland for hikers and backpackers. Its rugged beaches, rainforest valleys, alpine meadows, and mountaintop glaciers offer an amazing variety of hiking and backpacking opportunities. For alpine hikes, there are the trails at Hurricane Ridge and Deer Park. To experience the rainforest in all its drippy glory, there are the trails of the Bogachiel, Hoh, Queets, and Quinault valleys. Of these rainforest trails, the Hoh Valley has the more accessible (and consequently more popular) trails, including the trail that leads backpackers on the multi-day hike to the summit of Mount Olympus. Favorite hikes include the stretch of coast between La Push and Oil City and from Rialto Beach north to Lake Ozette and on to Shi Shi Beach.

The restored Victorian seaport of Port Townsend in the northeast corner of the peninsula offers a striking contrast to the wildness of Olympic National Park. Here, a restored historic commercial district on the waterfront is packed with interesting shops and good restaurants, while on the bluff above, the streets are lined with stately Victorian homes (many are bed-and-breakfast inns). Together, the town's two historic neighborhoods have made Port Townsend one of the state's most popular destinations.

The rural community of Sequim (pronounced *skwim*) has also been developing quite a reputation in recent years for a very different reason. The Sequim area lies in the rain shadow of the Olympic Mountains and receives fewer than 20 inches of rain per year (less than half the average of Seattle). Sure, the skies here are still cloudy much of the year, but anyone who has lived very long in the Northwest begins to

dream of someplace where it doesn't rain quite so much. In Sequim, these dreamers are building retirement homes as fast as they can. The dry climate has also proven to be an ideal environment for growing lavender, and fields of purple blossoms are sprouting all over the Sequim area.

Long before the first white settlers arrived, various Native American tribes called the Olympic Peninsula home. The Makah, Quinault, Hoh, Elwha, and Skokomish tribes all inhabited different regions of the peninsula, but all stayed close to the coast, where they could harvest the plentiful mollusks, fish, and whales. Today, there are numerous Indian reservations, both large and small, on the peninsula. On the Jamestown S'Klallam Reservation, you'll find a casino, and on the Makah Reservation, a museum of culture and history.

While at first it might seem that the entire peninsula is a pristine wilderness, that just isn't the case. When the first white settlers arrived, they took one look at the 300-foot-tall trees that grew on the Olympic Peninsula and started sharpening their axes. The supply of trees seemed endless, but by the 1980s the end was in sight for the trees that had not been preserved within Olympic National Park. Today, U.S. 101, which loops around the east, north, and west side of the peninsula is lined with clear-cuts and second- and third-growth forests for much of its length, a fact that takes many first-time visitors by surprise.

1 Port Townsend: A Restored Victorian Seaport

60 miles NW of Seattle, 48 miles E of Port Angeles, 40 miles S of Anacortes

Named by English explorer Captain George Vancouver in 1792, Port Townsend did not attract its first settlers until 1851. However, by the 1880s the town had become an important shipping port and was expected to grow into one of the most important cities on the West Coast. Port Townsend felt that it was the logical end of the line for the transcontinental railroad that was pushing westward in the 1880s; and based on the certainty of a railroad connection, real estate speculation and development boomed. Merchants and investors erected mercantile palaces along Water Street and

The Olympic Peninsula

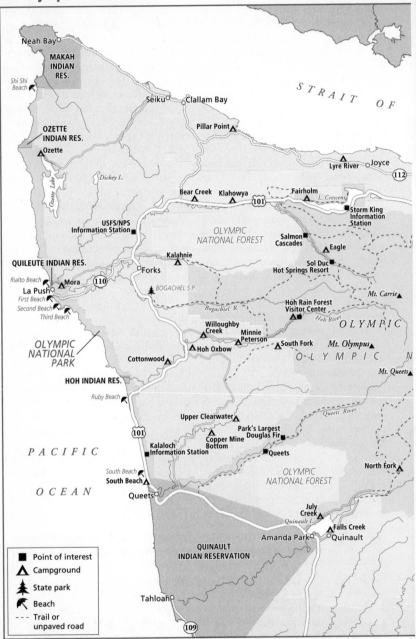

STRAIT OF

Neah Bay

MAKAH INDIAN RES.

Shi Shi Beach

Seiku
Clallam Bay

Pillar Point

OZETTE INDIAN RES.

Ozette

Lyre River
Joyce
112

Dickey L.

Bear Creek
Klahowya
Fairholm
L. Crescent
101
Storm King Information Station

Ozette Lake

USFS/NPS Information Station

OLYMPIC NATIONAL FOREST

Salmon Cascades
Eagle

Sol Duc Hot Springs Resort

Kalahnie

Mt. Carrie

QUILEUTE INDIAN RES.

Rialto Beach
Mora
110
Forks

Bogachiel S.P.

Hoh Rain Forest Visitor Center

La Push

First Beach
Second Beach
Third Beach

Bogachiel R.
Hoh River
OLYMPIC

OLYMPIC NATIONAL PARK

Willoughby Creek
Minnie Peterson
South Fork
Mt. Olympus
O L Y M P I C   N

Cottonwood
Hoh Oxbow

Mt. Queets

HOH INDIAN RES.

Ruby Beach

Upper Clearwater
Queets River

101

Park's Largest Douglas Fir

Copper Mine Bottom

Kalaloch Information Station

Queets

PACIFIC

North Fork

OLYMPIC NATIONAL FOREST

OCEAN

South Beach
South Beach

Queets

July Creek
Quinault L.
Falls Creek
Amanda Park
Quinault

QUINAULT INDIAN RESERVATION

Tahloah

109

■ Point of interest
▲ Campground
🌲 State park
🔱 Beach
--- Trail or unpaved road

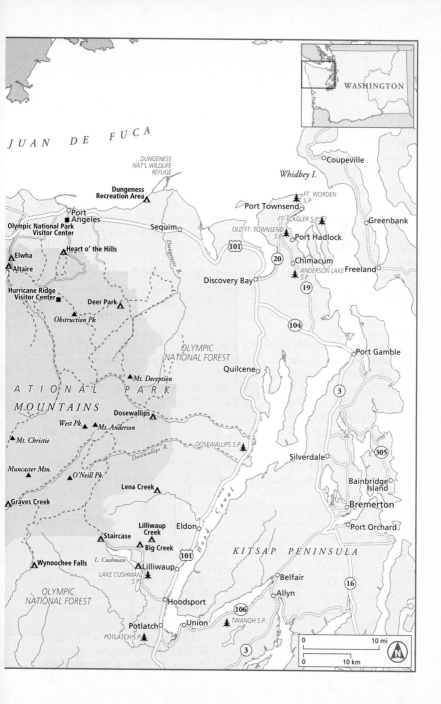

WASHINGTON

JUAN DE FUCA

DUNGENESS NAT'L WILDLIFE REFUGE

Coupeville

Whidbey I.

Dungeness Recreation Area

FT. WORDEN S.P.

Port Townsend

Port Angeles

FT. FLAGLER S.P.

Greenbank

Olympic National Park Visitor Center

Sequim

OLD FT. TOWNSEND S.P.

Port Hadlock

101

Elwha

20

Chimacum

Freeland

Altaire

Heart o' the Hills

ANDERSON LAKE S.P.

Discovery Bay

19

Hurricane Ridge Visitor Center

Deer Park

104

Obstruction Pk.

OLYMPIC NATIONAL FOREST

Port Gamble

Quilcene

3

ATIONAL PARK

Mt. Deception

MOUNTAINS

Dosewallips

West Pk. Mt. Anderson

305

Mt. Christie

Dosewallips R.

DOSEWALLIPS S.P.

Silverdale

Muncaster Mtn.

O'Neill Pk.

Bainbridge Island

Lena Creek

Bremerton

Graves Creek

Hood Canal

Port Orchard

Staircase

Lilliwaup Creek

Eldon

Big Creek

101

KITSAP PENINSULA

Wynoochee Falls

L. Cushman

Lilliwaup

LAKE CUSHMAN S.P.

Belfair

16

OLYMPIC NATIONAL FOREST

Allyn

Hoodsport

106

Potlatch

Union

TWANOH S.P.

POTLATCH S.P.

3

0   10 mi

0   10 km

elaborate Victorian homes on the bluff above the wharf district. However, the railroad never arrived. Tacoma got the rails, and Port Townsend got the shaft.

With its importance as a shipping port usurped by Seattle and Tacoma, Port Townsend slipped into quiet obscurity. Progress passed it by and its elegant homes and commercial buildings were left to slowly fade away. However, in 1976 the waterfront district and bluff-top residential neighborhood were declared a National Historic District and the town began a slow revival. Today the streets of Port Townsend are once again crowded with people. The waterfront district is filled with boutiques, galleries, and other interesting shops, and many of the Victorian homes atop the bluff have become bed-and-breakfast inns.

ESSENTIALS

GETTING THERE   Port Townsend is on Wash. 20, off U.S. 101 in the northeast corner of the Olympic Peninsula. The Hood Canal Bridge, which connects the Kitsap Peninsula with the Olympic Peninsula and is on the route from Seattle to Port Townsend, is sometimes closed due to high winds; if you want to be certain that it's open, call © **800/419-9085.**

Washington State Ferries (© **800/84-FERRY** or 888/808-7977 within Washington, or 206/464-6400; www.wsdot.wa.gov/ferries) operates a ferry between Port Townsend and Keystone (on Whidbey Island). The crossing takes 30 minutes and costs $8.20 to $10 for a vehicle and driver, $2.35 per passenger (discounted fares for seniors and youths).

From late April to early October, passenger-boat service between Port Townsend and Friday Harbor (in the San Juan Islands) is offered by **P.S. Express** (© **360/385-5288;** www.pugetsoundexpress.com), which will also carry bicycles and sea kayaks. One-way fares are $40 to $50 for adults and $30 to $40 for children; round-trip fares are $60 to $67 for adults and $41 to $49 for children.

VISITOR INFORMATION   Contact the **Port Townsend Chamber of Commerce Visitor Information Center,** 2437 E. Sims Way, Port Townsend, WA 98368 (© **888/365-6978** or 360/385-2722; www.ptguide.com).

GETTING AROUND   Because parking spaces are hard to come by in downtown Port Townsend on weekends and anytime in the summer, **Jefferson Transit** (© **800/371-0497** or 360/385-4777; www.jeffersontransit.com), the local public bus service, operates a shuttle into downtown Port Townsend from a park-and-ride lot on the south side of town. Jefferson Transit also operates other buses around Port Townsend. The fare is $1.25.

FESTIVALS   As a tourist town, Port Townsend schedules quite a few festivals throughout the year. In late March the town celebrates its Victorian heritage with the **Victorian Festival** (© 360/379-0668; www.victorianfestival.org). The end of July brings the **Centrum's Jazz Port Townsend Festival** (© 360/385-3102; www.centrum.org). The **Wooden Boat Festival** (© 360/385-3628; www.woodenboat.org), the largest of its kind in the United States, is on the first weekend after Labor Day.

To see inside some of the town's many restored homes, schedule a visit during the **Historic Homes Tour** (© **888/365-6978** or 360/385-2722; www.ptguide.com/homes tour), on the third weekend in September. During the **Kinetic Sculpture Race** (© **360/379-4972;** www.kineticrace.info), held the first weekend in October, outrageous human-powered vehicles race on land, on water, and through a mud bog.

EXPLORING THE TOWN

With its abundance of restored Victorian homes and commercial buildings, Port Townsend's most popular activity is simply walking or driving through the historic districts. The town is divided into the waterfront commercial district and the residential uptown area, which is atop a bluff that rises precipitously only 2 blocks from the water. Uptown Port Townsend developed in part so that proper Victorian ladies would not have to associate with the riffraff that frequented the waterfront. At the Port Townsend Visitor Information Center, you can pick up a guide that lists the town's many historic homes and commercial buildings.

Water Street is the town's main commercial district. It is lined for several blocks with 100-year-old restored brick buildings, many of which have ornate facades. Within these buildings are dozens of interesting shops and boutiques, several restaurants, and a handful of hotels and inns. To learn a little more about the history of this part of town and to gain a different perspective, walk out on **Union Wharf,** at the foot of Taylor Street. Here you'll find interpretive plaques covering topics ranging from sea grass to waterfront history.

Make your first stop in town the **Jefferson County Historical Society Museum,** 540 Water St. (© 360/385-1003; www.jchsmuseum.org), where you can learn about the history of the area. Among the collections here are regional Native American artifacts and antiques from the Victorian era. It's open Monday through Saturday from 11am to 4pm and Sunday from 1 to 4pm (in Jan and Feb, open Sat–Sun only). Admission is $3 for adults and $1 for children under 12. In 2005, this museum was located in a temporary space on the second floor of the Kuhn Building at the corner of Water and Polk streets. Hopefully, by the time you arrive, the restoration of the museum's historic city hall location will be completed.

The town's noted Victorian homes are in uptown Port Townsend, atop the bluff that rises behind the waterfront's commercial buildings. This is where you'll find stately homes, views, and the city's favorite park. To reach the uptown area, either drive up Washington Street (1 block over from Water St.) or walk up the stairs at the end of Taylor Street, which start behind the Haller Fountain.

At the top of the stairs, you'll see an 1890 bell tower, which once summoned volunteer firemen, and the **Rothschild House,** at Taylor and Franklin streets (© 360/379-8076 or 360/385-1103; www.jchsmuseum.org). Built in 1868, this Greek Revival–style house is one of the oldest buildings in town and displays a sober architecture compared to other area homes. The gardens contain a wide variety of roses, peonies, and lilacs. It's open May through September, Monday to Saturday from 11am to 4pm and Sunday from 1 to 4pm. Admission is $4 for adults and $1 for children under 12. A $5 passport gets you into both this historic house and the Jefferson County Historical Society Museum.

The most fascinating uptown home open to the public is the **Ann Starrett Mansion Boutique Hotel,** 744 Clay St. (© 360/385-3205), Port Townsend's most astoundingly ornate Queen Anne Victorian home. Currently operated as a bed-and-breakfast, this mansion is best known for its imposing turret, ceiling frescoes, and unusual spiral staircase. It's open for guided tours daily from 2 to 3pm. Tours cost $3.

Also here in the uptown neighborhood, at the corner of Garfield and Jackson streets, is **Chetzemoka Park,** which was established in 1904 and is named for a local S'Klallam Indian chief. The park perches on a bluff overlooking Admiralty Inlet and has access to a pleasant little beach. However, most visitors head straight for the rose garden, arbor, and waterfall garden.

Shopping is just about the most popular activity in Port Townsend's old town, and of the many stores in the historic district, several stand out. **Earthenworks Gallery,** 702 Water St. (© 360/385-0328; www.earthenworksgallery.com), showcases colorful ceramics, glass, jewelry, and other American-made crafts. **Ancestral Spirits Gallery,** 701 Water St. (© 360/385-0078; www.ancestralspirits.com), is a large space with a great selection of Northwest Native American prints, masks, and carvings.

FORT WORDEN STATE PARK

Fort Worden State Park, once a military installation that guarded the mouth of Puget Sound, is north of the historic district and can be reached by turning onto Kearney Street at the south end of town, or onto Monroe Street at the north end of town, and following the signs. Built at the turn of the 20th century, the fort is now a 360-acre state park where a wide array of attractions and activities assure that it's busy much of the year. Many of the fort's old wooden buildings have been restored and put to new uses.

At the **Fort Worden Commanding Officer's House** (© 360/344-4452), you can see what life was like for a Victorian-era officer and his family. The home has been fully restored and is filled with period antiques. In summer, it's open daily from 10am to 5pm, and in spring and fall, Saturday and Sunday from noon to 4pm (call for hours in other months). Admission is $2 for adults, free for kids under 12.

Here at the park, you can learn about life below the waters of Puget Sound at the **Port Townsend Marine Science Center,** 532 Battery Way (© 800/566-3932 or 360/385-5582; www.ptmsc.org). It has great tidepool touch tanks filled with crabs, starfish, anemones, and other marine life. There's also a fascinating exhibit on the area's terrestrial natural history, complete with fossils from around the peninsula. Don't miss the exhibit on glaciers that once covered this region. In summer, the center is open Wednesday through Monday from 11am to 5pm, and in fall through spring, Friday through Monday from noon to 4pm. Admission is $5 for adults, $3 for youths 6 to 17.

Fort Worden is also home to the **Puget Sound Coast Artillery Museum** (© 360/385-0373), which is open June through August, Tuesday to Sunday from 11am to 4pm, and September, October, April, and May on Saturday and Sunday from 11am to 4pm. Admission is $2 for adults and $1 for children.

For many people, however, the main reason to visit the park is to hang out on the beach or at one of the picnic areas. Scuba divers also frequent Fort Worden, which has

---

Kids **A Victory for Kids in a Victorian Town**

There aren't a lot of children with an appreciation for Victorian architects, so parents visiting Port Townsend may find themselves at the mercy of whining young ones. Don't despair. You can all take a time out from touring mansions and head out to Fort Worden State Park. Here you'll find a fascinating marine science center where kids can grab starfish and poke anemones. There's also a long beach, and even though the water is cold, the kids might not mind. Then there are trails through the woods and the very spooky old gun emplacements. Bring a flashlight and you can dig around in the dark corners of history.

an underwater park just offshore. In spring, the Rhododendron Garden puts on a color-ful floral display. Throughout the year, there is a wide variety of concerts and other per-formances at the **Centrum** (*©* **800/733-3608** or 360/385-3102; www.centrum.org). Also on the premises are campgrounds, a restaurant, and restored officers' quarters that can be rented as vacation homes.

PORT TOWNSEND FROM THE WATER (& AIR)

If you'd like to explore this area from the water, you've got several options. Three-hour sailboat tours ($75) are offered by **Brisa Charters** (*©* **877/41-BRISA** or 360/385-2309; www.olympus.net/brisa_charters). Several times a year, the **Port Townsend Marine Science Center** (*©* **800/566-3932** or 360/385-5582; www.ptmsc.org) oper-ates boat tours ($45) to nearby Protection Island, a wildlife refuge that is home to puffins, rhinoceros auklets, and other nesting seabirds. One trip a year is done on a 101-foot historic schooner.

From late May to early September, whale-watching cruises ($65 for adults, $49 for children ages 2–10) through the San Juan Islands are offered by **P. S. Express,** Point Hudson Marina, 431 Water St. (*©* **360/385-5288;** www.pugetsoundexpress.com), which also operates passenger-ferry service to Friday Harbor.

If you'd like to try your hand at paddling a sea kayak around the area's waters, contact **Port Townsend Outdoors,** 1017B Water St. (*©* **888/754-8598;** www.ptoutdoors.com). Rental rates range from $18 to $32 for 1 hour up to between $45 and $75 for the day. A variety of guided kayak tours are also offered. At the nearby **Port Ludlow Marina** (*©* **800/308-7991** or 360/437-0513; www.portludlowresort.com), south of Port Townsend, you can rent sea kayaks ($10–$15 per hour) and motorboats ($20 per hour).

OTHER AREA ACTIVITIES

While you're visiting the area, you might want to check out Port Townsend's two wineries, both located south of town. **Sorensen Cellars,** 274 S. Otto St. (*©* **360/379-6416;** www.sorensencellars.com), is open March through September, Friday through Sunday from noon to 5pm (or by appointment). To find this winery, turn east off Wash. 20 onto Frederick Street and then south on Otto Street.

Fair Winds Winery, 1984 Hastings Ave. W. (*©* **360/385-6899;** www.fairwinds winery.com), is the only winery in the state producing Aligoté, a French-style white wine. From Memorial Day to Labor Day, the winery is open daily from noon to 5pm; in other months, it's open Friday and Monday from noon to 5pm. To get here, drive south from Port Townsend on Wash. 20, turn west on Jacob Miller Road, and con-tinue 2 miles to Hastings Avenue.

MARROWSTONE ISLAND

You'll find another old-fort-turned-state-park on nearby Marrowstone Island, which is reached by driving south 9 miles to Port Hadlock on Wash. 19 and then turning east on Wash. 116. From Port Hadlock, it's another 11 miles to the northern tip of Marrowstone Island and **Fort Flagler State Park.** This large park has a campground, boat ramp, beaches, and hiking trails.

Between Port Hadlock and Marrowstone Island is Indian Island, most of which is an active military base. The waters off the island are popular with sea kayakers, and at the south end of Indian Island is a small park popular with windsurfers.

WHERE TO STAY
IN PORT TOWNSEND
Moderate

Ann Starrett Mansion Boutique Hotel ☺☺   Built in 1889 for $6,000 as a wedding present for Ann Starrett, this Victorian jewel box is by far the most elegant and ornate historic hotel in Port Townsend (or the entire state, for that matter). The rose-and-teal-green mansion is a museum of the Victorian era: A three-story turret towers over the front door, and every room is exquisitely furnished with period antiques. In fact, if you aren't staying here, you can still have a look during one of the afternoon house tours ($3). Note that although this hotel seems as though it would be a bed-and-breakfast inn, it does not serve breakfast; there are, however, plenty of good breakfast places in the area.

744 Clay St., Port Townsend, WA 98368. © 800/321-0644 or 360/385-3205. Fax 360/385-2976. www.starrettmansion. com. 11 units. $85–$185 double. Rates include continental breakfast. AE, MC, V. *In room:* No phone.

F. W. Hastings House/Old Consulate Inn ☺☺   Though not quite as elaborate as the Starrett Mansion, the Old Consulate Inn is another example of the Victorian excess so wonderfully appealing today. The attention to detail and quality craftsmanship both in the construction and the restoration of this elegant mansion are evident wherever you look. Despite its heritage, however, the Old Consulate avoids being a museum; it's a comfortable yet elegant place to stay. If you're here for a special occasion, consider splurging on one of the turret rooms. Of the other units, my favorite is the Parkside. For entertainment, you'll find a grand piano, a billiards table, and a VCR, as well as stunning views out most of the windows. A multi-course breakfast is meant to be lingered over, so don't make any early morning appointments. Afternoon tea, evening cordials and dessert, and a hot tub add to the experience.

313 Walker St., Port Townsend, WA 98368. © 800/300-6753 or 360/385-6753. Fax 360/385-2097. www.oldconsulate inn.com. 8 units. June–Oct $110–$210 double; Nov–May $99–$189 double. Rates include full breakfast. MC, V. Children 12 and older are welcome. **Amenities:** Jacuzzi. *In room:* Hair dryer, no phone.

James House ☺☺   With an eclectic blend of antique and new furnishings, this grand 1889 Victorian sits atop the bluff overlooking Admiralty Inlet. The entry hall has a parquet floor and a big staircase climbing straight up to the second floor. In the two parlors are fireplaces that make the perfect gathering spot on a cool evening. The views from the upper front bedrooms are some of the best in town (ask for the Master Suite, which has a balcony, or the Chintz Room, which has a deck). You can even see Mount Rainier on a clear day. If you don't like climbing stairs, opt for one of the ground-floor suites or the Gardener's Cottage. An additional private bungalow, adjacent to the James House, is done in a contemporary style and has both a water and mountain view.

1238 Washington St., Port Townsend, WA 98368. © 800/385-1238 or 360/385-1238. Fax 360/379-5551. www.james house.com. 12 units. May–Sept $135–$150 double, $150–$225 suite or cottage; Oct–Apr $110–$150 double, $165–$185 suite or cottage. Rates include full breakfast. Children over 12 welcome. AE, DISC, MC, V. **Amenities:** Massage. *In room:* Dataport, hair dryer, free local calls, high-speed Internet access.

Manresa Castle ☺☺ *Value*   Built in 1892 by the first mayor of Port Townsend, this reproduction of a medieval castle later became a Jesuit retreat and school. Today, traditional elegance pervades Manresa Castle, and of all the hotels and B&Bs in Port Townsend, this place offers the most historic elegance for the money. The guest rooms have a genuine, vintage appeal that manages to avoid the contrived feeling that so often sneaks into the room decor of B&Bs. The tower suite is my favorite room in the hotel and is worth a splurge. In this huge room, you get sweeping views from a circular seating area. An elegant lounge and dining room further add to the Grand Hotel feel of this unusual lodging. A recent renovation has given this grande dame a welcome face-lift. Oh, and by the way, the hotel is haunted.

651 Cleveland St. (P.O. Box 564), Port Townsend, WA 98368. © 800/732-1281 or 360/385-5750. Fax 360/385-5883. www.manresacastle.com. 40 units. $99–$109 double; $139–$189 suite. Rates include continental breakfast. AE, MC, V. **Amenities:** Restaurant (Continental/International); lounge. *In room:* TV.

Palace Hotel ✦   In the heart of the historic district, the Palace Hotel occupies a building that once served as a bordello, and today, Madame Marie's suite—a big corner room with a kitchenette—is the best room in the house. Most of the other rooms are named for former working girls. Miss Kitty's room is as nice as the Madame's and includes a cast-iron woodstove and the best views at the Palace. The Crow's Nest room is another interesting space, with a sleeping loft, nautical theme, and woodstove. *Note:* The hotel is up a steep flight of stairs from the street, and some rooms are up on the third floor. The bathroom shared by two rooms has a big claw-foot tub, so you won't do badly if you take one of them.

1004 Water St., Port Townsend, WA 98368. © 800/962-0741 or 360/385-0773. Fax 360/385-0780. www.palace hotelpt.com. 19 units, 2 with shared bathroom. $59–$69 double with shared bathroom; $99–$169 double or suite with private bathroom. Rates include continental breakfast except in summer. Children under 12 stay free in parent's room. AE, DISC, MC, V. Pets accepted ($10 per day). *In room:* TV, coffeemaker.

Inexpensive

The Belmont ✦   Built in 1885, The Belmont is the oldest waterfront restaurant and saloon in town, and on the second floor, you'll find four very spacious, if not exactly luxurious, rooms. The two in back open right onto the water and offer one of the best views in town. Exposed brick walls provide character, and three of the rooms have loft sleeping areas. Expect some noise from the saloon downstairs. The Belmont also rents out three suites across the street. These rooms are definitely not for the finicky, but they've got loads of character.

925 Water St., Port Townsend, WA 98368. © 360/385-3007. Fax 360/344-3213. www.thebelmontpt.com. 4 units. $49–$109 double. AE, DISC, MC, V. **Amenities:** Restaurant (Regional American). *In room:* Coffeemaker.

IN PORT LUDLOW

The Resort at Ludlow Bay ✦✦   Set on a tiny peninsula jutting into Ludlow Bay, this luxurious inn is one of the finest in the Northwest. The setting rivals anything in the San Juan Islands, and the inn itself conjures up the image of a New England summer home at the shore. Designed for romantic getaways, the guest rooms are spacious and plush, with whirlpool tubs, fireplaces, and down-filled duvets on the beds. Every room has a water view and from some you can see Mount Baker or the Olympic Mountains. Casual meals are served in the inn's lounge. Additional amenities include paved walking paths through the adjacent resort and a croquet lawn.

One Heron Rd., Port Ludlow, WA 98365. © 877/805-0868 or 360/437-7000. Fax 360/437-7410. www.ludlowbay resort.com. 37 units. $149–$249 double; $189–$269 suite; $199–$325 condo. Rates in the inn include continental breakfast. AE, MC, V. **Amenities:** Restaurant (New American); lounge; 27-hole golf course; 2 tennis courts; spa services; boat rentals; bike rentals; massage; coin-op laundry. *In room:* TV/VCR, dataport, fridge, coffeemaker, hair dryer, iron, free local calls, Wi-Fi.

WHERE TO DINE
IN PORT TOWNSEND

One place on nearly everyone's itinerary is **Elevated Ice Cream,** 627 Water St. (© **360/ 385-1156**), which scoops up the best ice cream in town. For pastries, light meals, and good coffee, try **Bread & Roses Bakery,** 230 Quincy St. (© **360/379-3355**).

For espresso, drop by **Tyler Street Coffee House,** 215 Tyler St. (© **360/379-4185**). For tea instead of coffee, check out **Wild Sage,** 227 Adams St. (© **360/379-1222**).

Expensive

Fins Coastal Cuisine ☆ SEAFOOD   On the second floor of a waterfront building, this restaurant is just far enough removed from the sidewalk cruisers to have a sophisticated atmosphere. The food is the most imaginative in downtown Port Townsend, with such creative dishes as seared sea scallops with roasted-beet carpaccio. However, if your tastes lean to simpler fare, you can also get salt-encrusted prime rib. Remember, this is seafood country, so you might want to try the Portuguese fisherman's stew or the salmon with saffron-potato hash instead.

1019 Water St. © 360/379-FISH. www.finscoastalcuisine.com. Main courses $8–$14 at lunch, $18–$30 at dinner. AE, DISC, MC, V. Mon–Thurs 11:30am–3pm; Fri–Sun 11:30am–4:30pm; Sun–Thurs 5–8:30pm; Fri–Sat 5–9pm.

Moderate

Silverwater Cafe ☆☆ *Value* NORTHWEST   Works by local artists, lots of plants, and New Age music on the stereo set the tone for this casually chic restaurant. Though the menu focuses on Northwest dishes, it includes preparations from around the world. You can start your meal with an artichoke-and-Parmesan pâté and then move on to ahi tuna with lavender pepper, ginger-lime prawns, or smoked chicken with brandy and apples. The oysters in a blue-cheese sauce are a favorite of mine. Vegetarians will find a half-dozen options.

237 Taylor St. © 360/385-6448. www.silverwatercafe.com. Reservations accepted only for parties of 6 or more. Main courses $6.50–$13 at lunch, $11–$20 at dinner. MC, V. Mon–Thurs 11:30am–8:30pm; Fri–Sat 11:30am–9:30pm; Sun 5–8:30pm.

T's Restaurant ☆☆ ITALIAN   Across the street from the Boat Haven marina south of downtown Port Townsend, this romantic, low-key place is a welcome alternative to the touristy restaurants downtown. The menu usually features plenty of daily specials. Be sure to start with the creamy oyster stew, which is made with pancetta and fennel. You'll find a wide variety of interesting pasta dishes from which to choose, but the rigatoni Gorgonzola is our favorite. Traditional Spanish paella is another tasty dish. Local oysters, mussels, and clams show up frequently on the fresh sheet and are hard to resist.

2330 Washington St. © 360/385-0700. www.ts-restaurant.com. Reservations recommended. Main courses $14–$25. AE, MC, V. Wed–Mon 5–9pm.

Inexpensive

Fountain Cafe ☆ *Finds* ECLECTIC   Housed in a narrow clapboard building, this funky little place has long been a favorite of Port Townsend locals and counterculture types on a tight budget. Eclectic furnishings decorate the room, which has a few stools at the counter. The menu changes seasonally, but you can rest assured that the simple fare will be utterly fresh and that the offerings will include plenty of shellfish and pasta. The Greek pasta is a mainstay that's hard to beat, and the clam chowder is excellent. The wide range of flavors here assures that everyone will find something to his or her liking.

920 Washington St. © **360/385-1364.** Reservations accepted only for parties of 6 or more. Main courses $8–$18. MC, V. Mon–Fri 11:30am–3pm; Fri–Sat 8am–3pm; Sun–Thurs 5–9pm; Fri–Sat 5–9:30pm.

Khu Larb Thai ✦ THAI   A half-block off busy Water Street, Khu Larb seems a world removed from Port Townsend's sometimes-overdone Victorian decor. Thai easy-listening music plays on the stereo, while the pungent fragrance of Thai spices wafts through the dining room. One taste of any dish on the menu and you'll be convinced that this is great Thai food. The halibut in lemongrass sauce is delicious. If you like fish, be sure to order this dish. The curry dishes made with mussels are also good bets. This place even has low-carb dishes!

225 Adams St. © **360/385-5023.** www.khularbthai.com. Reservations not accepted. Main courses $9–$12. AE, DISC, MC, V. Tues–Sun 11am–9pm.

IN PORT HADLOCK

The Ajax Cafe ✦✦ *Value* INTERNATIONAL   With no two matching glasses and no two chairs the same, this long-time local favorite is as eclectic a place as you'll find—and a lot of fun, too. On the waterfront in Port Hadlock in an old wooden storefront, the restaurant is out of the way and funky, and that's exactly why it's so popular. Silly hats hang from the ceiling, the restroom walls are hung with loud ties, and patrons are encouraged to don silly garb while dining. To top it off, there's live music on weekends. The menu runs the gamut from a seafood pasta to ribs spiked with Jack Daniel's whiskey. However, the locals rave about the steaks. If you like good times and good food, this is a "don't miss." The perpetual party atmosphere makes this a great place for a celebration.

21 N. Water St., Port Hadlock. © **360/385-3450.** www.ajaxcafe.com. Reservations recommended. Main courses $8–$21. MC, V. Tues–Sun 5–9pm. Closed Jan.

PORT TOWNSEND AFTER DARK

On weekend nights, you can catch live music at **Lanza's,** 1020 Lawrence St. (© **360/ 379-1900**), an Italian restaurant; and the **Public House,** 1038 Water St. (© **360/ 385-9708;** www.thepublichouse.com), which books an eclectic range of music and has the feel of a 19th-century tavern.

2 Sequim & Dungeness Valley

17 miles E of Port Angeles, 31 miles W of Port Townsend

In the rain shadow of the Olympic Mountains, Sequim (remember, it's pronounced *skwim*) is the driest region of the state west of the Cascade Range and sodden, moss-laden Northwesterners have taken to retiring here in droves. While the rains descend on the rest of the region, the fortunate few who call Sequim home bask in their own personal microclimate of sunshine and warmth.

The lack of rainfall and temperate climate also make this an almost perfect place to grow lavender plants, and today, parts of Sequim take on the look of Provence each summer when lavender plants are in bloom. There are U-pick farms, shops selling kinds of lavender products, and, of course, an annual lavender festival.

Before this area became known for its lavender farms, it was famous for its hefty crustaceans. The nearby town of Dungeness is set at the foot of Dungeness Spit, which, at more than 6 miles in length, is the longest sand spit in the world. However, it is for lending its name to the Northwest's favorite crab that Dungeness is most famous. The Dungeness crab is as much a staple of Washington waters as the blue crab is in the Chesapeake Bay region.

ESSENTIALS

GETTING THERE   The Sequim–Dungeness Valley lies to the north of U.S. 101 between Port Townsend and Port Angeles. **Jefferson Transit** (*©* **800/371-0497** or 360/385-4777; www.jeffersontransit.com) has service from Port Townsend to Sequim, and **Clallam Transit** (*©* **800/858-3747** or 360/452-4511; www.clallam transit.com) operates west from Sequim and around the peninsula to Lake Crescent, Neah Bay, La Push, and Forks.

VISITOR INFORMATION   For information, contact the **Sequim–Dungeness Valley Chamber of Commerce,** 1192 E. Washington St. (P.O. Box 907), Sequim, WA 98382-0907 (*©* **800/737-8462** or 360/683-6197; www.visitsun.com).

FESTIVALS   The **Irrigation Festival** (*©* **800/737-8462** or 360/683-6197; www.irrigationfestival.com), the oldest continuous festival in Washington, has been going on for more than 110 years and takes place in early May. In mid-July, when the lavender gardens are in full bloom, the town observes the season with its **Sequim Lavender Festival** (*©* **877/681-3035;** www.lavenderfestival.com).

EXPLORING THE AREA

Just east of Sequim on U.S. 101, you'll find the **7 Cedars Casino,** 270756 U.S. 101 (*©* **800/4-LUCKY-7** or 360/683-7777; www.7cedarscasino.com), which is operated by the Jamestown S'Klallam Tribe and is designed to resemble a traditional longhouse, with several large totem poles out front. Nearby, you can visit the tribe's **Northwest Native Expressions,** 1033 Old Blyn Hwy. (*©* **360/681-4640**), where both quality and prices are high.

In downtown Sequim, you'll find the **Museum & Arts Center,** 175 W. Cedar St., Sequim (*©* **360/683-8110;** www.sequimmuseum.org), which houses a pair of mastodon tusks that were found near here in 1977. The mastodon had been killed by human hunters, a discovery that helped establish the presence of humans in this area 12,000 years ago. The museum also has an exhibit on the much more recent culture of the region's Native Americans. It's open Tuesday through Saturday from 8am to 4pm; admission is free.

If you've got the kids with you, Sequim's **Olympic Game Farm** ⊛, 1423 Ward Rd. (*©* **800/778-4295** or 360/683-4295; www.olygamefarm.com), is a must. You'll get up close and personal with bison, Kodiak bears, zebras, wolves, elk, deer, and many other species of wild animals that have appeared in over 100 movies and TV shows. There are drive-through and walking tours, as well as a petting farm. The farm is open daily from 9am; admission is $9 to $15 for adults, $8 to $13 for seniors and children ages 6 to 12, and free for children 5 and under.

The biggest attraction is Dungeness Spit, which is protected as the **Dungeness National Wildlife Refuge** ⊛⊛ (*©* **360/457-8451;** www.fws.gov/refuges). Within the refuge is a half-mile trail to a bluff-top overlook, but it is the spit, where you can hike for more than 5 miles to the historic New Dungeness Lighthouse, that is the favorite hiking area within the refuge. Along the way, you're likely to see numerous species of birds as well as harbor seals. There's a fee of $3 per family to visit the spit. Near the base of the Dungeness Spit, you'll also find the **Dungeness Recreation Area** (*©* **360/683-5847**), which has a campground, picnic area, and trail leading out to the

---

Fun Fact K-E-L-K Radio

Sequim is home to a herd of around 100 Roosevelt elk who constantly wander back and forth across U.S. 101 to travel from the foothills to their grazing land. To reduce the number of automobile-elk collisions, several members of the herd have had radio collars put on them. When the elk with radio collars approach the highway, the signals emitted by the collars signal yellow "Elk Crossing" warning lights to flash.

---

spit. If you're not up for a 10-mile round-trip hike to the lighthouse, you can paddle out on a tour with **Dungeness Kayaking Tours** (© 360/681-4190; www.dungeness kayaking.com). A 4-hour tour to the lighthouse costs $90 per person. Kayaks can also be rented if you're an experienced paddler. Camping and water access are also available at **Sequim Bay State Park** (© 360/902-8844), about 3 miles southeast of Sequim.

Sequim has also become known for its many lavender farms that paint the landscape with colorful blooms each summer. Sequim's climate is ideal for growing lavender, and you'll likely pass numerous large fields of this fragrant Mediterranean plant as you tour the area. If you want to stroll among the flowers of a lavender field, you've got plenty of options. **Purple Haze Lavender,** 180 Bell Bottom Rd. (© 888/852-6560 or 360/683-1714; www.purplehazelavender.com), a U-pick farm east of downtown Sequim off W. Sequim Bay Road, is one of our favorites. April through September, the farm is open daily from 10am to 5pm and has a gift shop in a small barn. The farm also has a year-round shop in downtown Sequim. North of here, don't miss **Graysmarsh Farm,** 6187 Woodcock Rd. (© 360/683-5563; www.graysmarsh.com), with its beautiful lavender fields and U-pick berry fields. In season, you can pick strawberries, raspberries, blueberries, and loganberries.

Up near the Dungeness Spit, you'll find a great organic lavender farm, **Jardin du Soleil,** 3932 Sequim-Dungeness Way (© 877/527-3461 or 360/582-1185; www. jardindusoleil.com), which surrounds an old farmhouse with Victorian gardens. From April to September, the farm is open daily from 10am to 5pm; in October, November, December, February, and March, it's open Friday through Sunday from 10am to 4pm. In the same area, you can visit the **Olympic Lavender Farm,** 1432 Marine Dr. (© 360/683-4475; www.olympiclavender.com), which is open in July and August daily from noon to 5pm.

Although **Cedarbrook Herb Farm,** 1345 S. Sequim Ave. (© 360/683-7733; www.cedarbrookherbfarm.com), isn't specifically a lavender farm, it's still well worth a visit. Here you can buy herb plants as well as herb vinegars, potpourris, dried flowers, lavender wands, garlic braids, and the like. You'll find this farm south of downtown Sequim at the top of a hill overlooking the town. It's open Monday through Saturday from 9am to 5pm and Sunday from 10am to 4pm. Closed in January.

Off to the southwest of Sequim is **Lost Mountain Lavender,** 1541 Taylor Cutoff Rd. (© 888/507-7481 or 360/681-2782; www.lostmountainlavender.com). This farm is open daily from 10am to 6pm in June, July, and August; in other months, it's open Thursday through Monday from 10am to 5pm.

To find your way around the area's lavender farms, stop by the Sequim–Dungeness Valley Chamber of Commerce visitor center (see above) or, on the Web, check out **www.lavendergrowers.org.**

If you're interested in tasting some locally produced wine, drive out to the **Lost Mountain Winery,** 3174 Lost Mountain Rd. (℃ **360/683-5229;** www.lostmountain. com), which produces Italian-style wines with no added sulfites. To find the winery from U.S. 101, go south 3 miles on Taylor Cut Off Road and turn right on Lost Mountain Road. You can also stop at **Olympic Cellars,** 255410 U.S. 101 (℃ **360/ 452-0160;** www.olympiccellars.com), housed in a large barn on the west side of Sequim.

The Sequim-Dungeness Valley is also one of the best areas in the state for **bicycle touring.** The roads are flat, there are great views, and you don't have to worry as much about getting rained on. Also, the **Olympic Discovery Trail,** a partly paved and partly gravel bike path, crosses much of the Sequim Dungeness Valley and links Sequim to Port Angeles.

If you'd like to do some bird-watching while you're in Sequim, drop by the **Dungeness River Audubon Center,** Railroad Bridge Park, 2151 Hendrickson Road (℃ **360/681-4076;** www.dungenessrivercenter.org), which has guided bird walks on Wednesday mornings at 8:30am. The center is open Tuesday through Saturday from 10am to 4pm and from noon to 4pm on Sunday. The center is on the west side of Sequim (from U.S. 101, take River Rd. north to Priest Rd. to Hendrickson Rd.).

WHERE TO STAY

Dungeness Bay Motel ☞ Despite the name, this is more a collection of cottages than a motel in the traditional sense of the word. Set on a bluff overlooking the Strait of Juan de Fuca and across the street from the waters of Dungeness Bay, this place boasts great views and economical accommodations. Most units actually have views of both the water and the Olympic Mountains. My favorite is the large San Juan Suite, which comes complete with a fireplace. The summer sunsets here simply cannot be beat.

140 Marine Dr., Sequim, WA 98382. ℃ **888/683-3013** or 360/683-3013. www.dungenessbay.com. 6 units. Apr 15–Oct 15 $90–$145 double; Oct 16–Apr 14 $80–$135 double. 2-night minimum. DISC, MC, V. **Amenities:** Massage. In room: TV/VCR, kitchen, fridge, coffeemaker, hair dryer, high-speed Internet access.

Juan de Fuca Cottages ☞ Right across the street from the water and surrounded by wide green lawns, these well-tended cottages have excellent views. While most face the water, the best views are actually from the one cottage that faces the Olympic Mountains to the south. This cabin has skylights and a long wall of windows. Other units have skylights as well, and all have whirlpool tubs and kitchenettes. The cottages also have their own little private beach. Although prices seem high for what you get, each cottage can sleep at least four people.

182 Marine Dr., Sequim, WA 98382. ℃ **866/683-4433** or 360/683-4433. www.juandefuca.com. 6 units. May–Sept $145–$285 double; Oct–Apr $140–$270 double. 2-night minimum July–Aug. DISC, MC, V. **Amenities:** Massage. In room: TV, kitchenette, fridge, coffeemaker, hair dryer, iron, high-speed Internet access, Wi-Fi.

Sunset Marine Resort ☞ Finds On the east shore of Sequim Bay, this collection of waterfront cabins is a secluded little retro hideaway. It's decorated in shabby-chic style by the owners, who also operate a little shabby-chic shop in downtown Sequim. Cabins include a renovated ranger station and a boathouse that sits on pilings over the water. Other cabins date from the 1930s and 1940s. Five of the cabins have full kitchens. You can spend your day paddling around the bay or touring the north Olympic Peninsula or, better yet, just kick back and wait for sunset. Because these cabins are distinctive and relatively economical, they book up months in advance.

40 Buzzard Ridge Rd., Sequim, WA 98382. © **360/681-4166.** www.sunsetmarineresort.com. 6 units. June–Sept $125–$195 double; Oct–May $95–$165 double. 2-night minimum June–Aug and all weekends. MC, V. Pets accepted ($15). **Amenities:** Kayak and canoe rentals. *In-room:* Fridge, coffeemaker.

WHERE TO DINE

If you're in need of a light lunch, don't miss **Jean's Deli** ⊛, 134 S. Second St. (© **360/683-6727**). This sandwich shop is in a historic church building a block off Sequim's main street. For coffee, head for **Hurricane Coffee,** 104 W. Washington St. (© **360/681-6008**) or **The Buzz,** 128 N. Sequim Ave. (© **360/683-2503**), which is right across the street and serves coffee from our favorite Seattle roastery. Pick up tasty picnic fare at **Sunny Farms Country Store,** 261461 U.S. 101 (© **360/683-8003**) on the west side of Sequim.

Petals Garden Café ⊛ AMERICAN   Set at the top of a hill on the south side of the highway bypass around Sequim, this cheery restaurant is on the grounds of the Cedarbrook Herb Farm, which makes this place a must for avid gardeners. If you're not too hungry, try the salmon salad or the Thai prawn salad. If you've got a heartier appetite, opt for the pork osso buco or one of the filling pasta dishes. Desserts are a highlight, and the lavender cheesecake is a must.

Cedarbrook Herb Farm, 1345 S. Sequim Ave. © **360/683-4541.** www.petalscafe.com. Reservations not necessary. Main courses $10–$25. AE, DISC, MC, V. Sun–Thurs 11am–8pm; Fri–Sat 11am–9pm.

The 3 Crabs ⊛ SEAFOOD   The 3 Crabs is an Olympic Peninsula institution— folks drive from miles around to enjoy the fresh seafood and sunset views at this friendly waterfront restaurant overlooking the Strait of Juan de Fuca and the New Dungeness Lighthouse. For more than 40 years, this place has been serving up Dungeness crabs in a wide variety of styles. You can order crabs as a cocktail, in a sandwich, cracked, or as crab Louie salad. Clams and oysters also come from the local waters and are equally good. There's great bird-watching here, especially in winter.

11 Three Crabs Rd. © **360/683-4264.** www.the3crabs.com. Reservations recommended. Main courses $7–$22. DISC, MC, V. Daily 11:30am–9pm (until 7pm in winter).

3 Olympic National Park North & the Northern Olympic Peninsula

Port Angeles park entrance: 48 miles W of Port Townsend, 57 miles E of Forks

The northern portions of Olympic National Park are both the most accessible and most heavily visited. It is here, south of Port Angeles, that two roads lead into the national park's high country. Of the two areas reached by these roads, Hurricane Ridge is the more accessible. Deer Park, the other road-accessed high-country destination, is at the end of a harrowing gravel road and is little visited. West of Port Angeles within the national park's lowlands lie two large lakes, Lake Crescent and Lake Ozette, that attract boaters and anglers. Also in this region are two hot springs—the developed Sol Duc Resort and the natural Olympic Hot Springs.

Outside the park boundaries, along the northern coast of the peninsula, are several campgrounds, a beautiful stretch of coastline that is popular with kayakers, and a couple of small sportfishing ports, Sekiu and Neah Bay, that are also popular with scuba divers. Neah Bay, which is on the Makah Indian Reservation, is also the site of one of the most interesting little museums in the state. The Makah Indian Reservation encompasses Cape Flattery, which is the northwesternmost point in the contiguous United States.

Port Angeles, primarily a lumber-shipping port, is the largest town on the north Olympic Peninsula and serves as a base for people exploring the national park and as a port for ferries crossing the Strait of Juan de Fuca to Victoria, British Columbia. Here is the region's greatest concentration of lodgings and restaurants.

ESSENTIALS

GETTING THERE   U.S. 101 circles Olympic National Park, with main park entrances south of Port Angeles, at Lake Crescent, and at the Hoh River south of Forks.

Kenmore Air (© **800/543-9595** or 425/486-1257; www.kenmoreair.com) flies between Seattle's Boeing Field and Port Angeles (the airline offers a free shuttle between Seattle–Tacoma International Airport and Boeing Field). Rental cars are available in Port Angeles from **Budget Rent-A-Car** (© **800/527-0700;** www.budget.com).

There is a **bus shuttle** to Port Angeles from Seattle and Sea-Tac Airport on **Olympic Bus Lines** (© **800/457-4492** or 360/417-0700; www.olympicbuslines.com). Reservations are recommended. **Jefferson Transit** (© **800/371-0497** or 360/385-4777; www.jeffersontransit.com) has service from Port Townsend to Sequim, where you can transfer to **Clallam Transit** (© **800/858-3747** or 360/452-4511; www.clallamtransit.com), which operates from Sequim around the peninsula to Lake Crescent, Neah Bay, La Push, and Forks.

Two **ferries,** one for foot passengers only and the other for vehicles and foot passengers, connect Port Angeles and Victoria, British Columbia. The ferry terminal for both ferries is at the corner of Laurel Street and Railroad Avenue. **Victoria Express** (© **360/452-8088** or 250/361-9144; www.victoriaexpress.com) is the faster of the two ferries (1 hr. between Port Angeles and Victoria) and carries foot passengers only. This ferry runs between Memorial Day weekend and the end of September. One-way fares are $11 per person (children under age 1 ride free). **Black Ball Transport** (© **360/457-4491,** or 250/386-2202 in Victoria; www.cohoferry.com) operates its ferry year-round except for 2 weeks in late January or early February; it carries vehicles as well as walk-on passengers. The crossing takes slightly more than 1½ hours. One-way fares are $9.50 for adults and $4.75 for children ages 5 to 11; it costs $38 for a car, van, camper, or motor home and driver.

VISITOR INFORMATION   For more information on the national park, contact **Olympic National Park,** 600 E. Park Ave., Port Angeles, WA 98362-6798 (© **360/ 565-3131** or 360/565-3130; www.nps.gov/olym). For information on Port Angeles and the rest of the northern Olympic Peninsula, contact the **North Olympic Peninsula Visitor and Convention Bureau,** 338 W. First St. (P.O. Box 670), Port Angeles, WA 98362 (© **800/942-4042** or 360/452-8552; www.olympicpeninsula.org), or the **Port Angeles Chamber of Commerce Visitor Center,** 121 E. Railroad Ave., Port Angeles, WA 98362 (© **877/456-8372** or 360/452-2363; www.portangeles.org).

⌒Tips Don't Leave Home without It

You may not be planning on taking an international vacation, but spend any time in the Port Angeles area, and you'll be tempted to hop a ferry to Victoria, British Columbia. Just in case, bring along your passport on your Olympic vacation. You don't absolutely have to have a passport to cross into Canada and return to the U.S., but it makes things much easier.

FESTIVALS   Each year in late August, **Makah Days** are celebrated in Neah Bay (on the Makah Indian Reservation) with canoe races, Indian dancing, a salmon bake, and other events.

PARK ADMISSION   Park admission is $10 per vehicle. Another option, if you plan to visit several national parks in a single year, is the National Parks Pass or the Golden Eagle Passport, an annual pass good at all national parks and recreation areas. The pass costs $50 (plus $15 for the Golden Eagle upgrade) and is available at all national park visitor centers. If you're over 62, you can get a Golden Age Passport for $10, and if you have a disability, you can get a free Golden Access Passport.

EXPLORING THE PARK'S NORTH SIDE

Port Angeles is the headquarters for the park, and here you'll find the **Olympic National Park Visitor Center,** 3002 Mount Angeles Rd. (✆ **360/565-3130;** www. nps.gov/olym). Mount Angeles Road is on the south edge of town and leads up to **Hurricane Ridge.** The center has lots of information, maps, and books about the park, as well as exhibits on the park's flora and fauna, old-growth forests, and whaling by local Native Americans. It's open daily from 9am to 4:30pm.

From the main visitor center, continue another 17 miles up Mount Angeles Road to Hurricane Ridge, which on clear days offers the most breathtaking views in the park. In summer, the surrounding subalpine meadows are carpeted with wildflowers. Several hiking trails lead into the park from here, and several day hikes are possible (the 3-mile **Hurricane Hill Trail** and the 1-mile **Meadow Loop Trail** are the most scenic). At the **Hurricane Ridge Visitor Center** (✆ **360/565-3130**), you can learn about the area's fragile alpine environment. In winter, Hurricane Ridge is a popular cross-country skiing area and also has two rope tows and a Poma lift for downhill skiing. However, because the ski area is so small and the conditions so unpredictable, this ski area is used almost exclusively by local families. For more information, contact **Hurricane Ridge Public Development Authority** (✆ **360/457-4519,** or 360/565-3131 for road conditions; www.hurricaneridge.com). The Hurricane Ridge Visitor Center has exhibits on alpine plants and wildlife. In summer, deer graze in the meadows and marmots—relatives of squirrels—lounge on rocks or nibble on flowers.

A few miles east of Port Angeles, another road heads south into the park to an area called **Deer Park.** This narrow, winding gravel road is a real test of nerves and consequently is not nearly as popular a route as the road to Hurricane Ridge. However, the scenery once you reach the end of the road is just as breathtaking as that from Hurricane Ridge. As the name implies, deer are common in this area. For the best easily accessible mountaintop view on the Olympic Peninsula, continue driving uphill from the Deer Park Campground to the end of the road. Here you'll find the ½-mile **Rainshadow Trail,** a loop that leads through meadows to the summit of 6,007-foot Blue Mountain. The views of the Olympic Mountains and expanses of the Strait of Juan de Fuca are breathtaking. For a longer hike, follow **Grand Ridge Trail** toward Obstruction Peak. To reach Deer Park, turn south at the Deer Park movie theater.

West of Port Angeles a few miles, up the Elwha River, you'll find the short trail (actually an abandoned road) that leads to **Olympic Hot Springs** ✿. These natural hot pools are in a forest setting and are extremely popular and often crowded, especially on weekends. For more developed hot springs soaking, head to Sol Duc Resort, west of Lake Crescent.

Also west of Port Angeles, on U.S. 101, is **Lake Crescent,** a glacier-carved lake surrounded by steep forested mountains that give the lake the feel of a fjord. This is one of the most beautiful lakes in the state and has long been a popular summer getaway. Near the east end of the lake, you'll find both the 1-mile trail to 90-foot-high **Marymere Falls** and the **Storm King Ranger Station** (℃ 360/928-3380), which is usually open in the summer and at other seasons when a ranger is in the station. From the Marymere Falls Trail, you can hike the steep 2 miles up **Mount Storm King** to a viewpoint overlooking Lake Crescent (climbing above the viewpoint is not recommended). On the north side of the lake, the **Spruce Railroad Trail** parallels the shore of the lake, crosses a picturesque little bridge, and is one of the only trails in the park open to mountain bikes. As the name implies, this was once the route of the railroad built to haul spruce out of these forests during World War I. Spruce was the ideal wood for building biplanes because of its strength and light weight. By the time the railroad was completed, the war was over and the demand for spruce had dwindled.

There are several places on the lake where you can rent various types of small boats during the warmer months. At **Lake Crescent Lodge** ⊕⊕ you can rent rowboats, and at the **Fairholm General Store** (℃ 360/928-3020), at the lake's west end, rent rowboats, canoes, and motorboats between April and October. The **Log Cabin Resort** on the north side of Lake Crescent rents rowboats, canoes, and pedal boats.

Continuing west from Lake Crescent, watch for the turnoff to **Sol Duc Hot Springs** (℃ 360/327-3583; www.visitsolduc.com). For 14 miles, the road follows the Soleduck River, passing the Salmon Cascades along the way. Sol Duc Hot Springs were for centuries considered healing waters by local Indians, and after white settlers arrived in the area, the springs became a popular resort. In addition to the warm swimming pool and hot soaking pools, you'll find cabins, a campground, a restaurant, and a snack bar. The springs are open daily from early April to mid-October; admission is $11 for adults, $8 for children ages 4 to 12, and $3 for children 3 and under. A 4.5-mile loop trail leads from the hot springs to **Sol Duc Falls,** which are among the most photographed falls in the park. Alternatively, you can drive to the end of the Sol Duc Road and make this an easy 1.5-mile hike. Along this same road, you can hike the half-mile **Ancient Groves Nature Trail.** Note that Sol Duc Road is one of the roads on which you'll have to pay an Olympic National Park entry fee.

EXPLORING THE PENINSULA'S NORTHWEST CORNER

Continuing west on U.S. 101 from the junction with the road to Sol Duc Hot Springs brings you to the crossroads of Sappho. Heading north at Sappho will bring you to Wash. 112, an alternate route from Port Angeles. It's 40 miles from this road junction to the town of **Neah Bay** on the Makah Indian Reservation.

Between Clallam Bay and Neah Bay, the road runs right alongside the water and there are opportunities to spot sea birds and marine mammals, including gray, orca, humpback, and pilot whales. Between February and April, keep an eye out for the dozens of bald eagles that gather along this stretch of coast. In Clallam Bay, at the county day-use park, you can hunt for agates and explore tidepools. Near Slip Point Lighthouse, there are fossil beds that are exposed at low tides.

Neah Bay is a busy commercial and sportfishing port, and is also home to the impressive **Makah Cultural and Research Center** ⊕⊕, Bayview Avenue (℃ 360/645-2711; www.makah.com), which displays artifacts from a Native American village that was inundated by a mudslide 500 years ago. This is the most perfectly preserved collection of Native American artifacts in the Northwest; part of the exhibit includes reproductions of canoes the Makah once used for hunting whales. There's also a long-house that shows the traditional lifestyle of the Makah people. Between Memorial Day and September 15, the museum is open daily from 10am to 5pm, and between September 16 and Memorial Day, it's open Wednesday through Sunday from 10am to 5pm; admission is $5 for adults, $4 for students and seniors, free for children ages 5 and under.

The reservation land includes **Cape Flattery** ☞☞☞, which is the northwesternmost point of land in the contiguous United States. Just off the cape lies Tatoosh Island, site of one of the oldest lighthouses in Washington. Cape Flattery is one of the most dramatic stretches of Pacific coastline in the Northwest, and is a popular spot for hiking and ocean viewing. The 1.5-mile round-trip trail to the tip of the cape is one of my favorite hikes in the entire state and includes not only great views but boardwalks, stairs, and viewing platforms atop the cliffs overlooking Tatoosh Island. Keep an eye out for whales and sea otters. Bird-watchers will definitely want to visit Cape Flattery, which is on the Pacific Fly Way. More than 250 species of birds have been spotted here, and in the spring, raptors gather here before crossing the Strait of Juan de Fuca. For directions to the trailhead, stop by the Makah Museum. At the museum or Washburn's General Store (on the main road through the community of Neah Bay), you'll also need to purchase a $7 Recreational Use Permit that will allow you to park at the Cape Flattery trailhead. *Note:* Be aware that car break-ins are not uncommon here, so take your valuables with you.

A turnoff 16 miles east of Neah Bay leads south to **Ozette Lake,** where there are boat ramps, a campground, and, stretching north and south, miles of beaches only accessible on foot. A 3.25-mile trail on a raised boardwalk leads from the Ozette Lake trailhead to **Cape Alava** ☞☞, one of two places claiming to be the westernmost point in the contiguous United States (the other is Cape Blanco, on the Oregon coast). The large rocks offshore are known as haystack rocks or sea stacks and are common along the rocky western coast of the Olympic Peninsula. Aside from five coastal Indian reservations, almost all this rugged northern coastline is preserved as part of the national park.

EDUCATIONAL PROGRAMS

The **Olympic Park Institute,** 111 Barnes Point Rd., Port Angeles, WA 98363 (℗ **360/928-3720;** www.yni.org/opi), which is in the Rosemary Inn on Lake Crescent, offers a wide array of summer field seminars ranging from painting classes to bird-watching trips to multi-day backpacking trips.

OUTDOOR ADVENTURES

BICYCLING   If you're interested in exploring the region on a bike, you can rent one at **Sound Bikes & Kayaks,** 120 E. Front St., Port Angeles (℗ **360/457-1240;** www.soundbikeskayaks.com), which can recommend good rides in the area and also offers bicycle tours. Bikes are $30 per day or $9 per hour.

FISHING   The rivers of the Olympic Peninsula are well known for their fighting salmon, steelhead, and trout. In Lakes Crescent and Ozette, you can even fish for such elusive species as Beardslee and Crescenti trout. No fishing license is necessary to fish for trout on national park rivers and streams or in Lake Crescent or Lake Ozette. However, you will need a state punch card—available wherever fishing licenses are sold—to fish for salmon or steelhead. For more information on freshwater fishing in the park, contact Olympic National Park (℗ **360/565-3130**). Boat rentals are available on Lake Crescent at Fairholm General Store, the Log Cabin Resort, and Lake

---

Fun Fact **The Buried Past Unearthed in Port Angeles**

In August, 2003, as the Washington Department of Transportation was building a dry dock on the Port Angeles waterfront, workers uncovered the remains of a Klallam Indian village that dates back more than 2,700 years. The village, now known as Tse-whit-zen, is the largest Indian village ever unearthed in the state. Hundreds of human burial sites, unusual etched stones, and countless artifacts have been uncovered from the village site. It is hoped that one day the artifacts will be displayed at a museum here in Port Angeles.

Crescent Lodge. Fly fishermen can pick up supplies and equipment at **Waters West Fly Fishing Outfitters,** 219 N. Oak St., Port Angeles (✆ **360/417-0937;** www.waterswest.com).

If you want to hire a guide to take you out on the rivers to where the big salmon and steelhead are biting, try **Sol Duc River Lodge Guide Service** (✆ **866/868-0128** or 360/327-3709; www.solducriverfishing.com), which charges $380 per day for two people—but that rate includes your room, breakfast, and lunch.

If you're more interested in heading out on open water to do a bit of salmon or deep-sea fishing, numerous charter boats operate out of Sekiu and Neah Bay. In Neah Bay, try **King Fisher Charters** (✆ **888/622-8216;** www.kingfisherenterprises.com). It's $140 to $180 per person for a day of fishing.

HIKING & BACKPACKING   For several of the most popular backpacking destinations in Olympic National Park (the Ozette Coast Loop, Grand Valley, Royal Basin, Badger Valley, Flapjack Lakes, and Lake Constance), advance-reservation hiking permits are required or highly recommended between May 1 and September 30 and can be made up to 30 days in advance. Reservations can be made by contacting the **Wilderness Information Center,** 3002 Mount Angeles Rd., Port Angeles (✆ **360/565-3100**). Both a Wilderness Use Fee ($5 for a group of up to 12 people) and a nightly camping fee ($2 per person per night) are charged. For most other overnight hikes, you can pick up a permit at a ranger station or at the trailhead. If in doubt, check with a park ranger before heading out to a trailhead for a backpacking trip. Also keep in mind that some trails start at trailheads on national forest land; for these, you'll need a Northwest Forest Pass. Also, should you be planning to backpack along the coast, keep in mind that some headlands can only be rounded at low tide, and others cannot be rounded at all. These latter headlands have marked (though often steep, muddy, and difficult) trails over them. In some cases, these "trails" consist of cable ladders or handhold ropes. Be aware that you'll have to ford quite a few creeks and even a river depending on which section of the coast you hike. Always carry a tide table.

Most of the best backpacking trips in Olympic National Park are long and aren't easily turned into loop trips. If you want to do a one-way backpacking trip, you can arrange a shuttle through **Windsox Trailhead Shuttle,** 406 W. E St., Forks (✆ **360/375-2002;** www.windsox.us).

LLAMA TREKKING   If you want to do an overnight trip into the backcountry of the national park but don't want to deal with all the gear, consider letting a llama carry your stuff. **Kit's Llamas,** P.O. Box 116, Olalla, WA 98359 (✆ **253/857-5274;** www.northolympic.com/llamas), offers llama trekking in the Olympic Mountains.

Prices, based on a group of six to eight adults, are $35 to $75 per person for day hikes, and $75 to $180 per person per day for overnight and multi-day trips, with special rates for children. **Deli Llama,** 17045 Llama Lane, Bow, WA 98232 (© **360/757-4212;** www.delillama.com), also does trips of 4 to 7 days in Olympic National Park ($135–$175 per person per day).

SCUBA DIVING   The waters off the town of Sekiu are the Olympic Peninsula's favorite dive site. For advice, air, and dive charters, divers will want to stop in at **Curley's Resort & Dive Center** (© **800/542-9680** or 360/963-2281; www.curleysresort. com), on the main road through town.

SEA KAYAKING & CANOEING   Sea-kayaking trips on nearby Lake Aldwell, at Freshwater Bay, and at Dungeness National Wildlife Refuge, are offered by **Olympic Raft & Kayak** (© **888/452-1443** or 360/452-1443; www.raftandkayak.com), which charges between $42 and $99 per person. Sea-kayak rentals are available at **Sound Bikes & Kayaks,** 120 E. Front St., Port Angeles (© **360/457-1240;** www.sound bikeskayaks.com), which charges $12 to $15 per hour or $40 to $70 per day. For sea-kayaking trips on the Hoh and Quillayute rivers, out on the west side of the peninsula, contact **Rainforest Paddlers,** 4883 Upper Hoh Rd., Forks (© **866/457-8398** or 360/374-5254; www.rainforestpaddlers.com). Between May and September, this company does half-day kayak outings on the Hoh River ($44 per person), and between February and September, they do early morning and sunset paddles on the Quillayute River estuary ($59 per adult for morning trips and $69 per adult for evening trips).

SKIING/SNOWBOARDING/SNOWSHOEING   Cross-country skiing, downhill skiing and snowboarding, and snowshoeing are all possible in the winter at **Hurricane Ridge.** Here you'll find a tiny ski area with two rope tows and a Poma lift for downhill skiing and snowboarding. There are also many miles of marked, though ungroomed, cross-country ski trails here. For more information, contact **Hurricane Ridge Public Development Authority** (© **360/457-4519** or 360/565-3131 for road conditions; www.hurricaneridge.net).

There are 90-minute ranger-led **snowshoe walks** on Saturdays and Sundays from late December through March (conditions permitting). Snowshoes are provided, and a small donation requested. Call the park visitor center for details.

WHITE-WATER RAFTING   The steep mountains and plentiful rains of the Olympic Peninsula allow for some great white-water rafting on the Elwha and Hoh rivers. Contact **Olympic Raft & Kayak** (© **888/452-1443** or 360/452-1443; www. raftandkayak.com). Rates start at $49 for a 2- to 2½-hour rafting trip.

Moments **Lose Yourself in a Labyrinth**

At the Port Angeles Fine Arts Center, you can lose yourself in a labyrinth hidden in a little glade in the art center's sculpture-filled woods. Mind you, this is not a maze, and the objective isn't to get physically lost. A labyrinth is a convoluted pathway that is meant to be used as a path for walking meditations. So, go on, get lost.

EXPLORING AROUND PORT ANGELES

If you're curious about the general history of this area, you may want to check out exhibits at the **Museum of the Clallam County Historical Society,** 223 E. Fourth St. (② 360/417-2364), which is housed in a former Carnegie Library. It's open Monday through Friday from 10am to 4pm and admission is free.

The **Port Angeles Fine Arts Center** ⚔, 1203 E. Lauridsen Blvd. (② **360/417-4590** or 360/457-3532; www.pafac.org), is the town's only other museum and hosts changing exhibits of contemporary art. The museum also maintains an unusual sculpture park in the woods surrounding the center. Sculptures within the park are often barely discernible from natural objects and are fascinating. Between March and November, the gallery is open Thursday through Sunday from 11am to 5pm; from December through February, it's open Thursday through Sunday from 10am to 4pm. Admission is free.

If you'd like to get a close-up look at some of the peninsula's aquatic inhabitants, stop by the **Arthur D. Feiro Marine Life Center,** Port Angeles City Pier, 315 N. Lincoln St. (② **360/417-6254;** www.olypen.com/feirolab). In the center's tanks, you may spot a wolf eel or octopus, and at a touch tank, you can pick up a starfish or sea cucumber. The center is only open on a regular basis in summer—Tuesday through Sunday from 10am to 5pm. Admission is $2.50 for adults, $1 for seniors and children ages 5 to 12, and free for children 4 and under.

If you'd like to taste some local wine, stop by **Black Diamond Winery,** 2976 Black Diamond Rd. (② **360/457-0748**), which produces both fruit and grape wines and is open February through December, Thursday through Saturday from 10am to 5pm, and Sunday and Monday from 10am to 4pm (closed Thanksgiving and Christmas). You can also visit **Camaraderie Cellars,** 334 Benson Rd. (② **360/417-3564;** www.camaraderiecellars.com). The winery's tasting room is open May to October on Saturday and Sunday from 11am to 5pm. This winery gets its grapes from eastern Washington and makes a range of red and white wines.

WHERE TO STAY

Beyond Port Angeles, accommodations are few and far between, and those places worth recommending tend to be very popular. Try to have room reservations before heading west from Port Angeles.

IN PORT ANGELES

The Downtown Hotel　This little hotel in downtown Port Angeles isn't too fancy, but it sure is comfortable and a real bargain. Also, if you're planning on taking the ferry to Victoria, it's very convenient. On the second and third floors of a building with shops on the ground floor, this place is a lot like European hotels. Some of the rooms have shared baths, but these are quite large and attractively furnished. Guest rooms with private bathrooms are equally comfortable. Reproductions of old French advertising posters lend a European flavor to this place. One room has a kitchenette.

101½ E. Front St., Port Angeles, WA 98362. ② 866/688-8600 or 360/565-1125. www.portangelesdowntown hotel.com. 17 units. $45–$55 double with shared bathroom; $65–$95 double with private bathroom. DISC, MC, V. *In room:* TV.

Red Lion Hotel Port Angeles ⚔　If you're on your way to or from Victoria, there's no more convenient hotel than the Red Lion. This is Port Angeles's only waterfront hotel, and it's steps from the Victoria ferry terminal. Rooms are large, if without much character, and most have balconies and large bathrooms. However, you'll pay a premium for a room with a view of the Strait of Juan de Fuca.

221 N. Lincoln St., Port Angeles, WA 98362. ✆ **800/RED-LION** or 360/452-9215. Fax 360/452-4734. www.redlion.com. 186 units. Mid-June to Sept 30 $150–$170 double. Lower rates off season. AE, DISC, MC, V. Pets accepted. **Amenities:** Restaurant (Steak/Seafood) and lounge; outdoor pool; exercise room; Jacuzzi; business center; room service; coin-op laundry. *In room:* A/C, TV, dataport, fridge, coffeemaker, hair dryer, iron, Wi-Fi.

The Tudor Inn ⌁   In a quiet residential neighborhood not far from the waterfront, this 1910 Tudor home is surrounded by a large yard and pretty gardens and is our favorite Port Angeles B&B. On the ground floor you'll find a living room and library; in one, there's a gas fireplace, and in the other, a wood-burning fireplace. Either is a great spot for warming yourself if the weather should turn cold and damp. Upstairs there are five rooms furnished with European antiques, including sleigh beds and four-posters. Several rooms have good views of the Olympic Mountains, and these are worth requesting.

1108 S. Oak St., Port Angeles, WA 98362. ✆ **866/286-2224** or 360/452-3138. www.tudorinn.com. 5 units. Mid-May to mid-Oct $105–$150 double; mid-Oct to mid-May $95–$135 double. Rates include full breakfast. AE, DISC, MC, V. Children over age 12 are welcome. **Amenities:** Access to nearby health club. *In room:* No phone.

EAST OF PORT ANGELES

BJ's Garden Gate ⌁⌁   For the ultimate in luxury, book a room at this modern Victorian farmhouse on a bluff overlooking the Strait of Juan de Fuca. The inn is located on the west side of the Sequim Dungeness Valley and is surrounded by 3 acres of English gardens and the views stretch all the way to Victoria on the far side of the straits. All the rooms have double Jacuzzi tubs, fireplaces, and water views and are furnished with European antiques. There are also showers for two and fluffy down comforters to make the rooms both romantic and cozy. Innkeeper BJ Paton makes all her guests feel like royalty.

397 Monterra Dr., Port Angeles, WA 98362. ✆ **800/880-1332** or 360/452-2322. www.bjgarden.com. 5 units. $140–$220 double. Rates include full breakfast. MC, V. *In room:* TV/VCR, dataport, high-speed Internet access.

Domaine Madeleine ⌁⌁   Just 7 miles east of Port Angeles, this contemporary B&B is set on 5 wooded acres and has a very secluded feel. Big windows take in the views, while inside you'll find lots of Asian antiques and other interesting touches. Combine this with the waterfront setting and you have a fabulous hideaway—you may not even bother exploring the park. The guest rooms are in several different buildings surrounded by colorful gardens. All rooms have fireplaces and views of the Strait of Juan de Fuca and the mountains beyond. Some have whirlpool tubs; some have kitchens or air-conditioning. For added privacy, there is a separate cottage.

146 Wildflower Lane, Port Angeles, WA 98362. ✆ **888/811-8376** or 360/457-4174. www.domainemadeleine.com. 5 units. $145–$245 double. Rates include full breakfast. 2-night minimum mid-Apr to mid-Oct and holidays. AE, DISC, MC, V. Children 12 and older welcome. **Amenities:** Access to nearby health club; massage. *In room:* TV/VCR/DVD, dataport, hair dryer, iron, free local calls, Wi-Fi.

WEST OF PORT ANGELES

Lake Crescent Lodge ⌁   This historic property, 20 miles west of Port Angeles on the south shore of picturesque Lake Crescent, is the lodging of choice for national park visitors wishing to stay on the north side of the park. Wood paneling, hardwood floors, a stone fireplace, and a sunroom make the lobby a popular spot for just sitting and relaxing (especially on rainy days). The guest rooms in this main lodge building have the most historic character, but have shared bathrooms. Other rooms are mostly

aging motel-style rooms that lack the character of the lodge rooms. If you can plan far enough in advance, the best accommodations by far are the Roosevelt cabins, which have fireplaces and are the most comfortable. However, a couple of the Singer cabins (nos. 20 and 21) do have great views. All but the main lodge rooms have views of either the lake or the mountains, and the dining room has a good view across the lake. From early November to mid-April, the lodge is open only on weekends, and only the Roosevelt fireplace cabins are available. The dining room is not open in winter.

416 Lake Crescent Rd., Port Angeles, WA 98363. © 360/928-3211. Fax 360/928-3253. www.lakecrescentlodge.com. 52 units, 5 with shared bathroom. $68–$85 double without bathroom; $106–$145 double with bathroom; $132–$211 cottage. AE, DC, DISC, MC, V. Children 6 and under stay free in parent's room. Pets accepted ($12). **Amenities:** Restaurant (Continental); lounge; rowboat rentals. *In room:* No phone.

Sol Duc Hot Springs Resort   The Sol Duc Hot Springs have for decades been a popular family vacation spot, with campers, day-trippers, and resort guests spending their days soaking and playing in the hot-water swimming pool. The grounds of the resort are grassy and open, and the forest is kept just at arm's reach. The cabins have very little character and are basically free-standing motel rooms. Don't come expecting a classic mountain cabin experience. There's a restaurant, as well as a poolside deli and grocery store. Three hot-spring-fed soaking pools and a large swimming pool are the focal point, open to the public for a small fee.

Sol Duc Rd., U.S. 101 (P.O. Box 2169), Port Angeles, WA 98362-0283. © 360/327-3583. Fax 360/327-3593. www.visit solduc.com. 32 units. $119–$139 cabin for 2. Children under 4 stay free in parent's room. AE, DC, DISC, MC, V. Closed Oct to late Mar. **Amenities:** 2 restaurants (American, Deli); outdoor pool; 4 hot-spring-fed soaking pools; massage. *In room:* Coffeemaker, no phone.

CAMPGROUNDS

The six national park campgrounds on the northern edge of the park are some of the busiest due to their proximity to U.S. 101. **Deer Park Campground** 🕻🕻 (14 campsites) is the easternmost of these campgrounds (take Deer Park Rd. from U.S. 101 east of Port Angeles) and the only high-elevation (5,400 ft.) campground in Olympic National Park. Deer Park is reached by a winding one-lane gravel road. The national park's **Heart O' the Hills Campground** (105 campsites), on Hurricane Ridge Road 5 miles south of the Olympic National Park Visitor Center, is the most convenient campground for exploring the Hurricane Ridge area. On Olympic Hot Springs Road up the Elwha River, you'll find **Elwha Campground** (40 campsites) and **Altaire Campground** (30 campsites).

West of Port Angeles along Wash. 112, a couple of public campgrounds are on the shore of the Strait of Juan de Fuca. **Salt Creek Recreation Area County Park** 🕻, 3506 Camp Hayden Rd. (© 360/928-3441)(90 campsites), 13 miles west of Port Angeles, is one of the most scenic spots on this whole coast. Campsites are $16 per night. About 20 miles west of Port Angeles is the Washington Department of Natural Resources' **Lyre River Park** (11 campsites).

The only campground on Lake Crescent is **Fairholm** (88 campsites) at the west end of the lake. The nearby **Sol Duc Campground** (82 campsites), set amid impressive stands of old-growth trees, is adjacent to the Sol Duc Hot Springs.

Heading west from Lake Crescent on U.S. 101, there are several campgrounds along the banks of the Sol Duc River.

The national park's remote **Ozette Campground** (15 campsites), on the north shore of Lake Ozette, is a good choice for people wanting to day-hike out to the beaches on either side of Cape Alava.

National park and other campgrounds in this area don't take reservations. However, for general information, contact **Olympic National Park** (© **360/565-3130**) or **Olympic National Forest, Forks Ranger Station,** 437 Tillicum Lane, Forks (© **360/374-6522;** www.fs.fed.us/r6/olympic).

WHERE TO DINE
IN PORT ANGELES

For great espresso and the best pastries on the peninsula, don't miss downtown's **Itty Bitty Buzz,** 110 E. First St. (© **360/565-8080;** www.thebuzzbeedazzled.com), which is affiliated with The Buzz in Sequim.

Bella Italia ✦ ITALIAN   This downtown Port Angeles restaurant is only a couple of blocks from the ferry terminal for ferries to and from Victoria, which makes it very convenient for many travelers. Dinners start with a basket of delicious bread accompanied by a garlic-and-herb dipping sauce. Fresh local seafood makes it onto the menu in the form of smoked-salmon ravioli, smoked-salmon fettuccine, and steamed mussels and clams. There are some interesting individual pizzas and a good selection of wines, as well as a wine bar, an espresso bar, and plenty of excellent Italian desserts.

118 E. First St. © 360/457-5442. www.bellaitaliapa.com. Reservations recommended. Main courses $8–$22. AE, MC, V. Sun–Thurs 4–9pm; Fri–Sat 4–10pm.

C'est Si Bon ✦✦ FRENCH   Just 4 miles south of town, off U.S. 101, C'est Si Bon is a brightly painted roadside building. Judging from its exterior, you might not think it served delicious traditional French food. Inside, the building's colorful exterior paint job gives way to more classic decor: reproductions of European works of art, crystal chandeliers, and old musical instruments used as wall decorations. The restaurant serves deftly prepared Gallic standards such as French onion soup or escargot for starters. Follow with *coquille Saint Jacques* or a Dungeness crab soufflé, finish with a rich, creamy *mousse au chocolat,* and *voilà!* You have the perfect French meal. Specials feature whatever is fresh.

23 Cedar Park Rd. © 360/452-8888. www.cestsibon-frenchcuisine.com. Reservations recommended. Main courses $21–$33. AE, DISC, MC, V. Tues–Sun 5–11pm.

Michael's Divine Dining ✦ NORTHWEST/MEDITERRANEAN   In the basement of a building in downtown Port Angeles, Michael's is a great place for a meal whether you're in the mood for tapas and a cocktail, a designer pizza, or a big dish of paella. This latter dish is the house specialty and shouldn't be missed. For dessert, be sure to try the banana fritter and caramelized banana with chocolate sauce, and also keep an eye out for the lavender ice cream. On Saturday and Sunday, brunch is served.

117B E. First St. © 360/417-6929. www.michaelsdining.com. Reservations recommended. Main courses $9–$32. AE, DC, DISC, MC, V. Daily 11am–9pm.

Sabai Thai ✦ *Finds* THAI   Set away from the waterfront and not a tourist haunt, this cozy little Thai restaurant serves delicious food redolent of exotic spices. With its big saltwater aquarium and abundance of elephants in the decor, this is also a very pretty place. If you're feeling adventurous, start with the savory fried banana appetizer. The *chu chee pla* is a house specialty and features cod in a rich and spicy red curry sauce. The pad Thai is also excellent. To find the restaurant, drive away from downtown on U.S. 101 and turn right on Eighth Street.

903 W. Eighth St. © 360/452-4505. Reservations not necessary. Main courses $9–$14. MC, V. Tues–Sun 4–9pm.

Toga's International Cuisine 🔥 INTERNATIONAL/GERMAN   On the west side of Port Angeles, this restaurant is an unexpected treat and serves some very unusual dishes, the likes of which are not found elsewhere in the state. Chef Toga Hertzog apprenticed in the Black Forest and has brought to his restaurant the traditional *Jagerstein* style of cooking in which diners cook their own meat or prawns on a hot rock. With 24 hours' notice, you can also have traditional Swiss cheese fondue or a lighter seafood fondue. To start your meal, you might try the crabmeat Rockefeller or the sampler of house-smoked salmon, scallops, oysters, and prawns. For dessert, nothing hits the spot like the chocolate mousse.

122 W. Lauridsen Blvd. 🕿 360/452-1952. Reservations recommended. Main courses $18–$31. AE, DISC, MC, V. Tues–Sat 5–10pm.

WEST OF PORT ANGELES

Outside of Port Angeles, the restaurant choices become exceedingly slim. Your best choices are the dining rooms at **Lake Crescent Lodge** (open mid-Apr through early Nov) and the **Log Cabin Resort** (open Apr–Oct), both on the shores of Lake Crescent. Continuing west, you'll find food at the dining room of **Sol Duc Hot Springs Resort** (open Mar–Sept).

Way out west, near Ozette Lake, you'll find **The Lost Resort,** Hoko-Ozette Road (🕿 **800/950-2899** or 360/963-2899; www.lostresort.net), a general store with a deli, espresso, and a tavern serving lots of microbrews. There are also some campsites and cabins for rent here.

4 Olympic National Park West

Forks: 57 miles W of Port Angeles, 50 miles S of Neah Bay, 77 miles N of Lake Quinault

The western regions of Olympic National Park can be roughly divided into two distinct sections—the rugged coastal strip and the famous rainforest valleys. Of course, these are the rainiest areas within the park, and many a visitor has called short a vacation here due to the rain. Well, what do you expect? It is, after all, a rainforest. Come prepared to get wet.

The coastal strip can be divided into three segments. North of La Push, which is on the Quileute Indian Reservation, the 20 miles of shoreline from Rialto Beach to Cape Alava are accessible only on foot. The northern end of this stretch of coast is accessed from Lake Ozette off Wash. 112 in the northwest corner of the peninsula. South of La Push, the park's coastline stretches for 17 miles from Third Beach to the Hoh River mouth and is also accessible only on foot. The third segment of Olympic Park coastline begins at Ruby Beach just south of both the Hoh River mouth and Hoh Indian Reservation and stretches south to South Beach. This stretch of coastline is paralleled by U.S. 101.

Inland of these coastal areas, which are not contiguous with the rest of the park, lie the four rainforest valleys of the Bogachiel, Hoh, Queets, and Quinault rivers. Of these valleys, only the Hoh and Quinault are penetrated by roads, and it is in the Hoh Valley that the rainforests are the primary attraction.

Located just outside the northwest corner of the park, the timber town of Forks serves as the gateway to Olympic National Park's west side. This town was at the heart of the controversy over protecting the northern spotted owl, and is still struggling to recover from the employment bust after the 1980s logging boom.

ESSENTIALS

GETTING THERE   The town of Forks is the largest community in the northwest corner of the Olympic Peninsula and is on U.S. 101, which continues south along the west side of the peninsula to the town of Hoquiam.

Bus service from Sequim to Lake Crescent, Neah Bay, La Push, and Forks is operated by **Clallam Transit** (ℂ **800/858-3747** or 360/452-4511; www.clallamtransit.com). Bus service between Forks and Lake Quinault is provided by **West Jefferson Transit** (ℂ **800/371-0497** or 360/385-4777; www.jeffersontransit.com). There is service to Quinault Lake from Olympia and Aberdeen on **Grays Harbor Transit** (ℂ **800/562-9730** or 360/532-2770; www.ghtransit.com).

VISITOR INFORMATION   For more information on this western section of Olympic National Park, see section 3 of this chapter. For more information on the Forks area, contact the **Forks Chamber of Commerce,** 1411 S. Forks Ave. (P.O. Box 1249), Forks, WA 98331 (ℂ **800/443-6757** or 360/374-2531; www.forkswa.com).

FESTIVALS   Each year in mid-July, **Quileute Days** are celebrated in La Push (on the Quileute Indian Reservation) with canoe races, traditional dancing, a salmon bake, and other events.

EXPLORING THE PARK'S WEST SIDE

If you want to learn more about the area's logging history, stop by the **Forks Timber Museum,** south of town on U.S. 101 (ℂ **360/374-9663**). The museum chronicles the history of logging in this region, but it also has displays on Native American culture and pioneer days. It's open from mid-April to October, Tuesday through Saturday from 10am to 4pm; admission is by donation.

Also in the Forks area, there are quite a few artists' studios and galleries. You can pick up an **Olympic West Arttrek** guide and map to these studios and galleries at the Forks Chamber of Commerce (see above for contact information).

West of Forks lie miles of pristine beaches and a narrow strip of forest (called the Olympic Coastal Strip) that are part of the national park, but are not connected to the inland mountainous section. The first place where you can actually drive right to the Pacific Ocean is just west of Forks. At the end of a spur road, you come to the Quileute Indian Reservation and the community of **La Push.** Right in town there's a beach at the mouth of the Quillayute River; however, before you reach La Push, you'll see signs for **Third Beach** 𝕏𝕏 and **Second Beach** 𝕏𝕏, which are two of the prettiest beaches on the peninsula. Third Beach is a 1½-mile walk and Second Beach is just over half a mile from the trailhead. **Rialto Beach** 𝕏𝕏, just north of La Push, is another beautiful and rugged beach; it's reached from a turnoff east of La Push. From here, you can backpack north for 24 miles to Cape Alava; this is also a very popular spot for shorter day hikes. One mile up the beach is a spot called **Hole in the Wall,** where ceaseless wave action has bored a large tunnel through solid rock. On any of these beaches, keep an eye out for bald eagles, seals, and sea lions.

Roughly 8 miles south of Forks is the turnoff for the Hoh River Valley. It's 17 miles up this side road to the **Hoh Visitor Center** (ℂ **360/374-6925**), campground, and trailheads. This valley receives an average of 140 inches of rain per year—and as much as 190 inches per year—making it the wettest region in the continental United States. At the visitor center, you can learn all about the natural forces that cause this tremendous rainfall.

To see the effect of so much rain on the landscape, walk the .8-mile **Hall of Mosses Trail,** where the trees (primarily Sitka spruce, western red cedar, and western hemlock) tower 200 feet tall. Here you'll see big-leaf maple trees with limbs draped in thick carpets of mosses. If you're up for a longer walk, try the **Spruce Nature Trail.** If you've come with a backpack, there's no better way to see the park and its habitats than by hiking the **Hoh River Trail,** which is 17 miles long and leads to Glacier Meadows and Blue Glacier on the flanks of Mount Olympus. A herd of elk calls the Hoh Valley home and can sometimes be seen along these trails.

On your way up the Hoh Valley, you might want to stop in at **Peak 6 Adventure Store,** 4883 Upper Hoh Rd. (© **360/374-5254**), an outfitter that sells not only any outdoors gear you might have forgotten, but also Native American baskets and art by local artists. Right beside this store, you'll find **Rainforest Paddlers** (© **866/457-8398** or 360/374-5254; www.rainforestpaddlers.com), which offers easy rafting trips on the Hoh River ($44 per person for a half-day and $79 for a full day). The season runs from mid-February through September. More exciting rafting trips on the Elwha and Solduc rivers are also offered. This company also does guided sea-kayak paddles on the Quillayute Estuary. These latter trips depart from the La Push Marina and cost $59 to $69 for adults and $49 to $59 for children ages 5 to 10. Tours last 3½ to 4½ hours. Kayaks and bikes can also be rented from this company.

Continuing south on U.S. 101, but before crossing the Hoh River, you'll come to a secondary road (Oil City Rd.) that heads west from the Hoh Oxbow campground. From the end of the road, it's a hike of less than a mile to a rocky beach at the **mouth of the Hoh River.** You may see sea lions or harbor seals feeding just offshore, and to the north, several haystack rocks that are nesting sites for numerous seabirds. Primitive camping is permitted on this beach, and from here backpackers can continue hiking for 17 miles north along a pristine wilderness of rugged headlands and secluded beaches.

South of the Hoh River off U.S. 101, you can drive to the **world's largest western red cedar.** Known as the Duncan cedar, this tree stands 178 feet tall and is almost 20 feet in diameter. You'll find the tree about 4 miles off the highway on Nolan Creek Road. Near milepost 170, watch for road N1000 on the east side of U.S. 101 and follow this road to a right fork onto N1100. Then turn right onto road N1112, and right again onto N112.

U.S. 101 finally reaches the coast at **Ruby Beach.** This beach gets its name from its pink sand, which is composed of tiny grains of garnet. With its colorful sands, tidepools, sea stacks, and driftwood logs, Ruby Beach is the prettiest of the beaches along this stretch of coast.

For another 17 miles or so south of Ruby Beach, the highway parallels the wave-swept coastline. Along this stretch of highway are turnoffs for five beaches that have only numbers for names. Beach 6 is a good place to look for whales and sea lions and also to see the effects of erosion on this coast (the trail that used to lead down to the beach has been washed away). At low tide the northern beaches have lots of tidepools to explore. Near the south end of this stretch of road, you'll find Kalaloch Lodge, which has a gas station, and the **Kalaloch Ranger Station** (© **360/962-2283**), which is usually open in the summer and in other seasons when a ranger is in the station.

Shortly beyond Kalaloch, the highway turns inland again and passes through the community of **Queets,** on the river of the same name. The Queets River Valley is another rainforest valley, and if you'd like to do a bit of hiking away from the crowds, head up the gravel road to the Queets campground, from which a hiking trail leads up the valley.

A long stretch of clear-cut areas and tree farms, mostly on the Quinault Indian Reservation, will bring you to **Quinault Lake.** Surrounded by forested mountains, this deep lake is the site of the rustic Lake Quinault Lodge and offers boating and freshwater fishing opportunities, as well as more rainforests to explore on a couple of short trails (there is a total of about 10 miles of trails on the south side of the lake). On the north shore of the lake, across from the Lake Quinault Resort, you'll find a short trail leading to one of the world's largest red cedar trees, and on the south shore, just past the Rain Forest Village Resort, you'll find another short trail that leads to the largest Sitka spruce in the world. This is also a good area for spotting Roosevelt elk.

For more information on guided tours and other outdoor recreational possibilities throughout the park's west side, see "Educational Programs" and "Outdoor Adventures" in section 3, earlier in this chapter.

WHERE TO STAY
IN THE FORKS AREA

The town of Forks has several inexpensive motels and is a good place to look for cheap lodgings if you happen to be out this way without a reservation. These include the **Forks Motel,** 351 S. Forks Ave. (© **800/544-3416** or 360/374-6243; www.forksmotel. com), which has a pool; and the **Pacific Inn Motel,** 352 S. Forks Ave. (© **800/ 235-7344** or 360/374-9400; www.pacificinnmotel.com).

Manitou Lodge   This secluded B&B on 10 private acres is only minutes from some of the most beautiful and remote beaches in the Northwest. The best room in the house is the Sacagawea, which has a fireplace and king-size bed. A separate cabin houses two of the rooms. Guests tend to gravitate to the comfortable living room, where a huge stone fireplace is the center of attention (fires help chase away the chill and damp of this rainy corner of the Olympic Peninsula). Breakfasts are hearty.

813 Kilmer Rd. (P.O. Box 600), Forks, WA 98331. © **360/374-6295.** Fax 360/374-7495. www.manitoulodge.com. 7 units. $90–$170 double. Rates include full breakfast. AE, DC, MC, V. Pets accepted ($10 per day). Take Wash. 110 west from north of Forks; turn right on Mora Rd. and then right on Kilmer Rd. Children over age 5 welcome. *In room:* Coffeemaker, hair dryer, Wi-Fi.

Miller Tree Inn   Just a few blocks east of downtown Forks, this large farmhouse B&B is surrounded by pastures and large old trees. With its classic styling, it feels very civilized compared to the wilds of the Olympic Peninsula and is a welcome sight at the end of the long drive out to Forks. Best of all, there are rooms with jetted tubs and fireplaces. One room also has a kitchenette (a definite bonus in this neck of the woods). There's nothing fussy or pretentious about this place—just a comfortable, friendly inn catering primarily to outdoors enthusiasts. At the end of a long day of hiking, the hot tub on the back deck is very welcome.

654 E. Division St. (P. O. Box 1565), Forks, WA 98331. © **800/943-6563** or 360/374-6806. Fax 360/374-6807. www.millertreeinn.com. 8 units. Mid-June to mid-Sept $95–$180 double; mid-Sept to mid-June $85–$145 double. 2-night minimum on summer weekends. Rates include full breakfast. DISC, MC, V. Pets accepted ($10 per day). **Amenities:** Jacuzzi. *In room:* No phone.

Olympic Suites Inn   Just off U.S. 101 at the north end of Forks and back in the forest a bit, this modern motel is your best bet in the area if you don't want to stay at a B&B. The motel has the look and feel of an apartment complex (which it once was), and most of the rooms are suites with full kitchens. The Calawah River and a boat ramp are just downhill from the motel. Some rooms have limited river views and others look into the forest.

800 Olympic Dr., Forks, WA 98331. ℂ 800/262-3433 or 360/374-5400. www.olympicsuitesinn.com. 32 units. July–Aug $74 double, $79–$109 suite; Sept and mid-May to June $64 double, $69–$89 suite; Oct to mid-May $54 double, $54–$74 suite. Children under 5 stay free in parent's room. AE, DISC, MC, V. Pets accepted ($5 per day). **Amenities:** Coin-op laundry. *In room:* TV, refrigerator, coffeemaker.

Quileute Oceanside Resort ⍟

Right on the sands of First Beach on the Quileute Indian Reservation, this rustic resort has a very wide range of accommodations. The basic cabins don't even have hot water, but the deluxe oceanfront cabins have the best rooms anywhere on this stretch of coast. These cabins have whirlpool tubs, walls of glass, lots of cedar accents, full kitchens, and carved wood furniture with Northwest Coast Native American designs. These latter cabins make this place worth recommending. Other older units are passable at best and are most popular with surfers and fishermen.

330 Ocean Dr. (P.O. Box 67), La Push, WA 98350. ℂ 800/487-1267 or 360/374-5267. Fax 360/374-4153. www.ocean-park.org. 65 units. May–Sept $55–$78 double, $80–$220 1- or 2-bedroom cabin, $125–$180 3-bedroom units; lower rates other months. 2-night minimum summer weekends, 3-night minimum on holidays. AE, DISC, MC, V. Pets accepted ($10). *In room:* Kitchen, no phone.

ALONG THE PARK'S WEST SIDE, SOUTH OF FORKS

Kalaloch Lodge ⍟

As the national park's only oceanfront accommodations, this rustic, cedar-shingled lodge and cluster of cabins are perched on a grassy bluff above the thundering Pacific Ocean. Wide sand beaches stretch north and south from the lodge, and huge driftwood logs are scattered at the base of the bluff like so many twigs. The rooms in the old lodge are the least expensive, and the oceanview bluff cabins are most in demand. The log cabins across the street from the bluff cabins don't have the knockout views. For modern comforts, there are motel-like rooms in the Sea Crest House. A casual coffee shop offers breakfast and lunch, while a slightly more formal dining room serves rather unmemorable meals. The lodge also has a general store and gas station. Because this place is popular throughout the year, you should make reservations at least 4 to 11 months in advance. However, it is in demand due to its location, not the quality of the accommodations.

157151 U.S. 101, Forks, WA 98331. ℂ 866/525-2562 or 360/962-2271. Fax 360/962-3391. www.visitkalaloch.com. 64 units. June–Sept $139–$149 double, $169–$259 suite, $179–$269 bluff cabin, $159–$179 log cabin; lower rates other months. Children 5 and under stay free in parent's room. AE, DC, MC, V. Pets accepted in cabins ($13). **Amenities:** Restaurant (American). *In room:* No phone.

Lake Quinault Lodge ⍟⍟

On the shore of Lake Quinault in the southwest corner of the park, this imposing grande dame of the Olympic Peninsula has an ageless tranquillity. Huge old firs and cedars shade the rustic lodge, and Adirondack chairs on the deck command a view of the lawn. The accommodations include small rooms in the main lodge, modern rooms with wicker furniture and small balconies, and rooms with fireplaces. The annex rooms are the least attractive, but have large bathtubs. The dining room has the most creative menu this side of the peninsula. For diversion, there are lawn games and rainforest tours.

345 S. Shore Rd. (P.O. Box 7), Quinault, WA 98575. ℂ 800/562-6672 or 360/288-2900. Fax 360/288-2901. www.visitlakequinault.com. 92 units. Mid-June to late Sept and winter holidays $117–$183 double, $255 suite; late Sept to mid-June $70–$133 double, $199 suite. Children under 6 stay free in parent's room. AE, MC, V. Pets accepted in Boat House building ($10 per night). **Amenities:** Restaurant (Northwest); lounge; indoor pool; sauna; seasonal boat rentals; tour desk; massage. *In room:* Coffeemaker, no phone.

Lake Quinault Resort ★★ *Finds*   On the north shore of Lake Quinault, this little lodge offers the most comfortable and luxurious accommodations this side of the peninsula. Because this "resort" is on the sunny side of the lake, you can catch great sunsets after a day of hiking the rainforest or paddling a canoe around the lake. Adirondack chairs on the long covered veranda are the perfect place to kick back and enjoy those sunsets. Guest rooms are spacious and modern, with a bit of modern country decor and Northwest style. Several rooms have kitchens.

314 N. Shore Rd., Amanda Park, WA 98526. ✆ 800/650-2362 or 360/288-2362. Fax 360/288-2218. www.lakequinault. com. 11 units. Mid-June to early Oct $129–$169 double; early Oct to mid-June $69–$119 double. AE, DISC, MC, V. **Amenities:** Canoe rentals; concierge; massage. *In room:* TV/DVD/VCR, fridge, coffeemaker, hair dryer, iron, free local calls.

Rain Forest Resort Village ★ *Kids*   If you can't get a room at the Lake Quinault Lodge, this should be your second choice in the area. Although the cabins and motel rooms are, for the most part, pretty basic, they are comfortable enough (and actually as nice as some lodge rooms). All the cabins have fireplaces and some have either a kitchen or a Jacuzzi tub. Wide lawns slope down to the lake, and most rooms and cabins have water views. In summer, you can rent canoes for exploring the lake. A short trail leads from the resort to the world's largest spruce tree.

516 S. Shore Rd., Lake Quinault, WA 98575. ✆ 800/255-6936 or 360/288-2535. Fax 360/288-2957. www.rainforest resort.com. 28 units. Late June to Labor Day weekend $93–$101 double, $132–$195 cabin. Lower rates other months. Children 5 and under stay free in parent's room. AE, DC, DISC, MC, V. **Amenities:** Restaurant (American); lounge; boat rentals; coin-op laundry. *In room:* TV, coffeemaker.

CAMPGROUNDS

If you want to say you've camped at the wettest campground in the contiguous United States, head for the national park's **Hoh Campground** ★ (88 campsites) in the Hoh River Valley. Almost as wet is the national park's **Queets Campground** (20 campsites). This campground is 14 miles up the Queets Road from U.S. 101. Campsites at **Bogachiel State Park** ★ (42 campsites), on the Bogachiel River 6 miles south of Forks on U.S. 101, are set under huge old spruce trees. On Quinault Lake, there are three campgrounds. On the south shore are two national forest campgrounds—**Willaby** (31 campsites) and **Falls Creek** (31 campsites). East of Lake Quinault, up the Quinault River valley, are two more national park rainforest campgrounds—**North Fork** (7 campsites) and **Graves Creek** (30 campsites)—that provide access to a couple of the park's long-distance hiking trails.

Along the peninsula's west side, there are also several beach campgrounds. These include the national park's **Mora Campground** ★ (94 campsites) on the beautiful Rialto Beach at the mouth of the Quillayute River west of Forks. If you're prepared to hike in with your gear, you can also camp on Second Beach (half-mile hike) and Third Beach (1.5-mile hike). South of the Hoh River, along the only stretch of U.S. 101 that is right on the beach, you'll find **Kalaloch Campground** (175 campsites), the national park's largest campground and the only one that takes reservations. Make reservations by contacting the **National Park Reservation Service** (✆ 800/365-2267 or 301/722-1257; reservations.nps.gov). For general information on national park campgrounds, contact **Olympic National Park** (✆ 360/565-3130). For information on nearby national forest campgrounds, contact the **Olympic National Forest, Quinault Ranger Station,** 353 S. Shore Rd., Quinault (✆ 360/288-2525; www.fs. fed.us/r6/olympic).

WHERE TO DINE

In the town of Forks, you'll find several basic diners and family restaurants, but nothing really worth recommending. South of Forks, your best bets are the dining rooms at the **Kalaloch Lodge** and the **Lake Quinault Lodge.** If you happen to be hungry up the Hoh River, don't miss the juicy burgers at the **Hard Rain Cafe,** 5763 Upper Hoh Rd. (© **360/374-9288**).

River's Edge Restaurant ✪ *Finds* AMERICAN   Operated by the Quileute Tribal Enterprises in a renovated, converted old boathouse, this place has great water views and the best food in the area. Fresh seafood is the specialty, and with salmon-fishing boats unloading at the adjacent marina, you can bet the salmon is as fresh as it gets. Although preparations are generally quite simple, you may get a little mango salsa with your baked salmon. With its big breakfasts, this is a good place to start your day. Keep an eye out for bald eagles and brown pelicans.

41 Main St., La Push. © **360/374-5777.** Main courses $8–$23. MC, V. Summer daily 7am–9pm; other months call for hours.

5 Olympic National Park East & Hood Canal

Hoodsport: 35 miles NW of Olympia, 75 miles S of Port Townsend, 100 miles E of Lake Quinault

The east side of Olympic National Park is the least visited side of the park. There are no wild beaches, no roads up into alpine meadows, and no rainforests. There are also no crowds of tourists. However, there are many miles of rugged hiking trails that lead intrepid hikers to some of the best mountaintop viewpoints on the peninsula. There are also rushing rivers, state parks, and the wide salt waters of Hood Canal, which isn't a canal at all, but rather a natural body of water off Puget Sound. Long, narrow, and hook-shaped, Hood Canal has miles of pristine waterfront and has long been a popular spot for summer homes. Fishing and clamming are among the most popular activities along Hood Canal.

ESSENTIALS

VISITOR INFORMATION   For information on hiking in the area, contact **Quilcene Ranger Station,** 295142 U.S. 101 S. (P.O. Box 280), Quilcene, WA 98376 (© **360/765-2200;** www.fs.fed.us/r6/olympic).

FESTIVALS   The Olympic Music Festival (© **206/527-8839;** www.olympicmusic festival.org), held nearby in an old barn near the town of Quilcene, is the area's most important music festival. This series of weekend concerts takes place between mid-June and mid-September.

DRIVING THE SHORES OF HOOD CANAL

In Union, at the south end of Hood Canal, you can rent kayaks at **Kayak Hood Canal,** 5101 E. Wash. 106 (© **360/898-5925;** www.kayakhoodcanal.com), and paddle around in the vicinity of the luxurious Alderbrook Resort. Kayaks rent for $15 to $30 per hour or $35 to $70 for 4 hours. Guided tours are also available.

In Hoodsport, a few miles north of Union, you can pick up some locally made wine at the **Hoodsport Winery,** 23501 N. U.S. 101 (© **360/877-9894;** www.hoodsport. com), best known in Washington for its fruit wines, including raspberry, loganberry, and rhubarb wine. The tasting room is open daily, 10am to 6pm.

If the tides are right, there's no red-tide warning in effect, the season is open, and you've got the proper fishing license, you can dig for clams on the wide beach at **Dosewallips State Park** (© 360/902-8844), which has a campground. The park is 25 miles north of Hoodsport on U. S. 101. Parking is $5.

If you're a gardener and happen to be in the area in late spring or early summer, be sure to stop in at **Whitney Gardens & Nursery,** 306264 U.S. 101, Brinnon (© 800/952-2404 or 360/796-4411; www.whitneygardens.com), which has been in business for more than 50 years and is considered the premier rhododendron garden and nursery in the Northwest. The springtime floral displays produced by the gardens' 2,500 rhodies are enchanting.

HIKING OLYMPIC PENINSULA EAST

Off U.S. 101 south of Port Townsend are several dead-end roads that lead to trailheads in Olympic National Forest. These trailheads are the starting points for many of the best day hikes on the Olympic Peninsula and lead into several different wilderness areas, as well as into Olympic National Park. Many of these hikes lead to the summits of mountains with astounding views across the Olympic Mountains and Puget Sound.

West of Hoodsport are the popular **Lake Cushman** and the trailheads for the 2-mile round-trip hike along the scenic **Staircase Trail,** the 4.5-mile round-trip hike to the summit of **Mount Ellinor,** and the 16-mile round-trip hike to the **Flapjack Lakes,** which are a very popular overnight destination. Up the Hamma Hamma River Road, just north of Eldon, you'll find the trailhead for the hike to the beautiful **Lena Lakes** area. Up the Dosewallips River Road west of Brinnon, you'll find the trailhead for the very popular, 4-mile round-trip hike to **Lake Constance.** Two miles south of Quilcene, you'll find Penny Creek/Big Quilcene River Road, which leads to the trailheads for both **Marmot Pass** and **Mount Townsend**—two of the best day-hike destinations on the peninsula. Both of these trails are between 10- and 11-mile round-trip hikes. Because floods frequently wash out trail bridges and sections of access road and trails, you should always check to see if a trail is open before heading out on a hike.

WHERE TO STAY & DINE

Alderbrook Resort & Spa ☆☆☆   As soon as this lodge opened on the southern shore of Hood Canal, it was an instant classic. Deliciously luxurious, yet with rugged mountain-lodge styling, it conjures up simple lakeside summer camps of the past. It is this melding of classic comfort and contemporary luxury that makes this one of my favorite lodges in the state. Cedar shingles, log beams, slate floors, and big walls of glass all add up to rustic grandeur. Sure, it's a long way from most tourist attractions, but the setting is so picture-perfect and the lodge so classic, that you can't help thinking this is what national park lodges should be like. Rooms have a classic beach-cottage feel and are decorated with old Hood Canal photos. Many have cozy window seats overlooking the water, but my favorite rooms are those with balconies. Families should consider the cottages.

10 E. Alderbrook Dr., Union, WA 98592. © 800/622-9370 or 360/898-2200. Fax 360/898-4610. www.alderbrook resort.com. 94 units. Summer $170–$270 double, $240–$290 suite, $260–$330 cottage; other months $120–$240 double, $190–$260 suite, $210–$300 suite. Children under 13 stay free in parent's room. AE, DC, MC, V. Pets accepted ($200 refundable deposit plus $10 per day). **Amenities:** Restaurant (Northwest); lounge; indoor pool; 18-hole golf course; 2 tennis courts; exercise room; small spa; Jacuzzi; sauna; steam room; kayak rentals; concierge; room service; massage; laundry service. *In room:* A/C, TV, dataport, fridge, coffeemaker, hair dryer, iron, safe, high-speed Internet access.

9

Southwest Washington

Southwest Washington, which for the purposes of this book is defined as the area west of I-5 and south of U.S. 12, is sparsely populated and heavily dependent on the timber industry for its economic base. However, the region also has the state's busiest beach resort areas—the Long Beach Peninsula and the Central Coast area—as well as the often-overlooked city of Vancouver, which shares a name with the far more famous Canadian city to the north. Present-day Vancouver, Washington, is little more than a bedroom community for Portland, but it abounds in pioneer history.

Aside from two last rocky headlands at the mouth of the Columbia River, the coastline of southwest Washington is a tame strip of sandy beaches and windswept dunes. Grays Harbor and Willapa Bay divide this stretch of coast into three distinct strips of sand: North Beach, South Beach, and the Long Beach Peninsula. These three strands have far more in common with one another than with the wild, rock-strewn beaches to the north. Although they are far less spectacular than those to the north, the abundance of tourist accommodations along this coastal stretch makes these the favored beach vacation destinations of the state.

Summers along the coast tend to be short and often wet or foggy, and the coastal waters are too cold and rough for swimming (although surfing is fairly popular). Consequently, the traditional beach pursuits of swimming and sunning aren't high on vacation priority lists. Instead, these beaches rely on other activities to attract visitors. All up and down this coast, digging for razor clams is a popular pastime, though open seasons are now short and as closely regulated as the salmon-fishing seasons. The towns of Westport, at the north end of the South Beach area, and Ilwaco, at the south end of the Long Beach Peninsula, have become the region's main charter-boat ports, with Westport charter boats also doing double duty as whale-watching excursion boats. South Beach and the Long Beach Peninsula are also among the few regions in the country where cranberries are grown commercially. Long Beach, a beach resort town for more than 100 years, bills itself as the kite-flying capital of America and boasts the longest drivable beach in the world. While vacationing families fuel the local economy, oysters still reign supreme in Willapa Bay, one of the cleanest estuaries in the country.

This coast is also home to a few pockets of wildness. The Willapa National Wildlife Refuge and the Long Beach Peninsula's Leadbetter Point together host a vast number of bird species each year. Combined with the Grays Harbor National Wildlife Refuge to the north, they offer the best bird-watching in the entire Northwest.

Southwest Washington

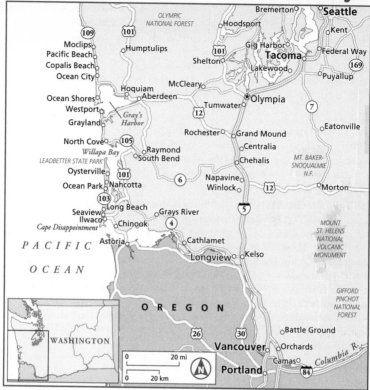

1 The Central Coast: Ocean Shores to Willapa Bay

67 miles W of Olympia, 67 miles S of Lake Quinault, 92 miles N of Long Beach

Washington's central coast, consisting of the North and South Beach areas and the Grays Harbor towns of Aberdeen and Hoquiam, is something of an anomaly. Though far from being the most scenic stretch of Washington coast, it contains the state's most popular beach destination, Ocean Shores, a modern beach development that consists of numerous oceanfront hotels and hundreds of vacation homes. Although not as scenic as the Olympic Peninsula coastline, this area is popular for its easy access to the cities of Puget Sound, and, because Ocean Shores is less than an hour east of Olympia, it is a popular weekend vacation spot.

The most scenic stretch of this coastline is the area known as North Beach, which consists of the beach north of the mouth of Grays Harbor. The farther north you go on this stretch of coast, the more spectacular is the scenery, even rivaling the beauty of the Olympic Peninsula's shoreline in some places. The South Beach area, so named because it occupies the south side of Grays Harbor, is an 18-mile stretch of flat beach bordered on the south by Willapa Bay. At the north end of South Beach is the town of Westport, Washington's busiest sportfishing and whale-watching port. Across the mouth of Willapa Bay from the South Beach area lies the northern tip of the Long Beach Peninsula.

Separating North Beach and South Beach is the large bay known as Grays Harbor, on whose shores are the two lumber-mill towns of Aberdeen and Hoquiam. These towns were once some of the most prosperous in the state, as their stately Victorian mansions and imposing commercial buildings attest. Unfortunately, they have yet to benefit from the prosperity that has overtaken the Puget Sound region, and historic commercial buildings stand empty and abandoned. Still, history is to be seen in these towns, though most people visit this region for the beaches, fishing, and clamming.

ESSENTIALS

GETTING THERE   U.S. 12 and Wash. 8 together connect Aberdeen with Olympia to the east, while U.S. 101 connects Aberdeen with Forks and Port Angeles to the north and Long Beach and Astoria to the south. Ocean Shores and the North Beach area are 20 miles west of Aberdeen on Wash. 109. The South Beach area is 20 miles west of Aberdeen on Wash. 105.

VISITOR INFORMATION   For more information on this area, contact **Tourism Grays Harbor,** P.O. Box 225, Aberdeen, WA 98520 (© **800/621-9625** or 360/533-7895; www.graysharbortourism.com); **Ocean Shores Visitor Information Center,** P.O. Box 382, Ocean Shores, WA 98569 (© **800/762-3224** or 360/289-2451; www.oceanshores.org); the **Washington Coast Chamber of Commerce,** 2616-A State Rte. 109, Ocean City, WA 98569 (© **800/286-4552** or 360/289-4552; www.washingtoncoastchamber.org); the **Westport-Grayland Chamber of Commerce,** 2985 S. Montesano Ave. (P.O. Box 306), Westport, WA 98595 (© **800/345-6223** or 360/268-9422; www.westportgrayland-chamber.org); or the **Willapa Harbor Chamber of Commerce,** P.O. Box 1249, South Bend, WA 98586 (© **360/942-5419;** www.visit.willapabay.org).

LEARNING ABOUT THE REGION'S HISTORY

Aberdeen and Hoquiam together comprise the largest urban area on the Washington coast and have long been dependent on the lumber industry that once made this a very prosperous part of the state. If you're interested in the region's history, stop by the **Polson Museum,** 1611 Riverside Ave., Hoquiam (© **360/533-5862;** www.polsonmuseum.org), which has rooms full of antique furnishings and also houses various collections of dolls, vintage clothing, Native American artifacts, and logging memorabilia. It's open in summer, Wednesday through Sunday from 11am to 4pm, and Sunday from noon to 4pm; in other months, Saturday and Sunday from noon to

---

Moments Pirates of the Caribbean North?

The wind in the rigging, the smell of the salt air. If you long for the life of a pirate or dream of being your own master and commander, then plan to visit Gray's Harbor on one of the rare occasions when the *Lady Washington* is here in her home port of Aberdeen. This tall ship, a replica of one of the ships Capt. Robert Gray sailed when he first explored the Northwest coast in 1788, was used in both *Pirates of the Caribbean* movies. You'll find the *Lady Washington* docked beside the Wal-Mart in Aberdeen at **Aberdeen Landing,** 320 S. Newell St. (© **800/200-LADY** or 360/532-8611; www.ladywashington.org). Dockside tours are scheduled when the ship is in port. Three-hour sail excursions are also offered occasionally.

4pm. Admission is $4 for adults, $2 for students, and $1 for children under age 12. The **Aberdeen Museum of History,** 111 E. Third St., Aberdeen (© **360/533-1976;** www.Aberdeen-museum.org), has similar displays and is open Tuesday through Saturday from 10am to 5pm and Sunday from 11am to 5pm; admission is by donation.

In the North Beach area, you can learn about both regional and natural history at the **Ocean Shores Interpretive Center,** 1033 Catala Ave. SE, Ocean Shores (© **360/ 289-4617;** www.oceanshoresinterpretivecenter.com), at the corner of Catala and Discovery avenues. The interpretive center is open from April through September, daily from 11am to 4pm.

If you aren't here during the whale-watching season, you can at least have a look at a couple of whale skeletons at the **Westport Maritime Museum,** 2201 Westhaven Dr., Westport (© **360/268-0078;** www.westportwa.com/museum). Housed in a 1939 Coast Guard station, the museum contains Coast Guard exhibits, displays on early pioneer life in the area, and, in a glass-enclosed building outside, the skeletons of a minke whale, a gray whale, and part of a blue whale. Between Memorial Day and Labor Day, the museum is open daily from 10am to 4pm (fall and spring, Thurs–Mon, noon–4pm; winter, Sat–Sun and holidays, noon–4pm), and admission is $3 for adults and $1 for children ages 5 to 14, free for children 4 and under. Nearby, you'll find the **Grays Harbor Lighthouse,** which was built in 1898 and is the tallest lighthouse in Washington. Tours of the lighthouse are operated by the Westport Maritime Museum and cost $3. The lighthouse is open the same hours as the museum. From the museum, you can walk the Maritime History Trail to reach the lighthouse.

FISHING, CLAMMING, WHALE-WATCHING & OTHER OUTDOOR ACTIVITIES

The stretch of coast known as North Beach begins in the vacation and retirement community of Ocean Shores and stretches north for 30 miles to Taholah, on the Quinault Indian Reservation. In the southern section of North Beach, in Ocean Shores, low windswept dunes covered with beach grass back the wide, sandy beach. Kite flying and horseback riding are among the favorite activities here. Also in Ocean Shores are 23 miles of canals and interconnecting lakes that are fun to explore by boat. Canoes can be rented at **Summer Sails** (© **360/289-2884**), located at Point Brown. For a game of golf, head to the **Ocean Shores Golf Course,** 500 Canal Dr. NE (© **360/289-3357;** oceanshoresgolfcourse.com).

North of Ocean City, high bluffs, haystack rocks, secluded beaches, and dark forests create a more dramatic coastline. Along this stretch of coast there is **beach access** at Ocean City, Griffiths-Priday, and Pacific Beach state parks. **Razor clamming** is one of the most popular activities on the secluded beaches of this area. To try your hand at clamming, you'll need a license, a shovel, and a tide table. With all three in hand, head out to the beach at low tide and start looking for clam holes. When you spot one, dig fast. Good luck! Also, before heading out to the beach, find out if clamming season is open by contacting the Westport-Grayland Chamber of Commerce (© **800/345-6223** or 360/268-9422; www.westportgrayland-chamber.org).

The 18 miles of coastline between Westport and Tokeland is called South Beach or the Cranberry Coast, and along this stretch of beach are plenty of places to access the sand and surf. Four state parks provide the best facilities and easiest access. **Twin Harbors State Park** is 2 miles south of Westport and is the largest of the four, with more than 3 miles of beach. **Grayland Beach State Park** is just south of the town of Grayland and has a campground and less than a mile of beach. Both of these parks have nature trails, picnic areas, and campgrounds. Just outside the marina area of Westport is **Westhaven State Park,** and just south of town is **Westport Light State Park,** where you'll find the popular Dune Trail, a paved 1.3-mile concrete boardwalk that parallels the beach and links Westport and Westhaven state parks. These latter two parks are day-use areas only.

In the South Beach area, charter fishing, clamming, and whale-watching are the big attractions, and most of the activity centers on the marina at Westport. Boats head out daily in summer in search of salmon, tuna, and bottom fish. If you'd like to try your luck at reeling in a big one, try **Deep Sea Charters** (© 800/562-0151 or 360/268-9300; www.oceansportfishing.com). Rates range from about $88 to $190 for a day of fishing. In the fall, salmon fishing is also popular right off the docks in the Westport Marina.

Each year between February and May, gray whales migrating to the calving grounds off Baja California, Mexico, pass by the Washington coast. The whales sometimes come so close to the mouth of Grays Harbor that they can be seen from the observation tower at the marina in Westport. However, for a closer look, you might want to head out on a **whale-watching** boat trip. Deep Sea Charters (above) has trips in March and April, and rates are $25 for adults and $18 for children.

Crabbing is another favorite area activity. To give crabbing a try, you'll need a crab ring (they can be bought for $20–$40 or rented for around $6 per day at the Westport Marina) and some bacon or chicken necks for bait. Find a spot on Westport's 1,000-foot-long pier, toss your trap over the side, and sit back and wait for the crabs to come to you—it's that easy.

All along the South Beach area between Grayland and Tokeland, you'll see **cranberry bogs** beside the highway. The cranberry harvest begins around Labor Day and continues on through October. To harvest the tart berries, the bogs are flooded, which causes the ripe berries to float on the surface of the water, where they can be easily scooped up mechanically.

Each year in late April and early May, Bowerman Basin in **Grays Harbor National Wildlife Refuge** ⊕ (© 360/753-9467; http://graysharbor.fws.gov) becomes a staging ground for tens of thousands of Arctic-bound shorebirds. This is one of the largest gatherings of such birds on the West Coast and one of the state's biggest annual events for bird-watchers. If you're a birder, don't miss this impressive event. The refuge is adjacent to the Aberdeen/Hoquiam Airport on the west side of Hoquiam.

Between early May and September, the **Westport Ocean Shores Passenger Ferry,** Silver King Motel, 1070 Discovery Ave. SE, Ocean Shores (© 360/289-3386), connects Ocean Shores with Westport Marina. The ferry operates daily between mid-June and Labor Day. From early May to mid-June and from Labor Day to late September, the ferry operates only on weekends. The crossing takes between 20 and 40 minutes, and the fare is $10 for a round-trip ticket. In Westport, the office is at 321 Dock St. (© 360/268-0047).

DRIVING AROUND WILLAPA BAY

Though it's only about 5 miles across the mouth of Willapa Bay to the northern tip of the Long Beach Peninsula, it's about 85 miles around to the town of Long Beach by road. Along the way you skirt the shores of Willapa Bay. There aren't too many towns on this bay, which is why this is one of the least polluted estuaries in the country and is a great place to raise oysters. Punctuating the miles of unspoiled scenery are oyster docks and processing plants.

As you pass through the town of Raymond, keep an eye out for the 200 steel-plate sculptures that comprise the **Raymond Wildlife-Heritage Sculpture Corridor.** The majority of these sculptures are silhouettes that can be seen along U.S. 101 in the most unexpected places. Included are sculptures of Native Americans, modern sea kayakers, bicyclists, and dozens of wild animals. Also here in Raymond, you'll find the **Willapa Seaport Museum** ⊛, 310 Alder St. (© 360/942-5666), a fascinating little museum dedicated to all things nautical. This is the best-designed museum on the coast and is well worth a visit. The museum is open Thursday through Sunday from 10am to 4pm; admission is by donation.

Right next door to the Willapa Seaport Museum, you'll find the **Northwest Carriage Museum,** 314 Alder St. (© 360/942-4150; www.nwcarriagemuseum.org), which is home to a large collection of immaculately restored antique carriages. On display is a wicker carriage, a hearse, and even a carriage that was used in *Gone With the Wind.* For the most part, these are luxury carriages once owned by the wealthy. The museum is open Wednesday through Saturday from 10am to 4pm. Admission is $3 for adults, $1 for children ages 6 to 17, and free for children 5 and under.

By some accounts, one out of every six oysters consumed in the United States comes from Willapa Bay, and in the town of **South Bend,** oystering reaches its zenith. South Bend claims to be the oyster capital of the world and holds its annual **Oyster Stampede** festival each year on Memorial Day weekend. If you just must have some oysters while in town, have a meal at The Boondocks (see below) or drop by **East Point Seafood,** U.S. 101, South Bend (© 888/317-8459 or 360/875-5419; www.eastpointseafood.com), at the north end of town.

South Bend's other claim to fame is its **county courthouse.** Though South Bend is the county seat today, back in 1893 it took a possibly rigged vote and armed force to wrest the title of county seat from Oysterville, across the bay on the Long Beach Peninsula. Construction of the new courthouse began 18 years later, and upon completion, the imposing structure was dubbed a "gilded palace of extravagance." The majestic courthouse, quite out of place in such a quiet backwater, stands on a hill overlooking town. The copper dome is lined inside with stained glass, and murals decorate interior walls. It's definitely worth a look.

WHERE TO STAY
IN OCEAN SHORES & THE NORTH BEACH AREA
If you can't get a room at any of the hotels listed below, contact **Ocean Shores Reservations** (© 800/562-8612 or 360/289-2430; www.oceanshoresreservation.com), which handles reservations at many area hotels, motels, resorts, and condominiums.

Ocean Crest Resort ⊛⊛ *(Kids)*   You simply won't find a more spectacular spot anywhere on the Washington coast. Perched high on a forested bluff and straddling a forested ravine, this hotel seems poised to go plummeting into the ocean below. The accommodations vary from small studios with no view to two-bedroom apartments with full kitchens and fireplaces. However, our vote for best rooms goes to the large third-floor, oceanview studios. These have cathedral ceilings, fireplaces, and balconies. The hotel's restaurant has one of the resort's best views, and the adjacent lounge is a great spot for a sunset drink. In addition to other amenities, the resort also has a playground. A wooden staircase winds down through the ravine to the beach.

4651 Wash. 109 (P.O. Box 7), Moclips, WA 98562. (© 800/684-8439 or 360/276-4465. Fax 360/276-4149. www.oceancrestresort.com. 47 units. June to mid-Sept $65–$189 double; mid-Sept to Oct and Mar–May $55–$142 double;

Nov–Feb $55–$122 double. Children 12 and under stay free in parent's room. AE, DISC, MC, V. Pets accepted ($18). **Amenities:** Restaurant (Steak/Seafood); lounge; indoor pool; health club; Jacuzzi; sauna; massage; coin-op laundry. *In room:* TV, coffeemaker, hair dryer, free local calls.

Quinault Beach Resort and Casino ⭐⭐   By far the most luxurious resort anywhere on the Washington coast, this large casino resort is a bit north of the rest of the Ocean Shores developments and thus feels a bit more secluded. With its modern Northwest lodge styling, it also has a far more contemporary feel than other area resorts. However, despite the attractive design and the miles of ocean beaches, it is still the in-house casino that is the main attraction. Don't worry, though—even if you aren't a fan of slot machines, you can actually stay here and almost not even notice the casino. All the rooms have gas fireplaces and are designed so that the fireplace separates the bed from the seating area.

78 Wash. 115 (P.O. Box 2107), Ocean Shores, WA 98569. ℂ 888/461-2214 or 360/289-9466. www.quinaultbch resort.com. 150 units. $100–$210 double; $280–$330 suite. AE, DC, DISC, MC, V. **Amenities:** 3 restaurants (Northwest, American, Sushi); 2 lounges; indoor pool; exercise room; full-service spa; Jacuzzi; limited room service; massage; casino. *In room:* A/C, TV, dataport, fridge, coffeemaker, hair dryer, high-speed Internet access.

IN HOQUIAM
Hoquiam's Castle ⭐⭐ *Value*   This stately Victorian mansion, built in 1897 by a local timber baron, is an amazing assemblage of turrets and gables, balconies and bay windows. Rooms here have names inspired by the castlelike setting (King's, Queen's, Princess's, Knight's, Maid's), and all are furnished in luxurious Victorian style. There are antiques throughout the inn and the quality of construction of this 10,000-square-foot mansion is evident in the wood floors and paneling, crystal chandeliers, and stained-glass windows. Guests can enjoy the city view from the turret, play the piano in the parlor, and sip tea on the front porch or sherry in the second-floor lounge. The inn even has its own ballroom.

515 Chenault Ave., Hoquiam, WA 98550. ℂ 360/533-2005. www.hoquiamscastle.com. 5 units. $125–$195 double. Rates include full breakfast. MC, V. Children over age 12 welcome. *In room:* Hair dryer, iron.

IN THE SOUTH BEACH AREA
Tokeland Hotel ⭐ *Finds*   On the north shore of Willapa Bay, the Tokeland Hotel has been welcoming guests since 1889 and, with its remote setting and simple interior decor, feels like a genuine step back in time. Lawns surround the wood-frame inn, and beyond these lies the water. The first floor is taken up by a large open lobby and dining room, off which is a small library with a fireplace. Up on the second floor, rooms are arranged on either side of a long hall and have painted wood floors. Antique furnishings lend an air of authenticity to the inn. Shared bathrooms all have claw-foot tubs. The inn's moderately priced dining room is the most popular restaurant for miles around and is particularly noteworthy for its Sunday dinner, which includes a delicious cranberry pot roast (open daily 8am–8pm; winter hours vary).

100 Hotel Rd., Tokeland, WA 98590. ℂ 360/267-7006. Fax 360/267-7006. www.tokelandhotel.com. 18 units, all with shared bathroom. $49–$65 double. DISC, MC, V. Pets accepted. **Amenities:** Restaurant (American). *In room:* No phone.

CAMPGROUNDS
On Wash. 109 north of Ocean Shores are two state park campgrounds. **Pacific Beach State Park** (64 campsites) is a small, exposed, and crowded patch of sand with little to recommend it other than good razor clamming nearby. More appealing is **Ocean City State Park** ⭐ (178 campsites), which at least has trees for protection against the wind. This is a good choice if you plan to bicycle along this stretch of coast. To make

---

---

a campsite reservation at either of these spots, contact **Washington State Parks** (© **888/226-7688;** www.parks.wa.gov/reserve.asp).

WHERE TO DINE

IN THE OCEAN SHORES & NORTH BEACH AREA

The best restaurants in this region are the dining rooms at the Ocean Crest Resort and the Quinault Beach Resort (see above for details).

IN ABERDEEN & HOQUIAM

Mallard's Bistro & Grill 🕊🕊 *Finds* CONTINENTAL   In downtown Aberdeen and owned by a Danish chef who cooked all over Europe before relocating here, this cozy little restaurant is one of the most unexpectedly enjoyable eateries in the state. In a town filled with burger joints and cheap Chinese restaurants, Mallard's dares to serve such creative fare as a delicious salmon with pinot noir sauce. The menu sticks mostly to traditional Continental fare, including coquille St. Jacques, and there are lots of good seafood preparations. The setting, with its many images of mallard ducks all around the dining room, is casual and homey.

118 E. Wishkah St. © **360/532-0731.** Reservations recommended. Main courses $15–$28. MC, V. Tues–Sat 5–9pm.

IN THE SOUTH BEACH AREA

Your best bet for a memorable meal in the South Beach area is the dining room at the historic Tokeland Hotel (see above for details).

Tokeland Hotel Dining Room 🕊 *Finds* AMERICAN   With its painted wood floors and wall of old wavy-glass windows looking out to the salt marsh, this restaurant has a more historical feel than almost any restaurant in the state. If you're anywhere on the central coast, be sure to have a meal here. Sunday suppers of cranberry pot roast are legendary, but any day of the week, you can get a sandwich made from the same tender pot roast. Plenty of good seafood dishes are made with local fish and shellfish. Also, save room for some blackberry cobbler.

100 Hotel Rd., Tokeland. © **360/267-7006.** www.tokelandhotel.com. Main course $7–$19. DISC, MC, V. Daily 8am–8pm.

2 The Long Beach Peninsula

110 miles NW of Portland, 180 miles SW of Seattle, 80 miles W of Longview/Kelso

With 28 uninterrupted miles of sand, the Long Beach Peninsula, a long narrow strip of low forest and sand dunes, claims to be the world's longest beach open to vehicles. For more than a century, all those miles of sand have been attracting vacationers from the Portland area and parts of southwestern Washington, and today the Long Beach

Peninsula is Washington's most developed stretch. There are dozens of resorts, motels, rental cabins, vacation homes, and campgrounds up and down the peninsula.

Each of the peninsula's towns has its distinct personality. In Seaview, there are restored Victorian homes. In Long Beach, go-cart tracks and family amusements hold sway. Klipsan Beach and Ocean Park are quiet retirement communities, while Nahcotta is still an active oystering port, albeit in a very attractive setting. Last is the tiny community of Oysterville, a National Historic District of restored homes and hands-down the prettiest community on the peninsula.

While kite flying, horseback riding, and beachcombing are the most popular beach activities here, digging for razor clams ranks right up there, too. Razor clams (and the area's oysters) also show up on plenty of area restaurant menus. Bivalves aren't the only type of seafood that attracts folks to the south coast, either. In Ilwaco, south of Long Beach, a fleet of charter fishing boats can take you out in search of salmon, tuna, or bottom fish.

Long Beach is one of the few beaches on the West Coast that allows vehicular traffic, so feel free to go for a drive on the beach. Just remember that the beach is a state highway and a 25-mph speed limit is enforced. There are beach-access roads up and down the peninsula, and once you're on the beach, be sure you stay above the clam beds (sand nearest to the low-tide area) and below the dry sand.

ESSENTIALS

GETTING THERE   The Long Beach Peninsula begins just off U.S. 101 in southwest Washington. U.S. 101 leads north to Aberdeen and south to Astoria, Oregon. Wash. 4 leads to Long Beach from Longview.

GETTING AROUND   Pacific Transit System (© **360/642-9418;** www.pacific transit.org) operates public buses that serve the area from Astoria in the south to Aberdeen in the north.

VISITOR INFORMATION   Contact the **Long Beach Peninsula Visitors Bureau,** P.O. Box 562, Long Beach, WA 98631 (© **800/451-2542** or 360/642-2400; www.fun beach.com), which operates a visitor center at the intersection of U.S. 101 and Pacific Avenue in Seaview.

FESTIVALS   Annual events on the Long Beach Peninsula include the **Northwest Garlic Festival** on the third weekend in June, the **Sand-Sations** sand-sculptures tournament in late July, the **International Kite Festival** in mid-August, the **Cranberrian Fair** in early October, and the **Water Music Festival** (chamber music) in late October.

SEEING THE SIGHTS

Fort Columbia State Park (© **360/642-3078**), a former military base that guarded the mouth of the Columbia River from 1896 until the end of World War II, is 9 miles east of Ilwaco on Wash. 103 near the Astoria-Megler Bridge, which is a 4½-mile-long span that connects Washington with Oregon. The views from the park's wooded bluff are breathtaking, and at picnic tables, you can enjoy the views. The park also has 5 miles of hiking trails. Its 1903-vintage buildings have been restored and house an interpretive center with displays on the history of the fort. There are also exhibits on the local Chinook Indian tribe. From Memorial Day through September, an interpretive center is open daily from 10am to 5pm, and the old commanding officer's home is open daily from 11am to 4pm. A couple of vacation rental homes are here. For reservations, contact Washington State Parks (© **888/226-7688;** www.parks.wa.gov/reserve.asp).

To learn more about the history of the area, stop by the **Ilwaco Heritage Museum,** 115 SE Lake St., Ilwaco (© **360/642-3446;** www.ilwacoheritagemuseum.org). This modern museum has displays on the history of southwest Washington and an excellent collection of Native American baskets and other artifacts. A railroad exhibit has a model railroad of Long Beach's Clamshell Railroad, with an actual passenger car. The museum is open Monday through Saturday from 10am to 4pm and Sunday from 1 to 5pm (Oct–Apr Mon–Sat 10am–4pm). Admission is $5 for adults, $4 for seniors, $2.50 for youths ages 12 to 17, $1 for children ages 6 to 11, free for children age 5 and under.

Also in Ilwaco is the historic **Colbert House,** which is operated by the Cape Disappointment State Park (see below). You'll find this restored home at the corner of Quaker and Spruce streets. It's open Friday through Sunday from 10am to 4pm, Memorial Day through September.

Anchoring the south end of the peninsula is forested **Cape Disappointment State Park** ✸✸ (© **360/642-3078**), at the mouth of the Columbia River. The park is a former military installation used to guard the river mouth, and many bunkers and batteries are still visible. Also within the boundaries of the park are the North Head and Cape Disappointment lighthouses. The North Head Lighthouse is open for tours in summer ($1 per person). This lighthouse suffers some of the highest winds on the West Coast, some as high as 160 mph. The Cape Disappointment Lighthouse was built in 1856 and is the oldest lighthouse on the West Coast. The park is also home to the **Lewis and Clark Interpretive Center** ✸✸ (© **360/642-3078**), which chronicles the 1805–06 journey of the two explorers; it's open daily from 10am to 5pm and admission is $3 for adults and $1 for children ages 7 to 17. Cape Disappointment, here in the park, was the end of the westward trail for Lewis and Clark. Also within the park are several picnic areas, hiking trails, a campground, and **Waikiki Beach,** the prettiest little beach between here and Moclips. This tiny cove backed by steep cliffs is named for several Hawaiian sailors who lost their lives nearby. The park is open from dawn to dusk, and admission is $5.

In the past 300 years, more than 2,000 vessels and 700 lives have been lost in the treacherous waters at the mouth of the Columbia River. Consequently, the U.S. Coast Guard has its **National Motor Life Boat School** here. Lifeboat drills can sometimes be observed from observation platforms on the North Jetty. This jetty, completed in 1917, was built to improve the channel across the Columbia Bar. A side effect of the 2-mile-long jetty was the creation of a much wider beach to the north. This widening of the beach accounts for the town of Long Beach's current distance from the waves.

If you're a kite flyer, or even if you're not, you may want to stop by the **World Kite Museum & Hall of Fame** ✸, 112 N. Third St., Long Beach (© **360/642-4020;** www.worldkitemuseum.com), which has displays on kites of the world. May through September, it's open daily from 11am to 5pm; October through April, it's open Friday through Monday from 11am to 5pm; admission is $3 for adults, $2 for seniors and children, or $8 per family.

Up toward the north end of the peninsula, you'll find the historic village of **Oysterville** ✸✸, an old oystering community that is a National Historic District and by far the quaintest little village on the peninsula. Old homes with spacious lawns cling to the edge of the marsh, creating a timeless scene. Oysterville had its heyday in the days of the California gold rush, when the village shipped tons of oysters to San Francisco, where people were willing to pay as much as $50 a plate for fresh oysters.

Today Oysterville is a sleepy little community of restored homes. In the town's white clapboard church, there are occasional music performances. **Oysterville Sea Farms** (© 800/272-6237 or 360/665-6585; www.oysterville.net) has a seafood and cranberry-products shop on the waterfront at the north end of the village.

Willapa Bay, which is one of the cleanest estuaries on the West Coast, is still known for its **oysters.** Up and down the peninsula, there are oyster farms and processing plants. To learn more about the history of the area's oystering industry, drop by the **Willapa Bay Interpretive Center** (© 360/665-4547) on the breakwater beside The Ark Restaurant in Nahcotta. The interpretive center is open Friday through Sunday, and holidays from 10am to 3pm, between Memorial Day and Labor Day, and it's free.

The peninsula is also a major producer of cranberries, and if you take a drive down almost any side road north of Long Beach, you'll pass acres of **cranberry bogs.** If you're curious to learn how cranberries are grown, stop in at the **Pacific Coast Cranberry Museum** ⊛, 2907 Pioneer Rd., Long Beach (© 360/642-5553; www.cranberry museum.com). Located on a demonstration cranberry farm, it has exhibits on all the stages of cranberry growing, both past and present. It's open from April to December 15, daily from 10am to 5pm. Admission is free.

AREA ACTIVITIES: KITE FLYING, BIRD-WATCHING & CLAMMING

Active vacations are the norm here on the Long Beach Peninsula, with plenty of activities to keep you busy. However, you won't be doing much swimming in the ocean. Although it gets warm enough in summer to lie on the beach, the waters never warm up much. Add to this the unpredictable currents, riptides, undertows, and heavy surf, and you have an ocean that's just not safe for swimming.

Instead of swimming, the beach's number-one activity is **kite flying.** Strong winds blow year-round across the Long Beach Peninsula, and with 28 miles of beach, you won't have to worry about kite-eating trees. You'll find several kite shops in Long Beach. Another very popular Long Beach activity is beachcombing. The most sought-after treasures are hand-blown-glass fishing floats used by Japanese fishermen.

Beach access is available up and down the peninsula, but the best beaches are at the peninsula's various state parks. The beaches of **Cape Disappointment State Park,** at the south end of the peninsula, are the most dramatic, while those at **Leadbetter Point State Park,** at the north end of the peninsula, are the most secluded. Just north of Ocean Park, there is beach access at the small **Pacific Pines State Park,** and south of Ocean Park, additional beach access at the west section of **Loomis Lake State Park.** This latter park is named for a popular fishing lake in the park's east section.

If you've ever dreamed of riding a horse down the beach, you can make your dream come true here in Long Beach. On South Tenth Street, just in from the beach, you'll

---

Kids **Believe It or Not!**

Children and other fans of the bizarre won't want to miss **Marsh's Free Museum** ⊛, 409 S. Pacific Ave., Long Beach (© 360/642-2188; www.marshsfree museum.com), a beachy gift shop filled with all manner of antique arcade games, oddities a la Ripley's Believe It or Not!, and, best of all, Jake the alligator man, who has been made famous by tabloids that rank this half-man, half-alligator creature right up there with aliens, Bigfoot, and the latest Elvis sighting.

find both **Skipper's Equestrian Center** (© 360/642-3676) and **Back Country Wilderness Outfitters** (© 360/642-2576; www.backcountryoutfit.com). A 1-hour ride will cost you $15.

Walking the dunes is a favorite Long Beach pastime. Between 17th Street South and 16th Street North, you'll find a pleasant 2-mile stretch of the **Discovery Trail,** a paved path that parallels the beach. The trail winds through grassy dunes that separate the town of Long Beach from the stretch of sand for which the town is named. For a half-mile of its length, the Discovery Trail parallels an elevated boardwalk that provides views of the beach and ocean over the tops of the dunes. In celebration of the Lewis and Clark bicentennial celebrated in 2005, the Discovery Trail was extended from the town of Long Beach south to Ilwaco, a distance of 8 miles. Along the stretch of trail in Long Beach, you'll find a whale skeleton, a basalt column, and a bronze statue of the gnarled tree on which Lewis and Clark carved their names. These monuments have been erected to commemorate Lewis and Clark's long-ago visit to this area.

If you'd just like to get away from the crowds and find your own piece of isolated shoreline, head to Leadbetter Point at the peninsula's northern tip. Here you'll find both **Leadbetter Point State Park Natural Area** and a portion of the **Willapa National Wildlife Refuge Complex** (© 360/484-3482; www.fws.gov/pacific/willapa). This area is well known for its variety of birds, and more than 100 species have been seen, including the snowy plover that nests at the point. Because the plovers nest on the sand, a portion of the point is closed to all visitors from March through September. However, you can still hike the trails, use the beach, and explore the marshes.

At Ilwaco, charter boats will take you out fishing for salmon, halibut, sturgeon, or bottom fish. Try **Pacific Salmon Charters** (© 800/831-2695 or 360/642-3466; www.pacificsalmoncharters.com) or **Coho Charters** (© 800/339-2646; www.coho charters.com).

Long Island, in the middle of Willapa Bay and accessible only by private boat, is part of the Willapa National Wildlife Refuge Complex (© 360/484-3482; www.fws.gov/pacific/willapa/), with headquarters about 9 miles up U.S. 101 from Seaview. The island is known for its grove of huge old red cedars and is popular with sea kayakers. There are a few campsites and some hiking trails.

WHERE TO STAY

If you're heading down this way with the whole family and need an entire vacation home, contact **Pacific Realty Property Management,** 102 NE Bolstad St. (P.O. Box 397), Long Beach, WA 98631 (© 888/879-5479 or 360/642-4549; pacificrealty rentals.com).

Among the most interesting accommodations in the area are the two former **lighthouse-keepers' homes** at the North Head Lighthouse in Cape Disappointment State Park. These vacation homes, which sleep up to six people each, can be rented through Washington State Parks (© 800/360-4240 or 360/902-8844; www.parks.wa.gov/vacationhouses) for between $123 and $345 per night, depending on the season. The two houses are in a clearing in the woods about 100 yards from the old lighthouse, and hiking trails lead from the grounds to the beach and through the park. Two more restored historic homes are at nearby Fort Columbia State Park. One rents for $123 to $183 per night and sleeps four people and the other rents for $185 to $371 per night and sleeps 12 people. Call the number above for reservations.

Boreas Bed & Breakfast Inn ✿✿   Although this inn is housed in a renovated 1920s beach house, you'd never guess it from the contemporary styling both outside and within. The inn is only a few blocks from downtown Long Beach and is separated from the ocean by grassy dunes. The upstairs rooms have the best views, but, with their spaciousness and private decks, the two downstairs rooms are also very comfortable. The downstairs Dunes Suite was formerly a sunroom and has two walls of windows. This suite also has a whirlpool tub in the bathroom. On the grounds, an enclosed gazebo houses a whirlpool spa.

607 N. Ocean Beach Blvd. (P.O. Box 1344), Long Beach, WA 98631. © 888/642-8069 or 360/642-8069. www.boreas inn.com. 5 units. $160–$170 double. Rates include full breakfast. AE, DISC, MC, V. **Amenities:** Access to nearby health club; Jacuzzi; concierge; massage. *In room:* Hair dryer, iron, Wi-Fi, no phone.

Moby Dick Hotel ☆ *(Finds)*   Though it looks like a big yellow bunker from the outside, the Moby Dick is actually a comfortable bed-and-breakfast inn. Built as a hotel back in 1930 (the year before the train stopped running), the hotel quickly fell on hard times but was later revived as a B&B. Today it's a casual place, eclectically furnished in a 1930s style. The location, at the north end of the peninsula, is removed from the beach strip of Seaview and Long Beach, and is convenient to the wild dunes and beaches of Leadbetter Park. You'll also be within walking distance of The Ark Restaurant (see below). Low rates, friendly atmosphere, and a tranquil setting make this a great choice. There is a sauna, and dinners are available. Breakfasts often include oysters from the inn's oyster beds.

Sandridge Rd. and Bay Ave., Nahcotta, WA 98637. © 360/665-4543. Fax 360/665-6887. www.mobydickhotel.com. 9 units, 3 with private bathroom. $85–$100 double with shared bathroom; $110–$140 double with private bathroom. Rates include full breakfast. 2-night minimum on summer weekends, 3-night minimum on festival weekends. AE, DISC, MC, V. Pets accepted ($10). **Amenities:** Restaurant (Northwest); sauna. *In room:* No phone.

Shelburne Country Inn ☆☆   This inn's tone perfectly captures that of a country inn. Step though the front door and you enter rooms filled with a pale light that is filtered by walls of stained-glass windows salvaged from an English church. In the main lobby, dark fir-paneled walls and a fire crackling on the hearth all extend a classic country welcome. Most guest rooms are on the second floor, but, on the ground floor, a couple of suites overlook the gardens and have their own decks. All the guest rooms are filled with antiques and, even if sometimes a bit cramped, all feel very luxurious and old-fashioned. The Shoalwater Restaurant here is one of the state's finest restaurants (see below).

4415 Pacific Hwy. (P.O. Box 250), Seaview, WA 98644-0250. © 800/INN-1896 or 360/642-2442. Fax 360/642-8904. www.theshelburneinn.com. 15 units. $125–$165 double; $185 suite. Rates include full breakfast. AE, MC, V. **Amenities:** Restaurant (Northwest); lounge. *In room:* Hair dryer, Wi-Fi.

CAMPGROUNDS

The only campground in this area worth recommending is **Cape Disappointment State Park** (235 campsites), at the southern end of the Long Beach Peninsula at the mouth of the Columbia River. This park has campsites on a small lake, as well as at the foot of North Head. Some of the sites in the latter area are tucked in amid massive boulders. For reservations, contact **Washington State Parks** (© **888/226-7688;** www.parks.wa.gov/reserve.asp).

WHERE TO DINE

For smoked salmon and oysters, fresh fish and crab, and fresh clam chowder, stop in at **Ocean Park Crab & Seafood Market,** 254th Street and Pacific Highway, Ocean Park (© **360/665-3474**).

The Ark Restaurant & Bakery ★★ NORTHWEST   At the north end of the Long Beach Peninsula, the Ark is an oyster lover's paradise. Set at the foot of a working dock and surrounded by oyster canneries and huge piles of oyster shells, the restaurant has its own oyster beds, as well as its own herb and edible-flower garden. You can be sure that whatever you order here will be absolutely fresh, and that's exactly what has kept the Ark afloat for decades. Of course, oysters are the top dinner choice, and the Ark's oyster platter comes with 16 oysters. Even if you aren't an oyster fan, you'll find plenty of delicious dishes on the menu; however, you had better like garlic, which is used liberally here. If you have a sweet tooth, save room for one of the Ark's excellent desserts.

3310 273rd St., Nahcotta. ✆ 360/665-4133. arkrestaurant.com. Reservations highly recommended. Main courses $9–$11 lunch, $12–$28 dinner. AE, DISC, MC, V. Aug–Sept 15 Tues–Sat 5–9:30pm, Sun 11am–2:30pm and 5–9:30pm (mid-Sept to Oct and late May to July closed Tues; mid-Mar to late May and Nov closed Tues–Wed; Dec to mid-Mar closed Tues–Thurs). Always call ahead to verify seasonal hours.

The Depot Restaurant ★★ ECLECTIC   This is the just the sort of restaurant you dream of finding on vacation: small, out of the way, casual and inexpensive, yet with excellent food. Located in the old Seaview train depot, this restaurant abounds in vintage character, from its linoleum floors to its wooden counter to its old-fashioned hanging lights. The menu is short and varied, and includes Willapa Bay oysters (of course) and clam chowder made with local clams. However, the more unusual preparations, such as scallops with truffle oil, are the real stars here. No matter what you order for an entree, be sure to start with the house salad made with mixed greens, candied walnuts, blue cheese, and slices of pear.

1208 38th Place at L St., Seaview. ✆ 360/642-7880. Reservations recommended. Main courses $16–$24. DISC, MC, V. Wed–Sun 5–9pm (Memorial Day–Labor Day Fri–Sat until 10pm).

Sanctuary Restaurant ★★ NORTHWEST/SCANDINAVIAN   A 1906 church in the community of Chinook, between Long Beach and the Astoria-Megler Bridge, now serves as one of southwest Washington's most memorable dining places. The church has changed very little since its days as a house of worship, and people still pack the pews, which are used for bench seating at the tables (should you happen to get a table on the altar, you may wind up in the minister's thronelike chair). The menu includes such staples as pan-fried oysters, but the traditional (Swedish meatballs) and more imaginative Scandinavian dishes are the real attractions here. The fish specialties shouldn't be missed, nor should the *krumkaka* (crumb cake) dessert. In back of the church, the affiliated Little Ocean Annie's serves fish and chips at lunch.

794 U.S. 101. ✆ 360/777-8380. www.sanctuaryrestaurant.com. Reservations recommended. Main courses $15–$22. AE, DISC, MC, V. Summer Wed–Sat 5–9pm, Sun 5–8pm; other months, call for hours.

The Shoalwater Restaurant/Heron and Beaver Pub ★★ NORTHWEST   The Shoalwater is one of the best restaurants in Washington and should not be missed on a visit to this corner of the state. Stained-glass windows salvaged from an English church suffuse the elegant dining room with a soft light, while furnishings evoke Victorian times. The menu changes frequently, but you'll find plenty of excellent oyster and clam dishes (made with local shellfish) at almost anytime of year. Since this is cranberry country, you may want to start with an appetizer of pâté with cranberry chutney and roasted-garlic crème fraîche. Here at the Shelburne Country Inn, you'll also find the casual Heron and Beaver Pub, which serves lighter fare at lower prices, and is open for both lunch and dinner.

In the Shelburne Inn, 4415 Pacific Way, Seaview. ✆ **360/642-4142**. www.shoalwater.com. Reservations highly recommended. Main courses $12–$30. AE, DC, DISC, MC, V. Daily 11:30am–3pm and 5:30–9pm.

UP THE COLUMBIA RIVER

Between the Long Beach Peninsula and I-5 at Longview lies one of the state's most enjoyable and little-known scenic drives. Wash. 4 passes through several small historic riverfront communities, and between Cathlamet and Longview, it runs right alongside the Columbia River, often at the base of steep hillsides or basalt cliffs. The quiet backwaters along this stretch of the river seem little changed by the passing of time.

Heading east from Long Beach on U.S. 101, you first skirt the south end of Willapa Bay, site of the Willapa National Wildlife Refuge. Each year in late April and early May, this area becomes a rest stop for thousands of birds heading north to summer breeding grounds in the Arctic. Roughly 20 miles east of the junction of U.S. 101 and Wash. 4, you'll come to the **Grays River covered bridge,** which was erected in 1905 and is one of two covered bridges in the state. The bridge is 2 miles off the highway.

Another 15 miles east, you'll come to the tiny community of **Skamokawa** (pronounced Skuh-*mah*-kuh-way), which is one of the only remaining Columbia River fishing villages dating from the early 20th century, when salmon canneries abounded along the Columbia River. Here you can visit the **River Life Interpretive Center** (✆ **360/795-3007;** riverlifeinterpretivecenter.org), which is housed in Redmen Hall, a restored 1894 schoolhouse. The center is right on Wash. 4 and is open Thursday through Sunday from noon to 4pm. Just east of Skamokawa lies the **Julia Butler Hansen National Wildlife Refuge** (✆ **360/795-3915;** www.fws.gov/pacific/willapa) that protects the rare Columbia River white-tailed deer, and to the west is the **Lewis and Clark National Wildlife Refuge** (✆ **360/795-3915;** www.fws.gov/pacific/willapa). For exploring the waterways of these refuges, contact the **Skamokawa Paddle Center,** 1391 W. State Rte. 4, Skamokawa, WA 98647 (✆ **888/920-2777** or 360/795-8300; www.skamokawakayak.com), with its wide variety of 1- and 2-day trips ranging from $99 to $195 per person. Classes and canoe/kayak rentals are also available.

East of Cathlamet begins the most picturesque portion of this drive, with the cliffs of Little Cape Horn marking the start of this scenic stretch. Due to its strong winds, the Little Cape Horn area is popular with windsurfers.

WHERE TO STAY

Skamokawa Inn ✦ *(finds)*   In the tiny historic fishing village of Skamokawa, this inn caters primarily to people coming to town to go sea kayaking with the affiliated Skamokawa Paddle Center. The inn's rooms, which are in a restored historic building, are modern, comfortable, and cheerful. Two have their own small balconies and river views. If you have family or friends along, consider the apartment in an adjacent house. The inn is located right on the water, with its own dock. On the ground floor, there's a general store with a casual dining room as well as a store. Canoes, kayaks, and mountain bikes can all be rented here.

1391 W. State Rte. 4 (P.O. Box 212), Skamokawa, WA 98647. ✆ **888/920-2777** or 360/795-8300. www.skamokawa kayak.com. 12 units. $80–$95 double; $145–$255 apt or suite. Rates include continental breakfast. MC, V. **Amenities:** Restaurant (American); watersports rentals; bike rentals. *In room:* TV, dataport.

3 Vancouver & Vicinity

6 miles N of downtown Portland, 120 miles SE of Long Beach, 40 miles S of Longview

Because Vancouver, Washington, is part of the Portland metropolitan area, and bears the same name as both a large island and a city in Canada, it is often overlooked by visitors to the Northwest. However, the city has several historic sites and other attractions that make it worth a stop. At Fort Vancouver, a Hudson's Bay Company (HBC) trading fort, much of the Northwest's important early pioneer history unfolded.

ESSENTIALS

GETTING THERE   Vancouver is located on I-5 just north across the Columbia River from Portland, Oregon. I-205 bypasses the city to the east, while Wash. 14 heads east up the Columbia Gorge.

With the Portland International Airport just across the river, Vancouver is also well connected to the rest of the world via numerous airlines, and served by Amtrak trains.

VISITOR INFORMATION   For more information on this area, contact the **Southwest Washington Convention & Visitors Bureau,** O.O. Howard House, 750 Anderson St., Vancouver, WA 98660 (© **877/600-0800** or 360/750-1553; www.southwestwashington.com), which operates a visitor's center in the Slocum House, Esther Short Park, 605 Esther St.

VANCOUVER'S HISTORICAL ATTRACTIONS

The city of Vancouver, Washington, was one of the first settlements in the Northwest and consequently has a long pioneer and military history. After the British gave up Fort Vancouver, it became the site of the Vancouver Barracks U.S. military post, and stately homes were built for the officers of the post. The buildings of Officers' Row and their attractive, tree-shaded surroundings are now preserved as the **Vancouver National Historic Reserve** 𝒌𝒌. Within the reserve, just east of I-5 (take the East Mill Plain Blvd. exit just north of the I-5 Interstate Bridge), you'll find not only Officers' Row, Fort Vancouver, and the Pearson Air Museum, but also the **Columbia River Waterfront Trail.** At the west end of this paved riverside trail, in a small park through a walkway under the railroad tracks, is the **oldest apple tree** in the Northwest. It was planted in 1826.

Fort Vancouver National Historic Site 𝒌𝒌   It was here at Fort Vancouver, a trading post operated by the British Hudson's Bay Company, that much of the Northwest's important early pioneer history unfolded. The HBC came to the Northwest in search of furs and, for most of the first half of the 19th century, was the only authority in this remote region. Fur trappers, mountain men, missionaries, explorers, and settlers all made Fort Vancouver their first stop in the Oregon country, which at that time also encompassed present-day Washington. Today, Fort Vancouver houses several reconstructed buildings furnished as they might have been in the mid-19th century. Throughout the year, there are a variety of living-history programs.

1501 E. Evergreen Blvd. © **800/832-3599** or 360/696-7655. www.nps.gov/fova. Admission $3 ($5 per family). Apr–Oct daily 9am–5pm; Nov–Mar daily 9am–4pm. Closed Thanksgiving, Dec 24–25, and Jan 1.

Pearson Air Museum 𝒌   A different piece of history is preserved at this small air museum on the far side of Fort Vancouver from Officers' Row. Established in 1905, this is the oldest operating airfield in the U.S. Dozens of vintage aircraft, including

World War I–era biplanes, are displayed in a large hangar, with an exhibit on the Russian plane that made the first transpolar flight.

1115 E. Fifth St. ℂ 360/694-7026. www.pearsonairmuseum.org. Admission $6 adults, $5 seniors, $3 children ages 6–12, free for children under 6. Wed–Sat 10am–5pm.

EXPLORING OUTSIDE OF TOWN

In the town of Washougal, 16 miles east of Vancouver on Wash. 14, you can visit the **Pendleton Woolen Mills Store,** 2 17th St., Washougal (ℂ **800/568-2480** or 360/835-1118; www.pendletonmillstore.com), and see how its famous wool blankets and classic wool fashions are made. The store is open Monday through Friday from 8am to 5pm, Saturday from 9am to 5pm, and Sunday from 11am to 5pm, with free mill tours offered Monday through Friday at 9, 10, and 11am, and 1:30pm. The mill closes for 2 weeks in both August and December.

Twenty-three miles north of Vancouver, in the town of Woodland, are the **Hulda Klager Lilac Gardens,** 115 S. Pekin Rd., Woodland (ℂ **360/225-8996;** www.lilac gardens.com). Between mid-April and mid-May, these gardens burst into color and the fragrance of lilacs hangs in the air. During this time, the gardens are open daily from 10am to 4pm. Admission is $2.

Ten miles east of Woodland off NE Cedar Creek Road, is the **Cedar Creek Grist Mill,** Grist Mill Road (ℂ **360/225-5832;** www.cedarcreekgristmill.com), the only remaining 19th-century gristmill in Washington. Built in 1876, the mill was restored over a 10-year period, and in 1989, once again became functional. When the mill is open, volunteers demonstrate how wheat is ground into flour. Hours of operation are Saturday from 1 to 4pm and Sunday from 2 to 4pm. Admission is by donation. Adjacent to the mill is one of Washington's two historic covered bridges.

WHERE TO STAY

The Heathman Lodge ★★ *Value*   Mountain lodge meets urban chic at this suburban Vancouver hotel adjacent to the Vancouver Mall. Just 20 minutes by car from downtown Portland, the hotel is well placed for exploring both the Columbia Gorge and Mount St. Helens. With its log, stone, and cedar-shingle construction, this hotel conjures up the Northwest's historic mountain lodges. As at Timberline Lodge on Oregon's Mount Hood, this hotel is filled with artwork and embellished with rugged Northwest-inspired craftwork, including totem poles, Eskimo kayak frames, and Pendleton blankets. Guest rooms feature a mix of rustic pine and peeled-hickory furniture, as well as rawhide lampshades and Pendleton-inspired bedspreads. Most rooms also have Tempur-Pedic mattresses.

7801 NE Greenwood Dr., Vancouver, WA 98662. ℂ **888/475-3100** or 360/254-3100. Fax 360/254-6100. www.heathmanlodge.com. 142 units. $79–$149 double; from $159-$350 suite. AE, DC, DISC, MC, V. **Amenities:** Restaurant (Northwest); lounge; indoor pool; exercise room; Jacuzzi; sauna; concierge; business center; room service; guest laundry; laundry service; dry cleaning. *In room:* A/C, TV, dataport, fridge, coffeemaker, hair dryer, iron, Wi-Fi.

WHERE TO DINE

Hudson's, the dining room at The Heathman Lodge (see above for details), is one of the city's best restaurants and serves three meals a day. When it's time for a pint of craft ale, head to **McMenamins on the Columbia,** 1801 SE Columbia River Dr. (ℂ **360/699-1521;** www.mcmenamins.com), a brewpub with a view.

Beaches Restaurant & Bar ★ *Kids* INTERNATIONAL   Sure, it's a long way to the beach, but why let that stop you from having a good time? That seems to be the attitude of this waterfront restaurant. The gardens are full of sand and a party atmosphere prevails most of the time. The menu is long and includes everything from good burgers to pizzas. With big walls of glass overlooking the Columbia River, sunset dinners are very popular. Despite the large size, service is usually good. To reach the restaurant from I-5, take Wash. 14 east and then take exit 1.

1919 SE Columbia River Dr. ⓒ **360/699-1592**. Reservations recommended. Main courses $7–$24. AE, DISC, MC, V. Sun–Mon 11am–9pm; Tues–Sat 11am–10pm.

10

The Cascades

Cloaked in places by dark forests of old-growth trees and stripped bare by logging clear-cuts in others, the Washington Cascades are a patchwork quilt of narrow valleys, rolling foothills, snowcapped volcanic peaks, and rugged mountain ranges. Lakes of the deepest blue are cradled beneath emerald forests. Glaciers carve their way inexorably from peaks that experience some of the heaviest snowfalls in the nation. (It's possible to drive or hike a short distance to the edge of several glaciers and listen to cracking and rumbling as gravity pulls at centuries-old ice.) The appropriately named Cascades send countless waterfalls cascading from the heights.

The I-5 corridor from the Canadian border south more than 150 miles to Olympia is the most densely populated region of Washington state, yet for millions of people who live here, gazing at mountain wilderness merely requires a look eastward on a clear day. Dominating the eastern skyline of the northern Puget Sound region are volcanic Mount Baker and the North Cascades. In the southern regions of the sound, Mount Rainier, another dormant volcano, looms grandly on the horizon. The easy accessibility of these mountains helps make the cities of Puget Sound so livable. With two national parks, a national volcanic monument, a half-dozen major ski areas, one of the largest networks of cross-country ski trails in the country, hundreds of lakes (including the third-deepest lake in the United States), a Bavarian village, and a false-fronted Wild West frontier town, these mountains offer a diversity of recreational and sightseeing activities.

Whatever the season, in good weather and bad, active Washingtonians head for the hills whenever they get the chance. Summer and winter are, however, the most popular seasons here. In summer, people come for the wildflowers and to go hiking, and in winter, they come for the skiing and snowboarding.

1 Mount Baker ★★ & the North Cascades Scenic Highway ★★★

Diablo Lake: 66 miles E of Burlington (I-5), 65 miles W of Winthrop; Mount Baker Ski Area: 62 miles E of Bellingham

Wolves and grizzly bears still call this wilderness home, and names such as Mount Fury, Mount Terror, and Forbidden Peak are testament to the rugged and remote nature of this terrain. Much of the region is preserved within the two units of North Cascades National Park, one of the least visited national parks in the country. This lack of visitors is easy to understand when you realize there is but one gravel road within the park boundaries, and it originates in the community of Stehekin on the north shore of Lake Chelan. Stehekin can only be reached by hiking trail, floatplane, or boat, which severely limits the number of vehicles that use this road. However, passing between the two units of the national park is the North Cascades Scenic Highway, which does provide access to viewpoints and trails that lead into the national park.

The Washington Cascades

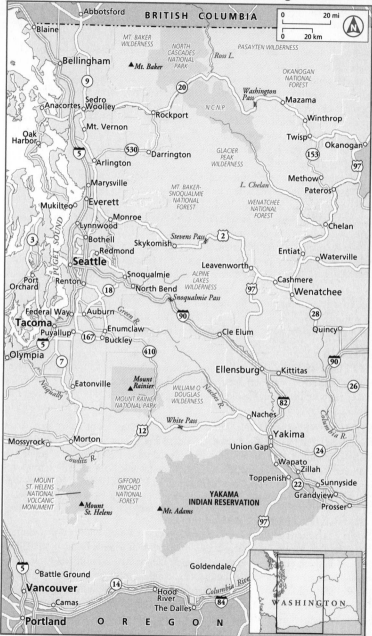

BRITISH COLUMBIA

Abbotsford

Blaine

MT. BAKER
WILDERNESS

NORTH
CASCADES
NATIONAL
PARK

PASAYTEN WILDERNESS

Ross L.

▲ Mt. Baker

9

OKANOGAN
NATIONAL
FOREST

Bellingham

20

Washington
Pass

Mazama

Sedro
Woolley

Anacortes

N.C.N.P.

Winthrop

Rockport

Mt. Vernon

Twisp

Okanogan

Oak
Harbor

5

530

Darrington

GLACIER
PEAK
WILDERNESS

153

97

Arlington

Marysville

MT. BAKER-
SNOQUALMIE
NATIONAL
FOREST

L. Chelan

Methow

Pateros

Mukilteo

Everett

WENATCHEE
NATIONAL
FOREST

Chelan

Monroe

Lynnwood

Bothell

Stevens Pass

2

3

Redmond

Skykomish

Entiat

Waterville

Seattle

Leavenworth

Port
Orchard

Renton

Snoqualmie

ALPINE
LAKES
WILDERNESS

Cashmere

Wenatchee

18

North Bend

97

Snoqualmie Pass

Federal Way

Auburn

Green R.

90

28

Quincy

Tacoma

Puyallup

Enumclaw

167

Buckley

Cle Elum

410

90

Olympia

5

7

Ellensburg

Kittitas

26

Eatonville

Mount
Rainier

WILLIAM O.
DOUGLAS
WILDERNESS

82

MOUNT RAINIER
NATIONAL PARK

Naches R.

Columbia R.

White Pass

Naches

Mossyrock

12

Morton

Yakima

Cowlitz R.

Union Gap

24

Wapato

Zillah

MOUNT
ST. HELENS
NATIONAL
VOLCANIC
MONUMENT

GIFFORD
PINCHOT
NATIONAL
FOREST

Toppenish

22

Sunnyside

▲ Mount
St. Helens

▲ Mt. Adams

YAKAMA
INDIAN RESERVATION

Grandview

Prosser

97

Battle Ground

5

Goldendale

Vancouver

14

Hood
River

Columbia River

WASHINGTON

Camas

The Dalles

84

Portland

OREGON

0 ———— 20 mi
0 ———— 20 km

273

There is very little road access in this area, but plenty of trails, and day hikers and backpackers can head into hundreds of miles of wilderness in national forest, park, and recreation areas.

Though numerous attempts were made over the years to build a road through the craggy, glacier-sculpted North Cascade mountains, it was not until 1972 that Wash. 20 finally connected the Skagit Valley communities on the west side of the North Cascades with Winthrop on the east side. Today the road is known as the North Cascades Scenic Highway, and it's one of the most breathtakingly beautiful stretches of road anywhere in the United States. Unfortunately, because of heavy winter snows and avalanches, the road is only open from April to November (depending on the weather). The scenic highway begins east of Sedro-Woolley, with more than a dozen campgrounds along its length.

Lying just outside the northwestern corner of North Cascades National Park is 10,778-foot Mount Baker, which on a clear day dominates the skyline to the east of Bellingham and the San Juan Islands. This is the northernmost of Washington's Cascade Range volcanoes, and, as such, rises high above the surrounding North Cascade peaks, which are geologically unrelated to Mount Baker. Because it is open to the winter storms that sweep up the Strait of Juan de Fuca from the Pacific Ocean, Mount Baker usually receives more snow than any other Cascades peak, and in the winter of 1998–99, a world record of 1,140 inches fell at the Mount Baker Ski Area.

The North Cascades Scenic Highway, with its mountain vistas and excellent hiking, attracts most people to this area, but Mount Baker's slopes are equally rewarding. In summer, hikers explore alpine meadows, and in winter, skiers and snowboarders sample some of the most legendary snows in the country.

ESSENTIALS

GETTING THERE   To reach Mount Baker ski area (and Heather Meadows and Artist Point in the summer), head east from Bellingham on Wash. 542 (the Mount Baker Hwy.). The North Cascades Scenic Highway is Wash. 20, and it leaves I-5 at Burlington.

VISITOR INFORMATION   For information on the Mount Baker area, contact the **Glacier Public Service Center,** Mount Baker Highway, Glacier (© **360/599-2714**). For information on the North Cascades National Park Complex, Mount Baker National Recreation Area, and Mount Baker–Snoqualmie National Forest, contact the jointly operated **Forest/Park Service Information Office,** 810 Wash. 20, Sedro-Woolley, WA 98284 (© **360/856-5700;** www.nps.gov/noca or www.fs.fed.us/r6/mbs).

VISITING THE MOUNT BAKER AREA

Wash. 542, known as the Mount Baker Highway, is a dead-end road that climbs to 5,140 feet in elevation at a ridge between 10,778-foot Mount Baker and 9,038-foot Mount Shuksan. The road ends at the aptly named **Artist Point** , an area of rugged beauty nearly unequaled in the state. Rising directly above Artist Point is flat-topped Table Mountain, up which there is a short but precipitous trail. Three miles before you reach Artist Point, you'll come to **Heather Meadows** and Picture Lake, in which the reflection of Mount Shuksan can be seen when the waters are still. Each year in July and August, the meadows of this area burst into bloom and attract crowds of weekend hikers who tramp the many miles of trails that radiate out from here. The 9-mile **Chain Lakes Loop Trail** is by far the most rewarding of the hikes in the area. It circles Table Mountain, passing numerous beautiful little lakes along the way. From July through September, the **Heather Meadows Visitor Center,** milepost 56 on Mount Baker Highway (no phone), has trail maps for the area and information on this region's unusual geology.

Two of the most rewarding hikes in the Mount Baker area actually originate not in the Heather Meadows/Artist Point area, but off side roads 1 mile east of the town of Glacier. These are the **Heliotrope Ridge Trail** ✯✯ (off Forest Service Rd. 39) and the **Skyline Divide Trail** ✯✯✯ (off Forest Service Rd. 37). Both of these trails climb up through meadows with excellent views of Mount Baker, and, from the Heliotrope Ridge Trail, there are also impressive glacier views. Also near Glacier, at milepost 41, is a short trail that leads to 100-foot Nooksack Falls.

To park at Heather Meadows, Artist Point, and other area trailheads, you'll need a Northwest Forest Pass. These permits cost $5 per day ($30 for an annual pass) and are purchased at ranger stations and national forest visitor centers.

While Kodak-moment meadows of colorful wildflowers are a big attraction throughout the summer, Mount Baker is better known as one of the nation's top snowboarding areas. Each winter, Mount Baker receives an average of more than 500 inches of snow, and in the winter of 1998–99, set a world record with 1,140 inches of snow. All this snow, combined with lots of extreme terrain, produces awesome skiing and snowboarding conditions. Consequently, **Mount Baker Ski Area** ✯✯ (© 360/671-0211; www.mtbaker.us) at Heather Meadows, is well known throughout the region for being the first ski area to open and the last to close each year. All-day lift tickets range from $32 to $40. Ski and snowboard rentals are available at the ski area, and snowboards can also be rented in the town of Glacier at **Mt. Baker Snowboard Shop,** 9996 Forest St. (© **360/599-2008;** www.mtbakersnowboard shop.com). Cross-country skiers will find a few miles of groomed trails at Mount Baker ski area, and more miles at the **Salmon Ridge Sno-Park** farther down the mountain. Telemark skiers and backcountry snowboarders enjoy terrain adjacent to Mount Baker ski area.

En route to or from Mount Baker, you can sample local wines at **Mount Baker Vineyards,** 4298 Mt. Baker Hwy., Deming (© **360/592-2300**); and stock up on gourmet picnic foods at the unexpectedly hip **Everybody's Store,** 5465 Potter Rd., Van Zandt (© **866/832-4695** or 360/592-2297; www.everybodys.com).

THE NORTH CASCADES SCENIC HIGHWAY

Wash. 20, the North Cascades Scenic Highway, is a bit slow in sharing its beauties. Though it runs along the Skagit River on the west side of the Cascades, not until the Ross Lake area does the scenery become truly grand. However, there are several distractions along the way before you reach the most scenic stretch of the highway.

North of Concrete, named for the cement it once produced, lie Lake Shannon and Baker Lake, the latter a popular summer camping and boating destination. From the road leading to **Baker Lake,** you can also access the **Mount Baker National Recreation Area,** which lies on the south side of Mount Baker. Several trails lead through lovely alpine meadows. The Railroad Grade–Paul Scott Trail is breathtaking.

Between Concrete and Marblemount, the highway parallels the Skagit River, and from December to February each year, hundreds of bald eagles descend on this stretch of the river to feed on dying salmon. Highway turnouts at the prime eagle-watching sites along this stretch of road provide opportunities to observe the eagles. To learn

Natural History Seminars

Want some training in how to track wildlife? Want to learn about Lummi Indian basketry? Delve into the mysteries of mycology? You can do any of these things if you sign up for the right class through the **North Cascades Institute.** Offering more than 50 natural history field seminars each year, the North Cascades Institute, 810 State Rte. 20, Sedro-Woolley, WA 98284-1239 (© **360/856-5700,** ext. 209; www.ncascades.org), is a nonprofit educational organization that offers a wide range of courses each year. While these seminars—many of which involve camping out—focus on the North Cascades region, there are programs throughout the state. The institute now has a beautiful environmental learning center on the shore of Diablo Lake.

more about them, stop by Rockport's **Skagit River Bald Eagle Interpretive Center,** Alfred Street (© 360/853-7077; www.skagiteagle.org), located 1 block south of Wash. 20 in the Rockport Fire Hall. The center is staffed Friday through Monday during eagle-watching season. This center can also provide information on the annual Upper Skagit Bald Eagle Festival that takes place each year in late January or early February. The best way to do your eagle watching is from a raft floating slowly down the river (no whitewater here). **Eagle-watching float trips** are offered by **Alpine Adventures** (© 800/723-8386 or 206/323-1220; www.alpineadventures.com); **Wildwater River Tours** (© 800/522-WILD or 206/939-2151; www.wildwater-river.com); and **Chinook Expeditions** (© 800/241-3451 or 360/793-3451; www.chinookexpeditions.com). Trips cost $59 to $79 per adult.

Right in the middle of the eagle-viewing area, you'll come to the town of Rockport. On its west side is **Rockport State Park,** where you can hike through a stand of old-growth Douglas firs, some more than 300 years old. Three miles east of Rockport, keep an eye out for **Cascadian Farm Home Farm Roadside Stand,** 55749 Hwy. 20 (© 360/853-8173; www.cfarm.com), which is open May through October and sells fresh organic berries, blueberry muffins and shortcake, homemade ice cream, organic produce, and sandwiches.

In Marblemount, the next town you come to, the North Cascades National Park Service Complex **Wilderness Information Center,** 7280 Ranger Station Rd. (© 360/873-4500, ext. 39), provides backcountry permits and information.

In the town of Newhalem, a picturesque Seattle City Light company town at the foot of the Gorge Dam, you'll find the **North Cascades Visitor Center** (© 206/386-4495, ext. 11; www.nps.gov/noca), the main visitor center for the North Cascades National Park Complex, which includes North Cascades National Park, Ross Lake National Recreation Area, and Lake Chelan National Recreation Area. The visitor center is filled with interesting exhibits on this remote national park. There are several short hikes in the area, and in the autumn, you can see spawning salmon at the base of the hydropower plant on the edge of town. Surrounding this powerhouse is an attractively landscaped garden reached by a swinging footbridge. Continuing east from Newhalem, the road passes through a deep, narrow gorge, where you can glimpse **Gorge Creek Falls** before reaching **Gorge Dam,** the first and smallest of the dams along this stretch of the Skagit River.

Beyond the Gorge Dam, you soon come to Diablo, another Seattle City Light company town. It stands at the base of Diablo Dam and is the starting point for one of the most fascinating excursions in this corner of the state—the 2-hour boat tour on turquoise-colored Diablo Lake. In places, steep cliffs rise directly from the lake waters and stunted conifers cling to rock walls. At times, this scenery looks as if it were lifted from a Chinese scroll painting. Diablo Lake Adventure tours are offered on Saturday and Sunday in June and September, and Thursday through Monday in July and August. Tours cost $25 for adults, $20 for seniors, and $12 for children ages 6 to 12. For information, or to make a reservation (highly recommended), call **Skagit Tours/ Seattle City Light** (© **206/684-3030** or 206/233-2709; www.skagittours.com). Dinner tours are offered.

Continuing on past Diablo, you cross the Thunder Arm of Diablo Lake and climb up to the spectacular **Diablo Lake Overlook** ★★. When the sun shines, the glacier-fed lake displays an astounding turquoise color due to suspended particles of glacial silt in the water. High above the lake, you can see glaciated Colonial and Pyramid peaks.

At the **Ross Lake Overlook,** several miles farther east, the dammed waters of this huge Ross Lake reservoir come into view. The lake, and in fact this entire stretch of highway from east of Marblemount to east of Ross Lake, is designated the **Ross Lake National Recreation Area.** The lake itself extends 24 miles north, with its northern shore lying 1½ miles inside Canada. The only access to the lake from the U. S. is by trail or water, and with its many shoreline backcountry campsites and East Bank Trail, it's a popular backpacker destination. Boaters in sea kayaks and canoes also frequent these remote waters. See "Where to Stay," below, for information on the Ross Lake Resort, which rents canoes and kayaks and has both a water-taxi service and a shuttle that will haul your kayak or canoe around Ross Dam. Trails lead down to the lake both at the dam (before the Ross Lake Overlook) and east of the overlook (access to the East Bank Trail).

Hikers in search of mountain vistas and wildflower-filled meadows should hold out for **Rainy Pass** ★★ (and hope that the pass is not living up to its name). Here you'll find an easy paved trail to **Rainy Lake,** which can be combined with the strenuous, but astoundingly soul-satisfying, **Maple Pass Loop.** The view from Maple Pass is one of the finest in the Northwest. The Pacific Crest Trail also crosses the highway at Rainy Pass. If you head north along the Pacific Crest Trail, you will climb to Cutthroat Pass, with more superb views. A few miles farther east, you'll find the trailhead for the short, but steep, hike to picturesque **Blue Lake.**

Roughly 20 miles before reaching the Wild West town of Winthrop, you come to the most breathtaking stretch of the North Cascades Scenic Highway. Here, at **Washington Pass** ★★★ (5,447 ft. in elevation), the granite peak of Liberty Bell Mountain rises 2,200 feet above. Across the valley are the jagged Early Winter Spires, a full 200 feet taller than Liberty Bell Mountain. Below the pass, the road has been blasted out of a steep cliff face in one huge switchback. The Washington Pass Overlook, with its short walking trail, provides an opportunity to enjoy these last awesome vistas of the North Cascades. With its in-your-face view of craggy peaks, this is the North Cascade Scenic Highway's big payoff and this sight alone makes the drive over the mountains worthwhile.

WHERE TO STAY
IN THE MOUNT BAKER AREA

The best accommodations at the foot of Mount Baker are to be had through **Mt. Baker Lodging,** 7463 Mt. Baker Hwy. (P.O. Box 2002), Maple Falls, WA 98266-2002

(© **800/709-7669** or 360/599-2453; www.mtbakerlodging.com), which rents out dozens of cabins, houses, and condos in a wide range of rates.

The Inn at Mt. Baker ☆☆ High on a hill at the end of a steep, 3,000-foot-long gravel driveway (don't worry, the inn really is up there), this B&B is by far the best place to stay along the Mt. Baker Highway. A head-on, jaw-dropping view of Mount Baker is the inn's focal point and all five of the guest rooms have mountain views, as does the Jacuzzi out on the patio. The inn is a large modern home, and all the rooms are spacious, with superb beds and oversize soaking tubs. The only drawback is that the hill leading up to the inn has been recently clear-cut. However, if not for that, you wouldn't have such a great view of Mount Baker.

8174 Mt. Baker Hwy. (P.O. Box 5150), Glacier, WA 98244. © 360/599-1776. Fax 360/599-3000. www.theinnatmt baker.com. 5 units. $125–$150 double. Rates include full breakfast. AE, DISC, MC, V. Children over 16 accepted. **Amenities:** Jacuzzi; massage. *In room:* No phone.

ALONG THE NORTH CASCADES SCENIC HIGHWAY

Ross Lake Resort ☆ *Finds* Although this is primarily a fishing resort, the fact that all the rooms are in floating cabins makes it unusual enough that even non-anglers might enjoy a stay here. Most of the cabins are small and rustic, but two large cabins have vaulted ceilings and modern amenities. If you're looking to get away from it all, this is the place—there's not even a road to the resort. To reach the resort, you must first drive to Diablo Dam on Wash. 20, then take a ferry to the end of the lake, where a truck carries you around Ross Dam to a boat landing, where a speedboat from the lodge picks you up. Alternatively, you can hike in on a 2-mile trail from milepost 134 on Wash. 20. There's no grocery store or restaurant here, so be sure to bring enough food for your stay. What do you do once you get here? Rent a boat and go fishing, rent a kayak or canoe and go paddling, do some hiking, or simply sit and relax.

Rockport, WA 98283. © **206/386-4437.** www.rosslakeresort.com. 15 units. $75–$213 cabin for 2. Boat rental required on weekends. Children under 4 stay free in parent's room. MC, V. **Amenities:** Watersports rentals. *In room:* Kitchen, fridge, coffeemaker.

Skagit River Resort/Clark's Cabins ☆ The first thing you notice when you arrive at this casual cabin resort is the rabbits. They're everywhere—hundreds of them in all shapes and sizes, contentedly munching the lawns or just sitting quietly. Although the bunnies are one of the main attractions here, it's the theme cabins that keep people coming back. Western, nautical, Victorian, Native American, Adirondack, and hacienda are among the choices of interior decor in these cabins. Other cabins are equally comfortable, but the theme cabins make this place just a bit different. These cabins are especially popular in winter when folks flock to the area to watch the bald eagles congregate on the Skagit River. There is also a bed-and-breakfast lodge here.

58468 Clark Cabin Rd., Rockport, WA 98283. © **800/273-2606** or 360/873-2250. Fax 360/873-4077. www.north cascades.com. 39 units. $69–$139 double. Children under 6 stay free in parent's room. AE, DISC, MC, V. Pets accepted ($10). **Amenities:** Restaurant (American); coin-op laundry. *In room:* TV, coffeemaker.

CAMPGROUNDS
In the Mount Baker Area

There are several campgrounds in the forests on the banks of the Nooksack River along the Mount Baker Highway. **Silver Fir Campground** ☆ (20 campsites) 13 miles east of Glacier is the closest campground to the Heather Meadows area, and the **Douglas Fir Campground** ☆ (29 campsites) 2 miles east of Glacier is the next best choice in the area. Reservations can be made at both of these campgrounds by calling the **National Recreation Reservation Service** (© **877/444-6777** or 518/885-3639; www. reserveusa.com). The most developed campground in the area is at **Silver Lake County Park,** 9006 Silver Lake Rd. (© **360/599-2776**), which is north of Maple Falls and has 92 campsites.

Along the North Cascades Scenic Highway

Heading over the North Cascades Highway from the west side, you'll find a very nice campground, with walk-in sites, at **Rockport State Park** ⊛ (62 campsites) just west of Rockport. This campground is set amid large old-growth trees and is on a first-come, first-served basis. Outside the town of Newhalem are **Goodell Creek** (21 campsites) and **Newhalem Creek** ⊛ (109 campsites), which is the site of the North Cascades Visitor Center. The next campground east is at **Colonial Creek** ⊛ (130 campsites) on the bank of Diablo Lake. This campground has some very nice sites right on the water.

East of Marblemount, a couple of small campgrounds are on the Cascade River Road, which leads to the trailhead for the popular hike to Cascade Pass. **Marble Creek** (22 campsites) is 8 miles east of Marblemount, and **Mineral Park** (22 campsites) is 15 miles east of Marblemount. Reservations at state park campgrounds can be made by calling **Washington State Parks Reservations** (© **888/226-7688;** www. camis.com/wa). Some National Forest campgrounds also accept reservations. For more information call the **National Recreation Reservation Service** (© **877/444-6777** or 518/885-3639; www.reserveusa.com).

WHERE TO DINE
IN THE MOUNT BAKER AREA

For microbrews and pizza, try the **North Fork,** 6186 Mt. Baker Hwy., Deming (© **360/599-2337**).

Milano's Market & Deli ⊛ *Value* ITALIAN   This casual deli and Italian eatery has long been a favorite of snowboarders and skiers coming down off the mountain after a day on the slopes. Fresh pasta dishes are the specialty here, and the menu usually includes four different types of ravioli (smoked salmon, mushroom, cheese, and meat). The desserts, including tiramisu, cappuccino chocolate torte, and polenta cake, are all big hits with the hungry downhill crowd.

9990 Mt. Baker Hwy., Glacier. © **360/599-2863.** Main courses $10–$18. AE, DISC, MC, V. Daily 10am–9pm (in winter, Sun–Thurs 10am–8:30pm).

ALONG THE NORTH CASCADES SCENIC HIGHWAY

In addition to the restaurant listed here, you can get decent, simple meals at the **Eatery Restaurant** at the Skagit River Resort, which is also in Marblemount.

Buffalo Run Restaurant ⊛ *Finds* AMERICAN   From the outside, this looks like any other roadside diner, but once you see the menu, it's obvious this place is unique. The restaurant's owners have a buffalo ranch and feature buffalo meat on the menu. There are buffalo burgers, buffalo T-bones, and even buffalo stroganoff. You'll also find elk, venison, and ostrich on the menu. Of course, there's a buffalo head (and skin) on the wall. You'll find the restaurant right in Marblemount. *Note:* At press time, this restaurant was for sale and might have quit serving buffalo by the time you visit.

60084 Hwy. 20 (milepost 106), Marblemount. © **360/873-2461.** www.buffalorunrestaurant.com. Main courses $7–$40. AE, DISC, MC, V. Summer Sun–Thurs 11am–9pm; Fri–Sat 11am–10pm (shorter hours other months).

2 Winthrop & the Methow Valley ✶✶

193 miles (summer) or 243 miles (winter) E of Seattle, 53 miles N of Chelan

Driving into Winthrop, you may think you've stumbled onto a movie set. A covered wooden sidewalk lines the town's main street, which has a saloon and blacksmith's shop. If it's a Saturday in summer, you may even see a staged shootout, but there are no cameras. This isn't a movie set—it's the real Winthrop.

Well, not *exactly* the real Winthrop. Back in 1972, when the North Cascades Scenic Highway opened, Winthrop needed a way to stop a few of the cars that started crossing the mountains on the new highway. Someone suggested that the town cash in on its Wild West heritage and put up some old-fashioned cow-town false fronts (based on old photos of the town). This rewriting of history worked and now Winthrop gets plenty of cars to stop. In fact, it has become a destination in its own right, known for its cross-country skiing in winter and mountain biking, hiking, and horseback riding in summer.

Winthrop and the Methow River Valley in which it is located really do have a Wild West history. Until 1883, there were no white settlers in this picturesque valley. The only inhabitants were Native Americans who annually migrated into the valley to harvest camas bulbs and fish for salmon. The Native Americans felt it was just too cold to live in the Methow Valley, but when the first white settlers showed up, they refused to listen to the Native Americans' weather reports and built their drafty log cabins anyway. Gold was discovered in the late 1800s and fueled a short-lived boom, but it was agriculture in the form of apples that kept the valley alive until the advent of tourism in the 1970s.

Why an Old West theme town? Possibly because Owen Wister, author of *The Virginian*, a Western novel that became a popular television series, was inspired to write his novel after coming to Winthrop to visit his former Harvard University roommate who ran a trading post here. You won't find trading posts anymore, but you will find two of the finest mountain lodges in the state.

ESSENTIALS

GETTING THERE   In summer, you can take Wash. 20, the North Cascades Scenic Highway, from I-5 at Burlington. However, in winter this road is closed and it's necessary to cross from north of Seattle on U.S. 2 to Wenatchee and then drive north on U.S. 97 to Wash. 153 at Pateros. If you're coming from north-central or eastern Washington, head east on Wash. 20 at Okanogan.

VISITOR INFORMATION   For more information on the Methow Valley, contact the **Winthrop Chamber of Commerce,** 202 Hwy. 20, Winthrop, WA 98862 (✆ **888/463-8469** or 509/996-2125; www.winthropwashington.com), which has its office on Winthrop's main intersection.

SPORTS & OUTDOOR ACTIVITIES

If you're here for the outdoors, then sooner or later you're going to need the **Mazama Store,** 50 Lost River Rd. (✆ **509/996-2855**), a general store for the multi-sport crowd. Not only are outdoor gear and clothing for sale, but there are gourmet groceries, Washington wines and microbrews, an espresso bar, and a deli.

FISHING   Fly-fishing is particularly popular in the Methow Valley, and the valley's fly-fishing headquarters is the **Mazama Fly Shop,** 50 Lost River Rd. (✆ **509/996-3674;**

www.methow.com/mazamastore/trout.html), which rents all manner of gear, gives you tips on where the fish are biting, and offers a guide service and classes.

HIKING Hikers will find miles of trails, including the **Pacific Crest Trail,** within a few miles of Winthrop, although the best hiking trails are farther west off the North Cascades Scenic Highway. For information, contact the **Okanogan/Wenatchee National Forest,** Methow Valley Ranger District, Methow Valley Visitor Center, 24 W. Chewuch Rd., Winthrop, WA 98862 (© **509/996-4000;** www.fs.fed.us/r6/okanogan).

If you want to head for the hills for a few days, but don't want to carry a pack, consider a llama trek. These can be arranged through **Deli Llama Wilderness Adventures,** 17045 Llama Lane, Bow, WA 98232 (© **360/757-4212;** www.delillama.com), which charges $135 to $175 per person per day; or **Pasayten Llama Packing,** P.O. Box 852, Twisp, WA 98856 (© **509/996-2326;** www.mtllama.com), which charges $125 per person per day.

HORSEBACK RIDING If you've come to Winthrop because you're a cowboy at heart, you'll probably be interested in doing some horseback riding. **Early Winters Outfitting** (© **800/737-8750** or 509/996-2659; www.earlywintersoutfitting.com) in Mazama offers rides ranging from an hour ($20) to overnight ($170) or longer.

HOT-AIR BALLOONING If you'd like to see the Methow Valley from the air, you can arrange a hot-air balloon flight through **Morning Glory Balloon Tours** (© **509/ 997-1700;** www.balloonwinthrop.com), which charges $175 per person for a 1-hour flight with a champagne picnic at the end of the flight.

MOUNTAIN BIKING With its many miles of gravel and dirt roads, and both national forest and **Methow Valley Sport Trails Association (MVSTA)** trails that are open to bikes in the snow-free months, the Methow Valley ranks as the best mountain-biking area in the entire state. Mountain-bike rentals and trail recommendations are available from **Winthrop Mountain Sports,** 257 Riverside Ave. (© **800/719- 3826** or 509/996-2886; www.winthropmountainsports.com), in downtown Winthrop, which charges $25 to $40 per day for rentals.

ROCK CLIMBING The best rock climbing in the state surrounds the Methow Valley, and if you'd like to hire a guide to lead you (or are interested in taking some climbing lessons), contact **North Cascades Mountain Guides,** 50 Lost River Rd., Mazama (© **509/996-3194;** www.ncmountainguides.com), which charges $100 to $210 per person per day for a day of guided climbing.

WHITEWATER RAFTING May through August is whitewater-rafting season on the Methow River. If you're interested, contact **Osprey River Adventures** (© **800/997- 4116** or 509/997-4116; www.methow.com/osprey). Trips are about $70 per person.

WINTER SPORTS ✦✦✦ With its sunshine and powdery winter snows, the Methow Valley is legendary in the Northwest for its cross-country skiing. The **Methow Valley Sport Trails Association** (© **509/996-3287,** or for trail conditions and pass information 800/682-5787; www.mvsta.com) maintains approximately 125 miles of groomed ski trails, which makes this the second-most extensive groomed trail system in the country. Trail passes are $16 for 1 day, $12 for a half-day, or $36 for 3 days. Children ages 13 to 17 pay around half-price, and children 12 and under ski free. Snowshoe passes are also available ($3 per day). The greatest concentration of trails for all skill levels are in the vicinity of Sun Mountain Lodge, while the trails around Mazama offer plenty of easy miles for distance skiing. The Rendezvous area trails are long and strenuous, but have huts that can be rented for overnight stays. For information on renting one of these huts, contact **Rendezvous Huts** (℃ **800/257-2452,** 800/422-3048, or 509/996-2148; www.methow.com/huts). Rental rates start at $25 per person.

You can pick up trail maps and rent equipment at **Sun Mountain Lodge** (℃ **509/996-4735**); **Winthrop Mountain Sports,** 257 Riverside Ave. (℃ **800/719-3826** or 509/996-2886; www.winthropmountainsports.com), in downtown Winthrop; **Mazama Country Inn,** 15 Country Rd. (℃ **509/996-2681;** www.mazamacountryinn.com); or **Jack's Hut at the Freestone Inn,** 17798 Wash. 20 (℃ **509/996-2752**). All of these offer a variety of lessons or can point you in the right direction for instruction.

If you happen to be out here with downhill skis or maybe want to do a little tele-mark skiing, try the small ski hill at **Loup Loup Ski Bowl** (℃ **509/826-2720;** www.skitheloup.com), 20 minutes east of Twisp on Wash. 20. It's open Wednesday and Friday through Sunday, and daily lift passes are $30. Although this ski area is small, it does have a quad chairlift. Experienced downhill skiers in search of virgin powder can, if they can afford it, do some heli-skiing with **North Cascade Heli-Ski-ing** (℃ **800/494-HELI** or 509/996-3272; www.heli-ski.com). A day of skiing that includes five runs and 10,000 vertical feet of slopes will cost $795 per person. How-ever, most people coming here for heli-skiing opt for a 3-day package that includes room, board, and skiing for $2,550 to $2,835 per person (based on double occu-pancy). Overnight yurt tours are also available.

If you're interested in taking a backcountry skiing course, contact **North Cascades Mountain Guides,** 50 Lost River Rd., Mazama (℃ **509/996-3194;** www.ncmountain guides.com), which offers 2-day courses for $280 per person.

OTHER AREA ATTRACTIONS

Though Winthrop is primarily a base for skiers, hikers, and mountain bikers, it also has a few interesting shops. If you're interested in the town's history, visit the **Shafer Historical Museum,** Castle Avenue (℃ **509/996-2712**), which consists of a collec-tion of historic buildings from around the area. It's open Memorial Day to Labor Day, Thursday through Monday from 10am to 5pm. Admission is by donation. To find the museum, go up Bridge Street from the junction of Wash. 20 and Riverside Drive and turn right on Castle Avenue.

The Methow Valley may not be wine country, but it does have a good little winery that is worth searching out. **Lost River Winery,** 699 Lost River Rd., Mazama (℃ **509/996-2888**), is almost 7 miles up the valley from the Mazama Store and open for tastings from May through September, on Saturdays from 11am to 4pm. In win-ter, call for an appointment.

WHERE TO STAY

If you're interested in renting a cabin or vacation house, contact **Methow Valley Central Reservations** (℃ **800/422-3048** or 509/996-2148; www.methowreservations.com).

IN WINTHROP

Hotel Rio Vista 🐾   As with all the other buildings in downtown Winthrop, the Rio Vista looks as if it has been built for a Hollywood Western movie set. Behind the false front, you'll find modern rooms with pine furnishings and an understated country decor. Step out onto your balcony for a view of the confluence of the Chewuch and Methow rivers and you'll likely see deer and bald eagles and many other species of birds. A hot tub overlooks the river. The Rio Vista also rents out a loft cabin up the valley near Mazama.

285 Riverside Ave. (P.O. Box 815), Winthrop, WA 98862. © 800/398-0911 or 509/996-3535. www.hotelriovista.com. 29 units. $55–$140 double. MC, V. **Amenities:** Jacuzzi. *In room:* A/C, TV, dataport, fridge, coffeemaker, hair dryer, Wi-Fi.

River Run Inn ⋆ Only a few hundred yards from downtown Winthrop, this motel on the bank of the Methow River feels as if it is miles from town. Its rooms all have balconies overlooking the river, with the mountains visible across the valley. Rustic peeled-log furniture made by a local craftsman gives the large rooms a Western feel. Aside from the riverside location, the best reason to stay here is the small indoor swimming pool and hot tub. The River Run Inn also rents out cabins and a large house.

27 Rader Rd., Winthrop, WA 98862. © 800/757-2709 or 509/996-2173. www.riverrun-inn.com. 15 units. $70–$110 double; $130–$170 cabin; $340–$475 house. MC, V. Pets accepted ($10). **Amenities:** Indoor pool; Jacuzzi. *In room:* A/C, TV, fridge, coffeemaker, free local calls.

Sun Mountain Lodge ⋆⋆⋆ *(Kids)* If you're looking for resort luxuries and proximity to hiking, cross-country skiing, and mountain-biking trails, Sun Mountain Lodge should be your first choice in the region. Perched on a mountaintop with grand views of the Methow Valley and the North Cascades, this luxurious lodge captures the spirit of the West, both in its breathtaking setting and its rustic design. In the lobby, flagstone floors and stone fireplaces lend a classically Western style. Most guest rooms have rustic Western furnishings and views of the mountains. The rooms in the Gardiner wing have balconies and slightly better views than those in the main lodge. If seclusion is what you're after, opt for one of the Patterson Lake cabins. The lodge's main dining room serves superb Northwest cuisine amid views that will take your breath away (see "Where to Dine," below). The lounge has the same great view. In addition to amenities listed below, the resort also is right on the valley's ski-trail system and has a ski shop, ski and snowshoe rentals, a ski school, horseback and sleigh rides, an ice-skating pond, lawn games, and a playground.

604 Patterson Lake Rd. (P.O. Box 1000), Winthrop, WA 98862. © 800/572-0493 or 509/996-2211. Fax 509/996-3133. www.sunmountainlodge.com. 115 units. Mid-June to mid-Oct $185–$400 double, $350–$700 suite, $275–$700 cabin; mid-Oct to mid-June $150–$300 double, $250–$500 suite, $200–$500 cabin. Children 12 and under stay free in parent's room. AE, DC, MC, V. **Amenities:** 2 restaurants (Northwest, American); lounge; 2 outdoor pools; 4 tennis courts; exercise room; full-service spa; 2 Jacuzzis; boat rentals; bike rentals; children's programs; concierge; activities desk; room service; massage; babysitting. *In room:* A/C, coffeemaker, hair dryer, iron, Wi-Fi.

IN MAZAMA

Freestone Inn ⋆⋆⋆ At the upper end of the Methow Valley outside the community of Mazama, the Freestone Inn is second only to Sun Mountain Lodge in its luxury and many amenities. The inn's main building, which sits on the shore of a small lake with a superb view of the mountains, is a huge log lodge complete with a massive stone fireplace and cathedral ceiling. Guest rooms are thoughtfully designed with gas fireplaces and double whirlpool tubs that open to the bedroom so you can lie in the tub and still see the fireplace. All in all, these are some of the most memorable rooms in the state. For more privacy, opt for one of the cabins. Families may want to rent one of the large lakeside lodges. The restaurant is one of the finest in the valley (see "Where to Dine," below). In addition to amenities listed below, the inn also has cross-country ski rentals and lessons (ski trails are adjacent), sleigh rides, and a fly-fishing and swimming lake.

31 Early Winters Dr., Mazama, WA 98833. © 800/639-3809 or 509/996-3906. Fax 509/996-3907. www.freestone inn.com. 39 units. Summer $165–$265 double; $195–$295 suite; $165–$315 cabin; $275–$485 lodge; winter

$120–$190 double, $155–$245 suite, $125–$260 cabin, $250–$435 lodge. Lower rates in spring and fall. Children under 13 stay free in parent's room. AE, MC, V. Pets accepted in cabins ($30 per night). **Amenities:** Restaurant (Northwest); lounge; outdoor pool; 2 Jacuzzis; watersports rentals; bike rentals; children's programs; activities desk; massage. *In room:* A/C, TV/VCR, dataport, fridge, coffeemaker, hair dryer, iron, high-speed Internet access.

CAMPGROUNDS

Lone Fir ✱ (27 sites) is the first real campground below Washington Pass. Continuing eastward on Wash. 20, you come to **Klipchuck** (46 campsites) and **Early Winters** (12 campsites) campgrounds. There are also several campgrounds west of Early Winters on the Harts Pass Road. **Harts Pass** ✱ (5 campsites) and **Meadows** ✱ (14 campsites), a little bit farther on this rough road, are both at high elevations and provide access to the Pacific Crest Trail.

In the Winthrop area, **Pearrygin Lake State Park** ✱ (163 campsites) is a good choice if you're in need of a hot shower. For reservations, contact **Washington State Parks Reservations** (② 888/226-7688; www.camis.com/wa). For information on all other campgrounds, contact the Okanogan National Forest's **Methow Valley Visitor Center,** 49 Hwy. 20, Winthrop, WA 98862 (② 509/996-4000; www.fs.fed.us/r6/okanogan). For national forest campground reservations, contact the **National Recreation Reservation Service** (② 877/444-6777 or 518/885-3639; www.reserveusa.com).

WHERE TO DINE
IN THE WINTHROP & TWISP AREAS

Down valley from Winthrop, in the town of Twisp, you'll find great baked goodies at **Cinnamon Twisp Bakery,** 116 N. Glover St. (② 509/997-5030).

Sun Mountain Lodge ✱✱ NORTHWEST   Although most popular with guests at this mountaintop resort, the dining room offers the best meals and best views in the Winthrop area. Consequently, whether you stay here or not, your visit to the valley won't be complete without a meal here, preferably one when the sun is shining so you can enjoy the view. The menu changes regularly, but you might start with chicken-curry soup or a mushroom strudel. After this, you could move on to pork tenderloin with herbed spaetzle or halibut baked in parchment.

604 Patterson Lake Rd. ② **509/996-4707.** Reservations recommended. Main courses $24–$48 dinner. AE, DC, MC, V. Mon–Thurs 7–11am and 5:30–9pm; Fri–Sat 7–11am and 5:30–9:30pm; Sun 7am–noon and 5:30–9pm.

Topo Café PAN-ASIAN   If you've tired of the burgers and steaks that are the mainstays of most area restaurants, try this stylish little restaurant in an old house on Winthrop's main street. The food is simply prepared Asian dishes with an emphasis on noodles and rice bowls. In the summer, be sure to sit out back on the deck overlooking the Methow River.

253 Riverside Ave., Winthrop ② **509/996-4596.** Reservations accepted for parties of 6 or more. Main courses $8.50–$13. MC, V. Mon–Thurs 5–8pm; Fri–Sat 5–9pm.

Twisp River Pub ✱ PUB FOOD   Set on the banks of the Methow River at the west end of town, this big pub is a favorite hangout of locals, including families. Good beers and hard cider are made on the premises, and there's plenty of decent pub food, including good burgers and soups. In summer, there is live jazz on the deck overlooking the river, and the rest of the year, there's usually live music at least one night a week. If you come down here from Winthrop for dinner, be sure to keep an eye out for deer crossing the highway. You'll find the pub beside the bridge at the Winthrop end of town.

Wash. 20 ℭ **888/220-3360** or 509/997-6822. www.twispriverpub.com. Main courses $6–$18. AE, DISC, MC, V. Oct–Apr Wed–Sun 11:30am–9pm; May–Sept daily 11:30am–9 or 10pm.

Winthrop Brewing Company ℛ *finds* AMERICAN   In a tiny, wedge-shaped old schoolhouse in downtown Winthrop, this local watering hole is Winthrop's favorite gathering spot. The walls are covered with old rifles and business cards with lipstick prints. There's a deck out back overlooking the river and in summer, a beer garden. On Thursday and Friday nights, there's usually some kind of live music going on. The beers are some of the best (and most unusual) in the state, and the menu is typical pub fare—pizza, burgers, fish and chips, steaks, sandwiches, chicken, fish, and ribs.

155 Riverside Dr. ℭ **509/996-3183**. Main courses $7.50–$16. MC, V. Daily noon–10pm.

IN MAZAMA

For gourmet groceries, decent deli food, and espresso drinks, drop by the **Mazama Store,** 50 Lost River Rd. (ℭ **509/996-2855;** www.methow.com/mazamastore).

Freestone Inn Dining Room ℛℛ NORTHWEST   The Freestone Inn is one of the two luxury lodges in the valley and its restaurant is, not surprisingly, one of the two best restaurants. Located mainly in the lobby of the lodge, the dining room benefits from all the rustic styling that goes with the cathedral ceiling, while the menu is decidedly modern in focus. A recent menu included among the appetizers grilled Dungeness crab cakes with roasted beet chutney and citrus-ginger aioli. Main courses likewise include plenty of hearty, innovative dishes, such as pan-seared trout with a quinoa crust, and lemon-garlic roasted chicken breast with pear-fennel succotash salad.

31 Early Winters Dr. ℭ **800/639-3809** or 509/996-3906. Reservations recommended. Main courses $10–$34. AE, MC, V. Daily 7am–4pm and 5–9pm (closed mid-week in spring and fall).

3 Lake Chelan ℛ

166 miles E of Seattle, 37 miles N of Wenatchee, 59 miles S of Winthrop

Formed when a glacier-carved valley flooded, Lake Chelan is 1,500 feet deep, 55 miles long, and less than 2 miles wide in most places. This landlocked fjord is the third-deepest lake in the United States (reaching 400 ft. below sea level) and the longest natural lake in Washington. Only the southern 25 miles of the lake are accessible by road, yet at the northern end, the community of Stehekin (reachable only by boat, plane, or on foot) has managed to survive for more than 100 years, despite not being connected to the outside world by road. Plenty of summer sunshine, clear water, and blue skies have made the lake one of the top destinations in eastern Washington, and today the town of Chelan has the feel of a beach town, despite the rugged mountain views all around.

At the lake's southern end, apple orchards cover the foothills, while at the northern end, forests and rugged slopes are home to mountain goats and black bears and come down to the water's edge. The southern end of the lake is the domain of ski boats and personal watercraft, but at the northern, remote end—as idyllic a locale as you could wish for—you'll feel cut off from the outside world.

ESSENTIALS

GETTING THERE   Chelan is on U.S. 97, the main north-south highway in central Washington. From Seattle, take U.S. 2 to Wenatchee and then head north.

GETTING AROUND Although not very convenient for visitors, the Link bus system (© **509/662-1155**; www.linktransit.com) services the Lake Chelan, Wenatchee, and Leavenworth areas.

VISITOR INFORMATION For more information on this area, contact the **Lake Chelan Chamber of Commerce,** 102 E. Johnson St. (P.O. Box 216), Chelan, WA 98816 (© **800/4-CHELAN** or 509/682-3503; www.lakechelan.com). For information on Stehekin on the Web, check out **http://stehekinchoice.com,** which is the website of the community newspaper. This site has lots of information on things to do in Stehekin.

EXPLORING CHELAN & LOWER LAKE CHELAN

Downtown Chelan's **Riverwalk Park,** which stretches along both shores of the lake, has a 1-mile paved path and is a pleasant spot for a walk. The park is also home to the **Riverwalk Pavilion,** where outdoor concerts are sometimes held during the summer. Lake Chelan history is on display at the **Chelan Museum,** corner of Woodin and Emerson streets (© **509/682-5644**). June through September, the museum is open daily from 10am to 4pm; in other months, call for hours. Admission is $2 for adults and $1 for students and seniors.

Chelan has long been one of Washington's main apple-growing regions, but with low prices for apples in recent years, local farmers have been searching for other ways to make money. Many have now set up farmstands, while others have planted vineyards and are now making wine. In downtown Chelan, be sure to stop by **The Harvest Tree,** 109 E. Woodin Ave. (© **800/568-6062**; www.theapplestore.net), a shop dedicated almost exclusively to apples and apple products. At **Blueberry Hills Farms,** 1315 Washington St., Manson (© **509/687-BERY**; www.wildaboutberries.com), you can pick blueberries or sit down to a slice of pie.

WINE TOURING

Lately, Chelan has been Washington's fastest-growing wine region. Wineries and vineyards have been popping up faster than champagne corks on New Year's Eve. The following are my current favorite wineries in the area.

Benson Vineyards Estate Winery About midway between Chelan and Manson, this winery was in the process of building an impressive new tasting room and barrel-aging cave when I last visited. With the area's most established vineyards, this winery should produce plenty of estate wines in the years to come.

754 Winesap Ave., Manson. © **509/687-0313**. www.bensonvineyards.com. Summer daily noon–5pm (call for hours other months).

Big Pine Winery This little winery out on the west side of Manson is also worth searching out. It makes decent chardonnay, merlot, and cab-merlot blends.

280 Summit Blvd., Manson. © **509/687-0889**. www.bigpinewinery.com. Summer, daily noon–7pm (call for hours other months).

C.R. Sandidge Wines Right in downtown Chelan, this is the winery of Ray Sandidge, one of Washington's most respected winemakers. Syrahs get most of the attention here, but the winery also produces viognier and a cab-merlot blend.

137 E. Woodin Ave., Chelan. © **509/682-3704**. www.crsandidgewines.com. Mon–Sat 10am–8pm, Sun 11am–6pm.

Tildio Winery Situated in the hills above Manson, this small winery does a nice, oaky chardonnay, as well as viognier, zinfandel, and sangiovese. Although this winery is a bit out of the way, it's pretty reliable and worth searching out. Co-owner and wine-maker Katy Perry formerly made wine for Chateau Ste. Michelle Winery and Tsillan Winery.

70 E Wapato Lake Rd., Manson. (ℂ 509/687-8463. www.tildio.com. Summer, daily noon–7pm (call for hours in other months).

Tsillan Cellars   On the south shore of Lake Chelan, this is the area's most impres-sive winery, although it doesn't necessarily produce the most impressive wines. Built to resemble a Tuscan villa, the winery has a gorgeous view of the lake. During the sum-mer, concerts are held in the small amphitheater.

3875 U.S. 97A (ℂ 877/682-8463 or 509/682-9463. www.tsillancellars.com. Apr–Oct daily 10am–6pm; Nov–Mar 11am–5pm.

Vin du Lac/Chelan Wine Company   This winery on the north shore of the lake pro-duces a variety of very well balanced wines under the Vin du Lac label. This tasting room is in a little yellow house, set amid vineyards and orchards, and has a deli case selling arti-san cheeses from around the region. Sandwiches and light meals are also served here.

105 Wash. 150., Chelan. (ℂ 866/455-9463 or 509/682-2882. www.chelanwine.com. Apr–Oct daily 11am–6pm; Nov–Mar, daily 11am–5pm.

Wapato Point Cellars   Right in Manson on the grounds of a condominium devel-opment, this winery may not produce the most memorable wines in the area, but dou-bles as a wine bar/bistro that's one of the best places for a light meal.

200 Quetilquasoon Rd., Manson. (ℂ 509/687-4000. www.wapatopointcellars.com. Summer daily from 11am–9pm; other months Thurs–Sun noon–6pm.

UP THE LAKE TO STEHEKIN ✹✹

If you have time for only one activity while in the Lake Chelan area, it should be an all-day boat ride up the lake to Stehekin, a community accessible only by boat, float-plane, or hiking trail, and located within the Lake Chelan National Recreation Area of the North Cascades National Park Complex. This remote community has been a vacation destination for more than 100 years and is set amid rugged, glacier-clad mountains at the far north end of Lake Chelan.

The **Lake Chelan Boat Company** (ℂ **509/682-4584;** www.ladyofthelake.com), with its dock 1 mile west of downtown Chelan on South Shore Road (U.S. 97A), operates three passenger ferries—*Lady of the Lake II, Lady Express,* and *Lady Cat*—between Chelan and Stehekin. The trip encompasses some of the most spectacular scenery in the Northwest as you travel from gentle rolling foothills to deep within the rugged North Cascades mountains. Wildlife such as deer, mountain goats, and even bears are frequently seen from the boats.

The *Lady of the Lake II* takes 9½ hours for the round-trip (including a 90-min. lay-over) and charges $32 per person, while the *Lady Express* takes about 6 hours (including

---

Three Cherries in Apple Country

If you want to try recouping your vacation costs while you're in the area, stop by the **Mill Bay Casino**, 455 Wapato Lake Rd. (ℂ **800/648-2946**) in the town of Manson, which is on the north shore of the lake. The casino is operated by the Colville Confederated Tribes.

a 60-min. layover) and charges $51. The *Lady Cat,* the fastest of the three boats, makes the round-trip in only 4 hours (including a 90-min. layover) but costs $96. Children ages 2 to 11 pay half-fare, and children under age 2 ride free. Unless you plan to stay overnight, you won't have more than 90 minutes to look around Stehekin unless you book a combination ticket that allows you to go up on one of the boats, spend 3¼ to 7¼ hours in Stehekin, and return on another boat. These tickets are only available in summer.

If you want to get to Stehekin in a hurry, you can make the trip by floatplane on **Chelan Airways** (*©* **509/682-5555;** www.chelanairways.com), which leaves from the dock next to the ferries. The fare is $139 round-trip. This company also offers flight-seeing trips for between $49 and $199.

A variety of day trips are also operated in conjunction with the passenger ferries of the **Lake Chelan Boat Company** (*©* **509/682-4584;** www.ladyofthelake.com). Tours include the popular bus ride to 312-foot Rainbow Falls ($7 adults, $4 children ages 6–11, free for children under 6), and a combination picnic lunch and narrated bus trip up the valley ($20 adults, $10 children ages 6–11, $5 children under 6). Hiking and biking tours are available.

Although a road (paved for the first 4 miles) once led 23 miles up the Stehekin Valley to Cottonwood Campground, a flood in 1995 damaged much of the road toward the upper end of the valley and another flood in October 2003 did even more damage. Currently, the road is only open as far as High Bridge (10 miles up valley). Although only one shuttle bus was operating in summer 2005 due to the floods, transportation up the Stehekin Valley Road is usually provided by two different buses. The National Park Service's shuttle usually operates between mid-May and mid-October. Reservations for this bus should be made by calling the **Golden West Visitor Center** (*©* **360/856-5700,** ext. 340, then 14). Between late May and early October, another bus runs four times a day between Stehekin Landing and High Bridge. No reservations are required, and the cost is $5. If you just want to ride as far as the Stehekin Pastry Company, the fare is only $1.

A wide range of recreational activities can also be arranged in Stehekin through the **Courtney Log Office** (*©* **509/682-4677;** www.courtneycountry.com), 150 yards up the road from the boat landing. Horseback rides are offered through **Cascade Corrals** (*©* **509/682-7742**) at Stehekin Valley Ranch. A 2½-hour ride costs $43. Whitewater rafting trips on the Stehekin River are operated by **North Cascades Kayaking and Rafting** (*©* **509/679-6164;** www.stehekinguideservice.com) and cost $40 for adults and $30 for children 12 and under. Sea-kayak tours are also offered ($30 for adults; $20 for children). Mountain bikes can be rented for $20 per day from **Discovery Bikes** (no phone; stehekindiscoverybikes.com) at the Courtney Log Office. Discovery Bikes also does a very fun Ranch Breakfast Ride that includes a hearty breakfast at Stehekin Valley Ranch and then a bike ride down the valley.

Along the length of the Stehekin Valley, there are many miles of excellent hiking trails, ranging from easy strolls along the river to strenuous climbs high into the mountain wilderness surrounding the valley. Many of the valley's trailheads can be accessed from the bus that usually runs up the valley, which makes this an excellent place for doing a variety of day hikes over several days. There are also many longer trails originating here in Stehekin, which makes this a popular starting point for backpacking trips. For information on hiking trails and to pick up permits for overnight backpacking trips, stop by the **Golden West Visitor Center,** which is operated by the

---

> *Fun Fact* **Hang in There, Baby**
>
> Chelan is one of the nation's top hang-gliding and paragliding spots. Strong winds and thermals allow flyers to sail for 100 miles or more from the Chelan Sky Park atop Chelan Butte.

National Park Service and is near the boat landing. It's open daily between mid-March and mid-October. Fly-fishing on the Stehekin River is also very popular and usually very productive. In winter, there is good snowshoeing at Stehekin, and snowshoes can be rented from **North Cascades Stehekin Lodge** (© **509/682-4494**).

SPORTS & OUTDOOR ACTIVITIES IN THE LOWER LAKE AREA

FISHING   Fishing is one of the top recreational activities at Lake Chelan, and in this deep lake's clear waters, you'll find chinook and kokanee salmon, lake (mackinaw) trout, rainbow trout, smallmouth bass, and freshwater lingcod. Although there is bank fishing for stocked rainbows in the lower lake, most other fishing requires a boat. Up in Stehekin, there is good fly-fishing for native cutthroat and rainbow trout. If you want to make sure you come home from Lake Chelan with some good fish stories, get in touch with Terry Allan of **Allan's Fishing Guide Service** (© **509/687-3084;** www. fishlakechelan.com). In 2001, Allan twice helped clients catch state-record lake trout. Guided fishing trips cost $155 to $175 for a day of fishing.

GOLF   Right on the edge of town, golfers will find the municipal **Lake Chelan Golf Course,** 1501 Golf Course Dr. (© **800/246-5361** or 509/682-8026; www.lake chelangolf.com), where greens fees range from $31 to $35. However, anyone out this way with golf clubs is probably headed to **Desert Canyon Golf Resort,** 1201 Desert Canyon Blvd., Orondo (© **800/258-4173** or 509/784-1111; www.desertcanyon.com), just 17 miles south of Chelan and voted the best public course in Washington. Greens fees range from $55 to $99.

HIKING   Beyond the ends of the roads at the south end of Lake Chelan lie thousands of acres of unspoiled forests and many miles of hiking trails. Access to the trails is from trailheads at road ends or from flagstops along the route of the *Lady of the Lake II.* However, the best trails begin in the Stehekin area. For more information on hiking and biking opportunities, contact the **Chelan Ranger Station,** 428 W. Woodin Ave., Chelan, WA 98816-9724 (© **509/682-2576;** www.fs.fed.us/r6/wenatchee).

MOUNTAIN BIKING   During snow-free months of the year, the extensive network of cross-country ski trails at Echo Ridge becomes a mountain-bikers' playground. The area has 20 miles of dirt roads and trails that are open to mountain bikes. The trailhead for this trail system is just under 10 miles from downtown Chelan. Take the Manson Highway (Wash. 150) west to Boyd Road, turn right and follow signs for Echo Valley Ski Area. From the ski area, continue on Forest Service Road 1821-100. Mountain-bike rentals are available in Chelan from **Uncle Tim's Toys,** Lakeshore Marina Park, 619 W. Wash. 150 (© **509/670-8467;** www.uncletimstoys.com). Bikes rent for $20 for 2 hours. Rentals are also available at Echo Valley.

WATERSPORTS   Opportunities for aquatic activities abound on Lake Chelan. Good places to swim include **Lakeside Park** on the South Shore Road, **Don Morse Memorial Park** on the edge of downtown Chelan, and **Manson Bay Park** in Manson.

Lake Chelan State Park and **25-mile Creek State Park,** both on South Shore Road, offer swimming, picnicking, and camping.

You can rent powerboats and personal watercraft from **Shoreline Watercraft Rentals** (© **800/682-1561** or 509/682-1515) and **RSI Sports** (© **800/786-2637** or 509/669-4779). Expect to pay around $35 per hour or $165 per day.

If you've got the kids along, you'll find it impossible not to spend some time at **Slidewaters,** 102 Waterslide Dr. (© **509/682-5751;** www.slidewaters.com), which has eight waterslides, an inner-tube river ride, a 60-person hot tub, and a swimming pool. Admission is $16 for adults, $13 for children under 4 feet tall. You'll find this water park just outside town off the South Shore Road.

WHERE TO STAY
IN CHELAN

Best Western Lakeside Lodge 🎣 *Kids*   With lake views from most rooms, indoor and outdoor pools, a whirlpool, and a public park with a beach adjacent to the property, this comfortable motel on the south shore of the lake is a good choice, especially for families. The guest accommodations range from standard motel rooms to spacious suites with full kitchens. Some of the rooms also have VCRs, and all have balconies or patios. If you're up for a splurge, request one of the large suites, preferably one on the top floor—these have high ceilings.

2312 W. Woodin Ave., Chelan, WA 98816. © **800/468-2781** or 509/682-4396. Fax 509/682-3278. www.bestwestern. com. 99 units. Mid-June to early Sept $149–$199 double, $169–$299 suite; early Sept to mid-Oct and early May to mid-June $99–$149 double, $129–$169 suite; mid-Oct to early May $79–$99 double, $109–$159 suite. AE, DC, DISC, MC, V. Pets accepted ($10 per night). **Amenities:** Indoor and outdoor swimming pools; 2 Jacuzzis; coin-op laundry. *In room:* A/C, TV, fridge, coffeemaker.

Campbell's Resort on Lake Chelan 🎣🎣   The Campbell Hotel first opened in 1901 and has remained Chelan's most popular lodging. On the banks of the lake in downtown Chelan, Campbell's today has 1,200 feet of sandy beach and 8 acres of lawns, which you wouldn't guess by looking at it from the less-than-appealing street side of the resort. Most of the rooms have been updated in the past few years, and though the main building's deluxe rooms (with furnishings and styling to equal any Seattle luxury hotel) are still the best rooms, many other rooms are looking good these days, too. Fortunately, every room has a lake view, and many, including several cottages, have a kitchen or kitchenette. The dining room is in the original 1901 hotel, and has the most elegant dining in town. There's a pub upstairs from the restaurant and a poolside beach bar in summer.

104 W. Woodin Ave., Chelan, WA 98816. © **800/553-8225** or 509/682-2561. Fax 509/682-2177. www.campbells resort.com. 170 units. Mid-June to Aug $190–$252 double, $260–$398 suite, $226–$296 2-bedroom family unit. Lower rates off season. AE, MC, V. **Amenities:** 2 restaurants (American); lounge; 2 outdoor swimming pools; exercise room; day spa; 2 Jacuzzis; watersports equipment rentals; children's programs; business center; babysitting; coin-op laundry. *In room:* A/C, TV, dataport, coffeemaker, hair dryer, iron, Wi-Fi.

Fun Fact **Chelan Fish Stories**

Not all the big ones get away. In 2001, Lake Chelan twice set the state record for Mackinaw trout. On December 31, 2001, a 35.7-pound fish was reeled in. Four months earlier, a state-record 33.65-pound fish was caught.

IN STEHEKIN

If you're heading up to Stehekin and plan to do cooking during your stay, bring your own food. Only limited groceries are available here.

North Cascades Stehekin Lodge ☆   Right at Stehekin Landing, the North Cascades Lodge is not fancy or luxurious, but is shaded by tall conifers and overlooks the lake. The variety of accommodations ranges from basic rooms with no lake view to large apartments. The studio apartments have kitchens and are the best deal, all with lake views. Between May and mid-October, the lodge's restaurant serves three meals a day; the rest of the year, three meals are served on weekends and lunch on weekdays. Snowshoe rentals are available in winter.

P.O. Box 457, Chelan, WA 98816. ℂ 509/682-4494. Fax 509/682-5872. www.stehekin.com. 28 units. Memorial Day weekend and June 15–Oct 15 $99–$146 double; Oct 16–June 14, excluding Memorial Day weekend $79–$126 double. Children under 6 stay free in parent's room. DISC, MC, V. **Amenities:** Restaurant (American); watersports rentals; bike rentals; activities desk; coin-op laundry. *In room:* No phone.

Silver Bay Inn & Resort ☆☆   Situated on the banks of both the lake and the Stehekin River, Silver Bay rents out two cabins and a house. The views are superb, and should you stay in the Lake View House, a spacious Northwest contemporary home on the banks of both the river and the lake, you'll find antiques, a big sunroom, and a deck with a view of the river. This house also has a separate room with a river view (the least expensive of accommodations). Be sure to bring your own food to cook. Bicycles, rowboats, and canoes for guests are free of charge, and allow you to explore the lake and the Stehekin environs.

10 Silver Bay Rd. (Box 85), Stehekin, WA 98852. ℂ 509/687-3142. www.silverbayinn.com. 4 units. $135–$295 double or cabin for 4. Lower rates off season. Minimum stay 2 nights (5 nights for cabins in summer). Children over 12 are welcome. MC, V. Pets accepted in off season ($10 per night). **Amenities:** Jacuzzi; watersports equipment; bikes; massage; laundry service. *In room:* Kitchen, fridge, coffeemaker, hair dryer, Wi-Fi, no phone.

Stehekin Valley Ranch ☆ *Kids*   If you're a camper at heart, then the tent cabins at the Stehekin Valley Ranch should be just fine. With canvas roofs, screen windows, and no electricity or plumbing, these "cabins" are little more than permanent tents. Bathroom facilities are in the nearby main building. For slightly more comfortable accommodations, opt for one of the permanent cabins. Activities available at additional cost include horseback riding, river rafting, sea kayaking, and mountain biking. The ranch is accessible by ferry or floatplane to Stehekin Landing; from there, you're taken 9 miles up the valley to the ranch in a Stehekin Valley Ranch shuttle bus.

P.O. Box 36, Stehekin, WA 98852. ℂ 800/536-0745 or 509/682-4677. www.courtneycountry.com. 12 units. Tent cabins $65–$75 per adult per night, $45–$55 per child 4–12, $5–$15 per child 1–3; cabins $75–$85 per adult, $55–$65 per child 4–12, $10–$20 per child 1–3. Rates include all meals and transportation in lower valley. MC, V by phone only for reservations. Closed mid-Oct to mid-June. **Amenities:** Restaurant (American); activities desk. *In room:* No phone.

CAMPGROUNDS

On Lake Chelan, there are two state park campgrounds at the southern end of the lake—**Lake Chelan State Park** (144 campsites) and **Twenty-Five Mile Creek State Park** (67 campsites)—both of which are crowded and noisy. At the north end of the lake, along the Stehekin Valley Road, there are 11 campgrounds, most of which are served by the shuttle bus from Stehekin. **Purple Point** ☆ (six campsites) is right in Stehekin and most convenient to the boat landing.

For reservations at the two state parks, contact **Washington State Parks Reservations** (ℂ 888/226-7688; www.camis.com/wa). For information on campgrounds in the Stehekin Valley, contact the **Golden West Visitor Center** (© **360/856-5700,** ext. 340, then 14; www.nps.gov/noca). For national forest campground reservations, contact the **National Recreation Reservation Service** (© **877/444-6777** or 518/885-3639; www.reserveusa.com).

WHERE TO DINE
IN CHELAN

If you're looking for a good cup of coffee, try **The Vogue,** 117 E. Woodin Ave. (© **509/888-5282**) in downtown Chelan. This espresso bar also sells local wines. For light lunches, don't miss the patio at **Vin du Lac/Chelan Wine Company,** 105 Wash. 150, Chelan (© **866/455-9463** or 509/682-2882); it's the prettiest spot in Chelan for a meal and also has the best view. For light, early dinners, head to **Wapato Point Cellars,** 200 Quetilquasoon Rd., Manson (© **509/687-4000**).

The Campbell House Café ☆ AMERICAN   Housed in the original 1901 Campbell Hotel, this is one of only two upscale restaurants in Chelan, and as such, stays pretty busy in the summer months. While the menu is not overly creative, it has more imaginative offerings than most places in town. The steaks and prime rib are your best bets. If you prefer burgers to scallops flamed with brandy, then you're better off upstairs at the casual pub, which serves inexpensive steaks and decent pub fare to go with its Northwest microbrews and single-malt Scotches.

104 W. Woodin Ave. © 509/682-4250. Main courses $12–$28. AE, DISC, MC, V. Mon–Fri 6:45–11am, 11:30am–1:30pm, and 5–9pm; Sat 6:45am–1pm and 5–9pm; Sun 6:45am–1pm and 5–8:30pm. Reduced hours in winter.

Capers ☆ CONTINENTAL   In a nondescript building in downtown Chelan, Capers may not boast a great location, but it does serve the best food in town. Crisp white linens may seem a bit out of place in this central Washington summer-vacation town, but sometimes a bit of formality adds a nice touch to an otherwise casual vacation. The menu includes a wide range of traditional favorites, including vichyssoise, filet mignon with a merlot-and-mushroom sauce, chateaubriand for two, and rock Cornish game hens. However, you'll also find some interesting, and very recommendable, game dishes such as pheasant-hazelnut-and-cognac sausage, rabbit in wine, and loin of venison. Just don't eat so much that you don't have room for the delicious pear poached in pinot noir.

127 E. Johnson St. © 509/682-1611. Reservations recommended. Main courses $18–$29. AE, DISC, MC, V. July–Sept Wed–Mon 6–9pm, Fri–Sat 5–10pm; Oct–June Thurs–Sun 5–8pm.

IN STEHEKIN

The dining options in Stehekin are slim, and if you plan to stay in a cabin or camp out, be sure to bring all the food you'll need. Otherwise, simple meals are available at **North Cascades Stehekin Lodge** (© **509/682-4494**), which is right at the ferry landing in Stehekin. Note that during the winter, the restaurant here is open for three meals a day only on weekends; weekdays, only lunch is available. When you just must have something sweet, you're in luck; the **Stehekin Pastry Company** (© **509/682-4677**), just 2 miles up valley from the boat landing, serves pastries and ice cream, as well as pizza and espresso.

4 Bavarian Leavenworth ☆☆ & the Wenatchee Valley

108 miles E of Everett, 22 miles W of Wenatchee, 58 miles SW of Chelan

You're out for a Sunday drive through the mountains, just enjoying the views, maybe doing a bit of hiking or cross-country skiing, when you come around a bend and find yourself in the Bavarian Alps. Folks in lederhosen and dirndls dance in the streets, a polka band plays the old oompah-pah, and all the buildings look like alpine chalets. Have you entered the Twilight Zone? No, it's just Leavenworth, Washington's Bavarian village.

Many an unsuspecting traveler has had this experience, but if you read about this town before your visit, you'll be prepared for the sight of a Bavarian village transported to the middle of the Washington Cascades. Whether you think it's the most romantic town in the state, a great place to go shopping, the perfect base for hiking and skiing, or just another example of *über*-kitsch, there's no denying that Leavenworth makes an impression.

ESSENTIALS

GETTING THERE   From I-5, take U.S. 2 from Everett, or if you're coming from the south, take I-405 to Bothell and then head northeast to Monroe, where you pick up U.S. 2 heading east. From U.S. 97, the main north-south route along the east side of the Cascades in the central part of the state, head west on U.S. 2. Wenatchee is at the junction of U.S. 2 and U.S. 97. Wash. 28 connects Wenatchee to the eastern part of the state.

Wenatchee's **Pangborn Memorial Airport** (© **509/884-2494;** www.pangborn airport.com) is served by **Horizon Air** from Seattle. Amtrak trains stop in Wenatchee en route between Spokane and Seattle.

VISITOR INFORMATION   For more information on this area, contact the **Leavenworth Chamber of Commerce & Visitor Center,** P.O. Box 327, Leavenworth, WA 98826 (© **509/548-5807;** www.leavenworth.org), or, when you're in town, drop by the Visitor Center, 220 Ninth St., inside the Obertal Mall. For more information on the Wenatchee area, contact the **Wenatchee Valley Convention & Visitors Bureau,** 25 N. Wenatchee Ave., Suite C111, Wenatchee, WA 98801 (© **800/572-7753** or 509/663-3723; www.wenatcheevalley.org).

GETTING AROUND   Car rentals are available in Wenatchee from Hertz and Budget. Although it is not very convenient for exploring this area, the Link bus system (© **509/662-1155;** www.linktransit.com) services the Leavenworth, Wenatchee, and Lake Chelan areas.

FESTIVALS   During the annual **Maifest** (mid-May) and **Washington State Autumn Leaf Festival** (late Sept), Leavenworth rolls out the barrel and takes to the streets and parks with polka bands, Bavarian dancing, and plenty of crafts vendors. In June, more music hits town with the **Leavenworth International Accordion Celebration** (www.accordioncelebration.com). In mid-September, the **Wenatchee River Salmon Festival** celebrates the return of salmon to the river, and in October there's **Oktoberfest.** In December, the whole town gets lit up in perhaps the most impressive **Christmas Lighting Festival** in the Northwest. Nearby Wenatchee celebrates its apples each year with the **Washington State Apple Blossom Festival,** with more than a week of festivities in late April and early May.

EXPLORING LEAVENWORTH

Leavenworth's main attraction is the town itself. Back in the early 1960s, this was just another mountain town struggling to get by on a limited economy. Sure, the valley was beautiful, but beauty wasn't enough to bring in the bucks. A few years after a motel with alpine architecture opened in town, Leavenworth decided to give itself a complete makeover. Today nearly every commercial building in town, from the gas station to the Safeway, looks as if it were built by Bavarian gnomes. What may come as a surprise is that they did a good job! Stroll around town and you'll convince yourself that you've just had the world's cheapest trip to the Alps. People here even speak German.

Anytime of year, the town's most popular tourist activity seems to be shopping for genuine Bavarian souvenirs in the many gift shops—you'll find cuckoo clocks, Hummel figurines, imported lace, and nutcrackers. In fact, if nutcrackers are your passion, don't miss the **Leavenworth Nutcracker Museum,** 735 Front St. (© **800/892-3989** or 509/548-4573; www.nutcrackermuseum.com), which has more than 4,000 nutcrackers of all shapes and sizes. The museum is open May through October, daily from 2 to 5pm, and November through April on weekends only. Admission is $2.50 for adults and $1 for children ages 6 to 17. The **Upper Valley Museum,** 347 Division St. (© **509/548-0728**), in a beautiful historic home, is a work in progress. When finally completed, it will showcase the history of the valley. Currently, the grounds are open to the public, and some small exhibits are in the old house. From May through October, the museum is open Friday through Sunday from noon to 6pm; the rest of the year, it closes at 4pm.

Classical music fans should be sure to see what's happening at the **Icicle Creek Music Center** ⚑ (© **877/265-6026** or 509/548-6347; www.icicle.org), which is at the Sleeping Lady resort and has programs throughout the year. There are also many musical performances and festivals in the small Front Street Park in downtown Leavenworth, where a large gazebo serves as a bandstand. If you're looking for something to do on a Friday night, drop by the **Community Coffeehouse,** Chumstick Grange Hall, 621 Front St. (© **509/548-7374**; www.leavenworthcoffeehouse.com), which has live acoustic music ranging from Celtic to contemporary to classical.

Downtown Leavenworth has seen an explosion of winery tasting rooms in the past few years. You can now wander from one tasting room to the next and sample wines from all over the state. At the tasting room of **Kestrel Vintners,** 843B Front St. (© **509/548-7348**), you can sample from one of my favorite little Yakima Valley wineries. It is open Sunday through Thursday from 11am to 5pm and Friday and Saturday from 11am to 6pm. At the **Leavenworth Tasting Room,** 939 Front St. (© **509/548-5166**), on the second floor of the Masterpiece Gallery, you can taste a sample from another of my favorite wineries—Willow Crest Winery—and Pasek Cellars, which is known for its fruit wines. The room is open daily from 11am to 6pm. **Silver Lake Winery,** 715A Front St. (© **509/548-5788**; www.silverlakewinery.com), also has a tasting room in Leavenworth where you can sample both Silver Lake and Glen Fiona wines. It's open daily 11am to 5pm (Jan–May, closed Tues–Wed). **Bavarian Cellars/Maison de Padgett Winery,** 208 Ninth St. (© **509/548-7717**), is open Wednesday through Monday from noon to 6pm and boasts the most unusual wine labels in the state. A few blocks west of downtown, you'll find **Gold Digger Cellars,** 285 U.S. 2 (© **509/548-9883**; www.golddiggercellars.com), with its winery up near the Canada border near the town of Oroville. This tasting room is open Sunday through Thursday from 11am to 6pm and Friday and Saturday from 11am to 8pm.

EXPLORING THE LOWER WENATCHEE VALLEY

As you drive east down the Wenatchee Valley from Leavenworth, you begin to see the valley's many apple and pear orchards. In summer and fall, you can taste the fruits of the valley at farmstands along U.S. 2. **Smallwood's Harvest** (© 509/548-4196; www. smallwoodsharvest.com), and **Prey's Fruit Barn** (© 509/548-5771; www.preysfruit barn.com) are the biggest and best farmstands along this stretch of road. Because apple prices have been so low in recent years, some orchards have planted vineyards, and wineries are proliferating in the area.

Eagle Creek Winery & Cottage, 10037 Eagle Creek Rd. (© 509/548-7668; www.eaglecreekwinery.com), is one of the closest wineries to Leavenworth, located off Chumstick Highway about 5 miles from town. May through October, the tasting room is open Saturday and Sunday from noon to 4pm; other months by appointment. Heading farther down the valley, you'll come to **Icicle Ridge Winery,** 8977 North Rd., Peshastin (© 509/548-7019; www.icicleridgewinery.com), with tasting rooms in a log cabin at a pear orchard, and also in downtown Leavenworth at 821 Front St., Suite B; both are open daily from noon to 5pm. In summer, the winery hosts jazz concerts. In Peshastin, you'll find **Wedge Mountain Winery,** 9534 Saunders Rd., Peshastin (© 509/548-7068; www.wedgemountainwinery.com), which specializes in bordeaux varietals. The tasting room is open Thursday to Monday from 10am to 6pm. For more information on area wineries, contact **Columbia Cascade Wine & Wineries** (© 509/782-0708; www.columbiacascadewines.com).

CASHMERE: AN EARLY AMERICAN TOWN

Just west of Wenatchee, you'll find the town of **Cashmere,** which has adopted an Early American theme. The town's main attraction is the **Aplets & Cotlets Candy Factory and Country Store,** 117 Mission Ave. (© 800/231-3242 or 509/782-2191; www. libertyorchards.com), where you can tour the kitchens that produce these unusual fruit-and-nut confections. Between April and December, the factory and store are open Monday through Friday from 8am to 5:30pm and Saturday and Sunday from 10am to 4pm; between January and March, they're open Monday through Friday from 8:30am to 4:30pm.

For a different sort of sweet treat, don't miss **Anjou Bakery,** 3898 Old Monitor Rd. (© 509/782-4360), just off U.S. 2 in the middle of a pear orchard on the outskirts of Cashmere. The ovens here produce great pastries and rustic breads.

Also worth a visit in Cashmere is the **Chelan County Historical Society Pioneer Village and Museum,** 600 Cotlets Way (© 509/782-3230; www.cashmeremuseum.com). Nearly 20 old log buildings have been assembled here and are filled with period antiques. Inside the main museum building, you'll find exhibits on the early Native American cultures of the region, pioneer history, and natural history. The museum is open from March 1 to October 31, daily from 9:30am to 4:30pm, and November 1 through December 21, Friday through Sunday from 10:30am to 3:30pm. Admission is $4.50 for adults, $3.50 for seniors and students ages 13 to 18, and $2.50 for children ages 5 to 12.

WENATCHEE

More apple-industry displays are part of the focus of the **Wenatchee Valley Museum & Cultural Center,** 127 S. Mission St. (© 509/664-3340; wenatcheevalleymuseum. com), but there are also interesting exhibits on local Native American cultures and the first transpacific flight. Model-railroading buffs will enjoy the HO-scale Great Northern Railway. The museum also hosts lectures, traveling exhibitions, and concerts, and at some concerts, the museum's 1919 Wurlitzer organ is played. It's open Tuesday through Saturday from 10am to 4pm. Admission is $3 for adults, $2 for seniors, and $1 for children ages 6 to 12.

An Apple a Day

Apples are the single largest agricultural industry in Washington—in fact, more than 50% of the fresh apples sold in the United States come from Washington. The combination of warm, sunny days and abundant irrigation water from both the Columbia and Wenatchee rivers have made Wenatchee the center of this apple-growing region.

Though it's only a dozen or so miles from the lush forests of the Cascades, Wenatchee is on the edge of central Washington's arid shrub-steppe region. To bring a bit of the mountains' greenery into this high desert, Herman Ohme and his family spent 60 years creating **Ohme Gardens** ★★, 3327 Ohme Rd., Wenatchee (© **509/ 662-5785;** www.ohmegardens.com), a lush alpine garden covering 9 cliff-top acres north of Wenatchee. The gardens wind along the top of a rocky outcropping that overlooks the Wenatchee Valley, Columbia River, and Cascade peaks. Rock gardens, meadows, fern grottoes, and waterfalls lend a naturalistic feel similar to that of a Japanese garden. The gardens are open from April 15 to October 15, daily from 9am to 6pm (until 7pm in summer). Admission is $7 for adults, $3.50 for children ages 6 to 17.

North of Wenatchee on the north side of the town of Entiat, watch for the **Columbia Breaks Fire Interpretive Center** (© **509/662-3035;** www.wildfirecenter.org), which has two old fire lookouts and the .5-mile Trail of Fire and Forest that explains the role of fires in western forests.

OUTDOOR ACTIVITIES: FROM GOLF TO WHITEWATER RAFTING

If your interests tend more toward hiking than to Hummel figurines, you'll find plenty to do around Leavenworth. The town is on the valley floor at the confluence of the Wenatchee River and Icicle Creek, and rising all around are the steep, forested mountainsides of the Stuart Range and Entiat Mountains. Spring through fall, there is rafting, hiking, mountain biking, and horseback riding, and, in winter, there is downhill and cross-country skiing and snowmobiling.

Just 25 miles north of town is **Lake Wenatchee,** a year-round recreation area with hiking and cross-country ski trails, horseback riding, canoe rentals, windsurfing, swimming, fishing, mountain biking, camping, and snowmobiling. **Lake Wenatchee State Park** (© **509/763-3101**) is the center of recreational activity.

If you need to rent some gear, contact **Leavenworth Mountain Sports,** 940 U.S. 2 (© **509/548-7864;** www.leavenworthmtnsports.com), which rents cross-country skis, snowshoes, and whitewater kayaks.

FISHING   Icicle Creek, which runs through Leavenworth, has a short summer salmon season for fish headed upstream to the Leavenworth Fish Hatchery. Lake Wenatchee is 5 miles long, the area's biggest lake, and it holds kokanee, as well as Dolly Varden and rainbows. To fish for kokanee, you'll need a boat. Several of the rivers and streams in the Leavenworth area are open to fly-fishing only.

GOLF   Golfers can play 18 holes at the **Leavenworth Golf Club,** 9101 Icicle Rd. (© **509/548-7267;** www.leavenworthgolf.com), which charges $25 to $30 for a round of golf and is located on the outskirts of town, or north of Leavenworth near Lake Wenatchee at **Kahler Glen Golf Course,** 20700 Clubhouse Dr. (© **509/763-4025;** www.kahlerglen.com), which charges $25 to $36 for 18 holes. However, the

Highlander Golf Club, 2920 Eighth St. SE, East Wenatchee (© **509/884-4653;** www.highlandergolfclub.com), with its Scottish links styling and awesome big-sky views, is the hottest course in the region these days. Greens fees range from $49 to $54 for 18 holes. If you want to practice your putting, check out the **Enzian Falls Championship Putting Course** (© **509/548-5269;** www.enzianfalls.com), located across from the Enzian Inn. It's a beautiful, bent-grass 18-hole putting course (not a tacky miniature golf course).

HIKING   Right in town, you'll find a pleasant paved walking path in **Waterfront Park.** Out at the **fish hatchery** on Icicle Road, there is also a mile-long interpretive trail with information on the hatchery. In winter, both of these areas have cross-country ski trails. Past the fish hatchery, up Icicle Canyon Road about 15 miles, you'll find the **Icicle Gorge River Trail,** an easy 4-mile loop trail along the banks of beautiful Icicle Creek. This is the prettiest easy hike in the area. Don't miss it. The trailhead is just past the Chatter Creek Ranger Station. In Tumwater Canyon, the narrow gorge that serves as a gateway to Leavenworth as you approach from the west, an easy hiking trail is along the Wenatchee River banks.

Just outside Leavenworth, in the **Alpine Lakes Wilderness** ⚘⚘⚘, lies some of the most spectacular mountain scenery in the state, and the trails that lead into this wilderness are among the most popular. They're so popular, in fact, that backpackers must reserve camping permits months in advance to stay overnight in such heavily visited areas as the Enchantment Lakes basin. Most of the trails in the area are best suited for overnight trips because they climb steeply and steadily for many miles before reaching the more scenic areas. For information on hiking trails in Wenatchee National Forest, contact the Leavenworth office of the **Wenatchee River Ranger Station,** 600 Sherbourne St., Leavenworth, WA 98826 (© **509/548-6977;** www.fs.fed.us/r6/wenatchee). Reservations for backpacking permits are accepted starting March 1; to apply, call the ranger station or visit its website. Permits go fast, so do apply early.

HORSEBACK RIDING   If you'd like to go horseback riding, contact **Eagle Creek Ranch** (© **800/221-7433** or 509/548-7798; www.eaglecreek.ws), which charges $26 for a 1½-hour ride and $39 for a 2-hour ride. Wagon rides are also available and cost $15 for adults, $7.50 for children ages 3 to 12. **Icicle Outfitters & Guides** (© **800/497-3912** or 509/669-1518 in Leavenworth or 509/763-3647 at Lake Wenatchee; www.icicleoutfitters.com), offers a similar variety of rides, with stables at Lake Wenatchee State Park and in Leavenworth on Icicle Road near the fish hatchery. A 1½-hour ride will cost you $37.

MOUNTAIN BIKING   From easy rides on meandering dirt roads to grueling climbs up mountaintops with spectacular views, the Leavenworth area has some of the best mountain-biking routes in the state. Mountain bikes can be rented at **Der Sportsmann,** 837 Front St. (© **800/548-4145** or 509/548-5623; www.dersportsmann.com), and **Das Rad Haus,** 1207 Front St. (© **509/548-5615;** www.dasradhaus.com). Expect to pay $30 to $40 per day for a mountain bike. Inquire at either of these shops about ride recommendations.

ROCK CLIMBING   Two miles west of Cashmere on U.S. 2, you'll find **Peshastin Pinnacles State Park,** Washington's only state park created exclusively for rock climbing. The **Snow Creek Wall,** about a mile up the trail to the Enchantment Lakes area, is another great climbing spot. The trailhead is located about 4 miles up Icicle Creek Road. Over on the west side of Stevens Pass, the **Index Town Walls** outside the tiny community of Index are the area's other great climbing site. For climbing gear and advice, stop by **Leavenworth Mountain Sports,** 940 Wash. 2 (© **509/548-7874;** www.eavenworthmtnsports.com).

WHITEWATER RAFTING & TUBING   The Wenatchee River flows right through Leavenworth and, just downstream from town, becomes one of the best whitewater-rafting rivers in the state. Rafting season runs from April to July. If you're interested, contact **Osprey Rafting Co.** (© **888/548-6850** or 509/548-6800; www. shoottherapids.com), or **River Riders** (© **800/448-7238** or 206/448-7238; www. riverrider.com). A half-day trip on the Wenatchee costs about $50 per person, and a full day is $65 to $75.

When there isn't enough water for rafting, a couple of local companies rent out big inner tubes and will shuttle you to or from the river. **Tube Leavenworth,** 321 Ninth St., Suite 102 (© **509/548-TUBE;** www.tubeleavenworth.com) charges $15 while **River Tubers,** 10866 U.S. 2 (© **800/448-RAFT;** www.rivertubers.com), charges $10. This latter company is located a couple of miles east of town. Either way, you get your money's worth and have loads of fun. Keep an eye out for trout in the river.

WINTER SPORTS   Some of the best downhill skiing and snowboarding in the state is available 40 miles west of Leavenworth at **Stevens Pass** 🦶🦶 (© **206/812-4510** for general information, or 206/634-1645 for snow conditions; www.stevens pass.com). Adult all-day lift tickets are $46 and night skiing is $28. There are plenty of intermediate and advanced runs, but not many beginner runs.

Head down the valley from Leavenworth and then up into the hills outside Wenatchee, and you'll find **Mission Ridge** ski area 🦶🦶 (© **509/663-3200** for snow reports, or 509/663-6543; www.missionridge.com), known for its powder snow (a rarity in the Cascades) and sunny weather. Adult lift ticket prices are $40.

Cross-country skiers can find plenty of groomed trails in the area. **Stevens Pass Nordic Center** (© **360/812-4510;** www.stevenspass.com/nordic) has mostly inter-mediate- and expert-level trails. These trails are open Friday through Sunday and on holidays, and a trail pass costs $15 for adults. The **Leavenworth Winter Sports Club** (© **509/548-5477;** www.skileavenworth.com) maintains 15 miles of groomed trails (including 3 miles of lighted trails for night skiing) at several locations around Leav-enworth. A trail pass runs $10 per day. This ski club also operates the beginner-level **Leavenworth Ski Hill,** a mile outside of town. Although small, this little ski hill does have a ski-jumping facility.

Skis can be rented at **Der Sportsmann,** 837 Front St. (© **800/548-4145** or 509/548-5623; www.dersportsmann.com), which charges $14 to $22 per day for cross-country skis and $25 for snowboards. Snowshoes ($12 per day) can also be rented. Rental equipment is also available at **Leavenworth Mountain Sports,** 940 U.S. 2 (© **509/548-7864;** www.leavenworthmtnsports.com).

If you'd rather experience the snow from a horse-drawn sleigh, you can do that, too. Sleigh rides are offered by **Red-Tail Canyon Farm,** 11780 Freund Canyon Rd., Leav-enworth (© **800/678-4512** or 509/548-4512; www.redtailcanyonfarm.com); and **Eagle Creek Ranch,** Eagle Creek Road (© **800/221-7433** or 509/548-7798; www. eaglecreek.ws). Rides cost about $15 for adults, and $7.50 for children.

WHERE TO STAY

EXPENSIVE

Mountain Home Lodge ✯✯   Set 2½ miles up a very steep, narrow road that is only paved in its lower stretch, this mountain lodge is surrounded by a 20-acre meadow and has a spectacular view of the craggy Stuart Range. In winter, the road up here is not plowed and guests are brought to the lodge by Snowcat. At that time of year, 40 miles of cross-country ski trails are the main attraction (cross-country skis and snowshoes are provided), but there are also guided snowmobile tours. In summer, hiking and mountain biking are the big draws. Guest rooms vary in size and each is individually decorated with themes that reflect the area's activities. However, The Hide Away, atop the lodge, is the best room in the house (excluding the suite). During the summer, when rates include only breakfast, gourmet lunches ($15) and dinners ($45) are available.

8201 Mountain Home Rd. (P.O. Box 687), Leavenworth, WA 98826. ✆ 800/414-2378 or 509/548-7077. Fax 509/548-5008. www.mthome.com. 12 units. Summer $110–$170 double, $230 suite, $350 cabin; winter $270–$355 double, $375 suite, $455 cabin. Summer rates include full breakfast; winter rates include 3 meals daily. 2-night minimum weekends and winter; 3-night minimum holidays. DISC, MC, V. **Amenities:** Restaurant (American); outdoor pool; tennis court; Jacuzzi; bike rentals; concierge; business center; room service; massage. *In room:* A/C, TV/VCR, minibar, coffeemaker, hair dryer, iron, high-speed Internet access, Wi-Fi.

Sleeping Lady ✯✯✯   Although primarily a conference resort, Sleeping Lady (the name comes from a nearby mountain) is one of the best-designed mountain retreats in the state. Set amid ponderosa pines and granite boulders, the small resort with red-roofed cabins looks much like the summer camp it once was. Guest rooms are done in a rustic contemporary style, abound in natural wood, and have high ceilings with exposed beams. The grounds, including a meadow on the bank of Icicle Creek, are beautifully landscaped and a delight to wander. Meals include produce from the resort's large organic vegetable garden, and throughout the year, classical music performances and plays are staged. The boulder-lined swimming pool is one of the most memorable pools in the state.

7375 Icicle Rd., Leavenworth, WA 98826. ✆ 800/574-2123 or 509/548-6344. Fax 509/548-6312. www.sleepinglady.com. 58 units. $280–$285 double. Rates include 3 meals. Children 4 and under stay free in parent's room. AE, DISC, MC, V. **Amenities:** 2 restaurants (Northwest, Deli); lounge; outdoor pool; exercise room; Jacuzzi; sauna; bike rentals; massage; coin-op laundry. *In room:* A/C, dataport, coffeemaker, hair dryer, free local calls.

MODERATE

Abendblume Inn ✯✯ *Value*   This alpine chalet, complete with flower boxes overflowing with blossoms, is a luxurious and romantic B&B overlooking Leavenworth and the surrounding mountains. From the hand-carved front door to the wrought-iron stair railing, an eye for detail is apparent throughout the inn. The large rooms with balconies overlooking the valley are the ones to book. In these, you'll find fireplaces, VCRs, and wonderfully luxurious beds and linens, but the bathrooms are the real attractions. Our favorite has a triangular tub for two, a pair of sinks, and heated marble floors. Nowhere in Leavenworth is there a more romantic room. Guests also have use of both indoor and outdoor spas.

12570 Ranger Rd. (P.O. Box 981), Leavenworth, WA 98826. ✆ 800/669-7634 or 509/548-4059. Fax 509/548-4059. www.abendblume.com. 7 units. $118–$225 double. Rates include full breakfast. AE, DISC, MC, V. Children under 12 not accepted. **Amenities:** 2 Jacuzzis; access to nearby health club; bikes; concierge; massage. *In room:* A/C, TV/VCR, coffeemaker, hair dryer, iron, safe, free local calls, high-speed Internet access, Wi-Fi.

Blackbird Lodge   Right in downtown Leavenworth overlooking the Wenatchee River, this hotel feels like a country inn, though it's within walking distance of the town's shops and restaurants. The exterior is Bavarian chalet, while the lobby has a mountain-lodge decor, with a slate floor and dark, woodsy touches. This styling alone sets the Blackbird apart from other moderately priced lodgings in town. The guest rooms are large, but otherwise standard motel-style rooms. However, the suites are both spacious and quite attractive; some have fireplaces or whirlpool tubs or both. The lodge also rents out a cottage.

305 Eighth St., Leavenworth, WA 98826. ✆ **800/446-0240** or 509/548-5800. www.blackbirdlodge.com. 21 units. $90–$120 double; $120–$225 suite. Lower midweek rates mid-Jan to mid-June. Rates include full breakfast. Children 12 and under stay free in parent's room. AE, DISC, MC, V. Pets accepted in cottage ($10). **Amenities:** Access to nearby health club; concierge; massage. *In room:* A/C, TV, free local calls.

Run of the River Inn & Refuge   Tranquil, luxurious, rustic, sophisticated—you simply won't find a more idyllic B&B anywhere in Washington. This contemporary log inn is set on 3 acres at a bend of Icicle Creek and has spectacular mountain views. With its hand-hewn log roof beams, rustic peeled-log furniture, and exposed stones, the inn has a timeless, mountain-lodge feel. All the accommodations are large suites, with special touches that make a stay unforgettable. There are fireplaces and double whirlpool tubs, balconies overlooking the river, and porch swings for quiet moments. Walking sticks, day packs, and picnic hampers are always ready for a day's outing, and the innkeepers provide tips on where to go and what to do in the area. With an emphasis on nature and outdoor recreation, this is the ideal base for exploring the nearby mountains.

9308 E. Leavenworth Rd. (P.O. Box 285), Leavenworth, WA 98826. ✆ **800/288-6491** or 509/548-7171. www.run oftheriver.com. 7 units. $205–$245 double. 2-night minimum May–Oct and Dec 1–20, and weekends throughout the year; 3-night minimum Dec 20–Jan 4 and 3-day weekends. DISC, MC, V. Children under 18 not encouraged. **Amenities:** Jacuzzi; bikes; concierge; massage. *In room:* A/C, TV/VCR, fridge, coffeemaker, hair dryer, iron, free local calls, high-speed Internet access, Wi-Fi.

INEXPENSIVE

Hotel Pension Anna   Though the guest rooms in the Pension Anna's main building are attractively appointed with pine furniture, including a four-poster bed in the honeymoon suite, the annex building contains the inn's two most outstanding rooms. This annex is a renovated church built in 1913 (and later moved to this site), and the Old Chapel Suite is a grand space that includes part of the old choir loft (now a sleeping loft). Ceilings 15 feet high give the room an expansive feel, and in the bedroom, you'll find an ornately carved headboard framed by draperies that reach to the ceiling. Though considerably smaller, the Parish Nook Room has an ornate king-size bed, marble-top bedside stands, and the original arched windows. Only slightly more expensive than a regular room, the Parish Nook is the inn's best deal.

926 Commercial St., Leavenworth, WA 98826. ✆ **800/509-ANNA** or 509/548-6273. Fax 509/548-4656. www.pension anna.com. 16 units. $89–$139 double; $179–$239 suite. Rates include full breakfast. Children under 6 stay free in parent's room. AE, DISC, MC, V. **Amenities:** Access to nearby health club; baby sitting. *In room:* A/C, TV, hair dryer, iron, free local calls, Wi-Fi.

CAMPGROUNDS

Tumwater (84 campsites) is the biggest campground in the Leavenworth area, yet is always full on summer weekends. Up Icicle Road on the west side of Leavenworth, there are seven campgrounds.

Lake Wenatchee is one of the most popular summer camping destinations in the state and there are lots of choices in the area. If you want creature comforts, such as hot showers, stay at **Lake Wenatchee State Park** (197 campsites), which is at the south end of the lake. This campground has a sandy beach and a great view up the lake. Farther up the south shore of the lake, the Forest Service's **Glacier View Campground** (23 campsites) provides a similar lakeside atmosphere with walk-in campsites. Right outside the entrance to the state park, you'll find the **Nason Creek Campground** (73 campsites), which has some nice sites right on this large creek. Northwest of Lake Wenatchee, there are several campgrounds along both the White River and the Little Wenatchee River.

For reservations at Lake Wenatchee State Park, contact **Washington State Parks Reservations** (© 888/226-7688; www.camis.com/wa). For information on all other campgrounds, contact the **Wenatchee River Ranger Station,** 600 Sherbourne St., Leavenworth, WA 98826 (© 509/548-6977; www.fs.fed.us/r6/wenatchee), or the ranger districts **Lake Wenatchee office,** 22976 Wash. 207, Leavenworth, WA 98826 (© 509/763-3103; www.fs.fed.us/r6/wenatchee). For national forest campground reservations, contact the **National Recreation Reservation Service** (© 877/444-6777 or 518/885-3639; www.reserveusa.com).

WHERE TO DINE
IN LEAVENWORTH

For delectable baked goods, drop by the **Homefires Bakery,** 13013 Bayne Rd. (© 509/548-7362; www.homefiresbakery.com), which is housed in an old log cabin off Icicle Road near the fish hatchery. For tasty crepes and cakes, check out **Pavz,** 833 Front St. (© 509/548-2103). If you're craving a good espresso, head to the Chevron station. That's right, Chevron, as in gas station. Here you'll find **Village Mercantile,** 920 U.S. 2 (© 509/548-7714), which not only serves the best lattes in town, but also is a great little gift shop that sells local wines.

Andreas Keller   GERMAN   Down in a *keller* (cellar) opposite the gazebo on Front Street, you'll find one of Leavenworth's true German experiences. From the waitresses shouting across the restaurant in German to the accordionist who plays in the evening and on weekend afternoons, everything about this place is Bavarian. Take a seat and you'll be surrounded by *Gemütlichkeit*. Rotisseried chicken and wursts are the staples here, washed down with Bavarian beer. Be sure to get something with the wine kraut; it's delicious (so is the German potato salad). It's casual and fun enough that even the kids will enjoy a meal here.

829 Front St. © 509/548-6000. www.andreaskellerrestaurant.com. Reservations recommended. Main courses $8–$17. MC, V. Sun–Thurs 11am–9pm; Fri–Sat 11am–10pm (may close earlier in off season).

Tips **Leavenworth's Polka Spot**

If you happen to find yourself in Leavenworth on one of those rare weekends when there is no festival going on, you can still take in some polka music at **King Ludwig's Restaurant,** 921 Front St. (© 360/548-6625; www.kingludwigs.com), which features live Bavarian music on Friday and Saturday nights.

Cafe Mozart Restaurant ☆☆ GERMAN/CONTINENTAL   Upstairs from the ever-popular Andreas Keller, this restaurant serves upscale German food, as well as French and American favorites, in a refined atmosphere. The cold-smoked Norwegian salmon and Dungeness crab cakes make good non-German starters. Follow this with Wiener schnitzel or Munich-style sauerbraten for a gourmet German meal. Mozart is played on the stereo, and on Friday and Saturday nights, there's live harp music.

829 Front St. ☎ 509/548-0600. www.cafemozartrestaurant.com. Reservations recommended. Main courses $9–$14 lunch, $15–$35 dinner. AE, MC, V. Mon–Sat 11:30am–2:30pm and 4:30–9pm; Sun 9am–noon and 4:30–9pm (Nov–May closed for lunch Mon–Thurs).

Visconti's of Leavenworth ☆☆ ITALIAN   If you think wurst is the best you can do in Leavenworth, think again. This classy Italian restaurant currently serves the best food in Leavenworth. For a totally Tuscan experience, try the panzanella (bread salad) followed by an 18-ounce rib-eye *bistecca*. The lemon chicken, spit roasted over apple wood, is another good bet. To start things out, be sure to have the pancetta-wrapped prawns. There's also a wine bar that's a great place to hang out if you aren't into hefting steins of hefeweizen.

636 Front St. ☎ 509/548-1213. Reservations recommended. Main courses $13–$33. AE, DISC, MC, V. Sun–Thurs 11am–9pm; Fri–Sat 11am–10pm.

5 The Snoqualmie Pass Route ☆☆

Snoqualmie Pass: 50 miles E of Seattle, 53 miles W of Ellensburg

While Seattle has become a sprawling city of congested highways and high housing prices, there is a reason so many put up with such drawbacks. Less than an hour east of the city lie mountains, so vast and rugged that you could hike for a week without ever crossing a road. In winter, The Summit at Snoqualmie Pass ski area is so close to the city that people head up after work for a bit of night skiing.

Between the city and this wilderness lies the Snoqualmie Valley, the Seattle region's last bit of bucolic countryside. Here you'll find small towns, pastures full of spotted cows, U-pick farms, and even a few unexpected attractions, including an impressive waterfall and, in summer, a medieval fair. While driving the back roads of the Snoqualmie Valley, keep an eye out for historic markers with old photos and details about the valley's past.

ESSENTIALS

GETTING THERE   Snoqualmie Pass is on I-90 between Seattle and Ellensburg.

VISITOR INFORMATION   For more information on the area, contact the **Snoqualmie Pass Visitor Center** (☎ 425/434-6111), just off I-90 at Snoqualmie Pass and operated by the National Forest Service. Information is also available through the **Cle Elum/Roslyn Chamber of Commerce,** 401 W. First St., Cle Elum, WA 98922 (☎ 509/674-5958; www.cleelumroslyn.org).

EXPLORING THE SNOQUALMIE VALLEY

Snoqualmie Falls ☆☆, the valley's biggest attraction, plummets 270 feet into a pool of deep blue water. The falls are surrounded by a park owned by Puget Power, which operates a hydroelectric plant inside the rock wall behind the falls. The plant, built in 1898, was the world's first underground electricity-generating facility. Within the park, you'll find two overlooks near the lip of the falls and a half-mile trail down to the base of the cascade. The river below the waterfall is popular both for fishing and for whitewater kayaking. This waterfall will be familiar to anyone who remembers the opening sequence of David Lynch's television series *Twin Peaks,* which was filmed in this area. To reach the falls, take I-90 east from Seattle for 35 to 45 minutes and get off at exit 27. If you're hungry for lunch, try the restaurant at **Salish Lodge,** the hotel at the top of the falls.

Snoqualmie Falls is located just outside the town of **Snoqualmie,** which is where you'll find the restored 1890 railroad depot that houses the **Northwest Railway Museum,** 38625 SE King St. (© **425/888-3030;** www.trainmuseum.org). The museum, an absolute must for anyone with a child who is familiar with Thomas the Tank Engine, operates the **Snoqualmie Valley Railroad** on weekends from April through October. The 65- to 75-minute railway excursions, using steam or diesel trains, run between here and the town of **North Bend.** Fares are $9 for adults, $8 for seniors, and $6 for children ages 2 to 12. Be sure to call ahead for a current schedule. The museum displays railroad memorabilia and has a large display of rolling stock. It's a big hit with kids!

Between Fall City and the town of **Carnation,** you'll pass several U-pick farms, where you can pick your own berries during the summer or pumpkins in the fall.

The Snoqualmie Valley is also the site of **Camlann Medieval Village,** 10320 Kelly Rd. NE (© **425/788-8624;** www.camlann.org), located north of Carnation off Wash. 203. On weekends between late July and late August, this reproduction medieval village stages the Camlann Medieval Faire and becomes home to knights and squires and assorted other costumed merrymakers. There are crafts stalls, food booths, and—the highlight each day—jousting matches. Medieval clothing is available for rent if you forgot to pack yours. Throughout the year, the village stages a wide variety of banquets, seasonal festivals, and weekend living-history demonstrations. Its Bors Hede restaurant is open Tuesday through Sunday for traditional dinners ($19 per person). Fair admission is $9 for adults and $6 for seniors and children ages 6 to 12. Admission to both the fair and a banquet is $40.

Thirty miles to the east of Snoqualmie Pass, you'll find the remote town of **Roslyn,** which was just a quietly decaying old coal-mining town until television turned it into Cicely, Alaska, for the hit TV show *Northern Exposure.* Although Cicely is but a fading memory now, visitors still wander up and down the town's 2-block-long main street soaking up the mining-town atmosphere. To learn more about the town's history, drop by the **Roslyn Museum,** 203 Pennsylvania Ave. (© **509/649-2776**). About the only other activity is wandering through the town's 25 cemeteries up the hill from the museum. These cemeteries contain the graves of miners who lived and died in Roslyn.

SPORTS & OUTDOOR ACTIVITIES
HIKING   Outside of North Bend rises **Mount Si,** one of the most frequently climbed mountains in the state. This mountain, carved by glaciers long ago, rises abruptly from the floor of the valley outside North Bend and presents a dramatic face to the valley. If you are the least bit athletic, it's hard to resist the temptation to hike to the summit, where awesome views are the payoff. Be forewarned, however, that it's a strenuous 8-mile round-trip hike, and you'll need to carry lots of water. To reach the trailhead, drive east of downtown North Bend on North Bend Way, turn left on Mount Si Road, turn right after crossing the Snoqualmie River, and continue another 2 miles.

Farther east on I-90, at Snoqualmie Pass and before you reach the pass, there are several trailheads. Some trails lead to mountain summits, others to glacier-carved lakes, and still others past waterfalls deep in the forest. Due to their proximity to Seattle, these trails can be very crowded, and you'll need a Northwest Forest Pass in order to park at national forest trailheads. Passes are available at the ranger station in North Bend. A Northwest Forest Pass is not necessary for parking at the Mount Si trailhead, which is on state land. For more information, contact the **North Bend Ranger District,** 42404 SE North Bend Way, North Bend, WA 98045 (© **425/888-1421;** www. fs.fed.us/r6/mbs).

HORSEBACK RIDING   If you're interested in spending a few hours or a few days in the saddle, contact **High Country Outfitters** (© **888/235-0111** or 509/674-4903; www.highcountry-outfitters.com), which charges about $90 for a day ride. Overnight and multi-day trips are also available.

MOUNTAIN BIKING   Iron Horse State Park/John Wayne Pioneer Trail, a railroad right-of-way that has been converted to a gravel path stretching more than 110 miles, provides one of the most unusual mountain-biking routes in the Northwest. The trail passes under Snoqualmie Pass by way of the 2½-mile-long Snoqualmie Tunnel, which is usually open to bicycles from May through October. To ride the tunnel, you'll need good lights, warm clothes, and rain gear (water constantly drips from the ceiling of the tunnel). To access the trail from the west side, take exit 38 off I-90. From the east side, take exit 62 off I-90.

SKIING   While much of the terrain is not very interesting and the snow can be frustratingly unreliable due to winter rains, **The Summit at Snoqualmie** (© **425/434-7669** or 206/236-7277 for information, or 206/236-1600 for the snow report; www. summit-at-snoqualmie.com) is the closest ski area to Seattle and consequently sees a lot of business both on weekends and for after-work night skiing. There are four ski areas (Alpental, Summit West, Summit Central, and Summit East) and 65 runs here. Rentals and lessons are available. Adult all-day lift tickets are $42. Call for hours of operation.

At Snoqualmie Pass, there are many miles of both groomed and ungroomed cross-country ski trails. **Summit Nordic Center** (© **425/434-7669** or 206/236-7277; www.summitatsnoqualmie.com/winter/nordic.html) offers rentals, instruction, and miles of groomed trails.

There are also several Sno-Parks (designated cross-country ski areas) along I-90 at Snoqualmie Pass. Some have groomed trails; others have trails that are marked, but not groomed. Be sure to get a **Sno-Park permit** ($8–$9 for a 1-day pass; $20–$21 for a season pass), which is required if you want to park at a cross-country ski area. Sno-Park permits are available at ski shops; pick one up when renting your skis.

In winter, **Bee Line Tours** (© **800/959-8387** or 206/632-5162; www.beeline tours.com) provides bus service from Seattle area hotels to The Summit at Snoqualmie ski area. Round-trip fare is $35.

WHERE TO STAY
ON THE WEST SIDE
Salish Lodge & Spa ★★★   Set at the top of 270-foot Snoqualmie Falls and only 30 minutes east of Seattle on I-90, the Salish Lodge & Spa is a popular weekend getaway spot for Seattle residents. With its country-lodge atmosphere, the Salish aims for

casual comfort and hits the mark, though the emphasis is clearly on luxury. Guest rooms, which are designed for romantic weekend escapes, have wood-burning fireplaces, oversize whirlpool tubs, feather beds, and down comforters. To make this an even more attractive getaway, there's the full-service spa. The lodge's country breakfast is a legendary feast that will keep you full right through to dinner, and at night you can choose from one of the most extensive lists of Washington wines at any restaurant in the state. By the way, if you were a fan of the TV show *Twin Peaks,* you'll immediately recognize this hotel.

6501 Railroad Ave. SE (P.O. Box 1109), Snoqualmie, WA 98065-1109. © **800/272-5474** or 425/888-2556. Fax 425/888-2420. www.salishlodge.com. 91 units. $209–$419 double; $499–$699 suite. Resort fee $15 extra. Children under 18 stay free in parent's room. AE, DC, DISC, MC, V. **Amenities:** 3 restaurants (Northwest, bistro, cafe); lounge with view of the falls; exercise room; access to nearby health club; full-service spa with Jacuzzis and saunas; bike rentals; activities desk; business center; room service; massage; laundry service; dry cleaning. *In room:* A/C, TV, dataport, minibar, coffeemaker, hair dryer, iron, safe, Wi-Fi.

ON THE EAST SIDE

Iron Horse Inn ✶   Railroad buffs won't want to miss an opportunity to stay at this restored Chicago, Milwaukee, St. Paul, and Pacific Railroad bunkhouse. The inn is filled with railroading memorabilia and each of the guest rooms is named for a railroad worker who once lived here. The rooms vary in size and are simply furnished with antiques. However, the most popular rooms here are the four cabooses on short lengths of track beside the inn. Two of the cabooses will sleep families with two or three kids.

526 Marie Ave. (P.O. Box 629), South Cle Elum, WA 98943. © **800/22-TWAIN** or 509/674-5939. www.ironhorse innbb.com. 10 units, 6 with private bathroom. $80 double with shared bathroom; $95–$105 double with private bathroom; $135 suite or caboose. Rates include full breakfast. Children under 2 stay free in parent's room. MC, V. **Amenities:** Jacuzzi. *In room:* No phone.

Prospector Inn at Suncadia ✶✶   Designed to conjure up an old mining building, this little lodge is the first of the accommodations to open in a huge new masterplanned resort community at the eastern end of Snoqualmie Pass. This lodge is just a glimpse of things to come and seems to be primarily a teaser for potential new-home and condo buyers. Still, the setting in the east side pine forests is pretty enough, although a bit out of the way for outdoors enthusiasts planning on hiking or skiing. The golf course is the main attraction here, so despite the woodsy setting, this is more golf resort than mountain lodge. Guest rooms are named for local mines. Most overlook the golf course and all have balconies and gas fireplaces.

P.O. Box 887, Roslyn, WA 98941. © **866/904-6300.** Fax 509/649-6420. www.prospectoratsuncadia.com. 18 units. Rates $245–$275 double; $325 suite. AE, DISC, MC, V. **Amenities:** 2 restaurants (American); lounge; 18-hole golf course; tour desk; business center; in-room spa services available. *In room:* A/C, TV, dataport, minibar, coffeemaker, hair dryer, iron, high-speed Internet access.

CAMPGROUNDS

Kachess Campground (120 campsites), near the north end of Kachess Lake, is the biggest campground in the area. Powerboating and fishing are the most popular activities here, but there are also some nearby trailheads providing access to the Alpine Lakes Wilderness. The Cle Elum Lake area offers the I-90 corridor's greatest concentration of campgrounds including **Wish Poosh** (34 campsites), **Cle Elum River** (23 campsites), **Red Mountain** (10 campsites), and **Salmon la Sac** (99 campsites), which is this area's biggest and busiest campground.

For information on campgrounds in this area, contact the **Snoqualmie Pass Visitor Center** (© 425/434-6111), just off I-90 at the pass. For national forest campground reservations, contact the **National Recreation Reservation Service** (© 877/444-6777 or 518/885-3639; www.reserveusa.com).

WHERE TO DINE
IN THE SNOQUALMIE VALLEY
The dining room at the **Salish Lodge** (see above) is by far the best restaurant on the west side of Snoqualmie Pass.

DINING & NIGHTLIFE IN ROSLYN
If you're heading to the hills and want to pack some great jerky, stop by **Carek's Custom Market** , 510 S. A St., Roslyn (© 509/649-2930). For nightlife or a simple meal, don't miss **The Brick Bar & Grill**, 1 Pennsylvania Ave., Roslyn (© 509/649-2643), which claims to be the oldest operating saloon in Washington and has a unique flowing-water spittoon under the bar. This place is an absolute classic. If it's good microbrews that you crave, wander up the street to the **Roslyn Brewery,** 208 Pennsylvania Ave. (© 509/649-2232), a more modern place. It's open Friday and Saturday from 1 to 7pm and Sunday from noon to 6pm.

6 Mount Rainier National Park ⋆⋆⋆ & Environs

Paradise: 110 miles SE of Seattle, 70 miles SE of Tacoma, 150 miles NE of Portland, 85 miles NW of Yakima

At 14,410 feet high, Mount Rainier is the tallest mountain in Washington, and to the sun-starved residents of Seattle and south Puget Sound, the dormant volcano is a giant weather gauge. When the skies clear over Puget Sound, the phrase "The mountain is out" is often heard around the region. And when the mountain is out, all eyes turn to admire its broad slopes.

Those slopes remain snow-covered throughout the year due to the region's infamous moisture-laden air, which has made Mount Rainier one of the snowiest spots in the country. In 1972, the mountain set a record when 93½ feet of snow fell in 1 year (and that record held until Washington's Mount Baker received 95 ft. in the winter of 1998–99). Such record snowfalls have created numerous glaciers on the mountain's flanks, and one of these, the Carbon Glacier, is the lowest-elevation glacier in the continental United States.

Snow and glaciers notwithstanding, Rainier has a heart of fire. Steam vents at the mountain's summit are evidence that, though this volcanic peak has been dormant for more than 150 years, it could erupt again at any time. However, scientists believe that Rainier's volcanic activity occurs in 3,000-year cycles—and luckily, it's another 500 years before there's another big eruption.

Known to Native Americans as Tahoma, Mount Rainier received its current name in 1792 when British explorer Capt. George Vancouver named the mountain for a friend (who never even visited the region). The first ascent to the mountain's summit was made in 1870 by Gen. Hazard Stevens and Philemon Van Trump, and it was 14 years later that James Longmire built the first hotel on the mountain's flanks. In 1899, Mount Rainier became the fifth national park.

ESSENTIALS
GETTING THERE   If you're coming from Seattle and your destination is Paradise (the park's most popular area), head for the southwest (Nisqually) park entrance. Take

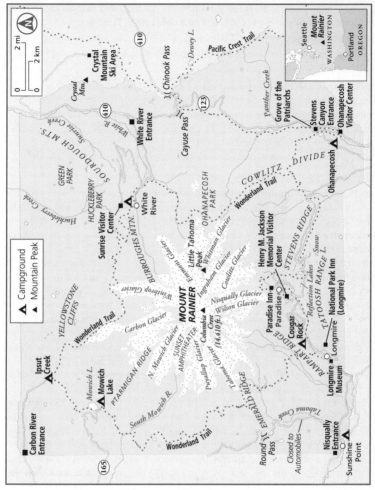

I-5 south to exit 127 and then head east on Wash. 512. Take the Wash. 7 exit and head south toward Elbe. At Elbe, continue east on Wash. 706.

If you're coming from Seattle and are heading for the northeast (White River) park entrance en route to Sunrise or Crystal Mountain, take I-90 to I-405 south. At Renton, take Wash. 169 south to Enumclaw, then pick up Wash. 410 heading east. Note that in winter, only the road from the Nisqually entrance to Paradise is open.

From the south, head north on I-5 to exit 68 and then take U.S. 12 east to the town of Morton. From Morton, head north on Wash. 7 to Elbe and then turn east on Wash. 706, which will bring you to the Nisqually (southwest) park entrance.

If you don't have a car, but still want to visit Mount Rainier National Park, book a tour through **Mt. Rainier Tours** (© **888/293-1404** or 206/768-1234; www.mt rainiertours.com), which charges $73 for adults and $49 for children ages 3 to 12 for a 10-hour tour. These tours spend most of that time in transit, but you get to see the mountain up close and do a couple of hours of hiking at Paradise.

VISITOR INFORMATION   For more park information, contact **Mount Rainier National Park,** Tahoma Woods, Star Route, Ashford, WA 98304-9751 (© **360/569-2211,** ext 3314; www.nps.gov/mora).

PARK ADMISSION   The park entrance fee is $10 per vehicle. Another option, if you plan to visit several national parks in a single year, is the National Parks Pass or the Golden Eagle Passport, an annual pass good at all national parks and recreation areas. The pass costs $50 (plus $15 for the Golden Eagle upgrade) and is available at all national park visitor centers. If you're over 62, you can get a Golden Age Passport for $10, and if you have a disability, you can get a free Golden Access Passport.

SEEING THE HIGHLIGHTS

Just past the **main southwest entrance (Nisqually),** is Longmire, site of the National Park Inn, the Longmire Museum (with exhibits on the park's natural and human history), a hiker information center that issues backcountry permits, and a ski-touring center that rents cross-country skis and snowshoes in winter.

The road then climbs to **Paradise** (elevation 5,400 ft.), the aptly named mountainside aerie that affords a breathtaking close-up view of the mountain. Paradise is the park's most popular destination, so expect crowds. During July and August, the meadows are ablaze with wildflowers. The circular **Henry M. Jackson Memorial Visitor Center** provides 360-degree panoramic views, and a short walk away is a spot from which you can look down on Nisqually Glacier. Many miles of other trails lead out from Paradise, looping through meadows and onto snowfields above the timberline. It's not unusual to find plenty of snow at Paradise as late as July. In 1972, the area set a world's record for snowfall in 1 year: 93½ feet! This record held until the 1998–99 winter season, during which La Niña climatic conditions produced a record-breaking 94 feet of snowfall on Mount Baker, which is north of Mount Rainier.

In summer, you can continue beyond Paradise to the **Ohanapecosh Visitor Center** (© **360/569-6046**), open daily from late June through September. Not far from this visitor center, you can walk through the **Grove of the Patriarchs** (see "Hiking & Backpacking," below). Continue around the mountain to reach the turnoff for Sunrise.

Driving counterclockwise around the mountain, you'll come to Cayuse Pass. A short detour from this pass will bring you to the picturesque **Chinook Pass** area, where there is a good 4.5-mile day-hike loop trail that begins at Tipsoo Lake and circles Naches Peak.

Continuing around the mountain, you'll come to the turnoff for the park's **White River entrance.** This road leads to some of the park's best day hikes, and a spur road leads to the White River Campground. At 6,400 feet, **Sunrise** is the highest spot in the park accessible by car. A beautiful old log lodge serves as the **Sunrise Visitor Center,** open daily from late June through mid-September. From here, you get a superb view of Mount Rainier, seemingly at arm's length, and **Emmons Glacier,** the largest glacier in the 48 contiguous states. From Sunrise, you can see Mount Baker to the north and Mount Adams to the south. Some of the park's most scenic trails begin at Sunrise, providing lots of options for day hikes.

If you want to see a bit of dense forest or hike without crowds, head for the park's **Carbon River entrance** in the northwest corner. This is the least visited region of the park because it only offers views to those willing to hike several miles uphill. About 3 miles up the trail, you'll come face to face with the Carbon River Glacier, which is the lowest-elevation glacier in the contiguous 48 states. At its lower end, this glacier plows through dense rainforest, an ominous and unforgettable sight. Continuing up this trail another 2 miles (following the glacier for much of the way) will bring you to beautiful wildflower meadows and close-up views of the northwest flank of Mount Rainier. The road into this area is in very bad shape. High-clearance vehicles are recommended.

OUTDOOR ACTIVITIES IN & NEAR THE NATIONAL PARK

After a long day of taking advantage of the park's outdoor activities, you may like to soak in a hot tub or get a massage. Contact the little woodland spa called **Wellspring** (© 360/569-2514) in Ashford, not far from the Nisqually park entrance. An hour in the hot tub costs $10 per person, while an hour massage costs $65. Alternatively, you can soak in a hot tub and get a massage, wrap, or body polish at nearby **Stormking,** 37311 Wash. 706 E., Ashford (© 360/569-2964; www.stormkingspa.com). Both places have cabins available for overnight guests.

HIKING & BACKPACKING   Hikers have more than 240 miles of trails to explore within the park, though the vast majority of park visitors do their hiking at only two places—Paradise and Sunrise. However, despite the crowds, these two alpine areas do offer the most scenic day-hiking opportunities.

At **Paradise** ★★, the 5-mile **Skyline Trail** ★★★ is the highest trail and climbs through beautiful meadows above the tree line. Unfortunately, the meadows, among the park's most beautiful, have been heavily damaged by hikers' boots over the past century, and now there are signs everywhere telling hikers to stay on the trails. Along the route of this trail are views of Mount Adams, Mount St. Helens, and the Nisqually Glacier. The **Lakes Trail,** of similar length, heads downhill to the Reflection Lakes, which have picture-perfect views of the mountain reflected in their waters. However, be forewarned that these lakes lie right alongside the road through the park, and are very popular with people who park by the roadside and get out of their cars for a brief stroll by the lakes.

At **Sunrise** ★★★ there are also numerous trails of varying lengths. Among these, the 5-mile **Burroughs Mountain Trail** and the 5.5-mile **Mount Fremont Trail** are both very rewarding—the latter even provides a chance to see mountain goats. The **Summerland Trail,** which starts 3 miles from the White River park entrance (the road to Sunrise), is another very popular day hike. This trail starts in forest and climbs 2,000 feet up into meadows with a great view of the mountain.

If you'd rather avoid most of the crowds, try the 2.5-mile round-trip trail to **Snow Lake,** which is set at the foot of Unicorn Peak. This trail involves only a few hundred feet of elevation gain. You'll find the trailhead between Paradise and Ohanapecosh. For a longer day hike, try the 11-mile round-trip hike to **Indian Henry's Hunting Ground,** which involves more than 2,000 feet of elevation gain. This trail starts from the Kautz Creek turnout east of Longmire. In 1947, a huge mudflow swept down Kautz Creek and buried the road here under 30 feet of mud. Up in the northwest corner of the park, the 6-mile round-trip trail from Mowich Lake to **Spray Park** is another breathtaking route that starts in the forest and climbs a little more than 2,000 feet into beautiful alpine meadows.

The park's single most memorable low-elevation hike is the **Grove of the Patriarchs Trail** ★★. This 1.5-mile round-trip trail is fairly flat (good for kids) and leads through a forest of huge old trees to a grove of 1,000-year-old red cedars on an island in the Ohanapecosh River. The trailhead for this hike is near the Stevens Canyon park entrance (southeast entrance).

Another interesting and easy, low-elevation walk is the **Trail of the Shadows,** a .75-mile loop trail in Longmire. This trail, which circles a wet meadow, leads past bubbling mineral springs.

There are also naturalist-led programs and walks throughout the spring, summer, and fall, and on winter weekends, there are guided snowshoe walks. Check the park newspaper for schedules.

The 95-mile-long **Wonderland Trail** 🎯🎯, which circles the mountain, is the quintessential Mount Rainier backpacking trip. This trail takes 10 days to 2 weeks to complete and offers spectacular scenery. However, there are also many shorter overnight hikes. Before heading out on any overnight backpacking trip, you'll need to pick up a permit at the Longmire Wilderness Information Center (© **360/569-4453;** fax 360/569-3131), the White River Wilderness Information Center (© **360/569-6030**), or the Wilkeson Wilderness Information Center (© **360/569-6020**) in the town of Wilkeson on the road to the Carbon River entrance to the park. For stays between May through September, reservations for backcountry campsites can be made beginning on March 15 (although reservation requests are not processed until Apr 1). Backcountry reservations cost $20 per party and can be made only by mail or fax.

MOUNTAINEERING Among climbers, Mount Rainier has a reputation as a training ground for making attempts on higher peaks, such as Mount Everest. If you're interested in taking a mountain-climbing class, contact **Rainier Mountaineering,** P.O. Box Q, Ashford, WA 98304 (© **888/892-5462** or 360/569-2227; www.rmi guides.com), which operates inside Mount Rainier National Park and offers 1-day classes for $165, 3-day summit climbs for $795, and a 5-day mountaineering seminar for $1,195.

WHITEWATER RAFTING The Tieton River, which flows down the eastern slopes of the Cascades to the east of the national park, is one of the state's most popular rafting rivers. However, the rafting season lasts for only about 3 weeks during the annual September drawdown of water from Rimrock Reservoir. Rafting companies with trips on this river include **Alpine Adventures** (© **800/723-8386** or 206/323-1220; www.alpineadventures.com) and **River Riders** (© **800/448-RAFT** or 206/448-RAFT; www.riverrider.com). Expect to pay $60 to $89.

WINTER SPORTS In winter, there's good cross-country skiing at Paradise, and at Longmire, you'll find a ski touring and rental shop at the National Park Inn (© **360/569-2411**). Skis rent for around $15 per day. Daily between Christmas and New Year's and on winter weekends, there are 2-hour **guided snowshoe walks** at Paradise, with snowshoes provided ($1 suggested donation). Snowshoes ($12 per day) can also be rented in Longmire, should you want to explore on your own. Snowboarding is popular throughout the year, though there is no lift to get you up the slope, and it's about a 1½-hour climb to the best snowboarding area.

Outside the park, near the town of Packwood, you can ski cross-country from hut to hut on a 50-mile trail system. For more information, contact the **Mount Tahoma Trails Association,** P.O. Box 206, Ashford, WA 98304 (© **360/569-2451;** www.ski mtta.com). Unfortunately, many of these trails are at such low elevations that snow cover is unreliable.

Just outside the park's northeast corner, off Wash. 410, is **Crystal Mountain** (© **360/663-2265** for general information, or 888/754-6199 for snow conditions; www.skicrystal.com), and most Washingtonians agree it's the best all-around ski area due to the variety of terrain. Lift-ticket prices range from $20 for night skiing to $45 for a weekend all-day pass. Call for hours of operation.

You'll also find downhill and cross-country skiing less than 20 miles from the southeast corner of the park on U.S. 12 at the small **White Pass Ski Area** 🖈 (© **509/672-3100;** www.skiwhitepass.com). Rental equipment is available. Lift rates range from $20 for an adult half-day midweek ticket to $40 for a full-day weekend ticket. Nordic track passes are $8.

OTHER ACTIVITIES & ATTRACTIONS OUTSIDE THE PARK

Between Memorial Day and the end of September, the **Mt. Rainier Scenic Railroad** (© **888/STEAM-11** or 360/569-2351; www.mrsr.com) operates vintage steam locomotives and both enclosed and open passenger cars along a 14-mile stretch of track between Elbe and Mineral Lake, just west of the park's Nisqually entrance. The trips last 1½ hours and cost $15 for adults, $14 for seniors, $10 for children ages 4 to 12, and are free for children under 3.

WHERE TO STAY
INSIDE THE PARK

Mount Rainier National Park's historic Paradise Inn is currently closed for major rehabilitation and structural improvements and is not scheduled to reopen until 2008. This project leaves visitors with only one lodging option within the park (except for camping).

National Park Inn 🖈   In Longmire at the southwest corner of the park, this rustic lodge opened in 1920 and is set in the dense forests blanketing the lower slopes of Mount Rainier. The inn's front veranda does, however, have a view of the mountain, and guests often gather here at sunset on clear days. The lounge, with its river-rock fireplace, is the perfect place to relax on a winter's night. Guest rooms vary in size and contain rustic furnishings, but are definitely not the most memorable part of a stay. The inn's restaurant has something for everyone, and (because the inn is popular with cross-country skiers and snowshoers) a gift shop at the lodge rents cross-country skis and snowshoes in winter. Because the park's premier lodging, the Paradise Inn, is currently closed for major renovations and won't reopen until 2008, you can expect reservations at the National Park Inn to be difficult to come by throughout 2006 and 2007.

Mount Rainier National Park, 55106 Kernahan Rd., Ashford, WA 98304. © **360/569-2275.** www.guestservices.com/ rainier. 25 units, 7 with shared bathroom. $98 double with shared bathroom; $132–$181 double with private bathroom. Rates from late Oct to late Apr include full breakfast. AE, DC, DISC, MC, V. Free parking. **Amenities:** Restaurant (American). *In room:* Coffeemaker, hair dryer, no phone.

OUTSIDE THE SOUTHWEST (NISQUALLY) ENTRANCE

Alexander's Country Inn 🖈🖈   Just outside the park's Nisqually entrance, this large B&B first opened as an inn back in 1912. Today, as then, it is one of the preferred places to stay in the area, offering not only comfortable rooms, but some of the best food for miles around. The first floor is taken up by the dining room, and on the second floor is a big lounge where you can sit by the fire on a cold night. By far the best room in the house is the tower suite, which is in a turret and has plenty of windows looking out on the woods (there's also a second, smaller turret suite). After a hard day of playing on the mountain, there's no better place to relax than in the hot tub overlooking the inn's trout pond. The inn also rents two three-bedroom houses.

37515 Wash. 706 E., Ashford, WA 98304. ℰ 800/654-7615 or 360/569-2300. Fax 360/569-2323. www.alexanders countryinn.com. 14 units. May–Oct $110–$120 double, $150 suite, $210 house; Nov–Apr $89–$99 double, $125 suite, $165 house. Rates include full breakfast. Children under 3 stay free in parent's room. MC, V. **Amenities:** Restaurant (American); Jacuzzi. *In room:* No phone.

Stormking ⭐ *(Finds)*   With three modern cabins, Stormking is a quiet getaway not far from the national park's main entrance. Three of the cabins are small and are best suited to couples, while the third is large enough for families and has a full kitchen. Our favorite cabin is set on the far side of a footbridge over a tiny pond and has a slate-floored entry hall, parquet floors, a woodstove, a stereo system with plenty of relaxing music, and a high ceiling. In the big bathroom, which has a flagstone floor and is filled with plants, you'll find a double shower amid the greenery. A hot tub is on the back deck, and all four cabins have hot tubs.

37311 Wash. 706 E. (P.O. Box 126), Ashford, WA 98304. ℰ 360/569-2964. www.stormkingspa.com. 4 units. $155–$195 cabin. 2-night minimum on weekends, holidays, and during the summer. MC, V. Pets accepted ($15). **Amenities:** Spa; massage. *In room:* TV, fridge, coffeemaker, hair dryer, no phone.

Wellspring ⭐⭐ *(Value)*   This little retreat definitely isn't for everyone, but it is the most unique of the area's accommodations. Private hot tubs and wood-fired saunas take the chill off even the coldest night, and massages are available to soothe aching muscles. Accommodations are an eclectic and fanciful mix. In the modern log cabins, you'll find feather beds, woodstoves, and vaulted ceilings. In The Nest, there's a queen-size bed suspended from the ceiling by ropes and situated under a skylight. In the Tatoosh Room, you'll find a large stone fireplace, a whirlpool tub, and a waterfall shower. There are also tent cabins (one has a tropical theme), and even a tiny treehouse room! Hot tubs and saunas are an additional $5 to $10 per person per hour. Several spa treatments are also available.

54922 Kernahan Rd. E., Ashford, WA 98304. ℰ 360/569-2514. 14 units. $85–$175 double. Rates for most rooms include continental breakfast. MC, V. **Amenities:** 2 Jacuzzis; 2 saunas; massage. *In room (except tent cabins):* Fridge, coffeemaker.

Whittaker's Bunkhouse ⭐   Though it definitely is nothing fancy, this lodge, a former millworkers' bunkhouse built in 1912, is the lodging of choice for climbers headed to or from the summit of Mount Rainier. The Bunkhouse is owned by Lou Whittaker, one of Mount Rainier's most famous climbers (and owner of Rainier Mountaineering), and in the lodge's espresso shop, you'll find many climbing photos and certificates received by Whittaker for climbing Mount Everest. The guest rooms are small and spartan, but have private bathrooms.

30205 Wash. 706 E. (P.O. Box 121), Ashford, WA 98304. ℰ 360/569-2439. Fax 360/569-2436. www.whittakers bunkhouse.com. 20 units. $110 double; $30 dorm. AE, MC, V. **Amenities:** Jacuzzi; espresso bar. *In room:* No phone.

OUTSIDE THE NORTHEAST (WHITE RIVER) ENTRANCE

Alta Crystal Resort at Mt. Rainier ⭐   This is the closest lodging to the northeast (White River) park entrance and the Sunrise area, and the resort, with its wooded grounds, stays busy both summer and winter (when skiers flock to Crystal Mountain's nearby slopes). After spending the day hiking or skiing, you can go for a swim or soak your body in a hot tub in the woods. Accommodations are in one-bedroom and loft chalet suites. All of the condos here have fireplaces.

68317 Wash. 410 E., Greenwater, WA 98022. © **800/277-6475** or 360/663-2500. Fax 360/663-2556. www.altacrystal resort.com. 24 units. $139–$269 chalet for 1–6 people. Children under 12 stay free in parent's room. AE, MC, V. **Amenities:** Outdoor pool; Jacuzzi; bike rentals; children's programs; room service; massage. *In room:* TV/DVD, dataport, kitchen, fridge, coffeemaker, hair dryer, Wi-Fi.

CAMPGROUNDS

There are six main campgrounds within Mount Rainier National Park, and because all the park's campgrounds stay full on summer weekends, you should either have a reservation or arrive early in the day. Reservations for Cougar Rock or Ohanapecosh campground can be made through the **National Park Reservation Service** (© **800/365-2267**; http://reservations.nps.gov). Campsite fees range from $8 to $15 per campsite per night. No electrical or water hookups are available. Only Sunshine Point Campground and, depending on snow level and road conditions, Ipsut Creek Campground, stay open all year. The rest are open summer through early fall, with White River Campground usually closing first.

Ohanapecosh (188 campsites), in the southeast corner of the park, is the largest, but is a long way from the alpine meadows that most visitors want to see. The closest campground to Paradise is **Cougar Rock** (173 campsites). **White River** ⚲ (112 campsites) is close to Sunrise, one of the most spectacular spots in the park. **Sunshine Point** (18 campsites) is near the Nisqually entrance. In addition to drive-in campgrounds and the many backcountry camps, there are two walk-in campgrounds that often have spaces available, even on weekends. **Mowich Lake** ⚲ (approximately 30 campsites) is in the northwest corner of the park not far from Ipsut Creek Campground, and the sites are only 50 yards from the parking lot.

For information on campgrounds in the national park, contact **Mount Rainier National Park,** Tahoma Woods, Star Route, Ashford, WA 98304-9751 (© **360/569-2211;** www.nps.gov/mora). For information on national forest campgrounds east of the park, contact the **Naches Ranger District,** 10237 U.S. 12, Naches, WA 98937 (© **509/653-1400;** www.fs.fed.us/r6/wenatchee); for those west of the park, contact the **Cowlitz Valley Ranger District,** 10024 U.S. 12 (P.O. Box 670), Randle, WA 98377 (© **360/497-1100;** www.fs.fed.us/r6/gpnf). For national forest campground reservations, contact the **National Recreation Reservation Service** (© **877/444-6777** or 518/885-3639; www.reserveusa.com).

WHERE TO DINE

Because the dining room at Paradise Inn is currently closed, while the lodge undergoes a major rehabilitation, your only option for a formal meal is the dining room at the National Park Inn. Expect this restaurant to stay very busy. For quick meals, there are snack bars at the Henry M. Jackson Memorial Visitor Center, at Paradise Inn, and at Sunrise Lodge. In Ashford, you'll find the **Copper Creek Restaurant,** 35707 Wash. 706 E., Ashford (© **360/569-2326**), which makes good berry pies.

Alexander's ⚲ AMERICAN Alexander's, which is also a popular B&B, is the best place to dine outside the Nisqually entrance to the park. Fresh trout from the inn's pond is the dinner of choice, but you'll also find steaks, pork chops, and pasta on the menu. Whatever you order, save room for the wild blackberry pie.

37515 Wash. 706 E., Ashford. © **800/654-7615** or 360/569-2323. www.alexanderscountryinn.com. Reservations recommended. Main courses $9–$24. MC, V. Daily 8:30–10:30am and 11:30am–8pm.

7 Mount St. Helens National Volcanic Monument ⓕⓕⓕ

Coldwater Ridge Visitor Center: 90 miles N of Portland, 168 miles S of Seattle

Named in 1792 by Capt. George Vancouver for his friend Baron St. Helens, Mount St. Helens was once considered the most perfect of the Cascade peaks, a snow-covered cone rising above lush forests. However, on May 18, 1980, all that changed when Mount St. Helens erupted with a violent explosion that was previously unknown in modern times.

The eruption blew out the side of the volcano and removed the top 1,300 feet of the peak, causing the largest landslide in recorded history. This blast is estimated to have traveled at up to 650 mph, with air temperatures of up to 800°F (425°C). The eruption also sent more than 540 million tons of ash nearly 16 miles into the atmosphere. This massive volume of ash rained down on an area of 22,000 square miles and could be measured as far away as Denver.

Today the volcano and 110,000 acres of both devastated and undisturbed forests have been preserved as Mount St. Helens National Volcanic Monument. Several visitor centers provide information on the eruption and the subsequent changes that have taken place here. At press time, the volcano was once again active, with a new cone forming inside the crater. This renewed activity, though not as dramatic as the 1980 eruption, made Mount St. Helens the only active volcano in the contiguous United States.

ESSENTIALS

GETTING THERE   Mount St. Helens National Volcanic Monument is accessed by three different routes. The one with the major information centers is Wash. 504, the Spirit Lake Highway, which heads east from I-5 at Castle Rock. The southern section of the monument is reached via Wash. 503 from I-5 at Woodland. The east side of the monument is reached via U.S. 12 from I-5 at exit 68.

VISITOR INFORMATION   For more information on the national monument, contact **Mount St. Helens National Volcanic Monument,** 42218 NE Yale Bridge Rd., Amboy, WA 98601 (ⓒ **360/247-3900;** www.fs.fed.us/gpnf/mshnvm).

ADMISSION   Admission to one monument visitor center (or Ape Cave) is $3 for adults and to two or more visitor centers (and Ape Cave) is $6. If you just want to park at one of the monument's trailheads and go for a hike, all you need is a valid Northwest Forest Pass, which costs $5 per day. If it's winter, you'll need a Sno-Park Permit ($8–$9 per day).

EXPLORING THE NATIONAL MONUMENT
MOUNT ST. HELENS WEST

The best place to start an exploration of the monument is the **Mount St. Helens Silver Lake Visitor Center** (ⓒ **360/274-0962;** www.parks.wa.gov/mountsthelens.asp), which is operated by Washington State Parks at Silver Lake, 5 miles east of Castle Rock on Wash. 504. The visitor center houses extensive exhibits on the eruption and its effects on the region. April through October, it's open daily from 9am to 5pm in summer (until 4pm in other months). Before reaching the center, you can stop and watch a 25-minute 70mm film about the eruption at the **Mount St. Helens Cinedome Theater** (ⓒ **360/274-9844;** www.thecinedome.com), at exit 49 off I-5; tickets cost $6 for adults, $5 for seniors and children.

Continuing east from the visitor center, at milepost 27, you'll come to the **Hoffstadt Bluffs Visitor Center** (ⓒ **360/274-7750;** www.mt-st-helens.com). This is primarily

Mount St. Helens National Volcanic Monument

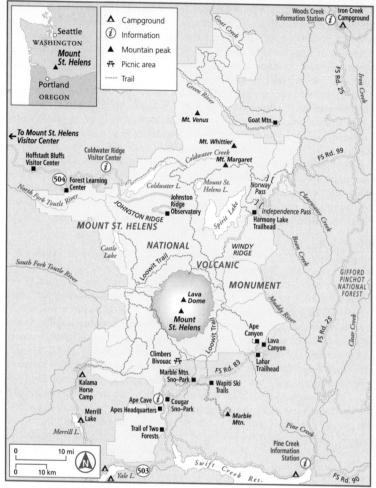

just a snack bar and takeoff site for 25-minute helicopter flights over Mount St. Helens ($114 with a three-person minimum), but there are also great views. From May to September, this visitor center is open daily from 10am to 7pm, but for shorter hours in other months.

A few miles farther, just past milepost 33, is the **Charles W. Bingham Forest Learning Center** (© **360/414-3439**), open mid-May through mid-October, daily from 10am to 6pm (until 5pm in Oct). This is primarily a promotional center for the timber industry, but, in a theater designed to resemble an ash-covered landscape, you can watch a short, fascinating video about the eruption. If you have young children, let them blow off steam at the great little playground. Outside the Hoffstadt Bluffs Visitor Center and the Forest Learning Center, you can usually see numerous elk on the floor of the Toutle River Valley far below.

The **Coldwater Ridge Visitor Center** (② 360/274-2114), at milepost 47 on Wash. 504, only 8 miles from the crater, is the second of the national monument's official visitor centers. It has interpretive displays on events leading up to the eruption and the subsequent slow regeneration of life around the volcano. You'll also find a picnic area, interpretive trail, restaurant, and boat launch at Coldwater Lake. From May through October, the visitor center is open daily from 10am to 6pm (in other months, hours are reduced).

Of the many visitor centers, none offers a more awe-inspiring view than that from the **Johnston Ridge Observatory** (② 360/274-2140), 10 miles past the Coldwater Ridge Visitor Center. Built into the mountainside and designed to blend into the landscape, this observatory houses equipment still used to monitor activity within Mount St. Helens. The observatory is open from early May to October, daily from 10am to 6pm. If you're up for a bit of hiking, the single best choice on this side of the monument is the **Boundary Ridge Trail,** which heads east from the Johnston Ridge Observatory, with a jaw-dropping view of the blast zone the entire way. This trail leads for many miles across the monument, so you can hike as much or as little as you want. There is a good turnaround point about 1 mile out from the observatory.

MOUNT ST. HELENS EAST

For a different perspective on the devastation wrought by Mount St. Helens's eruption, drive around to the mountain's east side and take the road up to Windy Ridge. Although it takes a couple of hours longer to get to this side of the mountain, you will be rewarded with equally amazing views, better hiking opportunities, and smaller crowds. To reach the east side of the mountain, take U.S. 12 east from exit 68 off I-5. In Randle, head south on Forest Road 25. The **Woods Creek Information Station,** on Forest Road 25 just before the junction with Route 26, has information on this part of the monument. South of Woods Creek, watch for Forest Road 99, the road to the Windy Ridge Viewpoint. This road crosses many miles of blown-down trees that were felled by a single blast, a reminder of the awesome power of nature. A quarter-century after the eruption, life is slowly returning to the devastated forest. At the **Windy Ridge Viewpoint,** visitors get one of the best close-up views of the crater. A staircase of 439 stairs climbs 220 feet up the hill above the parking area for even better views. Below Windy Ridge lies Spirit Lake, once one of the most popular summer vacation spots in the Washington Cascades. Today the lake is desolate and lifeless. The 1-mile **Harmony Trail** leads down to the shore of Spirit Lake and is a worthwhile hike; just keep in mind that it's a 600-foot climb back up from the lake.

MOUNT ST. HELENS SOUTH

The south side of the monument was the least affected by the eruption, and consequently does not offer the dramatic scenes of devastation as on the east and west sides. However, this area offers some good hiking and a couple of very interesting volcanic features. The first one you'll come to is the **Ape Cave,** a lava tube that was formed 1,900 years ago when lava poured from the volcano. When the lava finally stopped flowing, it left a 2-mile-long cave that is the longest continuous lava tube in the Western Hemisphere. At the Ape's Headquarters, you can join a regular ranger-led exploration of the cave or rent a lantern for exploring the cave on your own. This center is open daily from late June to Labor Day.

Of the trails on this side of the monument, the **Lava Canyon Trail** is the most fascinating. It follows a canyon that was unearthed by a mudflow that swept down this side of the mountain after the eruption.

On Wash. 503, the road leading to the south side of the monument, you'll find, in the town of Ariel, the **Lelooska Foundation** ✿✿, 165 Merwin Village Rd. (© **360/ 225-9522;** www.lelooska.com). Something of a Native American cultural center, this combination museum and art gallery features Native American arts and crafts from around the country, though the emphasis is on the work of Northwest artists. This is one of the finest Native American galleries in the state and is open on Saturdays from 11am to 3pm. Additionally, one Saturday evening each month in the spring and fall, there are performances of traditional Northwest Coast Native American masked dances, accompanied by traditional storytelling. The performances are held in a reproduction of a traditional cedar longhouse. Tickets are $8.50 for adults and $7 for children ages 12 and under, and advance reservations are required.

CLIMBING THE MOUNTAIN

If you're an experienced hiker in good physical condition, consider climbing to the top of Mount St. Helens. From the trailhead on the south side of the mountain, the hike takes 8 to 10 hours and can require an ice ax. Climbing permits ($15) are required, and because the climb is very popular, it is advisable to make a reservation (© **360/ 449-7861;** www.fs.fed.us/gpnf/mshnvm). Reservations are taken beginning on February 1, and summer weekends book up fast. If you don't have a reservation, you can try your luck by stopping at **Jack's Restaurant and Store,** on Wash. 503, 23 miles east of the town of Woodland. Each evening at 6pm, this store has a lottery of climbing permits for the next day. Between November 1 and March 31, permits are free and no reservation is necessary—but expect lots of snow. Currently, because of increased volcanic activity within the crater of Mount St. Helens, climbing to the crater rim is prohibited. Check with the monument before planning this climb.

A FEW UNIQUE WAYS TO SEE THE NATIONAL MONUMENT

For a bird's-eye view of the volcano, take a **helicopter flight** from the Hoffstadt Bluffs Visitor Center (© **360/274-7750**), for $114 per person. Rides are from June through September and last about 25 minutes. Alternatively, you can go up in a small plane with **C&C Aviation** (© **503/760-6969;** www.ccavn.com), which flies out of the Evergreen Airport in Vancouver, Washington ($90 per person; two-person minimum).

WHERE TO STAY

Blue Heron Inn Bed & Breakfast ✿✿   This modern inn on the road to the Coldwater and Johnston Ridge visitor centers is an excellent choice if you're searching for comfortable, modern accommodations in this area. Set on 5 acres of land across the highway from Silver Lake, the inn has an excellent view of Mount St. Helens. Lots of decks provide plenty of places for relaxing and soaking up the view, and during cooler weather, you can sit by the fire in the parlor. This inn is, by far, the best bet for accommodations in the area.

2846 Spirit Lake Hwy., Castle Rock, WA 98611. © **800/959-4049** or 360/274-9595. www.blueheroninn.com. 7 units. $159–$205 double. Rates include full breakfast. MC, V. Children over age 5 welcome. *In room:* A/C, TV, hair dryer, Wi-Fi.

CAMPGROUNDS

West of the monument, **Sequest State Park** (88 campsites), set amid impressive oldgrowth trees on Wash. 504 about 5 miles off I-5, is the closest public campground to Coldwater Ridge. This campground is set on Silver Lake adjacent to the Mount St. Helens Visitor Center. For reservations, contact **Washington State Parks Reservations** (© **888/226-7688;** www.camis.com/wa).

East of the monument, **Iron Creek** ⚲ (98 campsites), a Forest Service camp-ground, is the closest to Windy Ridge. This campground is set amid old-growth trees on the bank of the Cispus River.

South of the monument, the **Lower Falls Recreation Area** ⚲⚲ (42 campsites) on the Lewis River is a beautiful spot set beside the waterfalls for which it is named. For information on national forest campgrounds in the area, contact the **Cowlitz Valley Ranger District**, 10024 U.S. 12 (P.O. Box 670), Randle, WA 98377 (✆ 360/497-1100; www.fs.fed.us/r6/gpnf). For national forest campground reservations, contact the **National Recreation Reservation Service** (✆ 877/444-6777 or 518/885-3639; www.reserveusa.com).

WHERE TO DINE

There aren't a whole lot of dining options in the vicinity of the monument. Try the **Mount St. Helens Restaurant** at the Hoffstadt Bluffs Visitor Center (Spirit Lake Hwy. milepost 27) or the restaurant at the Coldwater Ridge Visitor Center (Spirit Lake Hwy. milepost 43).

8 The Columbia Gorge & the Mount Adams Area

Stevenson: 45 miles E of Vancouver, 25 miles W of White Salmon

The Columbia Gorge, which begins a few miles east of Vancouver, Washington, and extends eastward for nearly 70 miles, cuts through the Cascade Range and connects the rain-soaked west-side forests with the sagebrush scrublands of eastern Washington. This change in climate is caused by moist air condensing into snow and rain as it passes over the crest of the Cascades. Most of the air's moisture falls on the western slopes, so the eastern slopes and the land stretching for hundreds of miles beyond lie in what is called a rain shadow. Perhaps nowhere else on earth can you witness this rain-shadow effect so clearly. Between the two extremes lies a community of plants that's unique to the Columbia Gorge, and springtime in the gorge sees colorful displays of wildflowers, many of which occur naturally only here in the Columbia Gorge.

The Columbia River is older than the hills. It's older than the mountains, too, and this great age accounts for the river's dramatic gorge through the Cascades. The mountains have actually risen up *around* the river. Although the river's geologic history dates back 40 million years or so, it was a series of recent events, geologically speaking, that gave the Columbia Gorge its very distinctive appearance. About 15,000 years ago, toward the end of the last Ice Age, in what is now Montana, huge glacial ice dams burst and sent floodwaters racing down the Columbia. As the floodwaters swept through the Columbia Gorge, they were as much as 1,200 feet high. Ice and rock carried by the floodwaters helped the river scour out the sides of the once gently sloping valley, leaving behind the steep-walled gorge that we know today. The waterfalls that elicit so many oohs and aahs are the most dramatic evidence of these great floods. In 1986, much of this area was designated the **Columbia Gorge National Scenic Area** to preserve its spectacular and unique natural beauty.

As early as 1915, a scenic highway was built through the gorge on the Oregon side. However, while the Oregon side of the gorge has the spectacular waterfalls and scenic highway and gets all the publicity, it is actually from the Washington side, along **Wash. 14,** that you get the best views. From this highway, the views take in both the southern wall of the Columbia Gorge and the snowcapped summit of Mount Hood.

It is also on the Washington side of the gorge, in Stevenson, that you'll find the informative Columbia Gorge Interpretive Center.

Roughly 45 miles north of the Columbia Gorge rises Mount Adams, which, at 12,276 feet in elevation, is the second-highest peak in Washington. However, because it is so inaccessible from Puget Sound and can't be seen from most of Portland (the nearest metropolitan area), it remains one of the least visited major peaks in the state. Though few get to this massive peak, those who do often make the strenuous, though non-technical, climb to the mountain's summit.

ESSENTIALS

GETTING THERE   Wash. 14 parallels the Columbia River from Vancouver through the Columbia Gorge and into eastern Washington. Mount Adams lies to the north of the gorge and is accessed via Wash. 141 from White Salmon.

VISITOR INFORMATION   For more information on the Columbia Gorge, contact the **Columbia River Gorge National Scenic Area,** 902 Wasco Ave., Suite 200, Hood River, OR 97031 (© **541/308-1700;** www.fs.fed.us/r6/columbia), which also operates the **Skamania Lodge Visitor Center** in the lobby of **Skamania Lodge,** 1131 SW Skamania Lodge Dr. (© **509/427-2528**), in Stevenson, Washington. Information is also available from the **Skamania County Visitor Information Center,** 167 NW Second St., Stevenson, WA 98648 (© **800/989-9178** or 509/427-8911; www. skamania.org). For detailed information on the Oregon side of the Columbia Gorge, see *Frommer's Oregon* (Wiley Publishing, Inc.).

AN INTRODUCTION TO THE GORGE

Columbia Gorge Interpretive Center Museum 🐾🐾   Focusing on the gorge's early Native American inhabitants and the development of the area by white settlers, this museum is your single best introduction to the Columbia Gorge. Exhibits contain historical photographs by Edward Curtis and others, which illustrate the story of portage companies and paddle-wheelers that once operated along this stretch of the Columbia River. A 37-foot-high replica of a 19th-century fish wheel gives an understanding of how salmon runs have been threatened in the past and present. Displays frankly discuss other problems that the coming of civilization brought to this area. A slide program tells the history of the formation of the gorge. The center has an awesome view of the gorge.

990 SW Rock Creek Dr., Stevenson. © **800/991-2338** or 509/427-8211. www.columbiagorge.org. Admission $6 adults, $5 seniors and students, $4 children 6–12, free for children 5 and under. Daily 10am–5pm. Closed Thanksgiving, Christmas, and New Year's Day.

EXPLORING THE GORGE

Heading east from Vancouver, Wash. 14 passes through the industrial towns of Camas and Washougal before finally breaking free of the Portland/Vancouver metropolitan area. For much of the way, the highway stays close to the river, but at Cape Horn, an area where basalt cliffs rise straight out of the water, the highway climbs high above the river, providing one of the best views along this stretch of the highway. Several pull-offs let you stop and enjoy the views.

Roughly 35 miles east of Vancouver, you come to **Beacon Rock,** an 800-foot-tall monolith that has a 1-mile trail to its summit. The trail, which for much of the way consists of metal stairways and catwalks, was built between 1915 and 1918 by Henry Biddle, who saved Beacon Rock from being blasted into rubble for a jetty at the mouth of the Columbia River. Continuing east, you'll come to Stevenson, which is home to the Columbia Gorge Interpretive Center.

In the town of North Bonneville, a few miles west of Stevenson, you can swim in the mineral-water pool and soak in the hot tubs at **Bonneville Hot Springs Resort,** 1252 E. Cascade Dr. (© **866/459-1678** or 509/427-7767; www.bonnevilleresort.com), which charges $15 per day for the use of its pool and soaking tubs ($12 for seniors). Massages and other spa services are also available. East of Stevenson, in the town of Carson, you can also avail yourself of the therapeutic waters of the **Carson Hot Springs Resort** (© **800/607-3678**). This rustic "resort" has been in business since 1897 and has one building that looks every bit its age. However, it's just this old-fashioned appeal that keeps people coming back year after year. It's open daily from 8am to 7pm in summer and from 9am to 6pm in other months, and charges $12 for a soak and post-soak wrap. An hour's massage is $55. At press time, Carson Hot Springs was in the process of adding a new hotel and has plans to build a new pool and treatment facility. Expect major changes when you visit.

If you're up for a strenuous but rewarding hike, the 3-mile trail to the summit of 2,948-foot **Dog Mountain** provides views up and down the gorge. In spring, the wildflower displays in the meadows on Dog Mountain's slopes are some of the finest in the gorge. You'll find the trailhead on Wash. 14, 12 miles east of the Bridge of the Gods, a bridge that now spans the river at a site where a huge landslide once blocked the Columbia, creating a natural "bridge" across the river.

For a less strenuous, though no less scenic hike, drive 5 miles east of Bingen and turn left onto Rowland Lake Road. In just over a mile, you'll come to the roadside parking place for the **Catherine Creek** area. On the south side of the road is a 1.25-mile paved path that leads to several viewpoints. On the north side, an unpaved trail leads along Catherine Creek and connects to trails that climb up into the hills. *Warning:* Keep an eye out for poison oak. Also in this area is the recently opened Klickitat Trail, a former railroad bed that stretches for 31 miles up the Klickitat River and a side canyon of the river. Currently, this trail is gravel, but there are plans to pave the lower portion, which parallels the designated "Wild and Scenic" section of the river. A trailhead is right in the town of Lyle at its west end.

THE MOUNT ADAMS AREA

While Mount Adams's summit is popular with mountain climbers, at lower elevations there are also excellent trails for hikers and backpackers. The favorite summer spot for a hike is **Bird Creek Meadows** on the Yakama Indian Reservation north of the town of Trout Lake. These meadows are ablaze with wildflowers in July. Eight miles west of Trout Lake, you can explore several **ice caves.** The caves were formed by lava flows centuries ago, and year-round cool temperatures allow ice to build up within the caves. For more information on hiking on Mount Adams, contact the **Gifford Pinchot National Forest,** Mt. Adams Ranger District, 2455 Wash. 141, Trout Lake, WA 98650 (© **509/395-3400;** www.fs.fed.us/r6/gpnf).

THE EAST END OF THE GORGE

Between The Dalles Dam and the town of Goldendale (north of Wash. 14 on U.S. 97), a few unusual attractions are well worth a visit if you're exploring down at this eastern end of the gorge. In addition to attractions listed here, you'll also find four wineries in the area. **Waving Tree,** 2 Maryhill Hwy., Goldendale (© **509/773-6552**), is just outside the gates of Maryhill State Park near the Washington end of the Biggs

Bridge over the Columbia River. The tasting room is open May through November, daily from 9am to 5pm. **Maryhill Winery,** 9774 Wash. 14, Maryhill (© **877/627-9445;** www.maryhillwinery.com), has the best view of any winery in the Northwest and also produces some very good wines. **Cascade Cliffs Vineyard & Winery,** milepost 88.6, Wash. 14, Wishram (© **509/767-1100;** www.cascadecliffs.com), is set at the foot of 400-foot-tall basalt cliffs and produces, among other wines, one of the state's only barberas. **Marshal's Winery,** 150 Oak Creek Rd., Dallesport (© **509/767-4633**), just 2 miles up a gravel road, is a tiny, family-run winery that has produced some very quaffable cabernet sauvignons and merlots, as well as some unusual sweet wines.

Columbia Hills State Park ★ (Finds)

Between The Dalles Dam and Wishram on Wash. 14, Columbia Hills is the site of Horsethief Lake, a popular fishing area and campground. However, long before the area was designated a state park, this was a gathering ground for Native Americans, who fished for salmon at nearby Celilo Falls. The park isn't far from the famous Celilo Falls, which were, before being inundated by the waters behind The Dalles Dam, the most prolific salmon-fishing spot in the Northwest. Each year for thousands of years, Native Americans would gather here from all over the Northwest. These Native Americans created petroglyphs on rocks that are now protected within this park. The most famous of these is Tsagaglalal ("she who watches"), a large face that gazes down on the Columbia River. The only way to see the park's petroglyphs is on ranger-led walks on Friday and Saturday mornings at 10am. Reservations for these walks should be made at least 2 to 3 weeks in advance.

Wash. 14. © 509/767-1159. Admission $5 per car. Apr–Oct daily 6:30am–dusk. Closed Nov–Mar.

Goldendale Observatory State Park ★

If you happen to be an amateur astronomer, you won't want to miss a visit to the Goldendale Observatory. The central 24-inch Cassegrain reflecting telescope is one of the largest public telescopes in the country—large enough for scientific research—but instead, it's dedicated to sharing the stars with the general public. The observatory is out in this remote part of the state because this region's dry weather and distance from city lights almost guarantees that every night will be good for stargazing.

1602 Observatory Dr., Goldendale. © 509/773-3141. Admission $5 per car. Apr–Sept Wed–Sun 2–5pm and 8pm–midnight; Oct–Mar open by appointment Sat 1–5pm and 7–9pm, Sun 1–5pm. From downtown Goldendale, follow signs.

Maryhill Museum of Art/Stonehenge Monument ★★ (Finds)

Between 1914 and 1926, atop a remote, windswept bluff overlooking the Columbia River, eccentric entrepreneur Sam Hill built a grand mansion he called Maryhill. Though he never lived in the mansion, he did turn it into a museum that today is one of the finest, most eclectic, and least visited of the state's major museums. There is an acclaimed collection of sculptures and drawings by Auguste Rodin. An extensive collection of Native American artifacts includes the finest display of baskets in the state. Furniture, jewelry, and other items that once belonged to Hill's friend, Queen Marie of Romania, are also on display, as is a collection of miniature French fashion mannequins from just after World War II. Note that the Rodins and fashion mannequins are sometimes loaned out to other museums. The lush grounds surrounding the museum have sculptures, picnic tables, and plenty of shade trees, making this an ideal spot for a picnic (there's also a cafe inside the museum). A few miles east of Maryhill stands Hill's concrete reproduction of Stonehenge, which he built as a memorial to local men who died in World War I.

35 Maryhill Museum Dr. (Wash. 14). © **509/773-3733.** www.maryhillmuseum.org. Admission $7 adults, $6 seniors, $2 children 6–12. Mar 15–Nov 15 daily 9am–5pm. Closed Nov 16–Mar 14.

SPORTS & OUTDOOR ACTIVITIES

The Columbia Gorge is one of the nation's top windsurfing and kite-boarding spots, and if you're here to ride the wind, or just want to watch others as they race back and forth across the river, head to the **fish hatchery,** west of the mouth of the White Salmon River, or **Swell City,** a park about 3 miles west of the Hood River Bridge. **Bob's Beach,** in downtown Stevenson, is another popular spot.

When there isn't enough wind for sailing, there's still the option to go **rafting** on the White Salmon River. Companies offering raft trips on this river include **Zoller's Outdoor Odysseys** (© **800/366-2004** or 509/493-2641; www.zooraft.com), **Wet Planet Rafting** (© **800/306-1673;** www.wetplanetrafting.com), and **All Adventures Rafting** (© **877/641-RAFT** or 800/74-FLOAT; www.alladventures.net). Although the White Salmon can be rafted anytime of year, the most popular season runs from April through September. A half-day trip will cost around $55 or $60 per person.

If you're interested in a bit of horseback riding, contact **Northwestern Lake Riding Stables** (© **509/493-4965;** www.nwstables.com), at Northwestern Lake off Wash. 141 north of White Salmon. A 1-hour ride is $25.

WHERE TO STAY

IN STEVENSON

Bonneville Hot Springs Resort 🏕🏕   Although this hot-springs resort doesn't have any views to speak of, it is still one of your best bets for a memorable stay in the Columbia Gorge. With lots of stone-and-wood detail work used in the construction, this hideaway in the woods has the feel of a modern mountain lodge, although the furnishings are more classically European in styling. The focal point of the lobby is a huge river-rock fireplace. There's an 80-foot-long, mineral-water indoor pool, a full-service spa, and a big outdoor hot tub in a courtyard with an unusual stone wall and water cascading down it. Guest rooms have balconies (ask for one overlooking the courtyard), beds with ornate wood headboards, and attractive bathrooms. Some rooms have their own mineral-water soaking tubs.

1252 E. Cascade Dr. (P.O. Box 356), North Bonneville, WA 98639. © **866/459-1678** or 509/427-7767. Fax 509/427-7733. www.bonnevilleresort.com. 78 units. $135–$265 double; $325–$399 suite. Children under 4 stay free in parent's room. AE, DC, DISC, MC, V. **Amenities:** Restaurant (Continental); lounge; indoor pool; exercise room; full-service spa; 3 Jacuzzis; room service; massage. *In room:* A/C, TV, dataport, fridge, coffeemaker, hair dryer, iron.

Skamania Lodge 🏕🏕🏕   Boasting the most spectacular vistas of any hotel in the gorge, Skamania Lodge is also the only golf resort around. However, it is also well situated, whether you brought your sailboard, hiking boots, or mountain bike. The decor is classically rustic, with lots of rock and natural wood, and throughout the hotel, Northwest Indian artworks and artifacts are displayed. Huge windows in the lobby have superb views of the gorge. Of course, the river-view guest rooms are more expensive than the forest-view rooms (which overlook more parking lot than forest), but these rooms are well worth the extra cost. There are also rooms with fireplaces.

1131 Skamania Lodge Way, Stevenson, WA 98648. © **800/221-7117** or 509/427-7700. Fax 509/427-2547. www.skamania.com. 254 units. $119–$279 double; $229–$279 suite. Children under 17 stay free in parent's room. AE, DC, DISC, MC, V. **Amenities:** Restaurant (Northwest); lounge; indoor pool; 18-hole golf course; 2 tennis courts; exercise room; full-service spa; Jacuzzi; sauna; bike rentals; children's programs; activities desk; business center; room service; massage; babysitting; laundry service. *In room:* A/C, TV, dataport, minibar, coffeemaker, hair dryer, iron.

IN LYLE

Lyle Hotel ✪ *Finds*   At the east end of the gorge in the tiny town of Lyle, this old-fashioned hotel first opened for business in 1905. Today the rooms, though small and lacking private bathrooms, have a cozy, traditional feel, with quilts on the old wood or brass beds. Large windows let in lots of light. Best of all, there is an excellent restaurant on the ground floor, which makes this your best base for exploring the eastern end of the gorge.

100 Seventh St. (P.O. Box 114), Lyle, WA 98635. ℭ 800/447-6510 or 509/365-5953. www.lylehotel.com. 10 units, all with shared bathrooms. $64 double. Rates include continental breakfast. AE, MC, V. Pets accepted ($10 per night). **Amenities:** Restaurant (International); lounge; massage. *In room:* A/C, no phone.

WHERE TO DINE

The dining rooms of **Bonneville Hot Springs Resort** in North Bonneville, **Skamania Lodge** in Stevenson, and the **Lyle Hotel** in Lyle are by far the best restaurants on the Washington side of the gorge. See above for details.

IN STEVENSON

Walking Man Brewery ✪ *Finds* AMERICAN   Two blocks toward the river from Stevenson's main street, this little brewpub is a favorite hangout of windsurfers, hikers, and cross-country skiers. After a hard day of working your muscles, you owe it to yourself to have a good beer and pizza. The beer here is some of the best in the state, and the food isn't bad, either.

240 SW First St. ℭ 509/427-5520. Main courses $6–$12. DISC, MC, V. Wed–Fri 4–9pm; Sat 3–9pm; Sun 3–8pm.

IN BINGEN

Viento ✪ ECLECTIC   The name means "wind" in Spanish, an obvious bow to the blustery air that blows through the gorge. The menu here roams all over the globe, but there are comfort foods (including short ribs and a good burger), as well as such exotic dishes as Indian chicken kabobs, lamb steak rubbed with Moroccan spices, and vegetarian moussaka. Do start your meal with the pumpkin and chili soup. Next door, you'll find Gorge Wine Merchants, 218 W. Steuben St. (ℭ 509/493-5333; www.gorgewinemerchants.com), a great little wine bar.

216 W. Steuben St. (Wash. 14), Bingen. ℭ 509/493-0049. www.vientokitchen.com. Reservations recommended. Main courses $8.50–$17. MC, V. Wed–Thurs 5–9pm; Fri–Sat 5–10pm (until 10pm nightly in summer, also, Sun brunch 10am–2pm in summer).

11

Eastern Washington

For many people who live on the wet west side of the Cascades, life in Washington would be nearly impossible if it were not for the sunny east side of the mountains. Eastern Washington lies in the rain shadow of the Cascades, and many parts of the region receive less than 10 inches of rain per year. This lack of rain is also accompanied by plenty of sunshine—an average of 300 days per year. These statistics prove irresistible to folks from Puget Sound, who often head to eastern Washington to dry out.

There's little rainfall, but rivers such as the Columbia, which meanders through this region, have provided, with the assistance of dams such as the huge Grand Coulee Dam, sufficient irrigation water to make it a major agricultural area. Apples, pears, cherries, wine grapes (and wine), wheat, and potatoes are staple crops of a land where only sagebrush and bunchgrass once grew. The Columbia River created, thousands of years ago, the region's fascinating geological wonders— a dry waterfall four times larger than Niagara Falls and abandoned riverbeds known as coulees.

Down in the southeastern corner of the state, near the college and wheat-farming town of Walla Walla, the desert gives way to the Blue Mountains. It was near here that the region's first white settlers, Marcus and Narcissa Whitman, set up a mission in order to convert Native Americans to Christianity. They were later massacred by Cayuse Indians angered by the Whitman's inability to cure a measles epidemic. In recent years, Walla Walla has become one of Washington's fastest-growing winery regions. To the north of Walla Walla lie the Palouse Hills, a scenic region of rolling hills blanketed with the most productive wheat farms in the U.S.

Though Yakima attracts sun-seekers from the western part of the state, it is Spokane at the far eastern end, a few miles from Idaho, that is the region's largest city. With proximity to forests and mountains and a setting on the banks of the Spokane River, it appeals to outdoor activity enthusiasts. Its far easterly location, however, makes it seem more a part of the Rocky Mountain states than of the Northwest.

1 Ellensburg: A Glimpse of the Wild West

110 miles SE of Seattle, 36 miles N of Yakima, 75 miles S of Wenatchee

Ellensburg, which lies on the edge of cattle- and sheep-ranching country just east of the last Cascade foothills, is a town with a split personality. On the one hand, it is a small college town, site of Central Washington University. However, it is also a classic cow town best known as the site of the Ellensburg Rodeo, one of the West's top rodeos. A downtown full of historic commercial buildings further adds to the character of this town, and proximity to the mountains and ski area at Snoqualmie Pass make it a good base for summer hiking or winter skiing. Although the town isn't really

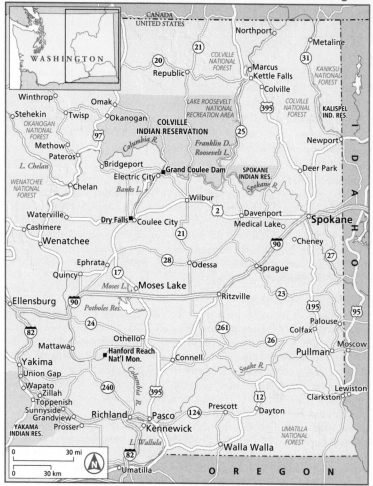

a destination per se, its proximity to Seattle and a sunny climate make it a quick escape from the Puget Sound rains.

Most of the buildings in the downtown historic district, one of the most attractive in the state, date from 1889, the year in which most of the town's commercial buildings were destroyed by a Fourth of July fire. If not for that, the town would likely have become the state capital (due to its central location). But with only one commercial building remaining, how could the government set up business in Ellensburg? Instead of becoming the capital, the town became the site of the state college that is now Central Washington University.

While the Ellensburg Rodeo is responsible for perpetuating this town's Wild West image, the Clymer Museum, devoted to the works of John Clymer, who illustrated more than 80 *Saturday Evening Post* magazine covers, does its share as well. Adding one last unusual ingredient to the eclectic milieu of Ellensburg is the Chimpanzee and Human Communication Institute, where chimps have been taught to use American Sign Language.

ESSENTIALS

GETTING THERE   Ellensburg is on I-90. Just east of town, I-82 leads southeast to Yakima and the Tri-Cities area (Wash. 821 is a scenic route south to Yakima). U.S. 97 leads north over Blewett Pass to Leavenworth and Wenatchee.

VISITOR INFORMATION   Contact the **Ellensburg Chamber of Commerce,** 609 N. Main St., Ellensburg, WA 98926 (© **888/925-2204** or 509/925-3137; www. visitellen.com or www.Ellensburg-chamber.com).

FESTIVALS   The third weekend of May has the Western Art Association's **Ellensburg National Art Show & Auction** (© **509/962-2934;** www.westernartassociation. org), with works by some of the nation's finest Western artists. On the last weekend in July, the city stages its **Jazz in the Valley** festival (© **888/925-2204** or 509/925-2002; www.jazzinthevalley.com), a 3-day binge of jazz and blues. The **Ellensburg Rodeo,** held on Labor Day weekend, is the town's biggest event and is one of the top 10 rodeos in the United States. For more information, contact the Ellensburg Rodeo and Kittitas County Fair, 609 N. Main St. (© **800/637-2444** or 509/962-7831; www.ellensburgrodeo.com).

EXPLORING THE TOWN

Ellensburg's most unusual attraction can be experienced at the university's **Chimpanzee and Human Communication Institute,** Dean Nicholson Boulevard and D Street (© **509/963-2244;** www.cwu.edu/~cwuchci), a research facility that stages what it calls **"Chimposiums."** At these programs, visitors learn about the primate communication project and get to observe several chimpanzees that have learned to use American Sign Language (ASL). Among these chimps is the famous Washoe, the first chimpanzee to learn ASL. The programs, held on Saturday and Sunday, cost $10 for adults and $7.50 for students; reservations are required.

The Western art of Ellensburg native John Clymer is displayed at the **Clymer Museum of Art,** 416 N. Pearl St. (© **509/962-6416;** www.clymermuseum.com). A member of the prestigious Cowboy Artists of America, Clymer is best known for producing more than 80 *Saturday Evening Post* covers. The museum is open Monday through Friday from 10am to 5pm (until 8pm on the first Fri of each month) and Saturday and Sunday from 11am to 4pm; admission by donation. In this same block, you'll find Ellensburg's oldest art gallery. **Gallery One,** 408½ N. Pearl St. (© **509/ 925-2670**), has works by regional, national, and international artists. For some unique local art, cruise by **Dick & Jane's Spot,** 101 N. Pearl St. (© **509/925-3224;** www.reflectorart.com). The house and yard are decorated with hundreds of colorful objects, including thousands of little reflective disks. However, the town's most famous artwork is the *Ellensburg Bull,* a cement statue that sits on a bench in a plaza in the downtown historic district.

Downtown, the **Kittitas County Museum,** 114 E. Third Ave. (© **509/925-3778;** www.kchm.org), has an interesting collection of Native American artifacts, and a large rock and mineral collection focusing on petrified wood. It's open Monday through Saturday, 10am to 4pm. Admission is by donation.

The Gorge at George

Although it is roughly 150 miles from Seattle to the community of George, Washington, the town each summer attracts tens of thousands of music fans who drive from Seattle and all over the Northwest to attend concerts (primarily rock) at a natural amphitheater overlooking the Columbia River. **The Gorge Amphitheatre**, 754 Silica Rd. NW, George (www.hob.com/venues/concerts/gorge), is in a spectacular setting that's surrounded by basalt cliffs. Tickets are sold through **Ticketmaster** (© **296/628-0888** in Seattle, 509/735-0500 in eastern Washington, or 509/453-7139 in Yakima; www.ticketmaster.com/venue/122913).

If you want to shop for some of the region's rare Ellensburg blue agate, stop by the **Ellensburg Agate & Bead Shop**, 201 S. Main St. (© **509/925-4998**). But be forewarned—this pale-blue semiprecious stone can be quite pricey.

Some 4 miles southeast of town, you'll find **Olmstead Place State Park** (© **509/925-1943**), a heritage site that preserves a pioneer homestead of the 1870s. Northwest of Ellensburg at exit 101 off I-90, in the town of Thorp, is the **Thorp Mill** (© **509/964-9640;** www.thorp.org), an 1880s gristmill open for tours from Memorial Day to Labor Day, Wednesday through Sunday, from 1 to 4pm.

Anyone wanting to cool off on a hot summer day should head for the waters of the nearby Yakima River, which allows for easy floating. **Rill Adventures,** 10471 Old Thorp Hwy. (© **888/281-1561** or 509/964-2520; www.rillsonline.com), rents rafts, with prices ranging from $60 to $90 per day. The section of this river south of town, through Yakima Canyon, is a popular stretch of river with tubers and canoeists, and is a favorite of fly anglers as well.

WHERE TO STAY

Cave B Inn at Sagecliffe 🐾🐾   Just 40 minutes east of Ellensburg, this oddly named luxury inn boasts the most dramatic setting of any hotel in the state. Perched on the edge of basalt cliffs 900 feet above the Columbia River, Cave B Inn makes the most of its location with huge walls of glass in the lobby and dining room and floor-to-ceiling windows in the guest rooms. Set in the middle of a large vineyard, the inn consists of several unusual, barrel-roofed stone buildings constructed with rock quarried right here on the property. Guest rooms range from large lodge rooms to spacious one- and two-bedroom "cliffhouses." While the rooms are all richly appointed, the gorgeous gorge views really steal the show. A winery serves as one of the main focuses at Cave B, but there is also a spa and a river-water "swimming hole" to round out the amenities. Under the direction of chef Fernando Divina, the inn's dining room gives a contemporary spin to the flavors of the Americas. If you're wondering why this hotel was built way out here in the middle of nowhere, you need only look next door to the Gorge Amphitheatre, which draws big crowds to summertime concerts.

344 Silica Rd. NW, Quincy, WA 98848. © **888/785-2283** or 509/785-2283. Fax 509/785-3670. www.cavebinn.com. 30 units. Mid-June to mid-Oct $195–$325 double, $225–$425 cottage; other months $95–$175 double, $125–$225 cottage. Children under 18 stay free in parent's room. AE, DC, MC, V. **Amenities:** Restaurant (New American); lounge; full-service spa; concierge; driving range. *In room:* A/C, TV, dataport, fridge, coffeemaker, hair dryer, Wi-Fi.

WHERE TO DINE

If you're in need of some espresso, drive up to the window at **D & M Coffee,** 408 S. Main St. (© **509/962-6333;** www.dmcoffee.com), in a 1920s gas station, or step inside the **D&M Coffee** at 301 N. Pine St. (© **509/962-9333**), in a building that was once a gas station. If you're looking for a place to hang out and have a beer or glass of wine, check out **Pearl's on Pearl,** 311 N. Pearl St. (© **509/962-8899;** www.pearls onpearl.com), a smoke-free bar and restaurant with live jazz, blues, and rock that attracts Ellensburg professionals and professors.

Valley Café ⊛ (Finds) INTERNATIONAL   Behind the shining black glass facade of this easily overlooked vintage cafe, you'll find a classic 1930s diner straight out of an Edward Hopper painting. Take a seat in one of the wooden booths and you'll swear you've stepped back in time. The menu, however, is quite contemporary, with dishes like roasted rack of lamb with a cabernet-balsamic reduction, seafood coconut curry, and cioppino. Lots of local wines are available.

105 W. Third St. © **509/925-3050.** Main courses $8–$24. AE, DISC, MC, V. Daily 11am–9pm.

The Yellow Church Cafe ⊛ AMERICAN   Though primarily an inexpensive college lunch place, this restaurant is well worth checking out for its setting in a little yellow church built in 1923. Saturday and Sunday breakfasts are among the most popular meals here, and the baked goods are favorite items. Pastas and salads are good, and the dinner menu includes inexpensive steaks and prawn dishes that are usually good bets. There are always interesting specials listed on the blackboard. If you can't find a table on the main floor, check up in the choir loft.

111 S. Pearl St. © **509/933-2233.** www.yellowchurchcafe.com. Main courses $7–$11 lunch, $9–$16 dinner. AE, MC, V. Mon–Fri 11am–8pm; Sat–Sun 8am–8pm.

2 Yakima & the Wine Country

150 miles SE of Seattle, 92 miles NW of Richland, 195 miles SW of Spokane

Considering the fact that Washington is notorious for its rainfall, it may seem hard to believe that eastern Washington's Yakima Valley receives only about 8 inches of rain per year. Located 3 hours from Seattle, Yakima is in another world—the sunny side of the Cascades. Despite the lack of rainfall, the area has become one of Washington's main apple-growing regions. Hops, used in making beer, are another important crop in the Yakima Valley, but it is grapes and the wines produced from those grapes that have been bringing the valley international attention for many years. On a visit to Yakima, you can sample the area's bounties at fruit stands, wineries, and microbreweries.

The city of Yakima lies at the western end of the Yakima Valley winery region, while at the eastern end is the Tri-Cities area comprising Richland, Kennewick, and Pasco. Although the Tri-Cities area has its share of wineries, it is best known for the Hanford Site, the huge military reservation where the first nuclear bomb was developed. Today Hanford is notorious for its many nuclear contamination sites, which luckily are well removed from any towns or vineyards, so there's no need to worry about glow-in-the-dark wine.

The land around Yakima was once the homeland of the Yakama people. The first white settlers, Catholic missionaries, arrived in 1847 and set up their mission south of present-day Yakima, and by the 1850s, growing hostilities between settlers and Native Americans had led to the establishment of Fort Simcoe, 38 miles west of Yakima. In 1880, when residents of Yakima City refused to sell land to the Northern Pacific Railroad, the railroad built North Yakima 4 miles away and moved 50 buildings from Yakima City to the new town site, which grew into the Yakima of today.

Despite the many wineries up and down the Yakima Valley, the region has never really caught on as a wine-touring destination and it has very few B&Bs or memorable restaurants. This is due to several factors. First, the wineries begin more than 20 miles away from Yakima, and so the city isn't exactly an ideal base for exploring this wine country. Also, the small towns scattered along the length of the Yakima Valley are basically farm towns and not what you would call quaint. In fact, Sunnyside has stockyards and their stench permeates the town. Vineyards are just part of the picture here, and you'll have to drive through a lot of unattractive scenery to reach the wineries. Despite that, a visit to the Yakima Valley is worthwhile so you can familiarize yourself with Washington wine.

ESSENTIALS

GETTING THERE   Yakima is on I-82 at the junction with U.S. 12, which connects to I-5 south of Centralia. You can also get to Yakima on U.S. 97 (from Ellensburg from the north and just east of The Dalles, Oregon, from the south).

The Yakima Municipal Airport, 2300 W. Washington Ave., on the southern outskirts of town, is served by Alaska Airlines.

VISITOR INFORMATION   Contact the **Yakima Valley Visitors & Convention Bureau,** 101 N. Fair St., Yakima, WA 98901 (© **800/221-0751** or 509/575-3010; www.visityakima.com). For information on Toppenish, contact the **Toppenish Chamber of Commerce,** 5A S. Toppenish Ave. (P.O. Box 28), Toppenish, WA 98948 (© **800/569-3982** or 509/865-3262; www.toppenish.net).

FESTIVALS   **Red Wine and Chocolate,** held each year over the Presidents' Day weekend, marks the start of the wine-tasting season at Yakima Valley wineries. The annual **Spring Barrel Tasting** on the last weekend in April is Yakima's biggest wine festival. During this event, the previous year's vintages are often tasted before being bottled. In late September, there's the **Catch the Crush** event, and then in November, there's **Thanksgiving in Wine Country.** Both are big wine-tasting weekends. Each year over the Fourth of July weekend, the **Toppenish Pow Wow & Rodeo** (© **509/865-5566;** www.toppenishrodeo.com) brings crowds of people to Toppenish to watch broncobusters and Native American dances. On the fourth full weekend in September, the skies over Prosser fill with hot-air balloons in the **Great Prosser Balloon Rally.**

WINE-COUNTRY TOURING

On the same latitude as France's main wine regions, the **Yakima Valley** is Washington's premier wine region. The valley sees sunshine on about 300 days of the year, which, combined with the rich volcanic soil, provides near-perfect grape-growing conditions. The only thing missing here is rain. Central Washington is virtually a desert, but irrigation long ago overcame this minor inconvenience, and today the area produces award-winning chardonnay, Riesling, chenin blanc, sauvignon blanc, semillon, gewürztraminer, cabernet sauvignon, merlot, lemberger, and muscat wines. Because of the clear weather here at harvest, and because freezing weather often arrives when there are still grapes on the vines, many wineries in the valley produce limited amounts of sweet, delicious ice wine made from frozen berries. Quite a few wineries also produce port-style wines.

The Yakima Valley wine country stretches roughly from Zillah (about 20 miles east of Yakima) to the Tri-Cities area (Richland, Pasco, and Kennewick), although the Tri-Cities area is officially in a Columbia Valley appellation. You can get a guide and map of the wine country from the Yakima Valley Visitors & Convention Bureau (see above) or the **Wine Yakima Valley,** P.O. Box 497, Prosser, WA 99350 (© **800/258-7270;** www.wineyakimavalley.org). This map covers the area from the city of Yakima east to Benton City's Red Hills region. For a map of Tri-Cities area wineries, contact the **Columbia Valley Winery Association,** P.O. Box 6644, Kennewick, WA 99336 (© **866/360-6611** or 509/628-8082; www.columbiavalleywine.com). However, even if you don't have a map, you can follow signs throughout the valley that point the way to various vineyards and wineries, or you can just follow Yakima Valley Highway/Wine Country Road (U.S. 12) between Zillah and Prosser, dropping in at whichever wineries strike your fancy. There are nearly 50 wineries in the valley, and you could easily spend a week here visiting them all. However, most people spend no more than a weekend in the area. We suggest picking no more than four or five to visit during a day of wine tasting. It's also advisable to have a designated driver.

The **Rattlesnake Hills Wine Trail** (© **800/882-8939** or 509/829-6027; www.rattlesnakehills.com) is an association of 15 Yakima Valley wineries that have issued a "Wine Trail Passport." This pass costs $5 and provides you with free tastings of reserve wines, as well as discounts on bottle purchases. Current members include Bonair Winery, Claar Cellars, Eaton Hill Winery, Horizon's Edge Winery, Hyatt Vineyards, Maison de Padgett Winery, Masset Winery, Paradisos del Sol, Piety Flats Winery, Portteus Vineyards, Sagelands Vineyard, Silver Lake at Roza Hills, Tefft Cellars, Two Mountain Winery, and Windy Point Vineyards.

YAKIMA

Kana Winery With a tasting room in a historic building in downtown Yakima, this is my favorite in-town winery. The 2002 Garnacha, made from grenache and tempranillo grapes, is particularly noteworthy and the 2002 Blau Franc, made from lemberger, is a good value.

10 S. Second St. © **509/453-6611.** www.kanawinery.com. Mon–Sat noon–6:30pm; Sun noon–5pm.

Yakima Cellars With its brick walls, wood floors, and soft lighting, this is the prettiest tasting room in Yakima. The winery produces a wide range of red wines, plus the occasional dessert wine, such as the 2002 Late Harvest Viognier.

32 N. Second St. © **509/577-0461.** www.yakimacellars.com. Tues–Fri noon–5pm; Sat–Sun 11am–5pm.

THE ZILLAH AREA

Also, if you want to pick up some fresh Yakima Valley fruit or indulge in a fresh peach sundae (in season, of course), drop by **Donald Fruit & Mercantile,** 2560 Donald-Wapato Rd., Wapato (© **509/877-3115**), which first opened in 1911 and is reached by driving north from exit 44 off I-82. This country store is also the tasting room for Piety Flats Winery.

Bonair Winery ✿ This small, family-run winery outside Zillah produces semisweet wines (including a couple of different meads) and inexpensive red wines. It makes a variety of dry wines, including decent chardonnay. Good values and a good sense of humor make this winery a must if you're *not* a wine snob.

500 S. Bonair Rd., Zillah. © **800/882-8939** or 509/829-6027. www.bonairwine.com. Mar–Nov daily 10am–5pm; Dec–Feb Sat–Sun 10am–5pm. Take exit 50 off I-82, go north to Highland Dr., and then turn right on Bonair Rd.

Claar Cellars · Although the Claar Cellars winery is north of the Tri-Cities area, its main tasting room is in Zillah, so as to reach more of the people touring the wine country. Claar Cellars produces only wines from estate-grown grapes, and the Rieslings and late-harvest Rieslings here can be quite good.

1001 Vintage Valley Pkwy., Zillah. ✆ **509/829-6810.** www.claarcellars.com. Daily 10am–6pm. Take exit 52 off I-82.

Eaton Hill Winery ✿   Housed in the old Rinehold Cannery building, this is the best place in the valley for a quick education in how different wines of one varietal can be, depending on how the grapes are grown and the wine is made. This winery focuses on cabernet sauvignon and chardonnay, and generally has a wide selection of vintages and varietals available.

530 Gurley Rd., Granger. ✆ **509/854-2220.** Daily 10am–4pm. Take exit 58 off I-82; go west on Yakima Valley Hwy. then right on Gurley Rd.

Hyatt Vineyards ✿ *(Value*   With wide lawns, valley views, and immaculately tended gardens, this winery is a good spot for a picnic (and it does a brisk wedding business). The white wines are good values, and there is a wide range of reds. A great reason to drop by is to try the black muscat dessert wines.

2020 Gilbert Rd., Zillah. ✆ **509/829-6333.** www.hyattvineyards.com. Daily 11am–5pm (call for winter hours). Take exit 50 off I-82, go north to Highland Dr., turn left on Bonair Rd., and turn right on Gilbert Rd.

Maison de Padgett Winery ✿✿   This place makes a wide range of wines, including malbec and sherry. If you think the odd labels, cute names, and unusual bottles are just a way to distract you from mediocre wines, you're wrong. Sure, there are some odd wines here, but also some superb (and pricey) vintages.

2231 Roza Dr., Zillah. ✆ **509/829-6412.** Mar–Nov Thurs–Mon 11am–5pm; Dec–Feb by appointment. Take exit 52 off I-82, go east on First Ave., turn left on Fifth St., which becomes Roza Dr.

Paradisos del Sol ✿✿   Barrel-aged dry white wines are one of the hallmarks of Paul Vandenberg, who has made wines for Portteus Vineyards (one of our favorites). The vintages are full-bodied, complex, and among the most distinctive in the state.

3230 Highland Dr., Zillah. ✆ **509/829-9000.** www.paradisosdelsol.com. Daily 11am–5pm. Take exit 52 off I-82, go east on First Ave., turn left on Fifth St., which becomes Roza Dr.; at Highland Dr., turn right.

Portteus Vineyards ✿✿   With excellent views across the valley, this winery produces some of the best reds in the Yakima Valley. Bold, full-bodied wines are the hallmark here. While most bottles are in the $20 to $25 range, the very drinkable Rattlesnake Red weighs in at under $15.

5201 Highland Dr., Zillah. ✆ **509/829-6970.** www.portteus.com. Mon–Fri 10am–5pm; Sat 11am–5pm; Sun noon–4:30pm. Take exit 50 off I-82, go north, and then follow Highland east almost as far as it goes.

Sheridan Vineyard ✿✿✿   Producing limited quantities of bordeaux blends and syrah from estate-grown grapes, this winery crafts some of the valley's most distinctive wines. The 2002 L'Orage blend was the most intensely fruit-driven red wine I've

---

Finds **Texas Tea?**

While in Zillah, don't miss the opportunity to see the **Teapot Dome gas station,** 14691 Yakima Valley Hwy. a national historic building constructed in 1922 in the shape of a giant teapot to call attention to a scandal in the administration of President Warren G. Harding. You'll find the teapot on the south side of I-82.

tasted from the Yakima Valley. Truly unforgettable. Hopefully, future wines will reproduce the flavors in this amazing vintage.

2980 Gilbert Rd., Zillah. © **509/829-3205**. www.sheridanvineyard.com. Apr–Nov Fri–Sat 11am–5pm, Sun noon–4pm. Take exit 52 off I-82 and go north over the freeway, turn left on Cheyne Rd., drive north to Gilbert Rd. and turn left.

Silver Lake at Roza Hills ⚝ This is one of the state's larger wineries, with tasting rooms here and in Woodinville (near Seattle). Producing a wide range of wines, Silver Lake keeps prices reasonable and often has great sales and discounts. The tasting room set in the hills on the north side of the valley has good views.

1500 Vintage Rd., Zillah. © **509/829-6235**. www.silverlakewinery.com. Apr–Nov daily 10am–5pm; Dec–Mar daily 11am–4pm. Take exit 52 off I-82 and go north over the freeway, turn left on Cheyne Rd., right on Highland Rd., and left on Vintage Rd.

Tefft Cellars ⚝ Tefft produces easy-drinking, moderately priced wines, including a good Italian-style red table wine, cabernet sauvignon, and merlot. It also makes an unusual cabernet port. Lots of good values are to be had here.

1320 Independence Rd., Outlook. © **888/549-7244** or 509/837-7651. www.tefftcellars.com. Daily 10am–5pm. Take exit 63 off I-82; go north on Outlook Rd. and west on Independence Rd.

Windy Point Vineyards This winery, perched atop a hill with an outstanding view from the glass-walled tasting room, is at the west end of the valley and makes an excellent starting point for a wine tour of the area. The family-owned place produces everything from Riesling to zinfandel. Good values can be found here.

420 Windy Point Dr., Wapato. © **509/877-6824**. www.windypointvineyards.com. Thurs–Mon 10am–5pm (Dec–Jan by appointment). Take exit 40 off I-82, go south on Yakima Valley Hwy. for 2 miles and turn left onto W. Parker Heights Rd., continue ½ mile to Windy Point Dr.

Wineglass Cellars ⚝⚝⚝ (Finds) This small husband-and-wife winery may be the most underrated and little-known winery in the state. Owners/winemakers David and Linda Lowe produce only about 3,500 cases of wine a year, and almost everything they make is deliciously complex and cellar-worthy. Be sure to sample the reserve wines. The cabernet sauvignons and merlots are the highlights here.

260 N. Bonair Rd. © **509/829-3011**. www.wineglasscellars.com. Fri–Mon 10:30am–5pm. Closed Dec–Presidents' Weekend. Take exit 50 off I-82, go north to Highland Dr., turn left on Bonair Rd.

SUNNYSIDE

If you need some cheese to go with your wine, drop by Sunnyside's **Darigold Dairy Fair,** 400 Alexander Rd. (© **509/837-4321**), a half-mile south of I-82 at exit 67. A sort of circus atmosphere prevails, and ice cream and sandwiches are available, as well as plenty of cheese. Dairy Fair is open Monday through Saturday from 8am to 7pm and Sunday from 10am to 6pm.

Apex Cellars ⚝ Just off the interstate in Sunnyside, you'll find, in a former Carnation building, one of the most versatile of the Yakima Valley wineries. Apex Cellars produces wines under three different labels (and in three different price ranges). Most tend to be soft, ready-to-drink wines.

111 E. Lincoln Ave., Sunnyside. © **800/814-7004** or 509/839-9463. www.apexcellars.com. Daily 9am–5pm (in winter, Thurs–Mon 11am–5pm and Tues–Wed by appointment). Take exit 67 off I-82, north on Midvale Rd. to Lincoln Ave.

PROSSER

Here in Prosser, at exit 80 off I-82, you can also stop in at **Chukar Cherry Company,** 320 Wine Country Rd. (© **509/786-2055**), and sample dried cherries and lots of dried fruits and candies. The shop is open daily from 8am to 6pm.

Alexandria Nicole Cellars ✿ The Alexandria Nicole tasting room in downtown Prosser is one of the prettiest tasting rooms in the valley; all the better, the winery has a tapas cafe here on Thursday through Saturday nights from 5 to 9pm. Most wines are priced around $20, and the viognier and both white and red blends left good impressions the last time I visited.

717 Sixth St., Prosser. © 509/786-3497. www.alexandrianicolecellars.com. Wed–Sun 11am–5pm.

Chinook Wines ✿ Dry wines, both red and white, are the focus at this Prosser winery, which is a husband-and-wife operation. The reds are big and bold and tend to be fairly pricey. In 2003, they produced a delicious cabernet franc.

Wine Country Rd. at Wittkopf Loop, Prosser. © 509/786-2725. www.chinookwines.com. May–Oct Sat–Sun noon–5pm. Take exit 82 off I-82 and go east on Wine Country Rd. (away from Prosser).

Columbia Crest ✿ About 25 miles south of Prosser on 2,500 acres of vineyards overlooking the Columbia River, this is one of the state's largest wineries. It's worth visiting for its dramatic setting and châteaulike facility.

Wash. 221, Paterson. © 888/309-WINE or 509/875-2061. www.columbia-crest.com. Daily 10am–4:30pm. Take Wash. 221 south from Prosser.

The Hogue Cellars ✿✿ In an industrial park just off the freeway, Hogue is one of the state's largest, most reliable wineries, so it's a good place to visit if you're on a budget or want to sample decent Washington state wine. This winery produces three levels of wine; the Genesis label wines tend to be the best values.

2800 Lee Rd., Prosser. © 800/565-9779 or 509/786-4557. www.hoguecellars.com. Daily 10am–5pm (Jan to Presidents' Day weekend, call for hours). Take exit 82 off I-82 and go east on Wine Country Rd. (away from Prosser).

Kestrel Vintners ✿ This winery in a Prosser industrial park produces a wide range of wines, most in the $20 to $30 range. The Lady in Red blend is a particularly good value. It also produces cabernet sauvignon, merlot, syrah, and chardonnay. Be sure to pay to taste the reserve wines, which can be extraordinary.

2890 Lee Rd., Prosser. © 888/343-CORK or 509/786-2675. www.kestrelwines.com. Daily 10am–5pm. Take exit 82 off I-82, go east on Wine Country Rd., and turn left on Bennitz Rd. and then right on Lee Rd.

Pontin del Roza Winery ✿ This small, family-owned winery is one of the oldest in the area and has been producing wines since 1984. It produces a variety of whites and reds, including good chenin blanc and sangiovese.

35502 N. Hinzerling Rd., Prosser. © 509/786-4449. Daily 10am–5pm. Take exit 80 off I-82 and go north, then go east on Johnson Rd. and north on Hinzerling Rd.

Snoqualmie Vineyards ✿ This is another of Washington's large wine producers; you'll find Snoqualmie wines in grocery stores all across the state. Predictably reliable wines at reasonable prices are the specialty. A good place to start if you're new to wine or aren't into spending a lot of money.

660 Frontier Rd., Prosser. © 800/852-0885 or 509/786-2104. www.snoqualmie.com. Daily 10am–5pm. Take exit 82 off I-82 and drive south on Frontier Rd.

(Tips Let's Do Lunch

Because good restaurants are few and far between in the Yakima Valley, you should consider bringing along picnic supplies when you go out wine tasting. Lots of wineries have patios, picnic tables, and great views.

Thurston Wolfe Winery 🝑 This small family winery, in an industrial park outside of Prosser, focuses its attentions on producing exclusively red wines—zinfandel, sangiovese, lemberger, and syrah—and Dr. Wolfe's Family Red can be a very good value. They also do a port. At press time, they were building a new winery that is expected to open by February 2006. Call for the new location.

2880 Lee Rd., Suite C. ✆ **509/786-3313.** Apr to early Dec Thurs–Sun 11am–5pm; Mar Sat–Sun noon–5pm. Closed early Dec to Feb. Take exit 82 off I-82, go east on Wine Country Rd. and continue 300 ft. past Hogue Cellars.

Willow Crest Winery 🝑🝑 Set high in the hills north of Prosser, this is one of Yakima Valley's smallest wineries, with a very limited variety. However, since winemaker David Minick likes to experiment, you'll often find some rather unusual vintages here, such as a syrah port and a syrah sparkling wine. At press time, this winery was about to open a new facility on Merlot Road at exit 80.

135701 W. Snipes Rd., Prosser. ✆ **509/786-7999.** www.willowcrestwinery.com. Late Apr–Nov daily 10am–5pm. Closed Dec–late Apr. Take exit 80 off I-82, go north on Gap Rd., then right on Snipes Rd.

Yakima River Winery Founded in 1978 as the third winery in eastern Washington, and located across the river from downtown Prosser, this is another of the old family-owned wineries in the valley. It specializes in lemberger and barrel-aged red wines, but also does port (including a shiraz port).

143302 W. North River Rd., Prosser. ✆ **509/786-2805.** www.yakimariverwinery.com. Daily 10am–5pm. Take exit 80 off I-82, go south toward Prosser, and turn right on North River Rd.

BENTON CITY

Chandler Reach 🝑🝑 This is one of the newer wineries in the valley, and at press time was still working on its new Tuscan villa–style winery and tasting room overlooking the Yakima River. However, the barrel-aging caves are complete and are a great place for tasting. Chandler Reach produces exclusively big red wines, with prices in the $20 to $25 range.

9506 W. Chandler Rd., Benton City. ✆ **509/588-8800.** www.chandlerreach.com. Fri–Sun 11am–5pm (call for winter hours). Take exit 93 off I-82 and go north.

Hedges Cellars at Red Mountain 🝑🝑 Focusing attentions on its cabernet sauvignon–merlot blend and an unusual sauvignon blanc–chardonnay blend, this winery has tasting rooms both at its Red Mountain vineyards and in the city of Issaquah near Seattle. It is one of Washington's more reliable wineries. The CMS cab-merlot-syrah blend is usually a great deal.

53511 N. Sunset Rd., Benton City ✆ **509/588-3155.** www.hedgescellars.com. Apr–Dec Fri–Sun 11am–5pm. Take exit 96 off I-82, go east on Wash. 224, and then turn left on Sunset Rd.

Kiona Vineyards 🝑 Down a gravel road in the valley's Red Hills region, this large winery produces a variety of easy-to-drink wines at moderate prices.

44612 N. Sunset Rd., Benton City. © **509/588-6716.** www.kionawine.com. Daily noon–5pm. Take exit 96 off I-82, go east on Wash. 224, and then turn left on Sunset Rd.

Oakwood Cellars   The view of Rattlesnake Mountain makes this boutique winery a good choice for a picnic on a day of tasting wines in the Benton City area. Oakwood Cellars produces a wide range of both reds and whites.

40504 N. DeMoss Rd., Benton City. © **509/588-5332.** Sat–Sun noon–5pm (closed 2nd weekend in Dec to Presidents' Day weekend). Take exit 96 off I-82; go east on Wash. 224, then left on DeMoss Rd.

Terra Blanca Vintners ⚘   Despite the name, which translates as "white earth," this winery's vineyards are on the slopes of Red Mountain, known for producing outstanding wines. Tannic bordeaux blends, syrah, and chardonnay are the main focus, viognier and several dessert wines are also produced. This is one of the only wineries in the state with barrel-aging caves.

34715 N. DeMoss Rd., Benton City. © **509/588-6082.** www.terrablanca.com. Daily 11am–6pm (Dec 25–Feb 14 by appointment). Take exit 96 off I-82; go east on Wash. 224, then left on DeMoss Rd.

THE TRI-CITIES AREA
Barnard Griffin ⚘   Good white wines, including semillon, fumé blanc, and chardonnay, can be had here, as well as dessert wines. Prices are quite reasonable.

878 Tulip Lane, Richland. © **509/627-0266.** www.barnardgriffin.com. Daily 10am–6pm. Take exit 3 off I-182 and turn left on Columbia Dr.

Bookwalter Winery ⚘⚘   Producing everything from light, drinkable picnic wines to complex, full-bodied cabernet sauvignon and merlot, this winery on the west side of Richland is one of the valley's more reliable operations. No matter what your tastes, you're likely to find something here that you'll like. During the summer, the winery has a bistro that serves light meals (with an emphasis on regional cheeses) and features live music several nights each week.

894 Tulip Lane, Richland. © **877/667-8300** or 509/627-5000. www.bookwalterwines.com. Summer, Mon–Tues 10am–10pm, Wed–Sat 10am–11pm, Sun 10am–6pm (call for hours in other months). Take exit 3 off I-182 and turn left on Columbia Dr.

TOPPENISH & ITS MURALS
Before or after visiting wineries around Zillah, you may want to drive into **Toppenish,** which was just a quiet little cow town until someone got the great idea of enlivening a few town walls with **historical murals.** Today, there are more than 60 murals depicting aspects of Toppenish history on walls all over town. If you stop in at almost any store in town, you can pick up a map to the murals. Though some murals have taken as much as a month to paint, each year on the first Saturday in June, crowds descend on the town to watch a new mural being created in just 1 day. One of the best ways to see the murals is on a horse-drawn trolley tour with **Toppenish Mural Tours** (© **509/697-8995**). For 1½ hours, tours cost $12 for adults, $10 for seniors, and $4 for children ages 12 and under.

Toppenish is within the boundaries of the Yakama Indian Reservation, which operates the **Yakama Nation Cultural Heritage Center** 100 Spilyay Loop (© **509/865-2800;** www.yakamamuseum.org), on U.S. 97 just outside town. This large building, designed to resemble a traditional Yakama winter lodge, contains a museum, library, gift shop, and restaurant (see p. 339 for restaurant details). Exhibits in the museum present the history and culture of the Yakama people. The Yakama are well known for their beadwork and you'll find pieces for sale in the gift shop. The center is open daily from 8am to 5pm; admission is $5 for adults, $3 for seniors and students, and $1 for children ages 10 and under.

Several other attractions in town provide glimpses into the area's history. The most entertaining is the **Northern Pacific Railway Museum,** 10 S. Asotin Ave. (© **509/ 865-1911;** www.nprymuseum.org; May–Oct Wed–Sat 10am–4pm, Sun noon–4pm; closed Nov–April; $3 adults, $2 children ages 17 and under accompanied by a parent), which is in the town's 1911 railway depot and also operates, a few times a year, 22-mile scenic railway excursions on the Toppenish, Simcoe & Western Railroad. Excursions are $10 for adults and $5 for children ages 4 to 17. The Yakima Valley is one of the world's main hops-growing regions, and here you will find the **American Hop Museum,** 22 S. B St. (© **509/865-HOPS;** www.americanhopmuseum.org), where you can learn all about this crucial beer ingredient. The museum is open May through September, Wednesday through Sunday from 11am to 4pm; cost is $3 for adults and $2 for students.

Fort Simcoe, 27 miles west of Toppenish in the Cascade foothills, was established in the late 1850s because of conflicts between Indians and settlers. Today, the fort is preserved as **Fort Simcoe State Park Heritage Site** (© **509/874-2372**) and is the site of surprisingly elegant quarters that were used for only a few years before becoming the Indian Agency headquarters and school. The park's buildings are open April through September, Wednesday through Sunday from 9:30am to 4:30pm. However, the grounds are open daily.

ATTRACTIONS & ACTIVITIES IN THE YAKIMA AREA

Local history is chronicled at the **Yakima Valley Museum** ★★, 2105 Tieton Dr. (© **509/248-0747;** www.yakimavalleymuseum.org), where a collection of restored horse-drawn vehicles is on display. There are also displays on the Yakama tribe and on former Supreme Court justice and environmentalist William O. Douglas, who was a Yakima resident. The museum's most enjoyable exhibit is a functioning replica of a 1930s soda fountain. The museum is open Monday through Saturday from 10am to 5pm; admission is $5 for adults, $3 for seniors and students. The museum also operates the **H. M. Gilbert Homeplace,** an 1898 Victorian farmhouse, at 2109 W. Yakima Ave. This historic home is open by appointment, and admission is $2.50.

Extending between Union Gap and Selah Gap, the **Yakima Greenway** follows the banks of the **Yakima River,** with 10 miles of paved pathways within the greenway. The easiest place to access the path is at Sherman Park on Nob Hill Boulevard. In summer, **kayaking, rafting, and tubing** are popular on this section of the river, and the **bird-watching** is good year-round.

If you'd like to see another scenic river stretch, head north to Selah and take Wash. 821 north through the **Yakima River Canyon.** The river has been around longer than the surrounding hills that have risen as the river slices through them.

Of Apples & Birdies

Golfers take note. Here in Yakima, you'll find a golf course with the world's only greens on an apple-shaped island. The **Apple Tree Golf Course,** 8804 Occidental Ave. (© **509/966-5877;** www.appletreegolf.com), on the west side of town is rated among the best golf courses in the state but is most noteworthy for its unusual apple island. Greens fees are $25 to $60.

ATTRACTIONS & ACTIVITIES IN THE TRI-CITIES AREA

If you're interested in learning more about the history (including the nuclear history), science, and technology of this region, pay a visit to the **Columbia River Exhibition of History, Science & Technology,** 95 Lee Blvd., Richland (© 877/789-9935 or 509/943-9000; www.crehst.org), adjacent to the attractive Howard Amon Park in downtown Richland. Do ask to watch the video on the great floods that scoured this landscape during the last ice age. The museum is open Monday through Saturday from 10am to 5pm and Sunday from noon to 5pm. Admission is $3.50 for adults, $2.50 for seniors, and $2.75 for students.

Upriver from the Tri-Cities area are both the Hanford Site (where the plutonium for the first nuclear bombs was made) and the Hanford Reach National Monument, which preserves the last free-flowing stretch of the Columbia River in the U.S. There are some remote areas of the monument accessible by vehicle, but the best way to see it is on the jet-boat tours offered by **Columbia River Journeys** (© 888/486-9119 or 509/946-3651; www.columbiariverjourneys.com). The 4-hour tours cost $54 for adults and $39 for children. Along the way, you'll see not only the wild shores of the Columbia River, but also the nuclear reactors of the Hanford Site. Tours are offered from May through mid-October.

WHERE TO STAY

For a list of bed-and-breakfast inns in the wine country, contact **Wine Yakima Valley,** P.O. Box 497, Prosser, WA 99350 (© 800/258-7270; www.yakimavalleywine.com).

IN YAKIMA

Birchfield Manor 🏵🏵 Just 2½ miles east of Yakima, Birchfield Manor is surrounded by pastures and is well known for elegant dinners (see below for restaurant review). Both upstairs from the dining room in the 1910 Victorian farmhouse and in a new building constructed to resemble a vintage home, you'll find antiques-filled guest rooms, most with good views out over the countryside. Several rooms have fireplaces, whirlpool tubs, and decks to take in the view. Breakfasts are nearly as legendary as the dinners and a great start for a day of wine-country touring. Note that the rooms in the new building have TVs and phones.

2018 Birchfield Rd., Yakima, WA 98901. © 800/375-3420 or 509/452-1960. www.birchfieldmanor.com. 11 units. $119–$219 double. Rates include full or continental breakfast. Children 8 and older welcome. AE, DC, DISC, MC, V. **Amenities:** Restaurant (Continental); outdoor pool; limited room service. *In room:* A/C, coffeemaker, hair dryer, iron, Wi-Fi, no phone.

Oxford Inn 🏵 East of I-82 on the banks of the Yakima River, these are Yakima's most pleasant and popular budget accommodations. As such, the inn regularly books up on weekends. The rooms are spacious, and many have balconies overlooking the river. Most also have refrigerators. Walkers and joggers will be pleased to find a 10-mile riverside walking/biking path going past the motel. Right next door, you'll find the affiliated Oxford Suites, which offers larger rooms and complimentary breakfast buffets.

1603 E. Yakima Ave., Yakima, WA 98901. © 800/521-3050 or 509/457-4444. Fax 509/453-7593. www.oxford innyakima.com. 96 units. $79–$89 double. Rates include continental breakfast. Children 10 and under stay free in parent's room. AE, DC, DISC, MC, V. Pets accepted ($20 nonrefundable deposit). **Amenities:** Outdoor pool; exercise room; Jacuzzi; courtesy airport shuttle; business center; coin-op laundry; laundry service; dry cleaning. *In room:* A/C, TV, fridge, coffeemaker.

IN THE TRI-CITIES AREA

Hampton Inn Richland/Tri-Cities 🐾🐾 *(Kids)*   On the banks of the Columbia River adjacent to Richland's Howard Amon Park, this inn claims the best location of any Tri-Cities area hotel. The walking paths and green lawns of the park are right next door, and good restaurants are a short walk. Rooms are well designed and comfortable, many with balconies overlooking the river. With the indoor pool and complimentary breakfast, this is a good bet for families.

486 Bradley Blvd., Richland, WA 99352. ℭ 800/HAMPTON or 509/943-4400. Fax 509/943-1797. www.hampton inn.com. 130 units. $92–$125 double; $250 suite. Rates include continental breakfast. Children under 18 stay free in parent's room. AE, DC, DISC, MC, V. **Amenities:** Indoor swimming pool; exercise room; Jacuzzi; courtesy airport shuttle; business center; coin-op laundry; laundry service; dry cleaning. *In room:* A/C, TV, dataport, fridge, coffeemaker, hair dryer, free local calls.

WHERE TO DINE

IN YAKIMA

For espresso, breakfast, pastries, and good bread to take along on a picnic, drop by **Essencia Artisan Bakery and Chocolaterie,** 4 N. Third St. (ℭ **509/575-5570**).

Barrel House 🐾 NORTHWEST   In downtown Yakima in a 1906 vintage building that was once a hotel and saloon, this casual wine bar and restaurant is a great end to a day of wine tasting. The food is reasonably priced and there are lots of local wines available by the glass or bottle. I like the Gorgonzola chicken, and the spicy shrimp scampi is another good bet. You'll find this restaurant on the same block as the Greystone Inn and Café Mélange (around the corner).

22 N. First St. ℭ 509/453-3769. www.barrelhouse.net. Reservations recommended. Main courses $14–$24. AE, MC, V. Mon–Thurs 11:30am–11pm; Fri 11:30am–midnight; Sat 4:30pm–midnight.

Birchfield Manor Country Inn 🐾🐾 CONTINENTAL   Birchfield Manor, a grand old farmhouse on the eastern outskirts of Yakima, doubles as both Yakima's best B&B (see above) and its best restaurant. The dining room looks as if a wealthy family cleared out the regular furniture and brought in a few extra tables for a holiday dinner. The menu changes with the season and includes a choice of five or six entrees. The house specialty is salmon in puff pastry with a chardonnay sauce, but other offerings are very tempting as well. The filet mignon with cabernet sauce and steak Diane with a brandy-cream sauce are two other standout dishes here. The dinner includes fresh-baked bread, an appetizer, salad, and, best of all, handmade after-dinner chocolates.

2018 Birchfield Rd. ℭ 800/375-3420 or 509/452-1960. www.birchfieldmanor.com. Reservations required. 5-course dinner $32–$49. AE, DC, DISC, MC, V. Seatings Thurs–Fri 7pm; Sat 6 and 8:45pm.

Café Mélange 🐾 ITALIAN   It's small and inconspicuous, but this restaurant has been one of Yakima's best, most popular restaurants. Pastas were long the specialty, but you can get more substantial meals. Try the duck with huckleberry-port sauce, available both as an appetizer and entree, or the delicious smoked-salmon ravioli with basil-cream sauce. A good wine list includes local wines.

7 N. Front St. ℭ 509/453-0571. Reservations recommended. Main courses $11–$14 lunch, $20–$26 dinner. AE, DISC, MC, V. Mon–Thurs 11:30am–2pm and 5–8:30pm; Fri 11:30am–2pm and 5–9:30pm; Sat 5–9:30pm.

Greystone Restaurant 🐾🐾 NEW AMERICAN   Housed in—you guessed it—a gray stone building, this restaurant has, for more than 20 years, been Yakima's favorite upscale, downtown dining establishment. With its historic character, lively little bar, and convivial atmosphere, this is an excellent place to end a day of wine tasting. Gravlax salmon, pan-fried oysters, and spicy south-of-the-border-style crab cakes all make good starters, before moving on to spicy prawns in Tabasco-cream sauce or bourbon-basted salmon. Desserts are pure comfort foods—brownies, ice cream, cheesecake. There's a long list of regional wines, also.

5 N. Front St. ✆ **509/248-9801**. www.greystonerestaurant.com. Reservations recommended. Main courses $13–$35. AE, MC, V. Mon–Fri 11am–2pm; Tues–Sat 5–10pm (bar opens at 4:30pm).

IN ZILLAH & TOPPENISH
Heritage Inn Restaurant ☆ *Finds* AMERICAN/NATIVE AMERICAN On the grounds of the Yakama Nation Cultural Heritage Center, this casual restaurant has noteworthy Native American dishes, like traditional Yakama salmon stew and fry bread. Even the salad bar comes with fry bread. There are buffalo burgers, buffalo steaks, and buffalo stew. For dessert, don't pass up the huckleberry pie.

Yakama Nation Cultural Heritage Center, 280 Buster Rd., Toppenish. ✆ **509/865-2551**. Main courses $5.25–$18. MC, V. Mon–Wed 8am–3pm; Thurs–Sat 8am–8pm; Sun 8am–2pm. Take exit 37 off U. S. 97 22 miles S of Yakima.

IN GRANDVIEW & PROSSER
If you're anywhere near Prosser at dinnertime on Thursday through Saturday, head downtown to the tasting room/tapas cafe at **Alexandria Nicole,** 717 Sixth St., Prosser (✆ **509/786-3497;** www.alexandrianicolecellars.com), where the menu includes small plates such as spanakopita, bacon-wrapped scallops, marinated olives, and stuffed portabella mushrooms. Live music is on Thursday nights.

Dykstra House Restaurant ☆ ITALIAN/CONTINENTAL This eclectic eatery, housed in a historic building dating from 1914, is primarily a lunch spot, but on Friday and Saturday nights, dinners are also served. Friday is Italian night and usually features familiar standards. Saturday night is a bit more eclectic, and there might be salmon in puff pastry, chicken Mediterranean, or pork loin. Lunches are equally unpredictable—you never know what will be on the menu, which makes a meal here all the more fun. There's a good selection of local wines.

114 Birch Ave. ✆ **509/882-2082**. Reservations required for dinner. Main courses $5.25–$7.25 lunch, $10–$24 dinner. AE, DC, DISC, MC, V. Tues–Thurs 10am–4pm; Fri 10am–4pm and 6–9pm; Sat 11am–2pm and 6–9pm.

IN THE TRI-CITIES AREA
If you're just in the mood for some pub food and a microbrew, head to **Atomic Ale Brewpub & Eatery,** 1015 Lee Blvd., Richland (✆ **509/946-5465**), which is just a block off Richland's George Washington Way in downtown Richland. One of my favorite places in the area for a light meal is the **Bookwalter Winery,** 894 Tulip Lane, Richland (✆ **877/667-8300** or 509/627-5000; bookwalterwines.com), which serves simple meat and cheese plates to go with the wines. There's live music on Wednesday through Saturday nights. See the listing above for hours.

Amici's ☆ *Finds* ITALIAN A half-block from Richland's riverfront Howard Amon Park, you'll find one of the most enjoyable little restaurants in central Washington. With only a handful of tables, Amici's is a cozy place with a suitably Mediterranean decor that is surprisingly chic. Plenty of wines by the glass and by the bottle make this restaurant a must if you're in the area on a wine-tasting trip. Classic Italian dishes are the mainstay of the short menu.

94 Lee Blvd., Richland. ✆ **509/942-1914**. Main courses $12–$19. MC, V. Mon–Sat 11am–10pm.

Katya's Bistro & Wine Bar ✿ NORTHWEST/ITALIAN   With a couple of river-front hotels nearby and the pretty Howard Amon Park just a couple of blocks away, this little second-story restaurant is another surprising find in downtown Richland. The menu is fairly long and quite creative for this area. Start with the Ukrainian borscht if it's still on the menu when you visit. Then move on to the veal roulade with crab. There's an extensive wine list that emphasizes local wines.

430 George Washington Way, Suite 201. ℂ **509/946-7777**. Reservations recommended. Main courses $14–$26. AE, DISC, MC, V. Mon–Thurs 11am–9pm; Fri–Sat 11am–10pm.

3 Walla Walla

50 miles E of Richland/Pasco/Kennewick, 155 miles S of Spokane, 39 miles NE of Pendleton

Although Walla Walla is perhaps best known as the home of the Walla Walla sweet onion, in recent years the town has become the epicenter of a burgeoning wine industry. New wineries have been popping up as fast as champagne corks on New Year's Eve, making this town the single best locale in the state for a few days of wine touring. The explosion of wineries has also brought on a downtown renaissance, with a restored historic hotel, new restaurants, and a few wine bars.

Before there was wine, it was onions that made Walla Walla famous (well, maybe not exactly famous). The Walla Walla onion is a big sweet variety, similar to the Vidalia onion of Georgia, and owes its sweetness not to sugar, but to a high-water and low-sulfur content. These onions, which can weigh as much as 2 pounds, are legendary around the Northwest as the best onions for burgers at summer barbecues. Between June and August, produce stands in the area sell big bags of these sweet onions. There's even a Walla Walla Sweet Onion Festival in mid-July.

This is also a college town with three schools of higher learning: Walla Walla College, Whitman College, and Walla Walla Community College. Due in large part to these colleges, the town wears a rather cultured air. The town's residential streets, lined with stately old homes and large shade trees, add yet another layer to Walla Walla's character. A stroll or drive through the town's old neighborhoods conjures up times past, when the pace of life was slower.

Walla Walla is also one of the oldest communities in the Northwest and was the site of both an early mission and one of the region's first forts. Before white settlers arrived, the area was home to several Indian tribes from which the town's name, which means "many waters" or "small, rapid streams," is derived.

ESSENTIALS

GETTING THERE   Walla Walla is on U.S. 12, 45 miles east of I-82/I-182 in the Tri-Cities area. From I-82 west of Richland, take I-182 to Pasco and continue south, then west on U.S. 12. From Pendleton, Oregon, and I-84, take Ore. 11 north. From Spokane, take U.S. 195 south to Colfax, continuing south on Wash. 26 and then Wash. 127. In Dodge, you pick up U.S. 12 and continue south to Walla Walla.

Walla Walla Regional Airport (ℂ **509/525-3100;** www.wallawallaairport.com) is served by Horizon Airlines.

VISITOR INFORMATION   Contact the **Walla Walla Area Chamber of Commerce,** 29 E. Sumach St. (P.O. Box 644), Walla Walla, WA 99362 (ℂ **877/WWVISIT** or 509/525-0850; www.wallawalla.org).

GETTING AROUND   Rental cars are available through Hertz and Budget.

FESTIVALS In early May, there's the **Walla Walla Balloon Stampede,** and in mid-July, the **Walla Walla Sweet Onion Festival.** Area wine festivals include the **Spring Release Weekend** over the first full weekend in May and the **Holiday Barrel Tasting** on the first weekend in December.

EXPLORING THE TOWN

The **Whitman Mission National Historic Site** (© 509/522-6357; www.nps.gov/whmi), 7 miles west of Walla Walla, just off U.S. 12, is dedicated to a tragic page in Northwest history. Missionaries Marcus and Narcissa Whitman were some of the first settlers to travel overland to the Northwest and arrived in this area in 1836. Although the Whitmans had come here to convert Indians, Marcus Whitman was also a doctor and often treated the local Cayuse people. During the mid-1840s, a wagon train brought a measles epidemic to the area, and the Cayuse, who had no resistance to the disease, began dying. Though Whitman was able to save his own family, most of the Cayuse who contracted the disease died from it. Legend has it that the Cayuse had a tradition of killing medicine men who could not cure an illness, and on November 29, 1847, several Cayuse attacked and killed the Whitmans and 11 other residents of the mission. The massacre at the Whitman mission prompted a war on the Cayuse and a demand for territorial status for what was at that time the Oregon country. In 1848, in response to pleas brought about by the Whitman massacre, Oregon (which at that time included present-day Washington state) became the first territory west of the Rocky Mountains.

Today, nothing remains of the mission, but a trail leads through the mission site and the building locations are outlined with concrete. An interpretive center provides historical background on the mission and has artifacts from the days when the Whitmans worked with the Cayuse. The site is open daily (except Thanksgiving, Christmas, and New Year's Day) until dusk; the visitor center is open from 8am to 6pm in summer and from 8am to 4:30pm in other months. Admission is $3 per person or $5 per family.

In town, you'll find the **Fort Walla Walla Museum Complex,** 755 Myra Rd. (© **509/525-7703;** www.fortwallawallamuseum.org). The museum is a collection of pioneer-era buildings, including log cabins, a one-room schoolhouse, an old railway station, and several other buildings. It's open April through October, daily from 10am to 5pm. Admission is $7 for adults, $6 for seniors and students, and $3 for children ages 6 to 12, free for children under 6. In addition to displays on pioneer life, there's a large collection of horse-era farming equipment, including an old combine pulled by 33 life-size fiberglass mules.

WINE TOURING

Although Washington's main winery region lies to the west of the Tri-Cities area, the Walla Walla area has seen a proliferation of wineries in recent years and has become the state's hottest wine region. The climate and soils are perfect for growing wine grapes, and the emphasis is now on syrah grapes. In fact, because Walla Walla is such an attractive town, this is a far more appealing wine-touring region than the Yakima Valley. In addition to the area wineries listed below, open to the public on a regular basis, some are only open by appointment or a couple of weekends a year. For more information on area wineries, contact the **Walla Walla Valley Wine Alliance,** 128 N. Second Ave., Suite 219, Walla Walla, WA 99362 (© **509/526-3117;** www.wallawallawine.com).

IN DOWNTOWN WALLA WALLA

Downtown Walla Walla continues to add more and more wineries and tasting rooms. I've listed my favorites below, but others that are open on a regular basis include **Ash Hollow,** 14 N. Second Ave. (℃ 509/529-7565; www.ashhollow.com); **Bergevin Lane,** 1215 W. Poplar St. (℃ 509/526-4300. www.bergevinlane.com); **Forgeron Cellars,** 33 W. Birch St. (℃ 509/522-9463; www.forgeroncellars.com); **Patit Creek Cellars,** 4 S. Fourth Ave. (℃ 509/522-4684; www.patitcreekcellars.com); **Spring Valley Vineyard,** 7 S. Fourth Ave. (℃ 509/337-6915; www.springvalleyvineyard.com).

Amavi Cellars ✿✿✿   This is one of the newer wineries in Walla Walla, a sister winery to the celebrated Pepper Bridge Winery. Although Amavi doesn't produce very many varietals, it makes complex and delicious wines. The tasting room, incorporating an 1890s log cabin, is next door to Canoe Ridge Vineyard.

635 N. 13th Ave. ℃ 509/525-3541. www.amavicellars.com. Mar 15–Dec 15 Tues–Sun 11am–5pm; Dec 16–Mar 14 Fri–Sun 11am–4:30pm. From U.S. 12, go south on W. Pine St. and then right on 13th Ave.

Canoe Ridge Vineyard ✿   Taking its name from a nearby vineyard region, this winery is in an old streetcar engine house outside Walla Walla. It has gone through changes in recent years, and the current releases are very drinkable.

1102 W. Cherry St. ℃ 509/527-0885. www.canoeridgevineyard.com. May–Sept daily 11am–5pm; Oct–Apr daily 11am–4pm. From U.S. 12, go south on W. Pine St. and then right on 13th Ave.

Fort Walla Walla ✿   The owners of this little winery were home winemakers until 2001 when they made the jump to producing their first commercial vintage. So far, they're putting in a good showing with their bordeaux and rhone varietals, and the place has been labeled a "new winery to watch" by *The Wine Spectator.*

127 E. Main St. ℃ 509/520-1095. www.fortwallawallacellars.com. Fri–Sat noon–4:30pm; Sun noon–4pm.

Morrison Lane ✿   If I told you the 2002 syrahs produced here tasted of cherry cough syrup, you might think that was a bad thing. However, as a kid, I loved cherry cough syrup and I love these syrahs even more. They're big fruit-driven wines with, unfortunately, big prices. In 2003, this winery began producing nebbiolo- and barolo-style wines, as well as barbaresco.

201 W. Main St. ℃ 509/526-0229. www.morrisonlane.com. Fri–Mon noon–6pm.

Patrick M. Paul Vineyards/Walla Walla Village Winery ✿   In business since 1988, Patrick M. Paul Vineyards has remained small and focused production on premium red wines. It is best known for the cabernet franc, but also produces cabernet sauvignon and merlot. The tasting room is downtown and is shared with Walla Walla Village Winery, which produces some very approachable red wines.

107 S. Third Ave. ℃ 509/526-0676 or 509/525-9463. May–Nov Mon–Tues and Fri–Sat 11am–5pm, Sun 1–5pm; Dec–Apr Sun–Tues and Thurs 1–5pm, Fri–Sat 11am–5pm.

Seven Hills Winery ✿   Housed in the same renovated woodworking-mill building as the Whitehouse-Crawford Restaurant, this winery produces some excellent red wines, including merlot and syrah. Most are in the $20 to $30 range.

212 N. Third Ave. ℃ 877/777-7870. www.sevenhillswinery.com. May–Aug Thurs–Sat 11am–4pm (call for appointment other months).

Waterbrook Winery ✿   Although Waterbrook Winery itself is in nearby Lowden, the tasting room is downtown Walla Walla. The focus here is on cabernet sauvignon and merlot in the $15 to $25 range. Whites include chardonnay, sauvignon blanc, and the less familiar viognier, all of which are quite drinkable and very reasonably priced. There are some good values to be had here.

31 E. Main St. 🕐 **509/522-1262**. www.waterbrook.com. Daily 10:30am–4:30pm.

Whitman Cellars 🐾 Winemaker Stephen Lessard formerly worked at Hedges Cellars, long one of my favorite large state wineries. Here, Lessard is producing consistent, aromatic wines with soft tannins. All are very drinkable.

1015 W. Pine St. 🕐 **509/529-1142**. www.whitmancellars.com. Daily 11am–5pm.

WEST OF WALLA WALLA

L'Ecole No. 41 🐾 Housed in a former elementary school and using children's art on its labels, this is one of the oldest wineries in the region. It started with semillon and merlot, and the semillon is still one of the best wines, though the chardonnays and cabernet-merlot blends are good, also. The semillon tends to be in the $15 to $20 range, while reds are often in the $30 to $45 range.

41 Lowden School Rd., Lowden. 🕐 **509/525-0940**. www.lecole.com. Daily 10am–5pm. On U.S. 12, 12 miles west of Walla Walla.

Reininger This westside winery focuses almost exclusively on red wines made from Walla Walla and Columbia Valley grapes. Wine from the latter fruit is priced lower and is usually meant to be drunk immediately, rather than be cellared.

5858 W. Hwy. 12. 🕐 **509/522-1994**. www.reiningerwinery.com Daily 10am–6pm. Located 8 miles west of Walla Walla on U.S. 12.

Three Rivers Winery This large winery may be the wave of the future for the Walla Walla wine business. Housed in a large building in the middle of the Walla Walla farm country, Three Rivers produces a wide range of wines from robust syrahs and sangioveses to late-harvest gewürztraminer.

5641 W. Hwy. 12 🕐 **509/526-9463**. www.threeriverswinery.com. Daily 10am–6pm. Located 8 miles west of Walla Walla on U.S. 12.

Woodward Canyon Winery 🐾🐾🐾 This winery is well known in the Northwest for its full-bodied reds and vineyard-designate chardonnays and is one of Washington's best wineries. While most of the wines come in at $30 to $50, the Nelms Road reds are usually priced around $20, a particularly good value. The tasting room is in a renovated old farmhouse adjacent to the winery.

11920 W. Hwy. 12, Lowden. 🕐 **509/525-4129**. www.woodwardcanyon.com. Daily 10am–5pm. On U.S. 12, 12 miles west of Walla Walla.

EAST OF WALLA WALLA

The Walla Walla Airport serves as a sort of incubator for small new wineries. Rents are cheap out here, so new winemakers can afford to go out on their own. Many of these wineries are only open on Saturday afternoon. Among my current favorites are **Buty,** 535 E. Cessna Ave. (🕐 **509/527-0901**; www.butywinery.com; open daily 11am–4pm), where winemaker Caleb Foster, who has worked for Woodward Canyon and Chateau Ste. Michelle, produces regional blends; **Russell Creek Winery,** 301 Aeronica Ave. (🕐 **509/386-4401**; www.russellcreek-winery.com; open daily 11am–4pm); **Syzygy,** 405 E. Boeing Ave. (🕐 **509/522-0484**; www.syzygywines.com; open Sat 11am–4pm); **Colvin Vineyards,** 720 C St. (🕐 **509/527-9463**; www.colvinvineyards.com), which is noteworthy for producing wines using carmenère grapes; and **Cougar Crest,** 202 A St. (© **509/529-5980;** www.cougarcrestwinery.com).

Dunham Cellars   Adjacent to the Walla Walla airport, this winery produces an exceptional red blend called Trutina, and its composition varies from year to year. The wines here are, mostly big, long-keeping reds. Expect to pay $20 to $45.

150 E. Boeing Ave. © **509/529-4685.** www.dunhamcellars.com. Daily 11am–4pm. Take the airport exit off U.S. 12 east of downtown.

Five Star Cellars ★★★   Can you say YUM? That's all I can think when I taste the wines produced by this little rising-star winery. Its stellar wines include super-silky reds that caress your tongue and fill your mouth with big dark fruit flavors. These out-of-this- world wines are priced around $30.

840 C St. © **509/527-8400.** www.fivestarcellars.com. Sat 10am–4pm. Take the airport exit off U.S. 12 east of downtown.

Tamarack Cellars ★★★   The first time I visited this winery, gregarious winemaker Ron Coleman played loud classical music in his barrel-aging room. He swore it helped to make great wine. The proof is in the glass. Red wines that caress the tongue and fill your mouth with fresh fruit flavors are symphonies for the palate.

700 C St. © **509/526-3533.** www.tamarackcellars.com. Sat 10am–4pm or by appointment.

Walla Walla Vintners ★   This small winery makes only red wines and in the past has produced some excellent cabernet sauvignon and merlot. It also makes cabernet franc and several red cuvees. Most wines are in the $28 to $35 range.

225 Vineyard Lane. © **509/525-4724.** www.wallawallavintners.com. Mar–Dec Sat 10:30am–4:30pm; Jan–Feb Sat 1:30–4:30pm. Located east of town off Mill Creek Rd.

SOUTH OF WALLA WALLA

Basel Cellars ★   No visit to Walla Walla is complete without a stop at this huge log lodge on a hilltop south of town. The wines are good, though pretty pricey, but even if you aren't in the market for a $48 syrah, you should stop by just to see the most impressive winery building in eastern Washington. By the way, you can rent this place out and even spend the night.

2901 Old Milton Hwy. © **509/522-0200.** www.baselcellars.com. Mon–Sat 10am–4pm. Drive south on Wash. 125 and then turn right on Old Milton Hwy.

Dusted Valley Vintners ★   Housed in a garage underneath the owner's home, this tiny winery is the absolute antithesis of nearby Basel Cellars, but produces some excellent wines, despite its low-key character. The chardonnay and viognier are standouts here, as is the Barrel Thief Super Tuscan.

1248 Old Milton Hwy. © **509/525-1337.** www.dustedvalley.com. Sat–Sun noon–5pm. Drive south on Wash. 125, and then turn left on Old Milton Hwy.

Pepper Bridge Winery ★★   Crafting ultra-premium wines from estate-grown grapes, Pepper Bridge is one of the state's premier producers of bordeaux-style wines, with the emphasis on cabernet sauvignon. A state-of-the-art gravity-flow winery ensures as little handling of the grapes as possible, which produces smoother, more cellar-worthy wines. Expect to pay around $50 per bottle here.

1704 J.B. George Rd. © **509/525-6502.** www.pepperbridge.com. Mon–Sat 10am–4pm. Drive south on Wash. 125, turn left on Old Milton Hwy, turn right on Pepper Bridge Rd., and then left on J.B. George Rd.

Rulo Winery ✮✮ *(Finds*   This small, family-run winery on the south side of town produces outstanding and reasonably priced syrah and viognier. This latter is a delicious, food-friendly white wine with a wonderful nose. Don't miss this winery, which also produces some outstanding chardonnays.

2525 Pranger Rd. ⓒ **509/525-7856.** www.rulowinery.com. Sat 11am–4pm. Drive south on Wash. 125, turn left on Old Milton Hwy., and then right on Pranger Rd.

Saviah Cellars ✮   Fruit-forward red wines with soft, silky tannins are the specialty of winemaker Richard Funk, who was a microbiologist in another life. The science background obviously helped Funk to better understand the winemaking process. Most of the wines are in the $30 range.

1979 JB George Rd. ⓒ **509/520-5166.** www.saviahcellars.com. May–Oct Sat 11am–5pm. Drive south on Wash. 125, turn left on Old Milton Hwy, turn right on Pepper Bridge Rd., then left on J.B. George Rd.

SPORTS & OUTDOOR ACTIVITIES

The land immediately surrounding Walla Walla is rolling farm country, but less than 20 miles east, the **Blue Mountains** rise more than 6,000 feet. Hiking, mountain biking, fishing, and hunting all are popular in these mountains. For more information, contact the **Walla Walla Ranger District,** 1415 W. Rose St., Walla Walla, WA 99362 (ⓒ **509/522-6290;** www.fs.fed.us/r6/uma).

WHERE TO STAY

Green Gables Inn ✮   On a quiet, shady street, this large 1909 home, with its three big front gables, is only a block from the Whitman College campus, which makes it a good choice if you are here on college business or to visit your kids. Two sitting rooms downstairs are furnished with antiques and have fireplaces at each end that make it quite cozy on a chilly evening. Guest room names are from the book *Anne of Green Gables.* Dryad's Bubble is filled with Maxfield Parrish prints and has a claw-foot tub, while in the master suite, you'll find a fireplace, whirlpool tub, deck, and mahogany furniture. The Carriage House easily sleeps four and has 1½ bathrooms and a kitchen.

922 Bonsella St., Walla Walla, WA 99362. ⓒ **888/525-5501** or 509/525-5501. www.greengablesinn.com. 5 units, 1 carriage house. $125–$155 double; $155 carriage house for 2, $35 each additional guest. Rates include full breakfast. AE, DISC, MC, V. Children over age 12 welcome in main house; younger children welcome in Carriage House. *In room:* A/C, TV/VCR, fridge, hair dryer, no phone.

Inn at Abeja ✮✮ *(Finds*   Set on a classically picturesque farm a few miles outside of town, this inn is surrounded by green lawns and big shade trees. The main house's wide veranda, hammocks under the trees, and colorful perennial gardens all add up to the quintessential farm getaway that you imagine when thinking of running away to your own green acres. Guest rooms are in a collection of converted outbuildings, including an old summer kitchen, a bunkhouse, and even the old chicken coop (which now has vaulted ceilings and its own kitchen). An on-site winery makes this place ideal as a base for a wine tour of the area.

2014 Mill Creek Rd., Walla Walla, WA 99362. ⓒ **509/522-1234.** Fax 509/529-3292. www.abeja.net. 5 units. $200–$270 double. Rates include full breakfast. MC, V. Pets accepted ($15). *In room:* A/C, TV, kitchen, fridge, coffeemaker, hair dryer, iron.

Marcus Whitman Hotel ✮✮   Opened in 1928, this historic high-rise hotel in downtown Walla Walla is the finest in this corner of the state, and is an excellent base for a local wine tour. Not only is there an excellent restaurant and wine bar on the premises, but several others are a few blocks away. Guest rooms are designed with a classic elegance to match the lobby, which is filled with dark wood paneling, ornate plasterwork, and lots of original details. Most of the guest rooms are in a modern addition, so if you absolutely must stay in the original tower, you'll have to spring for one of the luxurious suites. Other than the suites, the best rooms are the king executives, which are spacious and well designed.

6 W. Rose St., Walla Walla, WA 99362. (℃ 866/826-9422 or 509/525-2200. Fax 509/524-1747. www.marcuswhitman hotel.com. 91 units. $99–$159 double; $199–$254 suite. Rates include full breakfast. AE, DC, DISC, MC, V. Pets accepted ($20 fee). **Amenities:** Restaurant (Northwest); lounge; exercise room; concierge; business center; laundry service; dry cleaning. *In room:* A/C, TV, dataport, coffeemaker, hair dryer, iron, high-speed Internet access, Wi-Fi.

WHERE TO DINE

For breakfast, lunch, or snacks, **Merchants Ltd.,** 21 E. Main St. (℃ **509/525-0900**), has long been Walla Walla's favorite downtown establishment. Basically a huge, glorified deli, it even has live music on some evenings. When it's coffee time, try **Coffee Perk,** 4 S. First Ave. (℃ **509/526-0636**), a favorite downtown espresso place. If it's pub food and microbrews you're after, then head to **Mill Creek Brew Pub,** 11 S. Palouse St. (℃ **509/522-2440**).

Creek Town Cafe ✸✸ NORTHWEST   This immensely popular little restaurant is 10 blocks south of downtown in a new building with modern, wine-country character. Start your meal with the spinach salad, spicy calamari, or the unusual trout cakes. Entrees include intriguing dishes made with locally produced Monteillet goat cheese; give these a try. The menu changes regularly, but keep an eye out for crab cannelloni, cherry-balsamic duck breast, and beet ravioli. In summer, dine on the patio. Local wines are available by the glass.

1129 S. Second St. (℃ **509/522-4777**. www.creektowncafe.com. Reservations recommended both lunch and dinner. Main courses $7.50–$15 lunch, $17–$26 dinner. AE, DISC, MC, V. Tues–Sat 11am–2:30pm and 5–9pm.

Grapefields ✸✸ NORTHWEST   Riding the Walla Walla wine wave, this casual bistro, wine bar, and wine shop is a good choice whether you're looking for a formal dinner or a light meal. You'll dine surrounded by shelves full of local wine, and there's a long list of local wines by the glass, so you can fill in gaps in your day's tasting tour. The stone oven produces many of the best dishes, including creative pizzas and cracker bread appetizers. For something to accompany a robust red wine, try the lamb, which might be rubbed with mint and whole-grain mustard, or the filet mignon with cabernet-and-thyme sauce.

4 E. Main St. (℃ **509/522-3993**. Main courses $6–$12. AE, MC, V. Tues–Thurs 11am–9pm; Fri–Sat 11am–10pm; Sun noon–6pm.

26brix ✸✸✸ NORTHWEST   26brix is proof that this community is becoming the Napa of the North. Chef Mike Davis opened this restaurant after serving as executive chef at the luxurious Salish Lodge near Seattle and has now raised the bar for Walla Walla restaurants. Using the finest, freshest ingredients and classic French techniques, Davis lets subtle flavors express themselves in such dishes as tomato tartare with cucumber sorbet watercress salad, and a basil infusion and butter-poached lobster risotto with smoked tomatoes and Madras curry. The menu changes with the availability of ingredients, but expect to find Washington shellfish and salmon, Oregon bison, sweetbreads, foie gras, and even caviar.

207 W. Main St. ℂ 509/526-4075. www.twentysixbrix.com. Reservations highly recommended. Main courses $22–$42; 6-course tasting menu $85 ($115 with wine). AE, DC, DISC, MC, V. Mon and Thurs–Sat 5–10pm; Sun 9am–2pm and 5–9pm.

Whitehouse-Crawford Restaurant 🌟🌟🌟 NORTHWEST   Housed in what was once a woodworking mill, this stylish restaurant brought a touch of urban sophistication to remote Walla Walla when it first opened. The menu is as creative as you'll find anywhere east or west of the Cascades and changes daily. Start out with the warm spinach salad that comes with smoked trout and grilled onions. I usually opt for entrees from the wood oven, perhaps halibut with a sesame-cilantro pesto. Anything with the brick-oven flatbread is another good bet, as are any dishes with Walla Walla sweet onions. Even the burger here is said to be the best in town. There are plenty of excellent wines available and many can be ordered by the glass. You also can dine in the wine bar.

55 W. Cherry St. ℂ **509/525-2222**. www.whitehousecrawford.com. Reservations highly recommended. Main courses $12–$34. AE, MC, V. Wed–Sun 5–9pm.

4 The Palouse: A Slice of Small-Town Rural Washington

Dayton: 33 miles NE of Walla Walla, 62 miles E of Tri-Cities, 129 miles SW of Spokane

Between Walla Walla and Spokane lie the rolling Palouse Hills, which are among the most productive wheatlands in the nation. Before the settlement of the region by whites, Native American peoples had discovered that the Palouse, as it's known, offered ideal horse-grazing land. Horses had reached the Northwest sometime after the Spanish conquered the southern regions of North America, and by the time Lewis and Clark passed through the Palouse, the tribes of the region had become well known for their horses, which they bred for stamina and sure-footedness. On the site of present-day Dayton, there was even a Native American horse-racing track. Today these native-bred horses are known as Appaloosas for the Palouse Hills from which they came.

   Although the Lewis and Clark expedition passed through this area in 1806, it was not until the 1850s that the first pioneers began settling in the area. By the 1880s, the region was booming as a major wheat- and barley-growing region. Throughout the Palouse, small towns that have long been out of the mainstream of Northwest development are nestled along creek banks below rolling hills. Several of these towns are classic examples of small-town America, with attractive Victorian homes lining their shady streets. Between the towns, the roads wind uphill and down, through a distinctive zebra-striped landscape created by farming practices developed to reduce erosion on the steep hills.

ESSENTIALS

GETTING THERE   U.S. 12, runs from Walla Walla to Clarkston, the main route through the southern part of the Palouse. From Lewiston, Idaho, across the Snake River from Clarkston, U.S. 195 runs north through the Palouse to Spokane.

VISITOR INFORMATION   Contact the **Dayton Chamber of Commerce,** 166 E. Main St., Dayton, WA 99328 (ℂ **800/882-6299** or 509/382-4825; www.historicdayton. com). Contact the **Pullman Chamber of Commerce,** 415 N. Grand Ave., Pullman, WA 99163 (ℂ **800/365-6948** or 509/334-3565; www.pullmanchamber.com). Check out **www.palousescenicbyway.com**.

Fun Fact   **Go, Team, Go!**

In **Colfax** you can take a look at the **Codger Pole,** the largest chain-saw sculpture in the world. The pole depicts the members of two football teams that got together in 1988 to replay their 1938 game. You'll find the Codger Pole on John Crawford Boulevard just off Main Street.

EXPLORING THE PALOUSE

Among the many little towns along the route from Walla Walla to Spokane, **Dayton** is the prettiest. Its old-fashioned, small-town American feel is as genuine as it gets. Dayton was one of the most important towns in this region and is still the county seat of Columbia County. Its 1887 **Columbia County Courthouse** is the oldest county courthouse still in use in the state of Washington. It's open Monday through Friday from 8:30am to 4:30pm. The **Dayton Historic Depot,** 222 E. Commercial Street (© **509/382-2026;** www.historicdaytondepot.org), the oldest railway depot in the state (built 1881). From Memorial Day through Labor Day weekends, the depot is open for tours Tuesday through Thursday from 11am to 5pm, Friday and Saturday from 10am to 5pm, and Sunday from 1 to 4pm; call for hours in other months. Admission is by $3 suggested donation. All in all, Dayton has nearly 120 buildings on the National Historic Register. On the second Sunday in October, there is a historic homes tour. In nearby Waitsburg, where there are more Victorian homes, you can also tour the 1883 **Bruce Memorial Museum** (© **509/337-6157**), open June through September, Friday and Saturday from 1 to 4pm. It is filled with Victorian-era furnishings.

If you didn't get enough wine in Walla Walla, you'll find plenty more at the **Patit Creek Winery,** 507 E. Main St., Dayton (© **509/382-1357;** www.patitcreekcellars.com). This winery also has a tasting room in Walla Walla at 4 S. Fourth St. (© **509/522-4684**).

About 44 miles northwest of Dayton, you'll find **Palouse Falls State Park.** The spectacular falls here cascade 198 feet into a rock-walled canyon. Park admission is $5. South of town 21 miles, you'll find **Ski Bluewood** (© **509/382-4725;** www.bluewood.com), a small ski area in the Blue Mountains.

Some 12½ miles north of Colfax, **Kamiak Butte County Park** provides the ideal vantage point for surveying the vast Palouse. To reach this park, take Wash. 272 east 5 miles to a right turn onto Clear Creek Road. Continue another 7 miles and turn right on Fugate Road. Nearby is **Steptoe Butte State Park,** which also has good views of the surrounding landscape. To reach this park, drive 6 miles north from Colfax on U.S. 195 and turn east on Scholz Road.

A trip to the Palouse can also include an exploration of **Hell's Canyon,** which was carved by the Snake River and is the deepest gorge in North America. **Beamer's Hells Canyon Tours** (© **800/522-6966;** www.hellscanyontours.com), which operates out of Clarkston, Washington, offers a variety of day and overnight jet-boat trips up the Snake River. Prices range from $60 for a half-day tour to $105 for a full-day tour. Overnight trips are $280.

WHERE TO STAY

The Weinhard Hotel ☆   Constructed in 1889 to house a saloon operated by Jacob Weinhard, the nephew of Portland, Oregon, brewer Henry Weinhard, this brick building is now a comfortable, generally inexpensive Victorian inn. In the large lobby is a grand piano and, in one corner, board games and magazines. Guest rooms have high ceilings with overhead fans and at least one piece of antique furniture. The best room in the house has a whirlpool tub in the bathroom. Up on the roof, you'll find a terrace garden where you can enjoy a cup of espresso.

235 E. Main St., Dayton, WA 99328. © **509/382-4032**. Fax 509/382-2640. www.weinhard.com. 15 units. $75–$150 double. Rates include continental breakfast. DISC, MC, V. Pets accepted ($20). **Amenities:** Restaurant (American); concierge. *In room:* A/C, TV, dataport.

WHERE TO DINE
IN WAITSBURG

Whoopemup Hollow Café ★ *Finds* SOUTHERN   Named for a valley just outside of town and sporting wooden booths and classic Art Deco styling, this little gem of a restaurant is the biggest thing to hit Waitsburg since they built the flour mill. Serving Cajun and southern food, the Whoopemup may seem out of place in this quiet wheat-farming community, but people from Walla Walla make the 20-mile drive on a regular basis for the tasty food and reasonable prices. The jambalaya is the best I've ever had; don't pass it up. Desserts here are a highlight, so be sure to save room (if you can) for the red-velvet cake or cola chocolate cake.

120 Main St., Waitsburg. © **509/337-9000**. Reservations highly recommended. Main courses $8–$22. MC, V. Tues–Sat 3–9pm.

IN DAYTON

Patit Creek Restaurant ★★ FRENCH   This restaurant, in a little green cottage beside the road on the north side of Dayton, is worth the trip to this small Palouse town. Don't let the proximity to the highway worry you; stained-glass windows hide the passing traffic from diners and allow guests to focus on their food. Though lunches include everything from a smoked turkey sandwich to top-sirloin steak bordelaise (and all at reasonable prices), dinners are on a very different level. You might start a meal with chevre cheese–stuffed dates or a delicious smoked salmon cheesecake. The entree menu includes such dishes as a superb filet mignon *poivre verte* with green peppercorns, cognac, and cream; and sautéed duck breast with red wine, currants, and port demi-glace.

725 Dayton Ave. © **509/382-2625**. Reservations recommended. Main courses $9–$15 lunch, $19–$29 dinner. MC, V. Wed–Fri 11:30am–1:30 or 2pm and 4:30–8 or 9pm; Sat 4:30–8 or 9pm.

Weinhard Café ★ NEW AMERICAN   This cozy little cafe perfectly captures the spirit of a small-town restaurant, yet with big-city culinary aesthetics. The menu changes regularly and is never very long. At lunch, you might have a panini, a chicken quesadilla, or some spicy Indian pakoras. At dinner, expect the likes of halibut cakes with avocado–pumpkin seed salsa, pan-seared salmon with an ancho chili glaze and grapefruit-plum salsa, or pork chops with Gorgonzola stuffing. The wine list includes lots of Walla Walla wines.

258 E. Main St. © **509/382-1681**. www.weinhard-café.com. Reservations recommended. Main courses $7–$9 lunch, $12–$23 dinner. AE, DISC, MC, V. Tues–Sat 11am–2pm and 5 to 8 or 9pm.

5 Spokane

284 miles E of Seattle, 195 miles NE of Yakima, 155 miles N of Walla Walla

Spokane is the second-largest city in Washington, the largest city between Seattle and Minneapolis, and a center for both commercial and cultural pursuits. While Spokane is a very pleasant city with a beautiful park, excellent museum, a downtown historic district, great hotels, and excellent restaurants, it isn't really a tourist destination. However, its proximity to Lake Coeur d'Alene and several Idaho ski areas makes it a jumping-off point for explorations of the northern Idaho Rocky Mountains.

For thousands of years, Native Americans lived along the Spokane River, and it was at Spokane Falls that the Spokan-ee tribe congregated each year to catch salmon. When the first explorers and fur traders arrived in 1807, it was near these falls that they established a trading post where they could barter with the Native Americans for beaver pelts. Spokan House (the original spelling had no letter *e*), established in 1810 downriver from Spokane Falls, became the first settlement in the area, but not until 1872 was a settlement established at the falls themselves. When the Northern Pacific Railroad arrived in 1881, the town of Spokan Falls became the most important town in the region. However, in the summer of 1889, the city's downtown commercial district was destroyed by fire. Within 2 years, the city had fully recovered from the fire and also changed the spelling of its name.

Today, the Spokane River is still this city's greatest asset. Along the river you'll find numerous parks and a paved hiking/biking trail. The falls themselves are an impressive sight, despite being hemmed in by industrial buildings, and only a few miles from downtown, the Spokane River still looks wild and untamed.

ESSENTIALS

GETTING THERE   Spokane is on I-90, Washington's east-west interstate. U.S. 2 is an alternative route from western Washington. U.S. 395 is the main route from Canada south to Spokane. U.S. 195 connects to Lewiston, Idaho.

Spokane International Airport, 9000 W. Airport Dr. (© **509/455-6455;** www. spokaneairports.net) is located 10 miles west of downtown and is served by Alaska Airlines, America West, Big Sky Airlines, Frontier, Horizon, Northwest, Skywest/Delta Airlines, Southwest, and United/United Express.

Amtrak passenger trains provide service to Spokane. The station is at 221 W. First Ave. (© **509/624-5144**).

VISITOR INFORMATION   Contact the **Spokane Area Visitor Information Center,** 201 W. Main Ave., Spokane, WA 99201 (© **888/SPOKANE** or 509/747-3230; www.visitspokane.com).

GETTING AROUND   **Rental cars** are available from Avis, Budget, Dollar, Enterprise, Hertz, National, and Thrifty. If you need a taxi, contact **Spokane Cab** (© **509/568-8000**). Public bus service is provided by the **Spokane Transit Authority** (© **509/328-7433;** www.spokanetransit.com); the fare is $1.

FESTIVALS   Spokane's nickname is the Lilac City, and the city's biggest annual event is the **Lilac Festival** (© **509/535-4554;** www.lilacfestival.org), which is held each year in mid-May. On the first Sunday in May, the city holds its annual **Lilac Bloomsday Run** (© **509/838-1579;** www.bloomsdayrun.com), the largest timed foot race in the world (more than 50,000 runners participate).

WHAT TO SEE & DO

Spokane has made it easy for visitors to get a sense of what the city is all about by mapping out a Spokane City Drive that takes in all the highlights. The well-marked route meanders through Spokane and passes by the city attractions listed below. The drive also takes in some great vistas from the hills to the south.

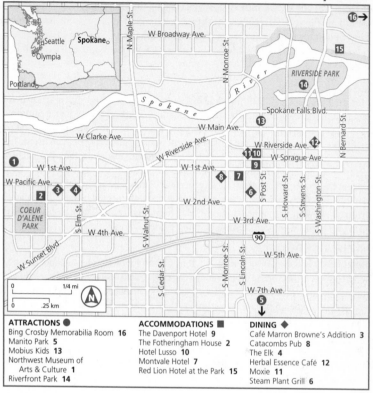

ATTRACTIONS ●
Bing Crosby Memorabilia Room **16**
Manito Park **5**
Mobius Kids **13**
Northwest Museum of
   Arts & Culture **1**
Riverfront Park **14**

ACCOMMODATIONS ■
The Davenport Hotel **9**
The Fotheringham House **2**
Hotel Lusso **10**
Montvale Hotel **7**
Red Lion Hotel at the Park **15**

DINING ◆
Café Marron Browne's Addition **3**
Catacombs Pub **8**
The Elk **4**
Herbal Essence Café **12**
Moxie **11**
Steam Plant Grill **6**

RIVERFRONT PARK

Created for the 1974 World's Fair Expo and set on an island in the middle of the Spokane River, 100-acre **Riverfront Park** ⭑ (© **800/336-PARK** or 509/625-6600; www.spokaneriverfrontpark.com) is the city's pride and joy. The land on which the park stands was once a maze of railroad tracks and depots, and the polluted river was nearly inaccessible to the public. The creation of the park helped rejuvenate downtown Spokane, and today crowds flock here to enjoy everything from summertime concerts to ice-skating in the winter. Activities for both adults and children abound. At the Howard Street entrance to the park, you'll find the **Rotary Riverfront Fountain,** a stainless-steel sculpture that's also a choreographed fountain in which people can play on hot days. The restored 1909 **Looff Carrousel** ⭑⭑, with its hand-carved horses, is one of the most beautiful in the country and also a big hit with kids. More contemporary entertainment is offered at the **IMAX Theatre** (© **509/625-6686**), where 70mm films are shown on screens five stories high. A family-fun center includes kiddie rides, miniature golf, and arcade games. Throughout the summer are many special events.

Serving as a spectacular backdrop for the park is the Spokane River, which here cascades over Spokane Falls, and is most impressive during the spring snow-melt season. The best view of the falls is from the lilac-colored gondolas of the **Spokane Falls**

SkyRide (© **509/625-6600**). Gondolas swing out over the falls before crossing to the far side of the river. Between early March and mid-October, the SkyRide operates daily with hours varying by the season; other months, it only operates Friday through Sunday and holidays. Rides cost $6 for adults, $5 for teens and seniors, and $4 for children ages 3 to 12.

MANITO PARK
Manito Park 🐾🐾 (© **509/363-5422**), Spokane's other major green space is a far more traditional place than Riverfront Park and is south of downtown, beginning at the corner of Division Street and 18th Avenue. Here at Manito, among rocks and pine forest, you'll find several of the most beautiful public gardens in the Northwest. Foremost of these is the classically proportioned **Duncan Garden,** a formal garden patterned after those of 17th-century Europe. Adjacent to this garden is the **Gaiser Conservatory,** which brims with exotic tropical plants. The perennial garden and rose garden are at their exuberant peaks in June and should not be missed. The lilac garden is also well worth a visit during the May flowering season. There is also the **Nishinomiya Japanese Garden,** a strolling pond garden.

MORE ATTRACTIONS
Bing Crosby Memorabilia Room 🐾   Bing Crosby got his start here in Spokane, where he spent most of his youth. When young Bing's aspirations soared beyond the bounds of Spokane and he made his name in Los Angeles, the members of his band who chose to stay safely at home must have long regretted their decision. All of Crosby's gold records, his Oscar, and plenty of other memorabilia (including a Bing-endorsed mousetrap and a Bing Crosby Ice Cream box) are on view. You can also take a look at Crosby's boyhood home, which is now home to the Gonzaga Alumni Association, 508 E. Sharp St.

Crosby Student Center, Gonzaga University, 502 E. Boone Ave. © **509/328-4220**, ext. 4297. Free admission. Mon–Fri 7:30am–midnight; Sat–Sun 11am–midnight. Closed holidays.

Mobius Kids 𝘬𝘪𝘥𝘴   Inside the River Park Square shopping mall, this little children's museum is filled with fun interactive exhibits that will keep your kids entertained for hours. They won't even realize they're learning important scientific principles. Adults have a lot of fun here, too.

808 W. Main Ave. © **509/624-5437**. www.mobiusspokane.org. Admission $5.75 adults and children over age 1, $4.75 senior. Mon–Sat 10am–5pm; Sun 11am–5pm. Closed Thanksgiving, Christmas, Easter.

Northwest Museum of Arts & Culture 🐾🐾   From the dramatic architecture and landscaping to the eclectic collections and exhibits, this museum makes a big impression. One of the most fascinating exhibits focuses on the region's Plateau Indians. Other galleries mount temporary art exhibits. Next door to the museum is the historic Campbell House; a tour of this old mansion is included in the admission price. With a well-balanced blend of history, art, and culture, this is one of the finest museums in the Northwest and should not be missed.

2316 W. First Ave. © **509/456-3931**. www.northwestmuseum.org. Admission $7 adults, $5 seniors and students, free for children 5 and under; open by donation from 5–9pm 1st Fri of each month. Tues–Sun 11am–5pm (1st Fri of each month until 9pm). Closed Easter, Memorial Day, July 4, Labor Day, Thanksgiving, Christmas.

WINE TOURING
The Spokane area is too cold to produce much in the way of wine grapes, but a handful of area wineries produce wines from Yakima and Columbia Valley grapes.

Arbor Crest Wine Cellars ✪   Northeast of downtown Spokane in the historic Cliff House atop a 450-foot-high bluff overlooking the Spokane River, this winery boasts one of the most spectacular settings of any winery in the state. Prices are reasonable, though the wines are not memorable.

4705 N. Fruithill Rd. ✆ **509/927-9463.** www.arborcrest.com. Daily noon–5pm. Take exit 287 off I-90, go north on Argonne Rd., turn right on Upriver Dr. and then left on Fruithill Rd.

Barrister Winery ✪✪✪   This winery and its tasting room are both in the up-and-coming downtown warehouse/arts district, and owned by a couple of lawyers who also happen to be great winemakers. Cabernet franc is their flagship wine, and in both 2002 and 2003, the winery produced outstanding vintages. However, they have also produced excellent syrah and merlot. Expect soft, silky tannins on the fruit-forward wines here. Prices are in the $25 to $30 range.

1213 W. Railroad Ave. ✆ **509/465-3591.** www.barristerwinery.com. Sat 10am–4pm. In downtown, drive west on Second Ave., turn right on Jefferson St. and then left onto Railroad Ave.

Caterina Winery   In the historic Broadview Dairy Building across the Spokane River from downtown, Caterina produces primarily moderately priced wines ($10–$20). On Friday and Saturday nights, the wine bar has live music.

905 N. Washington St. ✆ **509/328-5069.** www.caterina.com. Daily noon–5pm. From downtown, go north on Division St. and then left on N. River Dr.

Grande Ronde Wine Cellars/Mountain Dome   Showcasing the wines of two local wineries, this cellar room is a convenient place to taste a wide range of wines.

170 S. Lincoln St. ✆ **509/455-8161.** Wed–Sat noon–6pm. In downtown at corner of Second Ave. and Lincoln St.

Knipprath Cellars ✪   Housed in an old school building in a residential neighborhood on Spokane's east side, this small winery is most noteworthy for its port wines, one of which is flavored with chocolate and absolutely delicious.

5634 E. Commerce Ave. ✆ **509/534-5121.** www.knipprath-cellars.com. Thurs–Sun noon–5pm. Take exit 287, go north on Argonne Rd., turn left on Trent Ave., then turn right on Fancher Rd.

Latah Creek Wine Cellars   Housed in a Spanish mission–style building amid industrial complexes that back I-90, this winery seems more interested in its extensive gift shop offerings than its wines. Although it's known for its merlot, we've found the reds to have very odd flavors. A May wine is a specialty here.

13030 E. Indiana Ave. ✆ **800/LatahCreek** or 509/926-0164. www.latahcreek.com. Daily 9am–5pm. Take exit 289, go north on Pines Rd. and then turn right on Indiana Ave.

Lone Canary Winery ✪   A red, a rouge, and a rosso. These three red-wine blends are the main focus of winemaker Mike Scott, who formerly worked at Caterina Winery here in Spokane. The wines are each done in different styles–American, Bordeaux, and Tuscan. With their blends of different varietals, each of these wines is distinctly different from the other. All are under $20. A sauvignon blanc is also available.

109 S. Scott St. ✆ **509/534-9062.** www.lonecanary.com. Fri–Sun noon–5pm. From downtown, drive ½ mile east on Sprague Street and turn right on Scott St.

Robert Karl Cellars ✪   In a downtown warehouse just a few blocks from the heart of Spokane, this winery is the husband-and-wife operation of Joe and Rebecca Gunselman, who produced outstanding cabernet sauvignon in 2002.

115 W. Pacific Ave. © 509/363-1353. www.robertkarl.com. Sat noon–5pm. From downtown, drive north on Division St. and turn left on Pacific Ave.

Townshend Cellar ★★ *Finds*   This may be the most out-of-the-way winery in the Spokane area, but it is well worth searching out for its delicious port wines, including some made exclusively with huckleberries and some with grapes and huckleberries. This winery also makes good chardonnay and syrah, and a fun huckleberry blush that's made with viognier.

16112 Greenbluff Rd. © 509/238-1400. www.townshendcellar.com. Fri–Sun noon–6pm. From I-90, take exit 287, go north on Argonne Rd., which becomes Bruce Rd., turn left at the "T" intersection onto Day-Mt. Spokane Rd., go ½ mile and turn right on Greenbluff Rd.

SPORTS & OUTDOOR ACTIVITIES

Walkers, joggers, and cyclists will want to get in some exercise on the **Spokane River Centennial Trail** (www.spokanecentennialtrail.org). The paved trail starts at Nine Mile Falls west of the city and parallels the river for 37 miles to the Idaho state line, where it connects to the Idaho Centennial Trail for a final leg into Coeur d'Alene (a total of 61 miles of pathway). Bicycles can be rented at Riverfront Park.

Riverside State Park ★★ (© 509/465-5064) lies along the banks of the meandering Spokane River on the west edge of the city, with 32 miles of hiking trails, picnic areas, campgrounds, and access to the Spokane River Centennial Trail. Despite proximity to the city, the park has a surprisingly wild feel, and the river flowing through the park is one of the state's prettiest stretches of water. The Bowl and Pitcher Overlook, near the park headquarters, provides a vista of huge basalt boulders on the banks of the river. Adjacent to the park is the **Spokane House Interpretive Site,** which tells the story of the early fur trade in this area. It's open from Memorial Day to Labor Day, on Thursday, Friday, and Monday from 1 to 4pm, and Saturday and Sunday from 10am to 4pm. To find the park, drive north from downtown on Maple Street, turn left on Maxwell Street, which becomes Pettit Street; go past the Downriver Golf Course. Park admission is $5.

For a great view of the region, head northwest 30 miles to **Mount Spokane State Park** (© 509/238-4258), where you can drive to the top of the mountain. Hiking trails wander for miles through the forest here. Park admission is $5.

WHERE TO STAY

The Davenport Hotel ★★★   Far and away the state's finest hotel east of Seattle, this restored grande dame is an absolute work of art. Originally opened in 1914 and reopened in 2002 after a total restoration, the Davenport has an astonishingly ornate Spanish Renaissance lobby that is way over the top and lends the feel of a European palace. The many ballrooms, each of which draws on different European periods and

---

Kids **Cat Tales**

Fifteen miles north of Spokane is a wildlife park unlike any other in the state. **Cat Tales Zoological Park,** 17020 N. Newport Hwy., Mead (© 509/238-4126; www.cat tales.org), lets visitors get up close to tigers and other big cats from around the world. There's also a petting zoo where you might be able to pet a baby tiger. Treat bags can also be purchased, if you want to help feed the big cats.

countries for styling, continue the palatial feel of the hotel. However, the highlight is the Hall of the Doges, where you should be sure to sneak a peek while you're here. Guest rooms are as classically elegant as the lobby, with hand-carved furniture imported from Indonesia. This should be anyone's first choice of hotel in Spokane if cost is no object. In fact, the Davenport is reason enough to visit Spokane. At press time, there were plans to add a 319-room tower here by the fall of 2006.

10 S. Post St., Spokane, WA 99201. ⓒ 800/899-1482 or 509/455-8888. Fax 509/624-4455. www.thedavenporthotel. com. 283 units. $199–$239 double; $299–$1,950 suite. AE, DC, DISC, MC, V. Self parking $11, valet parking $16. Pets accepted. **Amenities:** 2 restaurants (Continental, American); 2 lounges; indoor pool; exercise room; access to nearby health club; full-service spa; Jacuzzi; concierge; business center; shopping arcade; 24-hr. room service; massage; babysitting; laundry service; dry cleaning. *In room:* A/C, TV, dataport, hair dryer, iron, safe, high-speed Internet access.

The Fotheringham House 🏆🏆

In the historic Browne's Addition neighborhood, this pretty Queen Anne Victorian home, built in 1891 by the first mayor of Spokane, is set behind a white picket fence and is surrounded by a colorful perennial garden. Inside you'll find an abundance of ornate woodwork and antique furniture. Most of the furnishings are period antiques, and in the large shared bathroom, you'll find the original claw-foot bathtub. Across the street is a shady park and historic mansions line the streets of the neighborhood.

2128 W. Second Ave., Spokane, WA 99204. ⓒ 509/838-1891. Fax 509/838-1807. www.fotheringham.net. 4 units, 1 with private bathroom. $95–$115 double. Rates include full breakfast. AE, MC, V. Children over age 12 welcome. Closed Jan. *In room:* A/C, hair dryer, no phone.

Hotel Lusso 🏆🏆

One of the most luxurious hotels in Spokane, the Lusso is far less ostentatious than the Davenport Hotel. Affecting a sort of contemporary Italianate styling, this boutique hotel has a very posh European feel. Because the hotel was created from two existing buildings, the rooms here are all a little bit different. Some of the standard rooms can be a bit small, but upgrades are possible in $20 increments. We'd suggest upgrading one or two levels. Most of the rooms have 12- to 14-foot ceilings that make even the smallest rooms feel big. For a splurge, there are penthouse suites, which have deluxe bathrooms with double whirlpool tubs surrounded by walls of glass. The Fugazzi restaurant is one of Spokane's hippest restaurants. There's also a separate lounge.

1 N. Post St., Spokane, WA 99201. ⓒ 509/747-9750. Fax 509/747-9751. www.hotellusso.com. 60 units. $171–$185 double; $214–$506 suite. Rates include continental breakfast. AE, DC, DISC, MC, V. Parking $12. **Amenities:** Restaurant (Northwest); lounge; access to nearby health club; concierge; room service; massage; dry cleaning. *In room:* A/C, TV, dataport, minibar, hair dryer, iron.

Montvale Hotel 🏆🏆

This little boutique hotel in downtown Spokane is the city's latest luxury hotel. In a building constructed in 1899, the Montvale has a small street-level lobby, but up one floor, there's a much bigger lobby with the feel of a living room in a rustic lodge or old-fashioned men's club. A large skylight bathes it in natural light, and a third-floor mezzanine frames the space. Guest rooms have a timeless, classic feel and meld antiques, antique reproductions, and classic and contemporary art. They have plush mattresses, flat-screen or wall-hung LCD TVs, and large bathrooms with both tubs and showers.

1005 W. First Ave., Spokane, WA 99201. ⓒ 866/668-8253 or 509/747-1919. www.montvalehotel.com. 36 units. $109–$175 double; $300–$400 suite. Rates include continental breakfast. AE, DISC, MC, V. Valet parking $12. **Amenities:** Concierge; dry cleaning. *In room:* A/C, TV, dataport, hair dryer, high-speed Internet access, Wi-Fi.

Red Lion Hotel at the Park 🌟🌟 *Kids*   Although this is primarily a convention hotel, its adjacency to downtown Spokane's Riverfront Park makes it the city's most conveniently located hotel for those on a family vacation. In addition to the fun in Riverfront Park, the hotel offers a resortlike, lagoon-style pool complete with a water-slide that kids love. A variety of rooms accommodate all travelers, even those without kids in tow, and anyone desiring extra luxury can opt for the executive rooms with bal-conies overlooking the pool or river.

303 W. North River Dr., Spokane, WA 99201. 📞 800/RED-LION or 509/326-8000. Fax 509/325-7329. www.westcoast hotels.com. 400 units. $109–$165 double; $160–$950 suite. AE, DC, DISC, MC, V. Pets accepted. **Amenities:** 2 restau-rants (Northwest, deli cafe); lounge; 2 swimming pools (1 indoor, 1 outdoor); exercise room; Jacuzzi; concierge; busi-ness center; limited room service; laundry service; dry cleaning. *In room:* A/C, TV, dataport, coffeemaker, hair dryer, iron, high-speed Internet access, Wi-Fi.

WHERE TO DINE

For espresso and muffins downtown, I always stop in at **Rocket Bakery,** 1325 W. First Ave. (📞 509/747-1834). Over by the Northwest Museum of Arts & Culture, the place for espresso is **Cabin Coffee,** 141 S. Cannon St. (📞 509/747-3088), just a few blocks from the museum. **The Milk Bottle,** 802 W. Garland Ave. (📞 509/325-1772), a few miles north of downtown, is a unique Spokane landmark. It's an old-time ice-cream parlor fronted by a three-story cement milk bottle. For the best break-fast in town, catch the train at **Frank's Diner,** 1516 W. Second Ave. (📞 509/747-8798; www.franksdiners.com). Actually, your gorgeously appointed 1906 railway car won't be leaving the station, but you can pretend.

And now for something completely different: At the **E.J. Roberts' Mansion,** 1923 W. First Ave. (📞 866/456-8839 or 509/456-8839; www.ejrobertsmansion.com), a beautifully restored mansion in the Browne's Addition neighborhood, you can take a gourmet cooking lesson from Chadwick the master butler. Classes are lots of fun and cost $25. There are high teas for $25.

Café Marron Browne's Addition 🌟🌟 MEDITERRANEAN   With its tree-shaded streets lined with grand old mansions, the Browne's Addition neighborhood just west of downtown is my favorite part of Spokane, and now it has a wonderful little neighborhood restaurant that is worth searching out. "Marron" means brown in French, so it shouldn't come as a surprise that this Browne's Addition restaurant is painted shades of brown and beige. The menu, however, is anything but beige. A recent menu included a colorful and flavorful salad made with watermelon, fennel, avocado, arugula, and parmesan. A couple of French classics—the steak *frites* and duck confit with stewed lentils—are among the standouts here. Not up for a big dinner? Just have a Gorgonzola burger. On warm sum-mer days, the front wall of the restaurant rolls up for alfresco dining.

144 S. Cannon St. 📞 509/456-8660. www.cafemarronbrownes.com. Reservations recommended. Main courses $9–$19. AE, DISC, MC, V. Mon–Fri 11am–10pm; Sat–Sun 8am–10pm.

Catacombs Pub 🌟 INTERNATIONAL   In the basement of the Montvale Hotel in downtown Spokane and only about a block away from the Davenport Hotel, this casual place comes pretty close to living up to its name. Stone walls and heavy ceiling beams set the tone; the only things missing are the old bones that catacombs are sup-posed to have. Designer pizzas are the specialty here, but there are also good salads. For dessert, don't miss the chocolate calzone.

110 S. Monroe St. 📞 509/838-4610. www.catacombspub.com. Main courses $9–$18. AE, DISC, MC, V. Mon–Thurs 11am–2pm and 5–11pm; Fri 11am–2pm and 5pm–1am; Sat 5pm–1am; Sun 5–11pm.

The Elk ✦ *Value* INTERNATIONAL   The Elk has been around since the early 1900s when it was the Elk Drug Company, supplying medicines and soda fountain treats to neighborhood residents. Today it has been restored and turned into a chic little pub serving the best of Northwest microbrews, along with such unusual pub fare as grilled lamb sandwiches and seared ahi sandwiches. The excellent and unusual, chicken Caesar soft tacos are our favorites for a light lunch in Spokane. During the warmer months, try to get a table out front on the sidewalk patio. This is one of Spokane's best bets for cheap eats.

1931 W. Pacific Ave. ✆ 509/363-1973. www.wedonthaveone.com. Main courses $7–$10. DISC, MC, V. Sun–Thurs 11am–10pm; Fri–Sat 11am–11:30pm.

Herbal Essence Café ✦ INTERNATIONAL   Popular both as a casual lunch spot for downtown office workers and a hip spot for dinner, this restaurant serves deliciously creative food. At lunch, try the south Philly smashed sub or the crab-and-artichoke sub. At dinner, the Jamaican chicken satay with mango barbecue sauce makes a zesty starter. For an entree, the top sirloin with huckleberry sauce and the elk chops with red currant-and-bacon demi-glace are both good bets. This place is just a couple of blocks from Riverfront Park.

115 N. Washington St. ✆ 509/838-4600. Reservations recommended. Main courses $6–$9.25 lunch, $15–$23 dinner. MC, V. Mon–Fri 11am–2pm and 5–9pm; Sat–Sun 5–9pm.

Moxie ✦ EURO-ASIAN   With its corrugated metal walls and glowing ceiling illuminated by red neon lights, this restaurant is one of the hippest dining spots in Spokane. The menu is just as hip as the setting with a contemporary blend of the lively flavors of Asia and the classics of Europe. Think tempura asparagus with ginger aioli and truffle ponzu sauce; seared yellow-fin tuna with red curry–coconut sauce; and Hawaiian-style grilled flat-iron steak. However, despite the Asian flavorings, it's the chipotle-glazed meatloaf that most people rave about here. Be sure to try the huckleberry shortcake.

816 W. Sprague Ave. ✆ 509/456-3594. moxiemoxie.com. Reservations recommended. Main courses $6–$12 lunch, $10–$30 dinner. AE, DISC, MC, V. Mon–Fri 11am–2pm; Sun and Tues–Thurs 5–9:30pm, Fri–Sat 5–10pm.

Steam Plant Grill ✦ *Finds* INTERNATIONAL   In a renovated former steam-generating plant that is now a historic landmark, the Steam Plant Grill is the most unusual restaurant in Spokane. The restaurant is surrounded by the girders, pipes, and boilers that once served to pump steam heat to the buildings of downtown Spokane. At lunch, the menu comprises burgers, sandwiches, and wraps. At dinner, there's more creativity, including a good basil-cream ravioli and southwestern-style salmon. The restaurant serves the microbrews of the Coeur d'Alene Brewing Company. Don't miss the smokestack dessert or smokestack room.

159 S. Lincoln St. ✆ 509/777-3900. www.steamplantgrill.com. Reservations recommended. Main courses $7–$11 lunch, $13–$29 dinner. AE, DISC, MC, V. Sun–Thurs 11:30am–9:30pm; Fri–Sat 11:30am–11pm.

SPOKANE AFTER DARK

As one of the largest cities in Washington, Spokane has a lively cultural and nightlife scene. To find out what's going on around Spokane, pick up a copy of *The Pacific Northwest Inlander,* a free weekly arts-and-entertainment newspaper. You'll find copies in restaurants, record stores, and bookstores. Also check with the **Spokane Arts Commission** (✆ 509/625-6050; www.spokanearts.org). Particularly noteworthy are concerts held throughout the year at the **Cathedral of St. John the Evangelist,** 127 E.

12th Ave. (© **509/838-4277;** www.stjohns-cathedral.org), a Gothic cathedral with an organ that has more than 4,000 pipes.

Ella's Supper Club, 110 W. First Ave. (© **509/747-7078;** www.spokanecenterstage. com), on the second floor of the historic 1909 Odd Fellows Hall, is a jazz bar with live music several nights a week. Silent movies are also projected on the wall of the Fox Theatre across the street from Ella's for a unique nightlife experience. Don't miss it. In the same building as Ella's is the affiliated **CenterStage** (© **509/747-8243**), a dinner theater. Also be sure to check the calendar at **The Big Easy,** 911 W. Sprague Ave. (© **509/BIG-EASY;** www.bigeasyconcerts.com), downtown's premier venue for touring rock acts.

6 The Grand Coulee Dam Area

85 miles W of Spokane, 92 miles NE of Wenatchee

Grand Coulee, formerly a wide, dry valley, is a geologic anomaly left over from the last Ice Age. At that time, a glacier repeatedly dammed an upstream tributary of the Columbia River and formed a huge lake in what is today Montana. When this prehistoric lake repeatedly burst through its ice dam, massive floods poured down from the Rocky Mountains. So great was the volume of water that the Columbia River overflowed its normal channel and, as these floodwaters flowed southward, they carved deep valleys into the basalt landscape of central Washington. As the floodwaters reached the Cascade Range, they were forced together into one great torrent that was so powerful, it scoured out the Columbia Gorge far downstream, carving cliffs and leaving us with today's beautiful waterfalls. With the end of the Ice Age, however, the Columbia returned to its original channel and the temporary flood channels were left high and dry. Early French explorers called these dry channels *coulées,* and the largest of them all was Grand Coulee, which is 50 miles long, between 2 miles and 5 miles wide, and 1,000 feet deep.

Located at the northern end of the Grand Coulee, Grand Coulee Dam is considered one of the greatest engineering marvels of the 20th century. Constructed during the Great Depression, it was the largest man-made structure on earth at the time of its completion in 1941 and is still the largest concrete dam in North America. The dam is 550 feet tall, 5,223 feet wide (almost a mile), and impounds the waters of the Columbia River, forming 151-mile-long Roosevelt Lake. Despite the name, the Grand Coulee Dam did not, however, fill the Grand Coulee with water. That did not happen until the 1950s when Dry Falls Dam was built at the south end of the coulee and waters from Roosevelt Lake were used to fill the Grand Coulee and form 31-mile-long Banks Lake. The waters of both Roosevelt Lake and Banks Lake have been used to irrigate the arid lands of eastern Washington, turning this region into productive farmlands. The Grand Coulee Dam is also a major producer of hydroelectric power.

ESSENTIALS

GETTING THERE The towns of Grand Coulee, Coulee Dam, and Electric City are at the junction of Wash. 155, which runs south to Coulee City and north to Omak, and Wash. 174, which runs west to Wash. 17 and east to U.S. 2.

VISITOR INFORMATION Contact the **Grand Coulee Dam Area Chamber of Commerce,** 306 Midway St. (P.O. Box 760), Grand Coulee, WA 99133-0760 (© **800/ 268-5332** or 509/633-3074; www.grandcouleedam.org).

WHAT TO SEE & DO

You can learn the history of the dam by stopping in at the **Grand Coulee Dam Visitor Arrival Center** (© 509/633-9265; www.usbr.gov/pn/grandcoulee), open daily from February through November. Here you can arrange for a free guided tour of the dam (tours are held daily on the hour 10am–5pm). Every night between the end of May and end of September, the **world's largest laser-light show** is projected onto the face of the dam. The accompanying narration is broadcast over the radio at 90.1 FM and tells the history of Grand Coulee and the dam. There's a self-guided walking tour through historic Coulee Dam, the government town built to house workers during the construction of the dam.

Lake Roosevelt, with 600 miles of shoreline, provides ample opportunities for watersports and fishing and makes up the **Lake Roosevelt National Recreation Area,** 1008 Crest Dr., Coulee Dam, WA 99116 (© 509/738-6266 or 509/725-2715; www. nps.gov/laro). Along the shores of the lake are 17 car or walk-in campgrounds and 10 boat-in campgrounds. About 21 miles north of Davenport, at the confluence of the Spokane and Columbia rivers, stands **Fort Spokane,** which was built in 1880. Four of the original buildings are still standing. An 1892 brick guardhouse serves as a visitor center, though the recreation area's main visitor center is the Grand Coulee Dam Visitor Arrival Center right at the dam.

Some 30 miles down the Grand Coulee, just south of Coulee City on Wash. 17, you can have a look at a natural wonder that's as impressive as the dam. **Dry Falls** are the remains of a massive waterfall created by the same floodwaters that scoured out the Grand Coulee. At their peak flow, the waters cascading 400 feet over these falls stretched 3½ miles wide (in comparison, Niagara Falls are only 1 mile wide and 165 ft. tall). Between mid-May and the end of September, you can learn more about the falls and floods at the **Dry Falls Visitor Center** (© 509/632-5214), at the Dry Falls Overlook on Wash. 17. If you're interested in going to the base of the falls, continue south 2 miles to **Sun Lakes-Dry Falls State Park,** which has a road leading back to the falls. Within this park, you'll also find a campground and lakes for swimming, boating, and fishing. Park admission is $5.

For a glimpse of another unusual waterfall, head 10 miles south of Coulee City on Pinto Ridge Road. Here you'll find **Summer Falls,** an impressive man-made waterfall that only flows between March and October. The falls are formed by the runoff water from the Grand Coulee's Banks Lake. The 165-foot-tall falls pour over a basalt cliff and into Billy Clapp Lake. To reach the falls from Coulee City, take Main Street to Pinto Ridge Road, drive 8.4 miles, turn left on a gravel road, and continue 1.3 miles.

Ten miles south of Sun Lakes State Park, you'll find **Lake Lenore Caves.** These caves were created by the same floodwaters that carved Dry Falls. In this case, the waters tore off chunks of basalt as they flowed past the cliffs above today's Lake Lenore. The caves were later used by wandering bands of prehistoric Indians. There are seven caves accessible along an established trail. To reach the caves trail from Coulee City, take Wash. 17 south 7 miles.

Continuing south will bring you to **Soap Lake,** an alkaline lake named for the soapsuds that gather on its shores. For centuries, the lake has attracted people who believe the waters have medicinal properties. Once a busy health spa, Soap Lake today is a quiet little town. However, it does have a couple of good lodges where you can soak in the lake's waters. A public town beach also provides lake access.

About 25 miles south of Soap Lake lies **Moses Lake,** popular with water-skiers. South of Moses Lake lie the **Potholes Reservoir** and **Columbia National Wildlife Refuge** (© **509/488-2668;** pacific.fws.gov/refuges/field/wa_columbia.htm). This area is a stark contrast of desert and water, with dramatic basalt outcroppings. To explore this region, drive south from Moses Lake on Wash. 17, west on Wash. 262, south on K2 SE Road (it becomes Morgan Lake Rd.), and west on Wash. 26.

WHERE TO STAY
IN COULEE DAM
Columbia River Inn ✯   Right across the street from Grand Coulee Dam Visitor Center, this remodeled motel is convenient for viewing the laser-light show (cross the street to the park). Guest rooms have attractive pine furnishings, small balconies with partial dam views, and some with whirlpool tubs.

10 Lincoln Ave., Coulee Dam, WA 99116. © **800/633-6421** or 509/633-2100. www.columbiariverinn.com. 35 units. $95 double; $105–$190 suite (lower rates in winter). AE, DISC, MC, V. **Amenities:** Outdoor pool; exercise room; Jacuzzi; sauna; coin-op laundry. *In room:* A/C, TV, fridge, dataport, coffeemaker, hair dryer, iron.

Four Winds Guest House ✯   In the picture-perfect company town that was built to house engineers and laborers working on the dam, this inn is in a former engineers' dorm where President Franklin D. Roosevelt once held a meeting during his visit to the dam site. The guest rooms are simply furnished in a traditional style that evokes the 1930s, when the dam was built.

301 Lincoln St., Coulee Dam, WA 99116. © **800/786-3146** or 509/633-3146. Fax 509/633-2454. www.fourwinds bandb.com. 10 units, 1 with private bathroom. $68 double with shared bathroom; $90 double with private bathroom. Rates include full breakfast. AE, DISC, MC, V. Children over age 8 welcome. *In room:* No phone.

Index